"The most basic question of ethics is not, How should we live? but rather, To whom do we belong? This important book tackles both of these questions in the light of discipleship-based biblical faith. Both David Gushee and Glen Stassen are activists as well as theorists, and this book reflects their passion for following Jesus even when it means swimming against the stream. Not all will agree with every solution proposed here, but no one can ignore this contribution to the evangelical conversation."

TIMOTHY GEORGE, DEAN OF BEESON DIVINITY SCHOOL, SAMFORD UNIVERSITY, AND EXECUTIVE EDITOR OF *CHRISTIANITY TODAY*

"*Kingdom Ethics* is a wonderful contribution to the community of Jesus' disciples. Guided by the dominant theme in Jesus' proclamation, the authors teach us that the issue is not the relevance of the kingdom of God to us but our obedient participation in its continuing activity. They accomplish this with accessible scholarship, perceptive cultural criticism and practical wisdom. Moreover, they manage the nearly impossible feat of introducing students to the range of issues in Christian ethics without losing the kingdom as the key to following Jesus. *Kingdom Ethics* should become an indispensable resource for discipleship in congregations, colleges and seminaries."

JONATHAN R. WILSON, PROFESSOR OF RELIGIOUS STUDIES, WESTMONT COLLEGE

"When two of today's leading evangelical Baptist ethicists team up, we would naturally expect a book that views the Christian ethic as our response to Jesus' call to discipleship. Drawing from the narrative approach and the focus on virtue or character ethics indicative of contemporary moral thinking, Stassen and Gushee engage with a wide range of formidable ethical questions, doing so, however, with Jesus' ethical teaching in the Sermon on the Mount always close at hand."

STANLEY J. GRENZ, DISTINGUISHED PROFESSOR OF THEOLOGY, GEORGE W. TRUETT THEOLOGICAL SEMINARY, BAYLOR UNIVERSITY

"Many Christians in America have accommodated themselves to the values of a secular culture, either acquiescing to a materialist/consumerist ethos (on the ideological right) or a relativist 'I'm OK, you're OK' ethos (on the ideological left). *Kingdom Ethics* is a clarion call to the church to be the body of Christ on earth, to live incarnationally and be as unique today as Jesus was in his day. Stassen and Gushee have reclaimed the centrality of Jesus and his teachings for the distinctiveness of the Christian and the church in the modern world. They have written an exciting book that clearly and concretely demonstrates the Christian ethos is not some kind of quixotic idealism but is truly a radical but practical way of living.

"At a time when Christians everywhere are asking 'What would Jesus do?' Stassen and Gushee have provided searching answers to the moral questions of the day. *Kingdom Ethics* is an outstanding contribution to the field that should be read by every serious Christian."

CARLOS R. PIAR, PROFESSOR OF RELIGIOUS STUDIES, CALIFORNIA STATE UNIVERSITY, LONG BEACH

"*Kingdom Ethics* is an excellent demonstration of how helpful it is to orient Christian moral reflection around Jesus' teachings and emphases. The authors' sustained engagement with the structure and substance of the Sermon on the Mount allows its grace-based guidance to speak powerfully to contemporary questions and concerns. Working adeptly with the Scriptures, Christian tradition and contemporary data, Stassen and Gushee have crafted an exceptional book.

"The chapters shine with insight and clarity. Complex issues are handled with careful analysis and pastoral sensitivity; the result is an ethics text that is courageous, thought-provoking and life-giving."

CHRISTINE D. POHL, PROFESSOR OF SOCIAL ETHICS, ASBURY THEOLOGICAL SEMINARY

"With *Kingdom Ethics: Following Jesus in Contemporary Context*, Stassen and Gushee invite us to confront anew the radical nature of Jesus' teachings as set forth in the Sermon on the Mount—teachings that often rub modern sensibilities the wrong way—yet teachings that are indispensable for Christian moral consciousness. The book challenges us to consider the Christian ethical life as one oriented to this message of the kingdom—a way of life characterized by prayer, passion and fidelity to specific practices consistent with the will of God, or as they put it, 'holistic character ethics.' Readers will find the discussion of such practices in their view of the Christian moral life to be informed, energetic and engaging."

SAMUEL K. ROBERTS, E. HERVEY EVANS PROFESSOR OF THEOLOGY AND ETHICS, UNION THEOLOGICAL SEMINARY-PRESBYTERIAN SCHOOL OF CHRISTIAN EDUCATION, RICHMOND, VIRGINIA

"*Kingdom Ethics* promises to become a cherished resource for a diverse audience of modern readers who hunger for the recovery of the ethics of Jesus for our times. Because of its balanced approach to theory and application, this book works equally well as a textbook for teaching and as a guidebook for living."

CHERYL J. SANDERS, PROFESSOR OF CHRISTIAN ETHICS, HOWARD UNIVERSITY SCHOOL OF DIVINITY, AND SENIOR PASTOR, THIRD STREET CHURCH OF GOD, WASHINGTON, D.C.

"*Kingdom Ethics* reaffirms and deepens the challenge raised a generation ago by John Howard Yoder to bring Jesus back into Christian ethics. This is an impressive book, scholarly yet accessible, wide-ranging yet consistently returning to the moral and theological vision of Jesus for guidance. There is much to learn from its careful construction of a kingdom-based character ethics, its clear-sighted approach to the methodology of Christian ethics and its intelligent examination of contemporary ethical issues. If ever there was a time the Christian community needed to recover the moral meaning of following Jesus, this is it, and *Kingdom Ethics* will go a long way in helping us do so."

CHRISTOPHER D. MARSHALL, TYNDALE GRADUATE SCHOOL OF THEOLOGY, AUCKLAND, NEW ZEALAND

"*Kingdom Ethics* is a profound call to Christian discipleship based on probing, incisive and illuminating reflection on the Sermon on the Mount. This is a very important book—a major contribution that provides a radically unique, compelling way of doing Christian ethics grounded in the teachings and practices of Jesus—and deserves to be used across denominational and cultural boundaries. I particularly hope that it will get serious attention from Asian American congregations as they seek to become faithful and prophetic communities of sojourners in the North American context."

JOON-SIK PARK, E. STANLEY JONES ASSOCIATE PROFESSOR OF WORLD EVANGELISM, METHODIST THEOLOGICAL SCHOOL, OHIO

"Gushee and Stassen make a compelling case for how the way of Jesus and his teachings in the Sermon on the Mount (in continuity with the prophet Isaiah) are normative for Christian life and practice. The general reader will appreciate the concrete, practical relevance and breadth of inquiry on issues like war and peace, sexuality, marriage and divorce, gender roles, race, economics, and the care of creation. The book will become a benchmark for the guild of scholars in Christian social ethics for the way it creatively engages the diversity of methodologies and perspective in our discipline with the question of what we do with Jesus."

DUANE K. FRIESEN, PROFESSOR OF BIBLE AND RELIGION, BETHEL COLLEGE, KANSAS

"Stassen and Gushee provide an exceptional guide through the thickets of the vexing ethical dilemmas thrust on us by our contemporary age. Their work is informed by solid biblical scholarship, up-to-date scientific insights and astute analyses grounded in the teaching of Scripture. Creative, comprehensive and lively, it is certain to give readers a more profound understanding of Christian ethics and ethical reasoning. "

DAVID E. GARLAND, ASSOCIATE DEAN FOR ACADEMIC AFFAIRS, PROFESSOR OF CHRISTIAN SCRIPTURES, GEORGE W. TRUETT THEOLOGICAL SEMINARY, BAYLOR UNIVERSITY

"Stassen and Gushee provide a book on Christian ethics that is both 'deep and wide.' It is deep in its focused attention on Jesus as the defining reality and continuing source for Christian living. It is wide in two ways. It is wide in its focus on both the teachings and practices of Christ. Second, the majority of the book is given to a creative search for how the life of faith, informed and inspired by the life of Christ, can find expression across the spectrum of contemporary moral challenges and conundrums. From bioethics to gender roles, politics to worship, and more, this book will inspire and inform those who take being Christian seriously."

DANIEL B. MCGEE, PROFESSOR OF CHRISTIAN ETHICS, BAYLOR UNIVERSITY

"*Kingdom Ethics* is distinctive in the way that it takes biblical perspectives seriously. Rather than letting contemporary issues and agendas limit the number of biblical texts that are considered relevant for ethics, it allows the Bible itself to define what matters most in contemporary life. While it doesn't shy away from arguing that particular actions or practices should be made illegal, it is far more interested in helping us understand why people should not desire them in the first place. Even better, it constantly encourages the reader to keep in view the kingdom vision that majors in constructive alternatives rather than mere ethical condemnations. All who are serious about glorifying God by the lives they live will benefit greatly from reading this book."

JOHN F. KILNER, PRESIDENT, THE CENTER FOR BIOETHICS AND HUMAN DIGNITY

"This is an important book for our times, when many Christians are once again looking to Jesus as someone who has something of unique significance to say about human life. For more than a century he has been regarded as someone to be right about, in one way or another. But his detailed teachings have for long not been taken seriously, within the church or out. They have been regarded as simply nothing essential to faith or to life. But he became the force he has been in the world precisely because those who initially took him seriously understood that who he is was a conclusive reason for regarding his specific teachings as the key to turning their concrete existence into a life in the kingdom of God—the only life suited to the human soul. The relevance of faith in him for the world of today and tomorrow will depend on those identified as his people reclaiming that same understanding of what it means for him to be Savior and Lord."

DALLAS WILLARD, PROFESSOR OF PHILOSOPHY, UNIVERSITY OF SOUTHERN CALIFORNIA, AND AUTHOR OF *THE DIVINE CONSPIRACY* AND *THE SPIRIT OF THE DISCIPLINES*.

"Groundbreaking, current, biblical, simply superb."

RONALD J. SIDER, PRESIDENT, EVANGELICALS FOR SOCIAL ACTION, AND PROFESSOR OF THEOLOGY AND CULTURE, EASTERN SEMINARY

"Working out of a self-confessed blend of baptistic traditions but including interpretive secondary materials from a broad range of different church traditions and scholarly perspectives, Glen Stassen and David Gushee creatively construct a Christian ethics modeled on an ethics of virtue. This model of virtue ethics is firmly grounded in the centrality of Jesus' proclamation of God's reign and its correlate moral teachings gathered in the Sermon on the Mount. The result is a rendition of Christian ethics that is focused on the cultivation of a person's virtuous character-in-community, and that is ecumenical in tone, experiential in nature, and salient in granting ethical insights, perspectives and guidance on contemporary moral issues. This book merits widespread use as a textbook for courses in Christian ethics in universities, colleges and seminaries, as well as a study guide for church-based educational programs desiring to engage class members in an informed and serious discussion of Christian moral life."

MURRAY W. DEMPSTER, PRESIDENT AND PROFESSOR OF SOCIAL ETHICS, VANGUARD UNIVERSITY

KINGDOM ETHICS

FOLLOWING JESUS IN CONTEMPORARY CONTEXT

Glen H. Stassen & David P. Gushee

InterVarsity Press
Downers Grove, Illinois

InterVarsity Press
P.O. Box 1400, Downers Grove, IL 60515-1426
World Wide Web: www.ivpress.com
E-mail: mail@ivpress.com

InterVarsity Press® is the book-publishing division of InterVarsity Christian Fellowship/USA®, a student movement active on campus at hundreds of universities, colleges and schools of nursing in the United States of America, and a member movement of the International Fellowship of Evangelical Students. For information about local and regional activities, write Public Relations Dept., InterVarsity Christian Fellowship/USA, 6400 Schroeder Rd., P.O. Box 7895, Madison, WI 53707-7895, or visit the IVCF website at <www.ivcf.org>.

Scripture quotations, unless otherwise noted, are from the New Revised Standard Version of the Bible, *copyright 1989 by the Division of Christian Education of the National Council of the Churches of Christ in the USA. Used by permission. All rights reserved.*

Chapter six appeared in an earlier form as "Recovering the Way of Jesus in the Sermon on the Mount," Journal of the European Pentecostal Theological Association, *2002. Used by permission.*

Jacob Zimmer's account in chapter eight of his visit to Littleton, Colorado, is used by permission.

Chapter twelve appeared in an earlier form as "Matters of Life and Death," Christianity Today, *October 1, 2001. Used by permission.*

Cover image: Scala/Art Resource, NY

ISBN 0-8308-2668-8

Printed in the United States of America ∞

Library of Congress Cataloging-in-Publication Data

Stassen, Glen Harold, 1936-
  Kingdom ethics: following Jesus in contemporary context / by Glen H.
Stassen and David P. Gushee.
      p. cm.
Includes bibliographical references and index.
  ISBN 0-8308-2668-8
  1. Christian ethics. 2. Jesus Christ—Ethics. 3. Sermon on the
mount—Criticism, interpretation, etc. I. Gushee, David P., 1962- II.
Title.
  BJ1251 .S8132 2002
  241—dc21
                                                                        2002014451

P	17	16	15	14	13	12	11	10	9	8	7	6	5	4	3	2	1
Y	16	15	14	13	12	11	10	09	08	07	06	05	04	03			

CONTENTS

ACKNOWLEDGMENTS

Glen Stassen

A deeply felt thank-you to Sondra Ely Wheeler, Christine Pohl and Beth Phillips, for their incisive comments and for friendship that goes well beyond the call of duty. To Larry Rasmussen and Jim Ball for help on environmental ethics. To Alan Culpepper, Richard Hays, Willard Swartley, David Garland, Marianne Meye Thompson, Donald Hagner, David Scholer, Christian Wolf, Gerald Borchert, Seyoon Kim and Rick Beaton for comments on the pivotal work on the Sermon on the Mount and the Isaianic context for the kingdom of God, without implying that they take responsibility. To Michael Westmoreland-White for research help, encouragement and criticism at countless points, and for writing the first draft for the chapter on Creation Care and the topic index. To Tammy Williams and Jeff Phillips for research assistance on violence. To the remarkably competent Susan Carlson Wood for the bibliography. To the Restaurant Theology Group and the Just Peacemaking Theory interdisciplinary group for insights, mutual enrichment and support. To Abbott Timothy Kelly and the monks of the Abbey of Gethsemani; Monsignor Alfred Horrigan; Bellarmine College; Bethel College; Berea College; Calvin College; Eastern Mennonite University; Judson College; Spalding University; Texas Lutheran College; Wheaton College; Associated Mennonite Biblical Seminary; the Baptist Theological Seminaries in Buckow, Sofia, Prague, Sioux Falls, Chicago and Taejun; and Louisville Presbyterian Theological Seminary for their invitations to lecture and dialogue on these themes. To former students—my overwhelmingly heartfelt source of professional pride—for all their encouragement that this recovery of the Sermon on the Mount for our living, and this grounding of the way of Jesus and the reign of God in the prophecy of Isaiah, are the way out from the churches' accommodation to Babylon's ideologies. To Dave Gushee, for "channeling the waterfall," sharing excitement in the process, and representing all my terrific former students.

David Gushee

Thanks go to former students Joshua Trent for invaluable research help and Autumn Ridenour for dialogue about each chapter. To Greg Cales and Michael Westmoreland-White for help on the truthtelling chapter. To Audrey Chapman, James Huggins and John Kilner for help on the biotechnology chapter. To the numerous students who have spoken with me about their experiences as children of divorce. To Nevlynn Johnson for numerous dialogues related to racial justice and reconciliation. To George Guthrie for dialogue about New Testament studies. To Second Presbyterian Church, Methodist Theological School in Ohio, the Evangelical Theology Group of the American Academy of Religion and my own students for listening to this project as it developed. Very special thanks from both of us to Christine Pohl and Sondra Wheeler, who read through and engaged with the entire manuscript in various stages. To Glen Stassen himself, for the years of teaching and mentoring, and for choosing me as his partner in this project.

PREFACE

The Problem: The Evasion of Jesus
and the Sermon on the Mount

━━━━━━

The church confesses that Jesus of Nazareth is the Messiah. He is God incarnate. He is the Savior. He is the Lord of the church and of the world. He is the center not only of Christian faith but also, Scripture asserts, of the universe itself, the one through whom all things were made: "He himself is before all things, and in him all things hold together" (Col 1:17). Christianity is a nonsensical enterprise apart from Jesus, its central figure, its source, ground, authority and destiny.

Here is the problem. Christian churches across the theological and confessional spectrum, and Christian ethics as an academic discipline that serves the churches, are often guilty of evading Jesus, the cornerstone and center of the Christian faith. Specifically, *the teachings and practices of Jesus*—especially the largest block of his teachings, the Sermon on the Mount—are routinely ignored or misinterpreted in the preaching and teaching ministry of the churches and in Christian scholarship in ethics. This evasion of the concrete teachings of Jesus has seriously malformed Christian moral practices, moral beliefs and moral witness. Jesus taught that the test of our discipleship is whether we act on his teachings, whether we "put into practice" his words. This is what it means to "buil[d our] house on rock" (Mt 7:24).

We believe that Jesus meant what he said. And so it is no overstatement to claim that the evasion of the teachings of Jesus constitutes a crisis of Christian identity and raises the question of who exactly is functioning as the Lord of the church. When Jesus' way of discipleship is thinned down, marginalized or avoided, then churches and Christians lose their antibodies against infection by secular ideologies that manipulate Christians into serving the purposes of some other lord. We fear precisely that kind of idolatry now.

We write to redress this problem. Our purpose is to reclaim Jesus Christ for Christian ethics and for the moral life of the churches. We intend to write an introductory interpretation of Christian ethics built on the "rock"—the teachings and practices of Jesus. And in the process we also intend to recover the Sermon on the Mount for Christian ethics. We think that the Christian life consists of following Jesus—obeying his teachings and practicing the way of life he taught and modeled. Jesus taught that as his disciples obey him and practice what he taught and lived, they participate in the reign of God that Jesus inaugurated during his earthly ministry and that will reach its climax when he comes again. So we are attempting to write an introduction to Christian ethics that focuses unremittingly on Jesus Christ, the inaugurator of the kingdom of God.

When we surveyed the available textbooks in Christian ethics, we were amazed to find that almost none learned anything constructive from the Sermon on the Mount—the largest block of Jesus' teaching in the New Testament, the teaching that Jesus says in the Great Commission is the way to make disciples and that the early church referred to more often than any other Scripture. Something was very wrong. Now we are pleased to think we are part of a trend to recover the way of Jesus for Christian discipleship. Recently, and from three different traditions, Dallas Willard has published *The Divine Conspiracy*, William Spohn has published *Go and Do Likewise*, and Allen Verhey has published *Remembering Jesus*. It is with great enthusiasm that we welcome these three elegantly written books, each of which takes the way of Jesus seriously. We are part of the same cause, and we hope all four books foretell a movement and will work together like a team of four horses pulling in the same direction.

Plan and Structure of the Book

We intend in this book to let Jesus, and especially the Sermon on the Mount, set the agenda for Christian ethics. This simple decision has surprisingly concrete consequences. Many current introductions to Christian ethics—not to mention current moral advocacy efforts in the churches—focus their primary attention on issues that Jesus did not discuss, while ignoring several that Jesus did continually address. While we acknowledge the need to consider present-day concerns that were nonexistent in Jesus' time, as far as possible we will try to allow Jesus' teachings to set our agenda. We want to focus our attention on what Jesus taught was essential to Christian discipleship. We think this is the best way to be a Christian—a Christ-follower. Such an approach also constitutes a check against the intrusion of present-day ideologies and the distorted agendas they promote.

Yet this is not simply a book on the Sermon on the Mount, but a book on Christian ethics. And further, we are not basing the biblical parts of the book only on the Sermon on the Mount: we regularly ground the interpretation in the Hebrew Scriptures of the Old Testament, and regularly look to the rest of the New Testament for confirmation. In fact, we see the background of Jesus' teaching about the kingdom of God in the deliverance passages of the prophet Isaiah, which brings far richer content to our understanding of the reign of God in Jesus' teaching. This particular grounding in the Hebrew Scriptures is one of the guiding insights of the book and is why this book is called *Kingdom Ethics*.

The book is divided into seven sections. Section one attempts to situate the ethic Jesus taught by considering the meaning of *the kingdom of God*, for this idea stood at the heart of his proclamation and self-understanding. Our approach to Christian ethics offers a sharp focus on God's reign, a focus we think well justified given Jesus' own proclamation. This discussion then lays the foundation for our treatment of the issue of character, beginning with a kingdom-centered rethinking of the Beatitudes and moving to a consideration of contemporary character ethics.

Section two considers the perennial themes of moral authority and moral norms in Christian ethics. All approaches to ethics, Christian or not, must offer some account of what will count as authoritative in determining moral truth and of how such truth is packaged and communicated. In this section, we attempt to show the way in which Jesus dealt both with moral authority and the shape and function of moral norms. This section will be our most obviously "methodological"—and yet the entire work is intended as a demonstration of a certain methodology in Christian ethics.

All remaining chapters deal with issues and themes raised by the Sermon on the Mount or suggested by the Sermon in relation to contemporary moral challenges. Section three focuses on various issues of life and death; section four considers sexual, gender and marriage ethics; section five explores the great themes of love and justice; section six looks at relationships of justice and love by exploring truth-telling, race, economics and creation care. Finally, section seven concludes the volume by considering Jesus' teachings on prayer, politics and moral practices.

Each chapter is in one way or another grounded in a portion of the Sermon on the Mount, but the Sermon does not form the exclusive basis of the ethic that is developed there, and we do not attempt to organize the book as a straightforward exposition of the Sermon. As in any worthy introduction to Christian ethics, we attempt to present the most relevant biblical texts, themes and motifs related to the issues under discussion. Because we are trying to stay as close as possible to the ethics that Jesus taught, we attend especially to those Old Testament texts that most strongly influenced Jesus' teaching and to New Testament materials that reflect the Sermon on the Mount and other Jesus-sayings as passed on to the early church. But we do consider the whole of the canon as authoritative for Christian ethics and do our biblical work accordingly.

Reasoned and Spirit-illuminated reflection on tradition, experience and social scientific data, among other resources, also offers insight on most moral issues we face, and plenty of that kind of moral archaeology can be found here as well. To claim as we do that Christian ethics must be built on the rock,

Jesus Christ, and on his teachings is by no means to claim that the rest of the Bible should be abandoned or that no other source of knowledge is relevant.

To make the book more readable, we have avoided footnotes and incorporated the notes in parentheses within the text, often with a shortened title even on first reference. A bibliography for further reading at the end of the book identifies the publication information for the books to which the parenthetical notes refer. We hope the discussion is interesting enough, and controversial enough, to lead you to want to read further.

Authorship, Agenda and Audience

We always appreciate it when authors tell us who they are, what their agenda is, and whom they are trying to reach. So we here briefly offer the same courtesy to our own readers.

Glen was raised a North American Baptist in Minnesota. He is now Lewis B. Smedes Professor of Christian Ethics at Fuller Theological Seminary. He took up that position in 1996, after twenty years of teaching at Southern Baptist Theological Seminary, as well as at Duke University, Kentucky Southern College and Berea College. David was raised a Roman Catholic in Virginia and became a Southern Baptist through a conversion experience at the age of sixteen. He is now Graves Professor of Moral Philosophy at Union University, located in Jackson, Tennessee. David began teaching at Union in 1996, after three years on the faculty of Southern Seminary and three years serving as managing editor of the publications of Evangelicals for Social Action and guest teaching at Eastern Baptist Theological Seminary.

This project was born during three overlapping years at Southern Seminary (1993-1996). David, originally a student of Glen's, returned to Southern to join him as his partner in the two-person Christian ethics faculty. Glen had the original idea for the book in 1995, and later David joined the project. We were both excited about our sense of calling to retrieve Jesus' teachings and redemptive actions for Christian ethics.

Circumstances change in ways none of us anticipate. In 1996 David moved to Union, where he has developed a program in Christian ethics within the Christian studies department, and Glen moved to Fuller. From a distance of two thousand miles, with the aid of e-mail, we completed our work—though it took a bit of time!

Our agenda is to write an excellent introduction to Christian ethics grounded in the teachings of Jesus. We have aimed for a book that can be used in college and seminary classes. However, by introducing several new kinds of arguments we also hope to advance the ongoing conversation about Christian ethics among professional practitioners of our discipline. And we have tried to write with sufficient verve to attract the thoughtful general reader as well.

Those interested in theological/political labels and categories may find this book hard to pin down. We think we are offering a Christian ethics that seeks to follow Jesus' lead as faithfully as possible. As such, it is simply *Christian* ethics. We are writing for all Christians who have an interest in following Jesus and want to recover, or deepen, what that means.

Our publisher is an evangelical Christian publishing company, and as authors we are certainly comfortable with that theological label. We happily embrace the authority of Scripture and the tenets of orthodox Christian faith, and have written this work on that basis. Both of us, though, relate widely to an array of Christian communities both in North America and abroad, and attempt to avoid ideological pigeonholing. We hope that anyone interested in the moral teaching of Jesus Christ and the contemporary moral witness of the Christian church will find much here that is of value.

The informed reader will likely notice the theological/ethical traditions and figures that seem to influence us most heavily, but it is good to be explicit about this as well. Both of us are Baptists—the kind of Baptists who connect both to the Anabaptist and to the Reformed strands of the Baptist tradition, as well as to the Great Awakening, revivalist and Pietist heritage of North American Baptist life. The Anabaptist strand offers especially strong emphasis on the teachings of Jesus and the Sermon on the Mount. The Reformed strand develops creational and covenantal themes, and has always emphasized the Hebrew Scriptures and the sovereignty of God over all of life, not only over the church or a narrow "religious" part of life. The revivalist and Pietist strands stress the role of heartfelt personal commitment to Christ as Savior *and* Lord, and the empowerment of the Holy Spirit. These themes are all critically important in our approach. Thus our approach seeks to be faithfully and concretely Trinitarian, in, we hope, a fresh way.

We also both find the historic black church tradition in the United States to be extraordinarily congenial and confess its deep influence on our thinking, especially in its emphasis on incarnational ethics and on justice. Recent years have found us impressed by the Pentecostal/charismatic wing of the church; its thinkers are beginning to offer important insights for Christian scholarship, some of which we incorporate here. Glen has been intimately connected with the Protestant churches of Europe, especially Germany, for many years; that influence is felt here. Finally, having been trained in mainline seminaries and universities, both of us are well acquainted with Catholic and mainline theological and social ethics and have studied closely the towering figures of those traditions. Thinkers such as Dietrich Bonhoeffer and H. Richard Niebuhr have clearly left their mark on this work.

All of this is to say that the Christian ethics we offer here is nourished by the grand tradition(s) of the church as a whole, with certain strands particularly prominent—in large part because of their recognition of the centrality of Jesus for Christian ethics. Our primary loyalty is to Jesus as Lord and Savior, not to traditions about him, but we are happy to draw on the best of those traditions where they are most insightful.

Finally, we want to emphasize to our readers that our voices intertwine throughout the work. David (sometimes using Glen's research) wrote the first draft of this preface and of chapters 4, 10-15, 18-20, and 22-24. Michael Westmoreland-White wrote the first draft of chapter 21. Glen wrote the first draft of all other chapters, except chapter 5, which was jointly drafted. Each of us interacted thoroughly with each other's draft chapters; the final product is genuinely our mutual work. For the sake of clarity, on those few occasions when we wish to offer a personal opinion or story in a chapter, we will identify the individual author by the first name (e.g., "I, David" or "I, Glen"). All future first-person references in that chapter will refer to the same author. Normally, however, we will speak in the coauthor "we" voice. But both of us accept full responsibility for every word you will read here. We invite you along as together we explore Christian ethics as following Jesus.

SECTION I:

The Reign of God
and Christian Character

The chapters in this section establish the biblical framework for our treatment of Christian ethics in this book and begin to apply that framework.

The embodied drama of the reign of God lies at the heart of the biblical record. Jesus came preaching and incarnating the long-promised and desperately awaited kingdom of God. We have chosen to ground our discussion of the Christian moral life right here, in God's reign, as Jesus proclaimed it. Our first chapter offers careful discussion of what we believe is a new insight about Jesus' proclamation of the reign of God and teases out implications for Christian ethics.

This kingdom focus opens up new vistas on a number of themes and issues in Christian ethics. In the remainder of this section, we offer two chapters on the question of character, a critical theme in both classic and contemporary ethics. The virtues of chapter two will be a recurring theme in several of the following chapters. The diagram of holistic character ethics in chapter three will provide some of the unity for the way of doing ethics in subsequent chapters. You will find yourself referring back to that diagram to help you notice and analyze the reasoning on varieties of questions as we proceed. It might look complex at first, but it will become increasingly familiar as its dimensions are illustrated in later chapters. We hope it will help you to develop an increasing awareness of the variables that shape your own ethics as well as the ethics of others you relate to and thus to increase both self-understanding and mutual understanding. Furthermore, clarifying those variables can help you make the self-corrections that seem right and thus grow in wisdom. This is the process of continuous *metanoia*, repentance and growth.

1

THE REIGN OF GOD

—

Jesus began to proclaim, "Repent, for the kingdom has come near."
MATTHEW 4:17

Jesus came to Galilee, proclaiming the good news of God, and saying, "The time is
fulfilled, and the kingdom of God has come near; repent, and believe in the good news."
MARK 1:14-15

He stood up to read, and the scroll of the prophet Isaiah was given to him. He unrolled the
scroll and found the place where it was written:
  "The Spirit of the Lord is upon me,
      because he has anointed me
          to bring good news to the poor.
  He has sent me to proclaim release to the captives
      and recovery of sight to the blind,
          to let the oppressed go free,
      to proclaim the year of the Lord's favor."...
  "Today this scripture has been fulfilled in your hearing."...
"I must proclaim the good news of the kingdom of God to the other cities also; for I was
sent for this purpose."
LUKE 4:16-19, 21, 43

Scholars agree with what any of us can see in the Gospels: Jesus came announcing that the kingdom of God was at hand (Mt 4:12-17; Mk 1:2-3, 14-15; Lk
4:14-21, 43). As Gordon Fee says, "The universal witness of the Synoptic tradition is that the absolutely central theme of Jesus' mission and message was 'the
good news of the kingdom of God'" ("Kingdom of God," 8). But scholars as
well as plain Christians have been puzzled about what Jesus meant when he
spoke of the kingdom. What did Jesus himself understand by the reign of God?
    In seeking to answer that question, New Testament scholars regularly focus

on the question of whether the kingdom is already present or whether it is a future transformation far beyond our present experience. Some scholars have argued that Jesus taught what has been called "realized eschatology," in which the reign of God has come in all of its fullness either in his coming or with the giving of the Holy Spirit. Others push the kingdom off entirely into the future, perhaps locating it at the time of Jesus' second coming to the earth at the end of the age.

The first option fails to account either for numerous New Testament passages about the kingdom that speak of its future consummation or for the continued sinfulness and misery that still characterize human life. Yet the second option fails to account for the celebration of the inbreaking or dawning of God's reign that characterized Jesus' ministry, or for the evidences even now of the impact of the living Christ and the transforming presence of God's Spirit. As Gordon Fee rightly says, what was unique and astonishing about Jesus was his claim that God's reign was "actually in process of realization in his coming." Here was someone who proclaimed that the time of mourning was now at an end; the "bridegroom" had arrived—the kingdom of heaven was "near" or "at hand," in and through himself. Let the party begin (Fee, "Kingdom of God," 8, 10)!

The kingdom, as Fee says, is *"both* a future event *and* a present reality"* ("Kingdom of God," 11). God's reign has been *inaugurated* in Jesus Christ, but its ultimate consummation remains a future event. There is reason both for exultant celebration at the initiation of God's long-promised salvation and for earnest hope for its final consummation, when "mourning and crying and pain will be no more" (Rev 21:4). Those who live their lives based on the conviction that the New Testament story is truthful, then, will understand themselves as living in the time between the times—the eon (of uncertain duration) between the inauguration and consummation of the reign of God. The preponderance of scholars conclude that *kingdom of God* refers both to the present beginning and to the much bigger dramatic overcoming in the future. Some argue for exclusive emphasis on one or the other end of the polarity, and there are different ways of putting the two ends together (see, e.g., the sevenfold typology in N. T. Wright, *Jesus and the Victory of God*, 208).

But we want to ask another question. We want to ask not only about the timing of the kingdom but about the characteristics, the marks, of the kingdom. Jesus said no one knows when the kingdom will come in the full, future sense (Mt 24:36; Mk 13:32); the point, he said, is not to know the timing, but to be ready for it (Mt 7:21-27; 22:4-15; 24:42—25:13; Mk 13:32-37; Lk 12:35-48). If we focus our attention on *when the kingdom comes*, and not on *what its characteristics are*, we neglect the practices that prepare for it. The result is academic debate or fatalistic speculation rather than faithful participation. *What its characteristics are* is crucial for Christian ethics, for Christian discipleship, for

Christian living and for the response of faith(fulness).

New Testament scholars Bruce Chilton and J. I. H. McDonald show that the kingdom of God is not about what God does while humans stand by passively; nor is it about our effort to build the kingdom while God passively watches. The kingdom of God is *performative:* it is God's performance in which we actively participate. For example, the parable of the seed growing secretly in Mark 4:26-29 reads like a commentary on Isaiah 28:23-29: the kingdom of God is like a man sowing seed, which grows while he sleeps; then the earth produces its harvest and he immediately puts in the sickle and harvests it (see Chilton and McDonald, *Jesus and the Ethics,* 19-20).

> At one end is the divine performance of the kingdom, an inceptive reality which attracts hope. At the other end is human performance, an enacted response which itself elicits action. Hopeful action and enacted hope characterize the parable as a whole, at each point in what is depicted. . . . The parable never concerns merely promise alone or action alone. Indeed, the creative interface between the two is of the essence of the Kingdom which is presented. . . . Just this aspect has long been recognized in research on the parables. In the parables of the treasure in the field and of the pearl, for example, an overwhelming discovery galvanizes the discoverers into unaccustomed action. The joyful news of the Kingdom effects joy in the discoverer, and he acts accordingly. . . .
>
> To read the parables is itself an acknowledgment that human action might be implicated in God's Kingdom; to believe them is actually to undertake appropriate action, the parabolic action of the Kingdom, in the present. Because the Kingdom is of a God whose claims are absolute, it necessarily addresses itself to people as a cognitive and an ethical challenge at one and the same time. (Chilton and McDonald, *Jesus and the Ethics,* 24, 31)

So Chilton and McDonald describe "the praxis of the kingdom": the reversal of worldly values and a new lifestyle of service, servanthood and humility; receiving the yoke of the kingdom in childlike fashion; and sacrificing human reliance on worldly support-systems. The one who enters the kingdom is healed from blindness and follows Jesus' way with faith-perception, seeking justice and surrendering false values such as wealth, status-seeking and power. "The focus of the new obedience is found in the twin commandment to love" (Chilton and McDonald, *Jesus and the Ethics,* 53, 73, 86-87, 91-92).

Jesus' koinonia (fellowship and service) "encompassed 'tax collectors and sinners' within its table fellowship" (Mk 2:15). That practice of including outcasts, "totally ignoring the strictly drawn conventions of religiosity, represented a theme of Jesus' ministry which became an issue in society" (Chilton and McDonald, *Jesus and the Ethics,* 96). Love to enemy as a strategy of the kingdom (Mt 5:44-48) "is much more than a general expression of goodwill towards humanity." It "presupposes a social context of the faith-community encountering opposition, even persecution in society," and is "characterized . . . not by exclusiveness or defensiveness but by an openness to others that, indeed, reflects the openness of God to his children." Therefore, the New Testament community "renounces retaliation in kind when violence is offered: the strategy of the Kingdom is always to 'do good to those who hate you' (Lk 6:27; cf. Rom 13:1; I Pet 2:15). In the context of the disciple-community around Jesus, this is tantamount to the rejection of the Zealot option" (Chilton and McDonald, *Jesus and the Ethics,* 102-3).

This ethical praxis is our way of participating in the kingdom. But we want to ask further about the character of God's action in bringing the kingdom. What did it mean to Jesus' hearers in the first century?

Curiously, the term "kingdom of God" was seldom used in the literature that has survived from the first century, except for the New Testament. Hence it is not easy to establish its meaning for people in Jesus' day. Surely Jesus was using a term that would have made sense to his hearers in first-century Palestine. Yet "in none of the kingdom material collected by J. Jeremias from the Apocrypha and Pseudepigrapha . . . is the kingdom announced" (Chilton, *God in Strength,* 277n).

Chilton wrote *Pure Kingdom: Jesus' Vision of God* in order to clarify the meaning of the kingdom. He surveys references to the kingdom in the literature of Judaism in the two centuries before and after Jesus, and concludes: "The language of the kingdom was obviously varied in early Judaism. There were several distinctive usages of the concept," and Jesus' understanding of the kingdom cannot be identified with any of them (*Pure Kingdom,* 30). So Chilton then decides to turn to the Psalms in order to seek an answer. He argues that five themes are important in relation to the theme of God as king in the Psalms: eschatology, transcendence, judgment, purity and radiance (*Pure Kingdom,* 32-41.) He then seeks to describe Jesus' mission and message as patterned after these five themes. But the pattern does not fit well, and even after the themes are modified in order to fit, the result seems surprisingly abstract and tangential to Jesus' teachings and actions.

We argue that seven clues point us not to the Psalms but to Isaiah as the place to look for the background of Jesus' teaching on the kingdom.

The New Testament scholar W. D. Davies has provided the first clue. Jesus' proclamation of the kingdom of God "is to be understood, as is made evident in the rest of the NT, in the light of the expectations expressed in the OT, and in Judaism, that, at some future date, God would act for the salvation of his people. . . . The ethical aspirations of the OT and Judaism, the Law and the Prophets, are not annulled; they are fulfilled (Mt. 5:17-18). This means that Jesus consciously accepted the ethical tradition of his people. . . . E.g., it has been possible to claim that in the figure of the Suffering Servant (Isaiah 53)

Jesus could have found the most profound emphases of his ethical teaching" (Davies, *Setting of the Sermon on the Mount*, 167-68). Contrary to some who seek to see Jesus more in a Hellenistic context, we believe it necessary to pay attention to the Jewish context (well put by Spohn, *Go and Do Likewise*, 20-23). This suggests we look especially for Old Testament passages that proclaim God's act for the salvation or deliverance of his people, perhaps especially in the prophet Isaiah.

A second clue is that many passages in Isaiah speak of the kingship or sovereignty of God, the coming reign of God, in the sense of God's delivering the oppressed and bringing salvation. And that is what we see in Jesus' proclamation of the kingdom: delivering the oppressed and bringing salvation.

A third clue is that we do not find Jesus citing the Qumran literature or the rabbis as authorities, but mostly the prophet Isaiah and the Psalms, and, to a lesser degree, Deuteronomy and Genesis (see, for example, the Scripture index in the back of a Nestlé edition of the Greek New Testament). The Gospel of Mark, which is the earliest Gospel, cites and alludes to Isaiah more than any other book, and more than all the other Old Testament prophets combined. In Mark, Isaiah is the only prophet named (Mk 1:2; 7:6), and "Isaiah shares many common motifs with Mark; a Spirit-filled figure who brings a new message of deliverance to an Israel that suffers from spiritual blindness and deafness" (Watts, *Isaiah's New Exodus*, 26-28, 60).

A fourth clue comes from the Dead Sea Scrolls, our most abundant source of literature from the period when Jesus lived. These scrolls show that Isaiah was much in use and well known in Jesus' time—more so than any other biblical book. The list of scrolls in Martínez's edition includes eighteen fragments from the prophet Isaiah. The index of biblical quotations in Dupont-Sommers's edition of Qumran writings has one reference to Genesis, two to Exodus, eleven to Deuteronomy, four to Psalms, one to Jeremiah, three to Ezekiel and fourteen to Isaiah (Dupont-Sommers, *The Essene Writings from Qumran*, 422-24). The actual number of references to Isaiah is in fact far more.

Fifth, in the specific New Testament passages where Jesus announced the kingdom of God, he seems to have used terms that come from Isaiah. In spite of Chilton's recent focus on the Psalms, his earlier study concluded that in each of the passages "which substantively record Jesus' announcement of the kingdom of God," Jesus referred to the prophet Isaiah in Aramaic translation. "In each case, . . . Isaiah has been seen to be of especial importance as preserving material which seems to have been a formative influence on the thought and language of [Jesus'] announcements" (Chilton, *God in Strength*, 277; see also Chilton, *Galilean Rabbi*, 129-30, 277). The New Testament passages are Matthew 8:11; Mark 1:15; 9:1; Luke 4:18, 19, 21; and 16:16. Chilton finds words and phrases in Jesus' kingdom proclamations that most likely come from

Isaiah 24:23; 25:6; 31:6; 40:10; 41:8-9; 42:1; 43:5, 10; 45:6; 49:12; 51:7-8; 53:1; 59:19; 60:20-22; and 61:1.

In Jesus' day, the use of Hebrew was something like the use of Latin in the Catholic church a half-century ago. It was no longer generally understood by the people. The people spoke Aramaic. Therefore, Jesus taught in Aramaic. In worship services a translator, called a meturgeman, would paraphrase the Hebrew Scripture passage into the language of the people. He did not give a literal translation but paraphrased it so that it would make the most sense to the hearers—something like Eugene Peterson's lovely paraphrase of the Bible, *The Message*. Out of this practice a written version in Aramaic finally came together in the fourth century. It contains paraphrases that were used in Jesus' day mixed with later material from the following three centuries. These documents are called the Targums.

What is intriguing is that in the Isaiah Targum four passages speak directly of "the kingdom of God," and one speaks of "the kingdom of the Messiah." Here may be an important sixth clue to what Jesus' contemporaries would likely have understood by the Aramaic phrase meaning "the kingdom of God." We cannot be sure which parts accurately reflect the words used in Jesus' time, although scholars like Chilton do make some likely assessments (*Galilean Rabbi*, 57-61 et passim; *Isaiah Targum*, xxiv et passim). Hence we must consider this an *additional* clue, an additional piece of intriguing evidence, that strengthens the indicators already seen in the previous clues. It does indicate the context where the rabbis thought they could use the phrase "the kingdom of God" as a fitting paraphrase. The fact that it is in the Aramaic version of Isaiah that we find "the kingdom of God" is highly suggestive, particularly in light of the rarity of the phrase in other first-century literature.

The Targum for Isaiah 24:23 paraphrases "The LORD of hosts will reign on Mount Zion" as "*The kingdom* of the LORD of hosts will be revealed on the Mount of Zion." Isaiah 31:4 says, "The LORD of hosts will come down to fight upon Mount Zion," and the Aramaic paraphrases this as "*The kingdom* of the LORD of hosts will be revealed to settle upon Mount Zion." Isaiah 40:9 says, "Here is your God," and the Targum says, "*The kingdom* of your God is revealed." Isaiah 52:7 says, "Your God reigns," and the Aramaic paraphrase says, "*The kingdom* of your God is revealed." Isaiah 53:10 says, "shall see *the kingdom of their Messiah*." This latter passage is well known as a salvation text: the suffering of God's servant is an offering for sin by which the servant's offspring will prosper and be made righteous. Chilton's study indicates that the Targums of chapters 24, 52 and 53 likely come from the early Tannaitic period, during or close to Jesus' time, and that chapters 31 and 40 are mixed—partly early and partly later (Chilton, *Isaiah Targum*, xxiv and notes on the particular passages).

What seems clear is that all these passages announce that God is being revealed, being disclosed before our very eyes. But Jewish piety so highly revered the revelation of the Lord that the Targum did not want to say directly, "God is revealed." Instead it said, "The kingdom of God is revealed." This means that the kingdom of God was understood as referring to the self-revelation of God and God's dynamic reign. It was not a place but an action. Furthermore, all five of the kingdom passages announce God's intervention *to deliver or save* us. And they praise God or express great joy that God is revealed as saving us. Chilton observes, "Especially in the Targum of Isaiah, the language of the kingdom is employed to render passages that in the Hebrew original speak of God intervening actively on behalf of his people. . . . The emphasis is on the dynamic, personal presence of God—not on the nature of God in itself, but on his saving, normally future activity" (*Pure Kingdom*, 11-12; Chilton and Evans, *Studying the Historical Jesus*, 268).

The seventh clue will come from the fruitfulness of Isaiah as background for Jesus' teaching and actions. We shall see this in many of the following chapters.

The Seven Marks of God's Reign

So we turn to the prophet Isaiah to ask about the characteristics of the deliverance that Isaiah prophesied. We ask, which passages in Isaiah rejoice that God will reign to deliver his people? Seventeen passages do: Isaiah 9:1-7; 11; 24:14—25:12; 26; 31:1—32:20; 33; 35; 40:1-11; 42:1—44:8; 49; 51:1—52:12; 52:13—53:12; 54; 56; 60; 61—62. These passages of God's deliverance describe what the kingdom of God means in Isaiah—the biblical book to which Jesus referred when he proclaimed the kingdom. So the next logical question is, do some characteristics of God's reign recur consistently in these passages; are there some themes that clarify the content of God's kingdom?

> *Deliverance* or *salvation* occurs in all seventeen deliverance passages in Isaiah; *righteousness/justice* occurs in sixteen of the passages; *peace* in fourteen; *joy* in twelve; *God's presence as Spirit or Light* in nine (and God's dynamic presence is implied in all seventeen). These five characteristics of the reign of God are remarkably consistent in the deliverance passages. We may conclude that these are characteristics of God's delivering action as described in Isaiah. In addition, *healing* occurs in seven passages. It may be seen as a mark in its own right, or as part of the themes of peace and restoration of outcasts to community, since major infirmities caused people to be treated as outcasts. *Return from exile* occurs in nine passages. Therefore, these also may be key ingredients in the reign of God as prophesied by Isaiah.

For one example, let us look at Isaiah 9:2-7:

> The people who walked in darkness
>   have seen a great *light*;
> those who lived in a land of deep darkness—
>   on them *light* has shined.
> You have multiplied the nation,
>   you have increased its *joy*;
> they *rejoice* before you
>   as with *joy* at the harvest,
>   as people *exult* when dividing plunder.
> For the yoke of their burden,
>   and the bar across their shoulders,
>   the rod of their oppressor,
>   you have broken as on the day of Midian. [deliverance]
> For all the boots of the tramping warriors
>   and all the garments rolled in blood
>   shall be burned as fuel for the fire. [peace]
> For a child has been born for us,
>   a son given to us;
> authority rests upon his shoulders,
>   and he is named
> Wonderful Counselor, Mighty God,
>   Everlasting Father, Prince of *Peace*.
> His authority shall grow continually
>   and there shall be endless *peace*
> for the throne of David and his *kingdom*.
>   He will establish and uphold it
> with *justice* and with *righteousness*
>   from this time onward and forevermore.
> The zeal of the LORD of hosts will do this.

The five major themes are clearly emphasized:
1. "Light," twice in verse 2, is often the symbol of God's presence in these passages.
2. "Joy," "rejoice" and "exult" in verse 3.
3. God's deliverance from oppression in verse 4; deliverance and dynamic presence in "Mighty God, Everlasting Father" and "The zeal of the LORD of hosts will do this" in verses 6-7.
4. Peace in verse 5: the instruments of war will be burned; "Prince of Peace" in 6; "there shall be endless peace" in 7.
5. "Justice and righteousness" in verse 7.

All of these characteristics mark the reign or kingdom of God, which itself is suggested in "authority rests upon his shoulders" in verse 6, and "his authority" and "his kingdom" in verse 7.

Now consider Isaiah 60:17-19:

> I will appoint *Peace* as your overseer
>   and *Righteousness* as your taskmaster.
> *Violence* shall no more be heard in your land,
>   devastation or destruction within your borders;
> you shall call your walls *Salvation*,
>   and your gates *Praise*.
> The sun shall no longer be
>   your light by day,
> nor for brightness shall the moon
>   give light to you by night,
> but the LORD will be your everlasting *light*,
>   and your God will be your glory.

For the third example, consider Isaiah 35:5-6 and 8-10:

> Then the eyes of the blind shall be opened,
>   and the ears of the deaf unstopped;
> then the lame shall leap like a deer,
>   and the tongue of the speechless sing for joy.
> For waters shall break forth in the wilderness,
>   and streams in the desert;
> the burning sand shall become a pool,
>   and the thirsty ground springs of water. . . .
> A highway shall be there,
>   and it shall be called the Holy Way;
> the unclean shall not travel on it,
>   but it shall be for God's people;
> no traveler, not even fools, shall go astray. . . .
> And the ransomed of the LORD shall return,
>   and come to Zion with singing;
> everlasting joy shall be upon their heads;
>   they shall obtain joy and gladness,
>   and sorrow and sighing shall flee away.

Here we see the themes of healing the blind and lame, return from exile, deliverance (ransom) and joy. These themes recur throughout Isaiah. In this book we aim to show that Jesus saw these characteristics as essential to the kingdom of God and thus central to his own ministry—and the work of all who would be his followers. We shall see that paying attention to Isaiah, whom Jesus so often cites, helps us notice what Jesus proclaims. Jesus himself confirms these as marks of God's reign.

Striking further confirmation can be found in Romans 14:17. It is highly unusual for Paul to use the phrase "kingdom of God." It is not his usual vocabulary. Here he is probably reporting the early Christian understanding that goes back to Jesus. It speaks of the very marks of the kingdom that we have seen in Isaiah. Paul has been opposing judgmentalism in arguments about what food we are allowed to eat (Rom 14:1-16). In verse 17 he declares: "The kingdom of God does not mean [judgmentalism about] food and drink, but *righteousness and peace and joy in the Holy Spirit*" (author's trans.). Of course, Paul's theology deserves much more extensive discussion. But in brief, we can say that in Paul's theology *righteousness* has to do with justice, *peace* is reconciliation both among people and with God, our *joy* is in God's salvation, and *the Holy Spirit* is God's presence. Paul is here saying just what we have found in the kingdom of God passages in Isaiah: the marks of God's reign are righteousness, peace, joy in God's salvation and the presence of God.

Jesus, the Kingdom and the Sermon on the Mount

Our argument thus far has been that Jesus came announcing the reign of God; that the prophet Isaiah—to whom Jesus frequently referred—offers a rich picture of the coming reign of God as a state of affairs characterized by God's salvation and deliverance, God's presence, justice and peace, and great joy.

Students of the Hebrew Scriptures will easily recognize the broader contours of the picture we are painting here. The Old Testament is characterized by the affirmation of God's sovereign kingship. God is sovereign as Creator and Sustainer of the earth and all that dwell therein; as Judge; as Redeemer of Israel; and in relation to all nations and peoples.

Yet the created turned against their Creator. The earth reels under the consequences of human rebellion. Human life is characterized by violence, injustice, unrighteousness and misery. Israel itself was shattered by cataclysmic wars, most notably the war with Babylon that destroyed Jerusalem and its temple, displaced the royal family and ended in the exile of her leading citizens, forcing Israel into a seemingly endless period of occupation at the hands of pagan armies—in Jesus' time, the Roman legions.

Thus the later Prophets are redolent with a deep yearning for *salvation*, in the deepest and most holistic sense of that word. In Isaiah, it is based on God's forgiveness, and it is eternal. It includes deliverance from oppression and injustice, from guilt and death, from war and slavery and imprisonment and exile. It includes peace and justice and forgiveness. The promise is that salvation is coming—for Israel and ultimately for the world, for societies, for families and for individuals. This is where the hope of a Messiah is located in the Hebrew Scriptures. The Old Testament hope of salvation is not merely for an eternal salvation in which our disembodied souls are snatched from this vale of tears. Nor is it merely for physical justice while fellowship with the presence of God's Holy Spirit is ignored. To the extent that Christians adopt any kind of body/soul, earth/heaven dualism we simply do not understand the message of Scripture—or of Jesus. God's salvation is the kingdom of God, and it means that—at last—God has acted to deliver humanity and now reigns over all of life, and is present to and with us, and will be in the future. The New Testament will bring a greater emphasis on eternal life, but it will not negate the holistic message of deliverance. The only possible response to this good news is great joy!

How could Jesus claim that in himself the reign of God had come, and yet evil had not yet been eradicated? He taught that we do not have the whole mustard bush, but we do have mustard seeds (Mk 4:30-32; Mt 13:31-32; Lk 13:18-19). The kingdom had come in God's presence through Jesus, in the justice of feeding the hungry, welcoming the stranger, visiting the sick, paying attention to the children (Mt 19:14) and forgiving debts (Mt 18:23-35); in the peacemaking of forgiveness and of welcoming the tax collectors, harlots and eunuchs (Mt 19:12; cf. Is 56:4), and proclaiming the gospel throughout the whole world as a testimony to the nations (Mt 24:14); in healing the blind, lame and demon-possessed (Mt 12:28); in the joy of the presence of the bridegroom (Mt 13:34; 25:1-13). When the disciples of John the Baptist asked Jesus whether he was the one who was to come, Jesus had just been healing some people. He replied: "Go and tell John what you have seen and heard: the blind receive their sight, the lame walk, the lepers are cleansed, the deaf hear, the dead are raised, the poor have good news brought to them. And blessed is anyone who takes no offense at me" (Lk 7:18-28). If we have in mind the marks of the kingdom as God's deliverance, presence, justice, peace, healing and joy, we recognize the mustard seeds with those characteristics. Fee says: "The presence of the kingdom in Jesus meant that the kingdom of God was of a radically different order from people's expectations. It was not "the overthrow of the hated Roman Empire" (Fee, "Kingdom of God," 11). It was present in Jesus as he performed the practices of the kingdom that Isaiah prophesied. "What has been 'fulfilled,' according to Jesus, was that *in his own ministry* the time of God's favor toward 'the poor' had come. In his healing the sick, casting out of demons, and eating with sinners—and thereby showing them God's unlimited mercy—the people were to understand that God's great eschatological day had finally dawned" (Fee, "Kingdom of God," 10).

This dialectical mustard seed/mustard bush understanding of the kingdom is matched by a corresponding ethic of joyful trust linked to sacrificial effort. On the one hand, Jesus taught that, as Fee says, "the kingdom was like seed growing quietly (Mk 4:26-29), like a minuscule mustard seed, whose beginnings were so small and insignificant that nothing could be expected of it, but whose final end—inherent in the seed and therefore inevitable—would be an herb of such dimensions that birds could rest in its branches" ("Kingdom of God," 12). The good news comes first—the kingdom has dawned in Jesus, and its final triumph is inevitable.

Yet, on the other hand, coworkers are needed. A Christian is (or should be) defined as one who humbles himself or herself and chooses to enter into discipleship, to follow Jesus' path, to build his or her life upon his teachings and his practices even at great cost, to pass those teachings and practices on to others, and thus to enjoy the unspeakable privilege of participating in the advance of God's reign. Jesus inaugurates the long-promised kingdom and thus offers holistic deliverance to the sick, the poor, the guilty and the rejected; incarnates and demands justice and righteousness; practices and teaches the way of peacemaking; and both experiences and imparts joy. Meanwhile, in his ministry and then through his living Spirit, Jesus offers the very presence of God. Disciples of Jesus Christ both taste the joy of kingdom living and are used by Jesus to advance the kingdom until he comes again. As Murray Dempster puts it, with reference to the theology of Luke:

> Luke made it clear in his prologue in the Acts that because of the transference of the Spirit the church continued to do and teach those things which Jesus began to do and teach (Acts 1:1). What needs to be underscored is that the message of the kingdom of God was the focal point of all those things that Jesus began to do and teach. ("Crossing Borders," 23; see also 149)

The same point is made in a somewhat different way in the Gospel of Matthew. At the end of that Gospel, Jesus gave his followers what we now call the Great Commission: "Go therefore and make disciples of all nations, baptizing them in the name of the Father and of the Son and of the Holy Spirit, and teaching them to obey everything that I have commanded you. And remember, I am with you always, to the end of the age" (Mt 28:19-20).

Christ-followers are here commissioned to "make disciples," which consists of introducing people to the triune God and then training them to practice the teachings of Jesus. In this introduction to Christian ethics we have chosen to focus on the Sermon on the Mount because the way of discipleship and the commands of Jesus are most explicitly taught in this Sermon. The way we are to make disciples of all peoples is to teach them the practices taught mostly in the Sermon on the Mount (Luz, *Matthew 1—7*, 214). And the Sermon on the Mount is a primer for kingdom ethics. The reign of God is mentioned explicitly nine times in the Sermon. Each of the Beatitudes announces a blessing of participation in the kingdom of God. The Lord's Prayer prays for the kingdom to come. Each of the main teachings in the Sermon on the Mount is actually a pointer to the way of deliverance that we are given when the kingdom breaks into our midst.

It is no coincidence that the Sermon on the Mount echoes throughout the Gospel of Luke, as well as in Paul's letters and the rest of the New Testament (Davies, *Setting of the Sermon*). In the first three centuries of the church, no other biblical passage was referred to as often (Kissinger, *Sermon on the Mount*, 6). There is no question that it was understood as the charter document for Christian living. Church leaders constantly quoted it when offering moral exhortation.

But today the Sermon on the Mount clearly does not occupy that central role except in a small number of Christian traditions. And, strangely, the way of Jesus as set forth in the Sermon on the Mount has been neglected in Christian ethics.

We believe that Jesus offered not hard sayings or high ideals but concrete ways to practice God's will and be delivered from the bondage of sin. In other words, he taught his followers how to participate in God's reign. He taught what the kingdom is like, what its characteristics are, and therefore what kinds of practices are done by those who participate in it and are ready for it. We believe that this approach to Christian ethics is most faithful to the biblical witness about what God in Christ intends to do in us and in the world.

In the Gospel of John, 14:26 and 15:26, Jesus promises that the Father will send the Holy Spirit in Jesus' name, and the Holy Spirit "will bring to your remembrance all that I have said to you," and "He will bear witness to me" (RSV). This means that we need to test what we believe is the guidance of the Spirit or other spirits in our experience by asking how well it corresponds with what Jesus has taught. We hope this book helps significantly in that testing process. Trusting these words, we are confident that the Holy Spirit will surely teach us the meaning of the Sermon on the Mount as we consider it carefully in chapters to come.

2

VIRTUES OF KINGDOM PEOPLE

Blessed are the poor in spirit, for theirs is the kingdom of heaven.

Blessed are those who mourn, for they will be comforted.

Blessed are those of a humbled spirit, for they will inherit the earth.

Blessed are those who hunger and thirst for righteousness, for they will be filled.

MATTHEW 5:3-6 AUTHOR'S TRANSLATION

Many are urging Christian ethics to shift its focus much more toward virtues and the formation of character, and away from rules and principles. They argue that it is not enough to teach rules and principles about right and wrong; we need to nurture the kind of character and virtues that lead people actually to do the right and avoid the wrong. Deeds are right or wrong; persons are virtuous or not virtuous.

> The rising popularity of virtue ethics . . . in popular culture . . . is evident in the success of William Bennett's works *The Book of Virtues* and *The Moral Compass* and in Hillary Rodham Clinton's *It Takes a Village*. This attention to the virtues is also reflected in the church: a recent catalog for a Christian book club devoted an entire page to Christian books on the virtues. . . . This turn to questions of virtue and character represents the recognition of failure in our ethical traditions and of the breaking down of morality in our culture. (Wilson, *Gospel Virtues*, 18)

Virtues are defined as qualities of a person that make that person a good person in community, and that contribute to the good of the community, or to the good that humans are designed for. They are qualities of character. For example, a good person has integrity and seeks justice. This general definition will become clearer when we see some examples, and we will explain the argument for an ethics of character and virtue further in the next chapter.

For now, we want to focus on a question that virtue ethicists are often strangely ambivalent or indefinite about: which virtues should Christians nurture? We begin our focus here because it is where Jesus begins in Matthew 5:3-12, the introductory verses of the Sermon on the Mount. These ten verses are called "the Beatitudes," because they each begin with "Blessed are you." They announce the *joys* of participation in the reign of God. We believe that the virtues taught by Jesus in the Beatitudes can guide us as to which virtues to emphasize.

The Beatitudes: The Idealistic Interpretation

Many have interpreted the Beatitudes idealistically, saying they are high ideals that Jesus is urging us to live up to: if only we would mourn, be pure in heart, be peacemakers and so on, then we would be rewarded. This is the ethics of *idealism*: "if only people would act according to these ideals, then good things would happen." Similarly, some say the Beatitudes are the entrance requirements for the kingdom of God: If we mourn, are pure in heart and are peacemakers—if we are virtuous—then we can enter the kingdom of God.

We now know from long historical experience with this "high ideals" interpretation that it creates serious problems:

It focuses attention on our own good works, rather than on God's grace. It makes the gospel into works-righteousness.

It causes feelings of guilt and resistance. So the more we emphasize these teachings as ideals to live up to, the guiltier we feel. Therefore, we ignore or evade Jesus' teachings. No wonder the Beatitudes and the Sermon on the Mount are so seldom taught, preached or lived.

If we think we do live up to these ideals, we fall into self-righteousness. We thank God that we are not like other people, who are not as virtuous as we are (cf. Lk 18:9-14). Our moralistic arrogance makes us hard to live with.

We understand them as a set of ideals floating above our heads, imposing an ethic on us from above us that does not fit our real struggles. They are foreign to our nature, like a suit of armor that does not fit our body, or a job that does not fit our gifts and interests. We try to make our reality fit the ideals, but it simply does not fit. This is a *heteronomous ethic,* imposed on us by an outside authority, and not fitting our nature or our real situation in history (Bonhoeffer, *Ethics,* 191-95).

This "high ideals" interpretation does not fit what Jesus in fact teaches. It imposes a foreign philosophy of idealism on the real Jewish Jesus who identifies with the realistic tradition of the Hebrew prophets, not the tradition of Greek idealism.

A Grace-Based Prophetic Interpretation

Biblical scholar Robert Guelich championed a grace-based and prophetic interpretation of the Beatitudes that pays special attention to Isaiah 61. This reflects more accurately Jesus' teaching in his own Jewish context as presented in the Gospel of Matthew. It is supported by strong evidence, and it rescues us from a sad history of interpreting Jesus' teachings as idealistic and then ignoring them in real life (Guelich, *Sermon on the Mount*, 63-87, 97-103, 109-11).

Guelich argued that the Beatitudes should be interpreted not as *wisdom teachings* but as *prophetic teachings*. Wisdom teachings emphasize human action that is wise because it fits God's way of ordering the world and therefore gets us good results. Prophetic (or eschatological) teachings emphasize God's action that delivers (rescues, frees, releases) us from mourning into rejoicing.

Is Jesus saying, "Happy are those who mourn, *because mourning makes them virtuous* and so they will get the reward that virtuous people deserve"? Or is he saying, "Congratulations to those who mourn, *because God is gracious and God is acting to deliver us* from our sorrows"?

The tradition of ideals or wisdom (1) speaks to people who are not what the ideals urge, and (2) promises them that if they will live by the ideals they will get the rewards of well-being and success. The Beatitudes are not like that. (1) They speak to disciples who already are being made participants in the presence of the Holy Spirit through Jesus Christ—we already know at least a taste of the experience of mourning, mercy, peacemaking and so on. And (2) they do not promise distant well-being and success; they congratulate disciples because God is already acting to deliver them. They are based not on the perfection of the disciples but on the coming of God's grace, already experienced in Jesus, at least in mustard-seed size (Mt 13:31; 17:20; Mk 4:31; Lk 13:19).

One clue is the way that several of the Beatitudes are based on Isaiah 61—the passage that Jesus read when he gave his inaugural sermon in Luke 4:18:

> The Spirit of the Lord is upon me
>   because he has anointed me;
> He has sent me to announce good news to the poor,
>   to proclaim release for prisoners
>   and recovery of sight for the blind;
> to let the broken victims go free,
>   to proclaim the year of the Lord's favour. (NEB)

Is this a passage about human effort to live up to high ideals? Is it urging us to become poor, prisoners, blind and victims so that God will reward us? Or is it a passage of celebration because God is acting graciously to deliver us from our poverty and captivity into God's reign of deliverance, justice and joy?

Look how the Beatitudes echo this prophetic passage of deliverance.

Table 2.1. The Beatitudes echo Isaiah 61

Isaiah 61		Matthew 5	
61:1, 2	good news to the oppressed ... the year of the LORD's favor	5:3	Blessed are the poor in spirit, for theirs is the kingdom of heaven.
61:1, 2	to bind up the brokenhearted ... to comfort all who mourn	5:4	Blessed are those who mourn, for they shall be comforted.
61:7	They will inherit a double portion in their land.	5:5	Blessed are the humble, for they shall inherit the earth.
61:3	They will be called oaks of righteousness.	5:6	Blessed are those who hunger and thirst for righteousness.
61:11	So the LORD God will cause righteousness and praise to spring up before all the nations.	5:10	Blessed are those who have been persecuted for ... righteousness, for theirs is the kingdom of heaven.

This confirms that the prophet Isaiah provides the context for Jesus' proclamation of the coming of the kingdom as deliverance. In Jesus' time, Isaiah 61 was understood as a prophetic and messianic passage of deliverance by God's Spirit. Dead Sea Scroll 4Q521 from the Qumran community illustrates this:

> 1 [for the heav]ens and the earth will listen to his Messiah, 2 [and all] that is in them will not turn away from the holy precepts. . . . 5 For the LORD will observe the devout, and call the just by name, 6 and upon the poor he will place his Spirit, and the faithful he will renew with his strength. 7 For he will honour the devout upon the throne of eternal royalty, 8 freeing prisoners, giving sight to the blind, straightening out the twisted. . . . 11 and the LORD will perform marvelous acts such as have not existed, just as he sa[id], 12 for he will heal the badly wounded and will make the dead live, he will proclaim good news to the meek [or poor], 13 give lavishly [to the need]y, lead the exiled and enrich the hungry.

Similarly, the Beatitudes concerning the merciful, the pure in heart and the peacemakers echo psalms that praise God's works of deliverance.

The Beatitudes are not about high ideals, but about God's gracious deliverance and our joyous participation. We believe that people have put too much emphasis on the virtues (poverty of spirit, purity of heart, peacemaking and so on), and not enough emphasis on what Jesus was emphasizing—God's presence, God's active deliverance, God's giving us a share in that deliverance and so blessedness and joy.

"Participative grace" is so important for understanding Jesus' good news and his way—and for understanding our approach in this book—that we want to pause here and set it out clearly. The theme of Isaiah 61 is grace, and echoes of this theme appear in the Beatitudes, in Jesus' inaugural sermon in Luke 4:16-22 and elsewhere in the Gospels. Grace is God's deliverance, his transforming initiative and not our human-effort, high-ideal, hard-striving achievement. It is a gift from God that we do not deserve; it is not self-righteousness that we achieve by our own good works. The New English Bible translates Luke 4:22 as "they were surprised that words of such *grace* should fall from his lips," and NRSV says they "were amazed at the *gracious* words that came from his mouth." The Greek has "words of grace" *(logois tēs charitos)*. God is bringing us deliverance; God is delivering grace.

Some have erroneously taken grace to imply passivity, disempowerment of those who receive God's grace: if God is giving grace, it means that we are doing nothing. And if we are doing something, if we are acting in conformity with God's will, it must not be grace. This sets God's grace and our discipleship in opposition, as rivals. Dietrich Bonhoeffer calls this "cheap grace" (*Cost of Discipleship*, 43, 59, 72, 78ff., 184, 191, 197, 206, 225, 238, 248ff., 300). It is grace without repentance, grace without concrete change in our way of relating to others, grace without cost to us. It is "easy believism," which characterizes many who claim to be Christians (Mt 7:15-27). And then people see God's grace and God's presence only in situations that extend beyond our control or where our knowledge does not reach. This moves God out to the periphery of our knowledge and action. Then the more we learn and the more we feel empowered, the less we need God. God becomes "the God of the gaps," the *Deus ex machina*, present only where we have not yet learned how to cope.

Instead, Bonhoeffer insists, Christ is in the center of our lives. When God acts to deliver us, we are thereby empowered, not disempowered. When the Holy Spirit comes into our lives, we are thereby empowered, not rendered powerless. A central theme in Bonhoeffer's writing is *participation* in what God is doing in Christ. Through God's grace in Christ, we become active participants in God's grace, and Christ takes shape in us (Todd, "Participation," 27-35). It is like the cripple by the pool of Bethesda or Bethzatha (Jn 5:2-9): he could not walk until Jesus delivered him; then he was empowered to move, to participate in the deliverance that Jesus brought.

Participation in delivering grace does not mean any kind of random empowerment. Grace is *Christomorphic,* not amorphic; it has a specific shape, a shape revealed in Christ. Its shape is the shape of the kingdom, of the Beatitudes, of the way of Jesus as seen in the New Testament and as grounded in the Old Testament. The shape of grace is Christ taking form in us. We participate by answering Jesus' gracious call: come follow me. This is not cheap grace, nor is it works-righteousness, in which we try to earn our way into the kingdom by our righteous deeds. This grace is a gift of deliverance, given only by God in his only Son, Jesus Christ, fully Lord and fully Savior. It comes through faith in Jesus Christ, worked in our hearts by the Holy Spirit. It is Spirit-led, participative, Christomorphic grace. Throughout this book, we hope to do a faithful job of making its patterns clear in the center of our lives in the twenty-first century. We want to point to the way of participation in Christo-morphic grace.

When Jesus proclaimed this message, Israel had been experiencing God as remote, transcendent or distant for about two centuries. During that time,' there were fewer prophets. Many of the writings of the period between the time of the prophets and the time of Jesus (such as the books of Esther, Tobit, Esdras and Maccabees) had less sense of God's active presence and instead emphasized angels, wisdom, magic and human cunning. Israel was experiencing moral corruption and foreign occupation, injustice and a lack of peace.

Now once again a prophet appeared who spoke for God—John the Baptist. Jesus had John baptize him, and immediately the heavens were opened. He saw the Spirit of God, which had seemed so absent, "descending like a dove and alighting on him. And a voice from heaven said, 'This is my son, the Be-loved, with whom I am well pleased,'" words that echo Isaiah 42:1 and Psalm 2:7. And from that moment on, Jesus was led by the Holy Spirit (Mt 3:16—4:1). Soon he began proclaiming that the kingdom of God was at hand!

Here in the Sermon on the Mount, Jesus was saying that we are blessed be-cause we are experiencing God's reign in our midst and will experience it yet more in the future reign. Each Beatitude begins with the joy, the happiness, the blessedness, of the good news of participation in God's gracious deliverance. And each Beatitude ends by pointing to the reality of God's coming reign: in God's kingdom, those who mourn will be comforted, the humble will inherit the earth, those who hunger for righteousness will be filled, mercy will be shown, people will see God, peacemakers will be called children of God, and the faithful will be members of the kingdom of God. And this experience was already beginning in Jesus.

An ethics of virtue must be subordinated to God's grace and deliverance, justice and righteousness, peace and presence. Virtues are only a part of the larger drama predicted in passages like Isaiah 61. They are a way of participating in that gracious deliverance.

Which Virtues?

Once we see the virtues that Jesus names in Matthew 5:3-12 as marks of the discipleship that participates in the larger drama of the reign of God, then we can see their unity more clearly. Let us examine the Beatitudes, one by one, seeking precision and accuracy in understanding and giving special attention to Jesus' references to the Hebrew Scriptures. We agree with Richard Hays: ethical positions should be "argued on the basis of deep exegetical engagement with the New Testament documents," rather than reading texts casually or superficially (*Moral Vision of the New Testament*, 291; cf. Hays chaps. 11-13).

The first Beatitude. Matthew 5:3 says, "Blessed are the poor in spirit, for theirs is the kingdom of heaven." Luke 6:20 says "Blessed are you who are poor; for yours is the kingdom of God." Which did Jesus teach? Poor or poor in spirit?

Our answer is both. Matthew and Luke are translating into Greek what Jesus quoted from Isaiah 61:1 in the Hebrew Bible. The Hebrew word combines both meanings—economically poor and spiritually humble. The Brown, Driver and Briggs *Lexicon* (776) gives the following meanings of the Hebrew word: poor, oppressed by the rich and powerful, powerless, needy, humble, lowly, pious. In one context it will have more of one meaning than another, but it carries this combination of connotations.

Jesus teaches that the spiritually humble, those who pray humbly without making any claims of being better than others, are the ones who participate in God's reign. The focus of the one who is poor in spirit is not on his or her own humility and virtue, but on God's grace and compassion. God says: "I dwell . . . with those who are contrite and humble in spirit, to revive the spirit of the humble and to revive the heart of the contrite," and, "This is the one to whom I will look, to the humble and contrite in spirit, who trembles at my word" (Is 57:15; 66:2; see Hagner, *Matthew 1—13*, 92).

But those who are really poor in spirit know much better than others just how unvirtuous they really are. Jesus' focus is not on how perfect the poor in spirit are, but on how God is love, how God is present to redeem, and how God will redeem. Humility means calling attention not to how lowly I am but to God's grace (Mt 5:16). It is giving myself over to God, surrendering myself to God.

In the Bible, the poor rely more on God. Just spend some time serving the poor in a homeless shelter and talk with people long enough to get to know them. The poor—as a whole—do have less pride that gets in the way and really do trust more in God.

Yet the key to understanding this is to focus on the character of God. The poor are blessed not because their virtue is perfect, but because God especially does want to rescue the poor. God knows that people who have power often use that power to guard their own privileges and to seek more power. The poor get pushed aside and dominated. If you are poor, just one illness, just one divorce or just one job loss can keep you from paying your bills and can get you evicted and homeless. This very night as I (Glen) write, the neighbor family across the street, with two teenage daughters, has just been evicted because the father lost his job and cannot find another; they are moving to a homeless shelter.

We see how God feels deep compassion for the poor and the outcast when we see how Jesus cared. Jesus was saying that God is working to deliver the poor from the misery and injustice that they experience. We see this in the way that Jesus and the disciples fed the poor, in the way the early church cared for the poor, and in the way some churches care for the poor now.

Jesus fulfilled Isaiah 61:1-2, bringing good news to the poor (Mt 5:3-5; 11:5; Lk 4:16-21; 7:22). He embraced the social and religious outcasts. His presence to them, his inviting them into community, his feeding them, his making them into disciples, was grace-based deliverance. This Beatitude is pointing to the good news that Isaiah's prophetic celebration of God's justice as deliverance of the poor, oppressed, humble, needy, weak and lowly, is happening in Jesus the Messiah and in the community practices of Jesus' followers. Because God is actively delivering the humble and the poor, Jesus' followers can rejoice—because as a community we participate in this deliverance. What greater meaning in life can there be than to participate, even in a little way, like a mustard seed, in the deliverance that God is bringing in Jesus?

Followers of Jesus participate in God's reign by humbling themselves before God, giving themselves over to God, depending on God's deliverance and following God in caring for the poor and oppressed. In a nutshell, *blessed are the humble before God, who cares for the poor and the humble.*

The second Beatitude. Matthew 5:4 says, "Blessed are those who mourn, for they shall be comforted."

Mourning, like *poor in spirit,* has a double meaning. It means the *grief,* the sadness, of those who have lost someone or something they care about deeply: the oppressed and the grieving mourn because they experience real loss and are sad. But it also means *repentance:* sinners mourn for their own sins and the sin of their community, and truly want to end their sinning and serve God. The prophet Amos pronounces God's judgment on those who do not mourn. They oppress the poor and crush the needy, and then say to their husbands, "Bring [wine], that we may drink!" They sin and then bring sacrifices to the temple, thinking their sacrifices cover their sins, when they continue to practice injustice. God pronounces woe on those who do not mourn: "Woe to those who are at ease in Zion. . . . Woe to those who lie upon beds of ivory, . . . who sing idle songs to the sound of the harp, . . . but are not grieved over the ruin of Joseph! . . . 'Surely I will never forget any of their deeds. Shall not the land tremble on this account, and everyone mourn who dwells in it? . . . I will turn your feasts into mourning'" (Amos 4:1-5; 5:6, 14; 6:1-7; 8:7-10; 9:5 RSV). When Jesus called for mourning, he meant the mourning of repentance that is sincere enough to cause us to change our way of living.

Both meanings come together once we see that the focus is on God. The Lord God will wipe away the tears from every face, and death and mourning will end (Is 25:8; Rev 21:4). God is already beginning to accomplish this deliverance in Jesus.

In a nutshell, *blessed are those mourn what is wrong and unjust and sincerely repent, for God comforts those who suffer and those who truly repent.*

The third Beatitude. Matthew 5:5 says, "Blessed are the humble, for they shall inherit the earth."

Here Jesus is quoting Psalm 37:11 (see below), which uses the same Hebrew word for *humble* that we saw in Isaiah 61:1, quoted in the first Beatitude. So this Beatitude has basically the same meaning: *"humble" in the sense of surrendered to God*, and *socially and economically poor or powerless*. If we are poor and surrendered to God, we are blessed, because in Christ God is delivering us, and we shall inherit the earth. Donald Hagner concludes: "In view are not persons who are submissive, mild, and unassertive, but those who are *humble* in the sense of being oppressed (hence 'have been humbled'), bent over by the injustice of the ungodly, but who are soon" to be delivered (*Matthew 1—13*, 92-93; Guelich, *Sermon on the Mount*, 81-82).

Clarence Jordan says it would be better to translate the word "tamed" rather than "meek," in the sense that their wills have been tamed by God's will: "In English, the word 'meek' has come to be about the same as 'weak' or 'harmless' or 'spiritless.'" A meek person is thought of as a doormat on which others wipe their feet and who is timid and fears what others will think. "But nothing could be more foreign to the biblical use of the word. It is used in particular to describe two persons—Moses (Numbers 12:3) and Jesus (Matthew 11:29). One of them defied the might of Egypt and the other couldn't be cowed by a powerful Roman official. . . . Both of them seemed absolutely fearless, . . . and completely surrendered to the will of God. . . . People may be called [tamed] to the extent that they have surrendered their wills to God and learned to do his bidding." They do not accommodate to the powerful and influential, but "surrender their will to God so completely that God's will becomes their will. . . . They become God's 'workhorses' on earth" (Jordan, *Sermon on the Mount*, 24-25).

The word has another connotation as well. Wherever the Greek word here translated "meek," or better, humble (*praÿs*), occurs in the Bible, it always points to peacefulness or peacemaking. Matthew 21:5 is a quote from Zechariah 9:9, where the entrance of the *nonviolent or peacemaking* Messianic king is described:

See, your king is coming to you,
his cause won, his victory gained,

humble and mounted on a donkey,
on a colt, the foal of a donkey.
He will banish the chariot from Ephraim
the war-horse from Jerusalem;
the warrior's bow will be banished,
and he will proclaim peace to the nations.
His rule will extend from sea to sea,
from the River to the ends of the earth. (REB)

The Swiss New Testament scholar Hans Weder concludes: "The blessing . . . stands historically in the context of the Zealot temptation. It is no accident that Christ in Matthew twice is designated as meek. Therein rightly lies the heart of his differentiation from the Zealots, from the violence-using battlers for the reign of God. Blessed the nonviolent. They will inherit the world" (*Die "Rede der Reden,"* 62). We add the clarification that in Jesus' time the zealous insurrectionists from whom Jesus differentiated himself and his movement were probably not yet called "Zealots." But Weder's point is still correct. Jesus fulfills "peace" as one of the marks of the reign of God.

Once again the several nuances of meaning come together into a unity when we see that the focus is on surrendering ourselves *to God*. The God to whom we surrender is "the God of peace" (Rom 15:33). God is the God who gives rain and sunshine to enemy as well as friend, and calls us to love our enemies (Mt 5:43-48). Martin Luther King Jr. said, "Jesus understood the difficulty inherent in the act of loving one's enemy. . . . He realized that every genuine expression of love grows out of a consistent and total surrender to God" (King, *Strength to Love,* 48). Jesus did not only teach this but himself brought God's love to his disciples and led those disciples to welcome tax collectors, Gentiles and outcasts into the fellowship. Followers of Jesus can rejoice because Jesus lets us begin to participate in this deliverance. In a nutshell, *blessed are those who are surrendered to God, who is the God of peace.*

The fourth Beatitude. Matthew 5:6 says, "Blessed are those who hunger and thirst for righteousness, for they shall be satisfied."

The key here is to understand the meaning of the word *righteousness*. New Testament scholars generally agree that righteousness and the kingdom are two central themes of the Sermon on the Mount—probably the two central themes. The question they usually ask is whether righteousness is something God gives us or something we do. Their widely agreed answer is both. "God brings righteousness as our deliverance, and we participate in it by doing righteousness" (see Guelich, *Sermon on the Mount,* 85-87). But the often overlooked question is, what does righteousness mean? What is its shape, its content? What are we hungering and thirsting after when we hope and long for righteousness?

The question is especially important because the English word *righteousness* communicates a false meaning. Because our culture is individualistic, we think of righteousness as the virtue of an individual person. And because our culture is possessive, we think of it as something an individual possesses. But righteousness that an individual possesses is self-righteousness. And that is exactly what the gospel says we cannot have (Rom 3).

The Greek word here, *dikaiosynē*, and its root, *dikē*, have the connotation of justice. Furthermore, Jesus is alluding to Isaiah 61, which rejoices three times that God is bringing righteousness or justice (vv. 3, 10, 11). The word there is the Hebrew *tsedaqah*. Jesus quoted the Bible in Hebrew or Aramaic, not in English or Greek. So we need to ask what *tsedaqah* means in Isaiah and elsewhere in the Law and Prophets. It means *delivering justice* (a justice that rescues and releases the oppressed) and *community-restoring justice* (a justice that restores the powerless and the outcasts to their rightful place in covenant community). That is why it appears so often in the Hebrew Bible in parallel with the other word for justice, *mishpat* (see Ps 37 and chapter seventeen below). And that is why the hungry and the thirsty hunger and thirst for righteousness; they yearn bodily for the kind of justice that delivers them from their hunger and thirst and restores them to community where they can eat and drink. It may be that only those readers who have experienced injustice, hunger and exclusion from community can fully experience the significance of what the Bible means by justice. But those are the kind of people who especially flocked to Jesus.

In the Old Testament, *righteousness* means preserving the peace and wholeness of the community, and is sometimes parallel with shalom, peace and, more often, justice. Its meaning is very close to social justice that delivers from alienation and oppression into a community with shalom (Is 32:16-17; Achtemeier, "Righteousness in the Old Testament," 80ff.). The ethical norm for righteousness is not a philosophical definition but the character of the LORD, Yahweh. Yahweh's character is seen supremely in delivering the people from the oppression of the Pharaoh in Egypt into the covenant community of the Promised Land. Hence the theme of deliverance that we have seen in Jesus' extensive references to Isaiah 61 and in the deliverance passages that proclaim the coming of the kingdom of God characterize the kind of justice/righteousness that we believe Jesus teaches and enacts.

> Thus Israel constantly appeals to Yahweh's righteousness for deliverance from trouble (Pss. 31:1; 143:11); from enemies (Pss. 5:8; 143:1); from the wicked (Pss. 36; 71:2); for vindication of her cause before her foes (Ps. 35:24). Yahweh is righteous insofar as he heeds these pleas. His righteousness consists in his intervention for his people, in his deliverance of Zion. . . . So her people should call on their God in the day of trouble (Ps. 50:15). For Yahweh maintains the cause of the afflicted and needy (Ps. 140:12). . . .

In short, Yahweh's righteous judgments are saving judgments (Ps. 36:6), and Deutero-Isaiah can therefore speak of Yahweh as a "righteous God and a Savior.". . .

Yahweh's righteousness is never solely an act of condemnation or punishment. There is no verse in the Old Testament in which Yahweh's righteousness means vengeance on the sinner. (Achtemeier, "Righteousness in the Old Testament," 82ff.; cf. Von Rad, *Old Testament Theology,* 377)

The Old Testament does sometimes speak of God's punishment, but then it uses other words like *wrath* or *vengeance.*

It is no accident that in the Sermon on the Mount Jesus emphasized giving to the borrower and the beggar; giving alms as service to God rather than for show; and not hoarding money for ourselves but giving it to God's kingdom and righteousness (Mt 5:42; 6:2-4, 19-34). Luke, in his parallel version of these teachings (Lk 6:20-26), and writing for Greek-speaking readers who would not have understood the Hebrew behind the word, does not use the word *righteousness* but emphasizes even more strongly coming to the aid of the poor rather than hoarding money for ourselves.

So, in a nutshell, *blessed are those who hunger and thirst for a justice that delivers and restores to covenant community, for God is a God who brings such justice.*

The fifth Beatitude. Matthew 5:7 says, "Blessed are the merciful, for they will be shown mercy."

The Greek word that the English versions translate as "merciful," *eleēmōn,* means *generous in doing deeds of deliverance.* Mercy is about an action; specifically, a generous action that delivers someone from need or bondage. It echoes Proverbs 14:21 (Hagner, *Matthew 1—13,* 93). *Mercy* in the Gospels can mean forgiveness that delivers from the bondage of guilt or (more often) an action of deliverance in the sense of healing or giving. When the Lord's Prayer specifically teaches forgiveness, it uses a different Greek word, *aphiēmi* (Mt 6:12), which probably translates an Aramaic verb meaning "to forgive" (Hagner, *Matthew 1—13,* 150). When Jesus walked down the road and a blind or crippled person called out, "Have mercy on me," he did not mean "Let me off easy," or "Forgive me," but "Heal me, deliver me from my affliction." That is why in Matthew 6:2 doing mercy, *eleēmosynē,* means giving alms to the poor.

Matthew's Gospel has a great deal to say about mercy. It is a fundamental demand (cf. 9:13; 12:7; 23:23) which is fleshed out both by Jesus' words (5:43-48; 18:21-35; 25:31-46) and by his example (9:27-31; 15:21-28; 17:14-18; 20:29-34). In much of this there is strict continuity with the Old Testament and Jewish tradition, for the disposition toward mercy—both an outward act and an inward feeling—was acknowledged as a human virtue as well as a divine attribute (Davies and Allison, *Critical and Exegetical Commentary,* 1:454).

"'Justice and mercy and faith'—these were the 'weightier matters of the law' neglected by Jesus' opponents," according to Matthew (Mt 23:23). "So perhaps throughout Matthew 'mercy' and its cognates imply that merciful action is the concrete expression of loyalty to God, and that what God demands is not so much activity directed Godward but lovingkindness benefitting other people ('I desire mercy not sacrifice')." "As 18:21-35 proves, disciples are able to show mercy because God has first shown them mercy (cf. Lk 6:36)." Mercy connotes the idea of loyalty within a covenant relationship. Matthew 9:13 and 12:7 "cite Hosea 6:6, in which mercy or steadfast love clearly involves covenant loyalty" (Davies and Allison, *Critical and Exegetical Commentary*, 1:454-55).

So the fifth Beatitude means, in a nutshell, *blessed are those who, like God, offer compassion in action, forgiveness, healing, aid and covenant steadfastness to those in need.*

The sixth Beatitude. Matthew 5:8 says, "Blessed are the pure in heart, for they will see God."

Hans Weder clears up a misunderstanding: "People often say that Jesus criticized the outwardness of forbidding certain foods and cultic purity in favor of an inner, spiritual purity. This may be an aspect, but is not the point. The point is expressed much more in Jesus' saying, in Mt. 15:11—'Not what goes into a person's mouth makes the person unclean, but what comes out of that person's mouth, that is what makes him or her unclean.' In this sentence two mutually exclusive ideas of purity stand opposite each other." The one leads to distancing oneself from others, shrinking away from outside influences and relationships. "Whoever blames impurity on outer influences does obeisance to the romantic thought of the original uncorruptedness of the heart."

"Jesus goes in a very different direction, not to the original nobility of the heart, but much more to the heart as the *origin* of impurity. Not the influences [inflows] make the person unclean, but much more the out-fluences [outflows]. . . . It is the impurity that I can by no means distance myself from, because it has its origin in me myself. I cannot wall myself from it, I can get rid of it at most through the creativity of God." The way to purity is in giving myself over to an "all-encompassing orientation toward God, Who creates all and therefore also purity. Therefore it says: blessed are those with pure hearts, for they shall see God" (Weder, *Die "Rede der Reden,"* 72-74).

Contrary to an Enlightenment or Greek split between outward action and inner heart, the biblical understanding is holistic: there is one whole self in relation to one God, the Lord of all. The heart is the relational organ. When God speaks to me, I receive it in my heart. When I act angrily toward someone, I do it with my heart. The real split is not between inner and outer, but between God-serving and idol-serving. It is between giving aid to the poor in order to be noticed and respected by others, and giving as service to God. It is between praying and fasting in order to be seen by others and praying and fasting as faithfulness toward God. It is between serving my desire for wealth and serving God's reign and justice.

> Purity of heart must involve integrity, a correspondence between outward action and inward thought (cf. 15:8), a lack of duplicity, singleness of intention, . . . and the desire to please God above all else. More succinctly: purity of heart is to will one thing, God's will, with all of one's being and doing. (Davies and Allison, *Critical and Exegetical Commentary*, 1:456)

So the sixth Beatitude means, in a nutshell, *blessed are those who give their whole self over to God, who is the only One worthy of the heart's full devotion.*

The seventh Beatitude. Matthew 5:9 says, "Blessed are the peacemakers, for they will be called children of God."

"'Peacemaker'. . . is the right translation, . . . for a positive action, reconciliation, is envisioned: the 'peacemakers' *seek to bring about peace*." Since the previous Beatitudes concern social relations, surely the meaning here is social, not simply peace between individuals and God, as is frequently claimed. "For Jesus as the bringer of peace, see Lk 2:14; 19:38; Acts 10:36; Rom 5:1; Eph 2:14-18; Col 1:2; Heb 7:2 (cf. Isa 9:5-6; Zech 9:10). In being a peacemaker, the disciple is imitating his Father in heaven, 'the God of peace' (Rom 16:20; cf. Rom 15:33; Phil 4:9; I Th 5:23; 2 Th 3:16; Heb 13:20)" (Davies and Allison, *Critical and Exegetical Commentary,* 1:457-58). We recall from chapter one that a mark of the kingdom is peace.

Donald Hagner writes: "In the context of the beatitudes, the point would seem to be directed against the Zealots, the Jewish revolutionaries who hoped through violence to bring the kingdom of God. Such means would have been a continual temptation for the downtrodden and oppressed who longed for the kingdom. The Zealots by their militarism hoped furthermore to demonstrate that they were the loyal 'sons of God.' But Jesus announces . . . it is the peacemakers who will be called the 'children of God.'. . . This stress on peace becomes a common motif in the New Testament (cf. Rom 14:19; Heb 12:14; Jas 3:18; 1 Pet 3:11)" (Hagner, *Matthew 1—13,* 94).

Being a peacemaker is part of being surrendered to God, for God brings peace. We abandon the effort to get our needs met through the destruction of enemies. God comes to us in Christ to make peace with us; and we participate in God's grace as we go to our enemies to make peace. This is why the peacemakers "will be called children of God." In a nutshell, *blessed are those who make peace with their enemies, as God shows love to God's enemies.*

The eighth and ninth Beatitudes. Matthew 5:10 says, "Blessed are those who are persecuted for righteousness' sake, for theirs is the kingdom of heaven." Matthew 5:11-12 says, "Blessed are you when people revile you and persecute you and utter all kinds of evil against you falsely on my account. Rejoice and be glad, for your reward is great in heaven, for in the same way they persecuted the prophets who were before you."

These two Beatitudes summarize and climax the others. They are about persecution for righteousness and for Jesus—as the prophets were persecuted. The Beatitudes should be interpreted in the context of the prophets with their emphasis on God's reign and God's call for righteousness and justice, and the suffering that they bore for calling Israel to covenant fidelity in their own day. As Matthew 5:17-20 makes clear, Jesus is teaching in continuity with the Law and the Prophets. In a nutshell, *blessed are those who suffer because of their practices of loyalty to Jesus and to justice.*

Simon Harak describes his own experience with two hundred people from twenty countries on a "Walk for a Peaceful Future in the Middle East." They walked to support nonviolence, not only nonviolence by themselves but by Israel and Palestine toward each other, and to support a solution in which each side would recognize the other as a legitimate state. They walked across the "Green Line," the border between the two territories, in the face of the heavily armed Israeli military forbidding them to cross the line. Harak describes his sense of love and even eagerness for the confrontation, because of his own deep commitment to nonviolence:

> It seems to me that this eagerness, this willingness to encounter and undergo physical suffering, is the primary passion for the virtue of nonviolence. Like all passions, this passion must be trained—and this passion especially, lest it become a wrong passion, a passion for self-*destruction*. . . . We do not need to read very far in Gandhi's work to see the value he places on "self-suffering." He says, for example, that "Suffering in one's own person is . . . the essence of nonviolence and is the chosen substitute for violence to others." *(Virtuous Passions)*

Harak then recalls the night when the home of Martin Luther King Jr. was bombed and his family narrowly escaped injury: King decisively led the way in training for nonviolence:

> When an angry crowd [of King's supporters] gathered around the King house, armed and calling for vengeance, King sent them home in peace. According to Andrew Young, King's refusal to accept retaliatory violence at that time definitively stamped the character of nonviolence on the civil rights movement.
>
> More pointedly, this passion to accept suffering into the self is characteristic of Jesus who was crucified. . . . The letter to the Hebrews tells us that Jesus "endured the cross, despising the shame" (12:2). And Christians are commanded to take up the cross as Jesus did and to suffer as he suffered. (Harak, *Virtuous Passions*, 130-31; see also Yoder, *Politics of Jesus*, chap. 7)

Donald Hagner concludes:

> What must be stressed here . . . is that the kingdom is presupposed as something

given by God. . . . Thus the beatitudes are, above all, predicated upon the experience of the grace of God. . . . Because [the recipients] are the poor and oppressed, they make no claim upon God for their achievements. They do not merit God's kingdom; they but await his mercy. This emphasis on God's mercy is essential at the beginning of Jesus' teaching, especially at the beginning of the present discourse with its description of the righteousness of the kingdom. . . . Here, as throughout God's dealings with humanity, grace precedes requirements. It is true that the beatitudes contain implied ethical exhortations. . . . Indeed, the traits of those who are proclaimed "happy" could well be taken as a description of the behavior of Jesus himself. Yet this ethical side of the beatitudes remains distinctly subordinate to the indicative aspect that is directly related to the announcement of the kingdom. (*Matthew 1—13*, 96)

Davies and Allison link the Beatitudes to the messiahship of Jesus:

The dependence of Matt. 5:3-12 upon Isa 61:1-3 . . . implicitly reveals the identity of the one who proclaims the sermon on the mount. . . . Jesus is the anointed one upon whom the Spirit of God rests. He is the Messiah. Moreover, he and his ministry are the fulfillment of Old Testament prophecy. (Davies and Allison, *Critical and Exegetical Commentary*, 1:466)

The shape of Jesus' fulfillment of Old Testament prophecy is the shape of the drama of the reign of God: God's presence, salvation, peace, joy and delivering justice. And the virtues of the participants fit the drama: we participate now and will be participating in God's merciful, compassionate deliverance. We

- are humble before God, and identify with the humble, the poor, and the outcasts.
- mourn with sincere repentance toward God, and comfort others who mourn.
- are surrendered to God, committing ourselves to following God's way, and making peace.
- hunger and thirst for delivering, community-restoring justice.
- practice compassion in action, covenant faithfulness toward those in need.
- seek God's will with holistic integrity, in all that we are and do.
- make peace with our enemies, as God shows love to God's enemies.
- are willing to suffer (just as Jesus suffered) because of our loyalty to Jesus and to justice.

This we are, and this we do, as a joyful response to God: "We love because he first loved us" (1 Jn 4:19). What greater meaning can there be than to be able to participate in the deliverance that God is bringing in Jesus Christ?

Virtues Elsewhere in the Biblical Drama

How do Jesus' virtues compare with the virtues that the apostle Paul teaches in six different places in his letters? The lists differ; clearly they do not imply that there is an exact set of seven or eight Christian virtues, no more and no less. Nevertheless, when we compare his lists, a highly interesting pattern of consistency emerges.

The virtues mentioned by Paul at least twice (see table 2.3) are love, compassion, kindness, humility, gentleness, patience, tolerance, unity, peace, joy, righteousness, forgiveness and endurance. These match the virtues that Jesus taught in the Beatitudes so closely that hardly any need discussion: Paul's virtues of tolerance, unity and patience, which he especially emphasized as needed for peacemaking in the churches, match the virtue of peacemaking in the Beatitudes. If goodness in Galatians 5 is like purity in 2 Corinthians 6, then we have a match for purity of heart in the Beatitudes. That leaves only Jesus' teaching, "Blessed are they who mourn," which we saw implies repentance. Surely Paul called for repentance often enough throughout his letters, even though he did not call it a virtue! Writing to churches two decades after Jesus, and before Matthew, Paul gave these virtues a slightly different meaning in his historical context. Nevertheless, the match is remarkably close.

First Timothy 4:12; 6:11; 2 Timothy 2:22; 3:10; 1 Peter 3:8; and 2 Peter 1:5-7 advocate basically the same virtues that we have seen already: love five times, faith three times, righteousness twice, godliness twice, purity and purity of

Table 2.2. Paul's virtues parallel the Beatitudes

Jesus' Beatitudes	Paul's virtues
humility and meekness	humility and gentleness
righteousness	righteousness
mercy	kindness, compassion, love, forgiveness
purity of heart	purity or goodness
peacemaking	peace, tolerance, unity, patience
suffering persecution for justice and Jesus' sake	endurance
(blessed are you)	joy

heart, endurance, perseverance, gentleness, peace, harmony, sympathy, compassion, kindness, humility, goodness, knowledge and self-control. They would add faith to our list of those mentioned twice or more (see Lohse, *Theological Ethics of the New Testament*, 82-88).

How do the virtues compare with the rest of the Bible, including the Old Testament? Benjamin Farley surveys the Bible, from Genesis through the later letters—James, Peter, John and Hebrews, but not Revelation—looking for virtues. The virtues that he finds seem to cluster together naturally.

One cluster centers in *humbly expecting God's deliverance*, just like the virtues of humility and surrender before God that we found in the Beatitudes. God's gracious redemption is the source for all the virtues, Farley emphasizes, just as Jesus based the Beatitudes on God's grace-based deliverance. In Farley's study, faith in God's redemption produces clusters of virtues like "waiting" faithfully and actively, accepting God's presence, action and ordering. Similarly, vigilance, equanimity, serenity, awareness of God's faithfulness, surrender, patience, self-control and temperance, refraining from vengeance, joy and humility all cluster around faithfully expecting and focusing on God's deliverance (Farley, *In Praise of Virtue*, 80-82, 85, 88, 114ff., 121-22, 125, 132ff., 138-39, 140, 153). Farley connects this with John Calvin's conversion experience of being tamed and brought to submission so that he became teachable by God's Word (cf. George, *Theology of the Reformers*, 173-75).

Second, Farley's biblical survey uncovers virtues of *mourning unto repentance* (Farley, *In Praise of Virtue*, 70, 78-79, 85, 117-18), the theme of the second Beatitude. He quotes Jeremiah 7:3-7 and comments that Jeremiah's sermon "compels the community to see that, central to biblical faith, is *a willingness to be reformed.* Thus *openness to reform* becomes a crucial biblical virtue," because it enables God not only to renew the self, "but to renew the just and collective commitments of the community of faith as well" (Farley, *In Praise of Virtue*, 78-79).

Third, the virtues of *justice, compassion and mercy for the powerless and outcast* recur especially frequently throughout the Bible (Farley, *In Praise of Virtue*, 55, 79, 83-84, 86, 114ff., 117, 119-20, 167-68).

Fourth, the virtue of purity of heart, or *integrity of inner and outer being and doing*, does not appear often in Farley's study of biblical virtues but is surely implied (*In Praise of Virtue*, 126 et passim).

Fifth, Farley does not notice the extensive biblical theme of *peacemaking* (although we see it in Cain and Abel, Jacob and Esau, Joseph and his brothers, Isaiah, Jeremiah, Hosea, Micah, the Sermon on the Mount, the Gospels, Paul, the book of Revelation). His one mention reduces peace to equanimity, an inner attitude (*In Praise of Virtue*, 132-33). When he thinks of purity or of peace, a split of inner attitudes from outward initiatives creeps into his assumptions, and so he does not notice the extensive biblical teachings (see the discussion

Table 2.3. Virtues in Paul's lists

Col 3:12-17	Phil 2:2-3	Eph 4:2-3, 32	Gal 5:22-23	Rom 14:17; 15:4-5	2 Cor 6:4-10
love	love	love	love		
compassion		compassion			
kindness		kindness	kindness		
humility	humility	humility			
gentleness		gentleness	gentleness		
patience		patience	patience		
tolerance		tolerance			
forgiveness		forgiveness			
	unity	unity		unity	
gratitude	like-mindedness				
wisdom					
peace		peace	peace	peace	
				righteousness	righteousness
			joy	joy in the Holy Spirit	joy
				endurance	endurance
				hope	
			goodness		purity
			faithfulness		understanding
			self-control		kindness
					patience

of the Enlightenment split above, under "purity of heart.")

A sixth extensive cluster of virtues in Farley's study is the virtue of *courage in suffering and willingness to resist the ethos of one's time* (Farley, *In Praise of Virtue*, 40, 65, 72), and determination, resoluteness and perseverance (*In Praise of Virtue*, 46, 72, 122-23). This matches Jesus' teaching on willingness to suffer and be persecuted because of loyalty to Jesus and to delivering justice.

Seventh, the *joy of being blessed by God's presence* that is the main point of the Beatitudes is, of course, a central biblical theme, and is rightly emphasized throughout Farley's book.

Farley adds the following virtues that he sees in the Ten Commandments: gratitude, respect, faithfulness, truthfulness and contentment. He also adds a number of what we will later call practices or application of virtues in action (141-42, 147, 150-56 et passim).

The conclusion seems clear: the virtues Jesus teaches in the Beatitudes are echoed in Paul's letters and are deeply rooted in the whole Bible. They are not merely an arbitrary selection; they are the heart of biblical virtues. They picture what it means to be a follower of Jesus. In fact, they picture Jesus' own virtues. And this picturing of Jesus is a crucial point: each virtue gets its meaning from Jesus' teaching and embodying the reign of God, in continuity with the prophets and the whole biblical drama.

How Shall We Relate Gospel Virtues to Traditional Virtues?

In reading through the literature of Christian virtue ethicists, one notices an ambivalence. It is a literature that values tradition, and so it tends to affirm the four traditional Greek virtues, courage *(andreia)*, justice *(dikaiosynē)*, temperance or modesty *(sōphrosynē)* and prudence *(phronēsis)*, supplemented by Paul's emphasis on faith, hope and love. But the authors seem uncertain. They do not argue persuasively for these particular virtues. "From the point of view of modern philosophical ethics, one of the things that must make attention to the virtues so unappealing is the lack of consensus about which virtues are morally central; and perhaps even more frustrating is the absence of any principle or method to determine what the primary virtues are or how they might be interrelated. . . . Certainly, no agreement exists about which virtues should be considered central" (Hauerwas, *Community of Character*, 121; cf. Spohn, *Go and Do Likewise*, 13). See also the parallel criticism of MacIntyre's lack of specifying shared virtues in Jean Porter (*Recovery of Virtue*, 83). Or Jonathan Wilson: "The tradition of virtue ethics comes from the Greek philosopher Aristotle's *Nichomachean Ethics*, but as many have pointed out, Aristotle's account is incompatible with Christianity. For instance, Aristotle has no place for the virtue of humility, and his account of friendship precludes the possibility of friendship between God and humanity" (Wilson, *Gospel Virtues*, 18-19). Furthermore, Aristotle said that friendship is possible only with people like us and equal to us. But Jesus' teaching emphasizes friendship with outcasts and the powerless. Aristotle also advocated other virtues including generosity, magnificence, high-mindedness, gentleness, truthfulness, wittiness, friendship and a proper amount of ambition but not too much. He chose these virtues by observing admired males in a hierarchical and warlike society that defended slavery and male superiority and did not believe in the God of Israel.

Hauerwas and Pinches reinterpret Aristotle's virtues to make them accord more with the Christian story. They point out that Thomas reinterpreted the four cardinal virtues so they would be guided more by love, but that his reinterpretation still retained some of Aristotle's patriarchalism. They say: "What Aristotle and Christians mean by being happy is quite different. . . . Aristotle suggests we can be happy only if we achieve a self-sufficiency that guards us against outrageous fortune. Christians claim, on the other hand, that we are happy only to the extent that our lives are formed in reference to Jesus of Nazareth." Furthermore, Aristotle's account is empty at the core; it begs for a Christ-centered narrative that will fill the emptiness (Hauerwas and Pinches, *Christians Among Virtues*, 16, 29).

John Milbank incisively criticizes Aristotelian virtue ethics as based on a homogeneous view of community and the need for war against those who differ. Instead, Christian belief in God calls for love of enemy and affirms participation in community of those who differ (*Theology and Social Theory*, 5-6, 405-17, 428). Aristotle's cardinal virtue of courage glorifies courage in warfare. Hauerwas and Pinches quote Jean Bethke Elshtain: "for the Greeks war was a natural state of affairs and the basis of society." So Thomas Aquinas transformed Aristotle's understanding of courage into the courage of the martyr and not the soldier, with the weapons of patience and faith. He redefined courage as persevering in doing what is "just"—with justice defined by compassion for the underdog (Hauerwas and Pinches, *Christians Among Virtues*, 151, 159-64). This resembles Jesus' commendation of a willingness to be persecuted for his sake and the sake of justice (see above).

Virtues are character traits that enable us to contribute to community—to the particular society in which we live. Peter Paris makes this clear: "The virtues of African and African American ethics are . . . determined by the goal of preserving and promoting community," or "the community's well-being" (Paris, *Spirituality of African Peoples*, 130-31, 134). Paris is studying African spirituality, whose orientation toward community is closer to the biblical understanding than American disconnected individualism. Character ethics intends to correct disconnected individualism, emphasizing virtues that contribute to the common good of the community. Similarly, John Milbank shows that the great African saint Augustine saw God's forgiveness, peace and justice as the order of reality that is normative for society. So his virtue ethics is a corrective for the good of society (Milbank, *Theology and Social Theory*, 409ff.). In biblical character ethics, the good we serve is the reign of God, and the reign of God is oriented toward community with God (God's presence and salvation) and community with our fellow human beings (peace and justice). The biblical virtues are keys to community well-being: peacemaking, hungering for justice, doing mercy, integrity, humility and caring for the poor and the mourning. And they are the way of participation in community with God.

Different kinds of society need different kinds of virtues (Wilson, *Gospel Virtues*, 122). The question for us, then, is which society, which politics, we live in. Jesus said we are blessed because we are living in the society of the mustard seeds. This does not mean that our society is just or that Jesus' society was just; in chapter seventeen we show that the Gospels show Jesus confronting injustice forty times. But in the midst of the injustice, God is planting mustard seeds of deliverance—in Jesus' actions, in the deeds and practices of the community of disciples, and in what God is doing beyond our awareness. This means that in spite of the injustice of our society, we are at the same time living where the mustard seeds of deliverance of God's presence, salvation, justice and peace are being planted. The biblical virtues fit that reign. All of us are also participants in one or more other societies: our hometown, our educational community, our church, our nation and the rapidly growing global community. We need to learn some virtues for making our contributions to those communities also (Jer 29:7). Those virtues differ. But our central virtues, by which the others are judged, are the virtues of the reign of God.

Today one may affirm the virtues of mutual respect, antidomination and participation in community that Michael Walzer advocates (Stassen, "Michael Walzer's Situated Justice," 382-87). These seem especially appropriate for a biblical Christian, and they do make coalition with a leading philosophy of our time that speaks to the needs and realities of a democratic, pluralistic, historically conscious, economically driven, postmodern society. One could include James McClendon's insightful and persuasive advocacy of the virtue of *presence* (McClendon, *Ethics*, 106-7). It fits perfectly one of the characteristics of the reign of God—God's presence. It strongly resembles Dietrich Bonhoeffer's advocacy of incarnationally entering into the reality of the other.

In several of his writings, Stanley Hauerwas emphasizes the virtue of *patience*—facing life's limits in an optimistic culture that tells us we can overcome all limits. Peter Paris develops and advocates six virtues that reclaim African American roots in African culture's God-centeredness and community-centeredness, with a strong emphasis that "a person becomes morally virtuous in order to make a substantial contribution to the preservation and promotion of the community" (Paris, *Spirituality of African Peoples*, 134ff.). Four of his

virtues—beneficence, forbearance, forgiveness and justice—are very close to
the virtues we have seen in Jesus, Paul and biblical tradition. Because of its emphasis on holistic community, reconciliation, forgiveness and God, African tradition produces virtues significantly closer to biblical virtues than Plato and
Aristotle do.

Like McClendon, Paris makes clear his six are not meant to be a complete
and exclusive list. As McClendon adds presence, and Hauerwas adds patience, one may add other virtues insofar as they are consistent with the gospel
and the basic Christian virtues. This would require extensive testing from the
perspective of fit with the Gospel narrative, and with a critical eye to their
function for justice and reconciliation in community. That testing could produce an insightful, creative and fruitful discussion. The study of Christian ethics is in part that very process of testing and validating.

3

HOLISTIC CHARACTER ETHICS

―

Happy are the pure in heart, for they will see God.

Do not store up for yourselves treasures in this world, where they are subject to the ravage
of such things as moth and corrosion and where thieves can break in and steal. . . .
For wherever your treasure is, there too will be your heart.

. . . If therefore your eye is generous, your whole person will be full of light; but if your eye
is covetous, your whole person will be full of darkness.

First take out the log from your own eye, and then you will see clearly enough to take the
speck out of your neighbor's eye.

MATTHEW 5:8; 6:19-23; 7:5 HAGNER TRANSLATION

*J*ersey Girl was a fun television movie. The central character, the "Jersey girl,"
lived with her working-class father, who taught her to be herself and to be loyal to her close friends rather than pretending she was someone she was not.
She was a delightful, loving, irrepressible human being, a teacher caring for little children in a preschool.

Her boyfriend, however, was trying to climb the corporate ladder of success, driving an expensive Mercedes, shafting a fellow employee to make
money, playing fast and loose with the truth to get ahead—and finally ditching
"the Jersey girl" because she was beneath the higher class status that he was
ambitious to attain.

She gave him so much grief! And love too. He didn't deserve the love. She
was true to her caring self and her caring father, and to her friends and roots
in working-class New Jersey. Her boyfriend was trying to cut himself off from
his roots and had lost his moral compass. He was manipulative and hard. She
confronted him with his own falseness, while demonstrating she was not just

his "girl," and jolted him into finding his roots again. He quit his job, crashed his car into a fire hydrant in front of the preschool where she taught—spraying a geyser of water all over the schoolyard, to the delight of the children—and joined her with the children in their learning and playing.

The profound point in this light story is that it takes *community* to shape a person with integrity of character. The Jersey girl derived her integrity from her community—her town, her family, her friends and her workplace. When her boyfriend tried to cut himself off from this community, she had the courage to confront him. It is a parable for our time: When you cut yourself off from your roots and your community and become an autonomous individual on the make, you lose your moral compass. Recovery of character requires confrontation by community.

Character ethicists say integrity of character is shaped when we see ourselves, our lives and our loyalties as *part of a larger drama* that shapes our community. The Jersey girl saw herself as part of a drama of mutual loyalty—with her father, her friends, her preschool children and her boyfriend. Her boyfriend saw himself as part of a drama of social and economic climbing. He gave his loyalty to his boss—as long as that gave him success. When his girlfriend got in the way of his climbing, he dropped her. But it finally crashed in on him that this drama of climbing was not good enough; in fact, it was not good at all. It was causing him to violate the more important loyalty of human community. The drama of autonomous individualistic climbing divorces us from what character ethicists call *the good*, or the *telos*, or the larger human purpose of life.

But this is what modern society does—it moves us away from our roots and our communities and teaches us to think of ourselves as self-made, autonomous individuals. It makes us too much like the social climber and too little like the Jersey girl. It teaches us "virtues" like self-containment, detachment from intimacy and community, efficiency, competitiveness and self-advancement. Success in modern society is measured by superficial criteria: appearance of competence, avoidance of suffering and cool apathy—concealing our anxieties and not committing ourselves to any social cause. The result is a loss of community and a resulting sense of alienation, a diminished sense of purpose, a deterioration of moral character and a dawning awareness that our society is in real moral trouble (Rasmussen, *Moral Fragments;* Clapp, *Families at the Crossroads;* Bellah et al., *Habits of the Heart*).

Character Ethics as a Better Way of Reasoning

To counter the corrosive force of modern atomistic individualism, several ethicists are arguing that we need to focus not only on right and wrong decisions but on what shapes the character of those who make the decisions and do the actions.

First, we need to emphasize that specific *practices* form character. For example, if a family, church or community makes an explicit practice of mercifully coming to the aid of people in need, its members are likely to learn mercy and compassion. Second, we need to emphasize the *virtues*—the marks of good character—for example, mercy or compassion. Third, we must stress that character is formed not by self-made individuals, but by the shaping, encouraging and correcting influence of *community.* Thus we must seek to develop the types of communities that form compassionate character. Finally, community and character depend on knowing that we are *participants in a larger history, a larger drama.* Because all four of these emphases are crucial to the development of character, we prefer to call this move in ethics not simply virtue ethics, but—using a more comprehensive term—*character ethics.*

Joseph Kotva sums up the case for character ethics in three points. First, we need character ethics because of *the widespread sense of moral decline,* which "stands behind calls for school prayer, character education, stronger criminal punishment, and the regulation of television violence" (*Christian Case for Virtue Ethics,* 6). Character ethics is a revolt against moral decline and against the modern rationalistic, Enlightenment-influenced market-oriented ethics that it blames for the decline. As Alasdair MacIntyre argues, rationalistic and individualistic ethics lacks attention to the practices and the communities that form character (*After Virtue*). Even earlier, in *The Revolution of the Saints* (1965), Michael Walzer argued that American society was living on borrowed moral virtues that it was not replenishing, and that Enlightenment liberalism was inadequate for replenishing character.

Walzer highlighted the attention that the Puritans gave to teaching moral virtues, before the time of the Enlightenment, in the sixteenth and seventeenth centuries. The Puritans ended monarchy, made the government accountable to its purpose of steering the ship of state toward justice, liberty and peace, brought democracy and religious toleration, and encouraged a new kind of moral character and civic virtue. "The saint's personality was his own most radical innovation. It was marked above all by an uncompromising and sustained commitment to a political ideal, . . . and by a pattern of rigorous and systematic labor in pursuit of that ideal" (Walzer, *Revolution of the Saints,* 2-3). Through scriptural teaching and church practice, the Puritans taught the virtues of discipline, duty, industriousness, self-control, rigorous pursuit of God's will, systematic obedience to God's commands, conscientious devotion to the common good, civic virtue and activism.

In the eighteenth century, Enlightenment liberals extended democracy, religious toleration and basic liberties, but they failed to nurture the kind of character needed for constitutional democracy to function in a healthy way. Their optimistic liberalism rested on the naive assumption that the political virtue of citizens was natural. "The result was that liberalism did not create the self-control it required." The liberal state depends on the kind of discipline that Calvinism provided, and it is not now growing the "saints" that society depends on—"persons whose good behavior could be relied upon" (Walzer, *Revolution of the Saints*, 302-3).

Second, we need character ethics because of *the "historical consciousness" of our time*. Stanley Hauerwas begins his primer in Christian ethics in this way: "All ethical reflection occurs relative to a particular time and place. Not only do ethical problems change from one time to the next, but the very nature and structure of ethics is determined by the particularities of a community's history and convictions" (*Peaceable Kingdom*, 1). In our time of globalization, we are increasingly aware of different moral rules held by people of different cultures. Ours is a time of global encounter and cultural diversity, and that requires adaptability. "Character ethics moves the focus from rules and acts to agents and their contexts." Therefore, it is more aware of social context, the dynamics of history, and "our need to respond to each situation's specific features" (Kotva, *Christian Case for Virtue Ethics*, 8-9).

Third, most modern individualistic and rationalistic ethical theories lack attention to the *formative influences of friendship, discipleship to mentors and bodily emotions*. In fact, these theories "are in some respects incompatible with and undermine those realities" (Kotva, *Christian Case for Virtue Ethics*, 10). Modern ethics seeks to base behavior on universal reason and impersonal duty. This systematically rules out considerations of particular persons, particular communities or personal feeling. But we are not Vulcans; we are not reasoning minds without feeling; we are *embodied* selves with passions. Our passions, emotions and desires "tell a lot about the kind of people we have become [and] help determine what actions we pursue and which we avoid." Therefore, character ethics "sees emotions and desires as ethically central" (Kotva, *Christian Case for Virtue Ethics*, 11-12).

And our character is shaped by other persons who are our models, our mentors, our mothers and fathers in the faith. Character ethics emphasizes *discipleship* to a teacher or master, or to persons who are models of righteousness. "It is in being guided by, following after, and imitating masters or worthy examples that we learn to recognize and *embody* the emotional and intellectual dispositions, habits, and skills designated by the virtues" (Kotva, *Christian Case for Virtue Ethics*, 80-81, 107-8, 110ff.; italics added). These emphases on embodiment and discipleship are two reasons why one way to describe the ethics we are proposing in this volume is *incarnational discipleship*. We are embodied selves, not minds without corporeal being or passions. And we are followers of the incarnate Jesus.

Ethics as incarnational discipleship points to the *incarnate Jesus, who taught the Sermon on the Mount and the kingdom of God, in the tradition of the prophets of Israel, embodied it in his practices and called us to embody it in our practices of disci-*

pleship. This Jesus is our Lord. This might seem obvious, but in fact many Christian ethicists reduce Jesus' lordship to a rule or a principle like the law of love. Because character ethics says that we learn our character and our sense of purpose from teachers or models, it can speak naturally of Jesus as manifesting the character that we are to imitate and the purpose of life that we are to pursue (Kotva, *Christian Case for Virtue Ethics,* 87, 89).

The Four Dimensions of Holistic Character Ethics

We want to develop character ethics in a systematic way by arguing that four dimensions are important: our passions/loyalties, our perceptions, our way of reasoning and our basic convictions. If an ethic lacks explicit attention to any of these dimensions, it either lacks the ability to take a clear stand on concrete ethical issues, or it takes the stand naively, unaware of and uncritical about its own crucial assumptions. It lacks the power to detect errors and weaknesses in that dimension of character, to know where to repent and change. It is like a soldier who rushes into battle with his helmet but forgets his sword and shield.

We want a character ethics with all four dimensions, because all four dimensions are crucial in Jesus' teachings and in biblical ethics generally. Furthermore, the four prove to be important across the wide range of ethical issues from abortion to peacemaking.

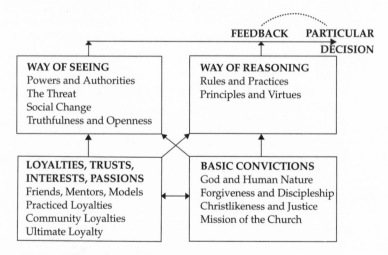

Figure 3.1. The Four Dimensions of Character

The Way of Reasoning Dimension

One dimension of character is having a way of ethical reasoning and being somewhat consistent in that way of reasoning. Character requires consistency, and character without reason is likely to be highly inconsistent. We shall devote chapter five to discussing various *ways of reasoning* in Christian ethics. Therefore, we only call attention to it here.

Let us simply say that character ethics both recognizes and affirms reasoning—but reasoning *with and through holistic character, which includes the virtues.* Virtues are character traits that are stable, consistent and reliable. Virtues aim toward discerning and doing what is good for our purpose in life as humans. They are developed by training and practice. They need a community where they are engendered, fostered and refined. And they derive from tradition—specifically Christian for Christian virtues—a tradition that provides the larger drama or narrative frame that makes sense of life (Porter, *Recovery of Virtue*, 70; McClendon, "Three Strands of Christian Ethics," 107; Hauerwas, *Community of Character*, 115). Thus those writers who emphasize character ethics rightly notice that any moral reasoning we do is undertaken through and with habits of mind and heart we already possess; reason does not function autonomously. Noticing this, character ethicists focus on the development of the kind of character that guides our reasoning aright (McClendon, *Ethics*, 329-32).

The Basic Convictions Dimension

Character ethics criticizes a rationalistic ethics that is grounded in allegedly universal philosophical premises and that accordingly neglects theological beliefs. Holistic character ethics is grounded in the larger drama or narrative of life that is crucial for character. We have already laid out our fundamental theological conviction that this larger drama of life is the reign of God, characterized by salvation, justice, peace, joy and God's presence. This is the narrative that Christ-followers are called to make their own, to inhabit and to orient their lives around. The first variable in the basic-convictions dimension is how one understands *the character of God*. In addition to emphasizing God's kingdom, Jesus often based his teaching in the Sermon the Mount on the character of God: God gives rain and sunshine to his enemies as well to the just; so love your enemies (Mt 5:45). God sees in secret and knows what you need before you ask (Mt 6:4, 6, 8, 18). God will forgive you if you forgive others, and otherwise will not (Mt 6:15). You cannot serve God and wealth (Mt 6:24). God cares for even the lilies of the field and the birds of the air, and surely cares for you (Mt 6:26-33). If you know how to give good gifts to your children, "how much more will your Father in heaven give good things to those who ask him!" (Mt 7:11). In sum, God is merciful and loves enemies. The delivering righteousness that Jesus taught therefore exceeded that of the Pharisees, for they excluded outcasts and the impure from their community of righteous practice.

The second basic-convictions variable is *human nature* (see figure 3.1 above). Different people understand human nature differently, and this influences their ethics more powerfully than they often realize. Jesus was realistic about human nature, diagnosing the vicious cycles that we get ourselves caught in (see chapter six below). At the same time he had a high view of the value of all human persons. He taught that God cares for each sparrow, but cares for each of us much more than the sparrows (Mt 6:26; Lk 12:6-7).

Next comes *forgiveness and discipleship*. Some traditions emphasize salvation by faith without works so exclusively that they deemphasize discipleship, and others do the reverse. How people relate the two themes has a powerful influence on their ethics. We will discuss this further below, in dialogue with Joseph Kotva.

The next set of variables is *Christlikeness and justice*. How one understands *Christlikeness*, the way of Jesus Christ, is crucial for Christian ethics. Furthermore, we need to relate the way of Jesus Christ to *the struggle for justice* in public ethics in the world. Some Christians limit the way of Jesus to relationships with other Christians within the church and so cut the way of Jesus off from relevance for the world. The result is to cause secularism: the gospel of Jesus Christ has no relevance in the world, so all our ethics in the world should come from secular sources. We call this "secularizing dualism." Other Christians believe we should impose the way of Jesus on the world whether the world agrees or not. This results in resentment and opposition by the secular world to the Christian faith, and thus this also causes secularism. We call this "secularizing domination" or authoritarianism. The trick is to figure out how and where the way of Jesus can be normative for public ethics by persuasion. We will deal with this throughout the book and explicitly in chapter twenty-three.

The final variable in the basic-convictions dimension is the understanding of *the mission of the church*. Jesus did not talk much about the church; the church had not yet begun. What had begun was the group of disciples and the groups of followers Jesus was developing in various communities as he traveled (N. T. Wright, *Jesus and the Victory of God*, 276, 295ff.). So when Jesus taught his way to the disciples, and when the New Testament speaks of the mission of the disciples, we are reading about the mission of the church. Character ethics emphasizes that how we understand the mission of the church shapes our ethics strongly. Character is shaped in community, and that means churches must be communities, not merely preaching stations. The New Testament word for this is *koinonia*, which combines the meaning of community and fellowship with the meaning of service. The church is a mission community, spreading the word and living it, different from the world but shining in the world, doing deeds that call attention to God's glory (Mt 5:13-16).

We believe these basic-conviction variables are central in Jesus' teaching in the Sermon on the Mount and how people understand them determines much of their ethics. So as the book proceeds, we will focus on how these pivotal basic-conviction variables shape people's ethics on issues like peacemaking, cloning, sex, marriage and divorce, economic justice, prayer and politics. If you keep these variables visually before you as you sort through these various issues, you will develop an increasingly articulate and self-aware ethics.

We want to give credit to Ralph Potter of Harvard University for identifying these variables as crucial to Christian ethics. Glen adapted and simplified them in his early argument for a holistic character ethics, and we have been testing the method ever since (Stassen, "Social Theory Model" and "Critical Variables in Christian Social Ethics"). Potter was influenced by the social theory of Talcott Parsons and by his own inductive study of moral arguments. He argued that these variables are not only peculiar to Christians but that non-Christians as well need an answer to the crucial questions that Christians answer with their understanding of God, human nature and so on:

> a) Ethical thought requires a ground of obligation, some answer to the existential question, "Why ought I be moral?" or . . . "What is human purpose?" Here the most important Christian loci are the doctrine of *creation and human nature*, and the shape and purpose of *God's action in history.* b) Ethics requires some content of obligation, and a way to handle discrepancy between the authority of ethical imperatives and the demands of worldly powers. For this question, interesting Christian loci are the meaning and political implications of Christian *love, justice, and the Sermon on the Mount.* c) Ethics assumes a source of power or motivation: how can I will what is obligatory on me? In Christian terms, what are we to be saved from, and what sort of goodness can we hope for?—i.e., *justification and sanctification.* . . . d) Ethics demands to know the channel or means of empowerment through which the motivating power of goodness becomes effective, especially in the face of conflict, change, and hope. [Quoting Potter:] "No portion of the theological paradigm is more significant than the section that treats of the . . . concept of *the mission of the church,* which is itself derived from the perception of what God is doing in the world through . . . creation and providential rule, . . . special revelation in Jesus Christ, and . . . witness through the Holy Spirit." (Stassen, "Social Theory Model")

This means that the particular variables that we focus on are chosen because Jesus emphasized them in the Sermon on the Mount, because Potter's systematic study has identified them as crucial for the logic of moral argument and because we have confirmed their importance in our own study.

This discussion of basic convictions reminds us of a link between Christian character ethics and the issue of worldview, under much discussion these days in Christian intellectual life. A worldview is that cohesive set of beliefs through which people view the world and thus, consciously or not, set their life-course. Christian thinkers in recent years have come to recognize that the cultural moral drift about which we are so concerned is a worldview issue. Underneath the coarsening of media, or sexual libertinism, or the press for euthanasia, for example, are broader worldview trends—the celebration of autonomy, the self-fulfillment ethos and so on. A community's ethics flows from, and includes, the core worldview convictions through which that community interprets reality and defines the good life.

Thus, the concept of worldview corresponds with the category of basic convictions that we offer. We are claiming that Christian ethics must be self-consciously grounded in well-conceived theological convictions, fundamentally the vision of the reign of God. This is our worldview, our driving metanarrative; if it is not, we are quite likely grounding our living on some other fundamental worldview and thus straying from our loyalty to Jesus Christ. Worldview (basic convictions) helps shape character, and character overflows into action.

The Passions/Loyalties Dimension

No human being is an autonomous mind, coming to moral conclusions through the purely dispassionate application of reasoning. The autonomous mind was an Enlightenment myth, launched by Descartes and now thoroughly discredited. Instead, we are embodied persons, with characteristic passions— "seized by fear, stricken by jealousy, falling in love, surprised by joy, moved with compassion" (Harak, *Virtuous Passions*, 2). To deny the place of passions in human life is to succumb to a vast illusion. And precisely because of the moral significance of passions, they must be brought into the light of day for consideration, even transformation.

> It is somehow wrong not to feel revulsion at rape, or to stay forever angry with imperfect parents. It is somehow right to rejoice at a friend's success, or to be moved by the plight of an abused child. So it seems upon reflection that our passions can be morally praise- or blameworthy after all. It is my central concern . . . to work out a moral theological account of that sense of the rightness or wrongness of passions, and, further, to consider ways to transform morally blameworthy passions, and to foster morally praise-worthy passions. (Harak, *Virtuous Passions*, 2)

We can change our emotions by changing our habits, by encouraging other emotions, or by understanding the causal history of our emotions. "Passions [are] the matter, the stuff of virtue. . . . One of the tasks of virtue is to impart to passions a dynamic, habitual constancy through time" (Harak, *Virtuous Passions*, 36, 39).

Passions are deeply related to our loyalties and interests—whom and what we *trust* the most or get passionate about. We bring into every situation in life our deepest loyalties; these are not checked at the door. Jesus emphasizes this dimension: "Do not store up for yourselves treasures in this world, where they are subject to the ravage of such things as moth and corrosion and where thieves can break in and steal. . . . For wherever your treasure is, there too will be your heart" (Mt 6:19-21 Hagner's translation). Jesus' realism warns us to be aware of our loyalties and vested interests.

The loyalties that shape our character may be divided into four levels: (a) We are shaped by our *loyalties to friends, mentors and models*, as discussed above. (b) We are shaped by loyalties to the *practices and means* that we regularly use to achieve our goals: economists clearly see how economic forces are causative; army officers see military strength as crucial; mothers see love as formative; pastors think sermons shape the world; ethicists know that what influences most are scholarly articles in obscure academic journals. (c) Loyalties to *communities* shape us powerfully; this is a central theme of character ethics. (d) According to research in the sociology of religion, *ultimate loyalty to God* turns out to be a significant force against racism and other false ideologies (e.g., Stassen, *Capital Punishment*, 210-13; Dittes, *Bias and the Pious*, 79-80, 87; Dittes and Switzer, *Driven by Hope*; Gushee, *Righteous Gentiles*, chap. 6). So we should pay attention to these four—persons, practices, communities and ultimate loyalty—as key variables in the loyalties dimension of character.

Perhaps the best way to understand the concept of *interests* is to watch ideological debates—who makes the arguments, how such arguments are made and especially the use of moral claims. It is no coincidence that, say, tobacco companies emphasize the moral significance of personal choice, or that oil companies tend to emphasize the moral virtue of further exploration of oil deposits rather than energy-saving strategies, or that politicians deeply indebted to corporate contributions oppose campaign finance reform as a violation of freedom of expression. We see reality through the filter provided by our self-interest and often make deeply distorted moral arguments without realizing that we are doing so. Jesus taught us to become people of such character as to make the reign of God our primary interest: "But strive first for the kingdom of God and his righteousness" (Mt 6:33). When our interests are aligned with God's interests, we will be able to reason more like Jesus did and move toward Christlikeness.

The Perception Dimension

It is surprising how differently people see what happens. In the Sermon on the Mount, Jesus taught that we see differently according to where we have invested our money. He said that our hearts are shaped by where we have our money invested, and then he immediately pointed to two different ways of *seeing*: "Wherever your treasure is, there will be your heart. . . . The eye is the lamp of the body. If therefore your eye is generous, your whole person will be full of light. But if your eye is covetous, your whole person will be full of darkness" (Mt 6:21-22 Hagner's translation). Hagner (*Matthew 1—13*, 158-59) explains that the words here in Near Eastern culture mean a sound versus unsound eye in the sense of generous versus greedy. Jesus is saying that our interests—whether we have invested our money in such things that thieves can break in and steal, or instead in kingdom concerns (such as missions to the lost and justice for the hungry)—shape our hearts or loyalties, and this shapes our way of seeing what is happening. Thus Jesus' teaching about the generous versus the greedy eye connects with the verse before it about where we have our money invested. And it connects with the verse after it about not being able to serve two masters, God and money.

Furthermore, the different ways people see what is happening shapes the ethical action that they advocate as much or more than how they reason morally. A Chinese proverb wisely puts it this way: "Ninety percent of what we see lies behind our eyes" (Birch and Rasmussen, *Bible and Ethics in the Christian Life*, 77). Jesus emphasized *seeing* much more than most ethics does, and we believe that ethics needs to become much more self-aware and self-critical about how we perceive. Jesus often taught about how we see, or do not see, what God is doing. He quoted Isaiah 6:9-10 about hearts grown dull and eyes that do not see, and said, "Seeing they do not see, and hearing they do not hear, nor do they understand" (Mt 13:13). He said, "Do you still not perceive or understand? Are your hearts hardened? Do you have eyes, and fail to see?" (Mk 8:17-18). He told of the priest and the Levite who saw the man who had been robbed and passed by the other side, but the Samaritan *saw him with compassion* and went to him (Lk 10:30-35).

Perception of the context of actions powerfully shapes what people do. Ethicists need to study how people select data and synthesize and interpret it. It is not enough to say, "Pay attention to the facts," or, "Vision is important to character," as they usually do. Treating the facts as givens, or not developing a critical theory for assessing how people interpret facts, locks us into biases about what is happening and what is possible, and blocks critical assessment of the theories that guide the selection, synthesis and interpretation of those facts. Therefore our method of incarnational discipleship not only pays realistic attention to our embodied passions and interests, but also attempts to identify variables that shape perceptions of what the facts mean in ethically controversial questions. We believe we have strong grounding both in Jesus' teaching and in the reality that how we see shapes what we do.

Four variables make crucial differences in how people perceive the context of action across the spectrum of ethical issues. To identify these variables for the perception dimension, Glen researched variables that shaped perception and misperception by national leaders in contexts of peace and war. National leaders leave a public record of their perceptions, and so we can see what variables influence their perceptions (Stassen, "Individual Preferences and Role Constraints" and "Social Theory Model"; Jervis, *Perception and Misperception*, xii). Then we have both tested to see whether these four variables identify formative differences in how people interpret varieties of ethical issues. We believe attention to them helps us notice how people differ and helps us sort the issues involved.

First is the *authority* variable. What people assume about the *powers and authorities* of their time and place has a powerful effect on their perception of the context of moral action. Some have such a high view of the present authorities that they believe we need one, unified, God-ordained authority that everybody should obey. They see the alternative as chaos, anarchy or insubordination. Others have a high view of God's justice as above and independent of human authority and are realistic about the sin of all, including authorities. Therefore they advocate that authority should not be vested in one place but that there should be separation of the powers, so that there are checks and balances against misuse of authority. They believe each of us is responsible to measure authority by standards of God's justice, and they see the alternative as authoritarianism. We will see that there is a strong relationship between how people understand the justice variable in the basic convictions dimension, and how they see the authority variable in the perception dimension.

Second, our perceptions are enormously influenced by how we understand the cause of whatever is wrong. Borrowing social science terminology, we call this the *threat perception*. This concept is closely related to basic beliefs about *human nature and sin*. Christians who believe that they are righteous and that others outside their community are sinners will probably locate the threat outside themselves and not feel called to real repentance. But Christians who emphasize Jesus' teaching that we need to take out the log from our own eye are more likely to search for ways that we might be contributing to the problem. They are more likely to ask how we might do some repenting and make some changes that can help heal what is wrong. This is the virtue of repentance (and humility) that we saw in Jesus' teaching of the Beatitudes. Christians who see sin as bondage (Rom 3:9; 6:12-23; 7:13-25) are more likely to look for ways of deliverance from systemic causes of the threat; Christians who see sin only as free choice are more likely to assign blame or to urge moral effort.

A third crucial variable that affects people's ethical perceptions is their understanding of the potential efficacy of various *strategies for social change*. This was clearly illustrated in the civil rights movement in the United States. When people and churches gave their support to the strategy of nonviolent direct action, the wall of segregation began to fall. A social structure that had been viewed as impervious to change crumbled because people began to *see* new possibilities. Eventually the strategy of nonviolent direct action spread to the toppling of communist dictatorships in East European countries, the dictator Marcos in the Philippines and apartheid in South Africa. It continues to spread (Buttry, *Bringing Your Church Back to Life*, 1994). People who understand the efficacy of various social change strategies will tend to feel empowered for creating change. This relates closely to how we understand *the mission of the church* in the theological belief dimension. Does the church have a pastoral calling to foster justice for people, should it support the status quo, or should it focus only on its own inward life?

Fourth, perceptions are much influenced by one's *information integrity: truthfulness* in facing reality and openness to evidence that calls people to change their perceptions. In the Sermon on the Mount, Jesus emphasized truthfulness and we shall devote a full chapter (eighteen) to it. Josef Pieper describes this virtue as "the kind of *open-mindedness* which recognizes the true variety of things and situations to be experienced and does not cage itself in any presumption of deceptive knowledge. What is meant is the ability to take advice, sprung not from any vague 'modesty,' but simply from the *desire for real understanding* (which, however, necessarily includes genuine humility). A closed mind and know-it-allness are fundamentally forms of resistance to the truth of real things" (Pieper, *Four Cardinal Virtues*, 16, italics added). This is closely related to the virtues of humility and repentance, and to our basic conviction about *forgiveness and discipleship*. People who are convinced they are righteous and have little need for forgiveness are likely to be more closed-minded and less open to evidence that they may be seeing things wrongly. A mind that seeks correction and a commitment to communicating truth accurately are crucial for accuracy in the perceptual dimension of ethics.

Character ethics often emphasizes these themes of perception, vision, discernment, seeing with faith and seeing with compassion. William Spohn is particularly insightful on the narratives of Jesus, the practice of prayer and the Eucharist, and conversion and nurture working together to correct our way of perceiving (*Go and Do Likewise*, chaps. 4-5). As Gilbert Meilaender puts it, "An ethic which focuses on virtue rather than duty will tend to make *vision* central in the moral life. . . . The way we describe our dilemmas and define our obligations depends on how we see the world. . . . An ethic of virtue is dominated by the eye, by metaphors of sight and vision" (*Theory and Practice of Virtue*, ix, 17). People's vision of the world frames their perception of dilemmas and obligations. We want to sharpen the focus by identifying variables that shape how people perceive the context in which ethics takes place. We want to seek self-critical awareness of how those variables work, and how they relate to Christian virtues and to basic Christian convictions. This will unfold as we study controversial questions in subsequent chapters. You will be the judge of whether our emphasis on self-awareness about the dimension of perception in character helps to increase your own awareness and your own character.

Jesus came preaching, "The reign of God is at hand; *repent, therefore,* and believe the good news." The good news of what God has for us is so good that the contrast with present actuality convinces us we need to repent; the good news is so forgiving that we are freed to be honest about where we need to repent; the judgment involved is so serious that we need to be serious about repentance. Therefore, a key move in a Christian ethics patterned after Jesus is to listen carefully to criticisms and learn from them. Christian ethics is continuous learning, transformational repenting, making corrections and growing in Christ. Jesus said, "You will know them by their fruits" (Mt 7:20). Therefore we take responsibility for our deeds and monitor the feedback from what we do. When we notice that we have done wrong, we stop to examine what led us to produce bad fruit. We can seek to identify where we went wrong and make corrections in our ethics. Repentance makes a correction. Identifying the variables that shape our ethics helps us to recognize what went wrong when attention to the fruits of our ethics tells us something did go wrong. Thus we are able to make corrections or repent more accurately so as to grow a more adequate ethic for further actions. In this way we grow character. (See figure 3.1.)

In the spirit of being open to criticism and making accurate corrections, we need to ask, what are some criticisms of character ethics that need to be heard and learned from?

Joseph Kotva: Is Character Ethics Salvation by Works?

Joseph Kotva, himself a virtue ethicist, criticizes virtue ethicists generally for failing to pay adequate attention to the theological or basic-convictions dimension. They fail to relate virtue to *sin, grace, discipleship and Jesus* (Kotva, *Christian Case for Virtue Ethics*, 50). "The themes of *forgiveness and reconciliation,* for example, are important in Scripture but are absent from most virtue accounts" (Kotva, *Christian Case for Virtue Ethics*, 61; see Hays, *Moral Vision of the New Testament*, 253-66, 291).

Ironically, this lack of theology and biblical exegesis may be a carryover from the modern Enlightenment ethics against which virtue ethicists are reacting. Enlightenment ethics was based upon Greek philosophical ethics, which concentrated on moral reasoning, and it neglected the Hebraic tradition with its attention to the other three dimensions—embodiment, convictions and seeing. In reacting against Enlightenment-influenced philosophical ethics, some virtue ethicists may still be mesmerized by its focus on the way of reasoning to the neglect of the other three dimensions. Overdependence on the Greek philosopher Aristotle may lead to neglect of the Hebraic or biblical tradition. Reformed, Anabaptist, and Pentecostal and Holiness traditions, as well as

Catholic and Orthodox renewal movements, now emphasize recovery of our Hebraic heritage. Our holistic ethics of character, with its attention to basic theological convictions and its explicitly Hebraic and prophetic base, systematically and intentionally corrects this weakness.

One crucial theological question is the relation between *forgiveness and sanctification (the life of discipleship)*. Character ethics emphasizes training character by regular practices in community, such as baptism, the Lord's Supper or Eucharist, and feeding the hungry (Yoder, *Body Politics*, chaps. 2 and 3). But many will ask whether this emphasis pays sufficient attention to the doctrine of salvation by grace alone. Does character ethics so emphasize practices that grow character that it skates too close to the thin ice of justification by works? Does *grace* mean God's forgiveness without our works, or does *grace* mean God's empowerment by the Holy Spirit to become new persons and live the Christian life of love?

Some Christians so emphasize forgiveness that they fear emphases on sanctification, discipleship, following Jesus and doing the will of God because these emphases might lead to trusting in our own works. This fear can result in Dietrich Bonhoeffer's "cheap grace," or "easy believism," in which following Jesus is ignored. It produces people who call themselves Christians but live no differently than unbelievers. By contrast, others so emphasize the empowerment of the Holy Spirit to live the Christian life that they diminish forgiveness for fear that it might lead to permissiveness. They emphasize discipleship, sanctification or holiness so strongly that there is a danger of self-righteousness or legalism. But Jesus strongly emphasized both forgiveness and doing his teachings (Mt 6:12-15; 7:15-27). We believe the solution is in radically emphasizing forgiveness so we are not afraid of failure if we commit ourselves to following Jesus fully, and in radically emphasizing following Jesus so we do know that we fail and need to live by forgiveness.

The apostle Paul employs many images to illustrate spiritual growth and moral progress. Paul speaks of walking, living and participating in Christ, and being in union with Christ. He pictures the Christian life as a race, for which we must train ourselves with regular discipline, and as aiming toward the goal of becoming more spiritually mature. To walk is "a common Semitic idiom for a pattern of behavior. . . . Instead of seeing morality primarily as discrete acts, judgments, and dilemmas, 'walking' or 'living' pictures morality as patterns of behavior and a continuous journey. . . . Paul's references to 'transformation' are also instructive. . . . He . . . sees Christ gradually reshaping us (2 Cor. 3:18; Rom. 8:29, 12:2). . . . Paul can even use faith as a synonym for obedience (Rom. 1:5, 8; 10:16; 11:23, 30, 31; 15:18; 16:19)" (Kotva, *Christian Case for Virtue Ethics*, 124-30; C. Wright, *Walking in the Ways of the Lord*; Hays, "Justification").

So Paul, the apostle of grace, strongly teaches the life of *being conformed to Christ*, of *participating in Christ*—themes Dietrich Bonhoeffer made central in order to maintain a balance between the extremes of cheap grace on the one hand and an overemphasis on works on the other (Todd, "Participation"). We have already seen that the theme of participation in the delivering reign of God is central in the Beatitudes. In a perceptive, sensitive and engaging study, William Spohn develops ways that *practices of spirituality* grounded in *concrete narratives of the way of Jesus Christ* are very important for shaping character in an *ethics of character* (Spohn, *Go and Do Likewise*).

Kotva argues that solid biblical and theological grounding is necessary for character ethics, and that such grounding transforms the content of the ethics. Virtues are not works we do ourselves, nor are they our own individual possessions; they are our participation in the living Christ. Life is life in Christ, and life in the Holy Spirit, through whom God pours his love into our hearts (Rom 5:5). "Sanctification involves a major affirmation that the earlier account of virtue theory does not mention: dependence on God's grace." Christian sanctification has its goal beyond this world, eschatologically; Aristotelian virtue ethics does not (Kotva, *Christian Case for Virtue Ethics*, 74, 76). But character ethics is right that "God's grace does not merely free us from sin. God's grace also frees us for a certain kind of life—one that exhibits" the fruits of the Spirit in community, not in isolation (91-92).

Without having set out to confirm the basic-conviction variables that we have identified, Kotva provides significant confirmation that these are the theological variables that are crucial for Christian ethics. Besides *grace, discipleship, forgiveness and reconciliation*, Kotva identifies other theological themes as essential for character ethics. He interprets theologians Hendrikus Berkhof, Millard Erickson, John Macquarrie, Norman Kraus and Edward Schillebeeckx as arguing that the goal or end of the process of sanctification is *Christlikeness*—being conformed to the image of Christ—with attention to Jesus' entire life, and not merely a particular principle such as love. *God's* gracious forgiveness and love, and our surrender and obedience before *God*, are important themes (Kotva, *Christian Case for Virtue Ethics*, 72ff.). *Human nature* is a crucial variable: considerations of the purpose of life, the good we prize, as well as the sin that impedes us (18, 52, 148). Furthermore, "Biblical *justice* is preoccupied with the needs of those who are poor, weak, disadvantaged, or oppressed (e.g., Deut. 24:17; Ps. 10:17-18; Isa. 10:1-2; Jer. 5:28; Luke 4:18-19)" (148). And all Christian virtue ethicists emphasize community, so a key theological theme for Kotva is *the mission of the church*.

Jean Porter: Does Character Ethics Abandon Principles?

Jean Porter makes clear that virtue ethics needs "ordering principles that a community must embody if its members are to be able to act in concert while each also seeks his or her own good as an individual." A principle is a general guideline, like equal treatment before the law, or justice to the poor, that applies not only to individuals but guides rules of action for a whole community or society, and so can also be used to measure the rectitude of an institution or an ideology. Virtues usually apply to persons, not to actions. Porter is saying that an ethic of virtues alone is inadequate; we also need an ethic of principles. Similarly, McClendon (*Ethics*, 1:163) advocates concrete rules as well; rules define practices. And Paris insists that "an ethic of virtue does not replace or preclude an imperative ethic of duty and obedience as prescribed by law" (*Spirituality of African Peoples*, 136).

If we reason only about virtues, then we become deaf and dumb with regard to principles that can guide us in assessing powers and authorities like governments, corporations, social and economic ideologies (e.g., racism, socialism) and political systems (tyranny, democracy). An ethic of virtues alone is a one-legged stool. So Porter points out that Thomas Aquinas, the great Catholic theologian who focused much attention on virtues, affirms principles as well as virtues:

> Aquinas' own theory of the virtues is very different from Hauerwas' theory, if only because Aquinas, unlike Hauerwas, grounds his theory of the virtues in a general theory of goodness and the human good. For this reason, it would be misleading to assume that the dichotomies between virtue theory and other sorts of moral theories that Hauerwas emphasizes are also present in Aquinas' work. . . . On Hauerwas' view, moral rules are precisely defined, rigid, and apply mostly to quandaries, whereas virtues are not precisely defined, are flexible, and apply to the whole of life. . . . If one means by a morality of rules a theory of morality according to which certain concrete kinds of action are identified as praiseworthy or blameworthy, then Aquinas certainly espouses a morality of rules as well as a morality of virtues. Indeed, his analysis of the moral value of actions and his analysis of the virtues fit together as two parts of one comprehensive theory of morality. Morally good kinds of actions are conceptually linked to the virtues, in that certain determinate kinds of actions are characteristic of particular virtues and tend to promote them in the individual." (Porter, *Recovery of Virtue*, 104-5)

In their more recent book, Hauerwas and Pinches affirm that their virtue ethics is not an alternative to rule- or principle-based ethics (*Christians Among Virtues*, ix). In fact, Hauerwas had said that earlier (*Community of Character*, 130). He is often understood as opposing rules and principles because he writes polemically and is tempted to throw out everything other kinds of ethics affirm, and he develops few rules or principles himself.

Fritz Stern: Is Character Ethics the Inward Emigration of Despair?

The Politics of Cultural Despair, by Columbia University historian Fritz Stern, is a study of three popular German philosophers of the late nineteenth and early twentieth century who reacted against the ethics of the Enlightenment and modernity and advocated a turn inward. These three—Paul de Lagarde, Julius Langbehn and Moeller van den Bruck—criticized the Enlightenment for being secular and atheistic, and for advocating universal categories that denigrated tradition and community standards. They reacted against the multiculturalism and lack of (homogeneous) community in modern cities. Instead they advocated a turn inward to traditional values, to homogeneous community and to cultivation of virtuous selves in homogeneous enclaves. This was "inward emigration"—emigration away from civic responsibility and toward likeminded self-righteousness. It was the politics of cultural despair.

    In their reaction against the secular culture of their time, these three philosophers turned cynical and despairing about the struggle for democracy, justice and human rights. They (wrongly) identified human rights as a product of the atheistic French Enlightenment and so rejected human rights. The concept of human rights is in fact the product of free-church Puritans in their struggle for religious liberty a century before the Enlightenment (Stassen, *Just Peacemaking: Transforming Initiatives,* 137ff.; Westmoreland-White, "Setting the Record Straight"). So at a critical period in German history, these philosophers persuaded their readers to withdraw their support from efforts to make democracy work. Their influence was a significant factor in the failure of Germany's attempt at democracy in the Weimar Republic and the takeover by Hitler and his fascists. Their advocacy of homogeneous community gave support to the rise of an authority figure to enforce like-mindedness and exclude people who were different. Through their erroneous critique of human rights as a product of the Enlightenment, when in fact it came from free-church Puritans a century before the Enlightenment, they undermined the standards of justice needed to recognize Hitler's evil and to organize opposition to Hitler's injustices. They unintentionally prepared the way for Nazism, Hitler, World War II and the Holocaust.

    Does character ethics, in its revolt against the ethics of the Enlightenment and modernity, also advocate homogeneous community? Is it another inward emigration of despair? Does it influence people to abdicate their God-given responsibility to pursue God's will in all of life, and instead to focus only on inward being? The character ethicist Gilbert Meilaender asks whether, in an increasingly narcissistic age, virtue ethics is part of a larger current of history toward

> an increasingly dangerous concentration upon self and self-development? . . . Self-consciousness about self is the fate which may too easily await a concentration upon virtue. . . . What about the danger of self-centeredness? Does not the very language of virtue suggest too much concentration upon self, too intense a devotion to self-cultivation? There is reason for concern here, especially when we

remember that the revival . . . of interest in the virtues has largely coincided with countless different versions of self-fulfillment and "developing one's own potential" within our culture. (*Theory and Practice of Virtue*, 13, 16, 39)

Hispanic Pentecostal ethicist Eldin Villafañe of Gordon-Conwell Theological Seminary has the same fear ("Politics of the Spirit," 162-63). If we advocate an ethics of virtue in the midst of a narcissistic culture that focuses on self-development and uses others as a means to self-fulfillment, will the culture use virtue ethics to foster narcissistic individualism? Will virtue ethics be used by culture to justify turning inward, away from concern for developing the structures of justice that are necessary for preventing the destructive collusion of sin and power?

Meilaender also warns of "the moral paralysis which comes from focusing upon self, from our illusions of self-mastery and our tendency to claim virtue as our possession. . . . As Luther thought he had learned from personal experience, too much attention to the examined life can be dangerous; it directs our gaze inward rather than outward to the promise" (*Theory and Practice of Virtue*, 107, 126).

The problem is exacerbated when some describe character ethics as an emphasis on being rather than doing. This is a fundamental error. Doing is crucial: fundamental to character ethics is that *practices shape character*. We are the kind of people we are because of what we do, what we *practice*. Again and again, Jesus emphasizes doing the word: Many will say "Lord, Lord," but will not be part of the kingdom; only those who do the will of God will enter. The wise person is the one who hears these words and does them; the foolish one hears these words and does not do them, and great will be the destruction (Mt 7:21-27). John Howard Yoder often reminded us that the New Testament speaks more about doing than about virtues (Hauerwas and Pinches, *Christians Among Virtues*, 113). Jesus proclaimed that concentrating on being righteous without lifting a finger for the weightier matters of justice, faithfulness and mercy brings disaster for the poor and judgment upon ourselves (Mt 23:23).

Joseph Kotva's Pennsylvania Mennonite church has combated virulent racism in the local culture with transformative practices. The church called forth one member's wonderful gift of quilting. She crafted a beautiful quilt of an African resurrected Jesus with arms outstretched, lovingly welcoming everyone who looks upon him. It covers the wall behind the pulpit during each worship service and welcomes all in whom the Holy Spirit brings about conversion, all who commit themselves to following Jesus. It portrays the theme in the Book of Acts of not being "hindered" from baptism by one's ethnicity (1955), and Yoder's explication of the practice of baptism as tearing down barriers (*Royal Priesthood*, 367 and 367n). When the occasion arises, the pastor and church members clearly explain that racist jokes or comments are not appropriate in a Christian community. Furthermore, this mainly white church now shares its space with a Latino congregation. Thus, *in regular church practices*, antiracism is clearly communicated as part of the commitment to follow Jesus Christ. Building this Christian commitment into the heart of the church's regular practice is much more effective than an occasional sermon or lesson. Like a parent, the church teaches more by practices explained by words than by words alone.

Antidotes to Inward Emigration

James McClendon argued that reducing ethics to the introspective conscience is a distortion, "an intense interiorization of Christian life." It focuses on our own choosing rather than on God's will as revealed in Jesus Christ (*Ethics*, 1:56-58). Here McClendon is joining with Dietrich Bonhoeffer, who makes similar criticisms in his *Ethics*. Both McClendon and Bonhoeffer criticize an "ethics of the gaps" that focuses on those extreme cases where we do not know what to do. Instead, they want us to focus on God's will in the center of our daily life. To overcome the reduction of ethics to an introspective struggle, McClendon developed an ethics with three strands: the body strand (including passions), the social strand (including social context) and the redemptive strand (including resurrection and eschatology). We agree. This is why we have developed our four-dimensional, holistic ethics. We believe all four dimensions (see figure 3.1, p. 59) are needed for a holistic ethic that is an antidote against inward emigration.

Most Christians participate in more than one community. They may participate in the community of their church, of their workplace, their circle of friends, their school and so on. We advocate that they also participate in a community that serves the needy or works for justice for the marginalized, as Jesus did. This will give them a new loyalty and a new perspective, and can enable them to engage in the kind of caring that we see in Jesus and the tradition that he embodied (Everett, "Vocation and Location," 91ff.). Their church may itself have such a mission group, or they may join a group of caring persons outside the church and make their witness as well as find their own compassionate character growing there. People are much less likely to be actively and effectively engaged in such caring action unless they are part of a group that does so regularly (Wuthnow, *Acts of Compassion*).

It is not enough to teach love in general. Many Christians rightly consider themselves loving persons and cultivate virtue in interpersonal relationships, but they lack awareness of how their participation in various economic and political structures promotes destructive policies, institutions and social practices. Character ethics desperately needs critical social theory or it can misuse people to turn them into virtuous supporters of an unjust society. Darryl Trimiew has pointed out that Robert E. Lee was known as a model of virtue. But he lacked a critical social theory that would have diagnosed the injustice of slavery. Therefore he dedicated his virtuous leadership skills to fighting a war to defend the system of slavery (Trimiew, "Limits of Virtue Theory").

Jesus did not concern himself only with the problem of individual sin. Out of concern for justice, Jesus confronted the religious and political authorities of his day who sought prestige for themselves without lifting a finger to relieve those who were excluded and oppressed (Mt 23:23; Lk 11:46; 13:10-16). This is why we emphasize *principles* of justice and human rights, the plumb line for measuring the powers and authorities (Amos 7:7-8). And it is why we assert the importance of *the way of seeing the social context* as crucial for an ethics of character.

Virtue does not only mean private morality. Character ethics emphasizes that every public institution has assumptions about what kind of character and virtues its participants should have. So character ethics tests institutions by what kind of people they develop (Hauerwas, *Community of Character*, 123). The standards of justice practiced in a society have an enormous influence on the moral virtues of persons in that society. The *Los Angeles Times* ran a series of articles on corruption, crime and poverty in Russia, describing how the economic system encourages ordinary Russians to make stealing a regular practice. During the Cold War, Europeans observed that the Americans they met were enculturated to have a strikingly hostile image of the Soviet Union as the enemy. Every Fourth of July, Americans celebrate their "independence"—an important part of the American ethos shaped by the narrative of U.S. history, which tells how America was founded in a revolutionary war. And Texans commemorate the Battle of the Alamo as almost a sacred story of the birth of Texas. American history is often taught largely as a history of wars (Juhnke and Hunter, *Missing Peace*). American television and children's video games are filled with violence.

These societal practices certainly influence moral character; the American homicide rate is far worse than in other comparable countries. Much of this societal influence on moral character operates at an unconscious level and goes uncorrected by persons who lack clear principles of justice and peacemaking with which to assess them. Without clear principles to correct injustice in society, persons become mere bystanders—and ultimately tacit supporters—of unjust and violent institutions and policies. Christians spend an hour or two in church each week but many hours in the society. Most Christians are not likely to be innoculated against the influence of the society's values by what they learn in church; the norm is simply to not talk about societal values while in church. To develop antibodies to false values, Christians need to develop their own bibically based social theories.

A holistic character ethics needs to develop a self-critical understanding of how we perceive *authority, change, threat and truthfulness* in our society. Without that, Christians will not understand how to act effectively to "seek the shalom of the city where you dwell" (Jer 29:7). They will emigrate inwardly into small enclaves of self-fulfillment. Their ethics will ignore powerful influences in the society that shape people's character and will lack the antidotes with which to correct secular ideologies. They will not know how to share in God's compassion for the mistreated. They will naively support an unjust status quo. They will have an ethics that focuses only on philosophical or theological generalities, or only on individualistic virtues, and act as if God is Lord only of theological doctrines, or of the private, individual life, and not of the power structures and struggles for justice. Those who do not understand the causative forces in society are condemned to repeat yesterday's injustices tomorrow.

The disciplines concerned with how society functions are primarily the social sciences. Studying social science is highly useful for Christian ethicists— both in order to learn from these disciplines themselves and also to understand the ethical assumptions that guide different schools of social science. Therefore, most Christian ethicists become critically aware of theories in at least one of the social sciences, such as sociology, political science, economics or international relations. A good Christian ethicist can discern ethical assumptions that inform methodologies employed by social scientists for selecting, synthesizing and interpreting data, and can thereby see how to interpret their conclusions critically.

Character ethicists emphasize narrative and interpret a society in terms of its master narrative. If they do that without critical study of social science, they may foster an idealistic interpretation that neglects power structures, economic arrangements and global forces: a society's master narrative often conceals its power relationships. We need to study power structures and organizational functions to uncover the real powers behind the thrones. For example, a narrative ethic without social analysis could interpret the boyfriend's problem in the movie *Jersey Girl* only in terms of the narrative of his individual ambition and would overlook the forces of economic globalization and corporate interest that inculcate and reward such self-centered values. Simply to criticize his narrative without understanding it in its global economic context is to focus on virtues without context, ideals without embodiment. This is a gnostic (disembodied) method, not the method of *incarnational* discipleship. Therefore, our perception dimension pays attention to assumptions about power and authority.

Validation by Historical Fruits

In our postmodern age, people want to know what difference the gospel makes for people's actual living. They doubt claims to "timeless truths." They experience different beliefs by people of different cultures, and different beliefs contending against each other within any one culture. They want to validate truth not by an authoritarian claim but by seeing how it works out in life. Unless we develop a clear understanding of validation of truth by its historical and experiential fruits, we are likely to fall into a subjective relativism. Evangelism requires first-hand witness to the difference Christian faith makes in actual lives. Jesus said it: "You will know them by their fruits." We believe that history is the laboratory in which our faith is tested. (H. Richard Niebuhr wrestled mightily with historical relativism. For eight steps in validating ethical truth, developed under his influence, see Stassen, Yeager and Yoder, *Authentic Transformation*, 156-62.) We have already cited Fritz Stern's study of the danger of inward emigration as one example of testing an ethic in the laboratory of history.

David Gushee studied those Gentiles who risked their lives to rescue Jews from the Nazis during the Holocaust. He asked what kind of virtues, what kind of influences, what kind of beliefs gave the rescuers enough clarity and strength to save the lives of Jews, when the vast majority of Christians and non-Christians either did nothing or else actively assisted the Nazis. He found that what mattered most was not any kind of self-proclaimed religious or political loyalty, but instead the kinds of moral practices in place among those whose help was sought. All four dimensions that we have identified turned out to be important.

Rescuers were more likely than nonrescuers to have grown up with parents who modeled responding "to others' needs in a caring and giving fashion," and who held firm opinions on moral issues and served as a model of moral conduct. Moral instruction whose content included tolerance, emphasizing the common humanity of all people, was a striking element of many rescuers' upbringing, as well as "a predisposition to regard all people as equals and to apply similar standards of right and wrong to them without regard to their social status or ethnicity" (Gushee, *Righteous Gentiles*).

Other common values included a commitment to justice, the obligation to care for people in need and the importance of being generous, loving, hospitable, concerned and helpful. Independence, self-reliance, competence and high self-esteem also cropped up frequently as the kinds of personal traits and moral virtues stressed by rescuers' parents. "Parental warmth and nurture that developed empathy in their children" were important. "Parents of rescuers relied less on physical punishment as a form of discipline than did parents of nonrescuers" and tended to reason with their children instead (Gushee, *Righteous Gentiles*).

Furthermore, Gushee's study found that "rescuers had more friends, coworkers, and neighbors who were Jewish than did nonrescuers." They also were more likely to have at least one friend, relative or community committed to rescue. Rescue was deeply affected by community ties and community character. Similarly, Murray W. Dempster shows how the early Pentecostals crossed the borders of race and class and that this figured strongly in their early radical social ethic—an ethic that, in the United States, they lost when they separated along race and class lines ("Crossing Borders," 63-80).

"A considerable number . . . acted on the basis of a political theory that enabled them to see through the deceptions of the fascist ideology and join together in an alternative view of justice in society." More than their neighbors, rescuers tended toward a belief in democratic pluralism and the full acceptance of diverse groups in national life. The inhabitants of the French village of Le Chambon, who hid as many Jews as there were villagers, had held an annual ceremony commemorating their Huguenot ancestors who were persecuted by the government. This helped give them a critical perspective on the government's injustice. As a community they had developed a commitment to justice and nonviolence.

Gushee concluded: "Character by itself is an empty vessel. . . . The churches must . . . also work more carefully to define the *kind* of character they want to produce." We must teach "the fixed perception that every other human being is my equal—in fact, my kin—and thus equally precious and worthy of a decent life. The Christian must be schooled to see that despite important differences among human beings, ultimately our common humanity bears more significance than that which divides us." We must teach open-heartedness—"an openness to receiving and interacting with the other's joy, pain, sorrow, or whatever else they bring to the encounter . . . a willingness to be vulnerable before and with the other . . . consistent alertness to the needs of the other." We must return central biblical teachings on compassion and love to the forefront of Christian proclamation and education (Gushee, *Righteous Gentiles*, chaps. 5-7).

A holistic ethic of character was crucial for those free-church Puritan Christians who acted to bring about religious liberty, democracy and human rights in the 1600s. It was crucial for those Christians who rescued Jews rather than passing by on the other side. It was crucial for those Christians who struggled to help the United States get free from the bondage of racial segregation and discrimination. It was crucial in Eastern Europe when communist dictatorships were toppled nonviolently, and in South Africa when apartheid was toppled. We believe it is crucial now as we are called to seek the shalom of the world in which we live. Will the twenty-first century bring the globalization of poverty and misery, or the globalization of peace and the sacredness of human life? Will we produce Christians who hide from that struggle or who participate with authentic Christian character and witness?

SECTION II:

The Way of Jesus
and Prophetic Authority

These chapters consider several knotty questions of methodology in Christian ethics.

Chapter four reflects on the question of authority—how we can reliably come to know God's will for the Christian moral life. We focus on how Scripture is to be interpreted for Christian ethics, emphasizing Jesus' statement in the Sermon that he came not to abolish but to fulfill the Law and the Prophets.

Chapter five takes up the matter of how moral reasoning takes place, addressing a number of perennial issues in ethical methodology. We argue that moral claims occur at four levels and that all are present in Jesus' recorded teachings. This four-level model then provides a grid for considering a wide range of important approaches to the language of moral reasoning. We also link the discussion of practices and virtues (chapters two and three) to this four-level approach.

Finally, chapter six further prepares the way for the more concrete discussions of the rest of the book by offering an approach to interpreting the Sermon on the Mount, the largest block of Jesus' recorded teaching and the central biblical passage we will consider in this volume. We trace how the evasion of the Sermon developed in historic Christian thought, the tragic consequences of that evasion and a discovery that rescues the Sermon from the realm of supposed "high ideals" and instead makes it a path to participation in the reign of God—as we think Jesus intended all along.

In each case, our focus on the kingdom of God as the context for all Christian moral reflection and practice brings new perspectives to these critical interpretive and methodological questions.

4

AUTHORITY AND SCRIPTURE

For truly I tell you, until heaven and earth pass away, not one letter, not one stroke of a letter, will pass from the law until all is accomplished. Therefore, whoever breaks one of the least of these commandments, and teaches others to do the same, will be called least in the kingdom of heaven; but whoever does them and teaches them will be called great in the kingdom of heaven. For I tell you, unless your righteousness exceeds that of the scribes and Pharisees, you will never enter the kingdom of heaven.

MATTHEW 5:18-20

Our goal in this chapter is to explore two key methodological issues in Christian ethics raised by what Jesus says about the law and the prophets here in Matthew 5:17-20. We will consider these related questions:

1. Where shall Christians turn for authoritative insight and direction in shaping their ethics? This is the question of *sources of authority*.
2. How shall Scripture be interpreted in Christian ethics? This is *the use of Scripture* question.

In answering these two questions, we will attempt to carry forward the method we have been applying so far—to consider important issues in Christian ethics on the basis of a consistent and informed focus on the teachings and practice of Jesus, in the context of the prophetic tradition of Israel, yet in dialogue with other important approaches both historic and contemporary. The result will be both a survey of the landscape and a proposal concerning what a Christian ethics that takes Jesus seriously might look like.

Sources of Authority for Christian Ethics

The issue of authority, in particular biblical authority, is a recurring question in church life and in Christian ethics. While the matter is frequently shrouded in controversy and in politicized rhetoric, it can and should be addressed forthrightly, in search of clear direction from Jesus.

If the church is functioning as it should, it will continually and very earnestly engage in a search for authoritative direction and insight concerning its
character and its conduct. It will desire above all else to know and to live out
the answer to the prophet's question, "What does the LORD require?" (Mic 6:8),
recognizing that the question needs to be asked again and again, rather than
once and for all. Christians whose lives are directed by this question need to
know where and to whom to turn in order to discover the answer. Those fonts
of insight and direction to which Christians turn are called the sources of authority for Christian ethics. Discussion of the sources of authority is a standard
feature of many ethics texts.

To illustrate the concept of sources of authority, consider once again the situation facing a Christian family confronted with the decision of whether or not
to take in persecuted Jews during the Holocaust. Here we flatly offer a broad
normative claim: where this family's commitment to Jesus Christ was operat-
ing as it should, their decision was made in light of—*under the authority of*—
their Christian faith and its moral resources. Where Christian faith is functioning as it should, it serves as the governing paradigm for life. Life is governed
by the narrative of God's coming reign in Christ and the way of life appropriate to it. Ultimately, in a growing Christian moral life this process becomes second nature. One is so absorbed into kingdom living and one's identity as
Christ's disciple that it essentially becomes impossible to respond to the circumstances of life from any other frame of reference.

One might say, then, that the sources of authority are the particular components of Christian identity that when woven together in the life of the church
constitute the rich tapestry of Christian moral conviction. Some of these sources of authority are unique to Christian faith, while others are generally available to all people within a particular historical situation, in which case their
"use" depends on their "user's" overall worldview and core convictions.

During the Holocaust, to continue our example, some Christians looked
primarily to the *Bible* for direction concerning how to respond to Jews in need
of help. Frequently, such people also prayed fervently in search of direct *divine guidance*, while others turned inward seeking direction from a religiously
informed moral *conscience*. Many looked for leadership from the *moral traditions* of their churches, while others turned for guidance to their current
church leaders. These five sources of authority, in some mix—and the mix itself
is obviously quite critical—can be seen as the most distinctively Christian
sources of authority.

Other Christians, though, turned to other sources of insight and direction.
For example, some looked not to church leaders but to other persons of significant moral authority in their lives, such as spouses, parents, teachers, cul-

tural figures, favorite politicians and friends. Some searched their nation's heritage for national values to which to appeal. If they felt a pull in the direction of rescuing Jews, some reflected carefully on the facts of their life-situation as they perceived them, and on their own and others' experiences related to both Nazis and Jews, before plunging into rescue. This latter group of sources of authority—and others surely could be named—are not distinctively Christian. Yet, in our view, they can and sometimes do function usefully as sources of authority for Christians when woven into a rightly ordered overall tapestry of moral authority.

This is what we mean by the sources of authority for ethics. People do not need to be told to hunt for guidance when they face important moral choices. They do it instinctively. The issue is not whether they will turn somewhere for guidance, but where they turn, to whom they turn, and what sources they will count as authoritative, not just in theory but in actual practice. Frequently, Christians reflect their cultural and ideological captivity by failing to consider distinctive Christian sources of authority or by proving unable to reflect on either these or general sources of authority with eyes able to see and ears able to hear. Many carry the name Christian and yet habitually fail to live their lives within the moral horizon actually established by Christian faith, or with reference to the fonts of moral conviction that exist within that faith.

Christian moral failure during the Holocaust itself provides stark illustration of this point. Many Christians failed to consider any particularly Christian sources of authority. They considered the risks to themselves, their neighbors' opinions, the view of the Jews presented by Nazi propaganda, the behavior of national leaders, their own experiences, their fears and so on, but nothing explicitly from the Christian tradition. This was true even of some who decided to rescue Jews.

Other Christians did consider such sources, like Scripture and prayer, but mangled them due to captivity to the power of anti-Semitism, nationalism and other "powers and authorities." For example, Scripture was interpreted by some to mean that God was punishing the Jews for "killing Christ" and should be aided in doing so. This act of interpretive mayhem was not unique, nor is similar interpretive mayhem today (Gushee, *Righteous Gentiles*, 118).

Perhaps worst of all, some of the sources themselves, notably tradition, were seriously flawed well before the Holocaust began. Anti-Semitism runs deep in the Christian tradition. This deeply distorted tradition was seriously in need of reformation and frequently led earnest seekers of guidance in precisely the wrong direction. For this the church itself has rightly been held accountable by its post-Holocaust Jewish dialogue partners. We can never again relate uncritically to our own sources of authority, our own narrative, as Darrell Fasching has perceptively reminded us (Fasching, *Ethical Challenge of Auschwitz and Hiroshima*).

Thus far we have made only the broadest of claims about the sources of authority. It is not enough to say that Scripture, tradition, divine guidance, conscience, church leaders and the others function as sources of authority. Christians need to know which among these sources they should really use, and how to order and rank the constellation of sources to which they do turn, not to mention how to make adequate use of each particular source. Different Christian traditions stand ready to give us different answers to these questions. About this we will say more later. But we think it important to be true to our focus on Jesus and first do what is less frequently done—consider how Jesus himself appeared to consider and employ the sources of authority.

Jesus and the Sources of Authority

The New Testament reveals that though Jesus made use of many of the sources we have named, the Bible (for him, the Hebrew Bible) served as the premier source of authority. In his teaching and preaching he constantly appealed to the Scriptures, quoting, alluding to or showing the impact of all aspects of his Bible. It is clear that Jesus immersed himself in the Scriptures, knew them well and lived out what he understood them to teach. Like so many other faithful Jews, he lived within the narrative horizon the Bible established. Other sources of authority found their place with reference to the Bible as he understood it.

Here it is important to return to Matthew 5:17-20 to correct a fundamental misunderstanding concerning Jesus' approach to the Old Testament, especially in the Sermon on the Mount. One of the most authoritative works on the Gospel of Matthew makes the following claim about Matthew 5:17-20:

> [This passage] plainly states that the six subsequent paragraphs are not to be interpreted—as they have been so often by so many—as "antitheses," "antitheses" that, in at least two or three instances, set aside the Torah. Instead Jesus upholds the Law. So that between him and Moses there can be no real conflict. (Davies and Allison, *Critical and Exegetical Commentary*, 1:481-82, 501)

In Luke 16:17, Jesus emphasizes the same point: "It is easier for heaven and earth to pass away, than for one stroke of a letter in the law to be dropped." Geza Vermes notes, "In the Lord's Prayer, Jesus followed 'Thy Kingdom come' with 'Thy will be done,' a divine will seen by Judaism of all ages as being expressed and manifested in the commandments received by Moses on Mount Sinai" and recorded in the Bible (*Jesus the Jew*, 148-49). So there can be little question that for Jesus the Scriptures are thoroughly authoritative for our ethics.

Jesus' discussion of the Pharisaic/rabbinic religious tradition makes the centrality and authority of Scripture strikingly clear, while also revealing his approach to tradition itself. In a key conversation with Pharisees and scribes,

Jesus quoted his favorite prophet, Isaiah, and also Moses. He juxtaposed "human tradition" (Mk 7:8)—the carefully developed "tradition of the elders" (Mk 7:3)—over against the Scripture, rejecting the former in favor of the latter where they conflict. He called Scripture the "commandment of God" (Mk 7:8) and the "word of God" (Mk 7:13), while offering no such attribution to tradition. In this particular conversation, he addressed the contrast between the fifth commandment ("honor your father and mother") and a contemporary tradition which was understood to relieve one from the obligation to support one's aged parents. On scriptural authority Jesus rejected the tradition.

For Jesus, then, a clear distinction existed between the Word of God and human tradition. This is the key point of Matthew 5:17-20. Here Jesus announces the authority and continuing validity of "the law [and] the prophets," here most specifically referring to these two commands God gave to Moses. He announces the purpose of his coming as fulfilling and accomplishing the law and the prophets, down to the very "stroke of a letter" (Mt 5:18). If Christian ethics is following Jesus, we have little choice but to follow his lead on this point, to affirm along with him the supremacy of Scripture as the central authoritative source for Christian ethics.

Yet it is important, in our view, not to see Jesus as unalterably opposed to the entire Pharisaic/rabbinic tradition. Jesus clearly cherished the Jewish religious tradition and participated in it in a wide variety of ways. But he insisted on subjecting that tradition to Scripture and to God's creative and redemptive intentions, sifting out what did not survive such a test. His sense of freedom to do so was an important part of the opposition he aroused. This reminds us that religious moral traditions do not exist in a vacuum but instead tend to be handed on to the people of faith by those considered authoritative interpreters of those traditions—even in decentralized religious structures. Thus these two sources of authority tend to be linked, unless alternative interpreters of the tradition arise to challenge those who currently control it, or unless access to the tradition is so radically democratized that no individual or group can be said to control it. Much denominational and confessional turmoil—and, at times, needed reform and change—arises at precisely this point.

The place of divine encounter in the life and ministry of Jesus is apparent, though Scripture records no direct example of Jesus' moral teaching flowing out of divine encounter. Jesus frequently retreats into prayer, especially before major decisions and experiences. We are told almost nothing about the content of those encounters. His teaching and preaching reflect the impact and centrality of Hebrew Scripture and should not be interpreted as coming to Jesus as unmediated direct divine revelation. Even his central teaching, concerning the kingdom of God, is a biblical concept, not something he discovered or created *ex nihilo* through encounter with God. Perhaps the most that can be said is that

Jesus sifted and interpreted Scripture, and saw his particular place in the drama of divine redemption, through the illumination provided by his uniquely intimate relationship with God the Father.

We have yet to say a word about Jesus' use of the other, "general" sources of authority. The Sermon on the Mount and numerous parables give ample evidence of his generous use of reasoning from human experience and observed facts of earthly existence. "Look at the birds of the air; they neither sow nor reap nor gather into barns, and yet your heavenly Father feeds them. . . . Can any of you by worrying add a single hour to your span of life? . . . Consider the lilies of the field, how they grow; they neither toil nor spin" (Mt 6:26, 28). One finds clear echoes of the wisdom tradition here. Thus it is possible to interpret Jesus' heavy use of such experiential or nature motifs as a dimension of the centrality and authority which he gave to Scripture, not as separate sources in their own right. Like the wisdom writers, Jesus was deeply impressed by evidences of God's providential design, care and sovereignty over earthly life.

Classic and Contemporary Voices in Christian Ethics

Christian ethics has repeatedly addressed the sources of authority question. It probably comes as no surprise that these voices offer us nothing approaching a unanimous point of view. Christians have identified and ordered the sources of authority in a wide variety of ways, with these decisions having an enormous impact on the understanding of Christian morality.

It is fair to say that every recognizably Christian tradition and moral thinker makes some use of the Bible, attributing a special significance to this particular book. While it is significant that Christian ethics uses the Christian Bible rather than the Bhagavad Gita, this bare fact tells us very little concerning the actual methodology or substance of Christian moral teaching. Some very basic parameters are established for Christian ethics because of the use of the Bible. But sharp differences in understanding the nature and authority of the Bible, and the place and use of other sources of authority, render the mere fact of some role for the Bible relatively insignificant.

One characteristic feature of Roman Catholic ethics, for example, has been an approach to the sources in which Christian moral tradition carries divine authority. The tradition (or Tradition) is understood to begin with Jesus Christ, who commanded the apostles to preach the gospel, which they then did orally and eventually in writing, under the inspiration of the Holy Spirit. Scripture is the first stage of authoritative written divine revelation, but church tradition is continuous with Scripture and is likewise Spirit-inspired and authoritative. "Both Scripture and Tradition must be accepted and honored with equal sentiments of devotion and reverence" (*Catechism of the Catholic Church*, no. 82, 26). Both Scripture and tradition are to be authoritatively interpreted by the magisterium of the Church ("the bishops in communion with . . . the Bishop of Rome," no. 85) which is responsible, along with the whole of the Church, for the holy task of preserving the "sacred deposit" of faith intact (no. 84).

The Catholic moral tradition, as well, has always been quite interested in gaining insight from other sources, such as the moral philosophy of ancient Greece or, in modern times, the best and most relevant scientific research available on any given question. This interest is rooted in a deeply held theological belief that God speaks to humanity not solely through the Bible (or church tradition) but also through the witness of the created order as discovered by the human mind.

The Protestant Reformers broke with Roman Catholicism precisely on the issue of sources of authority. The rallying cry of *sola scriptura* (Scripture alone) meant the rejection of the authority of the Catholic tradition in favor of a return to the Scriptures, and only the Scriptures, for theological and moral direction. Such an approach (at least officially) characterizes Lutheran and Reformed ethics, and certainly reflects the most commonly articulated point of view among contemporary evangelical Christians in North America.

However, the historic Methodist tradition, pioneered by John Wesley, as well as the Pietist and Pentecostal/charismatic expressions of Christian faith, are evangelical movements that offer different wrinkles on the sources of authority question. Wesley's use of sources has come to be known as the Wesleyan Quadrilateral—Scripture, tradition, reason and experience. All have a role to play in the formation of Christian faith and ethics, though Scripture occupies the central place. Likewise, classic Pietism places a great deal of emphasis on the encounter with God available through prayer and other spiritual disciplines. The Quakers, or Society of Friends, represent another Protestant movement that places extremely high value on direct religious experience. Meanwhile, Pentecostal and charismatic groups stress ecstatic religious experiences, especially in community, and the insights for living that are gained there. While at times experientially oriented movements have drifted from Scripture, on the contemporary scene their leaders normally proclaim the governing role of Scripture. Religious experience is subjected to Scripture, not the other way around (for example, Fee, *Gospel and Spirit*). But the meaning of Scripture is not rightly interpreted without the illumination and guidance of the Holy Spirit.

Modern trends related to the sources of authority in Christian ethics as an academic discipline are of two major types. First, there is the growing importance of findings in the social and natural sciences in shaping Christian moral teaching. Christian ethicists across the theological and ecclesial spectrum have recognized that it is impossible to do adequate reflection on the moral issues of our day apart from careful study of the relevant data.

A second trend has been a focus on human experience. This includes careful listening to the voices of real human beings, especially the broken and oppressed, whose lives offer considerable insight into the issues of our time. While every serious ethicist now examines the data/experience dimensions of moral issues with great care, one strand of Christian ethics goes further, essentially lifting these two sources up to a point at which they rival or eclipse the significance of Scripture and other sources. This development has occurred on the liberal and especially the liberation wings of Christian ethics, but its reverberations have been felt much more widely than that.

The other major trend with relevance for sources of authority has been the focus on character ethics discussed in the last two chapters. With reference to the sources of authority question, the effect has been a return to a focus on Scripture (understood primarily as narrative), interpreted authoritatively by the faith community as a whole (not the individual or church officials) and impacting both personal and ecclesial character (not primarily rules or principles, and not primarily society). This distinctive approach to Christian ethics will continue to have significant influence in the years ahead. We have sought to hear criticisms of this approach—including from its own advocates—respectfully, and to build corrections into our holistic version.

If we sift these classic and contemporary approaches by looking to Jesus and his way, several conclusions can be drawn.

First, we believe that while the Catholic tradition's emphasis on learning both from tradition and other sources of insight can be embraced, the equating of the authority of Scripture and of tradition must be rejected on the basis of Jesus' example. Church moral tradition should be understood as informative but not necessarily normative for contemporary Christian ethics. We should be fully aware of the shape of our moral tradition, though, for at least three reasons. First, it is a fact that all Christians stand within the Christian moral tradition in one of its particular expressions, whether they acknowledge it or not. If this is so, there is nothing to be gained by ignorance of that tradition and its impact on our character and conduct.

This leads to the second point. Once one gains a working knowledge of the Christian moral tradition(s), one is able to retrieve and appropriate aspects or strands of that tradition that are consistent with Scripture. Sometimes these will reflect the church's majority voice, while other times we will discover the need to juxtapose a healthier minority voice over against the dominant tradition; for there is no single, monolithic Christian moral tradition. Third, and related, we also need to be conversant with Christian moral tradition in order to know where we must repent, where our blind spots have been and are likely to be. The twenty centuries of Christian history thus far have left a mixed legacy of moral faithfulness and moral wrong. In the spirit of continuous repentance and openness to correction we are obligated to seek to learn from both. We need an approach to tradition that seeks humbly to "stand on the shoulders" of our forebearers in the church, retrieving every truthful and relevant moral insight while always prepared to reject traditions for the sake of the Word of God.

Are we thus adopting a *sola scriptura* Reformation position? We say yes to *sola scriptura* if that means that Scripture is the only authoritative and fully trustworthy source of authority for Christian ethics. The insights gained from all other sources must be sifted and interpreted by Scripture and must be rejected if they conflict with Scripture. The Bible is the "sun" around which all other sources of authority are brought into orbit.

Consider the implications of this approach for handling the issue of religious experience. The problem with religious experience as a source of authority for the moral life is its radical subjectivity. The same is true of claims grounded in the stirrings of moral conscience. Many are the devout Christian couples, for example, whose prayers seem to reveal different divine responses to the same search for moral direction. Such examples drive one back to the written Word, with which all interpreters can at least wrestle with a measure of objectivity and common ground (the deconstructionists notwithstanding). Yet once back to the Scripture, all of us know the nasty uses to which it is sometimes put when in the hands of Christians with cold hearts and mean spirits. Thus, we find ourselves drawn back to the importance of the guidance of the Holy Spirit and warmhearted Christian piety, especially in the context of vibrant and accountable Christian community.

Again, the example of Jesus provides the way through this conundrum. He adopted neither a coldhearted "bibliolatry" independent of a vital relationship with God nor an ungrounded and ethereal religious subjectivism. Instead, he sifted and interpreted the Scripture, and understood his role in God's redemptive plan, in light of the guidance of the Holy Spirit and a warm and disciplined relationship with God. It is hard to improve on that model, especially when we remember a basic theological truth: Jesus Christ is alive. He is risen, and because he is risen we have access to him today. This means that scripturally grounded encounter with the living Christ in the community of faith remains a legitimate source of authority for Christian ethics; Jesus is the living Word. We must be open to the fresh winds of God's Holy Spirit while remembering that the divinely breathed Scriptures cannot be contradicted by the One who breathed them.

This provides the clue we need for making appropriate use of the "general" sources of authority. If God is sovereign and the risen Christ is alive and speaking to his church, then nature, history, experience and so on—all that occurs on this planet—reveal something of the divine nature, will and purpose (Rom 1:20-

21). God is present and active, seeking to relate to human and other creatures as Creator, Judge and Redeemer (Stassen et al., *Authentic Transformation*). Thus it is perfectly appropriate, and indeed obligatory, for believing people to search the created order for clues concerning God's will and way for us. In the physical and social sciences, the creative efforts of musicians and novelists, the insights of those in other religious traditions, the flashes of awareness we gain through personal experiences, the meditations of the philosophers, we trust that we can find the truth of God. All truth is God's truth, as Arthur Holmes is so fond of saying, because God is sovereign (see Holmes, *Idea of a Christian College*). This is why it is not possible in principle to set limits on where God's truth might be discovered, and thus to place some ultimate outer boundary on the "sources of authority" for Christian ethics, as long as Scripture remains the final court of appeal.

Jesus, Scripture and Ethics

This conclusion brings us into direct encounter with the next issue: how this authoritative Bible is to be interpreted. If Scripture is to be so central a source of authority, we must devote considerable attention to understanding how it is to be interpreted for Christian ethics. As with biblical authority, the "use" of Scripture in Christian ethics has been a matter of considerable discussion in recent Christian ethics (Birch and Rasmussen, *Bible and Ethics in Christian Life*; Brueggemann, *Prophetic Imagination*; Goldingay, *Models for Interpretation of Scripture*; Hays, *Moral Vision of the New Testament*; Janzen, *Old Testament Ethics*; Fowl and Jones, *Reading in Communion*; Johnson, *Scripture and Discernment*; Ogletree, *Use of the Bible in Christian Ethics*; Siker, *Scripture and Ethics*; Spohn, *What Are They Saying About Scripture?*; Sleeper, *Bible and the Moral Life*; Swartley, *Israel's Scripture Traditions*; Wright, *Walking in the Ways of the Lord*). The issue is by no means as simple as many seem to think.

Among the "subissues" one must consider in this regard are the following:
1. What principle of selection, if any, determines which themes, sections, books or genres of that vast body of inspired and authoritative literature known as Holy Scripture will move to the center of biblical interpretation for Christian ethics?
2. When reading Scripture for ethics, what types of moral norms are we going to find there, derived from what type of literature? Laws, principles and rules, derived primarily from biblical commands, or community virtues and practices, derived primarily from biblical narratives? Or broad, foundational, theological commitments, derived from the overall picture of God presented in the Scripture?
3. How shall Scripture help us deal with contemporary issues that are not directly addressed in its pages?
4. Who is understood as the primary moral agent addressed by Scripture—

the human being, the society, the human family, the Christian, the Christian congregation, the international church?

5. How shall Old and New Testament ethical instruction be related to each other? Does Old Testament law still apply to the church? If so, how?

These are a handful of the most important questions that occupy ethicists and biblical scholars working in the "use of Scripture" vineyard, and most have been considered at various stages in the history of the church. We will not address all of them; some we will pick up in later chapters, some simply by implication. Again, our approach requires us to start by focusing our attention on how Jesus "used" his Scripture, the Hebrew Bible.

Jesus and Scripture

We have already sought to show that Matthew 5:17-20 and related passages demonstrate that for Jesus the Scriptures are authoritative; their authority is not abrogated but instead affirmed in his teaching and the conduct of his ministry. Indeed, we believe the Sermon on the Mount itself is best understood as a series of interpretations of teachings in the Torah (Genesis through Deuteronomy) and the Prophets (see Swartley, *Israel's Scripture Traditions*, for an example of outstanding scholarship from the Anabaptist tradition that pays insightful attention to the way Jesus' way is rooted in the Hebrew Scriptures). But—and this is a key point—Jesus brought to his interpretation of the Hebrew Bible a particular vantage point which governed his approach. Geza Vermes, who has studied Jesus' teachings and actions extensively from a Jewish perspective, concludes that Jesus was faithful to the Hebrew Scriptures and to Jewish piety *the way the great prophets of Israel were*. This point is absolutely critical to all that follows. Vermes argues that Jesus

> acknowledges the law of Moses as the foundation stone of his Judaism. This general attitude does not imply, however, that his concern matched that of mainstream Jewish thought and practice or Qumran Essenism. He was not preoccupied with particular precepts and their specific limits, with their traditional, or rational, or scriptural, or revelation-based exegesis, but focused his attention on the overall impact of the Torah on individual piety. . . . Jesus marched in the footsteps of the great prophets of Israel in placing an almost exaggerated accent on the *inward aspects* and *root causes* of the religious action. (Vermes, *Religion of Jesus the Jew*, 189, 195)

For Jesus, then, the Hebrew Scriptures were to be interpreted not through the grid of the rabbinic/scribal casuistry dominant in his day, but instead through that offered by the prophets of Israel (Davies and Allison, *Critical and Exegetical Commentary*, 1:484, 488, 491, 495). Thus Jesus focused on the Law and the Prophets, and on the Law as interpreted by the Prophets, especially

Isaiah. This was his hermeneutic, and it had at least four concrete expressions that placed him in direct confrontation with many in the religious leadership of his context.

First, Jesus interpreted the Torah as gracious divine covenant rather than as "law" as we might understand it. Jesus understood the Torah as an expression of God's grace just as the exodus was an expression of God's grace. "Without the liberating good news of the exodus there would be no Sinai of the divine commandments. . . . Its ways are the ways of grace, and all its paths lead to peace" (Lapide, *Sermon on the Mount*, 16). Every covenant recorded in the Old Testament is an expression of God's grace, not an imposition of oppressive burdens. Grace to all humankind with Noah as the covenant-partner; grace to Abraham and Sarah, and through them not only to a chosen people but all humanity; grace to the people of Israel at Sinai, through Moses, after grace in the exodus; grace to Israel in covenant with David and his line. So the covenants themselves are grace, promising a future with God's presence, guidance and blessing. They require obedient and faithful response, but it is no odious imposition to respond in obedience to such divine grace. The Torah, as Jesus said, is about the love of God and the love of neighbor (Mt 22:34-40, quoting Deut 6:5; Lev 19:18), in response to the prior love of God the Creator, Righteous Judge and Deliverer.

Second, interpreting Scripture through a prophetic grid leads to a greater emphasis on the moral than on the cultic aspects of the Law and thus of Hebrew Scripture. In Mark 12:34, when a scribe agreed with Jesus that the Law was summed up in love for God and love for neighbor, and that this "is much more important than all whole burnt offerings and sacrifices," Jesus said, "You are not far from the kingdom of God." The last phrase that the scribe affirmed—"much more important than all whole burnt offerings and sacrifices"—is the prophetic half of "the Law and the Prophets." Disdain for the sacrificial system (in particular) and religious observances (in general) as a false panacea, a substitute for moral integrity, is a common theme in the prophets, as evidenced by this famous passage (Amos 5:21-24):

> I hate, I despise your festivals,
>   and I take no delight in your solemn assemblies.
> Even though you offer me your burnt offerings and grain offerings,
>   I will not accept them;
> and the offerings of well-being of your fatted animals
>   I will not look upon.
> Take away from me the noise of your songs;
>   I will not listen to the melody of your harps.
> But let justice roll down like waters,
>   and righteousness like an everflowing stream.

It is interesting to note that Jesus is only once recorded as publicly affirming the sacrificial practices that occurred in the temple (Mt 5:23-24), and this is in the context of emphasizing the priority of moral rather than cultic practices. Generally he criticized temple practices as strongly as the prophets had done. His prophetic action at the temple is a signal example of this (Mt 21:12-17). His critique of the temple became part of the charge against him at his trial (Mt 26:61).

Third, Jesus had a prophetic rather than a legalistic understanding of the content of righteousness. For the prophets, true righteousness consisted of deeds of love, mercy and justice, especially to the most vulnerable. This undeniable prophetic emphasis had slipped from the center of rabbinic/scribal tradition, replaced with a focus on ritual purity and freedom from defilement in which Jesus had very little interest. This is what Jesus was referring to when he recognized the righteousness of the scribes and Pharisees, but said that our righteousness is to go beyond theirs (Mt 5:20). One need not list the hundreds of references in the Prophets that support this claim. Let us simply consider some of the most familiar of Jesus' teachings, many of which we will address later in this work as well.

A place to begin is with Jesus' "inaugural address" (Lk 4:18-19, quoting Is 61:1-2; 58:6), in which he embraced the poor, the captives, the blind and the oppressed as the foci of his ministry. Then there are his warnings to the rich to avoid hoarding money and instead do justice for the poor, the powerless and those in need (Mt 5:42; 6:2-4, 19-34; cf. Is 1:17), and the parables and stories that reinforce the point, such as the accounts of Lazarus and the rich man (Lk 16:19-31; cf. Nathan's confrontation with David over Bathsheba and Uriah in 2 Sam 12, and Elijah's clash with Ahab over Naboth's vineyard in 1 Kings 21) and the Sheep and Goats judgment (Mt 25:31-46). Jesus incarnated such concern through deeds of mercy to the hungry, the lame, the blind, the ritually unclean, the poor, the outcast, the sick, women, foreigners, lepers and so many more (compare these deeds with the ministries of Elijah and Elisha recorded in 1 and 2 Kings). There is his emphasis on expanding our circle of love by including strangers and enemies (Mt 5:43-48; 6:12-14; 7:1-5; Lk 10:25-37; cf. Lev 19:34). Again, we need to emphasize that these are hardly contradictions of the Law and the Prophets; they are all taught explicitly in both the Law and the Prophets. But Jesus was reclaiming their centrality in the face of a tradition that had defined righteousness on the basis of a different interpretive framework altogether.

Finally, as Vermes indicates, Jesus reflects a prophetic emphasis in his attention to what Vermes calls the "inward aspects" and "root causes" of behavior; in other words, his attention to the heart, or character. As the prophets wrestled with the people of their day, they repeatedly returned to the theme of the "heart." This is especially apparent in the prophet Jeremiah: "The heart is devious above all else; it is perverse—who can understand it? I the LORD test the mind and search the heart, to give to all according to their ways, according to the fruit of their doings" (Jer 17:9-10). "The days are surely coming, says the LORD, when I will make a new covenant with the house of Israel and the house of Judah. . . . I will put my law within them, and I will write it on their hearts; and I will be their God, and they shall be my people" (Jer 31:31, 33; cf. 4:14; 24:7; 29:13).

Jesus repeatedly called his listeners to turn from an emphasis on ritual defilement and outward purity toward an awareness of the inner wellsprings of real moral purity or defilement as they are expressed in behavior to others.

He said to them, "Then do you also fail to understand? Do you not see that whatever goes into a person from outside cannot defile, since it enters, not the heart but the stomach, and goes out into the sewer?" (Thus he declared all foods clean.) And he said, "It is what comes out of a person that defiles. For it is from within, from the human heart, that evil intentions come: fornication, theft, murder, adultery, avarice, wickedness, deceit, licentiousness, envy, slander, pride, folly. All these evil things come from within, and they defile a person" (Mk 7:18-23).

Jesus' emphasis on the heart is also apparent throughout the Sermon on the Mount, and he called the disciples to do righteousness not for show and prestige but for God (Mt 6:1-18; 7:6-12).

This emphasis on the heart should not be misconstrued, as it so frequently is, as a teaching that says that conduct does not matter; "only" one's heart or attitude matters. This frequent and disastrous interpretive move is in direct contradiction to Jesus' own teaching and that of the prophets. It allows Christians to dismiss the significance of how we actually live our lives in favor of an illusory sense of attitudinal moral goodness. Jesus, like the prophets, cared about the heart because he cared about the conduct that springs from the heart. The goal is total and loving obedience to God, and for this the heart must be made ready, through self-examination, repentance, forgiveness and regular engagement in practices of compassion and new commitment.

In sum, we are arguing that Jesus wholeheartedly affirmed the validity and continuing authority of the Law and the Prophets; that is, the Hebrew Bible. He was saying that we are obligated to obey them to the letter (Mt 5:17-20) and are called to be "perfect" in our righteousness (Mt 5:48)—*but not in the way that the scribes and Pharisees defined authority, obedience and righteousness*. It was a clash of interpretive grids—Jesus, on his own authority, on the basis of his prophetic reading of Scripture, against the reigning casuistic legalism of the major interpretive tradition of his day. He claimed authority to see meanings in the Scripture that this tradition and its authorized interpreters were not seeing, and these interpreters in their turn perceived Jesus' claim as a radical abrogation of Scripture and tradition, and a radical challenge to their own authority.

It is also instructive to notice how the key words in Matthew 5:17-20, at the beginning of the teachings of the Sermon on the Mount, are echoed in the ending, 7:15-27. They enclose the Sermon like matching bookends.

Table 4.1

Matthew 5:16-20	Matthew 7:15-27
5:19: Doing *(poieō)* the commandments	7:17, 19, 21, 24, 26: Doing *(poieō)* fruit and commandments
5:19: Kingdom of heaven	7:21: Kingdom of heaven
5:17: The Law and the Prophets	7:12: The Law and the Prophets
5:19: Those who do not do (who relax) the commandments	7:15: False prophets who do/bear *(poieō)* bad fruit
5:16, 20: Your good works give glory to my Father in heaven; your righteousness	7:21, 24: The one who does the will of my Father in heaven or who does these words

This striking symmetry of matching words and concepts at the introduction and conclusion of the Sermon on the Mount highlights the importance of these words and concepts. It says that (1) doing the commandments (rather than "relaxing" or failing to do them) (2) of the Law and Prophets (as interpreted by Jesus rather than scribal casuistry) (3) is authentic righteousness (rather than mere outer observance) and (4) is crucial for the kingdom of God (which is what Jesus and his disciples must be concerned about). It seems to us that we cannot improve on those four statements as a definition of Christian ethics as following Jesus.

Classic and Contemporary Voices in Christian Ethics

As we begin to interact with other voices in Christian ethics, we want to reaffirm that Christians are to have a very high view of the trustworthiness and authority of Scripture and place it above all other sources of authority for Christian faith and practice. Within that framework, we affirm with Jesus and historic Christianity the authority of the entire canonical witness. Just as Jesus demonstrated great familiarity and wide employment of the entire canon as he knew it, by analogy and imitation contemporary Christians must do the same. We will assume, again, as Jesus did, that the whole of the Bible can be trusted for that guidance and will not lead us astray. Here we reject any formal or functional truncation of the canon as an authoritative source of direction for the Christian life.

Martin Luther, for example, saw no real value in the Old Testament in terms of providing normative direction for the Christian moral life. He assumed that the Old Testament moral witness could be boiled down to the Law and then restricted the Christian's use of the Law to two functions: the theological use, for conviction of sin, and the civil use, for restraint of evil impulses in society. The rich and deep moral witness of the prophets was neglected altogether, and in general no positive moral guidance was gleaned.

Luther was quite direct and intentional in making this interpretive move, and many Christians today do the same. They assume or believe that the Old Testament equals "the Law," argue that Jesus came to abolish the Law and then conclude that the Old Testament is irrelevant for New Covenant people. Others functionally interpret the Scripture on the basis of this model, even though they do so unintentionally. But if Jesus is the bottom-line authority for Christian ethics, including our interpretation of Scripture for ethics, we are not free to move in this direction. Just as he read the Old Testament, and just as he employed it as providing substantive content for his ethics, we must do the same. Here Luther's fellow Reformer Calvin did better, as he acknowledged the so-called third use of the law as a source of authority for the content of the Christian moral life. But again, we would resist the winnowing down of the rich and diverse moral witness of the Old Testament into just one of its expressions, "Law."

Within this kind of "whole canon" hermeneutic, Christ must function as the norm for biblical interpretation (Westmoreland-White, "Reading Scripture in the Baptist Vision," 61ff.; Scalise, *Hermeneutics as Theological Prolegomena*). This is a common assertion but is frequently interpreted far too narrowly and abstractly. For example, many seem to assume that the meaning of Jesus Christ for the interpretation of Scripture is exhausted in the theological framework provided by his incarnation, death and resurrection. Thus, some Christians look to Scripture solely for preparatory, contemporary or retrospective reflections on the birth, death and resurrection of Jesus. The moral dimensions of the biblical witness are missed altogether, not to mention the moral teachings of Jesus himself. One sees this in most of the historic creeds of the church, which skip from Jesus' birth of the Virgin Mary to his death under Pontius Pilate, jumping completely over the entire conduct of his ministry. No one strand of Christian history is guilty of this, for it is common across denominational and confessional boundaries. Sustained attention to the actual moral teachings and example of Jesus is definitely a minority thread in the history of the Christian church after the first two centuries.

Instead, if Christ is the norm, then everything about his person and work is relevant to biblical interpretation for ethics. Indeed, to put it more strongly, if Christ is the pivot point of the advance of the kingdom, God's Son leading the redemption of the planet, we must study every aspect of his life and teachings, for he is the key to human history and all reality. So, because Jesus employed a prophetic hermeneutic we must do the same. Because Christ placed his mission and his teachings within the context of the kingdom of God, we must do likewise, and because Christ embodied his teaching in the way he treated people, we must do the same. None of this means an abandonment of the theological framework of incarnation, atoning death and resurrection; the opposite is the truth. Only an ethic that takes seriously the way of Jesus rightly respects Jesus as the Incarnate Lord, the Redeeming Savior, the Resurrected Christ, who has the authority to reveal to us the will of God. Any other approach functionally denies that Jesus is fully Lord, fully Savior and fully Christ.

Thus we must critique the work of those self-identified evangelical ethicists who draw little from any aspect of the person and work of Christ in the formulation of their ethics. When seeking biblical direction on contemporary moral issues, they frequently draw only from other aspects of the biblical witness, missing not only what Christ may have said or done that was relevant to the issue at hand, but also failing to apply a prophetic interpretive grid to the Scriptures they do consider. Of course, it is not only evangelical ethics that has been failing to take adequate account of the centrality of Jesus Christ.

The Bible is not flat; Christ is its peak and its center. No moral issue should be addressed apart from consideration of the meaning of Jesus Christ for reflection on that issue. We propose a Scripture and ethics hermeneutic that generally works in the following way:

1. Look first to Jesus—examining his incarnation/death/resurrection and his life/ministry/teachings.
2. Read all other Scriptures through the prophetic interpretive grid that Jesus employed and in light of all that we know of Jesus' witness on this issue.
3. Then look to other sources of authority for help on the basis of the same interpretive grid, remembering that Jesus is alive and continues to instruct his church through the witness of the Holy Spirit (Jn 15).

As one scans the horizon of church history for positive models that reflect the kind of approach we are taking here, two traditions stand out: (1) the believers' church tradition that James McClendon calls small "b" baptist, and especially their recent interpreters, such as J. H. Yoder, who emphasize the lordship of Christ over all of life, so incorporating an important truth from the Reformed tradition and Bonhoeffer, and (2) the historic black churches. While distinct in many ways, both focus primary attention on Jesus Christ, not overlooking his life and ministry, not missing his redemptive concern for the whole person and not misplacing his focus on suffering people, the poor and the oppressed. Both have lively interest in the whole Old Testament, and especially the prophets, not missing the centrality of Jesus' prophetic interpretive grid and not failing to apply it to the whole of Scripture. Both have considerable concern for the public good, while approaching public matters not from the perspective of pragmatic power politics but instead from the heights of the prophetic witness of Scripture.

Finally, both traditions consistently argue that obedience, deeds and practices are the key words, not merely assent to the right moral convictions. We share their belief that Christians must not simply assert the authority of the Scriptures, for that is not what Jesus did. He read the Scriptures as the functional daily authority for the conduct of his life and enjoined a similar approach on his followers. The goal is not to articulate the correct view of biblical authority but to hear and do the Word of God. Our commitment to the authority of Scriptures will be revealed in the laboratory of daily life. As Jesus put it: "You will know them by their fruits" (Mt 7:20).

We have argued that Scripture is the central source of authority for Christian ethics and that Jesus is the key to interpreting Scripture. Such convictions do not solve every problem or reduce the agony of every difficult moral decision. But they do give us a place to begin and a place to stand. We can see no satisfactory alternative. In the words of the old hymn, "On Christ the solid rock I stand, all other ground is sinking sand." Or in the words of the apostle Paul, "No one can lay any foundation other than the one that has been laid; that foundation is Jesus Christ" (1 Cor 3:11).

5

THE FORM AND FUNCTION
OF MORAL NORMS

▬

Do not think that I have come to abolish the law or the prophets; I have come not to abolish
but to fulfill.

MATTHEW 5:17

In this chapter we intend to look even more closely at the way Scripture informs our ethics. We want to propose that Christians (and, in fact, all human beings) organize and communicate their moral convictions—technically known as *moral norms*—at four different levels: the particular/immediate judgment level, the rules level, the principles level and the basic-conviction level. The same point in character language is the particular deed, the normative practice, the embodied virtue and the narrative base. It is vital to find congruence between these levels, so that ethics is neither too vague and abstract nor too legalistic and superficial. Scripture offers numerous examples of each of these levels of moral norms.

Our task in this chapter is threefold. First, we shall present this model as a way of organizing thinking about the nature of Christian moral norms. Second, we shall argue that the four levels belong together as incarnational, Hebraic, realistic, embodied narrative. Third, we shall explore each level of moral norms more deeply, considering approaches to Christian ethics that have seen one level or another as the heart of "doing" Christian ethics. Throughout the discussion, we will ground our own reflection on the witness of Jesus.

The issue of how Christian moral norms are to be understood is significant in at least two ways. First is the basic problem of communication: when discussing the biblical witness in ethics, or a particular moral issue, people often talk right past each other, and either confuse or anger each other, because they are talking on different levels, about different kinds of moral norms. Four friends can all be talking about abortion, for example, but not really communicating—because Sally is speaking at the rules level, Sam is addressing principles, Stephanie is doing theological basic-conviction reflection, and Stuart can be found at the immediate judgment level. This kind of communication breakdown happens every day.

Second, at a more technical level, Christian ethicists frequently differ over what kind of moral norms are most frequently found in Scripture, were most central for Jesus or are most significant for the Christian life. This turns out to be no mere technical squabble but a disagreement with practical consequences for Christian ethics and for behavioral norms. We need clarity about the nature of moral norms if we are to understand Christian ethics and communicate its insights clearly.

Four Levels of Moral Norms in Christian Ethics

Our approach to this issue has been influenced heavily by philosophical ethics, a field of inquiry that tries to clarify what people mean when talking about morality. Several decades ago, the philosophical ethicist Henry David Aiken defined four levels of moral norms. His proposal was adopted by Christian ethicist James Gustafson in a highly influential essay (Aiken, *Reason and Conduct*; Gustafson, "Context vs. Principle"). We believe Aiken and Gustafson's proposal helps correct some harmful errors in Christian ethics—especially concerning what we mean by *rules*.

1. The particular/immediate judgment level. Sometimes when we express a moral evaluation, we do not give any reasons. We just say, "That's wrong," or, "What a good thing to do!" Or, "Linda is a really good person!" These are examples of particular and immediate moral judgments, about actions (conduct) on the one hand and people (character) on the other. They are part and parcel of everyday life.

For example, Jesus once called Herod "that fox" (Lk 13:32). He meant "that vulture"! Jesus, like the prophets before him, often criticized the powerful for ignoring biblical mandates of justice, faithfulness and mercy, and covering it up with religious rationalizing.

But *in this particular passage*, Jesus criticized one particular ruler, Herod, and not all rulers who do injustice. He did not give any reasons for his criticism. He just said, "That fox." That is a moral judgment *on a particular and immediate level* rather than a general or universal level. If someone had asked Jesus why he said that, he could certainly have given reasons. Herod killed John the Baptist. Herod used his power, given to him by a foreign, Gentile, Roman Empire, to impose injustice on Israel. But in this one passage, Jesus only made *a moral declaration about one particular case—without stating any reasons that would apply to other cases.*

Sometimes when we make an immediate judgment about a particular act or a particular person, and do not give any reasons, we could give dozens of reasons if someone just asked us. Other times, we say, "I can't give you a reason. I just know it's wrong for him to say that to his own child. If anything is wrong, that is wrong!" This is a moral judgment about a particular case in which no reason is given and no reason apparently can be given. The person just knows, just intuits, just feels, that this particular action is definitely wrong. These are two types of ethical reasoning at the immediate judgment level: immediate judgments in which reasons could be given if asked, and those which are intuitive/emotive, for which no reason can be articulated. (This is a clarification and correction of the Aiken/Gustafson model developed in Stassen, "Social Theory Model" and "Critical Variables in Christian Social Ethics.")

> *Two things characterize a moral judgment at the particular, immediate level:*
>
> *(a) No reasons are given for the moral judgment.*
>
> *(b) The moral judgment applies to one particular case.*

Norms expressed at the immediate judgment level, whether grounded in Scripture, experience or other sources, can be useful in two different ways. First, when such judgments are examined, one can sometimes discover or extract the rule, principle or basic-conviction wellsprings from which they actually are derived. By asking why Jesus judged Herod to be a "fox," we can learn something about the deeper structure of his own moral convictions and norms with regard to justice, power, government and so on.

Second, we can sometimes apply particular and immediate judgments by way of *moral analogy.* Thus the immediate judgment that Jesus expressed concerning Herod may enable us to find in our own context a suitable analogy. One might say, "Herod was to Jesus' own context as X is to our own." The capacity of Scripture to function in this way is a critical part of its power for the church. For example, the parables of Jesus tell us particular, immediate stories and imply or sometimes directly articulate moral judgments and moral norms. We then reason by analogy from the particular moral judgment expressed/implied in that parable to our own situation. Thus, if I am to be to this needy minority child at my door as the good Samaritan was to the wounded Jew, what does this require me to do?

We imaginatively enter the particular story, place ourselves in the narrative in one or another role and then find ourselves drawn or driven to particular courses of action. The prophet Nathan offered this very style of reasoning when he confronted David about Bathsheba and Uriah; a rich man who steals a poor man's one lamb is analogous to a king who steals a man's wife and takes his life (2 Sam 12). David realized that the analogy was an accurate one and repented. To make correct analogies ourselves, we need to study the way the particular moral judgment functioned in the particular biblical context and then consider what moral judgment would function similarly in our social context (C. Wright, *Walking in the Ways of the Lord*, 36, 115, 161, 174; Goldingay, *Approaches to Old Testament Interpretation*, 55).

2. The rules level. In the Sermon on the Mount, Jesus taught a rule about instances when Roman soldiers compelled Jews to carry their packs a mile (Mt 5:41). In Roman law, soldiers had the right to require people to do this for them. The right was limited: they could require only one mile of this beast-of-burden duty. But it was resented, especially by rebels or freedom fighters like Barabbas, who urged people to resist the foreign occupation. Jesus opposed this strategy. Instead, he gave a different rule to those who would be his followers: when a Roman soldier compels you to carry his pack one mile, carry it two miles.

Two things characterize the reason we give at the rules level:

(a) A rule applies not just to one immediate case, but to all similar cases.

(b) A rule tells us directly what to do or not to do.

Jesus also quoted another rule, from the Ten Commandments: "Thou shalt not kill." He affirmed this rule, while adding several additional rules that undergird and support it: if you are unreconciled with someone, interrupt your worship of God to go make peace with that person; make friends with your accuser while on your way to court and so on (Mt 5:21-26).

These rules that Jesus taught do not apply only to one particular situation. Roman soldiers often compelled Jews to carry packs. Jesus said that when that happened, and it happened in numerous cases, his hearers should carry their packs a second mile. "Thou shalt not kill" applies to millions of cases, as does the command to go and make peace. So this is not simply a judgment about one particular case; it *applies to all similar cases.*

These rules *tell us directly and concretely what to do or not to do*: "Go the second mile" means "Don't carry the pack only one mile, but also a second mile." "Do not kill" tells us directly and concretely what not to do: do not kill. This is different from a general principle like "love your enemy," which does not tell us directly how we are to express our love for our enemy. In fact, this specific rule—carry his pack a second mile—is one concrete expression of the general principle "love your enemy." (And the spirit in which one carried that pack a second mile would reflect quite clearly the extent to which the principle of enemy-love was being demonstrated.) There are other possible expressions of love for the enemy, like praying for her and giving her something to drink when she is thirsty (Mt 5:44 and Rom 12:20). Both are rules Scripture commands that unpack the principle of love for enemies.

Or to consider an earlier example: if you are asked why you said it was wrong for that man to speak harshly to his child, you may respond with a rule: "With [the tongue] we curse those who are made in the likeness of God. . . . This ought not to be so" (Jas 3:9-10). The rule embedded in this text could also be articulated as "fathers [should] not provoke [their] children to anger" (Eph 6:4). It is natural to use a rule to support a particular judgment.

3. The principles level. Jesus also teaches principles. "Love your enemies" is one. Another is "Do to others as you would have them do to you" (Mt 7:12). Another is "Love your neighbor as yourself" (Mt 22:39). Another is "Love the Lord God with all your heart, and with all your soul, and with all your mind" (Mt 22:37). *Principles are more general than rules; they are one level deeper than rules. They do not tell us directly and concretely what to do.* They support rules—or criticize them. They provide the basis for rules—or show why certain rules need to be changed. So the principle "love your enemies," supports the rule "go a second mile." The principle supports the rule, and the rule spells out a direct application of the general principle.

Two things characterize the reason we give at the principles level:

(a) A principle supports rules—or criticizes them.

(b) A principle is more general than a rule; it does not tell us directly and concretely what to do.

So now we can understand the relation between the particular judgment level, the rules level and the principles level. Rules give reasons for particular judgments; principles give reasons for rules. Rules can also criticize particular judgments; principles can criticize rules. Rules serve principles, not the other way around.

This distinction helps us find our way through a sticky issue in Christian ethics: whether rules should be understood as "absolute" and whether we should admit there might be exceptions to rules. We join with many Christians and Christian ethicists in reacting against the permissiveness and moral relativism of our society and reaffirming the need today for clear, firm and sturdy moral rules. We do so primarily because we believe Jesus taught concrete, particular moral rules that he intended for his followers to obey. But we also do so for a very contemporary and practical reason: we have to live by rules or we get ourselves and others in trouble. Politicians, business leaders, pastors and so many others who do not have firm rules are harming our society and the church.

Some want to go a bit further, though. They say rules are absolute. They argue that we should do our ethics by absolute rules and are quite suspicious of anyone who would "open the door" to exceptions to moral rules.

There is certainly good reason for such a perspective. When you teach your children not to touch a pot on the stove, you do not immediately list a half-dozen exceptions. You don't say, "Do what seems right in the moment." You state a rule very firmly: "Don't ever touch pots on the stove."

The principles and reasons underlying this rule are clear: love for your children, a desire to protect them from harm, an awareness that boiling pots burn those who touch them without proper protection and so on. The rule is based on reasons and would be nonsensical apart from them. There is nothing intrinsic to stoves or pots that makes them bad or wrong to touch.

The problem is that *if rules are there for reasons, the reasons for which the rules exist sometimes can and must override the rules themselves.* Thus it is certainly true that the rule "don't touch pots on the stove" does not really apply if the pot is not hot and the stove is not turned on. Likewise, the rule does not apply in the same way when a child reaches an age in which he or she can begin to cook and begin working with hot pots on stoves. The principles on which rules are based need to be clearly understood, so we can know why the rule exists and thus when to make an exception to a rule.

I (Glen) taught in a college where students had to take two semesters of American history in order to graduate. A student from Ghana entered the school in the second semester of his freshman year and earned an A in History 102. He was not advised properly and never took the first semester of American history. He studied hard and was going to be ready to graduate after only three and a half years. Then came the time to register for his last semester. I realized that the one required course he still needed was the fall semester of American history. It would not be offered in the spring! This would mean he would have to come back to school the next fall in order to take just one course. That would keep him from returning home, where his family needed him because his father was dying of cancer. I went to the chair of the history department and pointed out that he was a business major and could take an elective course in the history of American labor-management relations, which would be more useful to him in his future work back in Ghana.

"But that would set a precedent," the chair said. He was imagining hundreds of students lining up at his door, asking for exemptions from American history. "But the reason for the rule about American history is to further students' education," I replied. "Labor Relations will further his education more; he will be more motivated to learn it, and it will be more relevant to his profession. He is an A- student and is not just trying to get out of something. He was given bad advice because he started his first semester in January." "No," said the chair. "It will set a precedent. A rule is a rule."

I realized we were talking on two different levels. I was trying to get him to think on the principles level: "The reason for the rule (the principle that the rule is based on) is to further students' education. Labor relations will further his education (achieve the principle) better."

The chair was talking on the rules level. His job as departmental enforcer encouraged him to stay at the rules level. I sensed what was going on and shifted to the rules level. I said, "Suppose we understand the rule to be that you have to take both semesters of American history unless you were given wrong advice, are an honors student from Ghana in your last semester whose father is dying of cancer, and can take another American history course instead?" "That could work; we can do that," he replied. He signed the permission; the student graduated, saved a semester's worth of money and achieved the underlying principle of being well educated.

This is a true story, with a detail changed to protect anonymity. It proves that Christian ethics can do some good. You can understand where other people are coming from.

Understanding that rules are based on principles enables us to affirm the strong need for rules without turning us into *legalists*—which can be defined in our model as *people who operate solely at the level of rules and thus detach them from the underlying principles that are their reason for existence.* We reject that approach to Christian ethics and thus any position that would say that moral rules, severed from their roots in principles and the character of God, are absolute and exceptionless.

4. The basic conviction level. There is yet one more level of moral reasoning. Suppose someone asks you what you base your commitment to the principle of covenant truth-telling on. You might say that you base it on God's command in Jesus Christ to "let your 'Yes' be 'Yes'" (Mt 5:37 NIV), or on God's covenant with us in the Ten Commandments: "You shall not bear false witness" (Ex 20:16), or on the fact that all people are made in God's image (Gen 1:26-28), so I owe truth to all people. But then suppose the next question is what you base your commitment to Jesus Christ on. You answer, "That is my rock-bottom life commitment. I don't base it on anything else. I base it on God." Now you have reached the basic conviction level.

For Christians, these are our most basic convictions about the character, activity and will of God, and about our nature as participants in that will. So now we have connected the way of moral reasoning with the basic convictions, which we identified in chapter three. These convictions are the ultimate ground of Christian ethics. At every other level of moral discourse, one can always dig deeper and find an underlying stratum of moral norms. Underneath particular judgments are rules; under rules are principles; under principles are basic convictions. But under core theological—basic—convictions, there is nothing deeper.

So when Jesus taught that we are to love our enemies, he gave a reason: "so that you may be children of your Father in heaven; for he makes his sun rise on the evil and on the good, and sends rain on the righteous and on the unrighteous" (Mt 5:45).

Two things characterize reasoning at the basic conviction level:

(a) A basic conviction is the basis for our principles, rules and overall ethical reasoning.

(b) You can't go deeper than basic convictions.

He taught similarly in 5:9, "Blessed are the peacemakers, for they will be called children of God." In the Sermon on the Mount, Jesus repeatedly grounded his teaching on God: God's mercifulness (Mt 5:7, 45; 6:14), knowledge of our needs (Mt 6:4, 6, 8, 18, 32; 7:11), providential care of the lilies of the field and us (Mt 6:30), judgment (Mt 5:22; 7:23, 27), sovereign ownership of all (Mt 5:34-35), and on our obligation to give glory to our Father who is in heaven (Mt 5:16). For Christians, *God's character, actions and will constitute the basic conviction level.*

Similarly, the Ten Commandments are grounded in God's grace. They are rooted in the events unfolded in Exodus 1—19: the revelation of God's name and character as the Lord, "I am that I am," present to hear the cries, see the needs and deliver the Hebrew slaves from their bondage and misery (Ex 3:1-12). By the twentieth chapter of Exodus it is clear that God has in fact heard those cries, delivered the Hebrews from the Pharaoh's oppression, and is bringing them miraculously to the Promised Land. This is the basis for the Ten Commandments—God's delivering grace. God begins the Ten Commandments by reminding the people of the revelation of the meaning of the name Yahweh to Moses in Exodus 3 and 6: The name of God is "Yahweh," which is often translated as "the LORD." This name means "I am," in the sense of "I am present to hear your cries with compassion and to deliver you from oppression, as I did for Abraham, Isaac and Jacob before you." To be sure we understand, Exodus 20:2 makes the point four times:
1. I am
2. the LORD

3. your God who brought you out of the land of Egypt
4. out of the house of slavery.

This revelation is the basis of the Ten Commandments. Each commandment is there because it reflects the gracious deliverance of God who hears the cries of those who are oppressed. We are to have no other God nor any graven image and are to keep the sabbath because God has delivered us and is our Lord. God wants us to remember the exodus and to give rest to all workers, including slaves, because we were once slaves in Egypt (Deut 5:14-15; Ex 20:8-11). God is known in compassionate delivering and creating action, not in some idol. We are to take care of our elderly parents, to not kill, not commit adultery, not steal (or kidnap, in the original meaning), not bear false witness, not covet, because God hears the cries of the elderly who cry out, the victims of slander who cry out, the murder victims who cry out, the victims of theft or kidnaping, and the persons victimized by adultery—and because this is God's covenant will. Knowing that the Ten Commandments are not just arbitrary legalistic dictates but are based on God who hears our cries and has compassion, gives them a much stronger grounding and helps us interpret them more meaningfully.

So now we have four levels of moral reasoning. Particular judgments depend on rules. Rules depend on principles. Principles depend on basic-conviction theological beliefs, which serve as the ultimate foundation, the rock-bottom, look-no-further basis for Christian ethics.

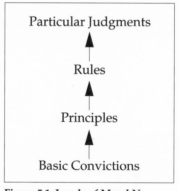

Figure 5.1. Levels of Moral Norms

Which Level Is Most Important?

Different approaches to Christian ethics tend to key in on one level of moral norms and present that level as the most important, often overlooking the role and value of moral norms at other levels. While these various approaches are frequently reviewed in introductory textbooks, normally they are not placed in proper context—as varying responses to the issue of the nature and levels of Christian moral norms. As we review these approaches, we will seek to extract positive gleanings that can be of use in a Christ-centered ethic.

1. A focus on the immediate judgment: situation ethics. Some Christian ethicists believe that every situation we face in life is so unique that it is wrong to try to make rules for living our lives—because rules, by definition, apply not just to one case but to all similar cases. Rules cause us to pay attention to what is (purportedly) the same about situations and to ignore what makes them different. That blinds us to the special circumstances, the unique individuals and the personal dimensions of every particular morally significant situation. Thus, the argument goes, we should stop making rules and attempting to apply them to all similar cases.

This is *situation ethics* (also called *situationism*). It reasons on the particular, immediate judgment level. It sees each case as so different from others that rules do not apply. "All abortions are wrong" means you treat all persons who consider an abortion the same. You do not pay attention to their particular needs. So situation ethics denies that we should have obligatory rules at all. We should just look at each situation and figure out in the unique moment what to do. Joseph Fletcher made situation ethics famous, or infamous, in the United States. He taught one principle: always do the loving thing. Rudolf Bultmann taught another kind of situation ethics in Germany, one he based on the theological conviction of "radical obedience." Even people who know very little about ethics tend to have heard the term "situation ethics" and to have some strong reaction to it. The term became a symbol, for many, of social and moral chaos.

The only kind of rules Fletcher recognized were "rules of thumb" or summary rules. A summary rule like "honesty pays," he said, teaches us only that in most cases in the past honesty has turned out to be the best, that is, the most effective policy. Consider the rule in football, "punt on fourth down." Usually that is the best policy. But there is no moral obligation to punt on fourth down. If there is only a minute to go in the game, and your team is down two points, and you punt because of the rule, you do not understand the meaning of a summary rule. You should calculate what is most likely to get you three points and win you the game. Just so, for Fletcher a rule like "honesty pays" carries no moral obligation. It just tells what usually works best. You should figure out in any particular case what will be the best for people. It may well include dishonesty.

Fletcher wrote a book, *Situation Ethics*, full of cases designed to show that if you follow the usual understanding of moral obligation and do what the moral rule says, you will do the wrong thing. Many found his reasoning persuasive.

Some Christians say, "It is not my business what other people do. I can't know or say what they should do. I just make my own decisions, and nobody else has any business telling me what I should do." This is a form of *moral subjectivism*—the belief that moral judgments are merely private and personal opinions or emotions, and as such are not appropriately subject to discussion and critique. Such a view is the cousin of situation ethics. It denies the existence of rules "out there" that apply to similar cases and says we are each so unique that we cannot reason about what is right and wrong in others' behavior.

We have all experienced, at some time or other, someone who insisted on enforcing a rule that seemed uncaring or lacking in compassion for the special needs of a person. Indeed, this was apparent in the story above about the student from Ghana. That story also revealed that situational considerations do indeed need to be taken into account in moral decision making. Good ethics involves thorough knowledge of all relevant factual and situational details in the matter under consideration, whether it be a decision about going to war or getting married or attempting in vitro fertilization. That is our point in emphasizing the dimension of "perception of the context," including the social context, in our holistic character ethics in chapter three.

Our four-level analysis helps to show how we can take account of situations without succumbing to situationism. The way to do so is to consider individual situations in all their richness and uniqueness yet apply relevant rules to them, rules grounded in broader principles and ultimately in the character and will of God.

During the heyday of situationism, one of the main factors behind its popularity was a reaction against the prohibition-heavy legalism so pervasive in American religion and culture. Situationists thought that the way to defeat legalism was to abandon rules. We disagree, on the basis of our four-level approach, which shows how rules can be important without being exceptionless and "absolute" and without leading to legalism. This is the first step in removing the persuasive power of situationism.

2. Rules alone: legalism. In his effort to reject situation ethics with full clarity, the ethicist John Jefferson Davis writes that "a protest against legalism in the Christian life can easily become a rejection of the binding moral authority of the specific precepts of God's written Word" (*Evangelical Ethics*, 6). To counter that dangerous trend, he moves far

In situationism:

(a) What is ethical is decided by the particular situation.

(b) Cases are unique; they can't be categorized by rules.

(c) Obligatory rules are a bad influence; they cause us to miss the uniqueness of the case and the person.

Problem: what if we need rules because without them people do wrong—because they are sinners, or just don't know enough?

in the opposite direction, advocating what he calls "contextual absolutism": "there are many moral absolutes, not just one absolute of 'love,' as in situation ethics. Examples of moral absolutes are provided by the Decalogue: idolatry, murder, blasphemy, adultery, stealing, and so forth are *always* morally wrong. . . . Contextual absolutism holds that in each and every ethical situation, no matter how extreme, there is a course of action that is morally right and free of sin" (*Evangelical Ethics*, 7).

But when one pays attention to the agonizing ethical challenges that sometimes emerge in real life, it is hard to adhere to this unbending commitment to "absolutes"—when that is taken to mean rules that tell you directly what to do in all similar cases without any exception under any circumstances and without any reference to the principles that undergird and support every particular rule. It is interesting to notice that in his brief list Davis omits the Decalogue's command not to bear false witness. Perhaps he simply did so as a literary convenience, to save space. But given his model, he could hardly have included it, since he had just approved of Rahab's act of lying to protect the Jewish spies (Josh 2:4-6). He also left the sabbath off. One wonders if he would approve of stealing an enemy's battle plan during wartime, and so would need to drop stealing off his list.

In legalism:

(a) What is ethical is defined and determined by **rules.**

(b) Rules are absolute and universal—for all cases.

(c) If there are exceptions, the rule must be redefined so it does not apply to such cases.

Problem: What if two rules conflict? What if the only way I can keep a murderer from killing someone is by telling a lie about where the person is?

By "contextual," Davis means that in some contexts prima facie duties (which means duties at first appearance, all other things being equal) are not *actual duties.* This is a long-established distinction in ethical thought, and one which helps to account for the vexatious but nonetheless compelling reality that moral rules are to be obeyed under all normal circumstances, but that sometimes, in a sinful and broken world, circumstances are not normal. Thus there can be a conflict between one's prima facie duty—do not steal—and one's *actual duty* in a particular situation—steal a loaf of bread to help keep a starving Jewish family alive during the Holocaust. Of course, the reason for the ever-present possibility of a gap between prima facie duties and actual duties is not only that we live in a sinful and broken world, but also that rules and principles sometimes conflict with each other, and so a decision for one rule or principle is a decision against another one.

Davis' approach articulates Christian ethics as *legalism*, with perhaps some contextual modification. It bases ethics on rules that apply to all similar cases and that tell us directly what to do or not to do, cut off from situational specifics or the grounding offered by principles. It reads the Bible looking for rules. It sees God primarily as the rule-giver.

The Brazilian sociologist Paul Freston offers an incisive critique of Third

World evangelical political involvement that speaks directly to the limits of a legalistic approach. Freston observes numerous examples of evangelicals gaining the power to hold political office but rapidly sliding into various "scandals and absurdities" involving the abuse of their newfound power. His diagnosis is as follows:

> The[y] [the scandals] . . . are not basically individual problems. They are deficiencies of teaching and of models of leadership. . . . Romans 12 talks of the transformation of the mind as the basis for a non-conformist Christian ethic. But when there is no teaching, we fall prey to conformity. And many churches do not teach ethical principles, but only casuistic rules. But the legalist who depends on rules, when he enters a sphere for which his church has not elaborated rules, becomes literally unruly. That is one reason why many evangelical politicians become corrupt: they are legalists and therefore people without principles. (Freston, "Evangelicals and Politics in the Third World," 125-26)

When evaluating a particular position with which one disagrees, it is always important to attempt to understand the forces that drive those who argue for that position. In particular, it is helpful to ask this question: what is it that the advocates of this view *fear* most of all? Legalists fear that acknowledging the possibility of making exceptions to rules will open the door to a disastrous moral relativism and subjectivism. Finally, to be frank, in some contexts it is also professionally dangerous to raise questions about the use of the phrase "moral absolutes."

In our view, the way to respond to these fears is to embrace moral rules within the context of our four-level model. The rules that Jesus taught are needed, they are binding, and they are to be obeyed. Exceptions are to be considered as a last, rather than a first, resort. A legitimate exception to a rule will exist only if it is grounded in a principle or another rule that Jesus also taught, or that is found in Scripture. And all actions and moral judgments must pass the basic-conviction test related to the character and will of God as revealed supremely in Jesus Christ.

3. The centrality of principles: principlism. Henlee Barnette, a leading Southern Baptist ethicist for many years, was dissatisfied with the extremes of both situationism and legalism, which were the main ethical options at the time he was teaching and writing (1950s-1970s). He coined a new term, *principlism*, to describe his own ethical reasoning (Barnette, *Church and the Ecological Crisis*). Principlism is also advocated by other ethicists under other names, such as *middle axioms* or *presumptions* (J. H. Yoder, *Christian Witness to the State*; Wogaman, *Christian Moral Judgment*). Barnette defines his norms as principles, not rules. For example, in an essay on euthanasia, he defines Christian love as "willing the well-being of God's creatures, creation, and oneself"—including love of enemies. Love is grounded in God, whose love is revealed in Jesus Christ (note the basic-conviction dimension). Jesus was not a legalist, Barnette argues; he taught principles, not rules. Love is not just an unstructured feeling or belief (contrary to situationism); it is expressed in specific principles (not rules—contrary to legalism) that give us guidance on complex issues.

For example, in an essay on what treatment to give and what to withhold for a terminally ill man whose cancer had spread—an essay in which he also writes of facing his own father's dying from cancer—Barnette writes that this decision should be based on the *principles* of justice, human dignity, double effect, well-being and truth, among others.

In principlism:

(a) What is ethical is defined and determined by **principles.**

(b) Principles support rules but also limit them.

(c) Rules are not absolute and universal; they can be overridden by principles, but only when the principles demand it.

(d) If two rules conflict, you decide by going deeper, to the principles level.

Problem: what if two principles conflict?

- The principle of *justice* requires that the kind of treatment given be based on the patient's basic right to *consent.* Justice also considers the ability of the family and the medical and insurance system to pay for prolonging the life of someone who is dying of incurable cancer.

- The principle of *human dignity* means the dying person should have the company of family members and friends when possible, and that measures should not be taken to prolong the last stages of dying from cancer.

- The principle of *double effect* means that he should be given enough pain medicine when the intended effect is to relieve his pain, even if a side effect will be to shorten his life.

- The principle of *well-being* means he should not be forced to prolong an intolerable life.

- The principle of *truth,* which Barnette always emphasizes strongly, means that the patient must receive accurate medical information.

So Barnette gives much more guidance for ethical decisions than Fletcher does, spelled out in relevant principles. He does not simply leave us to decide what is best in each case on the basis of intuitive response to a situation. His principles guard against the power of a family member or medical doctor to run roughshod over the patient's consent or dignity.

On the other hand, Barnette is not a legalist. He specifically states he is advocating no single absolute rule or set of rules about what should and should not be done. He argues that principles support rules but also limit them, and that rules are not "absolute" and universal, but instead can be overridden by principles when the principles demand it. The principles set the parameters of moral decision, leaving a range of particular actions to be determined in each particular case.

The value of principlism, then, lies in its attention both to the details of particular cases and to the broad principles that must govern any morally adequate response to particular cases.

Principlism can be critiqued, though, on two fronts. On the one hand, Jesus did teach some particular rules, as we have argued, such as "be reconciled to your brother or sister" (Mt 5:24). If we fear legalism above all, we may find it easier to disobey the direct commands of Christ by hiding behind broad principles. We may neglect the rich and demanding substance of Christ's moral teaching and thin out our ethics into a few vague generalities that do not require much of us in any particular moment. This has been a particular problem in mainline Protestant ethics, which has feared legalism above all. The other problem that can afflict principlism is the severing of principles from the basic convictions in which they ought to be situated. Principles cannot simply hang in the air, but instead must be grounded in God's character, will and reign.

Contemporary philosophical ethics, which has a huge impact on how the insights of ethics are integrated into the daily practices of business, medicine and other professions, has a particular problem at this point. For philosophical ethics, in secular settings, rejects the rooting of principles in any theological basic-conviction. Thus the principles exist, but without a satisfactory support system to nourish them. Why human dignity? Why justice? Why truthfulness? Why do these really matter, why are they binding upon us, apart from a theological narrative that gives such moral norms their meaning? And lacking any convictional basis like this, it becomes extremely difficult to fill out the content and meaning of the principles that are proposed. Thus we are led to the final level in our model, the theological basic conviction.

4. The theological ground for Christian ethics: contextualism and narrative ethics. One option remains: to focus Christian ethics at the theological basic-conviction level. Two groups of Christian ethicists do this, tending to downplay rules and principles in the process. The first is the *contextualists*, including H. Richard Niebuhr, Paul Lehmann and James Gustafson. The more recent group can be labeled *narrative* ethicists, including James McClendon, Stanley Hauerwas, Darrell Fasching and Katie Cannon. Though these groups differ in some significant ways, here we shall only summarize some of the arguments that they hold in common related to the form and function of Christian moral norms.

Advocates of a focus on the basic-conviction level begin by reminding us of an important reality: rules and principles get their meaning from the various contexts in which they are understood.

Imagine Sam Smith, a twenty-five-year-old businessman whose father was a loyal member of the armed forces and who was raised in a family and a church that celebrate the heroism of veterans and strongly support American military actions. Now imagine Bill Jones, also twenty-five years old, also a businessman. Bill, though, is married to a woman whose family was driven from their home and later killed during the war in El Salvador; Bill was raised in a Mennonite family and church deeply committed to their "peace-church" tradition. Now let us suppose that our nation is contemplating war against, say, North Korea or Iraq, and is heavily engaged in a debate about whether such a war would meet the criteria of just war theory. Sam and Bill are both Americans, both Christians, both men, both in business, both the same age, both thoughtful people, both well-informed. But due to their personal, church and theological contexts (and the loyalties that go with them), we can just about guarantee that even if they both make careful use of the rules of just war theory, they will reach opposite conclusions about what it teaches with regard to this particular military conflict.

Why is this so? Because human beings are not isolated individual decision-makers but instead members of groups, communities and societies in which they are embedded and to which they tend to be quite loyal (see chapter three). Thus, they respond to what they perceive to be happening from within the frame of reference provided by these contexts, not as isolated individuals weighing rules or principles, as if in a vacuum, moment by moment. That is a factual claim, but here is a normative one: Christian ethics must and should be done in the context of our faith-communities, and our faith-communities must do Christian ethics in the context of the theological narrative found in Scripture—in particular, the reign of God inaugurated in Jesus Christ.

Therefore, Christian ethics needs to focus on several kinds of contexts: the personal *faith context* that shapes us and our ethics, understood as "the story of my life" as a Christian person; the *church context* in which we together live out our Christian lives; and the *community/societal context*, which shapes our perceptions, attitudes and practices in myriad ways and within which ethical issues arise. We need acute insight and honesty to be able to name all of these contexts and correct them where needed, on the basis of the normative theological narrative that is to be foundational for our ethics as Christians.

We embrace the basic claim of the contextualists/narrativists, that the theological basic-conviction level is the most important one for Christian ethics, and are most at home in this understanding of Christian ethics. We cannot be satisfied with situationism, legalism or principlism, for all demand deeper grounding, the kind of grounding that Jesus gives when he roots moral precepts in the character of the delivering God.

However, to say this is still to say all too little. Many Christians recognize that ethics is grounded in theology yet still come out quite differently in the kinds of ethics they propose. We must acknowledge that different ways of approaching theology, both in terms of methodology and substance, lead to radically different ethical outcomes. And because Jesus taught that "you shall know them by their fruits" (Mt 7:20), it is legitimate to consider the ethical import of theological claims as part of the overall evaluation of their value and truthfulness.

Let us illustrate what we mean with several brief examples from historic and contemporary Christian theology. One classic tendency in Christian thought has been the development of a thoroughgoing *dualism* in which sharp dichotomies are drawn between body and spirit/soul, world and church, law and gospel, and so on. The tendency of this kind of theology has been to identify God with the former (spirit, church, gospel) and expel or radically alter the nature of God's presence and sovereignty in the latter (body, world, law). The goal of the church is to rescue souls from bodies, rescue the church from the world, and transport its passengers safely to the heavenly realms. The implication for ethics has tended to be a lack of emphasis on obeying the teachings of Jesus in real physical, this-worldly life, due to hopelessness about the possibility of obedience and, sometimes, simply a misguided belief that Jesus' teachings do not apply.

Old-style *dispensational* theology makes a similar error. In the classic dispensationalist reading of salvation history, the history of salvation was divided into several distinct "dispensations" or epochs. During the present dispensation of the church, the moral teachings of Jesus Christ (some of them, at least) do not apply. They will begin to apply in the era after Christ returns. This theological move has the profound moral

In contextualism and narrative ethics, as we interpret it:

(a) What is ethical is ultimately defined and determined by basic theological convictions and narrative contexts.

(b) Moral decision making is not just individual but helped by consultation and mutual admonition from the faith community.

(c) Rules and principles find their place within the context of core theological beliefs.

Problem: what if Christians cannot agree on the content of these foundational beliefs?

consequence of dissuading Christians from attempting to practice the teachings of Jesus as they stand, exactly contrary to what Jesus taught in the Sermon on the Mount (Mt 7:21-27)!

A more sophisticated and common misdirection of theology can be called *doctrinalism*. By this we mean an approach to the mission of the church which emphasizes the careful crafting of rigid doctrinal formulas as the heart of the Christian enterprise. This has been characteristic of many branches of the church. Right doctrine (orthodoxy) is carefully emphasized, while right living (orthopraxy) is utterly neglected. Doctrinalism robs the church of ethical seriousness through sheer neglect, imagining that calling Jesus "Lord, Lord," in just the right language will somehow lead to entrance into the kingdom of heaven (cf. Mt 7:21).

The fourth theological/ethical problem is *deism*, a stripped-down version of Christian faith that flowered during the Enlightenment. Deists embraced the view that God had set the world in motion but now was letting it run its course. They rejected any hint of the supernatural in the Scriptures and any evidence of God's continued involvement in his creation. Thus Jesus was viewed as a marvelous moral teacher but not as God incarnate, son of a virgin, miracle-worker, exorcist, kingdom-inaugurator or resurrected Lord. While an emphasis on the moral teachings of Jesus is obviously welcome, those teachings must be placed into a full-blooded biblical/theological framework. Jesus did not just say "Repent," but "Repent, for the kingdom of God is at hand" (Mt 4:17). The extraction of the moral teaching of Jesus from its theological narrative is a terrible mistake, for ultimately it drains the life out of both Christian theology and ethics. Not only the Deists have traveled this path; it is characteristic of many accommodationist approaches seeking to bring the gospel into conformity with prevailing cultural and intellectual winds (Eph 4:14-15). (A more extensive and very insightful typology of approaches can be found in C. Wright, *Walking in the Ways of the Lord*, chaps. 5 and 6.)

In placing so much emphasis on our version of the Christian theological narrative throughout this book, we have already illuminated the point we seek to make here about the significance of theological basic-conviction understandings for Christian ethics. We have said that Jesus came to inaugurate the reign of God. All areas of life belong under the will of the Sovereign Lord. Resistance continues but will ultimately be subdued. The church is that body of people who have joined with Jesus to win back the rebellious creation. The church is the beachhead of the kingdom, visibly bearing witness to God's reign. This is the basic-conviction theological narrative so foundational for our understanding of Christian ethics.

Our four-level analysis tells us that the particular beliefs and loyalties generated by the theological-narrative context that serves as our ultimate basic conviction for Christian ethics need to be spelled out in rules and principles in order to give us clear guidance. Rules and principles make clear what we understand to be the implications of the gospel story and our life stories for concrete ethics. They make our ethics transparent. They place our guiding norms up on the table where they can be seen, examined, criticized, repented of and corrected.

But that analysis also tells us that theological beliefs are not *postethical*, as the philosopher Aiken originally argued, but instead the essential basic convictions for the work of Christian ethics. As Aiken himself shows, rules and principles are grounded in what he called our "way of life" and what we call the narratives of our faith. Rules and principles are not suspended in midair, not for anyone, even if some choose not to acknowledge the ultimate grounding they are in fact employing (see Stassen, "Social Theory Model" and "Critical Variables in Christian Social Ethics").

We have discovered in discussions with students that their parents or those who raised them told them biblical, personal and ethnic stories that shaped them and shaped their family traditions in ways deeper than they and we have often realized, *and* that those stories usually had a concrete "moral," a lesson for living. For example, the story so often told by parents of the Depression era that "we had it hard, and survived by the grace of God and hard work," leads to the concrete moral that "you need to work hard to overcome obstacles too instead of spending your time complaining about your hard luck." Narratives teach morality.

The Bible is full of narratives. But the narratives do have rules and principles, often quite concrete and specific. The story of the exodus is central in the Hebrew Scriptures; and central to the story of the exodus is the covenant—the Ten Commandments and related laws. Jesus taught parables; but Jesus also taught the Sermon on the Mount. The cross is a narrative about Jesus' death; but it is also something we are to take up and follow Jesus with, concretely, in our lives, as every layer of the New Testament emphasizes (Yoder, *Politics of Jesus*, chap. 7).

So we want our rules and principles to be clearly *embodied* in narratives, church practices and faith-community understandings. Rules and principles are not suspended in midair; they get their meaning and have their context in the realistic, embodied, Hebraic narrative of both Testaments, and in their analogous function in a realistic, embodied way of living in our social context. And we want our narrative ethics to be concretely expressed, *embodied*, in principles, rules and concrete judgments about particular cases. Those are two reasons we call our method *incarnational discipleship*—rules and principles are incarnated in narratives, and narratives are incarnated in specific rules and principles (and particular judgments). Our method differs from some contextual and narrative ethicists who are biased against rules and principles; we say rules and principles are part of the narrative of God's incarnation in Jesus Christ.

The main point of our analysis is to correct the tendency of legalists and situationists to ignore the historically embodied narrative way of life of the people of God in both Testaments, and to correct the tendency of contextualists and narrativists to rebel against rules and principles. Wright, Goldingay, Janzen and Brueggemann, in their writings on the ethics of the Old Testament, are clear that the biblical paradigms include the several levels that we have analyzed in an integrated interconnection, although each identifies the several levels somewhat differently. (See especially C. Wright, *Walking in the Ways of the Lord*, 20-21, 36, 94ff., 115, 128, 176-77; Janzen, *Old Testament Ethics*, 26ff., 55-56, 58, 74-75; Goldingay, *Models for Interpretation of Scripture*, 55; Brueggemann, *Social Reading of Old Testament Prophetic Approaches*, 175-77, 186-87, 195, 210-12.) Our purpose is to show the integrated interconnection of those levels. Mainline neo-orthodox pastors have tended to preach sermons that are strong on the basic-convictions level but lack concrete guidance on the rules and principles level. Most people live on the rules and principles and particular-judgment level, and find such sermons too abstract to help them with daily living. Evangelical pastors with a legalistic bent have tended to preach rules about individualistic ethics with which the congregation already agrees, but without providing a clear enough relation to the embodied biblical narratives. We want to help heal those disconnections and to foster churches that teach discipleship in every aspect of life.

We want to be accountable for the *particular* actions we advocate and engage in, and to let our faith and our ethics be tested and corrected by how they work out in real life. We think this testing, correcting and repenting are helped if we make our ethics explicit, spelling out something like rules and principles as well as basic faith-grounding. It is like a scientific researcher spelling out her or his assumptions in a computer program so that others can see where the errors are and correct them. As Paul says in Romans 3:23, "all have sinned and fall short of the glory of God," and so all of us need to keep making corrections in our ethical theory and practice. It is a theme we learned from H. Richard Niebuhr: *metanoia*, or continuous repentance, or *semper reformandum* (the church is always to be reforming). We hope to keep learning and not to think we have arrived. The Holy Spirit does not simply affirm what we always believed but dynamically engages us in a process of continuous learning and correction. Keeping particular judgments, rules, principles and basic convictions in continuous conversation, continuous reformulation, continuous repentance, while always remaining accountable above all to God in Christ, in the power of the Holy Spirit, should be the church's experience. Meanwhile, we can gratefully trust in God's mercy to forgive us our many failings in moral discernment and action.

Teleology Versus Deontology

We want to explain one further distinction that is important for the way of reasoning in Christian ethics: the classic distinction between *deontological* and *teleological* reasoning. We are guided by William Frankena's *Ethics*. This succinct little book by a well-respected philosophical ethicist who is also a Christian has been used by many Christian ethicists to clarify our categories.

1. Teleological reasoning. The term *teleological* comes from the Greek word for end or goal *(telos)*. Actions are right or wrong depending upon whether or not they further progress toward an end *(telos)* or goal that is worth striving for. Another name for this is consequentialism (a term which tends to emphasize assessment of after-the-fact outcomes, whereas the term *teleology* tends to denote before-the-fact goals, visions and intentions). Actions are obligatory not in and of themselves but on the basis of their anticipated or actual consequences. The ends, or consequences, justify the means you choose. In fact, the end is the only thing that justifies an action.

Different kinds of teleological ethics advocate different good ends that we should strive for. *Utilitarianism* says we should do whatever achieves the greatest happiness or the welfare of the greatest number of people. *Perfectionism* or character-building says we should do whatever improves people's virtues and perfects their character. *Nationalism* says we should do whatever is best for the national interest. *Egoism* says we should do whatever is best for our own self-interest. The list could go on.

Joseph Fletcher, the situationist, advocates one principle that should guide our assessment of each situation. He calls it agape love, but he defines it as the greatest good for the greatest number of people. He gets this, not from the New Testament, but from utilitarianism. Thus Fletcher is a teleological thinker of the utilitarian type.

This utilitarian version of teleology has the problem of lacking any principle of just distribution that guards the rights of the minority. If we are to do whatever is best for the welfare of the greatest number, we have no basis for guarding minority rights. Teleological ethics can justify manipulating the truth, killing enemies and stifling minority religions or minority races if that is the most efficient way to advance the good consequences one seeks. A not very good example is John 11:50-53, where Caiaphas the high priest argues that "it is expedient for you that one man should die for the people, and that the whole nation should not perish. . . . So from that day on they took counsel how to put him to death" (RSV).

2. Deontological reasoning. The term *deontological* comes from the Greek word *deon*, which means "obligatory" or "binding." We are obligated to refrain from using wrong means to our ends. A deontological approach says that achieving a good end is not enough; we also have to pay attention to principles of justice and fairness in how we go about trying to achieve a good end. Actions are right and wrong because they fit justice or rightness or basic obligations. Murder is wrong because it violates the moral ground rules concerning the treatment of other human beings.

There are several types of deontological reasoning: human rights, divine command, Kantian, Rawlsian and natural law. We shall explain some of them when we deal with particular issues in some of the following chapters.

To be really clear, we need to say that most deontologists are also concerned about achieving good ends. This point is frequently overlooked or misunderstood. Fairness says it is wrong to discriminate against a minority race concerning who gets to go to good schools. That is an obligatory principle of justice, based not on some teleological goal but on what is just basically right. But once that *principle* is respected, then we should also pay attention to the *goal* of offering a good and effective education. It would be immoral, while avoiding discrimination, to cut off funding from all the schools so that everyone went to poor schools. A deontologist is concerned about achieving good ends as long as rules or principles of fairness or rightness are obeyed.

We want to be clear that the issue of deontology versus teleology is not the same as the issue of a rule-based legalism versus a nonlegalistic ethics. A deontologist would base the rule against murder on the principle of human rights and the sacredness of life, or because God commands us not to murder in the Ten Commandments. A teleologist of a utilitarian type could also advocate the rule against murder on the grounds that if murders are allowed, it will set back the welfare and happiness of a very large number of people, and the happiness of the greatest number will decrease. This is called "rule-utilitarianism." The difference between deontologists and teleologists is not whether they have rules, but whether they base their rules on the duty to do what is right or on the goal of achieving a good end.

Testing the hypothesis. Let us test our hypothesis on a basic ethical question: Why is murder wrong? We will assume that the respondents are all Christians.

Deontological perspectives

a. *situationist*—it was clear in this situation that murder would be a disobedient act, in violation of God's will for me.

b. *rule-oriented*—the Bible contains a rule against murder in Exodus.

c. *principlist*—murder violates the broad biblical principle of the sacredness of human life.

d. *basic-convictions*—murder is contrary to the loving and just character of God.

Teleological perspectives

a. *situationist*—Murdering this person in this situation would not lead to the greatest good for the greatest number of people.

b. *rule-oriented*—If I violate the rule against murder (or if that rule did not exist) it would not lead to the greatest good for the greatest number of people.

c. *principlist*—Murder undermines the biblical principles of the sacredness of human life and respect for human rights, and if these are undermined it will lead to bad consequences such as anarchy or tyranny.

d. *basic-convictions*—Murder violates God's intentions for human life, which include peace, justice and security.

We believe a Jesus-centered ethic takes divine commands seriously and is indeed vigorously deontological. But it understands the mandates and teachings of Jesus to be gracious and authoritative instruction concerning *how to do the will of God (deontological) and how to participate in the coming of the kingdom of God (teleological)*. Christians are to "go . . . be reconciled to your brother or sister" (Mt 5:24) both because Jesus taught this rule and we are obligated to obey it (deontological) and because initiatives such as these break the cycle of relational brokenness and bring about peace between human beings who had been estranged. And this peace is a part of the reign of God (teleological). So we obey Christ's teachings not only because he is our Lord, but because we trust that he above all knows what concrete behaviors advance the kingdom of God and wants us to know and do them as well. We do not look for exceptions to burdensome rules but instead look for ways to do the gloriously liberating things that he taught us to do.

The fact that a Jesus- and kingdom-centered ethic includes concerns about consequences for people and for the kingdom may trouble those who have dismissed the value of any concerns about good ends in their determination to oppose a teleological ethic. Yet "Seek ye first the kingdom of God" (Mt 6:33 KJV) is clearly concerned about a good end. Jesus presents a goal—verily, *the* goal—for which all Christians are to strive, and he sets us to work pursuing that goal. Actions that seek to forward the kingdom of God are obligatory; actions that hinder it are forbidden. Rightly understood, this kind of goal-oriented concern meshes with a healthy Christian deontology. After all, Jesus commanded complete obedience to the Law and the Prophets and offered a dire warning to any who would set these aside (Mt 5:17-20).

Christian ethics, then, must be sufficiently biblical to avoid reducing the moral life to a mere *decisionism* or *legalism* of abstract deontological absolutes. It must integrate those goals which the Scriptures urge the church to strive for as part of kingdom-seeking as well as those virtues of character which we are to seek to embody to get us there. The best overall term for the substantive content of Christian ethics is the broadest available—Christian ethics is about the entire "way of life" of the people of faith (Eph 2:10; cf. Deut 30:19-20). No aspect of moral existence is left out—decisions, practices, convictions, principles, goals and virtues are all included in the effort to "live your life in a manner worthy of the gospel" (Phil 1:27; cf. Rom 16:2; Eph 4:1; Col 1:10) as we seek the kingdom of God.

In this context the familiar language of "moral norms," language which has occupied us throughout this chapter, finally comes to feel too passive, static and theoretical. The church's moral task is not primarily to come up with the right beliefs about issues like euthanasia or peacemaking, and then make sure that every member holds these right beliefs. Nor is it to come up with the right set of timeless virtues and hope that every member will be virtuous. Instead, our central task is to discern which specific *practices* fit the kingdom of God and which attributes of community character are appropriate and fitting for people whose lives are surrendered to God. We want above all to be useful servants of the reign of God, and thus with all our heart we seek to discern and then to put into practice a total way of life that advances God's kingdom.

In our discussion of the Sermon on the Mount in the next chapter we will attempt to show that the moral teaching of Jesus in the Sermon is focused precisely in this way. He did not instruct his listeners merely in right beliefs about moral issues but instead trained his hearers in those behaviors, those *practices*, that characterize the reign of God, and offered concrete *transforming initiatives* that move us from here to there.

Practices, Virtues and Embodied Drama

In chapter three, we argued that character ethics needs rules and principles. We have now filled in that argument. But the question remains: how do *practices*, *virtues* and *narratives*, which are emphasized in character ethics, relate to these rule-and-principle levels of reasoning?

Practices are defined in three somewhat differing ways by John H. Yoder, Alasdair MacIntyre and James McClendon. Yoder names baptism, the Lord's Supper, calling out the gifts, the rule of Christ (making peace with one's antagonist) and the rule of Paul (community decision by respectful attention to the leading of each member) as normative practices. He describes a practice as a visible community action that is morally normative or authoritative because it is derived from the work of Jesus Christ in relation to the Holy Spirit and God the Father in the New Testament. It is God's gracious action in which humans participate and is commanded as mandatory, but it is not rigid or legalistic: it can be carried out in different ways in different contexts. Because the normative practices are not invisible, hidden mysteries, but visible community practices that a secular sociologist could observe and study, each has a dimension—like feeding the hungry as a normative part of the Lord's Supper in the New Testament (1 Cor 11:20-33)—that can be commended to secular society as ethically normative (Yoder, *Body Politics;* and see summary in Stassen et al., *Authentic Transformation,* 172-73).

MacIntyre defines a practice in a more general philosophical mode, as

> any coherent and complex form of socially established cooperative human activity through which goods internal to that form of activity are realized in the course of trying to achieve those standards of excellence which are appropriate to, and partially definitive of, that form of activity, with the result that human powers to achieve excellence, and the human conceptions of the ends and good involved, are systematically extended. (*After Virtue,* 187)

McClendon is influenced by both Yoder and MacIntyre, but criticizes MacIntyre's definition for setting practices as always good, over against institutions as always corrupting (McClendon, *Ethics,* 162, 172-73). He defines practices in a way that is closer to Yoder. Practices resemble a game like chess or football: they have as necessary elements *a goal, an allowed means, rules and the intention of really participating in the practice.* "The rules are not arbitrary additions we might very well discard. . . . It is exactly the rules that constitute" the practice (163). Practices are social in character, and people participate by playing roles defined by the practice (165-66). "Many virtues have their home in connection with particular practices whose pursuit evokes exactly those virtues" (169). "The lives of those who do engage in these practices must have at least enough continuity and coherence to permit the *formation* of those virtues and *sustaining* of those intentions—in a word, their lives must take a narrative form," particularly an embodied narrative like a drama (171). As his main example, he devotes chapter eight to analyzing the Christian practice of forgiveness, like Yoder's rule of Christ. (We also get our term *basic convictions* from McClendon, *Doctrine,* 4-12; *Ethics,* 22-23; *Witness,* 52ff.)

MacIntyre's definition seems strictly teleological: the object is to "realize goods" and "achieve excellence." Yoder's and McClendon's have deontological, mandatory actions.

If we accept McClendon's definition, we see that practices function primarily at the rules level. "Do this in remembrance of me," and "wait for one another" so that all are fed, are rules indicating directly what we are to do (1 Cor 11:24, 33). Practices are constituted by their rules, McClendon points out. Contrary to Fletcher, summary rules like "punt on fourth down" are not the only kind of rules in football. *Obligatory* rules *constitute* the game: "To disregard the *constitutive* rules . . . (say by trying to win by crossing the goal line over and over again before the game begins) is not a way to win at football; . . . it simply shows failure to understand what the rules are" (*Ethics*, 163-64). We notice further that practices are more concrete than general principles: they indicate directly what to do or not do. As morally normative, they support particular actions like feeding the hungry. So we can put practices at the level of rules.

Virtues are more general than rules. Being humble and yielded to God, being merciful and hungering for justice, and seeking to do God's will, do not tell us directly what to do in the way rules do. So virtues operate at the level of principles.

And the embodied drama that gives continuity and coherence to life and its practices functions at the level of basic convictions. For example, the embodied drama of Jesus' Last Supper with the disciples, his giving his body as a sacrifice for others and his blood as a covenant of grace, is what gives the deep theological meaning to the practice of the Lord's Supper, and to the community's feeding the hungry. That deeply symbolic practice embodies all the Christian virtues, certainly including the virtue of hungering for justice, as Paul makes clear in 1 Corinthians. Churches should practice the Lord's Supper or Eucharist in varieties of ways to portray different dimensions of its powerful meaning. And sermons should explicate different dimensions of the embodied drama that gives the practice coherence.

Duane Friesen's *Artists, Citizens, Philosophers: Seeking the Peace of the City* is an insightful integration of the levels of Christ-centered narrative, virtues and practices giving guidance to a theological ethic of the life of beauty, political engagement and intellectual inquisitiveness. It models the lordship of Christ over all of life, guided by an ethic of practices.

We speak of "embodied drama" and not simply of "narrative." Jesus did not just tell a story about someone giving his life for others but incarnated it in his own body and blood—and not as a private act, but as a community drama in which Christian disciples, Jewish power structure and Roman power structure participated. We all sinned. It is embodied *now* as the church enacts it and incarnates it in its worship and in its feeding the hungry. And it will be embodied in the *future* kingdom, which Jesus often portrays as a banquet to which many are invited who had not been thought includeable (Mt 22:9; Lk 14:23). (See McClendon, *Ethics*, 31ff., and the powerful argument in Cavanaugh, *Torture and the Eucharist*.)

6

THE TRANSFORMING INITIATIVES
OF THE SERMON ON THE MOUNT

But I say to you that if you are angry with a brother or sister, you will be liable to

judgment. . . . So when you are offering your gift at the altar, if you remember that your

brother or sister has something against you, leave your gift there before the altar and go;

first be reconciled to your brother or sister, and then come and offer your gift.

MATTHEW 5:22-24

When Dietrich Bonhoeffer was fifteen years old, he told his family that he had decided to go to the university and study theology. His older brother said: "Don't you know the church is corrupt and out of touch with the world today?" Dietrich replied: "If that's the case, I'll help reform the church!" By the time he was twenty-one years old, he had completed his doctoral dissertation. By the time he was twenty-four, he had been appointed lecturer in theology at the University of Berlin, and by age twenty-seven, he had written his second book.

But Germany was suffering from the Great Depression of 1929-1939, mass unemployment and civil unrest. It had only recently turned from a monarchy to a democratic government, and in 1933 Germans rejected their democratic government and handed the reins of power to Adolf Hitler, who was named chancellor on January 30. Hitler had promised to get the economy moving again. He had also enticed Christians to vote for him by promising to make Christianity "the basis of our whole morality." He assured Christians that they were the "most important factor safeguarding our national heritage" (Bethge, *Dietrich Bonhoeffer,* 262). He blamed Jews and Communists for Germany's problems. Jewish stores were boycotted on April 1, and Germans were warned against fraternizing with Jews. Germans who dated or married Jews were charged with "polluting the purity of the German race."

The first concentration camp was opened at Dachau in 1933. Hitler decreed an "Aryan clause" calling for the "racial purity" of the civil service and eventually of the church: No Christian of Jewish descent would be permitted to hold a position in the church.

The sad truth is that most Christians supported Hitler's anti-Semitism and discriminatory policies. Didn't Hitler speak about the need for Christian morality and about divine providence guiding Germany's history? Didn't Germany need a strong ruler who would get the economy moving again and defeat Germany's enemies? Christians were flattered by Hitler's claim to support Christianity, and they lacked the biblical commitment to standards of justice that would have warned them against his unjust plans.

Bonhoeffer was one of the very few Christian leaders to see from the start that Hitler was too authoritarian, too dictatorial, too unjust and too warlike. After Hitler's election, Bonhoeffer preached that Christians have only one Lord, Jesus Christ, and not some other lord, a secular authority. He gave a radio talk warning against the dangers of a leader who claimed absolute authority and trampled on basic human rights. Ominously, his talk was cut off before the climax, apparently by Hitler's censors.

How was Bonhoeffer able to see clearly when others were so wrong? How was he able to act courageously when others were so silent? He had not always seen so clearly. In 1929, when he had just finished his graduate studies, he had based his concrete ethics on nationalism, like other Lutheran theologians who ended up supporting Hitler. He claimed God had ordained the nation-state to guide us in politics, war and economics. In our social responsibilities, we should not follow Jesus but the realities of German politics (Tödt, "Kirche und Ethik," 447; Bonhoeffer, *Gesammelte Schriften* III, 48-58).

Bonhoeffer's big turning point came the next year, while he was studying at Union Theological Seminary in New York and involving himself in the life of the African-American Abyssinian Baptist Church in Harlem (Bonhoeffer, *Letters and Papers from Prison*, 275). He was converted by Jesus' Sermon on the Mount. It changed his life. He wrote about it in a letter to a girlfriend:

> I [had] plunged into my work in a very unchristian way. An . . . ambition that many noticed made my life difficult. . . . Then something happened, something that has changed and transformed my life to the present day. For the first time I discovered the Bible. . . . I had often preached . . . but I had not yet become a Christian. . . . I had never prayed, or prayed only very little. . . . Then the Bible, and in particular the Sermon on the Mount, freed me from all that. Since then, everything has changed. . . . It was a great liberation. It became clear to me that the life of a servant of Jesus Christ must belong to the Church, and step by step it became plainer to me how far that must go. (Bethge, *Dietrich Bonhoeffer*, 204-5)

Eventually Bonhoeffer became the lone faculty member in an underground theological seminary free from the Nazis' domination, and there his teaching emphasized the Sermon on the Mount and following Jesus. He wrote his classic on the Sermon on the Mount, *The Cost of Discipleship* (whose original German title means *Following Christ*). On the basis of the Sermon on the Mount, he sought to persuade others to oppose what Hitler was doing. Taking the Sermon on the Mount seriously meant love for the brother and love for the enemy, and it meant love must include all people—and that certainly included Jews. That meant Christians must oppose Hitler's anti-Jewish policies. Taking the Sermon on the Mount seriously also meant taking Jesus' teachings on peacemaking seriously. That meant he now had strong grounds for opposing Hitler's bellicose policies (Tödt, *Theologische Perspektiven*, 112ff.). He said that a clear and uncompromising stand based on the Sermon on the Mount was the only source of power strong enough to make Christianity a vital force for the people (Bethge, *Dietrich Bonhoeffer*, 413). And he said that a new sense of life as following Jesus in accord with the Sermon on the Mount would be the way toward restoration of the church after the Nazi debacle was finally over (Bonhoeffer, *Gesammelte Schriften* III, 25).

Karl Barth, who was one of the leaders of the Confessing Church, which opposed Hitler's takeover of the church, wrote: "From 1933 on Bonhoeffer was the first, indeed almost the only one, who focused so centrally and energetically" on defending Jews against Hitler's injustices (Tödt, "Kirche und Ethik," 447). While the Confessing Church concentrated on defending the church, it did little for Jews outside the church who were being deprived of their homes, their businesses and eventually of their lives. It was Bonhoeffer, standing on the basis of the Sermon on the Mount as concrete guidance for life, who spoke out against the Nazi anti-Jewish policies and urged the church to act in opposition. He helped smuggle fourteen Jews out of Germany into Switzerland and helped a Jewish professor named Perels to survive the concentration camp in Gurs (International Bonhoeffer Society, *Newsletter*).

It seems clear that Bonhoeffer's loyalty to Jesus Christ and his concrete understanding of Jesus' way as revealed in the Sermon on the Mount were major reasons why he was able to see so clearly what was wrong with Hitler. In his resistance to Hitler's injustices, the Sermon on the Mount was central.

Yet the curious and intriguing reality is that six years later when Bonhoeffer wrote his *Ethics*, he hardly even mentioned the Sermon on the Mount. Accordingly, his *Ethics* has been rightly criticized for lacking concrete normative guidance (for example, Rasmussen, *Dietrich Bonhoeffer*, 154-55, 160, 168). We believe this lack in one of Christianity's finest and most faithful leaders is deeply symbolic of a strange phenomenon that has diverted much church tradition from fully following Jesus. Let us explain something about our tradition, beginning from the beginning.

How the Tradition of Evasion and Dualism Developed

The Great Commission says: "Go, therefore, and *make disciples* of all nations, baptizing them in the name of the Father and of the Son and of the Holy Spirit, and *teaching them to obey everything that I have commanded you*" (Mt 28:19-20). The tradition begins by making clear that the way of discipleship includes practicing Jesus' commands. The way of discipleship and the commands of Jesus are most explicitly taught in the Sermon on the Mount. This is how the early Christians were taught how to be disciples (Luz, *Matthew 1—7*, 214). In the first three centuries of the church, the biblical passage most often referred to was the Sermon on the Mount (Kissinger, *Sermon on the Mount*, 6).

We see this clearly in one of the first Christian writers after the New Testament, Justin Martyr. About A.D. 154 Justin wrote his *First Apology*. When he presented what Christians stand for, he quoted fully from the teachings of the Sermon on the Mount—on chastity, marriage, truthtelling, loving your enemy, turning the other cheek, going the second mile, giving to the one who begs, not hoarding treasures or being anxious about possessions but seeking first the kingdom of God, letting your good works shine before others so that God is praised but not doing good works to be seen by others. He expected Christians to do these practices and live this way. He emphasized what Jesus emphasized: "Not every one who saith to me, Lord, Lord, shall enter into the kingdom of heaven, but he that doeth the will of My Father which is in heaven. . . . By their works ye shall know them. And every tree that bringeth not forth good fruit, is hewn down and cast into the fire." He said that as Christians carry out Jesus' teachings, this bears witness to the power of the teachings to transform the way people live: "And many, both men and women, who have been Christ's disciples from childhood, remain pure at the age of sixty or seventy years; and I boast that I could produce such from every race of men. For what shall I say, too, of the countless multitude of those who have reformed intemperate habits, and learned these things?" (Justin Martyr *First Apology* 167-68).

But then a crack appears, a hint of greater problems to come in subsequent church history. Justin addressed his *Apology* to Emperor Antoninus Pius and his son, trying to get their favor. Therefore, immediately after presenting these teachings from Jesus' way, he quoted Jesus' teaching in Matthew 22:17-21: "Render therefore to Caesar the things that are Caesar's, and to God the things that are God's" (RSV). He interpreted it dualistically: "Whence to God alone we render worship, but in other things we gladly serve you, acknowledging you as kings and rulers of men." Thus he limited Christian independence from the emperor to the matter of how we worship. Clearly Jesus' way as taught in the Sermon on the Mount concerns much more than our worship. It concerns sexual relations, marriage, truthtelling, loving enemies and investing our money. Yet here Justin introduced an incipient dualism. He was "apologizing" to the emperor—trying to persuade the emperor to be kind to Christians. In order to be subservient to the powers and authorities, he divided up Christian responsibility so that our *worship* belongs to God, while in *other things* we do what the earthly ruler says. That gave the emperor a blank check in matters outside of worship.

This was not Jesus' attitude. For Jesus, what belonged to God? Everything. Jesus was a Jew, not a dualist. He knew God is the Lord over everything. His teaching in Matthew 22:17-21 is an ironic Hebrew parallelism (Bornkamm, *Jesus of Nazareth,* 121-4). The second member of the parallelism, "Render to God the things that are God's," means "render *everything* to God." It gives an ironic twist to the first half of the teaching: God has sovereignty over Caesar; we render to Caesar only what fits God's will. But Justin was a Gentile, not a Jew, and a disciple of Socrates and Plato before his conversion, accustomed to a dualism in which the spiritual was split off from the earthly. In Platonic thought, God was outside the cave in which we live, in the eternal realm, not the earthly realm. Wanting to please the emperor, Justin here, perhaps unintentionally, gave the emperor authority over everything but the spiritual realm of worship.

Justin's order of teaching is the opposite of Jesus'. Having said a little coin can go to Caesar, *Jesus* climaxes his teaching by saying, in effect, "but God is Lord of everything." Having quoted Jesus' way in the Sermon on the Mount, *Justin* climaxes his teaching by saying, in effect, "but Caesar is Lord in everything but worship." It is this incipient Platonic dualism, combined with the desire to please the powers and authorities of this world—whether they be political rulers, concentrations of wealth, racist power structures, or habits, customs and self-interested practices—that creates in subsequent church history the devilish dualism in which whole swaths of life are moved out from under God's authority and placed under the authorities of this world. And then the way of Jesus gets fenced in to apply only to one narrowly limited realm—worship, inner attitudes or individual relations. Surely Justin, a sincere Christian, did not intend all that followed in subsequent church history from this seemingly small, innocent crack in our responsibility to God. But it did follow.

When Constantine became the first Christian emperor (306-337), the church downplayed whatever might suggest criticism of Constantine's way of ruling.

The disabling and ultimately tragic development is that the focus soon shifts from Jesus and the particular way he incarnated with his community, the way of his God, to the metaphysical relationship of the individual figure, Jesus, to the church's God, now become also the empire's God. . . . So one searches in vain in the classic creeds, those pure distillations of the faith, for anything at all about Jesus as the way in any moral sense, or of his community's way. (Rasmussen, *Moral Fragments and Moral Community*, 138-40)

Then came the Middle Ages. The people were mostly illiterate and could not read about Jesus' teaching or Jesus' way. They were told to let the clergy and the hierarchy tell them what they needed to believe. You can see pictorially what was emphasized about Jesus in the Middle Ages if you go to The Cloisters, the medieval art museum in New York City. The beautiful paintings and sculptures there depict only two themes: Mary and the baby Jesus, and Jesus on the cross—nothing about what happened between Jesus' birth and his death. It is like the Apostle's Creed: "born of the Virgin Mary, suffered under Pontius Pilate, was crucified, dead, and buried." The Sermon on the Mount and all of Jesus' prophetic teachings are hiding, unseen and unheard, behind that comma that zips him from his birth to his suffering under Pilate, with nothing in between but a comma.

The theologian Jürgen Moltmann (*Way of Jesus Christ*, 150), offers a constructive suggestion to fill this empty hole:

We cannot close this chapter on the messianic mission of Jesus Christ without offering a suggestion for an addition to these two ancient creeds of the church. The intention is not to alter the words of tradition; but one must know what has to be added in thought. After "born of the Virgin Mary" or "and was made man" in the Nicene Creed, we should add something along the following lines:

- baptized by John the Baptist,
- filled with the Holy Spirit:
- to preach the kingdom of God to the poor,
- to heal the sick,
- to receive those who have been cast out,
- to revive Israel for the salvation of the nations, and
- to have mercy upon all people.

In the Protestant Reformation, Martin Luther criticized the medieval church for splitting humankind into two classes. According to this two-class dualism, the teachings of the Sermon on the Mount were commands for monks and clergy, but for the rest of us, they were only optional advice if you wanted to be perfect ("counsels of perfection"). Luther insisted the teachings were for all Christians. But then he adopted something like Justin Martyr's Platonic dualism. The Sermon is for every Christian *in our inner attitudes*, but the outer self that has responsibilities to other persons should obey the authorities in the world and not the commands of the Sermon. The Sermon on the Mount was for our attitudes, not our actions (Luther, *Sermon on the Mount*, 364ff.). This is called a two-realms dualism. Like Justin, Luther was concerned with a ruler. His prince, Frederick, was defending him and his Reformation against the pope, who would have had him arrested for undermining the Catholic Church. Furthermore, Prince Frederick sat on his throne just opposite Luther as Luther preached, observing what Luther would say. Luther needed an ethic that said the Sermon would not undermine the authority and power of Frederick.

The church historian Jaroslav Pelikan shows that Luther's two-realms dualism marked a historic departure from the great preacher of the early Greek church, John Chrysostom, and the great preacher of the Roman church, Augustine (*Divine Rhetoric,* 145ff.). Chrysostom and Augustine taught that the commands of the Sermon were God's will for everyone—for disciples first, and through them, for all humankind; and were to be carried out in practice. Luther limited their application to Christians in their inner lives, not for Christians in their public lives or for all humankind (Pelikan, *Divine Rhetoric,* 79-80, 106-7, 110-14, 119, 123). The result was secularism: people were taught that the gospel has nothing concrete to say about how we live our lives in the public realm, except that our inner motive should be love. Having a motive of love, however, can be shaped into all kinds of ethics, especially when the secular ruler defines our actions in the public realm. Consequently the realm of religious faith gets reduced to ever-narrower parts of our lives. And laypeople see the gospel as less and less relevant to their lives. Secularism in Germany means only 5 percent of Lutherans are in church on an average Sunday morning.

The Bible, throughout its pages, teaches that there is only one God who is Lord of all of life. The Bible never splits life into one realm ruled by a secular ruler and the other ruled by God. Present-day Lutheran scholars and many Lutheran pastors are critical of the two-realms split and seek to correct it, as did Bonhoeffer, and as do we. (A brief history of interpretation of the Sermon on the Mount by an excellent Lutheran New Testament scholar is Luz, *Matthew 1—7,* 218-23; see also McArthur, *Understanding the Sermon on the Mount,* chaps. 3-4; Schnackenburg, *Bergpredigt,* 36-55; Baumann, *Sermon on the Mount;* and Kissinger, *Sermon on the Mount.*)

During the Reformation, John Calvin taught the sovereignty of God over all of life, and he developed a covenant ethic for life in the world that continues to be helpful today (Mount, *Covenant, Community, and the Common Good;* Mouw, *God Who Commands;* Smedes, *Mere Morality;* M. Stackhouse, *Covenant and Commitments.* M. A. Farley, *Personal Commitments,* gives a Roman Catholic version that has been helpful to us). He saw the Sermon on the Mount as Christ's interpretation of the Old Testament, not a contradiction of the Old Testament. He interpreted the Sermon as giving practical guidance and as intended to be obeyed. His practical emphases did sometimes reduce the Sermon to what he saw in the Old Testament, however, or to what he thought he could expect Christians to do. And he skipped over Jesus' teaching in Matthew 7 that we are not only to hear these words, but *do* them (Calvin, *Harmony of the Gospels*, 164-232).

The Anabaptists insisted on discipleship as following Jesus concretely, and they taught the Sermon on the Mount as authoritative for the whole life of Christians (outer as well as inner). But the Swiss and South-German Anabaptists did not see how they could expect the Sermon to apply to the kingdom of the world, and so they developed a "two-kingdoms ethic" in which they did not think the Sermon applied to non-Christians, and they did not develop an ethic for the outer kingdom. Menno Simons, however, clearly saw Christ as Lord over earthly rulers and did not hesitate to call rulers to do justice and act according to God's will as revealed in the Prophets and in Jesus. Present-day Anabaptist scholars are also emphasizing that Jesus Christ is Lord over all of life, not only over the church (Driedger and Kraybill, *Mennonite Peacemaking*, 73, 79, 90, 119ff., 175-76, 241).

The tradition of evasion continues in textbooks on Christian ethics. Until recently (see preface), we could find only two textbooks that draw *anything* constructive from the Sermon on the Mount. These two exceptions devote only a page or two to the Sermon. Remember, the Sermon on the Mount is the largest block of Jesus' teaching in the New Testament and was the manual for teaching what it meant to be a Christian in the early church. It is the central passage that stands for Jesus' way. When the way Christian ethics is taught and practiced conveys the understanding that the Sermon on the Mount does not contribute to Christian ethics, it spills over into the overall orientation toward Jesus' teachings as a whole. It conveys that Christian ethics is based on something other than following Jesus. It tends to result in a moralism and legalism that adopt authoritarian ideologies from the culture; or else in a culture-accommodating liberalism, permissivism and self-seeking individualism. (Richard Hays, *The Moral Vision of the New Testament*, which is a New Testament ethics rather than a Christian ethics textbook, does better.)

Why this evasion? What went wrong?

Not "High Ideals" but "Transforming Initiatives"

We have already identified a tendency to accommodate to powers and authorities in the culture and therefore to compartmentalize and marginalize Jesus. A key step in that accommodation is to teach that the Sermon consists of hard teachings, ideals too high for us to reach up to; lovely sentiments but impossible for practical living. Once that step is taken, then it is easier to argue that we need some other ethic that we can practice—which almost always turns out to be an ethic that accepts the authority of some secular power and authority.

Thus a tradition has developed that the pattern of the Sermon is *antitheses*, in which Jesus prohibits anger, lust, divorce, oaths, resistance to evil and commands that we renounce all rights. Then people realize that they cannot avoid ever being angry and so on. So they say these are hard teachings, high ideals, very strenuous demands. They praise them for being so idealistic and then conclude they cannot follow them in practice and adopt another ethic that comes from somewhere else. They compartmentalize Jesus' teachings as meant for attitudes but not actions, or for repentance but not obedience, or for another future dispensation but not the present time, or merely as illustrations of general principles like love but not meant to be followed in particular.

It is revealing to observe what they do when they come to Jesus' teachings in the conclusion of the Sermon on the Mount that say as clearly as possible that these teachings are meant to be *done*: "Every tree that does not bear good fruit is cut down and thrown into the fire. Thus you will know them by their fruits. Not every one who says to me, 'Lord, Lord,' will enter the kingdom of heaven, but only the one who *does* the will of my Father who is in heaven. . . . Every one then who hears these words of mine and *does them* will be like a wise man who built his house on rock. . . . And every one who hears these words of mine and *does not do them* will be like a foolish man who built his house on sand" (Mt 7:19-21, 24-27). When they come upon these words, they usually simply skip over them or interpret them to mean something else. Or they do not come upon the words, because they skip over the whole Sermon on the Mount. The result is what Dietrich Bonhoeffer calls "cheap grace": People congratulate themselves that they are forgiven, without repenting; that God is on their side, without their following the way of God as revealed in Jesus; that they are Christians, without it making much difference in their way of life (Bonhoeffer, *Cost of Discipleship*, 40, 45ff.). And the result plays into the hands of secular interests that do not want the way of Jesus to interfere with their practices. Morality becomes secularized. Jesus gets marginalized or compartmentalized. The church's ethic becomes vague and abstract.

We propose a way to rescue the Sermon from the antitheses interpretation as perfectionistic prohibitions. It is deceptively simple, but it makes a huge difference in how the way of Jesus in the Sermon of the Mount is interpreted and will guide our interpretation throughout the rest of this book. The pattern of the Sermon is not twofold antitheses but *threefold transforming initiatives*. Therefore, the emphasis in interpretation is to be placed not on an alleged idealistic prohibition but on the realistic way of deliverance through the transforming initiatives (for further evidence of these triads, see Stassen, *Just Peacemaking: Transforming Initiatives*, and "The Fourteen Triads of the Sermon on the Mount" [forthcoming in *Journal of Biblical Literature*, 2003]).

The easiest way to see the pattern is to begin with Jesus' first major teaching of the way he calls us to follow, Matthew 5:21-26. The tradition of antitheses has seen the teaching as following a twofold, or dyadic, pattern:

Traditional Righteousness	Jesus' Teaching
Matthew 5:21: You have heard that it was said to those of ancient times, 'You shall not kill; and whoever kills shall be liable to judgment" (author's translations in this chapter to follow the Greek verb forms more closely).	Matthew 5:22-26: But I say to you that every one being angry with his brother will be liable to judgment; whoever insults his brother will be liable to the council, and whoever says, 'You fool!" will be liable to the hell of fire. (Illustrations: So if you are offering your gift at the altar . . . make friends quickly with your accuser.)

Seeing it this way naturally places the emphasis on "Jesus' teaching." And, since it is clear that Jesus does give commands in the Sermon on the Mount, Jesus' teaching here is interpreted as a command not to be angry and not to call anyone a fool. But since we cannot avoid being angry, if we are truthful about ourselves, Jesus must not mean what he seems to have said. So it is a hard teaching, a high ideal, an impossible demand.

This is a misinterpretation. Jesus in fact gives no command not to be angry or not to call anyone a fool. In the Greek of the New Testament, "Being angry" in Matthew 5:22 is not a command, but a participle, an ongoing action. It is a diagnosis of a vicious cycle that we often get stuck in: being angry, insulting one another. It is simply realistic: we do get angry, we do insult one another, and it does lead to trouble. As New Testament scholar Dale Allison points out, early Christian tradition did not clearly know an injunction against all anger: Ephesians 4:26 says "Be angry but do not sin; do not let the sun go down on your anger." In Mark 1:41 the original text may have had Jesus "moved with anger," and Mark 3:5 explicitly says Jesus was angry—at the hardness of heart of those who would not say it was right to heal the man with the withered hand on the sabbath. Matthew 21:12-17 and Matthew 23 show Jesus angry, and in 23:17 Jesus calls his opponents fools, which would contradict 5:22 if that verse is read as a command. "For the most part later Christian tradition followed Eph. 4:26 and did not demand the elimination of all anger—only anger misdirected" (Allison, *Sermon on the Mount*, 64; cf. 64-71).

But Jesus does give commands here. There are five of them, all imperatives in the Greek. They all are found in what the above diagram tacks on as "illustrations." Yet Matthew 5:23-26 does not contain mere illustrations. It does not give "illustrations" of killing or being angry, or illustrations of a negative avoidance—not being angry. Jesus' commands here are *transforming initiatives* that are the way of deliverance from anger and killing. They are not mere illustrations; they are the climax of the teaching. Therefore, we propose that the teaching should be diagrammed in a way that does not underemphasize the climax of the teaching, but instead rightly highlights it as the third and climactic part of the teaching.

Traditional Righteousness	Vicious Cycle	Transforming Initiative
Matthew 5:21: You have heard that it was said to those of ancient times, "You shall not kill; and whoever kills shall be liable to judgment." (In the Greek, "shall not" and "shall be" are not imperatives, but futures; as translations of the Hebrew in the Ten Commandments, they do of course imply a command.)	Matthew 5:22: But I say to you that every one being angry with his brother will be liable to judgment; whoever insults his brother will be liable to the council, and whoever says, "You fool!" will be liable to the hell of fire. (No imperatives in the Greek.)	Matthew 5:23-26: So if you are offering your gift at the altar, and you remember that your brother or sister has something against you, *leave* your gift there. . . and *go*; first *be reconciled* to your brother, and then coming, *offer* your gift. *Make friends* quickly with your accuser. (Italics mark the Greek imperatives.)

We can see that the third member is the climax in three ways: It is where the commands, the imperatives, come. It is longer than the other parts of the teaching. And in biblical teaching, the third element of a teaching is where the climax regularly comes.

In fact, the Gospel of Matthew has about seventy-five teachings with a threefold or triadic pattern, and almost no teachings with a twofold or dyadic pattern. In each case, the third member of the triad is where the climax comes, as is typical of biblical teaching. It would be odd if Matthew's pattern in the Sermon on the Mount were only twofold teachings, when everywhere else he presents threefold and not twofold teachings.

So we want to propose the simple shift in perspective of putting the emphasis on the climactic part, where the imperatives are. We propose to label this part the *transforming initiative*. We mean this in three senses: it transforms the person who was angry into an active peacemaker; it transforms the relationship from one of anger into a peacemaking process; and it hopes to transform the enemy into a friend. Furthermore, it participates in the way of grace that God took in Jesus when there was enmity between God and humans: God came in Jesus to make peace. This is the breakthrough of the kingdom that we see happening in Jesus. It is the way of grace that Jesus is calling us to participate in. It invites us to deliverance from the vicious cycle of anger and insult.

As we shall show throughout the rest of this book, this pattern of transforming initiatives is followed consistently through the whole central section
of the Sermon on the Mount, from Matthew 5:21 through 7:12. And this
transforms our understanding of the whole Sermon. It means the emphasis
is not on some negative prohibitions that are hard teachings. The emphasis
is on positive transforming initiatives that are the way of deliverance based
in grace.

Thus we see the emphasis of Jesus' teaching throughout the Sermon to be
in the transforming initiatives, where the imperatives are. We see these initiatives as regular *practices* that are commanded by Jesus. Here, for example,
according to the first teaching (Mt 5:21-26), whenever we find ourselves in a
relationship of anger or insult, we are to engage in the *regular practice* of talking it over and seeking to make peace; that is, doing conflict resolution. And
so throughout the Sermon Jesus was giving us regular practices that participate in God's way of gracious deliverance from the vicious cycles in which
we get stuck. This connects with chapter five above: Jesus taught *practice
norms*. They are not mere inner attitudes, vague intentions, or moral convictions only, but regular practices to be engaged in. As we engage in them, we
learn better and better ways to practice resolving conflict: it is better first to
listen carefully rather than to begin by accusing or by stating our position. It
is better to point to my own problem, saying "I feel hurt by something you
said," rather than to speak judgmentally, as in "You often insult me." Conflict resolution is a shared community practice among followers of Jesus. We
learn from each other in the community how to go to our brother or sister
and seek to make peace. The same is true of the other moral practices taught
in the Sermon; we learn by doing.

This is not a "high ideal," to be admired from a distance, but an actual
practice. It is not an impossible teaching but is in fact practiced regularly by
many of us. It solves problems. It is the way of deliverance from vicious cycles
of anger and insult. Nor is it legalism. It is the way of grace—the way God
takes toward us in Christ, and the way we can participate in God's grace me-
diated through the community. It is part of what we celebrate in the Lord's
Supper: Jesus' death makes peace between us and God, and between us and
one another. And it is part of what the Christian community practices: making peace among us. Paul's letters are full of the practice of making peace in
the Christian community.

But let us step back a minute. Jesus does diagnose the vicious cycles that
cause killing. A key part of a medical doctor's healing is to diagnose the cause
of an illness. A key part of a scientist's method is to identify the causes of error
in an experiment and build in correction factors. A key part of an engineer's
planning is to identify crucial stresses or dangers and build in redundant

strength where needed. A key part of what the prophets and Jesus do is to identify the vicious cycles that cause unjust outcomes. None of these practicers of
wisdom assume we can ever eliminate all illness, all causes of error, all stresses,
all vicious cycles. Instead, the crucial first step is to name the sources of error.
So a key part of Jesus' message is repentance, naming the error and correcting
for it, taking the log out of our own eye. And then the all-important second step
is participating in the transforming initiative, the new practice, the corrective
pattern of behavior, the way of deliverance from captivity to the vicious cycle.
In parenting it is much more effective not simply to criticize children when they
do something wrong but to teach and model and practice together the new pattern that can replace the wrong pattern. That is what Jesus does.

So in Christian ethics, and in this book, we name the vicious cycles, rather
than overlooking them; and then we also name the transforming initiatives.

The Pattern of Transforming Initiatives in Matthew 5:38-42

Let us look at another teaching in the Sermon on the Mount, Matthew 5:38-42.
Again we see the threefold pattern:

Traditional Righteousness	Vicious Cycle	Transforming Initiative
Matthew 5:38: You have heard that it was said, "An eye for an eye and a tooth for a tooth."	Matthew 5:39: But I say to you, do not retaliate revengefully by evil means. (Not an imperative in the Greek, but an infinitive— probably with implied imperatival meaning.)	Matthew 5:40-42: But if anyone strikes you on the right cheek, *turn* the other also; and if any one wants to sue you and take your coat, *give* your cloak as well; and if any one forces you to go one mile, *go* also the second mile. *Give* to one who begs from you, and do not refuse one who would borrow from you.

Clearly the first statement is a traditional teaching, as we expected. In the
first member of these triads, Jesus offers a biblical quotation or some restatement of traditional Jewish moral teaching. Clearly the second statement is a vicious cycle—the cycle of revengeful retaliation. And again the transforming
initiative has the imperatives (which we have marked with italics).

We should explain our translation of the vicious cycle of Matthew 5:39 as
"do not retaliate revengefully by evil means." Usually it is translated, "do not
resist evil." But this seems wrong to anyone who thinks about it, because Jesus
often resisted evil, confronting Pharisees who excluded the outcasts, Peter who

told him not to suffer, the devil who tempted him not to follow God's will, the wealthy who hoarded their possessions, and the disciples who lacked faith.

In a seldom noticed insight, Clarence Jordan has pointed out that the Greek for "evil" can mean either "by evil means" or "the evil person." Either translation is equally good according to Greek grammar; the decision must come from the context. The context is that Jesus repeatedly confronts evil, but never by evil means, and never by means of revengeful violence. Therefore the context favors the instrumental "do not resist by evil means" (Jordan, *Substance of Faith*, 69; cf. Ferguson, *Politics of Love*, 4-5; Hagner, *Matthew 1—13*, 130-31; Lapide, *Sermon on the Mount*, 134; Swartley, "War and Peace in the New Testament," 2:26, 3:2338).

Furthermore, New Testament scholar Walter Wink ("Beyond Just War and Pacifism," 199) points out that the Greek word for "resist" or "retaliate" is used in the Greek translation of the Hebrew Scriptures (the *Septuagint*) and in the Greek sources of the time, Josephus and Philo, "for armed resistance in military encounters" in the majority of cases. Therefore the verse should be translated "do not retaliate or resist violently or revengefully, by evil means."

This is how the apostle Paul reported the teaching in Romans 12:17-21: "Do not repay anyone evil for evil. . . . Beloved, never avenge yourselves, but leave room for the wrath of God. . . . If your enemies are hungry, feed them; if they are thirsty, give them something to drink. . . . Do not overcome evil by evil means, but overcome evil with good." Paul also commanded transforming initiatives of peacemaking: feed a hungry enemy and water a thirsty one. The teaching is also echoed in Luke 6:27-36; 1 Thessalonians 5:15; and *Didache* 1:4-5; there is a somewhat similar teaching in 1 Peter 2:21-23. Not one of them refers to an evil person; not one of them speaks of not resisting evil; not one of them speaks of renouncing rights in a law court. All emphasize the transforming initiatives of returning good and not evil, using good means and not evil means; and Luke and the *Didache* give almost the same four transforming initiatives (cheek, coat, mile, begging). First Thessalonians 5:15 says, "See that none of you repays evil for evil, but always seek to do good to one another and to all." The evidence is overwhelming: this is not an impossible ideal of not resisting evil, but a naming of the vicious cycle of retaliation by violent, revengeful or evil means.

Furthermore, the emphasis should be placed on the four transforming initiatives in the third statement, with their four imperatives, and their greater length—surely the climax of the teaching. Each of these initiatives is like Martin Luther King's nonviolent direct action: it is nonviolent, and it is activist. Each resists evil by taking an action to oppose injustice, to stand up for human dignity and to invite to reconciliation. Turning the other cheek has been misunderstood in Western culture that thought there were only two alternatives—violence or passivity. But since Gandhi and King, we can appreciate Jesus' teaching better. In Jesus' culture, "to be struck on the *right* cheek was to be given a hostile, back-handed insult" with the back of the right hand. In that culture, it was forbidden to touch or strike anyone with the left hand; the left hand was for dirty things (Stassen, *Just Peacemaking*, 64-65, 68-69). To turn the other cheek was to surprise the insulter, saying, nonviolently, "you are treating me as an unequal, but I need to be treated as an equal." Jesus is saying: if you are slapped on the cheek of inferiority, turn the cheek of equal dignity (Garland, *Reading Matthew*, 73ff.; Luz, *Matthew 1—7*, 327-29; Stassen, *Just Peacemaking: Transforming Initiatives*, 63-70; Stassen, "Fourteen Triads of the Sermon on the Mount"; Wink, *Engaging the Powers*, 175-77).

As we will explain later, the other three transforming initiatives—the cloak, the second mile and giving to the beggar, are not merely giving in; they each go beyond what is demanded to take a nonviolent initiative that confronts injustice and initiates the possibility of reconciliation. For now, the point we want to make is that these are not impossible demands any more than nonviolent direct action was an impossibility in the civil rights movement or its continuing echoes in the overthrow of injustice by nonviolent direct action in the Philippines, Eastern Europe, South Africa and Latin America (Buttry, *Christian Peacemaking*, 63ff.). John Howard Yoder demonstrates that nonviolent direct action was practiced successfully by Jews resisting Roman oppression in Jesus' time (Yoder, *Politics of Jesus*, chap. 5).

Beyond this, notice that the four initiatives that Jesus teaches here use seven of the same Greek words used in the Septuagint version of the Suffering Servant passage, Isaiah 50:4-9: *resist, slap, cheek, sue, coat, give* and *turn away*. Isaiah 50:4-9 is a passage of participative grace, in which God gives deliverance, and the servant's actions participate in that deliverance. Here we quote only part of it, in order to show how it is based in the Lord who, in grace, gives deliverance:

The Sovereign LORD has given me an instructed tongue,
    to know the word that sustains the weary.
He wakens me morning by morning,
    wakens my ear to listen like one being taught. . . .
I offered my back to those who beat me,
    my cheeks to those who pulled out my beard;
I did not hide my face
    from mocking and spitting.
Because the Sovereign LORD helps me,
    I will not be disgraced.
Therefore have I set my face like flint,
    and I know I will not be put to shame.
He who vindicates me is near. . . .
It is the Sovereign LORD who helps me.
    Who is it that will condemn me? (NIV)

Furthermore, each of the four initiatives seems to look forward to Jesus' crucifixion and suggests our participation in Jesus' way of the cross. Davies and Allison (1:546) write: "Jesus himself was struck and slapped (26:67: *rapizō*) and his garments (27:35: *himatia*) were taken from him. If his followers then turn the other cheek and let the enemy have their clothes, will they not be remembering their Lord, especially in his passion?" And the Greek word that means "forces" or "compels" in the phrase "if someone *compels* you to go one mile," is the same word used when Simon of Cyrene is *compelled* to carry Jesus' cross, thus participating in Jesus' crucifixion with him (Mt 27:32). Jesus gave his life for us. When we go the second mile as an initiative of peacemaking, when we give to the poor, we are participating in the way of Jesus who was crucified for us. We are participating in the grace of the cross.

In chapter two, we saw that the Christian virtues, as taught by Jesus in the Beatitudes, include being surrendered or yielded to God, and how closely that is connected with being peacemakers. Jesus here explained what that means.

The Pattern of Transforming Initiatives in Matthew 5:43-48

Now let us turn to the next teaching in the Sermon on the Mount, the climax of the six teachings in this chapter, Matthew 5:43-48.

Traditional Righteousness	Vicious Cycle	Transforming Initiative
Matthew 5:43: You have heard that it was said: "You shall love your neighbor and hate your enemy."	Matthew 5:46-47: For if you love those who love you, what reward have you? Do not even the tax collectors do the same? And if you salute only your brethren, what more are you doing than others? Do not even the Gentiles do the same?	Matthew 5:44-45: But I say to you, *Love* your enemies and *pray* for those who persecute you, so that you may be sons of your Father who is in heaven; for he makes his sun rise on the evil and on the good, and sends rain on the just and on the unjust.

The traditional teaching comes not from the Old Testament but from the Dead Sea Scrolls (Davies, *Setting of the Sermon*, 252). The transforming initiative comes *second* rather than third, a shift in the usual order to indicate that this is the climactic conclusion of the first six triads in Matthew 6. And a summary verse, 5:48, is added, like the summary verse at the climax in 7:12. The transforming initiative is to participate in the kind of love that God gives regularly: as God gives sunshine and rain to enemies as well as friends, so are we to give love and prayers to our enemies as well as our friends. It could hardly be clearer that the transforming initiative is participation in God's active presence and God's grace. In practicing this kind of love, we are "children of our Father in heaven."

Those who want to make the Sermon on the Mount into impossibly high ideals interpret the summary verse, 5:48, as demanding moral perfection, as a Greek idealist ethics might. They assume that "Be perfect, therefore, as your heavenly Father is perfect" means moral perfection. But it would be odd in Hebrew and Aramaic to presume to speak of God as morally perfect in that Greek sense. Rather, the word here means *complete* or *all-inclusive*, in the sense of love that includes even enemies. This is the point that Jesus has been emphasizing in this teaching: the love of God's grace that includes the complete circle of humankind, with enemies in it as well, by contrast with tax collectors and Gentiles, who love only their friends. Its meaning is very much like Luke 6:36—"Be merciful, just as your Father is merciful." There Luke also has been emphasizing love that includes enemies. So we are not to think of Jesus as teaching impossible moral ideals, or idealistic moral perfection, but practical deeds of love toward enemies, including prayer for them. Those who have attempted heartfelt prayer for enemies know that it is indeed a transformative practice.

The Pattern Continues Throughout the Sermon

We have examined three of the teachings in the Sermon on the Mount and have seen that their basic pattern is threefold. They are not impossible ideals but transforming initiatives based on God's grace. They are the way of deliverance from the vicious cycles in which we get stuck. Thus we have taken a major step in overcoming the "hard teachings and high ideals" interpretation that has caused evasion of the Sermon. We have begun to see how the Sermon on the Mount consists of transforming initiatives that give real, practical, grace-based guidance for Christian ethics. This is a major step in the recovery of the way of Jesus for Christian ethics.

As we shall see in subsequent chapters, the pattern of threefold teachings, climaxing in grace-based transforming initiatives, continues throughout the central teachings of the Sermon on the Mount. For now, table 6.1 offers a road map, diagramming the Sermon on the Mount.

As we hope to show in subsequent chapters, the threefold transforming-initiatives structure can be verified in seven ways:

1. It is remarkably consistent throughout the fourteen triads, with strikingly few exceptions.
2. It fits the consistent tendency throughout Matthew's Gospel to prefer triads over dyads—with about seventy-five triads and almost no dyads.
3. Its emphasis on the third member of each triad, the transforming initiative, is confirmed by the Gospel of Luke. When Luke presents the parallel teachings, he most consistently presents the transforming initiative, while often

Table 6.1. The fourteen triads of the Sermon on the Mount

Traditional Righteousness	Vicious Cycle	Transforming Initiative
1. You shall not kill	Being angry, or saying, You fool!	*Go, be reconciled*
2. You shall not commit adultery	Looking with lust is adultery in the heart	*Remove the cause of temptation* (cf. Mk 9:43-50)
3. Whoever divorces, give a certificate	Divorcing involves you in adultery	(Be reconciled: 1 Cor 7:11)
4. You shall not swear falsely	Swearing by anything involves you in a false claim	Let your yes be yes, and your no be no
5. Eye for eye, tooth for tooth	Retaliating violently or revengefully, by evil means	*Turn the other cheek, give your tunic and cloak, go the second mile, give to beggar and borrower*
6. Love neighbor and hate enemy	Hating enemies is the same vicious cycle that you see in the Gentiles and tax collectors	*Love enemies, pray for your persecutors; be all-inclusive as your Father in heaven is*
7. When you give alms,	Practicing righteousness for show	But give in secret, and your Father will reward you
8. When you pray,	Practicing righteousness for show	But pray in secret, and your Father will reward you
9. When you pray,	Heaping up empty phrases	*Therefore pray like this: Our Father . . .*
10. When you fast,	Practicing righteousness for show	But dress with joy, and your Father will reward you
11. *Do not pile up treasures on earth* (cf. Luke 12:16-31)	*Moth and rust destroy, and thieves enter and steal*	*But pile up treasures in heaven*
12. *No one can serve two masters*	*Serving God and wealth, worrying about food and clothes*	*But seek first God's reign and God's justice/righteousness*
13. *Do not judge, lest you be judged*	*Judging others means you'll be judged by the same measure*	*First take the log out of your own eye*
14. Do not give holy things to dogs, nor pearls to pigs	They will trample them and tear you to pieces	*Give your trust in prayer to your Father in heaven*

not presenting the first two members of the teachings. (Where Luke parallels what Matthew reports is indicated by the italicized print in table 6.1.)

4. Once we see the triadic structure, the Greek verbs line up with remarkable consistency. The main verbs in the teachings of traditional righteousness are almost all futures or subjunctives, depending on the source in the tradition. The main verbs in the vicious cycles are all continuous process verbs—indicatives, participles, infinitives. The main verbs in the transforming initiative members are consistently imperatives.

5. The number three-times-fourteen was important to Matthew. The Sadducees and Pharisees saw a mystical significance in this number, and Matthew's rival group claimed their teachers were descended from a triad of fourteen generations. So Matthew began his Gospel by pointing out that there were three-times-fourteen generations from Abraham to Jesus (Davies, *Setting of the Sermon*, 303-4). It fits neatly that here, too, he gives us fourteen threefold teachings.

6. It gives a fruitful clue for the likely meaning of the hitherto baffling Matthew 7:6, on not giving our holy things to dogs and pigs, as we will show when we discuss that passage.

7. It shows that Jesus' teachings engage us in transforming initiatives that participate in the reign of God, the presence of the gracious God who acts in Jesus—who reconciles us with enemies, who is present with us in secret, who is faithful and trustworthy, and who brings deliverance from the vicious cycles that cause violations of the traditional righteousness. The second member consistently names vicious cycles; the Sermon is by no means based on an idealistic assumption that we do not get stuck in vicious cycles of sin. And the third member points the way of deliverance in the midst of this real world of sin. This corrects the idealism that sought to hallow Jesus' teachings by making them simply calls for hard, strenuous, even impossible human effort. Instead it suggests a hermeneutic (a way of interpretation) of grace-based, active participation in eschatological deliverance that begins now. The split between attitudes and actions, in which Jesus allegedly emphasized intentions and not actual practices, falls away. Legalism falls away too; Jesus is pointing to participation in the grace of the deliverance that characterizes the inbreaking of the reign of God. Jesus is indeed the prophetic Messiah who proclaims the inbreaking reign of God and points to specific ways of participation in the kingdom.

Healing the Split Between the Sermon and Ethics

Now we see how this triadic understanding could have helped Dietrich Bonhoeffer maintain his loyalty to the Sermon on the Mount in the midst of his agonizing struggle against the injustices of Hitler and the Nazis. Bonhoeffer interpreted each teaching primarily as renunciation of the vicious cycles, and he overlooked the transforming initiatives. This gave him a mostly passive understanding of the Sermon. Therefore, when he saw the need to do more in response to the evil and injustice of Hitler than passively renounce evil, the Sermon seemed not to give him the guidance he needed. Had he seen the transforming-initiative structure, he would have seen the Sermon as active initiatives, not only passive renunciation. Furthermore, it would have stood for the very justice that he needed over against Hitler's injustice. It would have pointed to the way of deliverance and the concrete guidance that he needed (see Stassen, "Healing the Split in Bonhoeffer's Ethics," forthcoming). Seeing the Sermon on the Mount as transforming initiatives can enable Christian ethics to return to following Jesus. We hope to show in this book how the Sermon on the Mount, along with other biblical teachings, points to the practices of deliverance in the midst of a world of sinful bondage to vicious cycles of despair and destruction—the guidance we need in our postmodern time.

Maybe it can help correct other causes of evasion of the Sermon on the Mount and the way of Jesus:

- When, in the early centuries, some Christian theologians began seeking to appeal to *Greek culture and philosophy* by adopting Greek metaphysics, they lost a sense of God's dynamic action in history. Greek metaphysics sees God as beyond history, dwelling in an eternal realm that does not change or move. So they lost God's grace breaking through the sinful course of life. In other words, they lacked a dynamic eschatology. Lacking a dynamic eschatology of God's dynamic rule, God's lordship, this Greek metaphysics misunderstood what Jesus pointed to as the breakthrough of the kingdom and God's grace-based gift of new life, and instead interpreted it merely as ideals for human effort. In chapters one and two we have already sought to show the kingdom of God as a grace-based gift. The reign is already beginning to occur as a way of deliverance that we can participate in. The transforming initiatives point us to exactly that participation in the way of deliverance, as we hope to show throughout the remaining chapters in this book.

- Some have interpreted the Sermon *legalistically*. They have seen it as consisting of prohibitions of anger, lust, divorce, oaths, resistance and concern about what we shall eat or wear. They did not see how they could obey those prohibitions. So it became, for them, "hard teachings" and an experience of guilt. Seeing the Sermon as transforming initiatives makes clear that Jesus was no legalist; Jesus was pointing to the breakthrough of the kingdom. Jesus was offering a way of life that participates in deliverance from vicious cycles that trap us. In chapter five, we began to see the difference between legalistic rules and grace-based practices, which is what the transforming initiatives are. We hope to show the difference this makes throughout this book.

- Many have not noticed the *justice* meaning of Jesus' emphasis on *righteousness*. To oppose Hitler's horrendous and systematic injustices, Bonhoeffer needed firm teaching on justice, and so do the rest of us who seek to resist injustices that we see. We will show this theme in the Sermon on the Mount, especially in chapter seventeen.

- Many evade the Sermon because they are living in *disobedience* to the way of Jesus. We genuinely hope this book will help change that. Our responsibility and our fervent commitment is to try to remove obstacles to Jesus' way of life that come from misinterpretation of Jesus' teaching. The rest is up to you, your community of faith and support, and the Holy Spirit.

SECTION III:

The Gospel of Life

This section addresses the value or sacredness of human life by considering war, violence, the death penalty, abortion, euthanasia and biotechnology.

Our fundamental claim in this section is that the kingdom of God consists of peace with justice, of life unmarred by killing. The good news of the gospel brings life and invites us to participate in bringing life and resisting death.

Certainly, meaningful distinctions can be drawn between the issues we consider in this section. War and the death penalty involve killing by the state; violence, abortion and euthanasia involve killing by individuals with or without the permission of the state. And whether certain developments in biotechnology involve killing at all is itself up for debate.

Yet what unites these issues, and this section, is the basic conviction that kingdom ethics resists killing, as Jesus did, and strongly affirms the value of human persons, as Jesus did. We saw these themes in the emphasis in the Beatitudes on the virtue of peacemaking, in peace as one of the most central characteristics of the kingdom of God, and in the three passages, Matthew 5:21-26, 38-42 and 43-48 that we studied in chapter six. The chapters in this section follow directly from each of these passages in Matthew.

7

JUST WAR, NONVIOLENCE
AND JUST PEACEMAKING

You have heard that it was said, "An eye for an eye and a tooth for a tooth." But I say to you, Do not resist an evildoer. But if anyone strikes you on the right cheek, turn the other also; and if anyone wants to sue you and take your coat, give your cloak as well; and if anyone forces you to go one mile, go also the second mile. Give to everyone who begs from you, and do not refuse anyone who wants to borrow from you.

MATTHEW 5:38-42

The world watched powerlessly on September 11, 2001, as the television showed, again and again, two planes plowing into the Twin Towers of the World Trade Center. Children, women and men who were passengers in those planes or workers in those towers died, many of them by fire. The terrorism that Michelle Tooley describes in her book *Voices of the Voiceless: Women, Justice, and Human Rights in Guatemala* was that day happening not only to people in Guatemala but also to people in New York City and in the Pentagon.

> Many women, especially indigenous women, became widows as their husbands were killed by the military forces of the government. . . . In addition to the deaths of husbands, sons and fathers disappeared or were forced into military service, never to be seen again. Daughters and mothers were violated by soldiers and members of the civil patrol. . . .Women watched powerlessly as soldiers entered their villages, burned houses and fields, kidnaped husbands and children. They watched as soldiers threw babies into fires or boiling water. They watched as half-dead husbands were buried alive. In front of children members of the military raped mothers and daughters. (Tooley, *Voices of the Voiceless*, 84)

The need for deliverance from terrorism and war came home to many who had been disengaged from the world's struggle for peace. The need for the gospel of the Prince of Peace, who wept over Jerusalem because it did not know the ways that make for peace, was understood in a new way around the world. Jesus gives us a powerful way of deliverance from the vicious cycles that lead to violent death and destruction. It is a message that the world desperately needs, and that Christians need to learn clearly so we can share it convincingly.

The discipline of Christian ethics now has three approaches to violence, war and peacemaking: just war theory, pacifism/nonviolence and just peacemaking theory. Like most Christian theological traditions, our discipline is divided over which one (or which combination) best displays Christian faithfulness to Jesus in a sinful world. In this chapter, we will begin by considering Jesus' way of peacemaking and its link to Isaiah's prophecies of the kingdom. We will present just war theory and pacifism in their best forms, as well as just peacemaking. We will eventually argue for just peacemaking as an obligatory dimension of Christian discipleship but will not attempt to resolve the just war/pacifism debate, which continues to be important even with a commitment to just peacemaking. Our goal is to provide the tools to help readers decide, by deep thought, listening prayer and biblical study, which model or combination you are called to embody. We urge that every church and educational setting teach the three models so that Christians are not simply blown about by every shifting wind and accommodated to secular forces.

The Basis for All Three Ethics: Jesus' Way of Peacemaking

In chapter one, we showed that peace is one of the five marks of the kingdom of God in Isaiah, and we claimed that Jesus fulfilled this prophetic hope. Now it is time to make that claim good. How did Jesus fulfill Isaiah's prophecy that the reign of God will bring peace?

To answer this question, we need to examine what Isaiah's prophecies of the coming of God's reign say about peace. Isaiah 26:12 prophesies, "O LORD, you will ordain peace for us." This declares the deliverance that the Lord will bring in the future and is presently working to accomplish, and that our actions are to participate in. Therefore, Isaiah 31:1-5 pronounces judgment on Israel for trusting in Egypt for military help instead of in the Lord. Egypt was notorious for encouraging an ally to join with it in fighting a war and then leaving the ally to fight alone and thus be betrayed into destruction. No military strength could produce security. Israel should trust in the powerful Spirit of the Lord, "poured upon us from on high" (Is 32:15 RSV). Trusting in the Holy Spirit does not mean being passive; it means being empowered to do God's will actively.

At the heart of the divine will is justice for the downtrodden. Once "the Spirit from on high is poured out on us, . . . [t]hen justice will dwell in the wilderness, and righteousness abide in the fruitful field. The effect of righteousness will be peace, and the result of righteousness, quietness and trust forever. My people will abide in a peaceful habitation, in secure dwellings, and in quiet resting places" (Is 32:15-18). In Hebrew, "righteousness" means "delivering justice"—the kind of justice that delivers the downtrodden from domination and brings the outcasts into community (see chapter seventeen). Peace, justice and compassion come as a single package; they depend on each other because they are part and parcel of God's will and God's action of deliverance:

> My covenant of peace shall not be removed,
>> says the LORD, who has compassion on you. (Is 54:10)

> I will appoint Peace as your overseer
>> and Righteousness as your taskmaster.
> Violence shall no more be heard in your land,
>> devastation or destruction within your borders. (Is 60:17-18)

> How beautiful upon the mountains
>> are the feet of the messenger who announces peace. (Is 52:7)

God's reign and mercy will bring peace through God's suffering servant, who will be so committed to peacemaking that he will do no violence:

> He will not cry or lift up his voice,
>> or make it heard in the street;
> a bruised reed he will not break,
>> and a dimly burning wick he will not quench. (Is 42:2)

The servant will bring peace through his suffering and death:

>> yet he did not open his mouth;
> like a lamb that is led to the slaughter,
>> and like a sheep that before its shearers is silent. . . .
> By a perversion of justice he was taken away . . .
> although he had done no violence,
>> and there was no deceit in his mouth. (Is 53:7-9)

God brings peace by delivering justice, by nonviolent suffering and by including the Gentiles in community rather than by hating and excluding them:

> I will give you as a light to the nations [i.e., the Gentiles],
>> that my salvation may reach to the end of the earth. (Is 49:6)

> Do not let the foreigner joined to the LORD say,
>> "The LORD will surely separate me from his people.". . .
> these I will bring to my holy mountain,
> and make them joyful in my house of prayer; . . .
> for my house shall be called a house of prayer
>> for *all* peoples. (Is 56:3, 7)

The passages in Isaiah prophesying the coming reign of God very clearly establish peace as a mark of the kingdom.

Did Jesus fulfill Isaiah's prophecies of the kingdom of God? Scholars confirm that in Jesus' time Jewish hatred of Rome was based on the religious drive for purity from corruption by foreign influences and power, on the political drive for independence and on economic resentment of the injustice of Roman taxes. Hatred and resentment often boiled up into guerrilla movements and insurrections against Roman rule. Violent resistance was supported not only by the insurrectionists, who were later called "Zealots," but by most groups in Israel, including most Pharisees. Jesus wept over Jerusalem, saying, "If you, even you, had only recognized on this day the things that make for peace! But now they are hidden from your eyes" (Lk 19:42). Instead of the way of peace, they knew the way of hatred of enemies, which would cause rebellion that would bring destruction.

Accordingly, Jesus prophesied—six times in the New Testament—that the temple would soon be destroyed. The very hatred that Jesus was trying to correct led his opponents to accuse him of seeking to destroy the temple, and so the high priest and the council decided to seek his crucifixion (Mt 26:61-66; Mk 14:58-64). They got the hated Romans to crucify the one who taught and practiced peacemaking toward the Romans. The hatred of enemies continued after he was crucified, and it boiled over into massive revolt in the year 66. Rome responded by crushing the revolt, destroying Jerusalem and demolishing the temple in the year 70.

Jesus had prophesied not only that the temple would be destroyed, but that people should flee into the mountains rather than waging war (Mk 13:14-23, 30). Because of his teachings and peacemaking practices, the Jesus movement became a Jewish peace movement, and so Christian Jews did not participate in the revolt but instead did flee Jerusalem (N. T. Wright, *Jesus and the Victory of God*, 151-60, 250-53, 268-71, 296, 385; Borg, *Conflict, Holiness, and Politics in the Teaching of Jesus*, 51-65, 70-71, 77, 79-83, 175ff.). So they were delivered from the war, and by their love they spread the gospel among the very Romans who were so hated. They showed the way of deliverance. Jesus' prophecy, which was fulfilled in the year 70, is at the same time a prophecy of the Second Coming of the Messiah with his deliverance.

In the Revelation to John the followers of the Beasts do violence, but the followers of the Lamb do not. Instead, a central theme throughout the book is that the followers of the Lamb do the deeds that Jesus taught (Rev 2:2, 19, 23, 26; 3:8, 10; 9:20-21; 12:17; 14:4, 12; 16:11; 19:8, 10; 20:4, 12-13; 22:11). Christians are given clear teaching against doing violence, echoing Matthew 26:52: "Whoever takes the sword to kill, by the sword he is bound to be killed" (Rev 13:10 NEB). The verse then gives a call for endurance and faith. Perhaps the most perceptive New Testament scholar on the book of Revelation, Richard Bauckham, concludes:

No doubt in the Jewish circles with which John and his churches had contact, . . . ideas of eschatological holy war against Rome, such as the Qumran community had entertained and the Zealots espoused, were well known. . . . Therefore, instead of simply repudiating apocalyptic militancy, [John] *reinterprets* it in a Christian sense, taking up its reading of Old Testament prophecy into a specifically Christian reading of the Old Testament. He aims to show that the decisive battle in God's eschatological holy war against all evil, including the power of Rome, has already been won—by the faithful witness and sacrificial death of Jesus. Christians are called to participate in his war and his victory—but by the same means as he employed: bearing the witness of Jesus to the point of martyrdom. (Bauckham, *Bible in Politics*, 233ff.)

And G. B. Caird writes:

Throughout the welter of Old Testament images in the chapters that follow, almost without exception the only title for Christ is **the Lamb,** and this title is meant to control and interpret all the rest of the symbolism. It is almost as if John were saying to us at one point after another: "Wherever the Old Testament says **'Lion,'** read **'Lamb.'** " Wherever the Old Testament speaks of the victory of the Messiah or the overthrow of the enemies of God, we are to remember that the gospel recognizes no other way of achieving these ends than the way of the Cross. (Caird, *Commentary on the Revelation of St. John the Divine,* 74ff, emphasis in original)

Hence when in Revelation 6:10 the martyrs cry out, "Sovereign Lord, holy and true, how long will it be before you judge and avenge our blood on the inhabitants of the earth?" they are "each given a white robe and told to rest a little longer." This fits Romans 12:19ff., where we are told never to avenge ourselves but to leave vengeance to God. The martyrs are told to wait patiently for God's victory rather than seeking to avenge themselves. They receive white robes that symbolize their innocence, in contrast with those who killed them.

Similarly, the two witnesses in Revelation 11:5, modeled after the prophets Moses and Elijah, slay with fire that comes *from their mouth,* as Christ in 19:15 slays with a sword that comes from his mouth. From their mouth comes the prophetic word, a figurative sword, like "the sword of the Spirit, which is the word of God" in Ephesians 6:17. So Christ is named "the Word of God" (Rev 19:13). The sword coming from the mouth is the prophetic word in Revelation 1:16; 2:12, 16; 19:15, 21; 4 Ezra 13:25-39; Isaiah 11:4; and Jeremiah 5:14, which says, "Because you have spoken this word, behold, I have given my words in your mouth [as] fire . . . and it will consume them" (Beale, *Book of Revelation*, 580).

Revelation 11:3-13 demonstrates that the prophetic witness and the martyrdom of the two witnesses "can achieve a result which the prophecy of the past has not achieved": the nations are converted and give glory to the God of heaven (Bauckham, *Bible in Politics*, 274, 279-82). "The Old Testament leads John to expect a Messiah who will be a lion of Judah, but the facts of the gospel present him with a lamb bearing the marks of a slaughter (5:5-6). The Old Testament predicts the smashing of the nations with an iron bar, but the only weapon the Lamb wields is his own cross and the martyrdom of his followers (2:27; 12:5; 19:15)" (Caird, *Commentary on the Revelation*, 293; cf. 243-45). So Revelation 12:10ff. says, "Now have come the salvation and the power of the kingdom of our God and the authority of his Messiah. . . . But they have conquered . . . by the blood of the Lamb and by the word of their testimony, for they did not cling to life even in the face of death."

Those who thought the right response to Roman enemies was to make war on them did have some support in the Old Testament. See, for example, the so-called holy war tradition as found in parts of Joshua, as well as Deuteronomy 20 and 1 Samuel 15, where the people of Israel are commanded to "utterly destroy all that they have; do not spare them, but kill both man and woman, child and infant, ox and sheep, camel and donkey" (1 Sam 15:3). But other passages in Isaiah, Micah, Hosea, Jeremiah and Jonah command peacemaking toward the other nations. The Hebrew Scriptures are a rich and diverse narrative. The people of Israel were a diverse people—originally an idolatrous people who worshiped and served many gods, including gods of war—who debated with each other how to interpret God's word to them. Jesus showed how to interpret that rich narrative. He never quoted passages that favor killing, war or national supremacy. He quoted only the passages that favor peacemaking. Our method of interpretation is to affirm Jesus Christ as fully Lord and fully Savior, and as the key to interpreting the Scriptures (chapter four above).

In chapter six we examined Matthew 5:21-26 and 5:38-42 in the Sermon on the Mount. We saw Jesus' way of deliverance through transforming initiatives of peacemaking. When something causes anger and divides us from another, we are to take the initiative of going to make peace. We are not to retaliate revengefully by evil means, but instead we are to take transforming initiatives of peacemaking. When the Roman soldiers demanded that Jews carry their pack a mile, the transforming initiative was not simply to refrain from doing violence, and not simply to comply with the demand, but to surprise the oppressors by taking an initiative of reconciliation. When sued (in court) for one's shirt, we are to give our cloak as well. This means we stand there naked, revealing the greed of the suitor in all its nakedness before the whole law court, thus confronting the injustice nonviolently and pressing for justice. When a beggar or a borrower asks for money, to give aid is also to take a nonviolent initiative to remove some of the gap between rich and poor. Each of these initiatives takes an action to oppose injustice, to stand up for human dignity and to invite to reconciliation. Each participates in the way of deliverance from vicious cycles of hate and resentment (Hays, *Moral Vision of the New Testament*, 319-29; Wink, *Engaging the Powers*, 175ff.; Stassen, *Just Peacemaking:*

Transforming Initiatives, 64-65, 68-69). We are to love our enemy, as God does.

Some have sought to limit Jesus' teachings only to individual relations. But Jesus was not only addressing private feelings but instead directly countering the resentful teaching of major political movements, including many Pharisees:

- They taught an apocalyptic future of triumph for Israel over the other nations; Jesus taught a prophetic eschatology of judgment on Israel as well as on other nations.

- They taught that Israel should be separated from all that is impure and so ostracized the lame, lepers, prostitutes, foreigners, sinners, Roman soldiers, tax collectors, children, women and the poor who could not pay the costly temple taxes and fees. They taught that the holiness of God meant that God is separated from all that is impure. By contrast, Isaiah taught that the holiness of God did not mean separation from the impure but redemptive compassion and inclusion of the outsider. Again and again, he spoke of God as One who redeems sinners rather than separates from sinners. Jesus fulfilled Isaiah's prophecies.

- They hated Samaritans; Jesus described the Samaritan as acting with compassion (Lk 10:33 and 37) and himself acted with compassion toward a Samaritan woman (Jn 4:1-26).

- They taught woes on the Gentiles; Jesus taught woes on this generation in Israel, not only Gentiles (Lk 10:13).

- They taught a zealot strategy of insurrection; Jesus advocated and enacted a politics of initiative toward the enemy and of repentance for one's own enmity (Mt 7:4).

- They hated Roman soldiers and Roman centurions and sought to kill them; Jesus welcomed them when they showed faith, just as he welcomed tax collectors and prostitutes when they showed faith.

Some make an argument from silence, saying that Jesus welcomed a centurion and did not tell him to put up his sword, so he must be blessing war-making for his followers. But this is an anachronism. In Jesus' day, the question was hardly whether his followers should join the Roman army or should instead refuse to do so; his followers were Jews, and Jews were certainly not invited to join the Roman army. The question for Jesus' followers was whether to make war on the Romans. Jesus taught them not to kill their enemies but to love them. He praised the faith of Gentiles, prostitutes, Samaritans, tax collectors and even a centurion.

Richard Hays has written what is widely regarded as the best New Testament ethics book (*Moral Vision of the New Testament*). Besides presenting much evidence in line with the above, he deals with the two verses (Mt 10:34 and Lk

22:36) in which Jesus warned the disciples that they could expect opposition, arrest, floggings and slander. Jesus said, "I have not come to bring peace, but a sword," and they should expect to need a sword. These are hardly advocating war-making but are warnings of impending persecution. When one of the disciples missed the point and took it literally, responding that they already had two swords, Jesus' response in the Greek "is impatient dismissal, indicating they have failed to grasp the point: 'Enough, already!'" When a disciple used a sword in the Garden, Jesus told him not to try to live by the sword, because that is the way of the vicious cycle of killing and retaliation (Hays, *Moral Vision of the New Testament*, 332-33). Hays concludes:

> Do the other texts in the canon reinforce the Sermon on the Mount's teaching on nonviolence, or do they provide other options that might allow or require Christians to take up the sword? When the question is posed this way, the immediate result—as Barth observed—is to underscore how impressively univocal is the testimony of the New Testament writers on this point. The evangelists are unanimous in portraying Jesus as a Messiah who subverts all prior expectations by assuming the vocation of suffering rather than conquering Israel's enemies. Despite his stinging criticism of those in positions of authority, he never attempts to exert force as a way of gaining social or political power. (329)

And Hays points out how consistent this is throughout the New Testament:

> There is not a syllable in the Pauline letters that can be cited in support of Christians employing violence. Paul's occasional uses of military imagery (e.g., 2 Cor. 10:3-6, Phil. 1:27-30) actually have the opposite effect: the warfare imagery is drafted into the service of the gospel, rather than the reverse. . . . "For though we live in the flesh, we do not wage war according to the flesh, for the weapons of our warfare are not fleshly" (2 Cor. 10:3-4). . . . The community's struggle is not against human adversaries but against "spiritual forces of darkness," and its armor and weapons are truth, righteousness, peace, faith, salvation, and the word of God. Rightly understood, these metaphors witness powerfully *against* violence as an expression of obedience to God in Christ. (331)

We add that these metaphors remind us once again of the characteristics of the kingdom of God: righteousness/justice, peace, salvation and the word (or presence) of God.

Jesus entered Jerusalem on a donkey at the time of the Passover, fulfilling Zechariah's prophecy of a Messiah of peace who stops war and commands peace to the nations (Zech 9:9-10). All four Gospels report this entry with different emphases, apparently coming from different traditions; yet all four, in different ways, emphasize the theme of peace-bringing as symbolizing Jesus' mission (Mk 11:1-10; Mt 21:1-9; Lk 19:28-38; Jn 12:12-18).

Jesus' next prophetic action was to clear the temple, stopping, for a brief time, the selling of sacrificial animals in the court of the Gentiles, citing Isaiah 56, which declares welcome to Gentiles in the temple (Mt 21:10-17). This was an act of inclusion toward Gentiles and thus love for enemies, in line with Isaiah—and with justice. The Greek in the first three Gospels says Jesus "drove out" or "sent out" the sellers and buyers (Mt 21:12; Mk 11:15; Lk 19:45). *Ekballo* means to drive out, expel, throw out, send out, take out, remove. It may or may not mean to do it by force. This is different from violence: one can throw someone out, even shove them out, without acting out of violence in the sense of injuring the person. John 2:15 says, "Making a whip of cords, he drove all of them out of the temple, both the sheep and the cattle." The Greek makes clear that Jesus used the whip of cords against the animals. Together the four passages imply force or power—as in turning over tables and charismatic power or force of conviction—but not violence, as in injuring people. "*Ekballo* (drive out), which occurs in LXX 2 Chr 29:5, in the account of Hezekiah's cleansing of the temple, suggests force (cf. LXX Hos 9:15)" (Davies and Allison, *Critical and Exegetical Commentary*, 2:137). "We are not here to think of Jesus as violent. . . . Jesus meant the action as an eschatological sign rather than a practical reform of the objectionable practices" (Hagner, *Matthew 14—28*, 2:600). Myers sees it as a likely reference to the judgment in Hosea 9:15 "upon the ruling class of Israel" (Myers, *Binding the Strong Man*, 299; see also Yoder, *Politics of Jesus*, 43). This incident must not be commandeered to read Jesus as an advocate of violence.

Jesus' next prophetic action was the Lord's Supper, in which he made clear that his way was the way of self-sacrifice and forgiveness, not the way of domination and violent insurrection.

In the Garden, Jesus resisted the temptation to refuse the cup of death. He did not want his disciple to use his sword in defensive rebellion, nor legions of angels to come fight a war of defensive rebellion (Mt 26:52-53).

> As Yoder has persuasively suggested, the temptation to refuse the cup is precisely the temptation to resort to armed resistance. Jesus, however, chooses the way of suffering obedience instead of the way of violence. . . . At the moment of Jesus' arrest, he admonishes the disciple who attempts armed resistance: "Put your sword back into its place; for all who take the sword will perish by the sword" (Mt 26:51-54). As Ulrich Mauser observes, "Jesus does not yield to the temptation to preserve his life by resisting evil with evil's own armor." (Hays, *Moral Vision of the New Testament*, 322)

And next came the crucifixion. This revealed the shocking sinfulness of the way of domination by violence—and other dimensions of our sin. From the cross, Jesus forgave those who crucified him, demonstrating and embodying the way of forgiveness rather than revenge.

The resurrection and Pentecost—and the spread of the gospel to all the nations that, prior to Jesus, had been hated and shunned by Jews as enemies—were God's vindication of Jesus' way over against sin, violence and the separation of the different tongues.

The witness is consistent and thorough: Jesus fulfilled Isaiah's prophecy that peacemaking would be a key mark of the reign of God. Jesus taught, lived and died the way of peacemaking, the way of deliverance from the vicious cycle of violence.

The Eight Rules of Just War Theory

The first Christian ethic for peace and war that we present—just war theory—originated with Ambrose and Augustine in the fourth century. Just war theory was developed in the context of an officially Christian Roman Empire that at the time was under threat of a barbarian invasion that ultimately proved devastating. It was an effort to make sense of the biblical witness but was also clearly inspired by Stoic philosophers who had already undertaken considerable development of a just war tradition.

Tested and revised through the centuries, just war theory has made its impact in international law, in military manuals for training the armed services and in the writings of philosophers. It makes the logical point that in order to justify the killing that occurs in war, there must be a reason so important that it overrides the truth that killing people is wrong. We share the view of Ralph Potter that just war theory, rightly understood, "is grounded in a strong presumption against the use of violence, a presumption established for the Christian by the non-resistant example of Jesus and for the rational non-Christian by prudent concern for order and mutual security. This presumption against resort to violence may be overcome only by the necessity to vindicate justice and to protect the innocent against unjust aggressors" (Potter, *War and Moral Discourse,* 61 and 53; cf. also Childress, Review of Walzer). "The moral theory of the 'just war' . . . begins with the presumption which binds all Christians: we should do no harm to our neighbors; how we treat our enemy is the key test of whether we love our neighbor; and the possibility of taking even one human life is a prospect we should consider in fear and trembling" (U.S. National Conference of Catholic Bishops, *Challenge of Peace,* no. 80). War may be justified by overriding reasons—but only by overriding reasons. What reasons count?

The reasons come in the form of criteria for when a war is just. All Christians—and others—need to know and remember the eight criteria of just war theory. Only if we know the rules that determine when war is just or unjust can we exercise our conscientious responsibility in deciding whether to support or oppose a war which a government proposes to wage on our behalf. The first seven rules concern the need for justice in deciding to go to war (*jus ad bello*), while the eighth concerns the need for justice in the methods used to wage war (*jus in bello*).

1. Just cause. The causes that can override the presumption against killing are stopping the massacre of large numbers of people and stopping the systematic and long-term violation of the human rights of life, liberty and community (Walzer, *Just and Unjust Wars*, xvi, 53, 101, 106, 108).

Some say that only the defense of one country from attack by another counts as just cause for war. Respect for borders does help prevent wars (Miller, "Just-War Criteria," 342ff.). But the widespread international sense has grown that when a country is massacring large numbers of its own people, there is a right of *humanitarian intervention* to stop the massacres. In East Pakistan (now Bangladesh), the Pakistani army was massacring the people. India invaded, stopped the massacres and then got out. Similarly in Uganda, the dictator, Idi Amin, was massacring large numbers of people. Tanzania invaded, deposed Amin, stopped the massacres and got out. By contrast, horrendous massacres also happened in Rwanda, but no country intervened until too late. The world, and the people of those countries, judged that India and Tanzania acted justly, and that someone should have intervened in Rwanda.

Some add the criterion that the side waging a just war must have a comparatively more just cause than the other side, in order "to emphasize the presumption against war" and to stress that "no state . . . has 'absolute justice' on its side." But most everyone thinks their own cause is more just than the other side's (U.S. National Conference of Catholic Bishops, *Challenge of Peace*, nos. 92-93). Therefore we stay with the somewhat more objective definition that war can be waged only to stop a systematic or long-lasting violation of the rights of life, liberty and community of large numbers of people. We would also add that the definition of a just cause for waging war must now be more conservative than prior to the Industrial Revolution, because today's weapons make war so much more destructive.

2. Just authority. To commit a nation to make a war in which many will die and be maimed is an enormous responsibility. No one can do that without just authority. Constitutional processes must be followed, so the people who will pay with their lives and resources will be represented in the decision. The U.S. Constitution grants the power "to declare war" to Congress, not the president (Article I, Section 8, clause 11). Presidents have sometimes sought ways to bypass Congress, notoriously in the Vietnam War, which eventually failed to maintain the support of Congress and the people. This necessitated the War Powers Act, limiting what the president can do. It is significant that in the Gulf War and the war on terrorism in Afghanistan, the two presidents Bush went to Congress to seek a congressional declaration before proceeding.

Furthermore, the approval of the United Nations or a representative international body or coalition should generally be sought, for two reasons. The cost in resources, wounded and dead will be borne by other nations as well. And nations that decide to go to war often are wrong. All sin (Rom 3:23), and that includes nations acting corporately. Therefore a nation needs the checks and balances provided by consulting with other nations. So both presidents Bush sought UN or international approval before the Gulf War and the attack on Afghanistan. President Clinton first got a United Nations declaration before invading Haiti in 1994, and that gave former President Carter the notice he needed to ask for a brief delay before overly rash action, to rush to Haiti before the warplanes arrived and to resolve the problem successfully by means of conflict resolution.

For these two kinds of just authority to function, both government truthfulness and freedom of the press are required so that people can judge situations accurately. Deceitful authority is unjust authority, especially when the deceit is in the service of getting people killed (see chapter eighteen).

3. Last resort. All means of negotiation, conflict resolution and prevention must be exhausted before resorting to war. The logic is clear: what justifies the killing in war is that it is the only way to stop the great evil that provides the just cause. If the evil can be stopped by a nonviolent resort, then there is no just cause for the killing.

In the Korean War, North Korea was already invading South Korea, so other resorts had been exhausted. In the Vietnam War, however, the U.S. government and the Saigon government refused negotiations, refused to hold the elections they had agreed to in the Geneva Accords and rejected involvement by the United Nations or World Court. They both knew the people of Vietnam and world opinion held the Saigon government to be unjust and would reject the war. Eventually, 80 percent of Americans agreed that the war was a mistake. In the Gulf War, Iraq accepted President Bush's terms for talks in Washington and Baghdad, but President Bush then refused to negotiate. Iraq then talked with Russia and agreed to get out of Kuwait immediately. But the United States attacked anyway (Stassen, *Just Peacemaking: Transforming Initiatives,* 242-45). As in Vietnam, the other resorts had not been exhausted, and most church groups that spoke opposed making the war. We believe it was a war that at that point could have been avoided. Apparently it was this war that turned Osama bin Laden down the path to the heinous evil of terrorism (see Watson et al., "On the Trail of the Real Osama bin Laden").

4. Just intention (final cause, or future aim). "The only legitimate intention is to secure a just peace for all involved. Neither revenge nor conquest nor economic gain nor ideological supremacy are justified" (Holmes, "Just War," 120).

After the attack on the World Trade Center and the Pentagon, the Pentagon initially code-named the war against terrorism "Infinite Justice." But *infinite* justice is not given to us this side of the second coming; all we can have is *better* justice. "Islamic leaders complained because only God can bestow infinite justice" (*Los Angeles Times*, September 21, 2001, A6). Faithful Christians say the same. When war is fought for grandiose ideological purposes, it usually means politicians want to whip up the fervor of people for a war, and the war turns into a crusade that kills many innocent people, justifies whatever means were used to destroy the enemy, jettisons rules against killing civilians and flows over the boundaries of just war. So the name was changed to the much better "Enduring Freedom." This name change functions as a nice symbol of the dimension of intentionality in just war thinking.

"Enemy states must be treated, morally as well as strategically, as future partners in some sort of international order" (Walzer, *Just and Unjust*, 116). The aim in war, "within the confines of the argument for justice," is a more secure world, "less vulnerable to territorial expansion, safer for ordinary men and women and for their domestic self-determinations." It is wrong to demand absolute conquest, because of the lives that will be taken, both on one's own side and on the enemy's side, in the pursuit of absolute ends. So the aim is not to be absolutely invulnerable, but less vulnerable; not absolutely safe, but safer. "Just wars are limited wars; there are moral reasons for the statesmen and soldiers who fight them to be prudent and realistic" (Walzer, *Just and Unjust*, 120-22).

5. Probability of success. It is wrong to enter into a war that will kill many people, depriving them of the right to life, liberty and community, in order to achieve a more important goal, if we will quite surely lose and not achieve that goal, and all those people will die in vain (Walzer, *Just and Unjust*, 110). "Lives have too frequently been needlessly lost in blind and futile" wars (Mott, *Biblical Ethics and Social Change*, 188). *The Pentagon Papers* revealed that the Pentagon had calculated in advance that there was not a reasonable chance of success in the Vietnam War—and they were right. By contrast, in World War II, the Korean War and the Gulf War, there was a reasonable hope of success.

6. Proportionality of cost. "Proportionality requires that the total good achieved by a victory will . . . outweigh the total evil and suffering that the war will cause. No one should prescribe a cure that is worse than the disease" (Clark and Rakestraw, *Readings in Christian Ethics*, 2:490). This is the rule that the U.S. Catholic bishops most emphasized when they condemned the Vietnam War as unjust. They said that its destructiveness far exceeded the good that was sought. Therefore they "called for its rapid conclusion, the rebuilding of Southeast Asia, pardons and amnesties for war resisters, the rehabilitation of veterans and prisoners of war, and forgiveness and reconciliation for all Americans" (Musto, *Catholic Peace Tradition*, 257).

7. Clear announcement. The government that is about to make war must anounce its intention to make war and the conditions for avoiding it. Stipulating the conditions for avoiding war enables the other side to know what it would take to avoid or stop the war. George W. Bush did exactly this in preparation for the attacks on Afghanistan in October 2001. Public announcement also enables the people to exercise their conscientious responsibility to weigh the justice and importance of the cause versus the killing that will be involved. It provides transparency so people may know what their government is doing in their name as it commits them to the horror of a war.

In Vietnam, the United States avoided declaring war, avoided announcing it and sneaked into a widening war by stages. The result was a war not supported by the people. In the Gulf War, by contrast, there was a national debate and a Congressional vote. The announcement was clear. That enabled Iraq to know war was surely coming, and they agreed to meet the conditions and get out of Kuwait. The fact that the United States made war in spite of Iraq's agreeing to meet the conditions must mean the announcement did not truthfully state the real conditions.

8. The war must be fought by just means. In a pragmatic culture like the United States, a frequent error is to emphasize the justice of *the cause* but then overlook the requirement that *the means* of fighting must be just. To correct this error, we need to emphasize *justice in war*, or in the traditional Latin, *jus in bello*. The rule of proportionality of cost must be applied not only to the decision to go *to war* but also to the means used *in the war*. In a world with so many nuclear weapons that their full use would result in "the almost complete reciprocal slaughter of one side by the other, not to speak of the widespread devastation that would follow in the world and the deadly after-effects from the use of such weapons," using the huge arsenals of nuclear weapons would cause far worse destruction than any alleged gain, and so any nuclear war would be unjust (U.S. National Conference of Catholic Bishops, *Challenge of Peace*, no. 101). The astonishing destructive power of many non-nuclear weapons now makes this dimension of proportionality a critical issue to consider in every war.

This criterion of *justice in war* "forbids direct, intentional attacks on nonmilitary persons" (Clark and Rakestraw, *Readings in Christian Ethics*, 2:490). "Individuals not actively contributing to the conflict (including POWs and casualties as well as civilian nonparticipants) should be immune from attack" (Holmes, "Just War," 121). All members of an enemy nation retain the sanctity of their lives, for they were created in the image of God. The only reason why just war overrides enemy soldiers' right to life is that there is no way of fighting without attacking soldiers. It is they who are making the war and thus opposing the just cause. Once soldiers have surrendered, they may not be killed or tortured. Noncombatants are not fighting the war, so their right to life forbids their being intentionally killed. "Any lethal force which is directed against noncombatants is therefore murder. Any terrorist violence against civilians is ruled out. . . . Torture can only be inflicted on a captive, who by definition" can no longer be an aggressor, "but rather is weak and helpless. Torture can constitute a greater assault on the dignity of human life even than killing. Torture is one of the surest indications of the denial of justice" (Mott, *Biblical Ethics and Social Change*, 190; cf. Walzer, *Just and Unjust*, 36, 47).

Bombing a military target like a tank or a weapons factory may have the indirect effect of killing some civilians. That is a realistic and allowable consequence of war (though nonetheless horrible), so long as it truly is unintentional and indirect, and its cost in lives is proportional to the gain. This is the principle of *double effect*—that is, the primary effect of the war is to kill soldiers and destroy military targets, but the secondary effect is some spillover death (to civilians) and destruction (to nonmilitary targets). Walzer adds that because civilians have the right to life, soldiers must take extra care to try to avoid killing them. He tells of French bomber pilots during World War II who flew low, at some risk to themselves, in order to bomb weapons factories more accurately and avoid hitting homes in German-occupied France. What these pilots knew about the right to life applies to all civilians because they are human (Walzer, *Just and Unjust*, 151-59; Childress, review of Walzer, 45).

Terrorism is the practice of attacking whoever happens to be in the target location—drug stores, shopping malls or tall office buildings—for the purpose of striking terror in civilians. It has no respect for the right to life of noncombatants and so is singularly evil. In order to guard the right to life and fundamental ethics, it is crucial not to fuzz the definition for ideological purposes. Some politicians label rebels against governmental order "terrorists." But "terrorist" is not the same as "rebel," "guerrilla" or "revolutionary." The guerrillas who shot at British troops from behind trees and stone fences during the American Revolution were not terrorists, nor are leftist guerrillas who shoot at military forces in Colombia. Only if guerrillas attack civilians randomly are they terrorists. Terrorism is particularly evil, and the term should be used precisely to name exactly the evil that it is. "We must condemn all reprisals against innocent people" (Walzer, *Just and Unjust*, 197-98, 215). The same applies to governments that attack homes, villages, neighborhoods and civilians. This is "state terrorism," as described by Michelle Tooley in the narrative with which this chapter began.

A war that fails even one of these criteria is unjust and by the logic of the just war theory we must oppose it. It is not enough to have a just cause if other possible resorts are not tried, nor is it adequate to have a just cause if the war is carried out by unjust means. It is easy to see how stringent application of just war theory places severe limits on war-making, in both senses—whether or not to fight a war, and how a war is fought.

How Not to Argue for the Just War Theory

Lurking at the door are powerful drives of revenge, hate, nationalism, racism, economic greed, powerlust, hateful stereotyping of the enemy, ideological crusades and self-righteousness (see Gen 4:7). These seek to use the just war theory as a rationalization for killing and pay scant attention to its actual logic and criteria. Whenever someone appeals to just war theory to argue that some wars are right, but does not judge the particular war under discussion by the criteria we have discussed, he or she is making use of ethical talk to rationalize the desire for war. When such toothless just war talk is used, it serves as a mask for other attitudes: Machiavellian "realism" about self-interest, crusade, Rambo attitudes, or a "war is hell" mindset that says once war has begun no rules apply (see Yoder, *Nevertheless*, 151-54).

We have sought to make clear that any legitimate Christian use of just war theory must be based on nonviolence and justice, as taught by Jesus. A Christian who supports just war theory should see it as the most effective way to minimize violence and injustice, not merely to rationalize making war. "Just war theory does not try to justify war. Rather it tries to bring war under the control of justice" (Holmes, "Just War," 119; cf. Cahill, *Love Your Enemies*, 237ff.). Michael Walzer bases it on justice as the right to life, liberty and community (*Just and Unjust*, xv-xvi, 53-54, 59, 61ff., 72, 108, 134-37, 254), and opposition to domination (29, 70-71). His emphasis on the right to life is a commitment to reduce killing and violence. Walter Wink calls the rules of just war theory "violence-reduction criteria" (*Engaging the Powers*, 220-27).

Lisa Cahill insightfully compares Augustine's basing just war theory on love of neighbor with Thomas's basing it on justice. Their logic is that war needs to be justified because it involves killing, and therefore the appeal to love or justice is necessary to override the strong presumption against killing. We acknowledge that some may base just war theory on the right of a state to make war and may then declare the presumption against violence to be irrelevant. But that has the rather direct consequence of declaring Jesus' way to be irrelevant, since Jesus' way affirms nonviolence. Furthermore, we believe it morally dangerous to place the right of the state above the requirement to justify what a state does morally. That weakens the checks and balances against dictatorship, nationalism, and empire. It becomes functional idolatry.

Just war theory should not be based on an argument that in a time of war Jesus is no longer Lord and his way is no longer relevant. *Privatism* argues that Jesus' lordship and teachings on peacemaking apply only to individual, private relationships and not to the obligation of governments to seek peace. Others argue that in our present sinful world, we must use just war theory *instead* of Jesus' teachings, as if Jesus' teachings were only for an ideal future eschatological world without sin. We have shown that Jesus' ethic regularly named the vicious cycles of the real, sinful world and opposed the teachings of political parties that wanted a war of insurrection against Rome. Jesus' ethic is precisely for this sinful world. Still others focus on the claim that the government has the authority to make war (usually citing Rom 13) and then fail to deal with the criteria for judging when this authority is exercised justly and when unjustly.

It seems to us that all these ways of marginalizing and compartmentalizing Jesus' lordship set up some other lord—the government, the need for retribution or nationalism—as lord over the rest of life. They are therefore idolatry. And they create secularism, because they teach that outside the private realm, or a future realm, or an ideal realm, Jesus is not relevant. Instead what are relevant are secular norms or authorities without critique from Jesus. Thus they remove just war theory from correction by gospel ethics, so that it serves some other lord and gets used dishonestly to justify wars that are not just. We argue that just war theory is not autonomous. Either it serves the purpose of reducing violence and seeking justice under Christ's lordship, or it serves some idolatrous loyalty such as rationalizing a war that we have an urge to make. Either Jesus is Lord over just war theory, or just war theory serves some other lord over Jesus.

Once Christians define just war theory as a way to try to decrease violence and injustice, they receive a second benefit: they are clearly affirming nonviolence and justice. So they can be more honest in affirming Jesus' teaching of peacemaking and justice. They no longer need to deny that Jesus teaches peacemaking in order to defend their loyalty to just war theory. That denial was a losing argument. Jesus' teachings are very clear. Just war theorists are wise to accept this truth. What they need to argue is not that Jesus' teaching does not apply. Rather, if they want to argue for just war theory, they need to argue that it is the most effective way to implement Jesus' way of peace and justice in a sinful world.

Nonviolence/Pacifism

For the first three hundred years of the Christian movement, the church was almost unanimously pacifist. Throughout church history numerous discipleship-oriented groups, such as Franciscans, Hussites, Waldensians, Anabaptists, Quakers, Brethren and the original Pentecostals, have also been pacifist. The number of pacifists within mainstream denominations has increased in recent decades due to greater emphasis on the Gospels and the greatly increased destructiveness of war.

A Christian pacifist is committed to making a clear witness to the way of Jesus. In this view, trying to make that witness while advocating killing enemies is wrong not only because it advocates killing people, but also because it disobeys Jesus and distorts Christian witness to his way. The clearest historical example of this distortion is the four centuries of Christian crusades against Muslims during the Middle Ages. Christian soldiers with crosses painted on their breastplates and banners, marching to kill Muslims, made a witness that turned Islam more militantly against Christian faith, with implications to this day.

This distortion of Christian faith was repeated by the Serbs at the close of the twentieth century as they rode their tanks into Kosovo, smilingly holding up three fingers as a symbol of the Trinity, on their mission to kill Muslims. A just war theorist will respond that the ethics of the crusade is precisely what it is opposing and seeking to correct. And the leading pacifist theologian of the last forty years of the twentieth century, John Howard Yoder, agrees that pacifists and just war theorists should be considered allies in the effort to oppose both crusades and the usual wars fought because governments decide such wars are in their interest without serious attention to the rules of just war theory (Yoder, *The War of the Lamb*). But he also criticizes just war theory for being used most frequently to justify wars that were fought for other reasons.

The first argument for Christian pacifism is that it takes the way of Jesus and the witness of the New Testament as authoritative for our witness. The point is to be faithful to the way of Jesus, and Jesus clearly taught nonviolence and exemplified it in his life and in his death on the cross.

Lisa Cahill has distinguished two kinds of Christian pacifists: One is committed to nonviolence as an obligatory rule: never make war or be violent. The other is committed to nonviolence as a way of life, a way of discipleship, not so much because of an obligatory rule, but because of loyalty to Jesus Christ and the presence as well as futurity of the kingdom of God. The way-of-life pacifist is committed not only to avoiding violence but to practicing peacemaking in a positive way in all relationships. Cahill argues that some just war theorists erroneously project their rule-and-exception ethic onto pacifism, arguing too simply against pacifism as a rule and thus miss the profound meaning of nonviolence as discipleship and a way of life (Cahill, *Love Your Enemies*, 210ff.; cf. our discussion of moral norms in chapter five).

We point out that the discipleship-pacifist may be slightly more flexible than the rule-pacifist. For example, Dietrich Bonhoeffer was committed to peacemaking and nonviolence as a way of life, but he opposed rule-absolutism. Accordingly, after much anguish, he supported the plot to carry out a coup against

Adolf Hitler in order to stop the killing that Hitler was causing. The advantage is that Bonhoeffer could be committed to discipleship and nonviolence, and *therefore*, still as a witness to Jesus' nonviolence, seek to stop Hitler from his violence. The danger is the slippery slope, possibly slipping into rationalization of war-making, and the confusion of witnessing to Jesus while seeking to quarantine or stop Hitler by the only means that seemed available, which involved killing him. Bonhoeffer emphasized his need for the grace and forgiveness of Christ for his own involvement in sin (*Ethics*, 154-64, 236ff. et passim).

John Howard Yoder distinguished twenty-eight varieties of pacifism (*Nevertheless*). He made clear that a *properly trained and disciplined* police force is logically different from an army preparing for war, so pacifists can logically support police work: (1) The threat of police violence is applied only to the offending party. (2) The police officer's violence is subject to review by higher authorities. (3) The authorized force is within a state whose laws the criminal knows apply to himself. (4) Safeguards seek to keep police violence from being applied in a wholesale way against the innocent. (5) Police power is generally great enough to overwhelm the offender so resistance is pointless (*Politics of Jesus*, 204; see further Winwright, "From Police Officers to Peace Officers").

Yoder pointed out that some who want to undermine pacifism confuse it with passivism. The two words have nothing in common. Pacifism comes from the Latin, *pax facere*, to make peace. Pacifists like Martin Luther King Jr. were and are admirably active in seeking ways to make peace. In fact, Christian pacifists on the whole have taken more initiatives and witnessed more clearly to initiatives to make peace than nonpacifists have. Many distort Jesus' teachings, claiming "turn the other cheek" means passivity. We have attempted to correct that interpretation and emphasize that Jesus' teachings are not mere prohibitions but are active, transforming initiatives.

Yoder is known for arguing that the point of discipleship is faithfulness, not effectiveness. To try to construct an ethics based on what is most effective in achieving a particular goal is to base ethics on complex calculations about what factors are likely to influence the outcome, on what historical surprises might occur, and on our own ability to control history. Calculations like these are based on the unknown, and on the self-interested and biased perceptions of decision-makers rather than on the suffering of those who will be impacted by the decisions. We are too limited in our knowledge and sinful in our perceptions to be able to control history. It is far wiser to act with faithfulness to what is right, and let God control the outcome (*Politics of Jesus*, chap. 12).

In "The Political Meaning of Hope" (Yoder, *War of the Lamb*), Yoder argues that Tolstoy, Gandhi and King all had a faith that the cosmos is governed by some kind of discernible moral cause-effect coherence. King liked to say that "the universe bends toward justice." If your rejection of violence is cosmically based, as for Tolstoy, Gandhi and King, and not merely pragmatic, the impact of that kind of commitment will in fact be greater effectiveness. Perseverance in the face of sacrifice and creativity in the face of dismay are heightened for those who believe that the grain of the universe is with them.

Furthermore, if God really is Lord, if the universe really does bend toward justice, then it makes sense to argue that faithful action is on the whole more effective. So in "Alternatives to Violence" *(War of the Lamb)*, Yoder offers arguments for the effectiveness of nonviolent direct action (cf. Sharp, *Politics of Nonviolent Action*, who documents over a thousand cases of effective nonviolent action). He argues that nonviolence should not be judged ineffective because sometimes it does not win. Military action works less than half the time, since for every winner of a war there is also a loser, and sometimes wars are so bad that both sides are losers. Nor should nonviolence be judged ineffective because sometimes people get killed; far more get killed in military action than in nonviolent action. In what he called the "King-Che discrepancy," Yoder noted that when Martin Luther King was killed, many concluded that nonviolence had thereby been refuted. But at the same time, few concluded that the fact that Che Guevara had been gunned down in the Bolivian mountains meant that guerrilla violence had been permanently refuted.

Yoder also argues that just war theory has failed the historical test. It has been used most regularly to bless whatever war a nation wanted to make. Seldom have churches used just war theory to condemn a war their own nation was making (Yoder, *When War Is Unjust* and *The War of the Lamb*). A partial answer to that criticism is that just war theory helped a great deal to clarify what was unjust about the Vietnam war (see Potter, *War and Moral Discourse* and Walzer, *Just and Unjust Wars*). It helped many see that nuclear war would be horribly wrong and must be avoided (National Conference of Catholic Bishops, *Challenge of Peace*). It helped to ensure that the focus of the bombing of Iraq, Kosovo and Afghanistan would be on military targets, not civilian targets (although we did learn after the Gulf War that military control of the news had given a false picture).

How Not to Argue for Nonviolence

Some pacifists have argued that Jesus' way is only for Christians. Christians must follow Jesus and renounce violence, but we cannot expect non-Christians to renounce violence. The gospel is only for Christians, and we have nothing to say to non-Christians. We can expect the government to do violence, because it is not Christian; that is not our problem. There is a long history of this stance among Christian pacifists.

But just like the argument for just war theory that marginalized Jesus as relevant only to private relations, this way of arguing for pacifism makes Jesus something less than fully Lord. It teaches that Jesus is not relevant to public ethics for non-Christians, and so produces secularism in the public realm.

Yoder and Bonhoeffer argued with thorough persuasiveness that Jesus really is Lord, and therefore the practices of peacemaking that Jesus taught for the church also have their normative relevance for the world. They are God's will. God is God over the whole world, not only over our private lives or only over the church (see Yoder, "Theological Point of Reference," in *War of the Lamb*, and the other books by Yoder in the bibliography).

This means that Christians, whether they are pacifists or just war theorists, are called to prod the government, and non-Christians, to adopt policies that are as nonviolent, as productive of nonviolence and as active in taking peacemaking initiatives, as possible. We cannot expect non-Christians to do this because of Christian faith; but because we believe the gospel reveals God's will, we must seek to persuade them to do peacemaking based on the ethics they do acknowledge.

Just Peacemaking Theory

During the 1980s, major church groups issued book-length statements calling for repentance and reversal of the nuclear weapons buildup. They all said the debate between pacifism and just war theory is inadequate. It narrows the discussion to the question of whether it is ever right to fight a war. But war is so destructive that we need an ethic of prevention, an ethic of initiatives that governments are obligated to take in order to prevent war and make peace. We need a positive theology of peacemaking.

Now a *just peacemaking theory* has arisen—a third paradigm for the ethics of peace and war. In the wake of the horror of World War II and the threat of World War III during the Cold War, plus the world devastation threatened by weapons of mass destruction even today, a worldwide awareness has arisen that we must develop effective war-preventing practices. It is a gift of God that ten such practices have developed in an interdisciplinary and ecumenical peacemaking literature, and where they receive support from the people and their governments, wars are being prevented. In the wake of the threat of terrorism, thoughtful persons are sensing that it is not enough to debate whether it is right or wrong to make war; we need to focus on effective ways to prevent terrorism and war.

The practices of just peacemaking are confirmed not only by empirical studies in international relations but also by the data in chapter eight on what works to decrease homicides. The data in both cases point to conflict resolution, preventive initiatives more than violent retaliation, nonviolent action strategies, economic justice, community organization, reduction in weapons and the development of groups that give spiritual support, as the effective way to prevent violence (for the data and further explanation of the practices of just peacemaking theory, plus the biblical foundations, see the two books in the bibliography under Stassen and the website <www.fuller.edu/sot/faculty/stassen>).

Just peacemaking theory fills out the original intention of the other two paradigms. It encourages pacifists to be what their name, derived from the Latin *pacem-facere,* means: peace-*makers.* And it calls just war theorists to enhance the content of their underdeveloped principles of last resort and just intention. It asks what resorts, exactly, must be tried before resorting to war? What actions must be taken to restore a just and durable peace? Furthermore, it fits Jesus' teaching of transforming initiatives of peacemaking. Jesus not only taught not to do violence; he taught *peacemaking initiatives.* Based both on Jesus' way of peacemaking and on the obligation to do what is effective in preventing war, the advocates of just peacemaking argue that these practices can and do guide us in shaping the future that is God's will and our need. They are obligations, and more. They are the way we are given to participate in the grace that God is giving in our time. The ten practices of just peacemaking are as follows:

1. Support nonviolent direct action. Nonviolent direct action as practiced effectively by Gandhi in India and Martin Luther King Jr. in the United States is spreading remarkably, ending dictatorship in the Philippines, bringing about nonviolent revolutions in Poland, East Germany and Central Europe, spurring democratic change in Latin America, South Africa and many other regions (Buttry, *Christian Peacemaking,* chap. 4). It is based on the way of Jesus (Mt 5:38ff.), and it is proving effective.

2. Take independent initiatives to reduce threat. Independent initiatives are designed to decrease the threat and distrust that undermine support for negotiated solutions. They (1) are visible and verifiable actions, not mere promises; (2) are accompanied by an announcement that their purpose is to decrease threat and distrust, and to invite reciprocation; (3) do not leave the initiator weak; (4) do not wait for the slow process of negotiations; (5) have a timing announced in advance that is carried out regardless of the other side's bluster; (6) come in a series: if the other side fails to reciprocate, small initiatives continue in order to keep inviting reciprocation. For example, the strategy of independent initiatives freed Austria from Soviet domination in the 1950s; produced the Atmospheric Test Ban Treaty of 1963 after Presidents Eisenhower and Kennedy halted atmospheric testing unilaterally; achieved dramatic reductions in nuclear weapons via the series of initiatives by President Gorbachev and the U.S. Congress, and then President George W. Bush's father; and led to breakthroughs by adversaries in Northern Ireland. After years of occupying southern Lebanon, the Israeli government announced in 2000 it would pull out all its forces and asked the Lebanese government to reciprocate by stopping insurgent groups from shooting at northern Israel. They pulled out on schedule, the shooting stopped, and the people of Israel, Lebanon and the world applauded the rare happy result from that region. At the time of this writing, a similar series of Israeli initiatives to pull out from occupying the West Bank and Gaza Strip, and to allow a viable, unified state of Palestine not severed by Israeli settlements and military roads, is desperately needed—to be reciprocated by the end of Palestinian terrorist attacks. The people of Israel and Palestine have too much distrust to support peacemaking unless one side takes a series of initiatives that show a will to make peace and create hope.

3. Use cooperative conflict resolution. Conflict resolution is becoming a well-known practice, seen dramatically in President Carter's achieving peace in the Camp David accords between Egypt and Israel, and in his peaceful resolution of conflicts with Haiti and North Korea. A key test of the seriousness of governments' claims to be seeking peace is whether they initiate negotiations or refuse them, and whether they develop imaginative solutions that show they understand their adversary's perspectives and needs. Jesus said that when there is anger between us and another, we must drop everything, go to the other, and make peace. It is a command, not an option (Mt 5:23ff.).

4. Acknowledge responsibility for conflict and injustice; seek repentance and forgiveness. This practice was initiated by Dietrich Bonhoeffer, and then by churches in Germany, confessing the sin of support for Hitler and his unimaginable violence and injustice. Since then, not only the German government, but also the U.S. government, Japan, and the Truth and Reconciliation Commission in South Africa have lanced the boil of festering historical injustices by acknowledging responsibility and seeking change and forgiveness (Mt 7:1-5; see chapter nineteen below for the application of this principle to racial issues).

The next two practices follow from the teaching of the prophets and Jesus that injustice is the cause of war's destruction, and that removing bitter injustice is essential for peacemaking.

5. Promote democracy, human rights and religious liberty. Spreading human rights, religious liberty and democracy is effective in building peace. As surprising as it seems, during the entire twentieth century, democracies with human rights fought *no wars* against one another. (We should be careful, however, not to use this for self-righteousness. At the time of this writing, the influence of enormous amounts of money so dominates the U.S. political process as to threaten to replace democracy by plutocracy—the rule of moneyed interests. One implication of the effectiveness of democracy and human rights in preventing war is the obligation to spread democracy and human rights, including through laws limiting the dominance of money in elections.) Work by churches and human rights groups to press for human rights has helped convert the dictatorships of Latin America to democracies or democracies-in-process, and the trend continues in Asia, Africa and Eastern Europe. Spreading peace is done by networks of persons willing to work together to gain public attention for protection against human rights violations.

6. Foster just and sustainable economic development. A just peace requires an equitable world economy in which extreme inequalities in wealth, power and participation are progressively overcome. East Asian economies, especially in Korea and Taiwan, have grown rapidly because their land reform distributed wealth more equitably and widely. That multiplied the number of customers for the businesses and thus stimulated the economy. By contrast, Latin America's wealth is owned by just a few rich families. Local businesses lack consumers for their products. Without a market, industries cannot grow (see chapter twenty).

The final set of practices implements Jesus' command to include enemies in the community of neighbors (Mt 5:43-48).

7. Work with emerging cooperative forces in the international system. Networks of international communication, international travel and migration, international church missions and international business are stitching nations together into an international society in which enemies are brought into continuous constructive interaction. Empirical evidence shows that the more nations are involved in these webs of interaction, the less likely they are to make war.

8. Strengthen the United Nations and international organizations. Acting alone, states cannot solve problems of trade, debt and interest rates; of pollution, ozone depletion, acid rain, depletion of fish stocks and global warming; of migrations and refugees seeking asylum; of military security when weapons rapidly penetrate borders; and of international terrorism. The problems are international. Therefore, the practice of supporting cooperative action via the United Nations and regional organizations is crucial. These organizations are resolving conflicts, monitoring, nurturing and even enforcing truces, and replacing violent conflict with the beginnings of cooperation. Empirical evidence shows that nations that are more engaged in these organizations more often avoid getting entangled in war.

9. Reduce offensive weapons and weapons trade. Weapons have become so destructive that war is usually not worth the price. The offense cannot destroy the defense before suffering huge retaliatory damage. Reducing offensive weapons and shifting toward defensive force structures strengthens that equation. It makes war less likely. For example, Soviet President Gorbachev removed half the Soviet Union's tanks from Central Europe and all its river-crossing equipment, thus reducing the threat of a Soviet attack on Europe. This freed NATO to agree to get rid of all medium-range and shorter-range nuclear weapons from Western Europe—the first dramatic step in ending the Cold War peacefully. The wars of Serbia against Bosnia, Croatia and Kosovo are the counter-examples that prove the rule: Serbians controlled the former Yugoslavian army and its weapons. They had the offensive weapons to make war without expecting a destructive counterattack, until world revulsion finally ended their onslaughts.

As nations turn toward democracy and human rights, their governments no longer need large militaries to keep them in power. They can reduce military spending and devote their economies to fighting inflation, paying debts and meeting basic human needs. Arms imports by developing nations in 1995 actually dropped to one-quarter of their peak in 1988. Nations with human rights and democracy, which do a better job of meeting the basic needs of their people, almost never breed terrorists. We have an opportunity in our time to move from authoritarianism to human rights, from war to justice, from high spending for offensive weapons to lower spending.

10. Encourage grassroots peacemaking groups and voluntary associations. Advocates of just peacemaking theory teach these effective practices, and their biblical grounding, in churches and other citizens' groups. And they test government actions, when governments claim to want peace, to see if they are taking these obligatory steps that do in fact lead to peace. They resist claims of politicians that we should vote for them because they claim to be Christian believers if they do not in fact do the things that make for peace, as Jesus taught.

The current struggle against terrorism demands of both Muslims and Christians fidelity in concrete practices of peacemaking and justice. We need to correct the bitter injustices and heal the festering resentments that breed terrorists. The growing worldwide people's movement of peacemaker groups constitutes a historical force that empowers just peacemaking. A transnational network of groups, including church groups, can partially transcend captivity to narrow national or ideological perspectives. They can serve as voices for the voiceless, as they did in churches in East Germany and in women's groups in Guatemala (see Tooley, *Voices of the Voiceless*). They can help to initiate, foster and support transforming initiatives that take risks to break out of the cycles that perpetuate violence and injustice. They can nurture the spirituality that sustains courage when just peacemaking is unpopular, that creates hope when despair and cynicism are tempting, and that fosters grace and forgiveness when just peacemaking fails.

How Not to Argue for Just Peacemaking Theory

Just peacemaking was developed by Christian ethicists, some of whom are pacifists and most of whom are just war theorists. It is supported by many from both traditions, because it asks and provides answers to questions that the usual debate between pacifism and just war theory does not answer: What steps should we be taking to prevent war? What practices make for peace? It does not try to answer the question that pacifism and just war theory answer: If just peacemaking fails, is it right to make war, or should we be committed to nonviolence? Everyone needs an answer to that question, because, short of the second coming, just peacemaking will not prevent all wars. And when war does come, we need to be solidly either just war theorists or pacifists. Otherwise we will be blown about by every wind of ideological interest (Eph 4:14).

Therefore, we urge you not to say, "I support just peacemaking theory. It is better than both pacifism and just war theory, and I support it and not them." We do urge you to support just peacemaking theory for what it actually contributes, and to teach it in your church and to demand its principles of your government. We urge you also to discuss both pacifism and just war theory carefully, in your Christian community, and seek in prayer and community to discern which is your calling. Then when all else fails, and the government is about to declare war, you can make a clear witness.

8

SOWING THE SEEDS OF PEACE

First go and be reconciled with your brother; then come and offer your gift. . . .

Love your enemies and pray for those who persecute you. . . .

Do not judge, or you too will be judged. . . . First take the plank out of your own eye, and then you will see clearly to remove the speck from your brother's eye.

MATTHEW 5:24, 44; 7:1, 5 NIV

Columbine High School became a symbol that brought youth violence to everyone's attention.

A Student's Visit to Columbine

From a distance I could read the marquee below the name of the high school building, advertising an "All Student Reunion." Outlining the words in the background were fluffy pink and white clouds.

I turned and walked up to the top of a small empty hill as the sun was about to set over the foothills of the Rocky Mountains. But the hilltop had not always been empty. The ground was dry and bare from the footsteps of thousands of people who had hiked to the top of it over the last year. And until they were recently removed, the hill had been decorated with thirteen white crosses.

Over the course of the evening hours, a number of people from the nearby park strolled up and down the hill. Some were high school students enjoying a summer day at the park. I asked one girl what had happened to the makeshift memorial of the crosses on the hill that I had seen on the news. She told me the park service that maintains the property had removed all the mementos. I was disappointed that there was no place for me to visit, no cards to read, no place to leave my tears of sympathy.

This young girl was well informed, and then it dawned on me—she was a Columbine High School student. She told me that the interior of the library and the cafeteria were being renovated to create an atrium as a permanent memorial to honor the victims.

She was in the cafeteria when she first heard loud bangs and saw smoke in the hallway. She thought some seniors were playing a prank by setting off fireworks. When students came running out of the smoke screaming for people to run, she found herself with a group of others running outside in terror, but not knowing what they were running from. From an elementary school across the street, they watched the TV news of gunshots in their own high school.

Over the course of the evening I met several students who were also there when it happened. A recent graduate was in the cafeteria eating lunch with her friends when they saw two students in black trench coats spray random gunfire. She ran and hid in a kitchen office with a group who were among the first to call the police. They kept the door closed by placing a desk in front of it. One of the killers knocked on the door and asked to be let in. He even said that he was a police officer. He kicked on the door a few times and then gave up and left.

A third student was in the library that day. He saw one student get shot in the knee and then another at point blank range, execution style. That's all he wanted to tell me.

It wasn't until days after the shootings that the community of Littleton, Colorado, and the students and staff of Columbine High School realized the full impact of what had happened. The names of the killed were not released, so they found out which of their friends were alive or dead by watching the news and televised funerals; if a friend was on TV, they knew the friend wasn't dead. Even those students who didn't lose close friends are still just as shaken. Some ask why they survived. Dylan and Eric (the students who did the shooting) had a web page outlining their motives and strategy, including a list of the students they targeted. Surprisingly, none on the list were killed. The randomness of the deaths seems beyond reason and comprehension.

Watching the news coverage on TV, reading the paper, even being here at the building itself and talking to survivors barely begins to give me an idea of the extraordinary horror of that day. The evil of this violence is simply unimaginable. Where was God on April 20, 1999? The old paradox of a presumed all-powerful and all-good yet seemingly absent divine being continues to be a source of anguish and confusion—as it always is in tragedies.

In his book *How to Handle Grief: Tracks of a Fellow Struggler*, written as he endured his daughter's diagnosis and death from leukemia, John Claypool was accused of heresy for stating to God: "You owe me an explanation." Indeed I too, like Abraham, Job, Amos and Jesus, will plead with God in the name of Cassie, Steven, Corey, Kelly, Matthew, Dan, Rachel, Isaiah, John, Lauren, Kyle, Daniel and William; I will anticipate an accounting of why thou hast forsaken us.

But for the students I spoke with today, the answer to "Where was God?" is clear. They credit God with the fact that two propane bombs that would have destroyed the entire building and everyone inside did not go off. Moreover, they credit God with the support and comfort poured out to the community. The cliques and groups among the student body vanished as everyone hugged and comforted one another. Friends, relatives neighbors, churches and even strangers in the neighborhoods provided meals, transportation and other physical needs to those suffering. The homes of the families of the victims were flooded with sympathy cards and flowers. Across the country millions prayed to God to grant peace, strength and consolation. On that tragic day as each child's life was suddenly cut short, hundreds of others injured, and thousands suffering emotional trauma, God's heart was the first to break, and God was the first to cry. Many survivors know exactly where God's hand was on April 20th, 1999: *by their side.*

As we sat and talked, they commented on the beauty of the setting sun resting between the mountaintops and the clouds. That they can recognize and accept beauty inspires me. I came here today anticipating visiting a memorial filled with dying flowers, wooden crosses and weather-torn paper cards, in a small effort to catch a glimpse of some of the pain that was caused here. I expected to be alone mourning the tragedy. Instead I found myself in the company of survivors who are struggling every second of their scarred lives to seek hope and peace.

And through faith in God, they are finding it. Thank God! (Jacob Zimmer, summer 2000)

Many besides Jacob (a youth and fellow church member with Glen a decade ago) have been trying to come to terms with the violent culture and the violent killings here in the United States. September 11, 2001—the day of the worst terrorist attack in American history—is now also a symbol of the violence that comes to us from beyond our shores.

In this chapter we focus especially on youth because

1. Youth do more than their share of the violence, and suffer more from it.
2. Churches can be surprisingly effective in reaching out to youth and combating youth violence.
3. Ministry to youth is a crucial mission of churches.
4. These years are when many make their fundamental decisions about life orientation, ethical commitments and their commitments to be followers of Jesus.
5. A focus on youth is a key strategy for spreading the gospel and growing churches.
6. Youth are our future.
7. Focusing on youth, whom we care about, may help people be preventive and not just punitive, as Jesus urges.

Perceiving What Works to Prevent Violence

We have seen that in the Sermon on the Mount Jesus named vicious cycles of violence. Jesus cared deeply about the sacredness of human life and pointed to the way of deliverance from violence—his transforming initiatives of peace-making. Jesus was here teaching about the kingdom of God; he was declaring: "Here is where God is."

Jesus can turn our discussion of violence in America from frustrated anger, powerless cynicism and self-defeating judgmentalism to transforming initiatives. Following Jesus, we want to focus on initiatives that actually do work to prevent violence. But immediately we realize that a culture of blame, a judgmental culture, wants to point the finger at the speck in someone else's eye (Mt 7:1-5). And political ideologies interpret the question of violence in a way that tries to turn the emotion of blame in ways that will be useful for their causes.

Jesus' teaching "Judge not" means "Do not condemn." It does not mean "Do not try to discern the difference between right and wrong." Jesus discerned that difference and called on us to do likewise (Hagner, *Matthew 1—13*, 169; Davies and Allison, *Critical and Exegetical Commentary*, 1:668-69). But what is not helpful is condemning others and unmercifully focusing attention on the specks in others' eyes. Jesus welcomed outcasts like sinners and tax collectors, lepers and adulterous women, without condemning them.

In the approach we outlined in chapter six, Matthew 7:1-2 is *traditional teaching*, and it is echoed throughout the New Testament (Mk 4:24; Lk 6:37-42; Rom 2:1; 14:4; 1 Cor 4:5; 5:12; and James 4:11-12; 5:9; Hagner, *Matthew 1—13*, 169). Here Jesus spells out the virtues of humility, continuous repentance and mercy that we saw in the Beatitudes (see chapter two).

The *vicious cycle* is named in Matthew 7:3-4. Davies and Allison (*Critical and Exegetical Commentary*, 1:673) put it perceptively: "Human beings unhappily possess an inbred proclivity to mix ignorance of themselves with arrogance toward others."

The *transforming initiative* (Mt 7:5) begins with taking responsibility for the biases in our way of seeing others, even violent others, in our social situation. Our own biases in perceiving and misperceiving our social situation are caused by our misplaced loyalties to other lords in our lives besides God (Mt 6:21-23), and by our self-righteous judgmentalism. Therefore, how we perceive and interpret what goes on around us is an ethical issue. In fact, we need to spend a lifetime taking the logs out of our own eyes. The standard is God's clear-sighted compassion: to be able to see ourselves and others clearly enough to be able to be of some help to them. Jesus often focuses our attention on blindness to God's present rule of mercy, over against seeing clearly with faith in God's powerful presence. We need an ethics of perception, a *perceptual ethics*.

As we discussed in chapter three, how you see shapes much of what you do. Remember that we found four variables that shape perception on all varieties of ethical issues:

1. threat—our assumptions about the cause of what is going wrong;

2. authority—how we see the locus, legitimacy and limits of powers and authorities;

3. social change—our attitude toward it and assumptions about how to bring it about;

4. information integrity, truthfulness and openness—our acquisition and communication of information.

The variable of *threat perception* is about *what* the cause of the problem is, *how urgent* it is, and *how extensively it is linked* to other problems or threats in society. How people perceive the causes of violence powerfully shapes what sort of solutions they advocate. So our question here is: What causes of violence can we identify that we can do something about?

People's attitude toward *authority* powerfully influences their perception of what causes violence and how to prevent it. People with an exaggerated authoritarian streak tend to see the solution to violence as imposing authority on people, having parents who punish more severely, having a criminal justice system that imposes harsher penalties and sometimes themselves using angry rhetoric, and even physical abuse or guns, to keep people in line. People with an exaggerated permissive streak, with an allergy to authority, tend to see the solution as individual autonomy, freedom, allowing people to do whatever they wish and tolerating wide varieties of what used to be thought of as inappropriate behavior. Where is the right balance?

People's attitude toward *social change*, and the kind of social change they advocate, shapes the kinds of solutions they advocate. What kind of social change can work to prevent violence, or at least decrease it?

We want to try to bring some light to this discussion by gaining insight from two sources. First, there have been extensive empirical studies of factors that influence how much violence happens in society and of what works to prevent it. We have surveyed these studies extensively and here present some of the research results, corroborated by multiple studies with different methodologies. Second, we ask how these results correspond with Jesus' teachings on the way of peace. Jesus wept over Jerusalem, saying, "Would that you knew the practices that make for peace" (Lk 19:41 author's translation). He pointed to those practices as the ways of God's deliverance. His focus was not merely on assigning blame, but on the transforming initiatives that prevent violence.

Some people do not think we can learn much from social science or from the Bible. "You can prove anything with statistics," they say. Or "You can prove anything with the Bible." And so they do not ask if something might be learned from studies or from the Bible that could correct some of their time-hardened perceptions. They refuse to seek ways of self-correction. Or they shrug their shoulders, saying they cannot understand, and then they sink into fatalism or cynicism. This demonstrates our fourth variable: *information integrity*, or *truthfulness and openness*.

There are *closed-minded* over against *inquisitive* approaches to information integrity. We are all sinners. We need to be inquisitive, always searching for new information and paying most attention to evidence that seems to contradict what we had previously thought. Scientists think contradictory evidence is where we can learn the most, because it can lead us to find improvements in our theories. Or it can confirm the theories and lead us to find improvements in our data-collection and data-interpretation methods. In Jesus' terms, it can help us notice the log in our own eye.

There are also *manipulative* uses of information, which are the opposite of *truthful* or *respectful* uses of information. We need as much respect for information as possible, because truth comes from God and we ourselves do not already have all the truth. In this chapter we shall examine research methods and results critically, and we shall look for results that are confirmed by multiple studies and different methods, that are statistically significant and that explain an impressive amount of the variance. We shall quote the studies extensively in order to portray their results as accurately as possible. Those are our criteria. But we have been surprised how much the results resemble the practices of peacemaking in just peacemaking theory.

One book summarizing research results seems to echo Jesus' emphasis on transforming initiatives: "This book was inspired by the fundamental belief that current policies aimed at addressing personal violence . . . are obsolete, ineffective, and deceptive to the public. . . . We are guided as well by the belief that, in the long run, *prevention* is cheaper, more effective, and more humane than the vast majority of our current efforts at detection, deterrence, punishment, or containment" (Wolfe et al., *Alternatives to Violence*, ix; see also Benson et al., *Fragile Foundation*). But the role of ideological blinders is also anticipated: "Unfortunately, new scientific evidence about the causes of violence or about the effectiveness of some intervention might also be rejected merely because its implications conflict with" many people's politically, ideologically or ethically formed values (Reiss and Roth, *Understanding and Preventing Violence*, 38-39). Let us try to do better here.

Take Direct Action Opposing Television Violence

"According to the American Psychological Association task force report on television and American society, . . . by the time the average child . . . who watches 2 to 4 hours of television each day finishes elementary school, he or she will have witnessed at least 8,000 murders and more than 100,000 other acts of violence on television" (Wolfe et al., *Alternatives to Violence*, 85). This is powerful conditioning.

Studies indicate that "exposure to media violence at a young age can have lasting . . . negative consequences. If aggressive habits are learned early in life, they may form the foundation for later antisocial behavior." One research team "concluded that early viewing of violence on television stimulates aggression and that early aggression is a statistical precursor to later criminal behavior. . . . Their analyses indicate that approximately 10% of the variability in later criminal behavior can be attributed to television violence" (Geen and Donnerstein, *Human Aggression*, 177-78; Benson et al., *Fragile Foundation*, 42). (Good social science pays attention not only to the statistical significance but to the amount of variance/variability that can be attributed to the cause it is investigating. *Statistical significance* says the result is not caused by mere random chance. *Variance* is how much of the outcome seems to be the result of the cause being investigated. The research team concluded television explains about 10 percent of the violence. So television is not the complete explanation. But 10 percent of the violence is a lot of violence.)

Christian ethicist Henlee Barnette has said: "Producers of violent films claim their programs filled with violence do not influence the behavior of children. But it is nonsense to argue that the media have no influence on viewers while they are paid billions to persuade people to purchase everything from Pablum to Slimfast" ("My Millennium").

What can be done? Parents can boycott TV shows that influence people to be violent. These are shows in which perpetrators of violence are rewarded or not punished; perpetrators are portrayed as admirable or similar to the viewer; violence is portrayed as being justified in the circumstances; violence is portrayed as a real event; violent acts are portrayed so they please the viewer; viewers are young children (see Geen and Donnerstein, *Human Aggression*, 185-91).

Beyond boycotting, parents can call and write TV stations and networks encouraging programs that model ethics and conflict resolution. During the 1980s, the three major television networks cut the number of hours they devoted to prosocial and educational programming for children by 80 percent. Yet we desperately need programs teaching prosocial concepts such as "sharing, empathy, concepts of right and wrong, deferred gratification, saving, opposition to stereotyping, and appreciation of different people, cultures, and religions" (Hampton et al., *Preventing Violence in America*, 133-34, 148-4).

"Parents can be taught to view television as a resource that needs to be *managed*." The process of establishing priorities and discussing program preferences as a family "makes children think about the issues of gratuitous sex and violence, concepts of right and wrong, and what constitutes viable entertainment. As such, it helps children form their own value systems within the family context" (Hampton et al., *Preventing Violence in America*, 152). It is like the nonviolent direct action modeled by Martin Luther King Jr.: boycotts as protest and as economic pressure for change, and direct action to affirm prosocial programs by contacting stations and managing television in our families.

When I (Glen) was the parent of three young children, I became deeply frustrated that my children were absorbing values from television that subverted the family's values and that my intelligent children were wasting their time on unintelligent programs. I noticed that when they watched more than two hours, they were significantly more likely to get into fights with each other, and so I tried persuading them to watch less and even expressed my own frustrated anger.

Finally, when the TV set stopped working, I called a family meeting. The rules for our family meetings come from 1 Corinthians 14:26-33: only one person is allowed to speak at a time, and everyone listens respectfully, not interrupting. Each has a chance to speak. The group seeks consensus on what the Spirit is leading us to decide. I began the meeting by offering the logical argument that the television was communicating values that undermined our family's values, was wasting our time, was below our level and was seducing us away from more useful ways of spending the hours we had. Therefore it made no sense to put out money to get the TV fixed. Instead we should agree on a worthy charity, and give the money there.

I thought the argument was admirably logical but hardly expected it to achieve consensus with three independent-minded and TV-addicted boys. After some discussion, our oldest son offered a peacemaking proposal: We would get the TV fixed but put a jar on top of it into which everyone would pay a nickel for each half hour of TV he or she watched. (A nickel then would be a dime now, and I was frugal in how much allowance I gave.) That would achieve two objectives: (1) It would pay for the repair, and surplus money generated could be given to a charity; and (2) it would induce us to make intelligent decisions about which programs were really worthwhile and to avoid others. As the discussion proceeded, we agreed that educational television and the news could be free. Because it was not an authoritarian imposition but an idea originated by one of the boys and decided by consensus, it worked. The TV was fixed and the jar was placed on it. The boys cut their amount of TV watching in half, selected more worthwhile programs and made good grades.

In the Sermon on the Mount, Jesus was pointing in the direction of a culture of peacemaking rather than violence. Curbing the influence of violent TV comports with the direction Jesus is pointing.

Undertake Early Training in Conflict Resolution

Research results indicate that "most violent events are preceded by escalation from verbal conflict through insults and threats" (cf. Mt 5:22: "if you are angry with a brother; . . . if you insult a brother, . . . and if you say 'You fool'"). Furthermore, research shows that teaching people to interrupt escalation by mediation and conflict resolution is effective and lasting if they are taught in the early grades. Teaching methods of conflict resolution is much less effective if it does not happen until high school, after habitual responses to conflict have been formed and reinforced by years of practice (Reiss and Roth, *Understanding and Preventing Violence*, 8, 108-9). It is more effective to teach conflict resolution and talking things through early in life, in the family, rather than, as parents, relying on physical dominance and bodily punishment.

"Research on maltreated children and adolescents clearly shows that in interactions with their parents, these children receive less verbal interaction, less approval, less instruction, less shared play, . . . and less reasoning during conflict situations." Research on violent adolescents also shows that their relationships have low amounts of positive emotional expression and communication. Furthermore, "what young people value *more than anything else* are relationships. They want good interpersonal ties and they want to be loved. The contest isn't even close" (Wolfe et al., *Alternatives to Violence*, 97-99). This finding parallels research on attachment, which shows that *warmth and sensitivity by the mother* produces secure attachments and positive child behavior and adjustment. But if children and youth do not learn from their parents to talk about feelings and to reason during conflict situations, then they are likely to be weak in that skill when they become adults. "[N]ot being able to effectively 'talk' it out, abusive individuals 'act' it out, using violent actions to regain control" (Wolfe et al., *Alternatives to Violence*, 95, 97).

This is similar to the findings about males who believe they should dominate. "Typically, fathers who sexually abuse their daughters maintain strict patriarchal family systems where they are the undisputed head of the household. . . . Many households in which violence occurs are characterized by patriarchal family structures where traditional sex roles are encouraged. Men raised in these households are more likely . . . to become violent as adults" (Hampton et al., *Preventing Violence in America*, 214, 216).

On the other hand, families in which the parent(s) are merely permissive, not showing care about how children behave or not being actively involved in teaching patterns and discipline, also tend to produce children with problems. Neither patriarchal authoritarianism nor laissez-faire autonomy works nearly as well as active parental involvement and caring, mutually respectful family cooperation, teaching patterns of behavior, right ways to do things, restraint and self-control (Berger, *Developing Person*, under "parenting styles.")

People might think that men who dominate their families by physical violence feel powerful. But in fact they usually feel relatively powerless. They lack skill in talking about their own emotions, and so they lack power to deal with those emotions. Researchers find that when women are being abused by the men in their life, teaching the women to respond in different ways is not often successful in stopping abuse. What works is to get the men into group counseling. There they can learn skills of talking with others about their feelings in a way that can achieve some positive response—and in a way that can achieve the intimacy they deeply need. And there they can learn restraint; they can learn to identify their own anger and not act it out but instead learn how to make peace.

A longer-term skill involves learning how feelings depend on perceptions and their associated interpretations. Therefore when something causes a person to be angry and to feel powerless, we need to learn to reinterpret it, withhold judgment until all the facts are in and see it from the other's perspective.

"Numerous studies have shown that violence in the home creates a pattern and expectation among children and youth that violence is an appropriate reaction to stress and an effective way to express anger. Children who are abused at home are much more likely to become violent youth" (Hampton et al., *Preventing Violence in America*, 164). African Americans are more likely to use physical violence in disciplining children, including belts, cords, switches, sticks and straps. Hispanic parents are less likely, and white parents are least likely to use physical violence in disciplining. This (and not something intrinsic to race), combined with disproportionate poverty, is a likely explanation of the different homicide rate among the three groups (Hampton et al., *Preventing Violence in America*, 64-65). A study of teenagers discovered "three factors most closely correlated with their perpetration of violence: exposure to violence and victimization in the community, degree of witnessing family conflict, and severity of corporal punishment used at home" (Hampton et al., *Preventing Violence in America*, 69). "Reinforcing positive social behavior, providing positive adult role modeling, and actually teaching children skills such as how to resist negative peer pressure and how to resolve conflicts peacefully are among the most promising approaches for preventing . . . violence" (Hampton et al., *Preventing Violence in America*, 171-72).

It is striking how closely this parallels Jesus' teaching on preventing murder in Matthew 5:21-24. If you realize that some hostility is arising between you and another, drop what you are doing and go, talk with that other, seeking to make peace. This is almost surely Jesus' interpretation of the first story of violence between brothers in a family, Cain and Abel (Gen 4). And a crucial step in conflict resolution is to try to understand how the other person is feeling and thinking. "Love your enemy," Jesus says. "Rejoice with those who rejoice, weep with those who weep," Paul says in Romans 12:15, where he is speaking of how to relate to enemies. He is saying we should identify with and affirm the interests of the other person. This requires talking together to learn the other's concerns: "Welcome one another, therefore, just as Christ has welcomed you" (Rom 15:7). Here again Paul is speaking of how to relate to those with whom we have strong disagreements. He means talk together, have meals together, fellowship together. It is the process of conflict resolution, acted out in practices of fellowship. Christians practice the skills of talking through their feelings and affirming the feelings of others. This needs to be a regular practice in church, in the family and in schools.

Foster Economic Justice

Economic deprivation is a major cause of homicides, especially when it gets worse than people expected. "The national homicide rate has peaked twice in this century; each peak was followed by a decline. The first peak was in the early 1930s," during the Great Depression. As jobs and real income steadily improved, "the [murder] rate then fell for the next 30 years, to reach a low in the early 1960s." When the post-Vietnam stagflation began, the homicide rate began to increase and hit something of a peak about 1989, during the period when the government was canceling job programs, real income of workers and of the poor was declining, and income was being shifted to the wealthy, so that the ratio of income of the wealthy to worker income doubled. Then in the 1990s, as real wages and employment steadily improved, the homicide rate declined steadily each year (Reiss and Roth, *Understanding and Preventing Violence*, 3, 51, 64, and chap. 2; Gurr, *Why Men Rebel*; Sider, *Just Generosity*, 42ff.).

This economic deprivation effect is confirmed in another way: "Rates of abuse—physical and sexual—are 6 times higher for children in families with income under $15,000 than for other children" (Reiss and Roth, *Understanding and Preventing Violence*, 10). Numerous other studies found that "homicides were disproportionately concentrated in areas of poverty. . . . This pattern has held up regardless of which ethnic group occupied the poor areas. . . . Race differences in violent crime rates tend to disappear when poverty is included as an explanation" (Reiss and Roth, *Understanding and Preventing Violence*, 132-33). It follows that job training, assistance to the working poor and greater justice in income distribution are effective ways to cut homicides.

This, too, corresponds with Jesus' teaching in the Sermon on the Mount. In Jesus' time, like ours, the rich were getting richer and the poor were getting poorer—losing their land and their economic base. Both Rome and the local government based in the temple system were taxing those with marginal incomes unjustly (see chapter seventeen). Jesus criticized this system, advocated forgiving debts and practicing the "jubilee" so people's land and means of work would not be taken from them; he emphasized almsgiving, which was the welfare system of the day; and he emphasized justice in using our money (see chapter twenty). In just peacemaking this is the emphasis on sustainable economic development and economic justice.

Focus on Early Detection and Prevention of Violence

How severely should we punish youth crime or how strongly should we push, instead, for positive preventive action? How people answer this is greatly influenced by their view of *authority* and *social change*. The reality of our political culture is that the urge to punish more severely causes laws and money to be invested in building more prisons and causes legislators and executives to pull money and policy away from preventive measures. It is as if those who make ideology for political candidates see prevention as the enemy of punishment. They cast it as softness versus toughness. If the cause of *the threat* of violence is seen as potential criminals not fearing punishment, then the solution advocated will be harsher punishment.

But if the cause of youth crime is personal and social disorganization, then the solution requires greater emphasis on personal and social reform. In that case the authority we need is the kind that works to get disorganized communities organized. Churches can make a big difference by organizing youth activities and youth groups, tutoring programs and job-finding programs. John DiIulio, an excellent social scientist and the first head of President Bush's faith-based initiative, has found a clear correlation between the presence of bars in neighborhoods and high crime rates, on the one hand, and between the presence of churches and low crime, on the other hand.

We saw in chapter six that Jesus warns in Matthew 5:39 that we should not retaliate or resist violently or revengefully, by evil means. We pointed out that this is confirmed by how the apostle Paul reports the teaching in Romans 12:17-21: "Do not repay anyone evil for evil. . . . Beloved, never avenge yourselves, but leave room for the wrath of God." This warns us that the self-righteous urge to blame, hate and punish—the urge to seek revenge—can distort our vision. It does not say there should be no punishment, but it does warn us about the distortion caused by the urge for revenge. Scapegoating is a widespread human phenomenon (Bailie, *Violence Unveiled*). Most of us know that in parenting, anger and the urge to punish children revengefully can cause failure in painful ways. It is more effective to demonstrate and explain the pattern that we want children to adopt, and then help them to practice it rightly. Some of that truth applies to crime. As Jesus said, revenge and hate are not the way of deliverance. Jesus taught instead the positive patterns that lead to deliverance: peacemaking, reconciliation and forgiveness.

During the 1980s, when government funding for job training and job placement was being sharply reduced, the urge to punish was given much greater prominence. Compassion was out; toughness was in. Prison terms were increased, youth were imprisoned with adults, and penalties for possessing illegal drugs were increased greatly. The death penalty was brought back into use.

Yet after ten years of this doubly punitive approach, by the end of the 1980s, the homicide rate hit its historic peak.

What does the research show? Better police-community relations and community policing do help decrease homicides, because police are able to catch criminals sooner. But increasing length of sentences and putting juveniles in adult prisons does not help. "While average prison time served *per violent crime* roughly tripled between 1975 and 1989, reported levels of serious violent crime" did not decrease (Reiss and Roth, *Understanding and Preventing Violence*, 6).

Imprisonment surely does help reduce crime. But the question is whether increasing sentences helps and how much (Reiss and Roth, *Understanding and Preventing Violence*, 291). A small fraction of criminals commits hundreds of crimes per year, and they do tend to get caught and to be given long sentences, because their record is so bad. Increasing sentences tends to apply to those criminals who commit few crimes, so it does not reduce the number of crimes much. "Incapacitation is subject to diminishing marginal returns, because most criminal careers are fairly short. . . . Increasing the chance of incarceration reduces crime levels more efficiently than does increasing the average time served." Increasing the chance of getting caught jails offenders earlier in their careers. It also increases the deterrence effect, because its effect comes sooner, while the longer sentence's effect comes much later (Reiss and Roth, *Understanding and Preventing Violence*, 293-94). Increasing the chance of getting caught requires increasing the police force, doing more community policing and improving police-community relations. This was the emphasis in the 1990s, and the homicide rate dropped every year during that decade. Putting people in jail for longer sentences does not cure the widespread culture of violence (Hampton et al., *Preventing Violence in America*, 197, 202-6).

Evidence suggests, further, that putting juveniles in adult prisons results in a "much lower probability of any treatment while in custody, and an increased risk of subsequent offending when released" (Elliott et al., *Violence in American Schools*, 10-11, 171). In this case the desire to be "tough on crime" simply produces more crime later.

Strengthen Community Organization

Community breakdown is a powerful cause of violence. When neighborhoods are not functioning well, violence is increased by the inability of parents "to distinguish neighborhood youth from outsiders, to band together with other parents to solve common problems, to question each others' children, to participate in voluntary organizations and friendship networks, and to watch neighborhood common areas. Single parents who work have less time for such activities and constant family turnover in large multidwelling housing units makes them more difficult to carry out" (Reiss and Roth, *Understanding and Preventing Violence*, 15).

When middle- and working-class families move out of ghetto areas, community networks of informal social control break down. The remaining residents experience high levels of family disruption and the breakdown of community networks of informal social control. Furthermore, "in studies of neighborhood rates of violent crime, measures of the density of multi-unit housing, residential mobility, and the prevalence of disrupted family structures generally accounted for more variation than did measures of poverty and income inequality" (Reiss and Roth, *Understanding and Preventing Violence*, 131-35).

Community disorganization within schools also causes school violence. A National Institute of Education study "reports higher rates of student violence in schools in which students perceive signs of ineffective social control: undisciplined classrooms, lax or arbitrary enforcement of school rules, and a weak principal." Identification with school values is important: "In secondary schools, violence rates increased with the percentages of students who did not aspire to good grades, who did not view their curricula as relevant, and who did not believe that their school experience could positively influence their lives" (Reiss and Roth, *Understanding and Preventing Violence*, 155-56).

The antidote is to strengthen neighborhood, school and community organization. In Boston, pastors of small African American community-based churches organized the TenPoint Coalition. They were seeing youth in Boston being murdered almost each week and finally asked drug dealers why this was happening. The drug dealers told Pastor Eugene Rivers: "When the kids come out of school in the afternoon, we are there and you are not. When they go out at night, we are there, and you are not. And the result is that we are winning, and you are not." The pastors decided they and their church members needed to get out in the streets and not wait for the youth to come to church. They developed and committed themselves to a ten-point plan. It involved youth evangelism in the streets, including evangelism with young drug traffickers. It involved recruiting church members to establish desperately needed mentoring and tutoring relationships with youth. They developed church programs to help youth prepare for and find jobs. Churches worked to involve youth in church youth activities and community service. Churches actually adopted gangs and showed they cared, working with them actively.

The city of Boston also developed a latticework of coalitions. Besides the TenPoint Coalition, Operation Cease Fire tackled youth firearm violence. Officials met with gang members and told them to cease the violence or face federal prosecution. Operation Night Light ensured that gang-involved youth complied with the terms of probation orders. The U.S. Attorney's Office broke several weapons trafficking operations and gained stiff federal sentences for key gang leaders. The police introduced decentralized neighborhood policing to address local problems. In the Youth Service Providers Network, police officers referred at-risk youngsters to social workers hired by the Boys and Girls Clubs of Boston. The social workers helped youth and their families locate programs tailored to the needs of the youth.

The result of these combined church, police and mentoring programs: 1997 homicide deaths among those twenty-four years of age and younger fell 70 percent from the average of the years 1991-1995; and among juveniles, firearm homicides were down 90 percent in 1997 compared to 1990. A 1997 survey revealed that 76 percent of residents felt safe at night in their neighborhoods, up from 55 percent in 1995. (See the website of the National Crime Prevention Council: <www.ncpc.org/boston.htm>.) This is dramatic confirmation of the just peacemaking practices that focus on building community. In just peacemaking practices, this is the emphasis on supporting forces that build community.

Reduce Handgun Availability

Marian Wright Edelman, director of the Children's Defense Fund (CDF), said in 1994 that 25 American children, the equivalent of an entire classroom, are killed by guns every two days (Hampton et al., *Preventing Violence in America*, 58). According to a CDF study, an average of 135,000 children per day take guns to school. "A 1991 study found that the United States had homicide rates among youth that were eight times higher than the rates in other industrialized countries" (Hampton, *Preventing Violence in America*, 160).

"In 1989 gun attacks resulted in about 12,000 homicides—about 60% of all homicides. In addition . . . 5.7 nonfatal gunshot injuries occur for every homicide. . . . For 1985, Rice and associates estimate the total cost of intentional and unintentional gun injuries at over $14 billion. In gun homicides for which the type of weapon was known, handguns accounted for nearly 80% in 1989, compared with 8% for rifles and 12% for shotguns" (Reiss and Roth, *Understanding and Preventing Violence*, 256-60). How many more deaths will it take to shock Americans into effective action?

A study of King County, Washington, between 1978 and 1983 found that 2% of the gunshot deaths occurred in self-protection; 98% were suicides, murders, or accidents. People justify handguns because they are intended for self-protection, but, overwhelmingly, their actual use is for self-destruction. Another study of 88 cases where young children in California fatally shot a playmate or themselves concluded that "75% occurred while children were playing with a gun or demonstrating its use" (Reiss and Roth, *Understanding and Preventing Violence*, 267). "Comparing experience in Seattle and Vancouver, two neighboring jurisdictions that are demographically and socio-economically similar but have different gun laws, Sloane et al. (1988) found no differences in . . . burglary and simple and aggravated assault rates—but Seattle, which has more permissive gun laws, had an overall homicide rate more than 60% higher and a firearm homicide rate 400% higher" (Reiss and Roth, *Understanding and Preventing Violence*, 268).

The 1977 Washington, D.C., law that prohibited handgun ownership by virtually everyone except police officers, security guards and previous gun owners was evaluated in three studies. "During periods of vigorous enforcement, the D.C. law did reduce the rates of gun robbery, assault, and homicide during the three years following implementation. The effect was especially strong for homicides arising from disputes among family members and acquaintances." There were "decreases of about one-fourth in D.C. gun homicides and suicides immediately after passage of the law. The effect . . . was not mirrored by trends in D.C. nongun homicides or suicides, or in gun homicides or suicides in nearby suburban areas that were not subject to the law" (Reiss and Roth, *Understanding and Preventing Violence*, 278). This latter comment indicates that other factors were not causing a decrease in homicides generally, apart from the effects of the law.

Notice that the issue is handguns, not hunting rifles. Handguns can be put in a pocket or a backpack and carried around the neighborhood or taken to school without being seen; rifles do not fit in a pocket. Rifles are hard to conceal and not likely to be used in robberies. They are more likely to be used in hunting or target-shooting, or even in defense. They have built-in transparency. There is almost no ambiguity about whether the rifle-carrier is armed. Handguns contrast on all these points. There is a similar issue with automatic weapons designed for killing people in war, not for hunting.

"[T]he gun-control debate concentrates on stranger crime rather than on the more common ways guns are used—that is, between or among acquaintances and family members" (Hampton et al., *Preventing Violence in America*, 44). Swords were what people used instead of handguns in Jesus' day. Jesus told his disciple to put up his sword: "All who take the sword will perish by the sword" (Mt 26:52). We showed in the last chapter that this is not merely one isolated proof text, but a theme in Jesus' teaching and practice.

The controversy over handgun control uncovers different understandings of the authority variable. Those who oppose handgun control tend to view authority as something imposed by force and power. On the one hand they seem to be libertarians, defending individual liberty to have handguns over against government authority to defend the right to life and to decrease killing. And on the other hand they seem to be authoritarian, defending their own authority to have the force and power to shoot intruders. What these opposites have in common is the assumption that authority is imposed by force.

On the other hand, those who favor handgun control tend to view authority as growing out of consent and cooperation. They see government having the legitimate obligation to defend the right to life against violence, based on the consent of the large majority who want handgun control. And they see our own safety as depending on working together to nurture a more healthy community with authority based on free discussion, consent and legitimacy. Both groups see authority as limited, but pro-handgun advocates see the constitutional provision allowing the people to form an armed militia as a crucial limit to governmental authority, while handgun control advocates see consent of the people within constitutional provisions as the crucial limit to governmental authority. In just peacemaking practice, this is called "reducing offensive weapons and weapons trade."

Encourage Spirituality and Other Forces for Resiliency

Another direction of research comes from noticing that in spite of a disruptive background, some youth still succeed and avoid serious trouble. Scholars label this "resiliency." Focusing attention on factors leading to resiliency shifts the focus from what causes some to turn out violent to what causes most to turn out nonviolent. Such a shift has been a recent trend among researchers. See, for example, the violence prevention program for workplaces designed by Joseph Kinney, focusing on "anchors" like a secure family life, stable finances, outside interests, religious life, friendships, emotional stability, a positive work history and lack of substance abuse (VandenBos and Bulatao, *Violence on the Job*, 273).

The Search Institute in Minneapolis shares this focus. They have identified forty factors that "help young people grow up healthy, caring, and responsible." They tested for these factors by asking over a million youth in the sixth to twelfth grades to rate themselves. And then they asked the same youth if they engage in specific kinds of "risky behavior." The self-report of the youth indicates that those who have a larger number of the forty assets are dramatically less violent and less engaged in self-destructive behavior. (This and the following information come from their website <www.search-institute.org> as well as Benson et al., *Fragile Foundation*.)

Twenty of the questions were designed to indicate "external assets." A youth who had all twenty external assets—which is unlikely—would give affirmative answers as follows: I have a family life with high levels of love and support, and positive communication with parent(s) in which I am willing to seek advice. I have support from three or more other caring adults and a caring neighborhood and community that value youth; a school that provides a caring, encouraging environment, with parent involvement in helping me succeed in school. Adults value youth and give youth useful roles in the community; and I serve in the community one hour or more per week. I feel safe at home, at school and in the neighborhood. My family has clear rules and consequences, and monitors my whereabouts; the school does also, and the neighbors also take responsibility. Parent(s) and other adults model positive, responsible behavior, and parents and teachers encourage me to do well. I spend significant time each week in lessons or practice in music, theater or other arts; in sports, clubs or organizations at school or in community organizations; or in activities in a religious institution, and I spend no more than two nights per week out with friends "with nothing special to do."

The other twenty questions were designed to indicate "internal assets": I am motivated to do well in school, actively engaged in learning, do at least one hour of homework every school day, care about my school, read for pleasure three or more hours per week and place high value on helping other people and on promoting equality and reducing hunger and poverty. I act on convictions and stand up for my beliefs, can resist negative peer pressure, tell the truth even when it is not easy, accept and take personal responsibility, and believe it is important not to be sexually active or to use alcohol or other drugs. I know how to plan ahead and make choices; have empathy, sensitivity and friendship skills; and have knowledge of and comfort with people of different cultural, racial and or ethnic backgrounds. I seek to resolve conflict nonviolently. My life has a purpose, and I am optimistic about my personal future.

The researchers conclude, "These assets are powerful influences on adolescent behavior, both protecting young people from many different problem behaviors and promoting positive attitudes and behaviors. This power is evident across all cultural and socioeconomic groups of youth. There is also evidence from other research that assets have the same kind of power for younger children."

The following chart summarizes what the researchers have found about the power of these assets. Among the key findings is that those with thirty-one or more assets have only one-tenth as many members who have engaged in violence and other self-destructive activity as the first group has.

Table 8.1. The more healthy assets, the less the risky behavior

Assets for Resilience	0-10	11-20	21-30	31-40
Problem Alcohol Use	53 %	30 %	11 %	3 %
Illicit Drug Use	42 %	19 %	6 %	1 %
Sexual Activity	33 %	21 %	10 %	3 %
Violence	61 %	35 %	10 %	6 %

It seems clear that we have a big stake in nurturing the kind of communities that provide the external assets and encourage youth to develop the internal assets. The Search Institute concludes:

> Yet, while the assets are powerful shapers of young people's lives and choices, too few young people experience enough of these assets. The average young person surveyed experiences only 18 of the 40 assets. Overall, 62 percent of young people surveyed experience fewer than 20 of the assets. In short, most young people in the United States do not have in their lives many of the basic building blocks of healthy development. (Benson, *Fragile Foundation*)

There are some criticisms that can be raised about the methodology and focus employed in the Search study (see Baumeister and Boden, "Aggression and Self," 132ff.). Nevertheless, the correlations they have found between the assets and avoidance of destructive behavior is dramatic. And the Search Institute has developed numerous helpful practical publications for nurturing these assets in families, churches, neighborhoods and schools. These assets resemble the practices in just peacemaking theory in the categories of "community" and "voluntary associations."

Little research has linked spirituality with adolescent development, and when it does, it usually focuses on social control rather than social support. Thomas and Carver's review of literature, however, "shows that religious involvement and commitment are consistently related to increases in the abilities and skills required for adequate functioning in society and to decreases in the likelihood of participating in activities that are devalued in society." They also show that a faith-mentor relationship can help youth set prosocial goals (Hampton et al., *Preventing Violence in America*, 122). The Search Institute concludes that "when parents act in ways that are congruent with their stated beliefs and provide a warm, supportive atmosphere for their youth at home and in the church, youth are likely to develop values similar to those of their parents . . . both *discussion* of values and *consistent demonstration* are necessary for this transfer to occur" (Hampton et al., *Preventing Violence in America,* 122, 124).

Robert Coles tells how an eight-year-old black girl's faith in God transformed a violent situation to one of peace:

> I was all alone and those [segregationist] people were screaming, and suddenly I saw God smiling and I smiled. . . . A woman was standing there [near the school door], and she shouted at me "Hey you little nigger, what you smiling at?" I looked right at her face and I said, "At God." Then she looked up at the sky, and then she looked at me, and she didn't call me any more names. (Hampton et al., *Preventing Violence in America,* 124-27)

9

RESTORATIVE PENALTIES
FOR HOMICIDE

—

For if you forgive others the wrongs they have done, your heavenly Father will also forgive
you; but if you do not forgive others, then the wrongs you have done will not be forgiven
by your Father.

MATTHEW 6:14-15 NEB

Visiting with families of a homicide victim convinces you quickly that murder leaves more than one victim. It is a devastating experience, and its effects last. We think of one family in Texas that desperately wanted the death penalty for the murderer of their son, hoping it would somehow make things right. They went to the trial, hoping it would provide some catharsis or release for their feelings of disbelief, shock, grief, disempowerment, endangerment, anger and resentment. The murderer did get sentenced to death, as they had hoped, but that did not assuage their inner turmoil. They even went to the execution, but it did not help either. Their nephew observes that the resentment and feeling of disempowerment and victimization are eating them alive. Their resentment is killing their spirits, making them into victims too.

By contrast, my (Glen) former pastor Jim Cook tells how tragic murders happened to two different persons in our church, but church members rallied around the families of the victims. They helped those families work through the agony and anguish to a remarkable sense of forgiveness and healing, through solidarity with fellow church members. It was a dramatic witness to the power of the gospel to heal, through the community of the church.

Similarly, Mary Sue Penn tells how Bill Pelke at first agreed with the death sentence given to Paula Cooper for senselessly murdering his grandmother during a petty theft (Stassen, *Capital Punishment*, 10ff.). But four months later,

Bill was distraught over the breakup of his marriage and his own imminent bankruptcy. As he was tearfully praying, God gave Bill insight into the needs of another:

> And it was at that point where I began to picture somebody with a whole lot more problems than I had. I pictured Paula Cooper slumped in the corner of her cell with tears in her eyes, saying, "What have I done, what have I done?". . .
>
> Then suddenly he pictured his grandmother. . . . But this time she had tears coming down her cheeks. "There was no doubt in my mind that they were tears of love and compassion for Paula and for her family. I was convinced that she wanted someone in our family to have that same love and compassion.
>
> "At that point I started thinking about forgiveness and how I was raised and what the Bible had to say. I recalled how Christ was crucified, nailed in his hands and his feet, with a crown of thorns in his brow, and he looked up to heaven and said, 'Father, forgive them, they know not what they're doing.' I basically thought that's where Paula fit in. I mean she didn't know what she was doing— that was a crazy act that took place in my grandmother's house."

So Pelke started to pray for God to give him love and compassion for Paula and her family. He decided then and there to write Paula and share his grandmother's faith with her. "I knew immediately that I no longer wanted her to die and I no longer had to try to forgive her—forgiveness at that point was automatic."

He has since exchanged more than two hundred letters with her. He has learned that Paula Cooper, a victim of child abuse who attended ten different schools by the time of her arrest, has received the equivalent of a high school diploma while in prison and has been taking college correspondence courses. She has told Pelke she feels remorse for the pain she caused him and his family. She knows she will have to live with her past actions. She wants to help young people avoid the pitfalls she experienced.

Forgiveness changed everything. It no longer made sense to Pelke to hold a grudge. Participating in groups that work to prevent murders is a far more effective way of empowerment than just accepting the role of powerless victim. So Bill Pelke joined Murder Victims' Families for Reconciliation. Together they seek to overcome their rage and hurt and to prevent murder.

This focus fits Jesus' teaching in the Beatitudes on the virtue of mercy. Recall that mercy in Jesus' teaching has two dimensions of meaning. Mercy means forgiveness that delivers from the bondage of guilt, as we see in the cleansing commitment to mercy that Bill Pelke experienced. And mercy means action that delivers from need, affliction and bondage, as we see in his joining a group that works to deliver us from the vicious cycles that cause homicide. Disciples who follow Jesus practice forgiveness, and they practice deeds of deliverance. They practice forgiveness even for murder, and they practice deeds that prevent murders. This is what Jesus teaches in Matthew 5:21-24, 38-42 and 43-48, as we saw in chapter seven. The way of deliverance is to turn concerns about murder and revenge into transforming initiatives that heal causes of murder at their roots and prevent more murders from taking place. Jesus' way is not a way of living in anger and resentment, but a way of deliverance from vicious cycles and into transforming initiatives that build community.

Many politicians turn legitimate concerns about murder and the desire for revenge into advocacy of the death penalty. Majority support for the death penalty in most polls that do not name an alternative has for decades led even politicians with doubts about this practice to offer public support for it.

But many careful statistical studies over decades have demonstrated that this is the way of powerlessness. They show clearly that despite the emotional satisfaction some draw from its existence, the death penalty does not reduce the murder rate. On the one hand it seems common sense that it must have a *deterrent effect* on those potential murderers who rationally calculate what the possible penalty might be before they make a rational decision to commit a murder. (Although, as District Attorney John O'Hair of Detroit, who has been a judge and prosecutor for thirty years, points out, "most homicides are impulsive actions, crimes of passion, in which the killers do not consider the consequences of what they are doing" [Bonner and Fessenden, "States Without the Death Penalty," A19]. The fact that only a small number of murderers are actually ever executed further reduces any deterrent value it might possess.)

On the other hand the evidence seems clear that the death penalty has a paradoxical *imitative effect* on other potential murderers: it sets an official governmental example that killing someone is a proper way to resolve feelings of resentment and to slake the desire for revenge. This ends up cheapening the value of human life and actually causes a boomerang effect that increases the murder rate. The *imitative effect* can be seen in four ways (Stassen, *Capital Punishment*, 2ff., 5ff., 62, 100 n. 13, 128, 130 n. 22; see also the Girardian theory of mimetic violence described in Bailie, *Violence Unveiled*):

1. After the government carries out an execution, the murder rate in the area where the execution takes place tends to increase.
2. Murder rates are higher in states that have the death penalty.
3. When a nation goes to war, the government unavoidably, though perhaps reluctantly, sets an example that killing enemies is the right thing to do. Homicide rates increase inside that nation during wartime.
4. Returning veterans who have participated in war unfortunately have a higher murder rate.

All four sets of data point to an *imitative effect*. The net effect of having the death penalty is an increase in the murder rate. An extensive study by *The New York Times* (Bonner and Fessenden, "States Without the Death Penalty," A1) showed that states without the death penalty have lower homicide rates than states with the death penalty. Ten of the twelve states without the death penalty have homicide rates below the national average, whereas half of the states with the death penalty have homicide rates above it. During the last twenty years, the homicide rate in states with the death penalty has been 48 percent to 101 percent higher than in states without the death penalty. Matching states that do have the death penalty with similar states that do not have it, such as South Dakota with North Dakota, Virginia with West Virginia, and Connecticut and Rhode Island with Massachusetts, shows the homicide rate higher in those states that do execute murderers.

In 1972 the Supreme Court temporarily banned the death penalty (in *Furman* v. *Georgia*) because it was racially and economically biased and essentially arbitrary in its application, but the majority of states changed their laws and resumed the death penalty after the Supreme Court again permitted it in 1976. In the twenty-one states that carried out their first executions by 1993, homicide rates declined a collective 5 percent over the four years after the execution. But rates declined 12 percent in states that had not had executions in the same years.

Turning victims' families toward advocating the death penalty turns their emotions toward what does not work. It heads them into resentful powerlessness even when executions are actually carried out. Worse, it diverts them away from proven methods that actually do work to prevent murders (see chapter eight above). Catching murderers, trying them promptly and imprisoning them both punishes murder and decreases the murder rate. We believe it is the best approach and that it fits with the way of Jesus, as we shall attempt to show.

The Key: Beginning with Jesus as Lord

One way to study biblical teaching on the death penalty is to begin with Jesus Christ as Lord, and with the commitment to be followers of Jesus, denying that there is some other lord we should follow instead. Then we ask first what Jesus taught on the death penalty as a response to murder.

Matthew 5:21-24 is about preventing murder. Jesus began by citing the traditional teaching of the Ten Commandments, "You shall not murder" (Ex 20:13). The Ten Commandments do not prescribe any specific penalty. Nor did Jesus prescribe the death penalty. He said, "You have heard that it was said . . . 'whoever murders shall be liable to judgment,'" but he avoided saying what the judgment will be. He did not quote Old Testament passages that prescribe the death penalty for murderers, like Exodus 21:12, Numbers 35:16-34 or Leviticus 24:17. Jesus is here consistent with a pattern we see throughout the Gospels: whenever he quoted an Old Testament teaching, he always omitted any parts of the teaching that advocate violence or nationalistic triumph against enemies. He avoided the violent parts of the teaching so systematically that it must not be happenstance. Jesus' teachings are always consistent with the sacredness of human life and with initiatives to heal vicious cycles of killing.

Then Jesus pointed to practices that cause murder: continuing in a growing anger and calling the brother fool in an escalation of rage (Mt 5:22). Here he was diagnosing, naming vicious cycles that lead to murder. As the way of deliverance from these causes of murder, he commanded us to make peace with the one who is angry with us or is accusing us (Mt 5:23-26).

Similarly, Matthew 5:38-42 is about preventing violent retaliation. The "law of retaliation" (lex talionis) is taught in only three places in the Old Testament; it is not right to characterize the Old Testament, over against the New, as emphasizing or consistently demanding retaliation. Notice what Jesus omitted in citing the three Old Testament passages: Exodus 21:23-24 says "life for life, eye for eye, tooth for tooth." Deuteronomy 19:21 says "life for life, eye for eye, tooth for tooth." Leviticus 24:20-21 says "eye for eye, tooth for tooth; . . . one who kills a human being shall be put to death." Jesus omitted "life for life" and "shall be put to death." Again, we see the pattern: he quoted Old Testament passages but specifically omitted the part that advocates the violent solution of taking the life of the murderer.

Then Jesus named the vicious cycle as violent or revengeful retaliation (Mt 5:39). Such revengeful retaliation leads to more killing. He said we should not be retaliating revengefully against evil or by evil means. He commanded us instead to take four transforming initiatives that deliver us from the vicious cycle of retaliation and that prevent killing (Mt 5:39-42).

If the Old Testament teaching of "life for life" is understood as a command to limit revenge by killing only the killer and not the killer's family, as most scholars believe, then Jesus was here taking a further leap in the same direction, limiting murderous revenge all the way down to zero. If "life for life" is understood as justifying or requiring the death penalty, then Jesus was directly opposing it. "Do not retaliate revengefully" (Mt 5:39). Either way, Jesus opposed taking a life as retribution for a life. The apostle Paul made this clear in Romans 12:19, which most New Testament scholars believe reflects Jesus' teaching against retaliation: "Beloved, never avenge yourselves, but leave room for the wrath of God; for it is written, 'Vengeance is mine, I will repay, says the Lord.'"

The third teaching is Matthew 5:43-48. Here Jesus taught that our response to our enemy is to be love, not hate. We are to give enemies love and prayer, not hate and vengeance, as God gives sun and rain to God's enemies.

If our only resource for thinking about the death penalty were Jesus' teaching in the Sermon on the Mount, if we forgot about all other customs, habits, practices and teachings, and had only Jesus' teaching as our Scripture, we would surely say that followers of Jesus are not people who seek retaliation by taking life for life, but instead they seek ways of deliverance from such vicious cycles of adding more killing to killing. They seek to take initiatives that deliver from the vicious cycles that lead to homicide (see chapter eight). Jesus' teaching is not the only resource we have in Scripture on this issue; but some interpreters act as if it is not there at all.

Jesus was confronted by the death penalty directly in John 8. The scribes and Pharisees made a woman stand before him to be judged. "Teacher, this woman was caught in the very act of committing adultery. Now in the law Moses commanded us to stone such women. Now what do you say? . . . They said this to test him, so that they might have some charge to bring against him" (Jn 8:3-5). If he had replied flatly, "God's mercy forbids the death penalty," they could have charged him with the blasphemy of disagreeing with Moses and stoned him. Jesus answered, " 'Let anyone among you who is without sin throw the first stone.' When they heard it, they went away, one by one; . . . and Jesus was left alone with the woman standing before him. Jesus . . . said to her, 'Woman, where are they? Has no one condemned you?' She said, 'No one, sir.' And Jesus said, 'Neither do I condemn you. Go your way, and from now on do not sin again' " (Jn 8:7-11).

Theologian Raymond E. Brown concludes: "The delicate balance between the justice of Jesus in not condoning the sin and his mercy in forgiving the sinner is one of the great gospel lessons" (Brown, *Gospel According to John*, 336ff.). Jesus released the woman from the death penalty. But he admonished her not to commit adultery again.

Bishop Lowell Erdahl says the accusers "were convicted of their own sins and accepted the fact that there is no justification for the vengeful execution of one sinner by another. If all Christians had followed their example, there would have been no blessing of capital punishment in Christian history" (Erdahl, *Pro-Life/Pro-Peace*, 114). He points out that this fits Jesus' consistent character and teaching. "The woman's accusers knew enough about Jesus to expect that he might oppose her execution. We too are not surprised. . . . We would be shocked if Jesus had said, '. . .Go ahead and kill this wretched sinner.'"

Genesis 9:6 as the Key?

Those who favor the death penalty and argue for it biblically often take as their key passage not Jesus' teaching but Genesis 9:6: "Whoever sheds the blood of a human, by a human (shall or will) that person's blood be shed" (e.g., House, "In Favor of the Death Penalty," 39-47; Murray in Clark and Rakestraw, *Readings in Christian Ethics*, 2:457-58; Vellenga in Stassen, *Capital Punishment*, 132). They take this verse to be a legal command, part of God's covenant with Noah and obligatory on all humankind. Because it is pre-Mosaic rather than a part of Jewish law, they argue, it is universally applicable and not limited to Israel. They avoid advocating what, interpreted as universal law, this passage would teach—that all killers, including accidental, manslaughter, defensive killing, killing with mitigating factors, or killing in war, must be put to death. Instead they advocate only what would correspond roughly with legal practice in the United States. Thus, it is fair to conclude that U.S. secular practice shapes their biblical interpretation, consciously or not.

They then let their interpretation of this passage govern how they interpret the rest of the Bible. They usually overlook the examples of murderers whom God did not want killed, like Cain, who murdered his own brother out of pre-meditated jealousy. Found out, he cried, "'I shall be a fugitive and a wanderer on the earth, and anyone who meets me may kill me.' Then the LORD said to him, 'Not so!' . . . And the LORD put a mark on Cain, so that no one who came upon him would kill him" (Gen 4:14-15). Similarly, Moses was seen in the act of murder and instead of receiving the death penalty was chosen by God to deliver his people from slavery (Ex 2:11—3:12).

David committed adultery with the beautiful Bathsheba and then had Bathsheba's husband killed, thus twice deserving the death penalty, according to the Mosaic law. Nathan the prophet confronted him, saying, "You have smitten Uriah the Hittite with the sword, and have taken his wife to be your wife." At this David confessed his sin, "and Nathan said to David, 'The LORD has put away your sin; you shall not die'" (2 Sam 12:9, 13 RSV). Accused of adultery, Tamar admitted she had committed adultery with her father-in-law, an act specifically requiring the death penalty. She was allowed to live, and her adultery produced an ancestor of David and Jesus (Gen 38; Mt 1:3; Lk 3:33). The book of Hosea tells how Gomer committed adultery repeatedly, and Hosea, not without great pain, forgave her, welcoming her back into their covenant relationship. In this forgiveness Hosea saw a picture of God's willingness to forgive his people for their "whoring" after other gods.

These interpreters also tend to bypass the fact that the first five books of the Bible also command the death penalty for owning an animal that kills people (Ex 21:29); kidnapping (Ex 21:16; Deut 24:7); giving false witness against a defendant in a death penalty trial (Deut 19:16-21); for a stubborn son's disobedience to his mother or father, or a child's cursing or striking a parent (Ex 21:15, 17; Lev 20:9; Deut 21:18-21); adultery (Lev 20:10); bestiality (Ex 22:19); homosexual practice (Lev 20:13); witchcraft and sorcery (Lev 20:27); sabbath-breaking (Ex 31:14); false claim to be a prophet (Deut 18:20-22); and blasphemy (Lev 24:15-16). Proponents of the death penalty either overlook these other crimes that require the death penalty or say that "Jesus freed believers from the judicial authority of the Law" (House, "In Favor of the Death Penalty, 60). But Jesus apparently did not free believers from the law of Genesis 9:6. They say Genesis 9:6 is a covenant with Noah, father of all who survived the flood, and so does apply to all; or is based on our being made in the image of God and so differs from all the other Old Testament Law (House, "In Favor of the Death Penalty," 39-40; Murray in Clark and Rakestraw, *Readings in Social Ethics*, 2:459-60).

Genesis 9:6 also dominates their interpretation of Jesus. In three ways they teach that Jesus added nothing to the conclusion they have reached from Genesis 9:6. (1) Jesus "said nothing specific about the death penalty" (House, "In Favor of the Death Penalty," 61; Murray in Clark and Rakestraw, *Readings in Social Ethics*, 2:460); "Capital punishment never became an issue for Jesus" (House, "In Favor of the Death Penalty," 65). (2) Jesus "centers on personal responses . . . the attitude more than the act" (House, "In Favor of the Death Penalty," 62). (3) His teachings were not "directed to the governmental authorities of his day" (House, "In Favor of the Death Penalty," 62).

House draws a threefold conclusion: Jesus (a) "accepted it [the death penalty] (b) as a valid exercise of governmental authority and (c) a proper part of the Mosaic Code" (63). This conclusion that Jesus accepted the death penalty is drawn by the same author who two pages previously said Jesus said nothing specific about the death penalty. The conclusion that Jesus accepted it "as a valid exercise of governmental authority" is drawn by the same author who one page earlier said Jesus did not direct his teachings to governmental authority. The conclusion that Jesus affirmed the Mosaic Code is drawn by the same author who three pages earlier said Jesus freed believers from the Mosaic Code. What might appear triply contradictory is explained by House's commitment to maintaining Genesis 9:6 as the universally valid law for present-day practice by governments. Therefore he fences Jesus off from saying anything that might suggest a different insight or interpretation of Genesis 9:6. And then he turns Jesus into confirming Genesis 9:6 as law for governments. Jesus is not allowed to say anything that could differ from his interpretation of Genesis 9:6 but is allowed to confirm that interpretation.

It is striking how different this is from the approach we are taking. The method of House and others systematically avoids learning anything positive from Jesus and instead takes Genesis 9:6 as the dominant authority. Thus Vellenga (in Stassen, *Capital Punishment*, 132-35) establishes the Old Testament's teaching on the basis of Genesis 9:6 and the law of retaliation passages in the Old Testament, and then states the New Testament adds nothing new: "The teachings of the New Testament are in harmony with the Old Testament." And Jesus' teachings "did not meddle with laws," did not say "that laws should be changed" and "were not propaganda to change jurisprudence." "Rather, the whole trend is that the church leave matters of justice and law enforcement to the government in power. . . . Natural law and order must prevail." Thus in two ways Vellenga fences Jesus off from saying anything new about the subject, and says that Christians must instead let the secular government in power set our standards.

Similarly, House fences off Jesus' teaching regarding the death penalty for the woman caught in adultery: He says it applies only to adultery, not murder. Furthermore, it is only about forgiveness, not about the death penalty.

By contrast, we take Jesus' teaching as the key and interpret Genesis through Jesus, not the other way around. Jesus echoed Genesis 9:6 when his disciple took up his sword to cut off the ear of one of the soldiers. Jesus told him to put up the sword: "All who take the sword, by the sword will die" (Mt 26:52, literal translation). Here Jesus interpreted the teaching not as a command that every sword-user should be given the death penalty, but as a proverb that predicts the likely consequence of relying on the sword: you are likely to end up getting killed (Hobbs in Clark and Rakestraw, *Readings in Christian Ethics*, 2:464; Smedes, *Mere Morality*, 119-20; Stassen, *Capital Punishment*, 129 n. 1; Yoder in Clark and Rakestraw, *Readings in Christian Ethics*, 2:472-76).

And indeed, careful examination of Genesis 9:6 leads some of the best biblical scholars to conclude that it is a proverb, not a command. As Claus Westermann, the Old Testament scholar who has written what is widely recognized as the most authoritative commentary on Genesis, explains, the embarrassment is that scholars do not agree whether Genesis 9:6 is a legal penalty, a prophetic admonition or a proverb (Westermann, *Genesis 1—11*, 467).

The disagreement has developed because the passage shows the influence of ancient traditional laws of revenge but has the form of a proverb and not a law. In other words, as it stands in Genesis, it does not command the death penalty but gives wise advice based on the likely consequence of your action: if you kill someone, you will end up being killed. Both Westermann in his commentary on Genesis and Hagner in his commentary on Matthew see Jesus as interpreting the meaning of Genesis 9:6 in Matthew 26:52. And Jesus clearly interprets it as a proverb, teaching "the generally true principle that violence begets violence" (Hagner, *Matthew 14—28*, 789). Both teachings in the original biblical languages are in chiastic order and teach proverbial wisdom. This fits the fact that nowhere in the Old Testament do we see an actual case where what seem like prescriptions of the death penalty for various offenses were carried out by an Israelite criminal law system. They actually function more like declarations of the great moral seriousness of these offenses. They do not function as criminal laws (McKeating, "Development of the Law," 61-67; "Sanctions Against Adultery," 58-59, 66-67).

John Howard Yoder also interprets Genesis 9:6 from the perspective of Jesus as Lord. He sees Genesis 9:6 as having its meaning both as a proverb and as a sacrificial expiation of sin (Clark and Rakestraw, *Readings in Christian Eth-*

ics, 2:474-80). A strong argument has also been made that the death penalty functions in U.S. society as a quasi-religious ritual of scapegoating and sacrificial expiation of sin (McBride in Stassen, *Capital Punishment,* 182ff.). Yoder argues that since Jesus' death is the once-for-all sacrifice for expiating sin, then it is heretical to insist that others pay the penalty of death as expiation for sin again. It is necessary to punish their wrongdoing; it is not necessary to require from them a blood sacrifice.

We should test "all things for whether they are compatible with Christ (1 Cor. 12:1-3, 1 John 4:1-2)." "Our interest should . . . be to discern, *in the midst* of this complexity, what the Christian gospel has to say" (Yoder, "Against the Death Penalty," 159). The culmination of the gospel story "is that the Cross of Christ puts an end to sacrifice for sin. . . . The Epistle to the Hebrews takes as its central theme the way the death of Christ is the end of all sacrifice" (Yoder, "Against the Death Penalty," 159, 176; Yoder in Clark and Rakestraw, *Readings in Christian Ethics,* 2:474ff.).

> Christians begin to deny their Lord when they admit that there are certain realms of life in which it would be inappropriate to bring Christ's rule to bear. Of course, non-Christians will insist that we should keep our *religion* out of the way of their *politics.* But the reason for that is not that Jesus has nothing to do with the public realm; it is that they want nothing to do with Jesus as Lord. . . . What we believe about Christ must apply to all our behavior, no matter how many of our neighbors remain unconvinced. (Yoder, "Against the Death Penalty," 144)

Was Jesus' Crucifixion Unjust?

Proponents and opponents of the death penalty also tend to interpret the cross differently. Opponents say Jesus' trial was unjust, and the plots by the authorities to have Jesus crucified were sinful. One part of the work of the cross in atoning for sin is its disclosure of the depth of sin in humankind: we are so sinful that we killed God's Son. As Jesus himself taught, "The tenants took his servants and beat one, killed another, and stoned another. Again he sent other servants, more than the first; and they did the same to them. Afterward he sent his son to them, saying, 'They will respect my son.' But when the tenants saw the son, they said to themselves, 'This is the heir; come, let us kill him and have the inheritance.' And they took him and cast him out of the vineyard, and killed him." Jesus then predicted judgment. "The chief priest and the Pharisees . . . perceived that he was speaking about them" (Mt 21:37-45).

All have sinned, profoundly—Christians, Jews and Gentiles. Jesus was betrayed by a disciple and deserted by the disciples; his crucifixion was demanded by Jewish authorities; he was crucified by Gentile Roman authority and soldiers. The Gospel accounts make clear that Jesus was falsely accused and unjustly condemned (for example, Jn 18:38). Ironically, Barabbas, who was actually guilty of the crime of insurrection that Jesus was falsely accused of, was freed in Jesus' place. This was clearly unjust. Jesus said from the cross, "Father, forgive them, for they know not what they do" (Lk 23:34). The reason they needed forgiveness is that they were doing terrible wrong. The New Testament witness is that God used their wrong to bring forgiveness and redemption, and this includes the disclosure of their sin and injustice in crucifying Jesus. Christians who remember that their Lord was unjustly and cruelly given the death penalty have a hard time being enthusiastic about imposing the death penalty on others. The cross on Christian churches signifies not that we should advocate more crosses for others, but that we are all sinners needing the mercy offered at the cross. We are not to seek vengeance (Rom 12:19). We are to love our enemies and seek to do mercy (Lk 6:35-36).

Proponents of the death penalty argue that the cross shows Jesus approved of the death penalty. Hence they usually avoid mentioning that this death penalty was sinful, a terrible wrong, unjust. If asked, they would surely agree that the cross discloses human sin, but they argue that it discloses the death penalty is right. William H. Baker (*On Capital Punishment*, 57ff.) refers to a conversation in John 19 between Jesus and the Roman colonial government authority, Pontius Pilate, as Pilate is about to sentence Jesus to death. Pilate asserted he has authority to crucify Jesus. Jesus answered, "You would have no authority over me, unless it had been given you from above; for this reason he who delivered me up to you has the greater sin."

Jesus was clearly saying that what Pilate was doing was wrong, a sin. Yet Baker argues that this shows God approves of the death penalty and governmental authority to order the death penalty. Baker and Pilate both *think* the conversation was about Pilate's secular authority. But read in context, John is clearly showing that Pilate misunderstood what the topic was. Jesus was speaking of God's power to bring about the hour of redemption, when he would die so that we would live. Pilate played a role in *this* death only because God was allowing it. He thought the topic was his power to command legions and kill people. Jesus was speaking of God's gift of redemption, not engaging in a discussion of whether God approves of the death penalty (Culpepper, *Anatomy of the Fourth Gospel*, 161, 172). As Raymond Brown says, "No one can take Jesus' life from him; he alone has power to lay it down. However, now Jesus has voluntarily entered 'the hour' appointed by his Father (12:37) when he will lay down his life. In the context of 'the hour' therefore, the Father has permitted men to have power over Jesus' life" (see Brown, *Gospel According to John*, 892-93).

The Gospels make clear that the governmental authorities acted unjustly in sentencing Jesus to death. By no means do they teach that giving the death penalty to Jesus was justice. Baker himself admits that "Pilate allowed a mis-

carriage of justice to take place." To use this miscarriage of justice as an argument for the rightness of the death penalty suggests desperation to find a New
Testament rationalization for a preconceived conviction.

All Death Penalties in the New Testament Are Unjust

Baker makes a similar argument concerning Acts 25:11, although he admits the
passage does not have "the express purpose of teaching anything about the subject of capital punishment" (*On Capital Punishment*, 62ff.). The point of the passage is the apostle Paul's defense against accusers who want to kill him. Paul
said: "*if* I . . . have committed anything worthy of death." He knew he did not
deserve the death penalty. The authorities twice explicitly declared they found
that "he had done nothing deserving of death" (Acts 25:25; 26:31). What Paul
said was not that he approved of the death penalty but that he was not afraid to
die. Likewise in Philippians 1:21 he said, "For me to live is Christ and to die is
gain." His defense told how he had once voted for the death penalty for Christians as blasphemers, and how he had now repented for his action (Acts 26).

Nowhere in the New Testament did the followers of Jesus advocate the
death penalty. The New Testament describes ten instances of the death penalty
being threatened or imposed. In each case the death penalty is presented as an
injustice: the beheading of John the Baptist (Mt 14:1-12); the crucifixion of Jesus
(Jn 18:38); the stoning of Stephen (Acts 7); the stoning of other Christians (Mt
21:35; 23:37; Jn 10:31-32; Acts 14:5); Herod's killing of James (Acts 12:2); the
threatened death penalty for Paul (Acts 25:11, 25; 26:31); the persecution of
Christians in the Book of Revelation. Furthermore, in the letter to Philemon,
Paul wrote persuasively "to save the life of the escaped slave, Onesimus, who
under Roman law was liable to execution" (Barnette, *Crucial Problems*, 129).

What we have seen so far must not be understood as New Testament versus
Old Testament. The direction of the Old Testament moves from the ancient
practice of the death penalty toward its abolition. We have seen that Genesis
9:6 is probably a proverb, not a command. Whichever way we interpret it, all
agree that it is based on the creation of every human person in the image of
God and strongly asserts God's command that we value the sacredness of the
life of human persons. This underlying value for the life of a human person
based on God's creation of all persons in God's image works through the Old
Testament to oppose actually carrying out a death penalty.

This explains why what look like commands in the first five books of the Bible for giving death for great varieties of offenses actually do not function as
commands to kill offenders, but as commands that these offenses be taken
with great seriousness. God wills that the first murderer, Cain, and Moses,
David, Tamar and Gomer not be killed. There is no example of the death penalty being carried out for adultery in the whole Hebrew Scriptures. Not one of

the books of the prophets or the later writings like Psalms, Proverbs, Ecclesiastes or Job affirms the death penalty for any offense whatsoever.

The Mishnah is the record of authoritative oral interpretation of the written law of the Torah by the Jewish religious leaders from about 200 B.C.E. to about 200 C.E. It makes the death penalty almost impossible. Death penalty trials required twenty-three judges. The biblical law (Deut 19:15) requiring at least two eyewitnesses to the commission of the crime "prevented many cases from being brought to trial at all, since such crimes are seldom committed with so much publicity." In the Mishnah the testimony of near relatives, women, slaves or people with a bad reputation is not admitted. If the judges find a witness testified falsely with malicious intent, the witness gets the penalty that would have gone to the defendant, as Deuteronomy 19:16-19 prescribes. "It is clear that with such a procedure conviction in capital cases was next to impossible, and that this was the intention of the framers of the rules is equally plain" (Moore, *Judaism in the First Centuries*, 2:184-87; Horowitz, *Spirit of the Jewish Law*, 165-70, 176).

The Mishnah brands a court that executes one man in seven years as "ruinous" or "destructive." It summarizes the teaching of authoritative rabbis: "Rabbi Eliezar ben Azariah says: Or one in even seventy years. Rabbi Tarfon and Rabbi Akiba say: Had we been in the Sanhedrin none would ever have been put to death. Rabbi Simeon ben Gamaliel says: [for the Sanhedrin to put someone to death] would have multiplied the shedders of blood in Israel" (Danby, *Mishnah*, 403; *Makkot* 1.10). With the much-debated exception of its execution of the Nazi war criminal Adolf Eichmann, modern Israel has never had capital punishment, which shows something of present-day Jewish understanding of the meaning of the tradition. The American Jewish Congress says that "capital punishment degrades and brutalizes the society which practices it; and . . . is cruel, unjust, and incompatible with the dignity and self respect of men."

Is Romans 13 About the Authority to Tax or the Death Penalty?

Proponents of the death penalty usually argue that the authority of the Roman government to impose the death penalty is specifically endorsed in Romans 13: "Let every person be subject to the governing authorities . . . for the authority does not bear the sword in vain! It is the servant of God to execute wrath on the wrongdoer. . . . For the same reason you also pay taxes, for the authorities are God's servants, busy with this very thing. Pay to all what is due them—taxes to whom taxes are due, revenue to whom revenue is due." They highlight "the sword" in the passage, and argue this means Paul is teaching that the Roman government has rightful authority to carry out the death penalty. This was the interpretation offered by Martin Luther and John Calvin, for example. It has a long lineage.

Yet once again, those who oppose the death penalty see Jesus' way as the norm for interpreting this passage. They say its context is Romans 12:14-21 and 13:8-10, which are Jesus' teachings about love and peacemaking as reported by Paul. Jesus' way is the key to the interpretation. Romans 13:1-7 is about owing nothing but love to our enemies, including the Roman government, and making peace with them; it is not about approving of killing people.

A team of New Testament scholars in Germany has studied Romans 13 and its historical context (Friedrich et al., "Zur historischen Situation," 131ff.). These scholars have concluded that Paul was not teaching about the death penalty but was urging his readers to pay their taxes and not to participate in a rebellion against Nero's new tax. An insurrection against taxes had recently occurred and had led to Christians, including Priscilla and Aquila, being expelled from Rome. Another insurrection was brewing. The Greek word for "sword" (*machaira*) in Romans 13:4 refers to the symbol of authority carried by the police who accompanied tax collectors. Paul was urging Christians to make peace, pay Nero's new tax and not rebel. He was not arguing for the death penalty, as he so often has been interpreted as doing. He was arguing *against* the violence of insurrection.

A Brief History of Church Teaching on the Death Penalty

James Megivern has written a history of the church's teaching on the death penalty. Gradually you realize the story is like a parable, a penetrating view into something much deeper. It reveals how the church departed from following Jesus and instead turned to other sources for its ethics, and it points the way for the church to recover its way and its life.

Megivern indicates that as the church became entangled in the death penalty, it got entangled in other kinds of ethics besides following Jesus. It shifted from an ethics of arguing from Jesus' teachings to an ethics of arguing from secular analogies, Roman law and philosophical principles—none of which took Jesus as normative or even mentioned Jesus' teachings.

The church started out opposing the death penalty and citing Jesus in its ethics. Clement of Alexandria, notorious for accommodating the gospel to the culture, writing after A.D. 202, was "the first Christian writer to provide theoretical grounds for the justification of capital punishment. In this he . . . appealed to a rather questionable medical analogy rather than to anything of specifically Christian inspiration": a doctor amputates a diseased organ if it threatens the body. This reduces the value of a human person created in the image of God to a part of the body that needs to be killed in order to save a life (Megivern, *Death Penalty*, 22). None of the passages Megivern quotes justifying the death penalty from the third century through the twelfth century even hint at any reference to the teachings of Jesus. The Bavarian Law, from the end of the seventh century, stands out brightly in contrast, citing Jesus in the Lord's Prayer: "For the Lord has said: 'The one who forgives will be forgiven.'" This beam of light from Jesus in the midst of the darkness led the Bavarian Law to be exceptional in clearly opposing the death penalty (46).

Persecution of heretics was a major source of entanglement with the death penalty. After Constantine became the first pro-Christian emperor in 312, "emperors passed at least sixty-six decrees against Christian heretics, and another twenty-five laws 'against paganism in all its forms.' The violence of the age was extraordinary, and Christians were becoming more and more deeply involved in it" (Megivern, *Death Penalty*, 28). "Once Christianity had become the state religion, the imperial values articulated in Roman law tended to overwhelm gospel values" (50). At first Augustine flatly rejected force against heretics. What caused him to change his mind by 408 was his persecution of the Donatists. The Theodosian Code, a decade after Augustine's death, has "120 laws that assign death as the proper penalty; they are the accumulation of all the earlier laws of the pagan empire plus the even stricter ones enacted over the previous century for the express purpose of 'Christianizing' the empire" (45). In 785, a law prescribed death for eating meat during the Lenten season, burning a cadaver in pagan style instead of burying it in a Christian cemetery or going into hiding rather than presenting oneself for baptism! "The whole issue of heresy thus continued to provoke the entanglement of churchmen ever more deeply in the use of the death penalty" (47, 59).

Megivern gives bloody examples of horrible violence by popes and the Inquisition, giving the death penalty to thousands and thousands of Christians, including Jan Hus, Joan of Arc, Albigensians, Waldensians, Franciscans, Knights Templars and Anabaptists. "This bizarre chapter in church history demonstrated that once the earlier tendencies were allowed to prevail, the trend toward diminished regard for human life led to the acceptance of violence and bloodshed as ordinary conduct, . . . even at the heart of the church" (*Death Penalty*, 138). In the witch craze of the seventeenth century, two to five hundred thousand people were executed across Europe and the New World (191-92).

In the fourth through eleventh centuries, the almost uninterrupted waging of war, including the Crusades, was the second source of entanglement that caused Christian values to be ignored. It was "a time of appalling ignorance and immorality among the clergy, who were thus unable to communicate much of the gospel to the masses" (Megivern, *Death Penalty*, 61). There were pogroms against Jews, and crusades killing them (67-68). Then there was the brutality of the wars of religion from 1559 to 1648, climaxing in the Thirty Years War, which both directly and by causing starvation, destroying sanitation and exacerbating the plague, killed one-third of Germany and Central Europe's population (Megivern, *Death Penalty*, 179).

The topic also shifted significantly to become a question of the God-given authority of the state. This approach runs deep in Christian history and remains common among Christians today. But to hold a sanguine view today of state power to execute is remarkably insensitive to brute historical fact. The pattern of injustice in the exercise of this power that was already apparent in Scripture and easily traced in early and medieval Christian history became a central feature of the (post-Christian) twentieth century. Much of the sorry story of that gruesome century is the history of government-sponsored murder—in the Soviet Union, Nazi Germany, China and other lands—as state-sponsored killings of all kinds claimed tens of millions of lives. In historically Christian Germany in the 1930s, leading Lutheran theologians Paul Althaus and Walter Künneth argued from the authority of the state as a God-given institution (Rom 13:4) to justify the death penalty. Little did they know at the time that they were underwriting a Nazi regime that would murder millions of its own people and millions of others. It is remarkable that Christians who are often so suspicious of governmental power can so readily offer uncritical support of the ultimate governmental power—power over life and death. The question that needs discussing is not simply whether the state has authority but whether this particular use of state authority is just or unjust, right or wrong, prolife or antilife.

Megivern credits the Waldensians six centuries before the Enlightenment, John Wyclif, numerous Anabaptist leaders and others of the Radical Reformation, and the Quakers, as "motivated by their understanding of the gospel to criticize the death penalty as an ungodly abomination long before the abolitionist movements began. Their objections designated it a violation of . . . the 'hard sayings' of Christ, which gave priority to love and forgiveness and rejected all revenge-taking among his followers. . . . 'Reform movements desirous of translating and distributing the Bible to the common people were invariably the wellspring. . . . There was no way to escape the impact of the Sermon on the Mount'" (*Death Penalty*, 193, 198).

Megivern also tells the story of the church's disentanglement from the death penalty since Pope John XXIII in *Pacem in Terris* insisted that "every human being is a person. . . . By virtue of this he has rights and duties of his own . . . which are *universal, inviolable, and inalienable*" (*Death Penalty*, 289). The other key was the return to Jesus' teachings against revenge and violence; Jesus' teachings reappear in the churches' ethics repeatedly during and since the turning against the death penalty (308ff., 385, 392). Now most published church statements on the death penalty oppose it (Melton, *Churches Speak on*

Capital Punishment). The Catholic Church, for example, has swung from ardent support of the death penalty to near-total opposition.

Is the Death Penalty in Actual Practice Unjust?

Walter Berns argues that justice means retribution. Therefore justice means we should care enough about moral and legal community to be angry and to give the death penalty as payback to heinous murderers who undermine that community (in Stassen, *Capital Punishment*, 14ff.). Similarly, Ernest van den Haag argues that justice means punishing guilty offenders according to what they deserve. Therefore justice demands that as many guilty murderers should be punished with the death penalty as can be so punished, even if the death penalty is unfairly given to blacks and the poor. The question for van den Haag is not whether there is discrimination, but whether those who do get the death penalty are guilty and deserve it (in Stassen, *Capital Punishment*, 101ff.).

First let us consider how discriminatory the death penalty really is in its current U.S. application. The data are quite clear and not much disputed. The Death Penalty Information Center summarizes two studies that show the continuing injustice of racism in the application of the death penalty (Dieter, "Executive Summary").

From the days of slavery in which black people were considered property, through the years of lynchings and Jim Crow laws, capital punishment has always been deeply affected by race. Unfortunately, the days of racial bias in the death penalty are not a remnant of the past.

Two of the country's foremost researchers on race and capital punishment, law professor David Baldus and statistician George Woodworth, along with colleagues in Philadelphia, have conducted a careful analysis of race and the death penalty in Philadelphia which reveals that the odds of receiving a death sentence are nearly four times higher if the defendant is black. These results were obtained after analyzing and controlling for case differences such as the severity of the crime and the background of the defendant.

A second study published in the *Cornell Law Review* in 1998 by Professor Jeffrey Pokorak and researchers at St. Mary's University Law School in Texas provides part of the explanation for why the application of the death penalty remains racially skewed. Their study found that the key decision makers in death cases around the country are almost exclusively white men. Of the chief District Attorneys in counties using the death penalty in the United States, nearly 98 percent are white and only 1 percent are African American.

These new empirical studies underscore a persistent pattern of racial disparities that has appeared throughout the country over the past twenty years. Examinations of the relationship between race and the death penalty, with varying levels of thoroughness and sophistication, have now been conducted in every major death penalty state. In 96 percent of these reviews, there was a pattern of either race-of-victim or race-of-defendant discrimination, or both. The gravity of the close connection between race and the death penalty is shown when compared to studies in other fields. Race is more likely to affect death sentencing than smoking affects the likelihood of dying from heart disease. The latter evidence has produced enormous changes in law and societal practice, while racism in the death penalty has been largely ignored.

A study of the inmates on death row in Kentucky found that 100 percent had a white victim, and none had a black victim, despite the fact that a thousand African Americans have been murdered in Kentucky since the resumption of the death penalty (Keil and Vito, "Race and the Death Penalty"). Nationally, 11 of those executed since 1976 were whites convicted of murdering a black victim; 158 were blacks convicted of murdering a white victim. It is hard to avoid the conclusion that our justice system treats the lives of whites as more valuable than those of blacks (see chapter nineteen).

The data for discrimination by economic class are even more clear. In his book arguing for capital punishment, Walter Berns admits that no affluent person has ever been given the death penalty in U.S. history (*For Capital Punishment*, 33-34).

I (Glen) have visited prisoners and have testified in numerous death-penalty trials. I have seen the jury-selection process work in such a way that even in western Kentucky, where the majority population is African American, no African American jurors were chosen. The prosecutors, judges and jury were all white. Almost all defendants were strikingly poor.

The data for *mistaken convictions* are also striking. In 1991, the Senate Judiciary Committee commissioned a study of the frequency of error in death penalty cases that was serious enough to cause guilty judgments to be reversed. Nearly 4,600 capital cases in all states with the death penalty between 1973 and 1995 were studied (Liebman et al., "A Broken System").

1. Nationally, the overall rate of serious reversible error in capital cases is 68 percent—nearly seven out of every ten cases. The report concludes that the error rate is so great that it leaves "grave doubt that all are caught" (1).

2. The most common errors, prompting the most reversals at the state post-convictions stage, are (a) "egregiously incompetent defense lawyers, mostly court appointed, *who did not even look for—and demonstrably missed—important evidence that the defendant was innocent or did not deserve to die*" (2; emphasis in the original). The appendix has many examples of lawyers sleeping through trials or appearing drunk in court; (b) police or prosecutors who did discover exculpatory or mitigating evidence, but suppressed it, keeping it from the jury (2).

3. Eighty-two percent of those convictions overturned at the state level were found to deserve less than death when errors were corrected on re-trial; 7 percent were found innocent of the capital crime (2). Only 11 percent of those capital convictions reversed on state review were still found to deserve death on retrial.

4. These high error rates exist all over the nation. Twenty-four states with the death penalty have overall error rates of 52 percent or higher. Twenty-two of the states have overall error rates of 60 percent or higher. Fifteen states have error rates of 70 percent or higher. Maryland, Georgia, Alabama, Mississippi, Oklahoma, Indiana, Wyoming, Montana, Arizona and California have error rates of 75 percent or higher (28).

5. In 1999 Governor Ryan (R) of Illinois imposed a moratorium on executions in his state following the release of twelve prisoners from death row due to proof of their innocence. The study found that Illinois' error rates in capital cases (66 percent) is slightly lower than the national average of 68 percent (3 and 28). The call for a moratorium on the death penalty due to widespread evidence of mistaken conviction is growing in strength across the nation—and across political lines.

The study concludes that the capital trial process is so error-ridden as to be not only unfair but also irrational. "Serious error in capital judgments has reached epidemic proportions" (20). After pages of discussing the high costs of this process, the study makes a strong conclusion: "If what were at stake was the fabrication of toasters, ... processing of social security claims, . . . etc., no one would tolerate this kind of error rate, which U.S. taxpayers have tolerated in their capital punishment system for decades. Any system with this much error and expense would be halted immediately, examined, and either reformed or scrapped" (121-23).

The death penalty condemns innocent people to die. The book *In Spite of Innocence* notes that since 1900 there have been 416 documented cases of innocent people being convicted and sentenced to death—not counting recent cases like the twelve people released in Illinois because their innocence was proved.

Berns and van den Haag assert that justice means retaliation against or punishment of those who are guilty. Biblically, however, while there is a retributive dimension to justice, the focus is given to deliverance of those in bondage and restoration to community. The normative picture of justice is the exodus of the oppressed from bondage to community. Fairness to the poor and powerless is emphasized. In the Beatitudes, Jesus teaches us the virtue of hungering and thirsting for *delivering justice* that restores the powerless and the outcasts to covenant community. In chapter seventeen, we will try to establish the biblical understanding of justice more firmly. It is a critical question, for the meaning of justice is actually one of the most contentious issues in ethics. Delivering justice, community-restoring justice, means restorative justice for both victims of crime and for perpetrators of crime.

We began this chapter by emphasizing restoration for the families of victims and by pointing to the cleansing experience of forgiveness. We conclude by pointing out that the death penalty discriminates against racial minorities, the poor and those wrongly convicted. Furthermore, unlike other penalties, once people are wrongly executed, there is no way for a court to reverse the error. And there is no way for them to repent and experience redemption, which is such a central biblical concern. Biblical justice pays special attention to the poor, the powerless and the oppressed. This is emphasized from the exodus of the oppressed Jews from Egypt through the redemption of the persecuted followers of the Lamb in Revelation. "You shall not pervert the justice due to your poor in their lawsuits. Keep far from a false charge, and do not kill the innocent and those in the right, for I will not acquit the guilty" (Ex 23:6-7).

Biblical justice does include punishment for wrongdoing. (The best study of punishment and New Testament ethics is widely believed to be Christopher Marshall, *Beyond Retribution: A New Testament Vision for Justice, Crime, and Punishment*, and we agree.) Most states have the option of imposing the punishment of life in prison without possibility of parole. When offered that alternative by polltakers, the majority of Americans support life imprisonment without parole over the death penalty. When offered the alternative of life without parole plus work in prison with income going to the family of the victim as a symbol of accountability and restitution, Americans favor that over the death penalty by two to one (Bowers in Stassen, *Capital Punishment*, 34ff.). This needs to be more widely known.

> **In the Sermon on the Mount, Jesus did not simply oppose evils such as killing, lying and hating the enemy;** *Jesus consistently emphasized a transforming initiative that could deliver us from the vicious cycle of violence or alienation.* **Simply to oppose the death penalty is unlikely to be effective. People feel too much anger about murder to give up the death penalty if there is not an alternative that takes injustice seriously and does something about the murderous violence in our society. The biblical clue is to look for transforming initiatives that can begin to deliver us from the cycles of violence that we experience. We identified such effective initiatives in chapter eight above.**

Some of the support for the death penalty has been because many have feared that the high rate of violence in U.S. society was a threat to the social order. As we focus attention on means of combating that threat that are effective in decreasing the homicide rate, support for the death penalty can be expected to decrease to a minority of the population, as it was only a minority during the presidencies of Eisenhower and Kennedy. Opinion polls indicate that a strong element of scapegoating in times of social frustration and polarization increases support for the death penalty. Only after the presidencies of Eisenhower and Kennedy, when society became so threatened by the polarization of the Vietnam War and Watergate, did majority support for the death penalty arise and sustain itself. If the United States stays out of such wrongful violence and attacks on civil order, and if partisan differences can become more civil, support for the death penalty is likely to continue to erode. This is especially true if the witness of Christians and others to the sanctity of human life becomes increasingly effective.

10

VALUING LIFE
AT ITS BEGINNINGS

▬

*You have heard that it was said to those of ancient times, "You shall not murder"; and
"whoever murders shall be liable to judgment.". . . So . . . go; first be reconciled to your
brother or sister, and then come and offer your gift."*

MATTHEW 5:21, 23

The theme of this section of our book is preventing violence and thus up-
holding the sacredness of human life taught by Jesus. Youth violence, war,
murder and the death penalty are key issues that have all been considered. We
have seen that Jesus does not just offer principled opposition to violence but
names vicious cycles that lead us to choose death rather than life and points to
the way of deliverance that disciples can practice. Jesus' teachings are always
consistent with the sacredness of human life and always practical in showing
us how to resist those forces that diminish and destroy life.

In this chapter we turn our attention to the controversial issue of abortion.
Most textbooks offer fairly standard and all-too-predictable ways of addressing this issue, closely related to the ideological/political perspectives of the
authors. Cultural/theological conservatives tend to oppose abortion as a violation of human dignity or the sacredness of human life; cultural/theological
liberals tend to favor abortion (rights) as essential for women's rights or a matter of personal liberty in a pluralistic society. In this chapter we will articulate
what we believe to be an approach that tries to follow Jesus, one which seeks
to cut across polarized ideological and political perspectives while learning as
much as possible from them, all in submission to the reign of God and the
teaching of Christ. We want to model an honest wrestling with issues rather
than simply to try to offer the "right" position.

Scripture and Abortion

Scripture does not record teaching from Jesus about abortion; nor, in fact, is there any passage in the whole of Scripture that tackles the issue directly. This reality should force all Christians toward a certain epistemological humility. Yet it would be a major mistake to think that lack of direct attention to particular issues means lack of relevant biblical materials.

We are grounding our overall approach to all issues in this section in our exegesis of the three teachings of Jesus concerning violence in Matthew 5:21-26, 38-42 and 43-48. In those passages we are taught to stop killing/harming one another; offered a diagnosis of how we get stuck in patterns leading us to keep killing and harming; and taught several transforming initiatives that can bring us back into an obedience that preserves and cherishes human life—all human life, just like the Father in heaven does (Mt 5:45, 48).

Of course, reviewing these key passages and considering their application to abortion demands our consideration of some perplexing questions: *Is the developing child a human being?* Is he or she part of the "one another" whom Jesus calls us to stop killing and harming? Or should the moral status of the conceived-yet-not-delivered child be understood differently? Here we see the basic-conviction variable of *the nature of human personhood* (chapter three) playing a pivotal role in the question.

We have no word from Jesus on such questions. There is no reference to the status of the unborn child in the rest of the New Testament. There is no teaching explicitly for or against abortion in the Old or New Testament. There *is* an explicit prohibition of abortion in the *Didache*, a very early handbook of Christian teaching: "Do not kill a fetus by abortion or kill a newborn infant" (*Didache* 2:2). Antiabortion teachings are also found in the *Epistle of Barnabas* and the *Apocalypse of Peter*, two other noncanonical but early Christian texts (Gorman, "Why Is the New Testament Silent About Abortion," 29). The early Christians were known for their rejection of abortion and infanticide in a morally degraded Greco-Roman context in which both practices were all-too-common. The *Didache* itself was heavily influenced by the Sermon on the Mount. This is a significant piece of evidence for our consideration.

Some Christian scholars find a different perspective in the Old Testament. Theologian Edmond Jacob says the Old Testament considers breathing at birth the mark of becoming a human person, and ceasing to breathe the mark of death (Jacob, *Theology of the Old Testament*, 158-63). Walter Brueggemann adds that God not only gives us our first breath, but that we depend on God to give us each breath that we breathe. "This means that the human person is, at origin and endlessly, dependent on the attentive giving of Yahweh in order to have life" (cf. Ps 104:29-30; Brueggemann, *Theology of the Old Testament*, 453). And of course it is at birth that we breathe. Certainly the crown of marriage was seen as the birth of children (Ps 127—128, etc.), and childlessness was viewed as a great tragedy (Gen 16—18; 1 Sam 1—2; Lk 1:5-7, 24-25). But the guy that werhdew + spield his seed on the ground. If a pregnant woman is injured + miscarries !

whether the Old Testament treats the developing child in the mother's womb as equivalent in status to the born child is hotly disputed. Let us briefly review some of the key passages.

Genesis 2:7 depicts the creation of the first man from the dust of the ground. God "breathed into his nostrils the breath of life, and the man became a living being." Some argue from this passage that *breath* is hereby declared the decisive mark of transition to full human personhood. In the womb, developing children receive oxygen through the placenta rather than breathing independently. It is only at birth that children take their first breath. Thus, the argument goes, full human status belongs either to those born people who have breathed on their own or, more conservatively, to those unborn who *could* breathe on their own if labor brought them forth prematurely. A counterargument here would be that—if we want to press this primeval history for this kind of moral norm, which we probably do not—only the first man and first woman came into existence through direct creation as adults. All the rest of us enter through conception and gestation, and thus the passage does not speak to the context in which human beings are now brought into existence.

Another critical issue concerns the interpretation of the legal provision in Exodus 21:22-25. The section of laws in Exodus 21:12-36 concerns compensation for personal injuries. In the New International Version, Exodus 21:22-23 reads: "If men who are fighting hit a pregnant woman and she gives birth prematurely but there is no serious injury, the offender must be fined whatever the husband demands and the court allows. But if there is serious injury, you are to take life for life." This translation could suggest that developing human life is sufficiently valuable that even a blow causing a premature (but successful) birth should be punished by a fine, and a blow causing more serious harm (miscarriage, presumably) invokes the *lex talionis* life-for-life principle. This is the most common interpretation of the passage in evangelical circles and would strengthen the biblical case for opposition to abortion (see Cottrell, "Abortion and the Mosaic Law," for an influential exposition of this view).

However, this turns out to be an interpretation shared by few English translations. The text is actually quite difficult. The first issue is how the Hebrew term *yatsa* is to be read. It literally means "come out." Men are fighting, they hit a pregnant woman, and her child *comes out*. That is all the text says. The next phrase, translated by the NIV as "but there is no serious injury," can be more literally translated as "and/but there is no harm." The word *serious* in the NIV is an interpretation. The same thing is true of the first phrase in Exodus 21:23: "any harm." That is all the Hebrew says. No adjective approximating "serious" is in the passage. It is unclear whether the coming out, or miscarriage, caused the baby to die, so that the fine is for the miscarriage and death of the baby; and whether the harm in addition to the miscarriage is to the woman or to the baby, so that the "life for life and eye for eye" is for additional harm to the woman or to the baby.

In short, the phrase that the NIV translates as "gives birth prematurely but there is no serious injury" can also be translated as "there is a miscarriage, and yet no harm follows." The RSV renders the phrase that way, and it was the Jewish rabbinic tradition as well. The KJV is ambiguous, saying "so that her fruit depart from her," not indicating whether the additional harm is to the woman or to the baby. The NEB has "so that she suffers a miscarriage but suffers no further hurt," and the NLT agrees. The Catholic New Jerusalem Bible says "and she suffers a miscarriage, though she does not die of it, the man responsible must pay the compensation. . . . But should she die, you shall give life for life." If this is correct, the meaning shifts dramatically. In context, a miscarriage is not defined as a serious injury or even (rather disturbingly) a "harm," and the punishment for causing a miscarriage is a fine rather than death. The unborn-yet-developing child has moral and legal standing sufficient to require a fine, but that standing is not equivalent to that of a born human being. On this view, the offender is apparently only hit with the life-for-life retribution if harm comes to the *mother herself* (for this view, see Simmons, *Birth and Death,* chap. 2).

This text seems to be sufficiently murky to fail as a foundation for any particular position on abortion, other than the minimal claim that reckless behavior causing a woman to deliver a child prematurely (dead or alive) was punishable, thus reflecting some valuation of the status of the unborn child and the legal rights of the mother and father.

Those who are opposed to abortion frequently cite Psalm 22:9-10; 139:13-16; and Jeremiah 1:5. Psalm 139:13-14 thanks God:

> For it was you who formed my inward parts;
>   you knit me together in my mother's womb.
> I praise you, for I am fearfully and wonderfully made.
>   Wonderful are your works.

In poetic language, these texts affirm that God forms/crafts the human being, that this forming/crafting takes place in the womb, and that God has knowledge of a person and his or her future even before birth. Prochoice Christians aver that these passages are not scientific treatises or treatises on the moral status of fetal life. They are about God's prevenient grace and knowledge. They affirm and celebrate prayerfully the goodness of God and a purposeful human life as ordained by God.

In the NIV Psalm 22:10 says, "From my mother's womb you have been my God," and some prolife Christians have taken this to mean from the moment of entry into the womb. But it is actually speaking of the time of birth out of the womb, not the time of entry into the womb. It is parallel with the preceding line, "From birth I was cast upon you," and it follows the verse that says:

Yet you brought me out of the womb;
you made me trust in you even at my mother's breast.

These passages are prayers of gratitude for God's prevenient grace and knowledge, and cannot be employed to settle the abortion issue. They are best read as exultant, awestruck celebrations of God's grace as experienced in the development of human physical life and personal identity. Their references to human development in the womb certainly teach that fetal life has deep meaning as God is involved in the process of bringing human persons to birth.

A final biblical word takes us back to the central narrative of the New Testament and to the center of our own approach to ethics: Jesus. The career of the Messiah begins with an angelic announcement to Mary—"You will conceive in your womb and bear a son" (Lk 1:31)—and a miraculous conception. The Holy Spirit comes upon Mary and she conceives. Mary opens her heart to welcome a child she has not conceived by human means, despite negative and potentially disastrous repercussions for herself (Mt 1:18-25; Lk 2:34-35). She visits her cousin Elizabeth, now carrying the future prophet John, and "the child leaped in her womb. And Elizabeth was filled with the Holy Spirit" (Lk 1:41) and exulted that "as soon as I heard the sound of your greeting, the child in my womb leaped for joy" (Lk 1:44). (It would be possible to treat this passing reference to John's "leap" as evidence of purposeful behavior on the part of a developing but not yet born child, though it is probably better to treat the event as reflecting the experience of every woman who has ever felt her baby move during the middle to latter stages of fetal development.)

Better yet exegetically is to notice that Luke 1:5—2:14 repeatedly celebrates the *joy* of God's miraculous *presence* and power acting to bring about the birth of Jesus and the deliverance of all persons whom God favors. It is *the joy of God's presence to deliver* that marks the kingdom of God both in Isaiah and in Jesus, as we saw in chapter one above. (For *joy*, see especially Lk 1:14, 19, 41-45, 46-55, 64, 68-79; 2:10-14, 18-20, 28-32, 38.) The words *joy* and *rejoice* occur nine times in the Greek (sometimes translated as "found favor," "blessed," "gladness" or "exulted"). *Holy Spirit* occurs six times, and a revelation of the *presence* of God in which the angel tells them to "fear not," or a vision is received, six times. *Peace, justice* and *righteousness, deliverance/salvation* and *kingdom* are also mentioned several times. Thus all the marks of the kingdom-deliverance that we noticed in chapter one are here. This is a wonderful celebration of God's prevenient grace, not of John's precocious intelligence. The coming of the kingdom is here being announced, with all the marks, exactly as we expected from our study of the deliverance passages in the prophet Isaiah!

What can we fairly say about the biblical evidence, saying neither too much nor too little? Perhaps the following:

- The human child is a deeply-to-be-desired creation and gift from God.

- The Bible recognizes the mystery and majesty of the process of fetal development and articulates God's role in forming the unborn child.

- God has knowledge of those who will be born even before they are born.

- The developing child in the womb was treated as worthy of some legal protection in Old Testament law.

- The incarnation began with the miraculous conception of Jesus and not just his birth.

- Mary showed hospitality to welcome a child she did not expect and whose presence brought great suffering into her life.

Reflecting on Fetal Personhood

A surprisingly high percentage of pregnancies end in miscarriage or stillbirth. By one estimate, more than 50 percent of conceptions never even reach the stage of uterine implantation; in such cases the woman may never even know she was pregnant (Harvey, "Distinctly Human," 13). U.S. census statistics record that in 1996, 16 percent of known pregnancies ended in spontaneous abortion or fetal loss—and 22 percent ended in elective abortion (U.S. Census Bureau, *Statistical Abstract 2000*, table 103). The process of bringing new human life into the world remains fraught with difficulties. It is a reminder of the curse on Eve in Genesis 3:16, for human beings certainly do have great pain in childbearing, not just in delivery but in everything associated with conceiving, nurturing, giving birth to and rearing babies. After three successful pregnancies, my (David's) wife and I lost two babies to unexplained fetal death at the halfway mark of pregnancy. No explanation—just grief. We soon learned of many who had similar experiences.

One might therefore say that fallen nature does its own violence to the unborn, a violence that no human is able to prevent. The ubiquity of fetal loss may have relevance to how we think about the moral status of the very early embryo or of the developing child more generally. But still, *elective abortion* and *spontaneous abortion* are morally very different events.

News of a pregnancy comes unexpectedly. The child is somewhere in the long, nine-month process of development, clinging for life along the uterine wall of her mother in a dependence so complete that it serves as a metaphor for every other kind of human dependence and vulnerability.

The mother—under whatever set of circumstances—engages the services of a specialist in ending fetal life. This specialist, most of the time, reaches into the woman's uterus with a scalpel and scrapes the fetus off the uterine wall and into oblivion. Abortions that occur later involve even more gruesome methods. *But all elective abortions involve the volitional destruction of a developing human life.* If left to develop without interruption, that developing human life will normally emerge after nine months, take his or her first breath and greet the world. But abortion terminates the development process and thus ends that existence.

Many Christians who oppose abortion insist on classifying this developing human life as a *human person.* They ground their argument against abortion in this way: abortion at any stage is a form of murder because it kills a member of the human species, one of that class of creatures called human persons, endowed by his Creator with immeasurable worth regardless of the developmental status of his particular functions or capacities. This view is called *essentialism,* the *species principle* or the *full-personhood* perspective.

This kind of argument has the great value of attributing the maximum possible moral status to developing human life, whether at the four-cell embryo stage, at eight weeks gestation or at six months. This entity, it is argued, is a person who must be both understood and treated as if he or she were just as valuable as any human being on the planet. This is a view much impressed by the scientific fact that the development process that runs from zygote to embryo to fetus to child to adolescent to adult is "an ordered serial development of different stages in the complete cycle of human life (Harvey, "Distinctly Human," 13).

One can point to various milestones in this development process, such as implantation in the womb (7 days), the appearance of the primitive streak (14 days), a heartbeat (22 days), quickening (felt fetal movement—around 20 weeks), viability (20-22 weeks), or birth with independent breathing (normally 38 weeks). But one can also point to all manner of milestones of development *after* birth: the first cry, the first word, the first step, the first day of school, the first date. . . . Indeed, in human life at its best development *never* ceases—until death—but even then we have reason to hope that a new kind of development of our humanity awaits us!

The full-personhood stance also has the virtue of preventing any gap from ever developing between the concepts of *human being* and *human person.* A number of very influential ethicists, such as the Princeton philosopher Peter Singer, make the argument that human personhood should be viewed as consisting of a number of specific and unique human functions, which can be summarized as a "developed capacity for conscious self-reflective intelligence" (Wennberg, "Right to Life," 36). In the technical literature on abortion this is sometimes called the *actuality principle* (or approach). Embryos and fetuses are just one among several types of human beings that lack such personhood capacities; others include those in a persistent vegetative state, newborns, the irreversibly comatose and the grossly retarded. It is argued that while the lives of all such *human beings* deserve a measure of respect, they do not have the same status as fully *human persons* and thus should be treated as having fewer rights. Singer, for example, envisions circumstances in which even *infanticide* would be morally permissible (see Singer, *Practical Ethics;* Preece, *Rethinking Peter Singer*), precisely because of the infant's supposed lack of personhood. Singer is also a "preference-utilitarian," for whom the end that justifies action is the greatest preference-satisfaction for the greatest number. Human persons have value insofar as they have complex preferences that can be satisfied. He thus illustrates the distinction between teleological and deontological reasoning that we explained in chapter five.

Gilbert Meilaender is one among many Christian ethicists who are deeply troubled by this horrifying use of the concept of personhood to exclude certain human beings from full membership in the human community (*Bioethics*, 31-33), as are we. The perception of all human beings as equal, and equally valuable, as persons worthy of respect and equal treatment before the law, is a relatively rare and recent achievement in human history. The concept that women, children, racial minorities, immigrants, refugees and the poor are to be treated not only equally but with *special concern* because of their frequent marginalization and vulnerability is a central biblical teaching rarely actualized in public life. Meilaender, whose own view is that personhood can be attributed to the fetus at approximately the second week of development, argues for the inclusion of "the weakest and least advantaged *members* of the human community" in our concept of personhood (*Bioethics*, 33, italics in original), including the developing human embryo.

I find that a version of the full-personhood view makes the most sense to me. I acknowledge that it is not possible to *prove* from Scripture or science that the embryo or early fetus is, before God, a person in the way that a born human being is a person. Personhood is a metaphysical notion beyond the possibility of proof. Theologians cannot even agree on the components of human personhood: are we a body/soul dualism, or inspirited bodies, or a tripartite body/spirit/soul composite, or a monistic unity, or something else? I also acknowledge that thoughtful Christian interpreters through the centuries have offered a variety of theories that have identified the emergence of recognizable personhood at various stages in the gestational process. Some prolife Christians have not wanted to acknowledge these very real conceptual variations and difficulties. However, on a matter involving the inclusion or exclusion of the developing human being in that category of creatures treated as full members of the human community—as persons—it seems best to err on the side of caution. I would much rather be wrong in attributing too much personhood to the fetus than in attributing too little. Surely the more pernicious tendency in human history has been to err on the side of too much exclusion from covenant community rather than too much inclusion, with disastrous and cruel results.

Yet it is possible to articulate a Christian stance opposing abortion but not embracing the full-personhood-from-conception position. Some Christian ethicists believe that this slightly "softer" claim about the moral status of unborn life may fit the biblical, scientific and experiential evidence a bit better. It is called the *potentiality* or *potential-personhood* approach (cf. Roberts, *African-American Christian Ethics*, 248; Clark and Rakestraw, *Readings in Christian Ethics*, 2:21-25).

A potentiality approach claims that "both potential and actual persons have a right to life" (Wennberg, "Right to Life," 37). A potential person is an entity that "will naturally and in due course develop into a person" (Wennberg, "Right to Life," 38) but is not yet a person. Fetal life thus represents potential rather than actual personhood. But potential personhood is morally significant. As Alan Donagan has put it: "if respect is owed to beings because they are in a certain state, it is owed to whatever, by its very nature, develops into that state" (Donagan, *Theory of Morality*, 171). Wennberg argues that an anencephalic fetus (in which no brain developed nor will develop) and an irreversibly comatose patient (or a persistent vegetative state patient) have membership in the human species but have no potential for ever having the crucial aspects of the image of God. If these patients are defined as full persons with all the human rights of full persons, the obligation for treatment is equal to that for full persons, and "this does seem odd."

This philosophical way of putting the matter can be sharpened with the more familiar biblical language we have been considering. The human child is a divine creation and gift from God, to be welcomed hospitably into the world, as Mary welcomed Jesus. And just like Jesus, the earthly career of every human being begins at conception, extends through gestation, and if all goes well transitions into the light of day at birth. Even if we do not define this entity as a person until (the vicinity of) birth, we are still duty-bound to acknowledge our moral obligations to her or him. It is interesting to note that the Jewish tradition historically opposed abortion except to save the life of the mother, even though the fetus was defined as only potentially a person (P. Ramsey, *Ethics at the Edges*, 46-47).

When a child is wanted, her mother and father tend to speak of her as such—their *baby*—from the moment a pregnancy is confirmed. This is morally quite significant. They cannot see her (except through technology), but knowing that she is there they do all they can to prepare to welcome her. And yet a *growing* sense of attachment to her is felt as the pregnancy progresses. The mother's belly rounds. The baby's first kick marks a major milestone. The last trimester of the pregnancy is a time of special caution and also great excitement. Life is dominated by preparations for the new family member.

Just as excitement heightens during the course of pregnancy, so does the grief associated with fetal loss. If the pregnancy ends in miscarriage during the first six weeks or so, the couple may be quite sad. Fetal loss at mid-term tends to be more painful. A late-term fetal loss or stillbirth, or the birth of a baby who is already dead, is one of life's most devastating experiences. Couples tend to bury lost late-term babies in cemeteries. Miscarriages are grieved, but not in this way. Perhaps these differentiations in response ought to be considered as we puzzle over how exactly to think of the moral status of the developing child.

Christians can resolutely reject abortion-on-demand without necessarily embracing the essentialist or full-personhood position. A potentiality approach can still affirm that abortion is a rejection of a divinely given, infinitely precious developing human being, through an act of volitional medicalized violence. Both full-personhood and potential-personhood views—and a variety of options that exist along a spectrum between them—demand that Christian disciples practice the welcoming and nurturing of human life. Likewise, a just society extends its respect and protection to the unborn, developing in complete vulnerability in their mothers' wombs. The fetus is certainly a form of life; it is a form of human life; it is (at least) developing into a human person. The burden of proof is certainly on anyone who would intervene in its life in order to destroy it.

Abortion is inconceivable apart from the reality of human sin. In the domain of the reign of God, there is no place for purposefully taking the life of any human. Death itself—especially premature death, especially intentional, violent premature death—is part of the brokenness of life apart from the reign of God. In biblical terms, death of any kind is a consequence of the fall (Gen 3:19), and violent death one of the most prominent evidences of the tragic rebellion of humanity against its Maker.

The church, as the beachhead of the kingdom of God, is to be that community which in its life gives evidence that intentional, violent and premature death from any source can be resisted and overcome, not just in the eschatological future but beginning now, in the eschatological kingdom present in mustard-seed form. The church cannot do this simply by holding appropriate positions on issues such as abortion. Nor is the primary task of the church to determine when these and other forms of killing might be permissible as exceptions to a general rule. This rule/exception casuistry has so dominated moral reflection in both Christian and secular ethics that it is sometimes hard to imagine any other way of dealing with a moral issue. But as we argued in chapter five, Jesus did not frequently adjudicate rules and exceptions.

Instead, in light of the coming kingdom of God, the task of the church is to participate in gracious transforming practices that reduce and in some cases eliminate various forms of killing. The church will stand at the forefront of creative and concrete efforts to reduce the sources and causes of the violent death that occurs all around us. Precisely because of our intoxication with the coming kingdom of God, we will be urgently engaged in addressing and overcoming the real human problems and vicious cycles that hinder its coming. This pattern applies as much to abortion as to any other issue.

Abortion: Two Narratives

Both Glen and I have had to grapple personally with the issue of abortion. For me, it was a situation in my family that first brought abortion into close personal proximity. One of my sisters became pregnant during her senior year in college. Prior to this experience she would have described herself as resolutely against abortion. Yet in the crisis, fearing that her future would be imperiled if she had a baby, she scheduled an abortion at a nearby clinic. For several difficult weeks the entire family, and not just my sister, wrestled with the very real issues raised by a crisis pregnancy.

Those issues were legion. How would my sister cope—emotionally, spiritually, physically—with raising a child on her own—or with abortion itself? Would adoption be the best choice? Would health insurance cover the maternity expenses? Would the father of the child be present? If so, would his presence be constructive? What would be the consequences for the baby of life without a father? Where would mother and baby live? How would my sister continue her education? Could she afford to do so? What kind of professional future could she have? Would day care for the baby be affordable? What impact would it have upon his or her development? What would be the impact on our family's reputation, especially in the local church? What would be the impact of either abortion or keeping the child on my sister's relationship to the rest of the family?

The shadows cast by such questions loomed large, so large that the real possibility of abortion became a matter of family discussion. That path was not taken—my sister, in great anguish of spirit, finally chose not to abort. My precious nephew Alex is a rambunctious ten-year-old, deeply loved by all of us. But it is now easier for me to understand why the abortion path is so frequently taken. Those who describe themselves as prolife often seem unwilling to reflect seriously on the real crises that drive women to consider abortion. When someone considers an abortion amidst an unplanned pregnancy, questions about how the baby will be raised, what will happen to the mother, and how the pregnancy will affect current relationships usually play the critical roles in the decision. This is precisely what we mean by "vicious cycles"—we get tangled up in forces and concerns that tempt us to disobey

God's will, sometimes because of concerns and pressures that we think are insurmountable. An ethic of transforming initiatives needs to show us how to address them.

For Glen, the circumstances surrounding his wife Dot's third pregnancy raised the issue of abortion in the most personal way imaginable. During the second month of her third pregnancy, Dot got sick with a fever and a rash. She had other symptoms: temporary foot drop, pain behind her ears and a throat culture that eliminated scarlet fever as a cause. All this pointed to rubella—German measles.

Glen and Dot wrestled with what to do. Rubella in the first three months of pregnancy is likely to do debilitating damage to a fetus. Glen consulted others and prayed. This was 1967, before the prolife movement, before he had read Christian ethics debates about abortion or heard the issue discussed in church. But he had already prayed intensely for their first two sons. He already had a strong sense that life is a gift from God. And one other thing: he had a not-very-well articulated hope that if things turned out badly, somehow they could cope. That had been his experience before.

Dot was a pediatrics nurse. She had taken care of so many indescribably, severely debilitated infants in much pain and with grim futures that she believed many of them would have been better off not having been born. Yet her own mother-loyalty to the baby in her womb caused her to block out much of the medical evidence about German measles.

When his son David was born, Glen pressed his nose against the top of the incubator, looking as intently as he could for any signs of damage. Two hours later, the pediatrician came to say the baby had several major problems from rubella. He had three serious problems in his heart. For his first month, he was almost too weak to nurse. It would take him one hour to drink just one ounce of milk, and then he and Dot would rest or sleep for an hour. That cycle went on twenty-four hours a day. By the end of the first month, David's heart went into failure. It was working so hard to pump the needed blood with all its defects that it was twice the normal size, and it could not keep this up. David was too weak to throw off an infection in his body so he could have major surgery. The odds were against his living. They pumped him full of antibiotics and operated. After the surgery, he kept losing weight for another two months.

Besides his heart, David's eyes and ears were damaged. He had brain damage and during his first year seemed so retarded that Glen thought he might never even learn to sit up. He was unable to chew or talk or even mumble until he was four and a half years old. The first word he said was "Dadda," sitting in Glen's lap and playing a rocking game blind children love to play, in the chair by the living room window. Glen remembers it vividly. He was so excited he spent the next year teaching David words for things and giving him high fives every time he said a word. He has become an advocate for every parent to spend regular time talking with infants, imitating their sounds, giving them encouragement, teaching them words and praising them for their efforts.

Now David Stassen has his B.A. and M.A. in German and his certificate from the University of Mainz in German translation, and he translates theological articles and books from German to English for publication or to help scholars do research.

But he is much shorter than his brothers, has had twelve operations and has significant handicaps. Life has had hard struggles, significant painful defeats and important victories.

The key to this story as Glen sees it is *all the help from caring others that was crucial to David's making it*: Heart surgeon Alan Lansing; fellow church members Jane Kent, Chris Conver, Monaei Schnur and Linda Compton; elementary and special education teachers Mrs. Hummel, Mrs. Woodie and Mrs. Kelly; numerous caring teachers at Perkins School for the Blind and Kentucky School for the Blind; Professor of German Alan Leidner; friend Kim Kosakowski; and so many others who went way beyond the call of duty. Apart from them, it would have been a tragedy. Together, these people formed a community of covenant faithfulness.

Glen has not only gratitude but also the deeply felt speechless sense of deliverance of the wounded, sad and desperate—that so many have come to rescue David and to rescue us: like Jesus' teaching "Blessed are the merciful," those who show compassion in action and covenant faithfulness toward those in need. Glen himself feels like the one who has been forgiven much and so is more grateful (Lk 7:43) and determined that there be help for others trying to cope. The best way to be prolife is to deliver people from the causes of abortions. See to it that potential mothers will have help raising their children or giving them a family through adoption. Make it possible for people to raise their babies and not to have to drop out of school, not to have to give up on a future. Help them have confidence that they can cope. So many people were crucial to their being able to cope, and to David making it. In more recent years, Dot has dedicated herself to working as a nurse in a high school for pregnant teenagers, with a baby nursery, helping them stay in school and raise healthy babies at the same time.

The Immediate Context of Abortion: Crisis Pregnancy

Two narratives cannot adequately summarize the entire context within which abortion arises. But together they point to several key aspects of that context.

First, the question of abortion arises almost exclusively as the result of a crisis in the life of the one (or ones) who face that question. Here we leave aside that small minority of women for whom abortions are a repeat experience, some of whom may have consciences so dulled that an abortion is a casual decision. The more common pattern is that the issue of abortion arises as a result of, and in the midst of, one of the most severe crises they will face in their entire lives. *Most think: I know I shouldn't consider abortion but in this crisis I feel trapped; abortion is my only way out.*

The precise nature of that crisis varies widely. It is mistaken to assume, for example, that abortion is solely the province of unmarried women or teenagers. As of 1996, the latest date for which complete federal statistics are available, women between the ages of 20 and 29 obtained 55 percent of abortions (U.S. Census Bureau, *Statistical Abstract 2000*, table 113). Fully 20 percent of all abortions are obtained by married women. Thus, while crisis pregnancies do frequently emerge in the lives of single teenagers, they also occur among married thirty-five-year-olds.

Antiabortion activists frequently charge that most abortions occur for reasons of "personal convenience" or cavalier self-regard. Yet this is to paint with far too broad a brush; it is in fact a heartless charge if applied indiscriminately to all who choose abortion. Important research by Frederica Mathewes-Green *(Real Choices)* indicates that the central driving force behind abortions resides in the network of relationships in which women are embedded. Put simply, if a pregnant woman cannot find in her intimate circle (parents, siblings, friends, lover/boyfriend/spouse) the love and support that she needs to carry her pregnancy to term, she is likely to seek an abortion. Such pregnant women usually have some idea of the trauma which an abortion will bring into both their emotions and their bodies. They are not eager to invite such trauma. Yet in the days of crisis they come to imagine what feels like one thing worse—the threat of rejection or even violence at the hands of those whose love means the most to them.

Mathewes-Green offers numerous poignant and even enraging stories of women who were given this simple "choice"—abortion or rejection. Such stories demonstrate that many powerless women are coerced into obtaining abortions. How contrary such sad tales are to the myth of abortion-on-demand as a major aspect of female autonomy and self-determination. Perhaps it plays that role for some. But it turns out that abortion, at least in many cases, is just another mechanism for the oppression of women. It underwrites male sexual predation and irresponsibility, leaving the burden of dealing with unwanted pregnancies in the hands—and bodies—of women alone. Socially structured gender inequality takes many forms; this is one of its most vicious.

Meanwhile, a small percentage of those who seek abortions do so for one of the several well-known "borderline" reasons. Some women's pregnancies result from the horrendous trauma of forced sex, such as rape or incest. Some pregnancies threaten the life or health of the mother. And some pregnancies involve serious fetal problems, as in the case of Glen and Dot's son David.

Women (or couples) living on the edge of malnutrition and financial collapse frequently view an unplanned pregnancy as a grave crisis. Women who do not believe they have the capacity to cope with raising a fourth or fifth child consider abortion. Women with serious mental or physical handicaps are sometimes simply unable to raise any child they might conceive. Other situations could easily be named. What these situations have in common is that for all of the women and/or couples involved, a pregnancy is a crisis—and all desire to find a way to resolve this crisis. For at least a period of time the "abortion option" looks like the "least worst" possibility.

The Centrality of Compassionate Help

How shall a Jesus-focused, kingdom-oriented Christian respond to the problem of crisis pregnancy and the broader issue of abortion? The place to begin is with the compassion of Jesus Christ. A transformative response begins here.

A woman panicking because of an unwanted pregnancy and perhaps reluctantly considering an abortion is a woman whom Jesus would have looked upon and loved (see Mk 10:21). One is reminded of the throngs who sought out Jesus when he attempted a temporary retreat from his ministry, and of his response: "When he saw the crowds, he had compassion for them, because they were harassed and helpless, like sheep without a shepherd" (Mt 9:36). Mathewes-Green says of women who have had abortions: "They needed personal support and encouragement more than any material aid" ("Why Women Choose Abortion," 25). Support, encouragement and compassion for the real women who face crisis pregnancies—this is the starting point of any Jesus-centered response to the abortion problem. Such compassion is a far cry from screaming "baby-killer" at women as they enter abortion clinics.

Compassion must then take the form of concrete help that participates in delivering needy persons from the situation in which they suffer. For Jesus, compassion led to action, both in his own conduct and in his teachings. The latter is perhaps nowhere better exemplified than in the parable of the compassionate Samaritan (Lk 10:25-37; for a full exposition, see chapter sixteen). The Samaritan both feels pity and takes a range of actions to help the bleeding man. He bandages his wounds, provides transportation, finds lodging, pays for the lodging, and arranges ongoing help. Only by this compassionate action is the victim provided with what he needs to recover. Remember that Jesus identified this kind of compassion-in-action as one of the virtues of his followers.

The application to the issue at hand is all too obvious. Women or couples facing crisis pregnancies need various forms of concrete help. Consider the case of a poor, single, pregnant fifteen-year-old who is alienated from her parents. She needs spiritual and emotional support, health care, adequate nutrition; she needs counseling and instruction in fetal development, parenting or adoption. Frequently she needs a place to stay because she has been kicked out of her home. She may need help with schoolwork and likely ongoing financial help until she can attain financial independence. Christian response to the issue of abortion begins right here. When Christians organize themselves to provide these forms of concrete help—whether as individuals, congregations or in larger group settings—their actions are consistent with the way of Jesus Christ.

For two years I served on the board of an organization called St. Elizabeth's Regional Maternity Center, based in the Louisville, Kentucky, area. On the basis of Christian conviction, St. Elizabeth's offers a comprehensive approach to meeting the needs of pregnant women. Its programming principle is simple—staff seek to determine the real, concrete needs of women facing crisis pregnancies and develop programs that meet those needs. This has led St. Elizabeth's into undertaking an exceedingly wide range of social, medical, legal, financial, vocational, educational, public-policy, psychological, moral and spiritual initiatives on behalf of those within its care (see <www.iglou.com/kac/stelizabeth.html>).

Dot Stassen's high school has social workers who help the girls cope with present challenges and plan their futures, nurses who teach them nutrition and childcare, a medical clinic so they can have their regular ob/gyn checkups without missing school, a day care in which the girls must help one hour per week so they also receive training in childcare, and evening programs for their sisters and their boyfriends to prevent further teenage pregnancies. The school, of course, has the usual academic courses as well; these are paid by the public school system, while the special services are paid by fundraising. As a result, the school has much lower than average problems like dropping out and drug use. And the babies average normal birth weight and healthiness, which is a dramatically better outcome than for most teenage pregnancies. The teenagers almost never get pregnant a second time, and they tend to finish school successfully. Ninety-nine percent of the teenagers do not have abortions. This public high school has to struggle for funding, and fears opposition by insensitive critics. But it is doing exactly what is really needed to prevent abortion.

Abortion and the Church

A second dimension of Christian response to the issue of abortion is the development of an ecclesial context in which abortion is generally unthinkable. The church is the beachhead of the kingdom, the place in which the reign of God begins to be made manifest here and now. A kingdom-focused church can be—must be—a place in which the scourge of abortion, except in the rarest of circumstances, has no place. This should be the case not primarily because one having an abortion in such churches would face negative sanctions, but because of the existence of a communal context which eliminates most of the circumstances within which crisis pregnancies arise—and which is permeated by an unshakable and joyful affirmation of the sacredness of every human life.

In such congregations it will be taught that sex is reserved for lifetime marriage. Sexual restraint will not only be taught, of course, but consistently, joyfully and faithfully practiced. Because most crisis pregnancies emerge in nonmarital contexts (80 percent), the mere practice of sexual chastity outside of marriage and covenant fidelity within marriage will have a revolutionary impact (see chapter thirteen). Some transforming initiatives are preventive—they head the crisis off before it ever develops.

If a crisis pregnancy does occur within the community of faith, such a congregation will rush compassionately to the side of the person(s) involved and offer all needed forms of assistance. Sometimes structured programs of assistance will exist, such as St. Elizabeth's; other times they will not. In either case, faithful congregations will offer the help that is needed and in so doing participate in saving lives and advancing God's reign. Such a congregation will also have the capacity to provide the enormous help needed by a pregnant victim of rape or incest, or by one who is carrying a seriously deformed child. They will surround the woman with love and support, enabling her to "love her child to life," as Mathewes-Green has so nicely put it ("If Wombs Had Windows"). It is quite possible that only such faith-based support can enable most of those facing such tragic circumstances to see the possibility of enduring them apart from abortion. The crisis of unwanted pregnancy must be met with the resources made available by a faith community characterized by the Christian virtues of love and mercy.

Permeating these and all other efforts to prevent abortion must be a resolute and consistently practiced commitment to the sacredness of human life at every stage and in every context. Congregations have the capacity to create a countercultural ethos of respect for life. Such an ethos governs the life of the committed community of faith in its daily expression, resisting the casual disregard for life characteristic of the broader cultural milieu and persisting even if the law permits abortion on demand. This countercultural ethos is precisely what the New Testament churches experienced (cf. Acts 2:43-45) and what the church is called to create and sustain today and in every era. Only as we affirm the God-given dignity and immeasurable worth of every human life at every stage of its existence does the church have a chance of resisting the currents of what John Paul II has rightly called "the culture of death" *(Gospel of Life)*. Only with such deeply held conviction can men and women facing life crises resist the seductive temptation, the short term answer, that abortion provides.

Many Christian ethicists offer careful and reasoned expositions of the prolife perspective, as well as efforts to respond to and prevail over prochoice arguments (a strong example is Beckwith; for the best of both sides of the argument, see Pojman/Beckwith). It is certainly the case that Christian leaders should in their teaching and preaching present the best case they can for their perspective and teach their congregants how to respond to widely held prochoice arguments. This is valuable—as long as no one operates under the illusion that the abortion issue will be settled simply by winning the argument on logical or rational grounds. Prolife Christian theorists have been attempting to do so for thirty years. Clearly, at a fundamental level the abortion "debate" is not really a debate but an uneasy *stalemate*, and women facing crisis pregnancies need the church's concrete help more than its antiabortion debating points. This is one reason why our focus in this chapter is not on winning arguments but helping women in crisis.

Abortion and the Law

A final question to consider in a discussion of abortion is the place of legal sanctions. Many who are concerned about abortion focus almost entirely on the public-policy arena. We have already sought to indicate why this is an inadequate approach to the Christian moral task. Yet the legal and public-policy issues still remain, and a response is required.

Current U.S. law on abortion is now characterized by a thirty-year-old precedent, *Roe v. Wade* (1973), which legalized abortion on the basis of a trimester model that is now both legally and medically obsolete. *Roe v. Wade* intended to limit abortion progressively as pregnancies proceeded, but for a variety of legal, cultural and practical reasons abortion became available essentially on demand. Succeeding decisions, including *Webster* v. *Reproductive Health Services* (1989) and *Planned Parenthood* v. *Casey* (1992), have upheld *Roe* v. *Wade*, though modifying it in the direction of allowing states to impose modest "speed bumps" intended to force reflection on the gravity of the decision and family involvement where minors are considering abortion. The principle of *stare decisis* makes it exceedingly difficult to reverse a settled body of legal precedent. The legal effort against that precedent will not be a short-term project. In fact, given overall trends in Western culture it seems quite unlikely that abortion on demand in the United States or any other Western country will be ended any time in the foreseeable future. The availability of the so-called RU-486 abortion pills for private use by women signals even greater difficulty in regulating or delegitimizing abortion.

Other laws are also relevant, though, when thinking about abortion. If abortion often arises as a desperate measure chosen by women who feel they really have no "choice" at all, we must explore more closely the failures in public policy that this desperation must signify; or, perhaps better, the failures in human behavior that public policy has inadequately addressed.

Unwanted pregnancies emerge from the act of sex, usually outside of marriage. State and federal public policies offer inadequate attention to preventing nonmarital sex and, where there is sex, conception. Further, public policy does little to encourage adoption or to make adoptions easier to arrange. Our stingy social welfare system provides some but not enough help to those for whom poverty is the key motivation to abort. Our broken health-care financing system leaves many mothers and babies without critical health care. Abortions emerging within the marriage relationship are also affected by inadequate health coverage of contraception and sterilization procedures. Our business practices are often unnecessarily inflexible and thus make it impossible for some to balance work and family. Stagnant wages at the low end of the economic system do not pay enough to support a family.

In tandem, abortion-on-demand and public policies such as those just mentioned *both* contribute to choosing death rather than life; they make abortion more appealing and make raising children in difficult circumstances more demanding.

So what should Christians advocate for public policy related to abortion? Here the issue becomes the role of the "powers and authorities" in the perception or "way of seeing" dimension of holistic character ethics (chapter three). In a later chapter (chapter twenty-three) we will articulate our perspective more fully on the role of the church in the public-policy arena and the extent to which it is appropriate for us to seek to bring the will of God as we understand it into the public policy of our nation. But because most moral issues we will address in this book have a public policy dimension, we need to say a few words about this issue now.

Christian discipleship cannot be coerced. The Christian commitment to religious liberty means there are very real limits on the extent to which Christians should seek laws that reflect the full range of our values and convictions. Further, in a democratic and pluralistic society, legislation needs to be proposed and passed on the basis of a public ethic that can be affirmed by persons of various faiths and no faith. This public ethic can be an expression or translation of specific Christian faith, but that faith has to be expressed in terms that others can adopt as well, or it is an inappropriate establishment of religion. The legitimacy and enforceability of any law or public policy depends critically on the role of public consent. Christians are often quite impatient with these limits on making our values into public law; but such constraints are part of the genius of democracy; they protect our own liberty of conscience, and supporting them fits with biblical principles of justice and love.

Yet law is a legitimate instrument for righting clear social wrongs even when opinion is at first starkly and vehemently divided. Legal change can, at times, lead to social changes which conform to kingdom principles, as in the case of the civil rights movement of the 1960s. Sometimes the law can help a society snap out of its temporary moral blindness with regard to moral principles of fundamental significance. The challenge is determining when a moral issue should be treated as a matter for legislation rather than an issue of private conscience and personal liberty.

For example, Glen and Dot joined with a few other parents of handicapped children, organized by the Kentucky Association for Retarded Persons, to sue the State of Kentucky so that they would act on their obligation to educate retarded and other handicapped children who could benefit from public education. For two centuries, Kentucky had not provided this education, so that each year thousands of children who desperately needed education had none. Now they do. Glen and Dot had seen what a tremendous difference the School of Hope in the basement of Berea Baptist Church was making for moderately retarded adults who had had no schooling in their entire childhood. They were learning simple reading, math, hygiene, personal skills, work skills and how to find their way around the city, and they were being paid for work in a sheltered workshop. It transformed their lives! We wanted this for other handicapped children throughout the state. The church led; the state followed. This was one step in making it more possible for parents to raise their children rather than having abortions; but it was more basically the recognition of a fundamental human right.

These considerations remind us that it is possible to take a morally prolife but legally prochoice perspective (for a philosophical analysis of this position, see Spiegel, "Can a Christian Be Morally Pro-Life and Politically Pro-Choice?"). Ardent advocates of the prolife position generally find this inconceivable. But a Christian could adopt this view for several reasons, including
1. justice and self-determination for women (see Mollenkott, "Reproductive Choice");
2. the value of personal freedom, freedom of conscience in particular;
3. an understanding of religious liberty/establishment of religion (see Steffen, Life/Choice, 133-37);
4. concerns about enforceability;
5. the potential consequences of an unregulated "back-alley" abortion regime.

There are a number of morally questionable or even clearly immoral practices that the state may finally, for a variety of reasons, choose not to forbid, such as drunkenness, smoking, adultery or abusive language. Christians are not to participate in these practices, often enforce these moral commitments within their own disciplined faith communities, but generally (at least these days) do not advocate laws against them. The Christian prochoice perspective understands abortion in a similar way.

We do not finally agree with this view. We think that abortion does cross the line into an issue the state must regulate. A Christian public ethic opposing abortion-on-demand can be based both on concern for the well-being of women and on respect for the value of developing human life. Abortion ultimately does not serve the best interests of women, who bear the scars of abortion in their own bodies and souls. At a very deep level, as Feminists for Life has long argued, abortion is a form of violence against women. Women—whose power to make truly autonomous choices is often illusory within their relational contexts—pay the personal, moral and social costs of both male and female sexual irresponsibility (and sometimes male sexual violence) by becoming complicit in destroying the lives developing within their own bodies.

Those lives themselves have value. Even the much-derided *Roe* v. *Wade* decision acknowledged that fetal life does have a moral claim on society, a claim that grows in significance during the course of fetal development. Both as a matter of culture and law, however, American society has demonstrated over these thirty years what amounts to a cavalier disregard for developing human life. With 1.2 to 1.5 million abortions a year, and 20 to 25 percent of all pregnancies ending in abortion, our society has woven abortion into its very fabric. The functioning of our culture is in a sad way dependent upon destroying a million-plus developing human beings a year. This devaluation of the value of human life is a worthy subject of legal reform. Notice that this way of making the argument does not hinge on theologically defining fetuses as persons or on any particular religious claim at all.

We believe deeply in freedom of conscience and religious liberty, but we believe that these precious freedoms do not override legitimate rights or the personal and social interests just articulated. Questions about enforceability and the consequences of limiting access to abortion are legitimate. This is why we believe that legal steps related to abortion must be taken incrementally.

We think the best way forward is to promote measures that discourage abortion or restrict it a little at a time (some of these measures were explicitly upheld by the *Casey* decision). They include the following: a twenty-four-hour waiting period for abortion, parental consent for a minor's abortion and requiring exposure to information on fetal development and crisis pregnancy services. The most promising current possibility of a more far-reaching type is to ban third-trimester abortions or "partial-birth" abortions. Such incremental steps are a way to seek some common ground in American life—as neither a full ban nor the present permissiveness currently do (see Sherlock et al., "Mediating the Polar Extremes").

As each such incremental measure is passed and assimilated, further restrictions could be considered. In this way government could gradually affirm an increasing interest of the state in limiting abortions (an interest which seems quite faint right now, despite the language of *Roe* v. *Wade*), and so build precedent for further limits in the future. The short-term goal would be to pass any measure that prevents or discourages abortion in even the smallest way. The mid-term goal would then be to begin to create a legal and cultural climate in which abortion is officially discouraged and increasingly limited to specific circumstances.

Meanwhile, a compassionate Christian approach will link support for such abortion-restricting measures to a wide range of other public policy initiatives related to abortion. These include the development and distribution of better nonabortive contraceptives, efforts to combat rape, sexual abuse, incest and other sexual violations of women, strong emphases on sexual morality and responsibility for both men and women, broadening availability of high-quality and affordable day care, altering business practices to include more job sharing and other arrangements conducive to balancing work and family obligations, making sterilization and contraceptive products a routine part of insurance coverage, major initiatives against the grinding poverty that still characterizes the lives of millions and leads to the kind of hopelessness that undermines personal responsibility, improved adoption services and laws, and, finally, support for all relevant government and nongovernmental services to pregnant women, new mothers and their children. Policymakers should ask the same question that effective crisis pregnancy centers and maternal care nonprofits now ask: what would be required to change the circumstances that now drive many to choose abortion? Systematic attention to those issues, perhaps through legislation leading to enhanced public-private partnerships, would be the most effective way to reduce abortion at its source. And, of course, as we have emphasized throughout this discussion, the Christian public-policy witness on abortion will have integrity only insofar as our communities of faith incarnate the possibility of life without abortion and lead the way in offering needed support to those facing crisis pregnancies. These are not mere wishes. During the 1990s, with moral education in favor of responsible sex and against abortion, with laws like *Webster*, and with the unemployment rate steadily dropping and the economy improving broadly so families could afford to raise children, the abortion rate slightly but steadily decreased. We are not without hope. Steadfast initiatives can and do make a difference.

We view abortion as a tragic sign of much that is wrong in the world as we find it. Every year the gift of new life for which so many couples yearn is met with a fatal rejection by millions of others. Doctors are paid to reach into the womb and destroy what grows there. Who can rest easy with this sorrowful and cruel reality? Each abortion is another victory for the reign of death and sorrow. We can do better. We can value life at its mysterious and miraculous beginnings by rescuing women (and thus the babies they carry) from those pressures that lead them to choose death rather than life.

11

VALUING LIFE AT ITS END

Go and tell John what you have seen and heard: the blind receive their sight, the lame walk, the lepers are cleansed, the deaf hear, the dead are raised, the poor have good news brought to them.

LUKE 7:22

Abortion involves ending a life before it has opportunity to see the light of day; it comes upon its victim without warning and without the victim's consent. It forecloses all of life's possibilities.

Euthanasia takes us to the other end of life. It usually involves the person's consent; it may even be requested earnestly. It comes when further opportunities for meaningful living are believed to be at an end.

Despite these very significant differences, abortion and euthanasia can be treated together as issues related to the sacredness of human life made in the image of God. Both involve the decision to end human life. In both cases, that decision often marks a failure of imagination, a failure of mercy and a failure to value life adequately due to the temptations presented in contexts of suffering and sorrow. In the end, both mark a failure to find ways to participate in the advance of God's reign. This chapter considers how Christians can value life at its end.

Jesus, Death and God's Reign

The hospital suites and nursing homes in which most North Americans now spend their last days are a far cry from the dusty villages in which most first-century Jews breathed their last. And so it might seem that a Jesus-following ethic has little to offer to the contemporary question of euthanasia. This conclusion would be a mistaken one. Yet the dramatic cultural and contextual gap between Jesus' world and our own cannot be denied or ignored. Jesus did not address the issue of euthanasia directly. And yet his life and his teachings speak to the issues that the contemporary practice of euthanasia raises.

Jesus spent a goodly portion of his brief ministry healing the sick. Three times he raised the dead (Mt 9:18-26; Lk 7:11-17; Jn 11:38-44). He sent out the twelve "to proclaim the kingdom of God and to heal" (Lk 9:2). After his ascension the early church continued to enjoy and exercise healing power. Some branches of the church continue to exercise that power today. How many of us, in the face of the suffering of loved ones, have wished such power was available to us!

Why did Jesus make such a priority of healing and even, occasionally, of raising the dead? It was not because he could somehow in one brief ministry end human suffering or death. Given what the Gospels record about the swarms of people seeking healing, it is far more likely that he barely made a dent in the sick population of first-century Palestine. And men, women and children went on dying as he walked the roads of Galilee and Judea—as they do today.

Three main reasons for Jesus' emphasis on healing can be identified. First, Jesus healed as evidence that God was acting in him to inaugurate the kingdom. The prophets promised that in the days to come, in the days of God's decisive intervention to redeem Israel, he would heal his people. "I have seen their ways, but I will heal them; I will lead them and repay them with comfort" (Is 57:18; cf. Jer 30:17; cf. Is 61:1-2 Septuagint/Lk 4:18-19; and other Isaiah passages cited in chapter one above). Healing was a sign of the inbreaking of God's reign; just as sin introduced suffering into the world, so redemption would bring healing. The fact that Jesus had the power to heal helped validate his identity as the one in whom God was acting to bring in the kingdom.

This theme is apparent, for example, in the important exchange between Jesus and two emissaries sent by John the Baptist, as recorded in Luke 7. To the emissaries' question, "Are you the one who is to come, or are we to wait for another?" Jesus replied, "Go and tell John what you have seen and heard: the blind receive their sight, the lame walk, the lepers are cleansed, the deaf hear, the dead are raised, the poor have good news brought to them" (Lk 7:20-22). Each reference alludes to a text in Isaiah about the messianic age (Is 29:18-19; 35:5-6; 61:1-2).

Jesus also healed and raised the dead as an expression of his compassion for the suffering he daily encountered, revealing God's character afresh. Luke 7 contains the moving narrative of Jesus' raising of the only son of the widow of Nain. "When the Lord saw her, he had compassion for her and said to her, 'Do not weep'" (Lk 7:13). And so he raised the young man, one of the most dramatic public miracles of Jesus' earthly ministry. One senses that in miracles like this we see no particular strategic purpose but instead simply an overflow of the divine compassion toward suffering humanity.

Finally, Jesus healed and raised the dead as a foreshadowing of the coming consummation of God's reign. Once there was a time before sin and suffering, mourning and death. Now life is lived with the daily reminder of what was lost. And yet God had promised through Isaiah the renewal of heaven and earth and an end to all this sorrow (Is 65:17; 66:22). The book of Revelation climaxes with this renewed creation in which "death will be no more" (Rev 21:4). In healing the sick, raising the dead and himself being raised from the dead (1 Cor 15:12-13), Jesus blazed the trail between here and a renewed creation. There will come a time when death shall be no more. Jesus is the path between here and there.

Paul declared death to be "the last enemy to be destroyed" (1 Cor 15:26). Death's own death knell was sounded with Christ's resurrection and thus death's defeat; and yet only at the end will death finally be completely subjected to the Son (1 Cor 15:20-28). Until then we must continue to deal with death and the misery it brings. Human life is precious; illness and death devour men, women and children made in God's image and sacred in God's sight. Death is an enemy of human wholeness, arguably the ultimate enemy. And yet as we experience the suffering that illness and death bring we can be confident that death has been defeated and that the full unveiling of its defeat is only a matter of time.

This particular mix of themes from within Scripture leads to a stance toward grave illness and death that is quite distinctive and has remained relatively consistent in Christian history. Both illness and death are seen as evidence of a disordered creation. It was not this way in the beginning, Scripture says; this was not God's intent; and the misery that illness and death bring to immeasurably precious human beings mark these as foes resulting from human sin rather than divine design.

So illness and death are enemies, and enemies that may be fought using the best of our divinely given human intelligence and creativity. What we now call "health care" is simply one aspect of the human response to a tragically disordered creation. The stewardship mandate of Genesis 1—2 comes to include responding energetically to the immense misery brought into existence by human sin.

It is fully in keeping with biblical truth, then, to fight illness and forestall death. Christians have long led the way in developing and offering health care in many parts of the world, believing—rightly—that in so doing they imitated Jesus' own compassionate fight against illness and death.

And yet, a boundary is set to these efforts by the biblical affirmation that death will not be destroyed or eliminated until the end of time. Christ has defeated death but humans still die, and will do so until he returns to bring an end to human history as we know it. There is a kind of fighting-off of death that evidences a failure to acknowledge its inevitability. Death claims us all, and even with the best modern medical care it cannot utterly be forestalled. The effort to keep alive a physical body indefinitely at any cost (sometimes pejoratively labeled *vitalism*) reveals a sad unwillingness to face the reality of the human condition. It may be evidence of an idolatry of human life and an unchristian fear of death that characterize modern Western culture. Extended life is not our Lord; God, the Giver of life and Caretaker of our afterlife, is our Lord.

The Christian hope of eternal life certainly contributes needed perspective. Whatever the details of one's eschatological timetable, belief in "the resurrection of the dead and the life everlasting," as the Nicene Creed puts it, is a central component of orthodox faith. A lively confidence in this resurrection enables us as Christians both to fight death and then to give up the fight without despair when we can sense that the time has finally come.

These biblical affirmations do not settle all moral questions related to euthanasia, but they do establish something of a horizon for our thinking. We know that human life is a gift from God, and that each human being is precious in God's sight, made in the divine image; that illness brings great suffering; that illness and death are evils resolutely to be fought; that we are free to use our best efforts to fight them, so reflecting God's will for human life; that in doing so we will win some victories but that all such victories are temporary until Jesus returns; that therefore we must be willing to give up the fight and simply care mercifully for the dying when that course is indicated. This horizon of convictions has led Christians to the vigorous practice of health care and to a peaceable acceptance of death when death becomes inevitable—but not a moment before. (For a thoughtful discussion of these theological issues, see Rae and Cox, *Bioethics*, 224-31. We found Verhey, *Remembering Jesus*, chaps. 4-7, especially moving and insightful.)

Gilbert Meilaender concludes his discussion of this context for Christian reflection about death in this way:

> If we are to talk about death in terms of this [Christian] story, it must remain ambivalent. We must say *both* that it is to be resisted *and* that, for every human being, it must at some point be acknowledged. We can say one of these to the exclusion of the other only if we remove death from the context of the story and define it in some other way. (in Boulton, *From Christ to the World*, 406)

Euthanasia: Defining Our Terms

Definitions help set the terms for moral reflection, for good or ill, and this is nowhere more apparent than with regard to the issue of euthanasia. The term *euthanasia* is derived from the Greek *eu* (good) and *thanatos* (death). Thus in its etymological sense *euthanasia* simply means "good death." Contemporary English dictionaries, though, generally define *euthanasia* not as a description of a certain kind of death but as an *act*. The Oxford English Dictionary defines *euthanasia* as "the action of inducing a quiet and easy death"; for Webster's it is "an act or practice of painlessly putting to death people suffering from incurable conditions or disease." While some bioethicists reject this kind of definition, we will see that it is actually pretty close to the mark.

What might be called the "standard account" in defining euthanasia involves drawing two key distinctions: the element of *decision or choice* on the part of the recipient of euthanasia, and the *way in which death is effected*. The box below schematizes the six main types of euthanasia if segmented in this way by the two parameters of choice and means.

Table 11.1. Types of euthanasia (standard account)

	voluntary	nonvoluntary	involuntary
active	voluntary/active	nonvoluntary/active	involuntary/active
passive	voluntary/passive	nonvoluntary/passive	involuntary/passive

Let us first consider the spectrum of choice-making that runs from voluntary to involuntary to nonvoluntary. *Voluntary euthanasia* is defined by nurse ethicist Megan-Jane Johnstone as occurring when "a fully competent patient makes an informed and voluntary choice to have a medically-assisted death, asks for assistance to die, and gives an informed consent for the actual procedure of euthanasia to be performed" (Johnstone, *Bioethics*; all definitions below found on 314). In essence, in this form of euthanasia, the patient *volunteers* to die and asks for and receives medical help in so doing.

Johnstone defines *nonvoluntary euthanasia* as "the act of killing a patient whose wishes cannot be known either because of immaturity, incompetency or both." Here the person does not have the ability to offer a judgment or make a decision one way or another. The two most common cases would be the infant or very small child, on the one hand, and the mentally incompetent, on the other (which could include the mentally ill, someone in a persistent vegetative state or the unconscious person). Nonvoluntary euthanasia would involve ending the life of someone in such a condition.

Involuntary euthanasia, on the other hand, is defined by Johnstone as "killing a patient without the patient's informed consent and/or contrary to that person's expressed wishes." In other words, the patient is judged to be mentally competent to make this decision for herself but is either not given opportunity to do so or is given that opportunity, chooses against euthanasia and has her choice overridden by someone else. Most discussions of involuntary euthanasia emphasize the latter dimension, which we think correct; involuntary euthanasia is killing someone who has a desire not to be killed and has made that desire plain.

Let us reflect further on these distinctions related to choice-making for just a moment before considering the matter of active versus passive euthanasia.

Typically, medical practitioners in the Western world today deal with the issue of decision making in health care by emphasizing *patient autonomy* as a baseline principle (see Beauchamp and Childress, *Principles of Biomedical Ethics,* chap. 3). Patients themselves must make health-care decisions if they are competent to do so, and those decisions must be respected. This fundamental but deeply contested principle underlies the definitions just offered.

However, many times patients facing life-threatening conditions are unable to make decisions for themselves. They are either temporarily or permanently incompetent (or their cognitive and decision-making abilities are agonizingly unclear). In such cases, decision-making authority is handed off. Someone else is permitted, even required, to act as a proxy decision-maker. This is sometimes called *substituted judgment*—someone stands in for the incompetent person and makes the decision in her or his place. Normally this surrogate decision-maker is the next of kin (parent, spouse, family members functioning collectively), but by law any competent adult can be designated as another adult's surrogate decision-maker if appropriate legal arrangements are made by the person in advance, such as obtaining a *durable power-of-attorney for health care.*

The rather clinical/legal language of *health-care surrogacy* partly masks the reality that the dying patient is not just a patient but a person, a dependent and vulnerable person who amidst her or his health crisis is a member of the human community and the community of a particular family. Even when the very ill person remains technically mentally competent, family members play a key role in health-care decision making. When the sick person crosses the line into unconsciousness or incompetence, the role of the family is only heightened. Now the decision may rest entirely on their shoulders. In consultation with health-care professionals, families become a community of care and life-and-death decision making. The felt burden of such decision-making is frequently enormous.

Studies show that surrogate decision makers in such situations understand their moral responsibilities in starkly differing ways. Much depends on the quality of relationships prior to the health-care crisis. Even when those relationships are loving and life-affirming, differences emerge. Some family members believe they are supposed to act as the person they represent would if able to decide for herself. They attempt to place themselves in the loved one's situation and intuit a decision from her or his perspective. Others understand their role as acting on behalf of the patient's (or the family's) best interests, broadly and reasonably considered—to choose a path that is best for Mom, say, rather than the path that Mom necessarily would have chosen for herself. Sometimes family members cannot agree on what to do because of these differences in understanding how to make these decisions. State laws reflect these ambiguities in the various ways they define the role of the health-care surrogate or guardian (see K. L. Hall, *Oxford Guide to United States Supreme Court Decisions*, 67-68). And, of course, surrogate decision makers are not mere empty vessels. They bring their own humanity and their own interests to the decisions they make; we all do. If they come to the situation in a loveless or self-interested manner, the rights and interests of the sick person become deeply threatened.

Another complexity related to health-care decision making has to do with the widespread use of *advance directives and living wills*. The federal Patient Self-Determination Act of 1990 permitted and in fact encouraged the use of advance directives in order to give patients more power over the course of their own health care. Typically, advance directives attempt to spell out a variety of health-care options and the choices that people would want to make and have honored if ever they were incompetent to make such decisions for themselves. Thus, advance directives attempt to deal with the informed consent and competence questions by making all relevant decisions *in advance* of the condition ever arising in which such decisions might be needed. It is an attempt to avoid or limit the use of proxy decision makers and extend patient autonomy both backward (to the moment the advance directive was made) and forward (to the moment the advance directive is needed).

Theoretically, universal use of advance directives would mean that uncertainty as to the patient's will would rarely arise and surrogate decision makers would rarely be needed. However, the profound flaw of advance directives is their inability to account adequately for such realities as the highly contextual nature of health-care decision making, the unique conditions created by health emergencies, the necessary and inevitable role of families and loved ones, and the professional and moral obligations of doctors, nurses and other health professionals. The use of advance directives can signal a lack of trust both in health-care providers and in family members, and can in some cases actually make the decisions facing both groups more difficult when the crisis comes.

Further, in a very real sense the person who writes up an advance directive at, say, thirty-five years old may not be the same person thirty-five years later when the emergency comes (Nuland, "The Principle of Hope," 5). Her values may have changed; what she counts as "a life worth living" may be very different than it was earlier in her life. These are some of the reasons why advance directives are sometimes ignored by families and by medical professionals in health-care decision making, and why the "who decides" question is not as easy to dispense with as one might gather from the use of advance directives.

However one defines euthanasia, the issue of decision-making authority and processes will remain. Contested as these issues are, they pale in comparison to the second distinction Johnstone and most other bioethicists make, that between *active* and *passive* euthanasia.

The classic distinction between active and passive euthanasia is normally understood as hinging on *the difference between acting and omitting action*. Johnstone defines active euthanasia as "involv[ing] a deliberate act . . . which results in the patient's death," while passive euthanasia is defined as "a deliberate omission or the withholding of certain life-supporting cares and treatments." Other definitions of passive euthanasia add "withdrawing" to withholding, getting at the fact that sometimes medical treatments are begun and eventually withdrawn rather than simply withheld altogether. Yet both fall within the rubric of passive euthanasia as classically defined in bioethics literature.

What would count as active euthanasia? The Nazis, for example, actively "euthanized" men, women and children in various medical centers by subjecting them to poison gas. It was the first use of gas chambers by that regime and led the way to later mass gassings at death camps. Of course, this was nothing other than state-sponsored murder of the old, sick and incompetent under the name of euthanasia. Active euthanasia could also involve giving someone a fatal overdose of any number of drugs, shooting them or offering a lethal injection; any number of means could be used, though usually the goal is a painless death. What makes an act active euthanasia is a combination of intent, act and outcome—the goal is to end the person's life and an act occurs with this intent in view that brings about death. The intervention, whatever it is, actually constitutes the medical cause of death.

Passive euthanasia, on the other hand—if we retain the term—differs significantly from the foregoing. Patients, their surrogates and medical professionals here decide to refrain from pursuing or continuing medical treatments that might extend life or prolong dying in the face of a terminal condition. An extra round of chemotherapy is cancelled; a patient is not resuscitated during a cardiac arrest; a ventilator is shut off for a person unable to breathe on his own. In these cases the medical condition actually becomes the cause of death; omitting curative medical treatment (though not pain relief or comfort care) allows the medical condition to take its course. Death is no longer fought. The patient is allowed to die.

It is important to place the highly visible issue of *physician-assisted suicide (PAS)* in this context and to sharpen definitions there as well. Assisted suicide would occur when one person helps another person end his or her life; PAS, then, involves a physician helping another person kill herself. It is a form of *voluntary active euthanasia*. Advocates of PAS often draw a further distinction between a physician's providing a person with the means to kill himself or herself (for example, by writing a prescription or providing particular drugs that the patient then ingests himself or herself) and a physician actually participating directly in the suicide (by administering the drugs personally). Recent law in the Netherlands allows both forms of PAS; state law in Oregon since 1997 has allowed only indirect physician participation but does permit PAS in that form—over ninety Oregonians have killed themselves with physician help by the time of this writing. Sherwin Nuland notes that the effort to keep physicians out of direct involvement with the suicides they are assisting has, in the Netherlands, actually resulted in various difficulties in completing the act in nearly 20 percent of reported cases—and thus, ironically, increased patient suffering (Nuland, "The Principle of Hope," 29).

Historically, a bright line has been drawn between "active" and "passive" euthanasia in Western countries, both legally and morally forbidding the former and (in recent decades, at least) permitting the latter under carefully limited conditions. Today, this line is blurring both theoretically and legally. Some argue that there is no significant moral distinction between active and passive euthanasia, and that both should be permitted if properly regulated.

Many thoughtful bioethicists reject the active/passive euthanasia terminology in part because of its very susceptibility to this kind of line-blurring.

Paul Ramsey was among the first ethicists to challenge and reject this distinction. He wrote in 1978 that euthanasia involves "choosing death as one among life's choices" (*Ethics at the Edges of Life*, 148)—which, in Christian thought, human beings are not permitted to do because it involves "throw[ing] the gift [of life] back in the face of the giver" (146). So-called active euthanasia, for Ramsey, is simply euthanasia—the immoral act of choosing death.

Likewise, so-called passive euthanasia should not retain that term. What actually happens exists in a different moral universe. This kind of end-of-life health-care decision involves *letting die* or, in Ramsey's words, "dying well enough." It differs in *intent*, because the actual intent is not the patient's death but instead "to avoid useless prolonging of the dying process" (Clark and Rakestraw, *Readings in Christian Ethics*, 2:97). It differs in *act* because nothing is done that involves choosing death; medical efforts *shift* from cure to care but never to killing. (Ramsey emphasized that the classic distinction between *omission* and *commission* here is not nearly strong enough to describe the difference between euthanasia and letting die.) And it differs in outcome in that while euthanasia has the direct consequence of ending a patient's life, letting die enables the patient to live as well as possible while dying of the disease that eventually takes his or her life.

> We prefer to use euthanasia vocabulary not as a mere technical matter but to guard the sacredness of human life at the end of life. Voluntary euthanasia would then be viewed as choosing death through suicide or self-killing. Nonvoluntary and involuntary euthanasia would be choosing another's death without their consent, which is nothing other than murder, regardless of one's motives. Withholding or withdrawing curative treatments would be defined as letting die—in order to die well. Health-care providers in "letting die" situations do not cease their activities but shift to comfort care (sometimes called palliative care). Family members support the dying person in his or her decision making or make the decision for the incompetent person. After the decision is made, they accompany the dying loved one through the journey toward death by their presence and love.

Of course, definitions do not settle ethical debates. The debate over euthanasia has swirled intensively in our nation since the 1970s and remains in play. Let us turn to tracking the debate as it has unfolded.

The Contemporary Debate

The euthanasia debate has shifted dramatically since the time it began in the 1970s. That shift reveals a great deal not just about ethics but about American society, politics and economics. We want to propose that, at least in the U.S. setting, the euthanasia debate has come in three rounds, all related to the shifting structure of health-care delivery and financing, with each raising significantly different issues.

Round one. The Karen Ann Quinlan case of 1975 sparked an extraordinary national debate about what became known as the *right to die* and led to a revolution in health-care practices. Quinlan was a twenty-one-year-old who collapsed after swallowing a mix of alcohol and tranquilizers at a party and was plunged into a persistent vegetative state. A persistent vegetative state is "a condition in which there is no awareness of the self or the surroundings though the patient appears at times to be awake. The condition results primarily from severe cerebral injury. . . . The electroencephalogram (EEG) is either very depressed or flat. . . . 'Personality, memory, purposive action, social interaction, sentience, thought, and even emotional states are gone. Only vegetative functions and reflexes persist.'" This is different from a coma, from which some persons emerge

(Clark and Rakestraw, *Readings in Christian Ethics*, 2:119-20).

With no reasonable hope of recovery, and convinced of the futility and horror of life in this state for their daughter, Quinlan's family requested that her respirator be disconnected. This the hospital would not do, however, until forced to do so after multiple rounds of legal battles ending in a 1976 New Jersey Supreme Court decision that favored the family's request. In an ironic twist, after Karen Ann was removed from the respirator she lived nine years before finally dying in a New Jersey nursing home in 1985. Public sympathy for the Quinlans and revulsion at the prospect of indefinitely being kept alive against one's will led to the Patient Self-Determination Act, living wills and other means to enhance patient autonomy discussed above.

A similar case that raised the issue of the removal of artificial nutrition and hydration, as well as the complex question of how exactly to define death, was the *Cruzan* case, finally determined in 1990. A 1983 car accident left twenty-six-year-old Nancy Cruzan in a persistent vegetative state, kept alive only by a feeding tube. Cruzan's family waged a legal battle to have her feeding tube removed. The case wended its way through the courts until settled by the Supreme Court in 1990. The Court ruled on a 5-4 vote that there did exist a liberty-based right for a competent patient to refuse or stop life-preserving medical treatment, including artificial nutrition, but the majority concluded that the Cruzans had failed to offer "clear and convincing evidence" that Nancy Cruzan had communicated such a decision with adequate clarity prior to her accident. The only evidence of such a stance on Nancy Cruzan's part was from an informal conversation with a friend a year before her accident. Note that the Court here was unwilling to extend families the power to substitute their own judgment for that of incompetent patients.

After the Supreme Court decision, the Cruzans did offer evidence that met the standards of the Missouri courts, which allowed their wishes to prevail in late 1990. The feedings ended, and Nancy Cruzan died a few days afterward. *Moral* debate over whether artificial nutrition and hydration should be classed with other medical treatments that can rightly be withheld or withdrawn, which began with this case, remains quite intense (see Meilaender and Rakestraw, in Clark and Rakestraw, *Readings in Christian Ethics,* 2.109-31), though the legal debate was settled in *Cruzan.*

Note the dynamics of round one of the euthanasia debate: doctors and hospitals were offering, even imposing, health care that family members and individuals considered overly aggressive and unhelpful and thus demanded the freedom to refuse. *The problem at the time was defined as physician and hospital paternalism in imposing too much care, and the solution was defined as an increase in patient and surrogate autonomy and decision making power.* Those familiar with the health-care system will recognize how far away those days now seem.

248 KINGDOM ETHICS

Round two. To some extent, this particular pattern still remained in what we might call round two of the euthanasia debate—the battle over physician-assisted suicide and active euthanasia. Having gained the right to be allowed to die, patients and their advocates began pressing for a right to *active euthanasia*, even to physician assistance in suicide. This move was made by employing several of the same arguments applied in the successful push for a right to be allowed to die. Patient autonomy has been central to the case made for assisted suicide. As well, advocates make their appeal on the basis of the loss of dignity and the great suffering of many terminally ill and dying persons, claiming that society has an obligation to reduce such suffering or at least to enable the suffering to make the decision for themselves to end their own lives (for a summary of pro-euthanasia arguments, see Johnstone, *Bioethics,* 316-18).

For its advocates, success in round two would be state laws or court judgments establishing a right to active euthanasia or to assistance in suicide. For a time in the 1990s, it appeared that this goal would in fact be reached. Not only did Oregon pass such a provision by referendum in 1994—implemented in 1997, after court battles—but other states were also due to consider similar referenda. Further, two U.S. Appeals Courts decided cases in favor of a right to assisted suicide in the mid-90s. In *Vacco* v. *Quill,* the court based its decision on the Equal Protection Clause of the Fourteenth Amendment, while in *Glucksburg* v. *Washington,* the Due Process Clause of that same amendment was cited.

In 1997, however, the Supreme Court dashed the grandest hopes of PAS advocates with a 9-0 decision dealing with both cases just mentioned. With regard to *Vacco,* the Court (in a decision written by Chief Justice William Rehnquist) refused to accept the equal protection argument which had sought to erase the distinction between active and passive euthanasia and to claim a right to the former to match the right to the latter. In discussing *Glucksburg,* the decision rejected the claim that the concept of personal autonomy provided a sufficient basis to assert a due process right to commit suicide or be assisted in suicide. Further, the decisions offered positive reasons for the ban on physician-assisted suicide, such as the integrity of the medical profession in its healing role, the possibility of abuse and the value of human life. While this is certainly not the end of round two of the euthanasia debate, it marks a decisive turning point. Unlike abortion, assisted suicide will not become a federally-guaranteed right. It will be dealt with state by state.

Round three. The unexpectedly stark resistance of the Court to physician-assisted suicide reflected sensitivity to social and economic trends in health care that are coming to dominate the euthanasia debate of the early twenty-first century. Whereas in 1975 patients were concerned about *too much* health care directed at the terminally ill or dying, today we hear a loud chorus of concern about *too little* health care.

A hot term these days is "futile care theory." Physicians, hospitals and some bioethicists are arguing that when a doctor believes that the quality of a patient's life is too low to justify life-sustaining treatments, the doctor is entitled to refuse care based on its *medical futility*, even if the treatment is wanted by the patient or surrogate (for a balanced discussion of this issue, see Rae and Cox, *Bioethics*, 238-40). In the mid-1990s, some hospitals began quietly developing policies based on futile care theory to determine when doctors or hospitals might refuse to provide the health-care services patients or families requested. Legislation to similar effect has been proposed in various states and in Congress.

One can easily see a reasonable basis for some safeguards here. Patient autonomy ought not mean a right to demand an appendectomy to treat a sore throat or an amputation to deal with a headache. Medical professionals do have both professional and moral obligations to refuse to offer frivolous or harmful care to their patients. Doctors and nurses are not health-care automatons but instead moral agents in their own right. If they are asked to render genuinely frivolous or futile care, they need some way to object and refuse (see Johnstone, *Bioethics*, on the concept of *conscientious objection* in health care, chap. 15).

However, anecdotal evidence emerging these days shows that it is in large part the unjust economics of health-care delivery that are driving the development of futile care theory. Whereas in 1975 a hospital might have forced unwanted treatment on a patient, today that same hospital is far more likely to be tempted to *withhold* needed care, *especially if the patient is indigent, uninsured or underinsured* (see Rae and Cox, *Bioethics*, 217-20). The economic injustice of our society is brutally apparent in the health-care system; the current and quite legitimate fear is that our elderly, dying, expensive-to-care-for, disabled, incompetent and powerless patients will be quietly shuffled off to a premature death—because no one in the decision making loop finds it to be in their best interests to arrive at any other outcome (see W. Smith, " 'Futile Care' and Its Friends"). Or, for that matter, they may be told directly that they have a *duty to die* based on the demands of distributive or intergenerational justice.

Perhaps now we can see how the incipient round three of the euthanasia debate helped to determine the outcome of round two. Among those most strenuously and vocally opposed to the legalization of PAS were disability-rights groups, such as the provocatively named "Not Dead Yet," which saw in the potential legalization of assisted suicide a real threat to the very survival of people such as themselves. They rightly feared that a quiet conspiracy of health insurers, hospitals, doctors and perhaps unsympathetic family members might find a way to hasten them into the next world before their time and without their consent. Their concerns were buttressed by evidence from the Netherlands that this is precisely what has been going on there for some time, as legally tolerated voluntary euthanasia has become the occasion for considerable involuntary euthanasia (see Johnstone, *Bioethics*, 305-6; Rae and Cox, *Bioethics*, 248-52; Nuland, "Principle of Hope," 28). And so they objected, loudly, and their objections were heard.

What does our Jesus-following ethic conclude about the issue of euthanasia as the debate has played out in American society?

First, we believe round one of the euthanasia debate was rightly decided. The Quinlan and later Cruzan cases both rightly established a right to refuse unneeded or unwanted medical care at the end of life. The absurdity of extending the physical shadow of human life via increasingly intrusive and quite fruitless medical interventions was rightly understood. A Christian vision for both living and dying places limits on this sometimes frantic scramble. The time does come when health-care providers must turn their attention from hopeless efforts to cure the incurable to provision of the finest comfort care they can offer. Families need help as well, often both medical and pastoral help, in perceiving when the time has come for their loyalty to their dying loved ones to take the form of compassionately letting them die.

Second, round two of the euthanasia debate in America was also rightly decided. Despite the arguments of James Rachels and others, the historic distinction between active and passive euthanasia (between killing and letting die) must not be effaced but instead strengthened (see J. P. Moreland article, "James Rachels and the Active Euthanasia Debate," 2:102-8). The role of the health-care professional is to cure if possible, to care always, and never to harm or to hasten death. There is no right to assisted suicide that can be conjured up from the founding documents or principles of medical responsibility.

The way to meet the legitimate needs of the suffering and dying is through enhanced pain management *(palliative care)*, hospice care and other creative and loving efforts to assure, as far as possible, a good process of dying. The physician Sherwin Nuland, himself an advocate of very limited access to assisted suicide, argues that recent advances in palliative care "have in the past few decades reached a level of effectiveness such that suffering thought at first to be intractable can almost always be relieved" ("Principle of Hope," 2). The tragedy—even scandal—is that most doctors are unaware of these advances and are thus unable to put them to work for their patients: "The know-how is available, but too many physicians do not know how" (Nuland, "Principle of Hope," 4). The *fear* of dying a long and agonizing death (not necessarily a patient's current pain, but the fear of a sick and often depressed person that their pain will become worse) is perhaps the fundamental driving force behind the drive for euthanasia. The path ahead for Christian physicians and other concerned Christians is clear—to care for the dying in such a way that the desire for euthanasia is forestalled.

Meilaender may have been right when he claimed in 1976 that the distinction between killing and letting die is grounded in the Christian faith and may be increasingly unintelligible to the wider society (Boulton, *From Christ to the World*, 406). The challenge to Christians is to help make it intelligible nonetheless, and to provide various means by which people can be spared the temptation of choosing death either for themselves or their loved ones.

Third, round three of the euthanasia debate demands vigilance on the part of concerned Christians against the surreptitious or overt abandonment of the vulnerable under the economic pressures of our unjust health-care financing (non)system. While it is true that patient autonomy, including the right to demand health-care services, is not absolute, the greater danger at this time (and, really, most times, as Reinhold Niebuhr never tired of reminding us) is the abuse of *institutional* rather than *individual* power. Christ-followers hunger and thirst for community-restoring justice, including justice in health care.

Until Jesus returns and brings an end to illness and death at last, God's will is that each very sick human being be treated with dignity and compassion, receive needed curative treatments, enjoy family community, benefit from pain relief—and die only when their time has really come. Failures in family life, in the health-care system and in the broader society may tempt us and others to end life prematurely. But that is precisely what it is—a temptation. Christians must hold the line against the encroachment of euthanasia and assisted suicide, and, most obviously, an involuntary euthanasia that is simply murder by another name. We can best do so by offering compassionate care that meets the needs of the ill and the dying, and their families.

NEW FRONTIERS
IN BIOTECHNOLOGY

—

Take care that you do not despise one of these little ones; for, I tell you, in heaven their angels continually see the face of my Father in heaven.

MATTHEW 18:10

On June 26, 2000, scientists Francis Collins and Craig Venter joined Bill Clinton at the White House for the stunning announcement that the human genome had been decoded. The president declared: "Today, we are learning the language in which God created life." Having learned that language, human beings will spend much of the twenty-first century, for better or worse, attempting to speak it.

The cracking of the genome is just one of the scientific breakthroughs currently converging to earn our nascent twenty-first century Jeremy Rifkin's label: "the biotech century." Animal cloning, advances in genetic engineering and the discovery of the regenerative powers of stem cells are among the other major advances of our time. A new and constantly developing vocabulary—genetic therapy, xenotransplantation, designer babies, reproductive cloning and so on—strains the ability of even the most thoughtful to keep up.

A sense of the gravity of recent scientific advances appears to have created a brief opening for public deliberation prior to the onward rush of technological application. If this will be the biotech century, its first few years may be the only chance nonspecialists have to play any role in determining the direction or limits of technological advances. This moment marks a rare opportunity. Christians must participate in what is already an international conversation on the part of nearly every literate sector of society about what humanity will look like once we become fully fluent in the lexicon of human genetics. For persons of biblical faith to play a constructive role in that conversation will test our theological depth, scientific literacy, moral vision and political savvy.

What Has Jesus to Do with Biotechnology?

Bruce Birch and Larry Rasmussen have written the following:

> While there is much in human nature that binds all of us together across vast stretches of time and culture, and much moral wisdom and folly which makes its way from age to age, it is yet undeniable that Christian ethics today must find its way amidst moral questions which never appeared on the horizon of biblical ethics. (*Bible and Ethics in the Christian Life*, 12)

Among the issues they list are biotechnology and bioethics, gene splicing and cellular engineering, genetic counseling and gene patenting. And this was in 1989! Undreamt of at the time of the formation of the canon, these kinds of issues pose significant and complex challenges to those today who attempt to govern their lives according to biblical faith. How do we live according to Jesus' way when Jesus had nothing to say—when he *could* have had nothing to say—about certain issues that demand our response today? Are we here bumping up against a fatal flaw in our Jesus-centered Christian ethic?

We propose several elements of a response:

1. Despite the gap between Jesus' context and our own, the theological basic-convictions dimension remains unchanged. In other words, the basic biblical narrative that we have been working with throughout this volume is still true and still applicable in an age of great biotech innovations—or any age.

   God is the sovereign Creator and ruler of the universe. The earth groans under the impact of human sin. God has acted decisively in Jesus Christ to reestablish his effective reign. Jesus taught ways to untangle ourselves from the webs of sin we create and to move toward obedience to God's will, which include attention to compassion in action and to hunger for delivering justice. Followers of Jesus are diligent students of Jesus' teachings and practices, seeking to fulfill the mission of the church to participate in the advance of the kingdom until Jesus returns.

2. The transforming initiatives rendering of Jesus' teachings, we believe, offers insight into all areas of human life. No matter what issues emerge, it will be possible (though not always easy) to identify the basic contours of God's will, the vicious cycles and patterns of sin we get into, and transforming or creative initiatives that can help us move ahead in joyful obedience.

3. Jesus taught and modeled a way of life that offers fundamental norms that apply to all kinds of different issues, not just the particular concerns he had opportunity to address in his context. In section five of this book, we will identify the two central norms of this type as justice and love. There is no issue to which these norms do not apply. They might be described as the cardinal principles of Christian ethics. Recall the discussion in chapter five

of the form and function of moral norms, and the key role of principles in moral thought and action.

4. In his healing ministry, Jesus intersected with many of the same concerns that today drive biotechnological innovations. It is appropriate to look at Jesus' attitudes toward illness, death and healing in search of relevant patterns, practices and principles. The discussion of these issues in chapter eleven should be remembered in this chapter as well.

5. New moral issues remind us of the value of other sources of authority in Christian ethics. We are reminded that moral insight is gained and developed in various ways, including tradition, scientific observation and human experience. In a quest to understand newly expanding human powers and to discern the appropriate moral limits to place on these powers, any helpful source of insight must be considered.

   A unique role is played by the church's bioethicists. By now, bioethical issues, including biotech concerns, have been the subject of several decades of critical reflection in Christian ethics. The ancient tradition of Christian medical ethics has branched off several subspecialties in response to new developments; a very small number of specialists on such issues as cloning, stem cell research and genetic ethics devote most of their research to these specialized concerns. This work is an aspect of the moral discernment task of the broader Christian community. We always need to listen to the best thinking of the faith community as a whole; issues like cloning or stem cells remind us of this.

6. The corporate character of the church as a whole is critical in shaping responses to new moral issues as they emerge. It is a major theme in Birch and Rasmussen's volume—Christian moral decision making has everything to do with the individual and corporate character of the church.

   To use the language we have been employing in this volume, we might say that what needs to happen is a thoughtful encounter between Christ-followers, bound together in community, already practiced in a discerning way of life dedicated to seeking the kingdom, with the new issues demanding Christian response. Certain options, certain trajectories under consideration, will be rejected (or embraced) by such a community according to whether or not they "fit" with the moral vision and moral character of this particular people—whether or not they are permitted to proceed in the broader culture.

The New Science and Its Applications

DNA and the genome. In 1953 researchers James Watson and Francis Crick described the structure of deoxyribonucleic acid (DNA), the genetic material found in all living organisms. DNA contains the codes for all inherited characteristics, not only for human beings but for all life. Genes are segments of DNA, formed at conception when the mother's genes and the father's genes unite to create a new and genetically distinct person. The human genome has twenty-three pairs of chromosomes containing an estimated thirty thousand genes.

In 1990 the U.S. government began sponsorship of the Human Genome Project, led by Collins, which sought to map the position of all human genes. Intense competition from Venter's private Celera Genomics accelerated the effort's progress. While years of genetic sleuthing lie ahead, the overall trajectory is clear—the genetic code has been at least partially cracked, and over time the particular functions of more and more genes will be identified. It is a major breakthrough in human knowledge. Scientists are also now seeking to decode and map the million or so human *proteins* that are generated by our genes; this is called the human proteome. Some project that *proteomics,* with its much more detailed information about cellular processes, will ultimately dwarf *genomics* in its significance.

Applications of the new genetic knowledge are already upon us. For some years already, medical professionals have offered *genetic counseling* that includes *genetic screening and testing. Genetic therapies* are under investigation and clinical trials have begun, though thus far results have generally been minimal. Currently we stand at an awkward in-between stage where medicine can identify some genetic abnormalities without being able to do much about them—opening the door to *genetic discrimination* and *selective abortion* of those adjudged to be genetically flawed.

Genetic engineering. Mention of genetic therapies brings into view an earlier breakthrough in DNA research. Known as recombinant DNA technology, this work involves manipulating and modifying DNA. It has been going on since the 1970s. Scientists are able not only to understand the link between some particular genes and their associated traits, but also to act directly upon the genetic material itself. Sometimes called genetic engineering, this work has gone much further than most nonscientists know.

Consider developments related to plants, food and animals. The United States has grown 3.5 trillion genetically modified (GM) or engineered plants since 1994. *Biopharming* attempts to engineer animals, plants and crops with particular pharmaceutical uses for humans. Genetically altered or modified food is now widely produced. More than one hundred million acres of the world's best farmland were planted with GM crops in 2000, and it appears that bioengineered foods are becoming an irreversible part of the world's food supply, even where they are not labeled as such or even welcomed.

Meanwhile, work proceeds on altering animal characteristics and experimenting in various ways with animal species. One application is *agricultural biotechnology,* which aims to identify desired animal genes, engineer animals accordingly and mass produce the desired animals through cloning. Such efforts are intended to create "super-naturally" strong, healthy and productive farm animals, to develop products for human health and to test therapies for human diseases. Thus far, many of these animals suffer gross abnormalities or simply die as failed experiments.

And of course, the big issue is the manipulation of *human* DNA. Scientists may one day be able to modify and engineer the human the way they now manipulate plants and animals. This effort is broadly labeled *human genetic intervention* and is generally broken down into four options (though these categories are disputed—see below). *Somatic therapy* would aim to repair a defect in the gene of a living individual; *germline therapy* would alter a person's reproductive DNA and thus prevent genetic errors from being passed on to any future generation. *Somatic enhancement* would engineer improvements in desired genetic traits for an individual; *germline enhancement* would engineer such improvements for future generations.

Cloning. It was within the context of genetic work related to animals that Dolly, the cloned sheep, was birthed in 1997. Dr. Ian Wilmut, a researcher at Edinburgh's Roslin Institute, was working on improving the genetic engineering of sheep when he became the first scientist to discover how to clone an adult mammal. Cloning involves extracting the nucleus of an adult cell and inserting it into an egg cell that has been stripped of its own nucleus. Wilmut figured out how to reprogram this cell to begin cell division as an embryo, thus creating an entirely new animal via asexual reproduction (this process is called *reproductive cloning*). After 277 tries, Dolly was born, the first asexually replicated adult animal. Since Dolly, at least six other animal species have been cloned, though at the cost of frequent fetal deaths, gross anomalies, mutations and other deviations. Animal cloning is being explored for medical research and agricultural biotechnology, and some argue for cloning to save endangered species.

Thus far, it *appears* that no one has successfully cloned an adult human and brought that clone to birth *(reproductive cloning)*. But we cannot be sure. Proposals endorsing human cloning have been floated, and some flamboyant researchers are promising to go ahead with cloning no matter what governments or public opinion might prescribe. Meanwhile, the matter is under serious discussion in mainstream medical and bioethics journals. The most commonly cited scenarios for human reproductive cloning include its use as a form of assisted reproduction (for couples with unusable sperm and eggs, homosexual couples, couples who risk passing on serious genetic disorders and single people). It is also sought by those hoping to conceive a child whose tissues would match that of a sick or dying child in need of treatment, or as a replacement for a dying or dead child or other loved one. Various other motives for reproductive cloning are under discussion.

Stem cells. In 1998 scientists discovered that a particular kind of cell, the stem cell, showed extraordinary promise for human healing. Embryonic stem cells are primordial cells that have not differentiated for particular uses by the body's 210 kinds of tissues but may be able to be used anywhere the body needs them for transplantation and replacement tissue. They show great promise for the treatment of cancer, Alzheimer's, Parkinson's, burns and a host of other conditions. Embryonic stem cells are further differentiated into totipotent, pluripotent and multipotent cells, depending on the embryo's stage of development.

Stem cells were originally discovered through research on human embryos. Available embryos came primarily from aborted fetuses and from some of the thousands of embryos not needed after couples employed assisted reproductive services. Today, some propose cloning as the best source of embryonic stem cells, particularly because the cloning of one's own cells is most likely to produce cells that will not be rejected by the body during treatment. This kind of cloning is called *therapeutic cloning*. In January 2001 Great Britain's Parliament made that nation the first to permit human cloning for precisely this purpose. Meanwhile, it has been discovered that umbilical cords, placentas and several portions of the adult body also carry stem cells; research and early therapies using these sources of stem cells are proceeding. Non-stem-cell-related strategies for *regenerative medicine* are also being explored.

Discerning the Signs of the Times

How shall Christians respond? Our faith offers us a way of perceiving reality. Can biblical faith offer a meaningful analysis of what is going on around us?

The science-technology-commerce connection. A quite concrete observation starts us toward an answer: it is not humanity-in-general that discovered and first practiced animal cloning, but a particular research scientist at a biotech firm in Scotland. It is not a vague spiritual force that is pushing today for embryonic stem cell research, but particular researchers and corporations.

At one level, the driving force behind the remarkable innovations we are considering here is simply the sprawling biotech industry itself, already doing more than eighty billion dollars worth of business in the United States alone. Like all industries in a capitalist economy, it exists to maximize profits and expand global markets. The private rather than public control of critical technological innovations is one of the most significant features of the biotech era and distinguishes this particular challenge from that raised in the last century by atomic and nuclear weapons, harrowing enough as that was.

Western Christians rarely offer sustained moral critiques of the dynamics of free-market capitalism but instead generally give ourselves over to our culture's grandest idol; the very idol (Mammon) that Jesus so constantly warned his listeners about (see chapter twenty). But the need for a sharp-eyed realism about economic life is more important now than ever, in an era of rapacious globalization. Developments in the biotech business simply demand such realism if any kind of moral response is to be offered. Powerful market forces, including that perennial desire for profit, tangle human beings up in patterns of conduct that ultimately prove destructive. We need at least to be willing to consider that this is what is happening in the biotech industry today.

Consumer demand. Suzanne Holland has written, "It is axiomatic in capitalism that the market exists both to create and to satisfy desire" ("To Market, to Market"). The biotech industry would not be awash in investor money were there not an expected demand for its products. Clones, genetically engineered embryos and stem cells are potential products all related to fundamental aspects of human desire or human need, such as the quest for health and success, the easing of suffering, the reproduction imperative and even the desire for immortality. The biotech industry both stimulates consumer desires and responds to the market demands of those who can afford to satisfy them. It is hard to bet against an industry that speaks to such primal human concerns, especially when the consuming public has been so exquisitely trained to seek happiness through the marketplace. Yet where shall it end? Daniel Bell argued in the 1960s that the "cultural contradictions of capitalism" would ultimately be self-devouring, as the unleashing of a consumerism impatient with any restraints would ultimately destroy the cultural virtues needed to sustain capitalism itself. Now we have reason to wonder whether it is not just a particular society but humanity itself that will finally be devoured by the unintended consequences of laissez-faire biotechnology—the ultimate vicious cycle.

Moral fragmentation. Ultimately, the direction that biotechnology takes will be an international decision. Yet the challenge of somehow actually having a coherent international moral conversation is staggering. Just how staggering is apparent when one thinks about how difficult it has been in recent decades for us to have a serious *national* conversation in the United States. Larry Rasmussen has written: "Our society currently lives from moral fragments and community fragments only, both of which are being destroyed faster than they are being replenished" (*Moral Fragments and Moral Community,* 11). A morally fragmented nation such as our own may lack the basic requisites for even having a conversation—a shared framework of meaning, a minimal level of trust, commitment to a common purpose and an agreed-upon vocabulary. Yet to fail to have a conversation and arrive at national (or international) decisions is to default to existing forces of power and interest, and quite likely to stumble into disaster.

Worldview dynamics. This leads us to a still deeper reality. Certainly the biotech industry wants to make money, and consumers want its products. But consumers are more than economic actors; we are creatures with a consciousness, whose actions and motives are themselves driven by broader presuppositions. In other words, we are worldview-holders, and those worldviews themselves are grounded in the particular stories we tell and believe. This is the theological basic-convictions dimension we have been considering throughout this volume.

Among some of those who press most aggressively for unrestrained development of biotech advances, we can identify worldview elements such as naturalism, atheism, utilitarianism and scientific utopianism. Many among us, quite tragically, live without the working hypothesis of God. Instead, many believe that we are on our own in a godless universe. Our task is simply to make human life as good as it can be until the next meteor hits. We must use our intelligence and skill to maximize happiness and minimize misery, for ourselves as individuals *(hedonism)* or, more nobly, for humanity as a whole *(utilitarianism)*. Even after Auschwitz and Hiroshima, many continue to dream of a society where most misery has been eliminated by science and technology (a belief sometimes called *techno-utopianism*). On this theme, Alison Caddick has written: "Today we are increasingly joined in the worship of the new technological dream. . . . We . . . move in this direction as we are emotionally drawn to its immense transcendent power" ("Bio-Tech Dreaming," 29).

The *libertarian* ideology whose nexus consists of *individualism, privacy, choice-making* and *autonomy* is also hugely significant here. If there are no divinely established limits on human conduct, no givens to human nature, no immutable deontological moral code and no binding obligation to pursue the common good, then human beings must be set free to pursue the good life as they define it with as much liberty as possible—constrained only by the legitimate interests of their neighbors and the limits of their own economic resources. No choice for self-realization that is not immediately harmful to another, it is believed, should be denied to the individual.

The combination of these factors means that a powerful contingent among us argues for the largely unrestrained pursuit of biotechnology as a matter of individual and reproductive liberty; in a pluralistic and fragmented society/ world lacking moral consensus; in pursuit of goods and benefits that the marketplace vigorously promotes and serves; in the context of an explicit or implicit belief that human beings are alone in this universe and must make our own choices without reference to a divine Creator; and in pursuit of a dream of overcoming our species' limits through human power and scientific progress.

That last item is worth lingering over. If the proverbial alien were to visit our planet today, he would see a species of extraordinary abilities that demonstrates little hesitation in transgressing historic understandings of what it means to be human (or animal, for that matter—the manipulation and exploitation of animal life deserves much more attention than it has received, and for this sensitivity Peter Singer is in fact to be commended). Some thinkers these days are suggesting triumphantly that our species is about to evolve right past *homo sapiens* to what Gregg Easterbrook has called *homo geneticus* ("Medical Evolution"). Some are trumpeting our power to gain control over human evolution. We will rebel against nature, leave the limits of the past behind and remake humanity itself. Yet right now, as bioethicist Audrey Chapman has suggested (*Unprecedented Choices*, 76), the nations as a whole are not sure they ought to pursue this siren song. They seem to be pausing for a moment at the brink, waiting to hear any reasons as to why they should not plunge unrestrainedly into the remaking of humanity.

Crafting a Moral Response—Stem Cells

It is not yet clear whether the potential health benefits of various stem cell therapies will actually be as dramatic as some researchers now suggest, but there is no reason to limit stem cell research and application as long as the source of such cells is morally unproblematic. The use of adult stem cells, umbilical cord cells and placenta cells in research and medical treatment, for example, raises no moral problems if one is open to the work of medicine at all. Stem cells from these sources are already being used in some therapies. Indeed, Christians should support initiatives like the bill proposed in 2001 by Representative Chris Smith (R-NJ) to establish a National Stem Cell Donor Bank involving only these cell sources. Such a donor bank would have the advantage of making stem cell research a fully legitimated public initiative and would make such cells far more widely available than is currently the case.

The use of embryonic stem cells raises very different issues, however. Such cells can originate from three primary sources: cloning, manipulation and destruction of an already existing embryo (most often a frozen leftover from assisted reproduction efforts), and voluntarily aborted fetuses. Researchers in several countries have cultivated *stem cell lines* (originating from a variety of sources) which they hope can provide an ongoing supply of fresh stem cells for research and medical use. Each of these sources of embryonic stem cells raises the question of the moral status of embryonic and fetal life. As such, this issue dovetails with the sacredness of the life of a human that we saw in the abortion question and must be considered in similar terms.

Let us begin with the (apparently rare) case of the use of aborted fetuses for stem cell extraction. We believe that research using electively aborted fetuses, where it occurs, involves the researcher in complicity with a prior wrong. This concept of complicity is difficult, but essentially it involves partnership or co-operation in wrongdoing, even if one had no role in the original wrong itself, and even if one's own motives are beyond reproach. Nazi scientists, for example, conducted all manner of horrific experiments on concentration camp prisoners. Knowledge with some medical value was occasionally gained. Yet the medical community, in order to avoid complicity with evil, generally rejected use of this knowledge due to the circumstances of its acquisition.

As for unused frozen embryos, of which it is estimated that there are a hundred thousand in the United States alone, the moral problem is simply the manipulation and ultimately the destruction of a human life at its earliest and most defenseless stage. A prior problem exists, of course; the routine practice in the largely unregulated assisted reproduction industry of producing many more embryos for infertile couples than they normally could ever use. There are various economic and practical considerations leading to this practice but it makes a fine example of the law of unintended consequences. Twenty years ago, at the dawn of assisted reproduction, no one imagined that two decades later a city's worth of embryos would await an uncertain future in icy limbo. Now they just sit there, a vulnerable target for mass experimentation and destruction—and for the utilitarian argument that because they are destined for destruction some good should be made of them.

So-called therapeutic cloning—human cloning in order to produce embryos intended for experimentation and research—is the most morally troubling of all potential sources of stem cells. This is so because (a) it involves the morally dubious practice of cloning itself and could surreptitiously lead to reproductive cloning, and (b) it *intentionally* manufactures human life with full intention of its ultimate destruction, rather than just using aborted fetuses or frozen embryos that happen already to be in existence.

Some researchers are pressing for therapeutic cloning because they believe it shows the greatest promise of producing usable embryonic stem cells. At a moral level, they argue that therapeutic cloning is different from reproductive cloning, in that embryonic development is cut off quite early, before the embryo could even have nested in the wall of the uterus, which is the third essential ingredient in (potential) human personhood: sperm plus ovum (fertilization) plus nesting in the uterus (implantation). Thus a therapeutic clone has potential, but it does not yet have the essential ingredients to form a human person. They conclude that a clear line can be drawn between therapeutic and reproductive cloning.

In offering a moral evaluation our triadic model may be helpful. The relevant traditional teaching is "do not murder." The vicious cycle we are in involves the temptation to respond to the very real miseries and maladies humans endure in a utilitarian manner by manipulating and destroying nascent lives in the hope of ameliorating those miseries. Some are destroyed so that others might live and flourish. Because a three-day-old embryo is not recognizably "human," and because it cannot speak for itself and represent its own interests, we are tempted to reduce it purely to a clump of cells usable as a means to a beneficent end.

In response to this very difficult challenge, Christians are called to advance transforming initiatives that go as far as possible to meet the human needs at stake but resolutely resist the temptation to destroy the developing life of a human person to get there. Our stance is analogous to the argument of Samuel Roberts (*African American Christian Ethics*, 248): "Human life is sacred, even if it is the result of medical initiatives. . . . To use this method to achieve a cure for sickle-cell anemia is fraught with much ethical turmoil, and, on the face of things, could not enjoy moral justification in my judgment."

As a matter of public policy, then, Christians and others who value fetal life have a right and obligation to press for the exemption of embryonic stem cells from the research efforts now being undertaken. This is especially the case in light of the availability and apparent promise of other sources of stem cells and other paths to the goals of regenerative medicine. Discovery of cures for such maladies as Parkinson's disease, Alzheimer's and sickle-cell anemia would be one of the great accomplishments in the human stewardship of the created order; but we are not morally permitted to pursue even this lofty goal via the destruction of human life at its earliest stage.

President George W. Bush attempted to resolve this issue in the U.S. setting—at least, the issue of federal involvement in stem cell research—by permitting federally funded research only on the sixty or so stem cell lines that existed at the time of his decision in August 2001. This decision opened the door to federal funding of embryonic stem cell research but refused to permit those funds to be used in the destruction of new embryos. While the decision was in its way politically ingenious, at a moral level it is more problematic. It does involve the federal government in complicity with prior wrongdoing and may have the consequence of creating a momentum for the later loosening of regulations under pressure or under a different president. And it must be remembered that our laissez-faire political economy means that all kinds of morally odious embryonic stem cell research will continue unregulated because it does not involve federal funding.

Cloning

A fascinating thing happened during the international human cloning debate that broke out after Dolly made her appearance—one could watch large sectors of the human community draw a line in the sand and say, "This crosses a line; this must not happen." A number of governments around the world rushed to ban reproductive cloning. Secular scientists, philosophers and physicians made arguments against it. Religious voices did not stand alone.

This does not mean that powerful and articulate voices within the biotech world and elsewhere are not actively making the best case they can for reproductive cloning. Nor does it mean that the research has halted. It is quite possible that someone will attempt reproductive human cloning, or that someone already has. But it may mean that the human family will actually rouse itself to draw an effective line before cloning becomes a fait accompli.

The best case against reproductive human cloning has been made by Leon Kass of the University of Chicago, head of the president's bioethics advisory council. Kass summarizes his case in the following four points: it constitutes unethical experimentation, it threatens human identity and individuality, it turns procreation into manufacture, and it means despotism over children and the perversion of parenthood.

Cloning is unethical experimentation because, among other reasons, the subject is nonconsenting, and because animal cloning so far reveals a very high failure rate and a very high incidence of major disabilities and deformities. No ethical scientist would proceed with human reproductive cloning under current conditions.

Cloning threatens human identity and individuality by permitting the intentional genetic replication of a person whose life is already in process. Says Kass: "He [the clone] will not be fully a surprise to the world; people are always likely to compare his doings in life with those of his alter ego" ("Preventing a Brave New World," 34).

Cloning turns procreation into manufacture by enabling the selection in advance of a total genetic blueprint. Things are *made* but people are *begotten*. In cloning, that boundary line is erased. "In natural procreation, human beings . . . give existence to another being that is formed exactly as we were, by what we are. . . . In clonal reproduction . . . we intend and design" a particular human child (Kass, "Preventing a Brave New World," 34). (Kass rightly notes that baby manufacturing actually has been underway ever since in vitro fertilization began.)

Cloning means despotism over children and the perversion of parenthood by turning children into genetically engineered possessions intended to fulfill parental wants rather than, as Sondra Wheeler puts it, human beings welcomed hospitably as a kind of stranger whom we can never possess ("Making Babies?"). Some argue that many children are already brought into the world for some parental reason other than the sheer desire to welcome new life. The right response to this is simply to reject (at last!) the commodification or instrumentalization of children however they are born rather than to extend such trends any further. Vicious cycles are to be ended, not extended.

A number of other arguments against reproductive cloning can be adduced. It would mark the first time that humans have reproduced through asexual replication, radically altering the nature of human procreation and eliminating dual genetic origin. In a law review essay Cathleen Kaveny has shown how dramatically cloning would confuse family lines and relations. If distributed purely by the market based on ability to pay, it would contribute to distributive injustice. It would weaken the relationships between men and women by further effacing the marriage/sex/reproduction link and for the first time enabling reproduction without any kind of involvement of representatives of two sexes. It would deepen the misery of children after divorce, as Mom has to look at hated Dad's young clone all day long (Kass, "Preventing a Brave New World," 34).

Cloning would contribute to our epidemic narcissism by enabling self-creation without any involvement of another; it would enable multiple self-cloning and thus the creation of a household freak show. It could be used without someone's consent. Or, alternatively, particular genotypes could be marketed by the famous or simply by corporate interests for those wanting an illusory guarantee of their children's success. Finally, in the end cloning does not meet any legitimate human need. Many kinds of reproductive technology exist for the infertile. And the effort to bring back a dead child through cloning (commonly cited in the pro-cloning literature) would mark a horribly sad and misguided attempt to salve a grief that cannot be salved, and at the cost of exploiting another human being created in the image of one's own projections, expectations and desires.

Human reproductive cloning clearly should be banned. The United States, which has the largest biotech industry in the world, must join dozens of other nations in banning cloning before the genie is out of its bottle. As of now, we are lagging irresponsibly behind. And we should push for an international agreement, because the problem cannot be solved by one government alone.

Genetic Therapies

The issue of various kinds of genetic therapies may be the most morally difficult of the three we are considering here.

As we noted earlier, a distinction between somatic therapies and enhancements and germline therapies and enhancements has been recognized in this field since the 1980s, with ethicists generally saying yes to somatic therapies and no to germline therapies and any kind of genetic enhancement efforts. But now questions are being raised about the scientific accuracy and moral relevance of these distinctions. An American Association for the Advancement of

Science (AAAS) study group has suggested abandoning the terminology and instead distinguishing only between inheritable and nonheritable genetic modifications. Let us consider first nonheritable genetic modifications, both to address disease and to enhance genetic capacities.

Francis Collins has written that the goal of genetic medicine right now is actually much more modest than the press reports would suggest: to identify gene variants that *may* (in combination with other genetic and environmental factors) increase people's risk of developing various illnesses ("Heredity and Humanity," 28). On the basis of this information, researchers hope, it will eventually be possible to design individualized programs of preventive medicine and disease treatment. Assuming that *somatic therapies* (nonheritable genetic modifications) of this type are safe before they are used, there does not seem to be any persuasive moral reason to resist such therapeutic advances. They would mark an important new advance in health care.

What about germline (or other inheritable) genetic modifications that would be intended to prevent the expression of genetically transmitted maladies? Several points argue in favor of germline therapy: some maladies might be cured, it might be the only way to attack some diseases, and prevention costs less than cures. If, for example, the gene for Tay-Sachs or Huntington's disease could be eliminated from the reproductive DNA of all those who carry it, these truly terrible diseases themselves could presumably be wiped out.

There are several concerns. One is simply scientific. If, as Collins argues based on the best current information from the genome project, the role of genes is complicated and undeterministic, and genes interact unpredictably with environment and free will, then the supposed promise of germline interventions may be vastly overstated. We may simply be in over our heads and end up doing more harm than good both for individuals and for the human race. The AAAS report states flatly that inheritable modifications cannot now be carried out safely on human beings ("Human Inheritable Genetic Modifications," 7).

Further, modification of inheritable characteristics would affect not just the individual but all of his or her offspring; more broadly, routine interventions of this type would affect the overall gene pool of the human race. Another concern is distributive—unless we create a health-care regime in which everyone gets access to germline therapies, then one can easily imagine the development of a two-tier society divided between the genetic haves and the genetic have nots. There is also the overall resource allocation issue; in a society with forty million uninsured for health coverage, how can we proceed with such exotic therapies for the few? Existing patterns of social advantage and power would only be exacerbated. There is the concern that efforts to eradicate genetic diseases will contribute to the social stigmatization of those who have them. Finally, it is hard to see how a firm line can be maintained against germline enhancement if we permit germline therapy. For these reasons and others, the AAAS report takes a markedly cautious stance on any use of inheritable genetic modification.

The issue is all the more acute if one considers germline *enhancement*. Here prepackaged excellence of various types would be imposed upon the next generation. All of the criticisms leveled against cloning—especially experimentation on nonconsenting subjects, parental despotism, reduced individuality and baby manufacturing—are even more relevant here. And the concerns about germline therapy are only heightened, as the built-in risks of germline manipulation must be measured against a much more dubious good than the prevention of inheritable diseases.

A variety of interesting approaches for resolving these issues is under consideration among ethicists. One helpful proposal for a new way to draw the line was made in a book called *From Chance to Choice: Genetics and Justice* (Buchanan et al.). The authors flatly propose that the purchase of what might be called "narcissistic excellence enhancements" should be prohibited by law. This would apply either to somatic or germline interventions. However, they argue for a socially arrived-at account of a small core of very basic human capabilities and for access on the part of all citizens in all health plans to genetic therapies (if they want them) that might be helpful in arriving at such capabilities. In a sense, this is the model that already prevails in health care (though it is deeply corrupted by unequal access due to flaws in how we distribute health-care services). It would simply be extended to genetic medicine. James Peterson likewise argues for a reconsideration of the absolute rejection of germline interventions, though in a spirit of very cautious deliberation and incremental application of new therapies (*Genetic Turning Points,* 306-21).

Eventually the fundamental distinction on this issue may be between narcissistic excellence enhancements and legitimate genetic therapies as an accepted dimension of health care. While the current incompleteness of knowledge related to inheritable genetic modifications demands at least a moratorium on any application of such interventions, research should be permitted to continue. It is possible to imagine a situation in the future in which very carefully targeted genetic maladies are nationally and even internationally eliminated through rigorously tested therapies made available to all who need and want them.

It may be, though, that this distinction between therapy and enhancement will be impossible to maintain in practice, and that humanity (some of us, anyway) will not be able to restrain itself from crossing this threshold. But it seems a good place to draw the line. We are called to heal the ill and advance *human* life, not to engineer ourselves into some other kind of species altogether.

Conclusion: At the Threshold

We argued above that the world, especially the biotech industry, asks the church this question: *Tell us why we should not proceed to remake humanity now that we are developing the power to do so.* Our answer is this: You rightly perceive a mandate to alleviate human suffering. You will have our support as you press such legitimate efforts. But you must pursue this mandate within the boundaries of human well-being under the sovereignty of God. These boundaries include limits on the means you may use to accomplish the goal you pursue. Human beings may not be manufactured, engineered or destroyed; the vulnerable may not be experimented on or otherwise used without their consent; legitimate benefits of your innovations may not be restricted to the privileged; and you may not make your decisions without the consent of the rest of humanity. Certainly Christians must make this their public witness and live according to such principles in their own personal decision making.

Audrey Chapman asks: "Will society have the wisdom, the powers of discernment, and the appropriate commitments to apply its new knowledge and capabilities for ethical ends?" (*Unprecedented Choices*, 2). May God graciously guide our steps, that the answer to that question will reflect wise exercise of our stewardship.

SECTION IV:

Male and Female

In this section, we take up a number of vexing questions pertaining to human relationships and sexuality. Topics include marriage, divorce, premarital sex, birth control, homosexuality and gender relations in family, church and society.

This section offers a good test of our kingdom-focused methodology. Many classic Christian treatments of these issues offer approaches rooted in natural law or orders of creation. We think that retaining our focus on Jesus' teachings yields fresh insights. The Sermon on the Mount offers critically important pericopes explicitly focused on marriage, divorce and sex, and carries implications for the entire way we think about male-female relations and roles. This section of the book is also important in focusing heightened attention on the fundamental biblical concept of covenant.

13

MARRIAGE AND DIVORCE

—

It was also said, "Whoever divorces his wife, let him give her a certificate of divorce." But I say to you that anyone who divorces his wife, except on the ground of unchastity, causes her to commit adultery; and whoever marries a divorced woman commits adultery.

MATTHEW 5:31-32

I (Dave Gushee) know a man who at the age of twenty, freshly returned from the trauma of war, married the first woman with whom he became involved. He was her third husband. She soon proved unfaithful, sleeping with his friends and coworkers, and making little effort to hide it. But this man had been taught that it was wrong to divorce and believed that people should not walk away from their problems. Finally, after seven miserable years, he ended the marriage. He later met another woman, fell in love and married again. They have now been happily married for over forty years and have raised four children.

Story two: In seminary, my wife and I became very close to a couple who were newlyweds, as we were. Together we experienced seminary and together we prepared for lives of ministry. How warmly I remember double dates with this couple and the love that they freely and openly shared with each other.

Seminary ended, and we parted ways. Ten years passed, and both couples had three children. After a while we learned that our friends had begun to have marital troubles. Then there was progress. Then more trouble, and counseling, and finally a decision on the wife's part to end the marriage. My wife pleaded with her to reconsider. There had been no adultery, no cruelty, no drug abuse, no violence. Problems centered around an accumulation of small resentments, leading to a slow choking out of the love this wife once had for her husband.

And so they divorced, adding three small children to the other million or so who each year have to adjust to having two families, two homes and two lives,

painfully observing that the mother they love and the father they love no longer love each other. Some years later I attended my friend's wedding. I will not
soon forget the beauty of the ceremony, nor the way the new stepmother made
every effort to craft out of this brokenness one family. Nor will I soon forget
the brave effort on the part of three young-yet-old, happy-yet-sad children to
participate in the remarriage of their father and the reconfiguring of their most
intimate world, yet again.

A third story: During my first year of teaching at Union University I encountered a deeply troubled young lady whose family history was a patch-
work of marriage, separation, divorce and cohabitation. In her short lifetime
she had experienced five marriages on the part of her mother and four on the
part of her father. She was a product of the original marriage, and it was clear
that she had long ago been left behind in the affection of her parents. Indeed,
that puts it far too nicely, for she also told of occasions of abuse at the hands of
some of the many (supposed) grownups who moved in and out of her life during her childhood. By the time I met her she was profoundly damaged. It will
be a very long road back to health.

Asking the Wrong Questions

One of the purposes of this book is to reframe the way in which questions in
Christian ethics are defined and addressed. Narratives such as these help us to
think more richly about what is at stake when we address moral issues. They
call our attention to matters we might otherwise be tempted to neglect. And
they move us beyond a cold and merely deductive ethic (Curran, *Catholic Moral Tradition Today*, chap. 6), driving us toward Jesus in search of both the right
answers and the right questions.

When it comes to divorce, these functions of narrative are highly significant. They remind us first that the issue of divorce *must* be addressed by the
churches. With few exceptions, American Christianity has simply capitulated
before the divorce epidemic that has swept the nation over the past thirty-five
years. The churches have at times attempted to help sweep up the broken pieces of American family life through ministry to the divorced. But they have had
little significant theological or moral response to offer to divorce itself: they
have not initiated any strategic counterattack.

But they also remind us that divorce requires the most sensitive handling.
As will be seen in this chapter, a contingent of evangelical biblical scholars has
not been silent. These scholars have sought to interpret biblical teachings on
divorce as faithfully as possible even as the culture has changed dramatically.

However, these scholars and churches tend to reflect a highly legalistic approach to biblical interpretation and application. They focus on rules and exceptions rather than the character of God, scriptural principles that reflect that

character, real human situations that reflect our bondage to sin, and transformative practices. They tend to ask the permissibility questions: *Under what circumstances is it morally permissible to get divorced or remarried?* Is it permissible for a divorced person to serve as a minister? Should a minister participate in marrying someone who has been divorced? They demonstrate little sensitivity to the human context in which all Christian ethics is done. What results is moral teaching torn asunder from contact with human experience, sometimes culminating in irrelevance or even cruelty.

In this chapter we will attend to fine points of biblical interpretation. We will ask about rules that are to govern the Christian life in the area of marriage. But we will do so in the context of a different moral paradigm. We will seek to do Christian ethics in the way of Jesus, and as we do the center of gravity of our ethic of marriage and divorce will shift considerably.

On Divorce: The Matthean or Markan Jesus?

On the issue of marriage and divorce, we are fortunate to have available the explicit teaching of Jesus. Unfortunately, the texts are notoriously difficult to interpret. The many church traditions concerning the treatment of divorce are nearly all traceable to this small body of teaching, portions of which can be found in each of the three Synoptic Gospels (Mt 5:31-32; 19:3-12; Mk 10:2-12; Lk 16:18; cf. 1 Cor 7:10-16). This relatively small body of scriptural teaching has given rise to a staggering array of different interpretations and ecclesiastical traditions.

There are four Gospel texts to consider. One, from the Sermon on the Mount, is the header for this chapter. One is a one-sentence summary of an element of Jesus' teaching (Lk 16:18). Two heavyweight texts remain: Matthew 19:3-12 and Mark 10:2-12.

The two latter passages are similar in many ways. Both record an encounter of Jesus with the Pharisees in which they seek to "test" him publicly. Both concern the issue of whether divorce is in keeping with Jewish law. In both, Jesus refused to answer the question on the terms in which it was addressed. Instead, he went behind the provisions of the Jewish law to the original intentions of God the Creator. In both he made a strong statement enjoining his listeners to obey God's will for marriage and thus refrain from divorce. In both he drew some kind of connection between the acts of divorce and remarriage, on the one hand, and adultery, on the other. Finally, in both he dealt with questions from his disciples after concluding his tangle with the Pharisees.

The differences, however, are significant: Matthew's Pharisees asked not merely whether divorce was lawful, but whether it was lawful *kata pasan aitian*, a phrase best translated as "for any and every reason" (Mt 19:3 NIV). Matthew's Pharisees were not asking if divorce per se was lawful, for according to Old Testament and rabbinic law it clearly was, as reference to the "certificate of dismissal" (Deut 24:1-4) indicates. They were asking Jesus to take sides in an ongoing rabbinic debate concerning the legally and morally legitimate grounds for divorce. Jesus initially refused to be drawn into that debate. But in his climactic public word on the subject, the Matthean Jesus included an *exception clause* to the divorce/remarriage/adultery combination. "Whoever divorces his wife, except for *porneia*, and marries another commits adultery" (Mt 19:9). It appears that Jesus was in fact now siding with one of the rabbinic parties, the more conservative one, on the issue of divorce. Or was he?

These variations in Matthew's account make for an instructive case study in biblical exegesis and its link to Christian ethics. Those who take the Matthean text as the starting point tend to be most readily drawn into a legalistic reading of Jesus' teaching on divorce and remarriage. They are most likely to frame the question in the way we outlined above, "On what grounds is it permissible?"; that is, they are most likely to frame the question *exactly the way the Pharisees did*. Most of those who follow the Markan reading, however, find this more difficult to do. For in Mark—as in Luke—no exception clause is given. Jesus backs us into a corner. Either we believe Jesus was giving us a new rule to which there are no possible exceptions—*no* divorce is legitimate, *every* remarriage is an act of adultery—or, in the face of "the bizarre and even cruel dilemmas" this interpretation creates, we are forced to shift the paradigm (Smedes, *Mere Morality*, 179). Our approach here reflects the latter perspective. Whatever Jesus was saying, his focus was not laws and rules and their exceptions. He wants us to ask a different question.

Marriage, Creation and the Kingdom

It should not be a surprise that Jesus responded to his questioners by appealing to God's intentions for marriage in creation. We have noted throughout that the heart of Jesus' mission and teaching was the inbreaking of the kingdom of God. As it came, that redemption would be demonstrated by glorious evidences of the doing of God's will. Over the centuries, God's intention at creation had become obscured. But now came the time of the end, in which God's eternal will would once again be seen and done.

So when Jesus was asked about divorce, he turned to the creation accounts. He was not interested in focusing on the Deuteronomic legislation that was at best a concession to human *sklērokardia* (Mk 10:5)—hardheartedness—or on the layers of further concessions that had built up around this first concession. Instead, he demanded that his listeners, and especially his followers, remember God's creational purposes for the marriage relationship. He wanted his listeners to regain a sense of the tragedy involved in the shattering of even a single marriage. He wanted them to plunge into the new (renewed) kingdom era, in which God's purposes in creation were now, after a very long wait, coming to fruition in and through himself.

What then, according to Jesus, does kingdom living entail in the area of marriage? The Markan text, undistracted by the exception clause, is a good place to find out.

1. Marriage is a male-female covenant partnership established by God for God's purposes. The creation story lies at the heart of Jesus' approach to marriage. Jesus first said that "God made them male and female," referring to Genesis 1:27. In that passage, God made humankind in the divine image, and both male and female were image-bearers. In its original biblical context, the "image of God" primarily refers to particular God-given tasks vis-à-vis the rest of creation (Gen 1:26-31). Male and female together represented God by accomplishing the purposes of God on God's behalf and at God's command. As Vigen Guroian puts it, "Through marriage and family God enables human beings to participate in his creative activity and redemptive purposes" (Guroian, "Ethic of Marriage and Family," 323). These purposes include *procreation*—propagating the human species, populating the planet and by extension, childrearing itself (Gen 1:28; cf. Mal 2:15). They also include the exercise of day-to-day *stewardship* over the creation and its creatures. The picture is of men and women together doing the work of God in God's creation. God's purposes also include relational *intimacy* and sexual *union* (Gen 2:24). Together these activities *deepen and strengthen the covenant relation* between husband and wife, to fulfill God's will for bonding and community (Grenz, *Sexual Ethics*, 55-56).

The New Testament witness on both discipleship and marriage builds on this understanding without fundamentally changing it. The central purpose of marriage, as of all of life, is to seek first the reign of God (Mt 6:33). Disciples of Jesus Christ are to live not for themselves but for God and God's purposes. As in "regular" life, so in marriage—as spouses lay down their own lives for God and for each other, as they lose themselves in the way of the cross (Lk 9:23-25), they find the richest possible fulfillment in marriage. But if they make marriage solely an avenue for their own self-fulfillment, they are likely to find anything but fulfillment therein.

Since the institution of marriage was established by God for God's purposes, God's concern extends to every marriage, whether the married couple has any sense of that concern or not. "[God] is the witness of all weddings, whether invited or not. Marriage is a sacred occasion whether the couple recognize it or not" (Geisler, *Christian Ethics*, 279).

2. Marriage is the joyful companionship of male and female in a one-flesh (re)union. In his next statement Jesus made reference to what is frequently called the "second" creation story. In this story (Gen 2:18-25), the man *(ha* *adam)* was "alone"—and God declared this state of affairs "not good" (Gen 2:18). So God decided to create an *ezer kenegdo* (helper-partner—Gen 2:18, 20). Not just any kind of creature would do, but only an equal partner, as the inadequacy of the animals demonstrated. Finally God drew woman from the very body of man and brought her to him, eliciting from him a cry of joyful satisfaction: "This at last is bone of my bones" (Gen 2:23). Woman was taken out of man; from one there came two. But in marriage, as Genesis says and Jesus quoted, the two become one again; they are reunited as they "cleave" to one another in a "one-flesh" union of unashamed sexual, personal and relational intimacy (Gen 2:24-25; Mk 10:7-9). Those who have enjoyed marriage at its peak know that this one-flesh (re)union is one of the most profound of God's gracious gifts to human beings.

3. Marriage is a covenant relationship intended to be faithful and permanent. With clarity and finality, Jesus said, "let no one separate" what God has joined together (Mk 10:9). God intends marriage to be permanent. It lasts until one spouse dies (cf. Rom 7:1-3; 1 Cor 7:10-11). While it does not extend into eternity (Mt 22:30), it is a lifetime commitment. Jesus did not tell us exactly why this is so. If we think teleologically, in terms of the divine purposes for marriage— procreation and childrearing, stewardship of the earth, covenant partnership, seeking the kingdom—we can readily intuit the superiority of permanence over transience in the marriage relationship. Meanwhile, if one thinks in terms of God's concern for our own well-being and happiness, it is also apparent both intuitively and experientially that stable and joyful lifetime marriages contribute to human well-being far better than the alternatives.

The Scripture *is* clear and explicit in its understanding of the significance of permanence in marriage. This theme is struck not only by Jesus but throughout the Bible. It is here that we see the significance of the language of *covenant* as it relates to marriage. The entirety of salvation-history, as the Scripture tells the story, is a series of irrevocable (Rom 11:29) covenantal relationships between God and human beings, beginning with Noah (Gen 9).

A covenant, as Scripture understands it, is a sacred, God-witnessed, public, mutually binding, irrevocable relationship between two parties who willingly promise and undertake to live by its terms. God chooses to relate to all creatures, to Israel and to the church, through covenants. How striking and significant it is, then, that the inspired Scriptures also choose the language of covenant to describe the nature of the marriage relationship and unashamedly use divine-human covenantal imagery to depict that relationship (Ezek 16:8; Hos 2:19; Mal 2:14-16; Eph 5:21-33). For the theme of covenant in marriage, see books in the bibliography by Anderson and Guernsey *(On Being Family)*, Grenz *(Sexual Ethics)*, Mount *(Covenant, Community, and the Common Good)*,

Smedes *(Mere Morality)*, and Stackhouse *(Covenant and Commitments)*.

It is this understanding of marriage that Jesus wanted to lift up before his hearers. Kingdom living in the area of marriage entails building and preserving joyful, companionable, just, faithful, permanent covenant partnerships committed to fulfilling God's purposes for marriage as an institution. Where a marriage such as this exists, God's will is done and God's kingdom is advanced. Where a marriage such as this is saved from a temptation that could ruin it, or a conflict that threatens it, or a rupture that poisons it, God's will is done. Jesus was saying to his followers: do God's will for marriage and stop asking when it is permissible to do less.

So Jesus redirects our attention. He sidesteps the legalistic questions we want to ask: when is it permissible to divorce? can ministers be remarried? If Christian ethics is following Jesus, the divorce question should be asked in something like the following way: *How shall we participate alongside God in creating, nurturing and preserving marriages that reflect God's intent for this holy covenant and that last for a joyous lifetime?* This leads directly to two other questions: *What are some of the attitudes and behaviors that destroy marriages? What concrete practices must we develop as spouses and churches that can help deliver us from marital discord and alienation and thus strengthen and preserve marriage?*

If our suggestion about the overall structure of Jesus' teaching is correct, then we should be able to look to him for answers to the questions we just posed. Indeed, according to our triadic reading of the Sermon on the Mount, we should be able to find (a) some statement of *traditional piety* or a teaching concerning God's will in the area of marriage, (b) teaching concerning the *vicious cycles or mechanisms of bondage* we get into that block us from doing God's will and (c) *transforming initiatives* that will deliver us from these vicious cycles. This approach may yield some fresh perspective on these difficult texts.

Traditional Piety: The Use and Abuse of the Divorce Certificate

Let us first consider the brief text on divorce in the Sermon on the Mount (Mt 5:31-32). Often this text has been read legalistically, with special emphasis on the exception clause and the linking of divorce, remarriage and adultery. But if we look instead for the traditional piety/vicious cycle/transforming initiative triad, what we first find is the following traditional piety: "It was also said, 'Whoever divorces his wife, let him give her a certificate of divorce.'" Here we do have a fragment of traditional Jewish piety and practice. What are we to make of it?

The reference is to Deuteronomy 24:1-4, the most important of four Old Testament texts which address the issue of divorce in legal terms (the others are Deut 22:13-21; 22:28-29; Lev 21:7, 14; cf. Is 50:1). Interestingly, a careful reading of the Deuteronomy 24 text shows, as Charles C. Ryrie has argued, that it does not mandate the practice of divorce, endorse it or even explicitly permit it ("Biblical Teachings on Divorce and Remarriage," 233). Instead, that text *assumes* the occurrence of divorce as a cultural practice: "Suppose a man enters into marriage with a woman, but she does not please him because he finds something objectionable about her, and so he writes her a certificate of divorce, puts it in her hand, and sends her out of his house" (Deut 24:1).

The text goes on to describe one particular variation on that scenario, in which the unfortunate woman in question is divorced by her first husband, marries a second husband and is also divorced by him. The issue is whether she can marry the first husband again; the answer is no, since she "has been defiled" (Deut 24:4). It is clear from both the Old Testament and the Talmud that the Jewish people did in fact employ this "certificate of divorce" method of dissolving marriages. The certificate was a more or less formal legal document that included the husband's official confirmation that he had divorced his wife and she was now free to remarry. The woman had no legal right to initiate divorce or to keep herself from being divorced by her husband.

The primary purpose of this law seems to have been to offer some minimal protection for abandoned women in a profoundly patriarchal society. As such, it is consistent with a host of other Old Testament laws likewise intended to look out for the interests of the vulnerable. In ancient Israel, a woman abandoned by her husband had no means to support herself and no prospect of a man's support, for no one was permitted to marry her. This regulation at least clarified a woman's status and in principle allowed her a second chance at marriage. Of course, a divorced woman's *actual* prospects for remarriage were probably not good. This regulation did not fundamentally alter the powerlessness and extreme vulnerability of women. If divorce came to be viewed as routine, women would be at great risk. This appears to be precisely what did happen.

In the later history of rabbinic interpretation and Jewish practice at the time of Jesus, this same text took on a heightened significance. Indeed, the situation for women and for marriage had worsened. Most commentators make note of the debate, as recorded in the Mishnah, between the rabbinic schools of Hillel and Shammai (with commentary from Akiba) on the issue of divorce:

> The School of Shammai say: A man may not divorce his wife unless he has found unchastity in her, for it is written, *Because he hath found in her **indecency** in anything*. And the School of Hillel say: [He may divorce her] even if she spoiled a dish for him, for it is written: *Because he hath found in her indecency in **anything***. R. Akiba says: Even if he found another fairer than she, for it is written, *And it shall be if she find no favour in his eyes*. (Gittin 9:10, in Hays, *Moral Vision of the New Testament*, 353)

The italicized words are drawn from Deuteronomy 24:1. The rabbinic debate concerned the appropriate interpretation of these words; in particular, of the Hebrew *erwath dabar* (Deut 24:1), an awkward phrase that literally reads "nakedness of a thing." They were asking about the legitimate grounds for divorce, as "commanded" (Mt 19:7) by Moses in Deuteronomy 24. Of course, this very effort indicated a misunderstanding of the import of the passage in its original context. A text that was intended to protect women from being casually divorced was now being examined in search of commands and permissions enabling men to know when they might initiate divorce.

What did the rabbis find? The "conservative" approach, as reflected in the teaching of Shammai, viewed divorce as morally legitimate ("lawful") only in cases of a wife's "indecency"; that is, some form of inappropriate sexual behavior (probably, though not necessarily, unchaste behavior short of adultery, which was officially punishable by death). The prevailing opinion, however—and, apparently, the prevailing practice—appeared to be that of Hillel, who interpreted the phrase broadly to mean "anything displeasing." Both Philo and Josephus knew and approved this view. Thus women could be divorced for failing to measure up to the beauty of a rival (Akiba), for failures in the kitchen (Hillel) or for any reason whatsoever. Thus the certificate of dismissal had been disastrously transmuted into a means of disobedience to God's will. Jesus called his hearers back to God's original intention for marriage: permanence, mutuality and peacemaking (Lapide, *Sermon on the Mount*, 64, 67-68).

Vicious Cycles: Rethinking the Divorce/Adultery Connection

The corruption of the "certificate of dismissal" practice is not the only mechanism of bondage identified by Jesus. He continued: "Anyone who divorces his wife, except on the ground of unchastity *[porneia]*, causes her to commit adultery; and whoever marries a divorced woman commits adultery" (Mt 5:32).

Similar sayings are reported in the Matthew 19 passage as well as in Mark and Luke:

Whoever divorces his wife, except for unchastity, and marries another commits adultery. (Mt 19:9)

Whoever divorces his wife and marries another commits adultery against her; and if she divorces her husband and marries another, she commits adultery. (Mk 10:11-12)

Anyone who divorces his wife and marries another commits adultery, and whoever marries a woman divorced from her husband commits adultery. (Lk 16:18)

It must first be noted that this aspect of the teaching of Jesus on divorce is hotly disputed. We must also be very much aware of what *we* bring to these texts.
North American readers bring a cultural context in which divorce and remarriage are part of the fabric of society and church. Thus as we read them today
these teachings are among the most difficult for us to accept of anything Jesus
said. We must beware of what might be our immediate tendency to neuter them.

We should first consider their literary similarities and their differences.

1. The Matthean texts. Notice the way in which these two passages differ from
each other.

> Matthew 5:32—"Anyone who divorces his wife . . . causes her to commit adul-
> tery; and whoever marries a divorced woman commits adultery."

> Matthew 19:9—"Whoever divorces his wife . . . and marries another commits
> adultery."

The Matthew 5 text has the following logic: "If I divorce you, I cause *you* to
commit adultery; and, if someone marries you (my ex-wife), *he* commits adultery." In the Matthew 19 text, the logic is: "If I divorce you and marry someone
else, *I* commit adultery."

An important exegetical issue in these Matthean texts is the significance, if
any, of the passive verb tense in Matthew 5 *(moicheuthēnai)*. Some interpreters
suggest this word should be understood to have the meaning that if I divorce
my wife, she is *viewed by others* (stigmatized) as having committed adultery
(Davis, *Evangelical Ethics,* 86-87). This makes a certain amount of sense on its
face, yet the interpretation is hindered by the use of active verbs in other discussions in these texts of the divorce/adultery connection. A more likely interpretation of the passive verb in Matthew 5:32 has to do with the woman's
powerlessness in Jewish legal context. She can be divorced by her husband
but cannot initiate divorce; another man can take her as his wife, but she is
not viewed as taking a man as her husband. The whole situation *happens to
her,* rather than being the result of her decisions. Another possibility is that being divorced causes the woman to commit adultery by putting her in a desperate situation in which she must make a new and illegitimate marriage in
order to survive.

Meanwhile, both Matthean texts differ from Mark and Luke in a critical
way: their inclusion/addition of some form of the so-called exception clause—
"except for unchastity" *(parektos logou porneias* in Mt 5). This clause has generated much discussion, as we shall see below.

2. Mark. The Markan text has the following logic: "If I divorce my wife and
marry someone else, *I* commit adultery *against her*" (presumably, my former
wife). It also contains an element not to be found either in Matthew or Luke;

the reciprocal application of the same teaching to the woman—"If *she* divorces me and marries another man, *she* commits adultery." Richard Hays points out the astonishing character of Mark's formulation of Jesus' sayings here:

> This declaration posits a fundamental redefinition of adultery; in Jewish law and tradition, adultery was a property offense, a form of stealing a man's property by "taking" his wife. Thus, adultery could by definition be committed only against a man, for the husband was not in any reciprocal sense regarded as the sexual property of his wife. Jesus' teaching, however, changes the rules of the game with one bold stroke. (Hays, *Moral Vision of the New Testament*, 352)

Jesus shattered the tradition by going back behind it to God's intention. Marriage is a mutual relationship with reciprocal rights. Either husband or wife can be faithful or faithless in marriage, and both are accountable for their behavior. In terms of the issue of a woman initiating divorce, which was normally impossible for Jewish women to do, many interpreters believe that Mark adapted the tradition to speak to the legal situation facing the readers of his Gospel in the Greco-Roman world, just as Matthew adapted the tradition to speak to his own Jewish Christian readers.

3. Luke. Luke's rendering of the same teaching also has an important difference, combining nuances found in both Matthew and Mark. Its logic is the following: "If I divorce you and marry another woman, I commit adultery; if someone marries *you [my ex-wife]*, *he* commits adultery." The first clause parallels the similar passages in Matthew 19 and Mark 10; the second parallels the final clause in Matthew 5.

All of these texts share the conviction that marriage is a lifetime covenant commitment and divorce a tragic violation of that commitment. This is what is most important about them. All of them also draw some connection between divorce, adultery and remarriage. Divorce and remarriage, which were quite common in first-century Jewish life, are somehow equated with adultery—a sin for which the Law mandated death. Surely these words are original to Jesus, and surely they attracted the astonished attention of his original listeners!

The Gospel writers differ in how exactly they record this divorce/remarriage/adultery connection. Their differences likely have to do with how oral and perhaps written traditions were redacted and used in the particular contexts of the Gospel writers' communities. We think it most likely that Mark offers the rendering closest to Jesus' original words, though perhaps adapted to his Hellenistic Gentile readers, and that Matthew clearly adapted his material for his Jewish Christian readers. Luke was a Gentile writing primarily for a Greco-Roman audience, but he situates Jesus' teaching on divorce within a polemic against the Pharisees' interpretation of Jewish law.

In any case, the slight but real differences in nuance among these four passages have bedeviled many generations of interpreters. They have also given rise to a variety of ecclesiastical traditions that have each sought to be faithful either to one of the versions above or to an attempted harmonization of all of them.

The historic Roman Catholic tradition read the evidence to permit *separation*, not divorce, on the ground of adultery, never to permit the actual dissolution of a marriage (i.e., divorce) and never to permit remarriage. Martin Luther drew a distinction between the legitimate grounds for separation, on the one hand, and divorce, on the other, permitted genuine divorce where biblically justifiable, and permitted remarriage where divorce was legitimately grounded.

Today, some conservative Protestant interpreters argue that neither divorce nor remarriage are *ever* morally permissible (Feinberg and Feinberg, *Ethics for a Brave New World*, 306-7). At least one argues that divorce is never morally "justifiable" but that remarriage is permissible after appropriate repentance (Geisler, *Christian Ethics*, 287, 291). Others argue that separation or divorce are morally permissible on the grounds of adultery, but that remarriage is never morally acceptable (Heth and Wenham, *Jesus and Divorce*, 52). Still others believe that divorce is morally permissible on grounds of adultery, and that where this is the case remarriage is morally permissible, at least for the victimized party (Erasmian view, quoted in Feinberg and Feinberg, *Ethics for a Brave New World*, 308). Others agree with this last position but broaden the grounds to include desertion by an unbelieving spouse (Trull, *Walking in the Way*, 313-14) or by one *acting like* an unbeliever—both based on 1 Corinthians 7:12-16 (discussed below); some remain open to divorce based on other offenses against marriage, such as physical abuse or various forms of gross immorality (Keener, *And Marries Another*, 104-10). Others speak in broad terms about "situations in which the divine intent [for marriage] has been effaced by sin and failure" (Grenz, *Sexual Ethics*, 109). The most open evangelical position is to argue that divorce is morally legitimate whenever a marriage "dies" and cannot be resuscitated, and that remarriage is permissible in any and every case in which the remarriage is well-advised (Smedes, *Mere Morality*, 178-82). And this list of options, make no mistake, is not an exhaustive one!

We submit that regardless of the particular outcome of each argument outlined above, most of them fall prey to that rule/exception moral reasoning style that characterized the Pharisees rather than Jesus. Perhaps that is one reason why most are ignored as Christian people actually make their decisions about divorce. It may be that church discipline and the practical demands of morally serious congregational life require the formulation of a position on divorce and remarriage that has, to some extent, a rule-type structure based on the fine parsing of these texts. But the kind of argumentation one finds in most evangelical treatments of divorce seems, on the whole, off-center and incomplete. Perhaps the very diversity of scholarly and churchly opinion helps to support this claim.

We would like to suggest consideration of the divorce/adultery connection in terms of the triadic structure of Jesus' moral teaching. We think that in linking divorce and remarriage with adultery Jesus was not writing a new law but instead claiming that divorce and remarriage are linked with adultery as cause is to effect; and, perhaps, as effect is to cause. In other words, there is a vicious cycle connecting them:

First, divorce and remarriage cause adultery in that the freedom to end one's marriage in order to start another one can create vulnerability to the temptation to "covet another man's wife" (Ex 20) rather than to remain committed to one's own. If marriage really is a one-man/one-woman bond that is indissoluble except by death, then I have no choice but to dig deep and recommit to the "wife (or husband) of my youth" rather than to seek out greener pastures. But if my marriage is easily dissolved, then I can escape my troubles through a new partner. Interestingly, the search for a new partner frequently takes the initial form of adultery in the narrow sense—a first act of sexual infidelity with a candidate for replacement partner. The next step, frequently, is adultery in the broad sense—the breaking of covenant with my original partner, in order to make a new relationship with my new partner (for a related view, see Smedes, *Mere Morality*, 180).

Second, the shattering of one's original marriage commitment frequently leads to weaker marriage commitments the second and third and fourth times around. Once the sacred meaning of the marriage covenant has been broken, especially through adultery, second and third marriages are less likely to be able to recover or recreate that meaning. They are inherently more precarious, as the statistics show. If you (and I) had affairs that ended both your first marriage and mine, and we did so with impunity because we were not happy with our spouses, what is to prevent one of us from doing the same thing in the course of this marriage? Why should I trust you when you could not be trusted before? Why should you trust me? What is the meaning of our commitment to each other?

> An underlying theme in our argument for covenant ethics is the deep need in our self-centered society for reestablishment of relationships of trust rather than distrust and manipulation. We need to recover the concept of covenant in the many levels of commitment and faithfulness into which we enter in various spheres of our lives, and of which marriage is the most formal and explicit. We desperately need relationships of trust; we desperately need to discern relationships of covenant and not mere manipulation in our relationships with others.

Third, divorce causes adultery through its impact on children. Divorce inevitably alters the relationship of children with their parents. The likelihood of some abandonment of covenant commitments between parent and child is quite high. Consider the ex-spouses who use their children as pawns in divorce proceedings; the father who fails to pay child support; the mother who moves a thousand miles away to marry another man and disappears from a child's life. Thus divorce and remarriage are linked with adultery in the broad sense of covenant-breaking. Further, children who experience the divorce of their parents begin their own dating/mating process at a profound experiential disadvantage. They can overcome this disadvantage, but without conscious attention they are more likely to struggle in marriage than the child of a happy, intact home. Thus divorce cycles into more divorce as the sins of the parents are visited upon the children and the children's children. If the children have seen faithlessness and relational instability modeled in their childhood, they have only negative models from which to draw.

We suggest that when Jesus linked divorce and remarriage with adultery, he was thinking concretely about vicious cycles of faithlessness and relational impermanence. He wanted to set his followers free from bondage to these cycles so that they could experience the joy of marriage as God designed it.

The Notorious Exception Clause

We have yet to consider the Matthean exception clause. This clause proves vexatious in traditional, rule-oriented interpretation of Jesus' teaching on divorce. It is also difficult to assimilate within the framework of our own approach to these texts.

The predominant approach to the Matthean "exception clause" is revealed in its historic name: to treat *parektos logou porneias* (Mt 5:32)/*mē epi porneia* (Mt 19:9) as an exception to the general prohibition of divorce. On this reasoning, for Matthew divorce (and perhaps remarriage) is morally impermissible except when one partner sins against the marriage through some act of *porneia*. This is to function as the rule for the community of faith.

Several different interpretations have been offered for the meaning of the term *porneia* here. Traditionally it has been translated as "adultery" (NIV— "marital unfaithfulness"). Thus, many have believed that Jesus' teaching prohibits divorce for any cause other than adultery on the part of one of the spouses; but that when that occurs, divorce (and perhaps remarriage) is permissible. In Jewish context, this would place Jesus in the neighborhood of the Shammaite position on divorce. Many church bodies have taken this view.

Yet not all are convinced. Some have argued that the term cannot mean adultery, as we understand it, because in the Jewish context adultery was punishable by death. The continuing application of the death penalty for adultery, at least at times, is perhaps illustrated by the story of the woman taken in adultery in John 8—though the story is not included in the earliest manuscripts of that Gospel (for a contrary view, see Hays, *Moral Vision of the New Testament*, 354).

More significant is the choice of the word *porneia* rather than *moicheia*, which is the Greek word for adultery. *Porneia* is generally used to denote sexual sin in a broad sense, including premarital intercourse ("fornication") and other forms of "unchastity," or "sexual immorality," as the NRSV renders the term when it is used in Matthew. That there is a distinction for Matthew between the two terms is indicated by Matthew 15:19, an enumeration of evil actions in which *both moicheia and porneia* are separately named (the NRSV translates the former as "adultery" and the latter as "fornication" in this case).

Some interpreters have argued that the use of the term *porneia* has the significance of broadening the legitimate grounds for divorce. On this reading, divorce can be morally legitimate not only in cases of adultery but, more broadly, whenever a spouse behaves indecently or unchastely, at least as a pattern of behavior. One can think of a wide range of sexually immoral or inappropriate behaviors short of adultery that constitute a fundamental offense against the marriage covenant—such as repeated use of pornography, exhibitionism, sexual contact with others short of intercourse and so on. One senses that the implicit goal of some of these interpreters is to loosen up the rules a bit in the interests of humanity and charity. Others simply believe the Greek word *porneia* is best translated in the broad sense of sexual unchastity (Cornes, *Divorce and Remarriage*, 296-97).

A most interesting suggestion comes from another direction altogether. Some have argued that *porneia*, in Matthew, must be understood as *premarital unchastity*, in light of Matthew's singular rendering of the nativity story (cf. Mt 1:18-25). In this story Joseph learns that his betrothed is pregnant; he first assumes she has had intercourse with a man, and thus makes plans to *apolysai* ("dismiss" NRSV; "divorce" NIV) her. The word can legitimately be translated either way. The narrator describes him, and by extension his conduct, as "righteous." No critique is offered of his plan to end the betrothal quietly. Then, of course, the angel intervenes and the story goes from there. Some have suggested that *this exception* is what Matthew has in mind with his exception clause. Divorce is not permissible except when a betrothed woman has been guilty of *porneia* (cf. Jn 8:41, in which Jesus' opponents label him as a product of *porneia*). In such cases the proper word can only be *porneia* rather than *moicheia*, because betrothal—though a serious commitment to marriage—is not yet marriage (Isaakson, in Piper, "Divorce and Remarriage," 8-10).

This account of the exception clause in Matthew might also help to explain the very existence of the clause in Matthew and only in Matthew, an issue with which every interpreter struggles. For it is only Matthew's Gospel that tells the story of the "righteous" Joseph's plan to dismiss his betrothed.

Thus only Matthew would have felt the need to explain to his readers that Joseph was in fact righteous in planning to dismiss Mary, even though every other episode of divorce is morally illegitimate.

It may be that the best way to interpret the uniquely Matthean exception clause is simply to see it as his rule-based adaptation of Jesus' unconditional teachings against divorce. Hays sees Matthew as the consummate "ecclesiastical politician" and "reconciler of differences," who adapted Jesus' teaching in order that it might function as a rigorous yet merciful rule of life for his community. If this is the way the exception clause is read, then a broad rendering of its meaning—sexual unchastity generally as grounds for divorce, where necessary—makes the most sense (Hays, *Moral Vision of the New Testament*, 355-56).

Marital Peacemaking: Rethinking the "Pauline Privilege"

We have seen a statement of traditional piety and of a mechanism of bondage in the arena of marriage and divorce. Next we would expect to find some statement of a transforming initiative to break this bondage and enable God's will to be done. But it is not here. Nothing in Matthew 5:31-32 takes the form of the expected transforming initiative. Thirteen of the fourteen teachings in the heart of the Sermon on the Mount (Mt 5:21—7:12) have the threefold, triadic structure, but here it is clearly missing. This is puzzling. At least it demonstrates the objectivity of our three categories: Clearly there is a traditional piety, clearly there is a vicious cycle, and just as clearly there is no transforming initiative.

But in 1 Corinthians 7:10-11 we do find a teaching of Jesus that offers a transforming initiative that can prevent divorce. The passage reads as follows: "To the married I give this command—*not I but the Lord*—that the wife should not separate from her husband (but if she does separate, let her remain unmarried *or else be reconciled* to her husband), and that the husband should not divorce his wife" (1 Cor 7:10-11, italics added).

It is important to understand the context of this passage. Paul was responding to questions from the Christians in Corinth. The entirety of 1 Corinthians 7 contains his responses to their queries concerning issues of sexuality and marriage. Earlier in the chapter he wrote of the mutual sexual rights belonging to both husband and wife and urged them not to abstain from sexual relations (1 Cor 7:2-6). It is possible that a movement was developing in which some believed that holiness required sexual asceticism; Paul rejected this firmly.

That is the likely context for the passage we are considering here. Women in the community were considering divorce in the interests of holiness and devotion to the Lord. In particular, women in mixed marriages were considering divorce because they found it hard to reconcile sexual relations with an unbeliever and holy participation in the body of Christ (cf. 1 Cor 6:12-20). The text also gives evidence that marital discord in such marriages, not just concern for holiness, was an issue.

In response, Paul offered here what he described as a Jesus-saying: spouses should not separate from each other; but if they do, they should "remain unmarried or else be reconciled." In other words, if separation has occurred, do not divorce; if divorce has occurred, do not remarry. Instead, seek reconciliation while there is yet a chance for it. Now we have an explicit teaching of Jesus—reported by Paul—of the sort that we expected—mandating transforming initiatives to heal strained marriages.

At the heart of a troubled marriage is relational brokenness and alienation. Sometimes alienation results from one major act that damages the marriage, such as an impetuous affair. Normally, though, marital alienation results from a slow "clogging of the marital arteries" through a buildup of resentment due to unresolved conflicts. So-called irreconcilable differences and marital breakdown, to which most divorces are attributed, do not happen overnight. The miracle of forgiveness is its ability to "unclog" the arteries of human relationships and remove the built-up resentments, and thus enable peaceable interaction once again in a reconciled relationship.

> Reconciliation does not happen by itself. It is the end product of the cycle of peacemaking that Jesus teaches throughout the Sermon on the Mount: acknowledging that we are trapped in a vicious cycle, seeking to participate in God's gracious deliverance, taking the initiative to go to the other, *seeking reconciliation*, refusing to take vengeance, affirming the other's valid interests, repenting rather than judging, forgiving rather than withholding forgiveness, praying for the adversary and, above all and in all, love. These steps are perhaps *nowhere* more applicable than in the marriage relationship. We think Jesus taught that husbands and wives should take initiatives such as these to make peace with one another, and that this teaching is recorded here.

The same emphasis on reconciliation is continued in 1 Corinthians 7:12-16, in which Paul offers instruction not described as a Jesus-saying but which, as always for Paul, is an attempt to be faithful to Jesus' teaching as it applies to a new context. Here the Christian in a religiously mixed marriage is instructed to stay in what is clearly a deeply strained relationship, in search of reconciliation. "If any believer has a wife who is an unbeliever, and she consents to live with him, he should not divorce her. . . . For the unbelieving husband is made holy through his wife, and the unbelieving wife is made holy through her husband. Otherwise, your children would be unclean; but as it is, they are holy" (1 Cor 7:12, 14).

It is most interesting to see the contrast between this response to religiously mixed marriages and that of the Old Testament leader Ezra during the Restoration period of Israel's history, just after the exile. In that case, Ezra commanded the Israelites to divorce their foreign wives and abandon the children of those marriages on account of the danger of idolatry and religious impurity (Ezra 10). Paul, on the other hand, emphasized the *possibilities* rather than the dangers of a mixed marriage (once one is in such a marriage—Paul disapproves the initiation of a mixed marriage; see 1 Cor 7:39). Under the impact of Jesus' teaching he focused on reconciliation between the spouses rather than the danger of religious impurity. Indeed, he turned the matter around and seemed to make the extraordinary suggestion that the unbeliever receives the spillover effects of the believer's right standing with God, rather than the other way around (Hays, *Moral Vision of the New Testament*, 357-61; cf. Maston, *Bible and Family Relations*, 214-15). Paul was primarily interested in reconciliation, not only between the spouses, but between the unbeliever, the children and God.

We think this is a critical passage for a Christian approach to marriage and divorce, understood in "participation in the kingdom" style rather than in the rule/exception style of moral reasoning. The passage has, though, primarily been used in the latter way. The focus has rested on 1 Corinthians 7:15: "But if the unbelieving partner separates, let it be so; in such a case the brother or sister is not bound."

This passage, following historic Roman Catholic tradition, has come to be called the Pauline Privilege. Interpreted in casuistic style, it has been understood to mean that *desertion or abandonment of a marriage by an unbelieving spouse* constitutes one further exception to the rule that prohibits divorce. Thus some readers believe that the legitimate grounds for divorce are actually two: adultery and desertion. Others see these as legitimate grounds for separation but not divorce. Many see them as grounds for divorce *and remarriage*, at least for the innocent party, on the basis of the Greek term *ou dedoulōtai* in verse 15, usually translated "is not bound" (literally "is not *enslaved*"; cf. Davis, *Evangelical Ethics*, 90).

As with the rule/exception paradigm in the case of *porneia* in Matthew 5 and 19, some interpreters seek to broaden the application of this new exception. Thus, for example, brutal physical abuse of a spouse, though not explicitly named here, is seen as a legitimate ground for divorce because such behavior is unchristian and thus *equivalent* either to abandonment or to behaving as an unbeliever. Likewise, endangerment of spouse or children through criminal behavior, substance abuse or gross immorality is considered akin to abandonment of the marriage covenant. John Jefferson Davis has zeroed in on the meaning of "consent" *(syneudokei)* in 7:13 to argue that some forms of behavior, such as physical abuse, constitute a de facto failure to *consent* to live in a viable marriage (Davis, *Evangelical Ethics*, 90-91).

Efforts such as these are important attempts to adjust the rule/exception paradigm in a way that accounts for, and responds humanely to, the misery of so many marriages in our time. There is value in such an approach, as long as it is remembered that this is not where the central weight of this passage should be found. The focus of 1 Corinthians 7:10-16 is not rule/exception casuistry but the drive for reconciliation. We should read this passage first as a mandate for reconciliation; only then can we talk about what happens when reconciliation fails. "It is to peace that God has called you" (1 Cor 7:15). This means first the peace of marital reconciliation. Only secondarily, and as a tragic exception, does it mean the cold, sorrowful peace of divorce.

Conclusion

We have discovered the heart of Jesus' teaching on marriage and divorce: *What God has joined together, keep together! Go and be reconciled!* This way of framing the issue leads to a far more fruitful set of Christian moral practices in the area of marriage. These practices focus concretely on *marriage building and divorce prevention* rather than on the development of a sophisticated casuistry of exceptions to the norm of lifetime marriage or a similarly tortuous casuistry of judgments concerning which categories of human beings might offer or receive the ministry of the Christian churches.

To discuss in any detail the marriage building practices needed today goes beyond what we can do in this chapter. We close, however, with our top ten best practices list. To move toward obedience to Jesus' teaching, we need to work on

1. shaping whole, healthy, committed Christian disciples with the skills and character necessary to succeed at marriage;
2. radically reorienting the church's moral vision vis-à-vis marriage away from self-centeredness and toward a kingdom vision;
3. developing relational and conflict resolution skills useful in marriage and in other aspects of church life as well;
4. emphasizing and modeling sexual purity and fidelity while deemphasizing the expectation of a marital sexual utopia;
5. nurturing a climate of relational equity and justice in marriage, which is critical to long-term success in married life;
6. creating and maintaining support relationships of intimacy and accountability as well as processes to intervene in severely stressed marriages;
7. recovering a covenantal understanding of marital permanence;
8. emphasizing second-chance discipleship and a future orientation rather than focusing on excluding persons for past mistakes;
9. lifting up models of healthy marriage at each developmental stage and perhaps employing such persons as mentors to younger couples;
10. nurturing a radically countercultural ecclesial ethos in which discipleship is understood to include *lifetime* marriage and all married disciples are helped to get there.

14

SEXUALITY

—

You have heard that it was said, "You shall not commit adultery." But I say to you that
anyone who looks at a woman with lust has already committed adultery with her in his
heart. If your right eye causes you to sin, tear it out and throw it away; it is better for you
to lose one of your members than for your whole body to be thrown into hell. And if your
right hand causes you to sin, cut it off and throw it away; it is better for you to lose one of
your members than for your whole body to go into hell.

MATTHEW 5:27-30

T he issue of the proper expression of human sexuality is a perennial one—
not only in Christian ethics but in every ethical system, indeed every human
society. There has never been a social order that has not reflected upon and
prescribed rules and principles for this powerful and mysterious dimension of
personhood. And as far as we know there has never been a social order in
which sexuality has not spilled messily over the boundaries established for it.

Sexual ethics looks very different depending on one's context in life and
one's understanding of human nature. When I (David) was a Christian teenager, sexual ethics was framed primarily in terms of the moral norm of abstinence
from intercourse over against the tremendous and growing urge to transgress
that norm. At that stage in life, prior to a deep covenant relation with my life
partner, and during the teenage wrestle with parental authority, human nature
and ethics were mostly about obeying and disobeying rules.

The onset of serious dating relationships in the late teen years, followed by
the relationship that would lead to my marriage at age twenty-two, shifted the
focus somewhat. While abstinence remained the central moral norm the
church offered, there was the ever-so-slight recognition of a deeper meaning—
the purpose of relationships as mutual service, loyalty, trust, giving ourselves
for each other, love in a covenant sense—and the legitimate place for limited
sexual bonding for the couple soon to be married. The "how far is too far" dis-

cussion commenced, though of course never in the Sunday sermon. But the focus deepened to a more important question, "Whom can I trust to live my life with, to be faithful to and to be faithful to me?"

Once the wedding was upon us, concerned adults handed us books on sexual fulfillment in marriage. The norm shifted dramatically from abstinence to enjoyment, from withholding sex to mutual fulfillment in sex. It was quite a change. Not long thereafter the focus of moral instruction deepened yet more to fidelity to one's spouse in marriage.

Now, eighteen years into marriage, the norms of fidelity and mutual fulfillment in sex remain joyfully central. Yet, at a broader level, longer experience with life reveals the astonishing multiplicity of sexual problems and sins. The most frequent is the sense that "my mate does not care much about my own concerns, needs and goals, so why should I keep investing my loyalties in my mate?" More drastically, adultery, child sexual abuse, rape, pornography, sadism, incest, pedophilia—these are among the offenses against God's will in the area of sexuality that have crossed my path as minister and teacher. And, of course, sexual sin is not all *out there*—it lies *in here*, too.

We began by observing that sexual ethics looks very different depending on one's context in life and one's understanding of human nature. We are paying attention to the variables in holistic character ethics of *loyalties* and *perceptions of one's context*, and one's understanding of *human nature* (chapter three), to begin to notice something about sexuality. The more I matured, the more sex became a question of bonding and not only rules. Rules were still important, but they began to be understood in the deeper context of bonding with mutual trust and mutual support. Human nature is such that we need and seek bonding, a trust relationship, mutual caring, loyalty and faithfulness (Gen 2:24). The drama of Adam and Eve in Genesis 2 and 3 tells us something profound about ourselves: in our search for love, we are wounded, exiled and alienated persons driven to find reconciliation, faithful community and mutual affirmation that overcomes our alienation and isolation. We can search for acceptance in covenant relationships where we experience faithfulness and loyalty that transcend life's failings and disappointments, or we can search in momentary relationships based on ability to attract and ended when we find another more attractive. In the latter case, the search for reconciliation and community leads only to a deeper distrust, to me-ism, self-seeking and the drive to find what we are missing in life by impressing others rather than by loyalty to others. The result is a deeper alienation.

In our consumer culture, there is a superficial understanding of sex as self-satisfaction in the moment, like a purchase on a whim, which participants can decide will mean nothing afterwards. But this flies in the face of psychological knowledge and regular experience. We have a much deeper understanding in the gospel, and the world needs it desperately. Jesus' realism is that how we relate our inner selves to other persons is what shapes us as well as defiles us (Mk 7:21), and sex surely does relate our inner selves to other persons: this is the realistic biblical-Hebraic understanding of one-flesh union (1 Cor 6:12-20; Gen 2:24). We become who we are in the way we relate to others, in our practices, and this is true at depths we cannot control in our sexual relating. The consumerist-momentary-encounter understanding is contradicted by insights from Freud and depth psychology, as well as our social experience. Sex is not merely a moment of pleasure, like eating a candy bar, but a character-shaping action. And how a society practices its sexuality shapes not only the people in the society but the society itself. If a society relates sexually in contexts of self-seeking, manipulation, distrust and betrayal, it tends to become a society of self-seeking, manipulation, distrust and betrayal. This is simply the reality of human nature.

So Jesus teaches about sex in the context of covenant relationships. Classic Christian theology argues that every aspect of the human person is both created good and corrupted by sin; that there is no feature of the human being that is not basically good but damaged and "fallen." The various uses, misuses and abuses of sexuality give ample evidence of the truthfulness of this important Christian doctrine. In broad perspective, then, sexual ethics is not just about what behavior I can and cannot do, must and must not do, at various stages in my life and in various relational contexts. Sexual ethics has to do with sexual integrity, with sexual character—with the total reclaiming of human sexuality for the covenant purposes for which God created it. It is important that sex, with its deep personal longings, take place in a context of faithfulness, forgivingness, mutually respectful justice and enduring loyalty—faithful and lasting covenant—and not in a context of rivalry, fear of not being accepted, manipulation for self-satisfaction and eventual abandonment. The latter leaves deep scars.

How we relate sexually is a critical arena for Christian proclamation and instruction, but one that is often neglected due to fear of giving offense or simply embarrassment and shame. Perhaps our discussion can provide some needed resources.

Matthew 5:27-30: Interpreting the Passage

As presented by Matthew, Jesus' teaching on sexuality in the Sermon on the Mount comes as the second triad of six in Matthew 5, just after the teaching on anger and making peace, and before the discussion of divorce.

When this passage is viewed as an antithesis, something like the following approach is taken. The Old Testament command not to commit adultery is intensified, or even abrogated, by Jesus' new and deeper teaching—that it is not only the action of illicit sex or adultery that Jesus forbids, but the very thought of it. His teaching represents a radical internalization and interiorization of the adultery command. However, the argument goes, because it is impossible to be human (or at least male) without lusting after others, Jesus' teaching must be understood as a harsh prohibition or an impossible ideal for us to strive for through hard human effort (or to laugh off in complacent resignation).

We instead argue for a triadic interpretation. Jesus first offered a restatement of the traditional Hebraic teaching, then explicated the traps or vicious cycles of sin in which we get caught and finally articulated a strategy of transforming initiatives that would enable his listeners to do the will of God in this area of human existence.

Traditional teaching: no adultery. The command against adultery, as is well known, is found in the covenant of the Ten Commandments (Ex 20:14; Deut 5:18). Thus when Jesus quoted this particular traditional teaching he reached into the very heart of the biblical moral witness to covenant ethics. Given what we have already claimed about Jesus' approach to Scripture, we do not believe he was abrogating the Old Testament command. And the triadic structure of the teaching makes that clear; he was not teaching an antithesis "anti" the teaching of Moses.

> Covenant is a central concept in the theological ethics of the Hebrew Scriptures. Some scholars believe it did not become important until the writings of the prophets, but it certainly is important for them and for the Old Testament as it exists (Brueggeman, *Theology of the Old Testament*, 418), and Jesus pointed often to the teaching of the prophets. But covenant alone is inadequate; first comes narrative. First comes the exodus; then come the Ten Commandments. First comes the grace of God's demonstration of faithfulness in a history of deliverance from domination, and a history of providential care; the covenant is based on this grace and faithfulness. The covenant is based on God's character, and it takes its shape from God's character as revealed in God's action. God cares for the needy, delivers the weak and the oppressed, acts with mercy and forgiveness and righteousness and justice, and is faithful; therefore, in the covenant relation with God, we are to care for the needy, deliver the oppressed and act with mercy, forgiveness, righteousness, justice and faithfulness (Birch, *Let Justice Roll Down*, 125-26, 174-77, 182, 245-48).

In the Old Testament, the centrality of covenant fidelity in marriage is revealed not only in its moral teachings but also in the metaphorical use of the language of covenant fidelity. Jeremiah (Jer 3:8-9; 5:7; 23:14), Ezekiel (Ezek 16:32; 23:37) and especially Hosea (Hos 1:2; 2:2) use the language of adultery, including the same Hebrew word *(zanah)*, to decry the infidelity of Israel to her covenant with God. In fact, the emphasis on covenant faithfulness to God may have preceded and influenced the emphasis on covenant faithfulness in marriage. The Old Testament describes polygamy, concubinage (even for Levite priests!) and mandatory divorce of foreign wives under Ezra even after the time of the prophets. The comparison of the divine-human and the husband-wife relationship is developed in a profound way by Paul (Eph 5:21-33), while the use of the term *adulterous* to describe infidelity to God is found both on Jesus' lips (Mt 12:39; 16:4) and in James (Jas 4:4).

But also, from the other side, narrative alone is inadequate; the narrative of God's faithfulness leads to a mutual entry into covenant with concrete stipulations of the kinds of actions and ways of relating that fit the covenant relationship. Grace without covenant becomes cheap grace (Brueggemann, *Theology of the Old Testament*, 419-20; cf. 164ff., 373ff., especially 417ff., and 451ff.). When we understand sexual relations by means of a covenant understanding of God's character and will, it means two things: (1) We are made for community, for bonding in covenant relationships, and not merely for self-advancement in a consumerist and profit-seeking market. (2) Our sexual relationships are in tune with the grain of the universe and our own natures if they care for the needy, deliver the oppressed (for we are both needy and we both do get oppressed even in relationships of love; and our covenant with each other is for a larger purpose of service to others, not only for ourselves), and are merciful, forgiving, just and faithful. (For a survey, analysis and annotated bibliography on covenant ethics as it applies to many spheres of life, not only sex, see Ottati and Schuurman, "Covenantal Ethics").

Faithfulness to covenant commitments links the two kinds of relationships. It is clear very early in the biblical record that faithfulness will be a fundamental requirement for any individual or people that would relate to God (Ex 20:3). Faithfulness is the very first commandment given at Sinai to the Jewish people, and its violation (idolatry) is repeatedly decried and severely punished wherever it occurs throughout the Old Testament.

Likewise, sexual faithfulness lies at the heart of the marriage relationship. Most moral commands of both Old and New Testament enjoin *in*clusivity: the people of God are to welcome and include the stranger, the alien, the widow and orphan. They are to share liberally with those in need. Inclusivity rules— except in the marriage bed. Here there must be *exclusivity* of rivals in order for both partners to be *included* in a trusting, loyal, mutually affirming, problem-overcoming, alienation-healing, covenant bond. As the church father Tertullian wrote, "All things are common among us but our wives" (in Wogaman,

Christian Ethics, 44). Adultery (*moicheia* in the Greek) is a kind of sexual inclusivity in marriage, in which the covenant promise of sexual exclusivity is abandoned. Neither the redefinition of marriage to allow sexual inclusivity nor any blessing of the violation of a promised sexual exclusivity is contemplated in the New Testament. Few teachings are more clear.

Considered in contemporary context, sexual intercourse risks the conception of children. Children conceived outside of marriage are at risk of abandonment, neglect or violent death, and the emotional/moral development of children caught in a home characterized by marital infidelity is likely to be hindered (Grenz, *Sexual Ethics*, 98). Further, because of the mysterious emotional/psychic bonding that normally occurs in sex, adultery grievously wounds the spirit of the victimized partner and damages or destroys the bond that exists with the spouse. Because of God's passion for justice, many biblical commands are intended to protect the innocent from harm. The command against adultery should be viewed in that light, in terms of harm to children, to the injured spouse and ultimately to the adulterer.

In any case, the biblical revelation is clear. There must be sexual exclusivity in marriage. There can be no adultery. It is true, of course, that the Old Testament contains evidence of much falling short of the full meaning of this command. The polygamy practiced by the patriarchs, the kings and others opened the marriage relationship up to what might be called sanctioned adultery in favor of the man in a patriarchal society. The biblical record also includes repeated examples of the difficulty of sustaining polygamous relationships in the face of the inevitable jealousies and intrigues among wives and children competing for their husband's/father's attention and blessing (consider the patriarchal narratives in Gen 12—50). Though this point is argued by some, it is important to note that polygamy is at least implicitly ruled out by the teaching of Jesus (cf. Mt 19:1-9), whose words called his listeners back to God's original intention for sex and marriage—the joyful lifetime union of one man with one woman.

Vicious cycles: the lustful gaze and the lonely heart. Jesus reaffirmed the biblical command against adultery. Precisely because of the significance of that command, he went on to point out the path the human heart sometimes takes on its way to the command's violation. That is, he moved from a statement of the command to shrewd observation diagnosing ways in which we get stuck in patterns of behavior that lead us into sin.

His statement is compact. "I say to you that everyone looking upon a woman with the intent to desire her has already committed adultery with her in his heart" (Mt 5:28 author's translation). This single sentence is among the most damagingly misunderstood in the entire scriptural record. Much hinges on a proper translation of the key phrase *pros to epithymēsai*. Most modern translations miss the critical dimension of *intent* that is implicit here. For example, the NRSV reads "everyone who looks at a woman with lust"; compare the NIV— "anyone who looks at a woman lustfully." The KJV actually captures the nuance more adequately: "whosoever looketh on a woman to lust after her." Donald Hagner has it just about right: "everyone who looks at a woman with the purpose of lusting after her" (*Matthew 1—13*, 119). Guelich translates the phrase "in order to desire having her (sexually)," emphasizing the aspect of possession of what belongs to another (*Sermon on the Mount*, 193-94).

This small matter of exegesis and translation is no small matter at all. The more common and less accurate translation has contributed greatly to an idealistic/unrealistic rendering of Jesus' teaching. If Jesus is saying that the first spark of attraction one has to another person is the equivalent of the act of adultery, then surely the average adult—especially the average male—has committed many such acts. If so, the teaching of Jesus is intended simply to shame us or to show us how far we are from the perfection he demands.

However, this is not the nature of Jesus' teaching. If we read his teaching instead as concrete direction concerning how to do God's will and thus enjoy kingdom existence here and now, then he must mean something like what the Greek text actually seems to say. Jesus is identifying an act of human will (or a pattern of human willfulness) which leads us in the direction of violating God's will and thus ensnaring ourselves in misery.

An accurate description of this process or pattern of behavior would begin with the acknowledgment that precisely because we are embodied sexual selves, sexual attraction is an inescapable dimension of human existence. We are drawn mysteriously to the physical beauty and form of others, certain others in particular. When we encounter people who for whatever reason of face, shape or form are particularly appealing to us, we frequently experience a momentary *frisson* of excitement, a spark of attraction. This appears to be part of the created order and should not be identified as sinful (cf. Allison, *Sermon on the Mount*, 73-74). (It should also be noted that we are sometimes drawn to the inner beauty of others; a different path that can have the same result. We will develop this theme a bit later.)

The issue then becomes what happens from that point of "sparking." With one person, that man or woman who becomes our spouse, that spark is appropriately fanned into flame in due course, with full sexual communion reserved for the marriage bed. (Neither Jesus nor the other New Testament writers ever speak disparagingly of sexual desire *within* the marriage relationship—see Schrage, *Ethics of the New Testament*, 98). With all *other* persons, however, prior to marriage or in the midst of marriage to our spouse, that spark is to be noted and duly redirected to other purposes or to our spouse.

The vicious cycle of sexual sin, particularly adultery, begins with the decision of the will not to redirect that spark of attraction. Instead, the spark is gradually fanned into an ever hotter flame. That process frequently begins precisely as Jesus indicated here: one looks upon another with the intent to desire them. So the quick notice of another's beauty lingers and becomes what Dallas Willard (*Divine Conspiracy*, 161) calls "the look." The look, or lustful gaze, is so pleasing that we look for further opportunities to encounter the same person for the same purpose. Our private thoughts turn to fantasies of sexual encounter with this person. We purpose in our hearts to make contact with the object of our desire in order to create a sexual opportunity. We make this phone call and arrange this particular set of circumstances and have that particular kind of conversation. We seize the opportunity we have created and finally have the sexual encounter long fantasized and desired. Of course, what I am discussing here can move well beyond a one-time attraction and become a pattern of behavior, beginning with the lustful look. We can become people characterized by "eyes full of adultery" (2 Pet 2:14), a way of living which one might describe as the antithesis of sexual integrity.

In the marvelous chapter of Job (Job 31) that I have elsewhere called "the code of a man of honor" (Gushee and Long, *A Bolder Pulpit*, 118-19), Job defends himself against the charge that his sin has brought down upon him the disasters that he is experiencing. That defense includes a careful explication of the ways in which Job has resisted the path to adultery. It begins with his internal commitment "not to look lustfully at a girl" (Job 31:1 NIV). In a stark parallel to Jesus' teachings, Job made a decision of the will not to linger over the beauty or form of a woman not his wife, not to covet or lust after her. He continues:

> If I have walked with falsehood, and my foot has hurried to deceit . . . if my step has turned aside from the way, and my heart has followed my eyes, and if any spot has clung to my hands, then let me sow, and another eat. . . . If my heart has been enticed by a woman, and I have lain in wait at my neighbor's door; then let my wife grind for another, and let other men kneel over her. For that would be a heinous crime. (Job 31:5-11)

We observe that the punishment Job hypothetically invites upon himself is that involuntary labor and sexual servitude happen *to his wife*. This is hardly an example of what we call Christ-following discipleship, and in fact Jesus' contrast with this view of womanhood demonstrates our hermeneutical principle of following Jesus' way of interpreting the Scripture. But in the first part of Job's statement, we see a realistic phenomenology of the progression from visual sexual attraction to adultery, along with a rigorous commitment to avoid that path. The lustful gaze leads to a decision to enter upon falsehood and deceit, which adultery is, by definition; and a web of falsehood and deceit almost always surrounds adultery. The heart turns away from covenantal commitments and instead follows the eyes. That turn of the heart then leads to practical action—steps to sin (waiting outside the neighbor's door for him to leave), finally culminating in adultery.

No wonder Jesus refers to this—admittedly in compact fashion—as committing adultery in one's heart. It is not the initial spark of attraction that is equivalent to adultery, but instead the downward spiral of behavior resulting from a heart that has turned from covenant fidelity to covenant breaking. This is the vicious cycle that leads to adultery, and many there are who lack only the opportunity to act on the path to which they have already given their hearts.

But sexual temptation does not always take the form we are outlining here. It does not always begin with a physical attraction that flowers into physical misconduct. Many times, the desire for love, for meaning or for acceptance is the path that leads to illicit sex. That hunger of the lonely heart for community is a powerful, instinctive and God-resembling aspect of human nature. Community denied; love denied; needs denied; meaning denied—these create a painful vacuum that easily lends itself to the quest for either love or sex as a substitute for love.

Gender differences are often significant on this issue. Most men are more frequently tempted via visual sexual stimulation than women appear to be. Of course, no generalization of this type is without exception. The old saw that women give sex to get love and that men give love to get sex contains a seed of truth that should not be ignored. Jesus' brief words on sexual sin in this passage are directed to men and indeed seem more relevant to men. But there is more than one path to illicit sex, and it may be that *visual* stimulation and response is less profound or important than *relational* enticements based on fundamental human needs gone begging. If a new woman finds my conversation fascinating, my skills or strength admirable, and my presence exciting, while my wife, who once did also, now takes them for granted, I may be more susceptible to temptation than I had believed possible. Belief that I am above reproach often goes before the fall. It drops my defenses and lets me enter into tempting practices.

Transforming initiatives: reversing the vicious cycle. Having reaffirmed the command against adultery and identified the traps that turn our hearts toward sexual sin, Jesus offered a hyperbolic statement of the transforming initiatives that can free us from the traps and keep us on the path of joyful obedience. There are four imperatives: *tear out* the eye and *throw it away, cut off the hand* and *throw it away* (Mt 5:29-30; for an interesting parallel, see Mt 18:8-9, cf. Mk 9:42-48).

No one seriously believes that Jesus intended to teach his followers to pluck out their eyes and cut off their hands if these bodily members lead them into sin. What Jesus *did* mean by these stark statements is a matter of debate. Some read him simply as reinforcing the seriousness of his teaching; that is, do whatever is necessary to avoid committing adultery, of the heart or any other kind. Dallas Willard (*Divine Conspiracy*, 167) puts the matter memorably:

> Of course being acceptable to God is so important that, *if* cutting bodily parts off could achieve it, one would be wise to cut them off. . . . But so far from suggesting that any advantage before God could actually be gained in this way, Jesus' teaching in this passage is exactly the opposite. The mutilated stump could still have a wicked heart. The deeper question always concerns who you are, not what you did do or can do. What would you do if you could? Eliminating bodily parts will not change that. (italics in original)

Willard is certainly correct in the claim that a heart turned toward adultery cannot be healed by self-mutilation, literal or figurative. However, we see a slightly different intention in these striking teachings. Along with Hagner (*Matthew 1—13*, 121) and Guelich (*Sermon on the Mount*, 241-42), what we see is instruction in preventive initiatives that can be taken to forestall the descent into sexual sin. Or, as Davies and Allison put it, these are "verses which vividly demand radical sacrifice for the purpose of avoiding occasions of sin" (*Critical and Exegetical Commentary*, 523).

"If your right eye causes you to sin, tear it out and throw it away." It is certainly the heart that is the ultimate source of sin, but it is just as certainly our eyes that we use to participate in that sin. No, we are not supposed to gouge out our eyes. But we are supposed to deal in a very disciplined manner with visual cues that take us in the wrong direction, especially if that is the primary source of our sexual temptation.

Consider the example of sexually explicit media. If I want to live in obedience to God's command and avoid doing anything that might begin to turn my heart, I will be very careful about the media that I set before my eyes (or my ears, for that matter). We live in a society in which sexual titillation is of course one of the most successful forms of media around. Further, sexual content has become more and more explicit and more and more widely available. The internet has now made sexually graphic material accessible at the click of a mouse, radically intensifying the visually available temptation to sin now available in the average home.

So I do not gouge out my eye. I might, however, "gouge out" the premium movie channel on my cable television subscription. I might "gouge out" much of the sexual content of my internet provider by acquiring a filtering program. And when traveling, I might "gouge out" the pay-porn movie options by notifying the front desk upon arrival of my preference that this be done. In other words, taking care to restrict what appears before my eyes is not legalism but instead simply a concrete expression of a will to live as a kingdom citizen. If my heart is not right on this matter, no such steps can keep my thoughts pure. However, there is a two-way connection between eyes and heart; the heart is affected by what the eyes see, and enough of the wrong kind of stimulation can lead the heart astray (cf. Lloyd-Jones, *Studies in the Sermon on the Mount,* 249 and our four-dimensional understanding of character in chapter three). This is simple realism. As we saw in chapter two, in the words of Davies and Allison, "Purity of heart must involve integrity, a correspondence between outward action and inward thought (cf. 15:8), a lack of duplicity, singleness of intention."

The reference to the right hand (simply "hand" in the parallel texts, in which the word "foot" is also included) is most interesting in this context. To discuss this matter honestly will require some direct words about subjects not often discussed candidly in Christian circles. To wit: one aspect of the transition from spark of attraction to adultery is masturbation (only Davies and Allison among the major commentators see this meaning as the evangelist's intention; *Critical and Exegetical Commentary,* 1:525-26). Its purveyors know that pornography is essentially a masturbatory device. While we are not arguing that self-touching is in every case wrong, it can be one component of the fantasizing that helps turn a feeling of attraction into a plan of action. When that is so the "right hand" is in a sense causing one to sin, and this is not harmless. There is a definite difference between masturbation as an occasional sexual release and masturbation as a dangerous and sometimes quite compulsive form of sexual fantasy in the process of being willed into reality. In the latter case especially the appropriate initiative is to "cut off" this kind of action.

Another quite relevant contemporary application of this statement has to do with the nature of the touching that occurs between unmarried men and women. The issue is usually handled as a matter of premarital rule-setting for the dating relationship. Yet it is also relevant in terms of the level of physical intimacy that develops between adults who are married but not to each other.

A variety of rule-schemes or broader principles have been proposed. For the unmarried young person, the fundamental questions ought to be what kind of touching (a) constitutes *de facto* sexual relations even if intercourse is avoided and (b) makes it *more* difficult to adhere to a commitment to abstinence from intercourse (a commitment which rightly understood is rooted not solely in a rule/act-focused morality but also in concern for the well-being of those with whom the unmarried are in relationship). For the married, the issue is perhaps best framed as what kind of touching (a) represents a form of infidelity to the marriage relationship, even if intercourse is avoided, and (b) tempts one down the path to extramarital sex. Avoiding such touch is one way to incarnate the transforming initiative that Jesus speaks of here.

Where sexual temptation impinges via a relational rather than physical or visual path, transforming initiatives take a different form. Careful monitoring of the intimacy and mutual meeting of needs in marriage, with both husband and wife sincerely trying to meet each other's needs for affirming and affectionate relationship, is the best way to prevent seeking of sexual relationships outside of marriage. (What Paul says in 1 Cor 7:3-5 should be applied to needs for relational intimacy as well as needs for sex.) By this we do not mean that a person should view the failure of his or her spouse to meet his or her needs as an excuse for looking elsewhere. No couple completely matches in interests and mutual affirmations. Jesus puts the responsibility on oneself, not on the other, for seeking ways to meet the other's needs.

Further, both spouses need to watch closely the development of an undue or dangerous intimacy with others outside of their relationship. Honest conversation about unmet needs in the relationship and the nature of relationships with others—especially during the inevitable times of strain and difficulty in married life—is an important discipline and can become a marriage-saving initiative in times of trouble. Practicing talking about intimate needs can improve a couple's skills in such needed conversation. Look at it as learning to play basketball or tennis; you cannot do it skillfully the first time, or even the first hundred times. But you can improve with practice.

The apostle Paul twice urged his readers to flee *(pheugō)* sexual sin (1 Cor 6:18; 2 Tim 2:22). When in doubt, run as fast as you can in the opposite direction of the temptation coming your way. Such instruction reflects the same intensity as Jesus' teaching here in Matthew 5. The matter is serious. It is serious because sex is easily misused. And it is serious in its consequences, not just for individuals and couples but for families, churches, society and the advancement of the reign of God through all of the above.

Situations and Applications

Historically, Christian teaching about sexual morality has addressed a number of particular situations and issues. These issues have included both the perennial and the ephemeral, both concerns emerging out of permanent aspects of human nature and those that reflect passing trends in culture or technology. Let us touch on a couple of issues of both types. This discussion will also give us a chance to bring historic and contemporary voices in Christian ethics into our treatment of sexuality.

Singleness and sexuality. The Jewish moral tradition assumed that all who were of sound mind and body would marry. There is no explicit provision made in the Old Testament for any kind of voluntary singleness. The New Testament presents a different picture. The church has historically believed that Jesus was unmarried and celibate, and the New Testament records one cryptic teaching in which he appears to endorse the celibate life (Mt 19:10-12). Meanwhile, the apostle Paul endorsed celibate singleness as preferable to marriage in terms of one's freedom for "unhindered devotion to the Lord" (1 Cor 7:35), and made clear that this was his own situation in life (1 Cor 7:7). While Peter and other apostles were clearly married, the apparent celibate singleness of the two towering figures of the New Testament has cast a long shadow over Christian moral teaching about sexuality. It provides a much stronger affirmation of the vocation of singles than traditional culture does. Churches need to affirm singles and not make singles second-class members unless they want to make Jesus and Paul second-class members of Christian tradition (see Clapp, *Families at the Crossroads*).

The impact has been felt most profoundly in the Catholic tradition. To unravel the skein of theological and moral reflection that led to the particular shape of Catholic moral theology in the area of sex would take us too far afield. Suffice it to say that the combination of Greek philosophical influences, the New Testament (through a particular interpretive grid) and the work of key Christian thinkers such as Augustine led to profound ambivalence concerning sexuality. Sex as a good aspect of creation sometimes gave way to despair over sex in all of its disastrous fallenness or a grudging toleration of sex as the means of procreation (see Gudorf, *Body, Sex, and Pleasure*, 129-31; Smedes, *Mere Morality*, chap. 2).

What emerged amounted to a toleration of sexual expression as a second-best alternative and a concession to sin. A two-tier ethic developed in which those seeking holiness would choose celibate singleness, which ultimately became an obligatory part of the lifestyle of the "religious," such as priests, monks and nuns. The more common but second-best path was for men and women to follow Catholic sexual teachings in the context of monogamous marriage. This was certainly a way of life to be preferred over sexual debauchery, and it was endorsed by the church. And yet the vision of the higher way of ascetic celibacy remained intact.

Martin Luther broke decisively with this aspect of Catholic thought. Just as convinced of the disastrous ramifications of sexual sin as was the entire Catholic moral tradition, he believed that the appropriate implication of this reality was that (nearly) all should marry and thus have a safe and legitimate outlet for the sexual fire that rages within. Though Luther said that "intercourse is never without sin," he managed also to construct a positive biblical theology of marriage grounded in creation (Cahill, *Between the Sexes*, 123-24). He himself married and had several children.

Following Luther, Protestant sexual ethics has tended to reject the legitimacy or at least the wisdom of the life of celibate singleness. In a striking reversal of Catholic tradition, the normative Protestant minister is married with children, and any other configuration is looked upon with suspicion. Many are the single ministers who have encountered difficulties in finding employment on precisely these grounds. Some Protestant leaders have even used 1 Timothy 3:2 (in which the elder is described—in some translations—as "the husband of one wife") to argue that marriage is morally obligatory for all ministers or pastors. However, the problem that Paul in that verse was warning against was not singleness but polygamy or promiscuity.

We believe that the Bible makes room for both celibate singleness and faithful monogamy as equally legitimate expressions of human sexuality for those who would follow Jesus (Grenz, *Sexual Ethics*, chap. 9). In light of the whole of the biblical witness there is no reason for proclaiming one or the other the higher way. This is a matter within the range of Christian liberty and God's calling in view of the gifts of each particular person in each particular context.

The contemporary church is full of all kinds of people: never-married, married, divorced, remarried, widowed and so on. Neither marriage nor singleness should be viewed as a requirement for ministry leadership. Among the laity are those who are single for life or single for a time in life. Clear instruction is available in the Bible for those in this wide variety of life situations and callings, and singles should not be "singled out" for second-class Christian status.

In contemporary society most singles are not celibate. In recent polls a shrinking minority of Americans claim that sex outside of marriage is always morally wrong. Many assume that adult singles will be sexually active and generally approve this as long as their sexual engagements are consensual and "safe." In biblical days a woman married between ages twelve and fourteen, and a man between sixteen and twenty-one. We ask singles to remain celibate for much longer than ever before in history. Dating was unheard of only a few generations ago. Long periods of unchaperoned intimacy with others, combined with a culture that presumes that sex is ubiquitous, challenge the traditional ethic as never before. The Christian sexual ethic has not faced such a challenge in Western society since the earliest days of the church's history.

Some voices within the church also argue for a reconsideration. In a 1987 article Karen Lebacqz called for an ethic that would tie the level of sexual expression to the level of vulnerability in the single's relationship. This would not rule out sexual intercourse for singles but would establish "appropriate vulnerability" as the measure by which to assess its rightness or wrongness (in Clark and Rakestraw, *Readings in Social Ethics*, 2:149-54). This is not an ethic that supports casual sex for singles but it does open the door to sex within somewhat more committed relationships. Some on the liberal end of the spectrum essentially embrace mutually pleasurable sex as a significant good in itself.

We believe our emphasis on the covenant character of human nature can help. Singles can make covenants with God, self and others that define their vocation in life as fulfilled in work and service commitments, and in mutually supportive relationships with others. We believe it can enrich life greatly to notice and nurture covenant relationships with close friends, fellow workers, fellow church members and relatives. The content and implicit or even explicit stipulations of faithful friendships, cooperative relationships and mutual bondings vary with the length and character of the relationships. We have at least implicit covenant relationships with our students and with each other, and with other friends, that are enormously important to our sense of gratitude for life, even though these are obviously not the same as our covenant relationships with our spouses, our parents or our siblings. To notice and nurture the various kinds of covenant relationships we enter into transforms and deepens our sense of life's blessings.

Of all the great moral questions facing humanity and the church today, the sexual behavior of, say, a forty-something couple who love each other faithfully and are moving toward marriage is not really at the top of the list. But the importance of combating a permissive ethic of egoistic self-fulfillment across the board, from sex to economic accumulation to consumption of the world's resources to nationalistic disregard of other nations, and instead developing a covenant ethic of truthful commitment and mutual support *is* at the top of the list. And how we act sexually does powerfully influence how we relate in other spheres. Practices do shape character, and sexual practices shape character powerfully. An ethic grounded in Scripture, including the teachings of Jesus, cannot move in the direction of the sexual revolution. Nor are we sanguine about the social and personal impact of the shattering of the once-assumed relationship between sex, marriage and childbearing (see Dawn, *Sexual Character*, esp. 23-24). So we do not embrace the adoption of a "mutual pleasure" or "mutual love" redefinition of Christian sexual ethics.

Birth control, childlessness and sterilization. Sexual intercourse leads to the conception and birth of children, and a whole host of moral issues associated with this miraculous dimension of human experience under God's sovereignty. Today a discussion of reproductive ethics, as one might call it, raises issues both new and old.

The entire Christian moral tradition assumes that it is God's will for children to be conceived and nurtured within the security and stability of marriage and family life. In a day in which fully one-third of all children in the United States and Canada are born outside of the marriage relationship, the church must not be intimidated into giving up its historic loyalty to covenant commitment and accommodate to individualistic privatism. We can develop and teach a deeper covenant morality without stigmatizing children born out of wedlock.

A vigorous reaffirmation of the wisdom of biblical teaching is needed. It is best for all parties, but especially for the children born of the sexual relationship between a man and a woman, that sex be limited to the publicly recognized and socially sanctioned marriage relationship. Even when functioning at only a minimal level of satisfaction, a marriage provides a context of stability, care and social identity for children. *This is who I am; this is my name; this is who my parents are; this is who is responsible for my care; this is whom I can count on to be faithful to my needs and to whom I am faithful and attentive; this is where I live; this is my place in the world; these are my ancestors; this is whom I want to grow up to imitate*—these are affirmations available to the child fortunate enough to be born and raised in the context of a family anchored in a marriage relationship (see Whitehead, *Divorce Culture*, chaps.4, 7). This is true as a general rule despite the miserable exceptions all of us could name in relationship to family breakdown and abuse.

Christian sexual ethics has not, then, wrestled with whether to endorse childbirth outside of marriage, at least not until recently. Other issues have been more controversial. For example, there is the matter of whether Christian couples are free to choose not to conceive children (the issue of *voluntary childlessness*). Voluntary childlessness was essentially unthinkable in the age prior to highly effective birth control and sterilization techniques, at least for those couples with a sexual relationship. But in the past forty years or so the voluntarily childless couple has become a social reality. So let us consider the issues of birth control and voluntary childlessness in tandem.

Catholic sexual ethics, under the impact of a natural law approach deeply influenced by Aristotle, has for centuries rejected the validity both of "artificial" birth control and of voluntary childlessness for the Christian couple. The entire structure of Catholic sexual ethics has been built upon the concept of fulfilling rather than thwarting what the church believed to be the fundamental God-given purpose of the human reproductive apparatus, which is to reproduce the species. For centuries procreation was viewed as the primary purpose of sex, with the covenant-strengthening (mutual love, mutual aid) function of sex a meaningful but secondary end (see Curran and McCormick, *Readings in Moral Theology No. 8*, pt. 2). Voluntary childlessness means that couples are having sex (presumably) but purposely thwarting reproduction, which is viewed in a natural law approach as something like growing an apple tree while purposely throwing away all the apples.

Classic Protestant sexual ethics joined Catholic ethics in recognizing that marital sex is a remedy for promiscuous sexual desire and a means of deepening and strengthening the couple's covenant unity, but generally rejected the subordination of these ends to the procreative purpose of sex. Thus space was opened for the later possibility of blessing the use of birth control within marriage; the issue of permanent voluntary childlessness raised somewhat different questions.

In recent decades Protestant and Catholic sexual ethics have converged quite a bit. Catholic ethics has elevated the significance and goodness of the relational/unitive/covenant dimension of sex in marriage. Meanwhile, both strands of Christian tradition have recently been more willing to grant the possibility that sexual pleasure itself is a God-given good for humans to enjoy rather than merely a means to other ends. As noted, this is a focus of much contemporary Christian ethical reflection from across the theological spectrum. Yet official Catholic teaching remains opposed to (artificial) means of birth control and to voluntary childlessness. Protestant thinkers generally see no compelling moral objection to birth control within marriage and are more willing to consider the prospect that some Christian couples might be called to a life of voluntary childlessness (Grenz, *Sexual Ethics*, 126-33, 147).

Birth control within marriage allows the Christian couple to attempt to make responsible decisions related to family size and spacing. As well, we believe there is the real possibility that some couples are called to voluntary childlessness in order to maximize their kingdom impact (by way of analogy to the call to celibate singleness) or perhaps because they do not have a temperament or life situation to which children ought to be exposed. To the objection that the creation mandate to be fruitful and multiply is normative here, we reply that this mandate applies to the whole of the human family but need not apply to every single human being—and that as a whole, the human family has more than fulfilled its terms. That mandate was given when the world population totaled to two persons and taught when Palestine was sparsely populated. Once the population grew, the mandate was never taught again, in the time of the prophets or the time of the New Testament. Today the earth's population is six billion and growing exponentially, and without access to birth control, it would grow even more rapidly.

When a couple is convinced that their childbearing days are over, they frequently turn to modern technology for sterilization. In principle, sterilization—whether of the man (through a vasectomy) or of the woman (through a tubal ligation)—raises the same kinds of moral questions that birth control in general does, only in a more acute form. It relieves a couple of ever having to worry about other forms of birth control and in some cases increases sexual satisfaction in marriage. Those who oppose all birth control, especially technological measures, oppose sterilization techniques even more strongly. The official Catholic position remains consistent at this point (Curran and McCormick, *Readings in Moral Theology No. 8*, pt. 3). Those open to birth control tend to be open to birth control through sterilization, especially in our time when the growing world population combined with overconsumption are seen by many Christians to be threatening the life of the planet.

Homosexuality. The contemporary struggle over homosexuality in church life (not to mention society) is perhaps the context in which conflicting historic and contemporary Christian approaches to sexual ethics are most readily apparent.

Jesus is not recorded to have said anything about homosexual behavior, homosexual persons or homosexuality as a phenomenon, at all. Given that our method attempts to place its emphasis where Jesus placed his, this is a matter of some significance. It is at least arguable from the fact of Jesus' silence—and the limited discussion in Scripture in general—that the contemporary fixation on homosexuality in some Christian circles is misplaced (Hays, *Moral Vision of the New Testament*, 381). Many widely used evangelical ethics texts reflect what we see as a disproportionate emphasis on homosexuality (see Davis, *Evangelical Ethics*; Rae, *Moral Choices*; Geisler, *Christian Ethics*). This lack of proportion helps to fuel the distressing and unfortunate perception, partly grounded in reality, of a conservative evangelical Christian crusade against homosexuals.

Of course, context matters, both in Jesus' time and in our own. Jesus was a Jew speaking primarily to Jews, and both the Old Testament and the Jewish tradition offered no legitimation whatsoever for homosexual behavior. God created male and female, joined the male and the female in marriage (Gen 2:18-25), and commanded them to "be fruitful and multiply" (Gen 1:28). As Donald Wold has written, "Creation provided the positive male-female model for sexual union" (*Out of Order*, 8).

Homosexual contacts between men are mentioned in Old Testament law twice (Lev 18:22; 20:13), in both cases to include them among a long list of sexual behaviors forbidden as "abominations" against holiness that brought divine wrath on the offender and danger to the entire community (Wold, *Out of Order*, 8). Two instances of attempted homosexual rape (there is no real doubt that this is what these incidents are describing—Nissinen, *Homoeroticism in the Biblical World*, 46, versus Bailey, *Homosexuality and the Western Christian Tradition*, 3-5) are offered in the Old Testament (Gen 19, Sodom; Judg 19, Gibeah). These incidents, especially the story of Sodom and Gomorrah, have had a profound impact on the Western imagination; they are often interpreted as license for hatred of homosexuals. This disastrous tendency ignores the fact that later biblical references to Sodom's fate emphasize the city's sin of inhospitality to God's messengers, not homosexuality (Ezek 16:49; Mt 10:5-15 and par.).

Three references to homosexuality can be found in the New Testament: 1 Corinthians 6:9-10, 1 Timothy 1:10 and Romans 1:26-27. The first two are included among lengthy vice lists that cover a wide range of sins. In 1 Corinthians, the function of the list is to combat a dangerous antinomian libertinism—in other words, to make absolutely clear that behavior does indeed matter in the Christian life despite the centrality of grace. In 1 Timothy, the discussion concerns the legitimate use of the law to condemn a wide range of flagrantly immoral practices, among which homosexual behavior is included. On the question of whether the terms used in these texts (*malakoi* and *arsenokoitai*) actually refer to homosexuality at all, the great majority of scholars now agree that they do (see Soards, *Scripture and Homosexuality*, 19; Wold, *Out of Order*, chap. 13, vs. Boswell, *Christianity, Social Tolerance, and Homosexuality*).

The most systematic treatment of homosexuality in Scripture is found in Paul's discussion in Romans 1. Our method is to interpret Scripture in context, not merely quote a verse, and let Jesus be Lord of our interpretation. Here Paul made the case for the gospel of Jesus Christ by first establishing that human beings are in sinful rebellion against God, under God's judgment and in desperate need of the salvation Christ's atoning death has made available. Making use of the fundamental distinction between Gentiles and Jews so prevalent in Jewish thought in Paul's own day, the apostle diagnosed spiritual need among the two groups.

For Gentiles, the problem was pagan "ungodliness and wickedness," shown in not honoring and giving thanks to God the Creator, knowledge of whom was available in creation. Instead of acknowledging and serving the one Creator God, they "exchanged the truth about God for a lie and worshiped . . . the creature rather than the Creator" (Rom 1:25). The rampant immorality of the Gentile world, Paul argued, was symptomatic rather than foundational, consequence rather than cause, flowing from this rebellion against God (Hays, *Moral Vision of the New Testament*, 384-85). In detailing what he clearly considered a shocking morass of immoral and unnatural behaviors, he lifted up both male and female homosexual acts for special attention (Rom 1:26-27). (A pagan Greek ethos taught that males are superior to females and homosexual relations with males superior to heterosexual relations with females.) Then Paul detailed a lengthy list of other pagan/Gentile vices—not a random list, but vices of hostility, the opposite of the virtue of peacemaking (Rom 1:29-31). These deviations from divine moral law and the created order had offended God and had both manifested and merited divine wrath.

Then Paul turned the tables on his Jewish readers, who were heartily agreeing with his judgment of the ethos of the pagan world. For Jews, the problem was that "you have no excuse, . . . when you judge others; for in passing judgment on another you condemn yourself, because you, the judge, are doing the very same things" (Rom 2:1). And then Paul diagnosed the parallel sin of his fellow Jews, who rather than being grateful for God's grace, rebelled against God's grace and put their trust in their own self-righteousness to save them and so turned, like the Gentiles, into hostility toward their fellow humans. Paul quoted the prophet Isaiah (Is 59:6-8), just as Jesus did: "Their mouths are full of cursing and bitterness. Their feet are swift to shed blood; . . . and the way of peace they have not known" (Rom 3:13-17; cf. Lk 19:41-42). The pattern in both cases was failure to live in gratitude to God, instead putting trust in human efforts, and consequential hostility to fellow humans.

Paul's point was that "the righteousness of God through faith in Jesus Christ" was "for *all* who believe. For *all* have sinned and fall short of the glory of God. . . . Or is God the God of Jews only? Is he not the God of Gentiles also? Yes, of Gentiles also" (Rom 3:22-23, 29, italics added). Christ's "sacrifice of atonement" (Rom 3:25) had made forgiveness and reconciliation with God available for all, Gentile and Jew. And this—reconciliation, justification by grace through faith for all—was the point of Paul's argument. There was no room for boasting or judging (Rom 2:1-24; 3:27-28; and see the climax of the letter, Rom 14:1—15:13). Salvation was by grace given in Jesus Christ through faith in Jesus Christ, and not by some human merit that could lead to boasting and judging others. This points back to Jesus' teaching in the Sermon on the Mount that we should not be judging others (Mt 7:1-5). Jesus' command means that we are not to be judging in the sense of condemning others, since we are all sinners saved by grace; however, we can and must be discerning about what is right and wrong.

Much has been made in recent literature of the link between idolatrous cults and homosexual behavior. Boswell and others have argued, for example, that Levitical passages related to homosexuality are cult-related and have nothing to do with sexual behavior in other contexts, thus invalidating their applicability to contemporary discussions of homosexuality. Perhaps the strongest arguments that "abomination" refers to idolatry and not specifically to sex are offered by Countryman (*Dirt, Greed, and Sex*, 11-65) and Edwards (*Gay/Lesbian Liberation*). Wold offers a careful refutation of this view, arguing that it is mistaken to narrow the meaning of the Hebrew vocabulary in this way (Wold, *Out of Order*, chap. 7; cf. Nissinen, *Homoeroticism in the Biblical World*, chap. 3; Grenz, *Welcoming but Not Affirming*, chap. 2). He argues at some length that the theological foundation of the biblical prohibition of homosexual practice seems to go deeper.

The debate in contemporary church life is, of course, not about cult prostitution or violent homosexual rape. There is no one on the Christian landscape arguing for the acceptance of such behavior. But there are some who claim that our own context poses a very different question than the one Paul was addressing.

One way to frame the current question is the following: What shall we say to, and about, men and women who (a) experience their sexual desire as being insistently directed to members of the same sex; and (b) desire to bond with a member of the same sex in the same kind of permanent faithful monogamy that some heterosexuals enjoy?

Much of what drives the quest among Christians for some kind of openness to legitimating homosexual behavior that occurs in this kind of context (monogamous, permanent) is sensitivity to the experiences, indeed the honest perplexity and profound suffering, of people who are in precisely this situation. In other words, personal loyalties and commitments are at play, and not dispassionate biblical exegesis or moral reasoning. We have already claimed that it is critical to look for this dimension of how moral judgments are made and positions taken, both by those we agree with and those we do not (see the loyalties and passions dimension of character in chapter three). And we affirm sensitivity to human suffering as a Christlike virtue.

Beyond this, the current discussion tends to reflect the shift in the fundamental approach to reasoning about sexual ethics that we suggested has been occurring in recent Christian ethics. If the axis of authority shifts, even subtly, from Scripture to personal experience, if all arguments related to nature are rejected, if pleasure and relational satisfaction or even faithful covenant bonding are the highest values in sexual ethics, if celibacy is unrealistic or oppressive for some, as Paul indicates in 1 Corinthians 7, the groundwork is laid for the kind of overall revision of Christian sexual ethics that has in fact been occurring in recent decades.

Arguments for the legitimation of homosexuality in particular take many forms these days (see Schmidt, *Straight and Narrow?* 56-58). We have already alluded to efforts to reread key biblical texts on homosexuality and their flaws. Some make a different move, highlighting biblical principles of love, mutuality, justice and even hospitality (see Rudy, *Sex and the Church*), and arguing that these are the relevant norms in sexual ethics. Our view is that this argument is successful in demonstrating how homosexual persons should be treated and how normative sexuality should be experienced but not in directing a revision of biblical sexual morality on the issue of homosexual acts or practices. Arguments from science related to the etiology of homosexuality are another popular avenue of approach (for a skeptical medical/scientific analysis, see Satinover, *Homosexuality and the Politics of Truth*). Even if it could be demonstrated that homosexual inclinations were genetically rooted, in combination with childhood experience, Christian moral thought offers no right to sexual gratification (Hays, *Moral Vision of the New Testament*, 401) regardless of the origin or object of sexual desire. Of course, some ethicists these days simply argue for the irrelevance, error, dangerousness or "counter-revelatory" value of Scripture in relation to the issue of homosexuality (Gudorf, *Body, Sex, and Pleasure*, 9; cf. Comstock, *Gay Theology Without Apology*) and having cleared away that obstacle freely embrace homosexual behavior. This of course is quite different from our approach to scriptural authority (see chapter four).

Homosexual conduct is one form of sexual expression that falls outside the will of God, one manifestation of what Hays calls "the disordered human condition" (388) under the impact of sin. Yet homosexual persons are precious, made in the image of God and bearers of all the dignity that God affords to all humanity. Christ-followers are never permitted to treat homosexuals as less than what God has declared all people to be. Spending one's life crusading against homosexuals, as some Christians do, hardly fits with the virtues of love, kindness, humility, peace and patience that are to characterize the follower of Christ. Looking for ways to deny homosexuals personal safety and security, access to jobs, housing, government service or other basic rights of participation in American society is abhorrent. On the other hand, supporting efforts by churches to enable homosexuals to deal with their sexuality in a redemptive way within the parameters offered by Scripture is certainly to be encouraged and fits with the transforming initiative approach we are taking to Jesus' teachings. We must love homosexual persons while remaining clear in our convictions about God's intentions for human sexuality—and equally clear that all of us stand guilty and in need of redemption.

Concluding Thoughts: How Much Does Sex Matter in Kingdom Perspective?

This tour of issues sexual in Christian ethics seems to beg a final question: how much does sex matter from a kingdom perspective?

It is certainly possible to overstate the significance of sex, and this is a mistake that the Christian moral tradition has made more than a few times, both on the negative and more recently on the positive side. Sexual ethics is just one part of kingdom living, and if the amount of attention Jesus gave to it relative to other subjects is taken seriously then it is not the most important moral issue on the landscape.

But sex does matter. It matters because there is no aspect of human personhood that God does not seek to redeem or that does not need redemption. God created us as sexual beings and had certain ends in mind when he did so. The tradition, as we have seen, affirms that our sexuality is intended not only for procreation but also for partnership and mutual pleasure. As well, the sexual dimension of our personhood is carried into every moment, and thus (regardless of actual sexual behavior) our sexuality affects every relationship and every interaction. Redeemed sexuality is part of the reign of God and depraved sexuality marks a setback for that reign wherever it appears.

Human beings require stable, rightly ordered sexual relationships in order to flourish. This does not mean that all are called to physical sexual activity, but that all are called to the expression of their God-given sexuality within the bounds of God's covenant will. Much of what is offered in music, television or film has to do with some variation on this theme—the quest for satisfaction, intimacy and wholeness in this area of life. Of course, the media offer many deeply erroneous perspectives on what this might look like. Ultimately, though, wise people come to recognize that covenantal relationships characterized by love, fidelity and justice are the path to the wholeness all seek.

Christians, as people devoted to the kingdom, want all aspects of their personhood rightly ordered. The reign of God is first experienced in the individual and corporate experience of Christian living. Believers who enjoy the blessing of sound, stable, covenantal sexual/family relationships and are characterized by sexual integrity are in the best position to advance God's reign with energy and focus. Undistracted by frustrated or misdirected sexuality, they can turn their attention to the advance of God's cause in a broken world.

15

GENDER ROLES

###

But the angel said to the women, "Do not be afraid; I know that you are looking for Jesus who was crucified. He is not here; for he has been raised, as he said. Come, see the place where he lay. Then go quickly and tell his disciples, 'He has been raised from the dead, and indeed he is going ahead of you to Galilee; there you will see him.' This is my message for you."

MATTHEW 28:5-7

The finest ethics student of her graduating class sat in my (David's) office with her fiancé. The discussion turned to the issue of her future. Prior to her engagement, Alisha (not her real name) had been seriously considering applying to the top tier of seminaries to study toward a doctorate in Christian ethics and then a teaching and writing career. As her professor, I was convinced of her ability to accomplish these goals.

But now that she was engaged Alisha was rethinking her future. She was aware that some members of her fiancé's family and friendship network were unsupportive of her pursuing graduate studies. They told her (and Jim, her fiancé) that a wife was to support her husband's career rather than to pursue her own. Some expressed doubts as to the biblical acceptability of a woman teaching men in a church or academic setting. Given that Jim was himself a minister, some argued that the role of a minister's wife was itself a full-time job. Jim, who was supportive of Alisha's career aspirations and tentative sense of calling, was also receiving the implicit and sometimes explicit message that a "real man" does not follow his wife as she pursues her career; she follows him as he pursues his.

Meanwhile, Alisha was plagued by doubts about her ability and her calling. As an evangelical woman, she was also concerned about employment opportunities in schools that otherwise might be theologically congenial. She also knew that church ministry opportunities, if she were interested in that path, would be hard to come by within her denomination (Southern Baptist). For these reasons she agonized over whether she was "really" called to pursue graduate studies. She heard conflicting advice from various mentors and leaders. Her struggle was acute and raises significant issues for Christian ethics.

The "Women's Issue" in Historical Perspective

Does a Jesus-centered Christian ethic have anything distinctive to say to Alisha about her options? Do we have a word about how men and women ought to understand and live out their respective roles in society, home and church? One could hardly imagine an issue that has been worked over more thoroughly; is there anything new to be said?

We think so. But before we move ahead to offer it we must comment on the professional and personal carnage that this issue has created in the recent history of evangelicals in North America, including the coauthors of this volume. Every generation of Christian scholars and church leaders, it seems, faces one or more defining doctrinal or moral issues. Which issues emerge in which contexts to become do-or-die concerns cannot be predicted in advance. Hindsight tends to reveal that historical, cultural and ecclesial circumstances at times converge to create a "perfect storm," into which the unsuspecting Christian scholar sails. Few emerge unscathed. In the 1930s in Germany the issue was Nazism; in the 1920s in the United States it was the fundamentalist/modernist controversy; in the mid-nineteenth century it was the issue of higher biblical criticism; in the sixteenth century it was the Reformation and its offshoots; in the early church it was the issue of whether Gentiles had to become Jews to become Christians!

The role of women in church and society became a defining issue in American evangelicalism in the 1980s and 1990s. The same issue crested in mainline Protestant circles in the 1960s and 1970s. It has not failed to roil the waters in Roman Catholicism since at least the 1960s.

Historical perspective is critical here. Classic political and philosophical liberalism, with its emphasis on autonomy, self-expression, equality, freedom, rights and participation, and its questioning of received religious and moral traditions, held within it the germ of a revolution in women's roles. That revolution did not come immediately, but the changes it would ultimately bring became apparent as early as the first decades of the nineteenth century. The so-called first wave of the women's movement pressed for basic social reforms in the situation of women in Western countries, including the United States. Christian leaders were among the most vocal opponents of these reform proposals. It took until 1920, it must be remembered, for women to be granted the right to vote in this nation—after a ferocious political struggle. In historical terms, that is a relatively recent event.

The second wave of the women's movement, which began in the 1960s, pressed for further reforms in both law and custom and the full equality of women in American life. By the end of the 1960s the women's movement had won critical victories that forced open a society previously reluctant to grant full economic, social and political participation to women. By now, it is sometimes easy to forget, we live in a society in which the full force of law prohibits any kind of discrimination against women—in education, employment, housing, political participation and so on. While women still encounter various configurations of power that hinder the full realization of this promised equality, the situation for women today barely resembles that which existed even forty years ago. In chapter three, we identified one's perception of social change as a crucial variable that affects our ethical outcomes on many issues; that is certainly evident in this case. It probably affects us in several ways of which we are not even aware.

The response of the Christian churches to the movement for women's rights has not been uniform. The story of that response tracks closely with the story of the church's response to modernity itself. Some sectors of the church embraced modernity in nearly every respect. Some embraced modernity selectively and rejected it selectively. And some sectors attempted to dig in their heels and hold off the forces of modernity with every ounce of strength they had. The same pattern could be seen in relation to the gender roles debate.

The "gender roles" question hit evangelicals, including Southern Baptists, in the 1980s because it was no longer historically or culturally possible for these groups to avoid an issue that had swept the society and affected other churches for at least twenty years. The gender issue emerged not because, all of a sudden, evangelical scholars decided the women's question might be interesting to study, but because forces of social change demanded an evangelical response. And the way in which the issue came to be framed was not a matter of theological or philosophical necessity but clearly reflected contingent historical realities.

The Contemporary Landscape

The result, twenty or so years later, is a deeply split Christian witness on this issue. We are sure that the readership of this volume will reflect that split.

Some readers will inhabit a faith-community context or intellectual frame of reference in which the very question of distinct gender roles or any limits on women's activities in any setting is seen as hugely anachronistic, highly insulting or at best deeply misleading. What women and men have in common is far more significant, on this view, than any intrinsic differences in psychology or anatomy that *might* be posited. Both men and women are free, autonomous, independent choice-makers. Both must be free to develop their potential to the fullest. No bar must be placed that would limit either women or men from any field of endeavor they might choose to pursue. Men and women are fundamentally equal in value, potential, rights and every other attribute that matters morally. Let us call this the *secular egalitarian* perspective on gender roles. It has been the dominant stance among the intellectual elite in Western civilization since the 1960s and characterizes large segments of the religious landscape as well. It represents the full acceptance of liberal and modernist presuppositions.

On the other end of the spectrum will be readers who are situated in contexts in which the secular egalitarian perspective is wholly and vigorously rejected. Numerous faith communities and families can be found in which very definite and well-defined gender roles are an important part of everyday life. Here the emphasis is not so much on what men and women have in common but instead on their (supposedly) God-given and intrinsic differences and the role distinctions that flow from those differences. Men are viewed as having been placed by the Creator in some form of leadership over women in home or church or society. Much emphasis is laid on the significance of structures of authority at all levels of human existence. Theoreticians of this perspective vary quite a bit in the arenas of application in which male leadership is most important. Most emphasize home and church while drawing back (in recent years at least) from envisioning an entirely male-led social order. While the most popular self-designation for this family of perspectives is *complementarian*, let us for clarity call this the *male leadership* perspective (see Piper and Grudem, *Recovering Biblical Manhood and Womanhood;* Kassian, *Feminist Gospel*).

Mainline Christians in the U.S. setting have at least in theory settled this matter in favor of the egalitarian perspective. The level of "secularism" in that egalitarianism has varied, but a male leadership perspective is by now simply unthinkable, and female seminarians and clergy are ubiquitous. But a fissure within evangelicalism on the issue has been clearly apparent since the mid-1980s; while it appears the majority of self-identified evangelicals do take some version of the male leadership position, a significant and influential minority has embraced an evangelical version of the egalitarian view. The preferred self-designation in this latter camp is *biblical egalitarian* or *biblical feminist* (see Scanzoni and Hardesty, *All We're Meant to Be;* Hull, *Equal to Serve;* Spencer, *Beyond the Curse*), and the movement as a whole insists that this perspective is biblically grounded rather than a capitulation to secular feminism or modernity. The focus of biblical egalitarianism is on a rereading of Scripture rather than its abandonment in favor of other sources of authority. The two sides have been deadlocked for quite some time, forming competing organizations (Council on Biblical Manhood and Womanhood, and Christians for Biblical Equality), issuing rival statements and scrapping for influence over the direction of future evangelical thought and practice. They do not much like each other, and relatively rare are the evangelical colleges and seminaries that have for long managed to hold together staffs with ardent adherents of both positions.

Here is where we come in. We have attempted not to belabor our own "social location" in this volume. But readers probably need to know that we both experienced firsthand the battle over gender as it played out in Southern Baptist life, and especially in Southern Baptist Theological Seminary, from 1985 to 1995. In 1985, when I was a student and Glen Stassen a professor at Southern, biblical egalitarianism was widely held. In 1993, when I was hired to teach alongside Glen at Southern, a somewhat more conservative trustee composition led to the administration's decision to accept faculty adherents of either the male leadership or the egalitarian view. By 1996, when for a variety of reasons we both decided to leave Southern's faculty, adherence to a male leadership/complementarian view—more precisely, a declaration of agreement with the statement that the Bible permits only men to serve as senior pastors of local congregations—became obligatory for all who would be hired, advanced or tenured. Agreement on all doctrinal points but this one was insufficient. The issue had become a faculty *status confessionis*.

Personally, I must admit here that thinking honestly, clearly and above all biblically about this issue proved nearly impossible in the political maelstrom of the controversy years. I was always aware that any comment I might make about the issue would be subject to rigorous political/religious parsing by partisans of the various positions. Concerns about my own professional future as a brand-new academician were acute (and still have an impact I must watch out for). There is an important lesson here about the kind of ecclesial and academic context that is required for faithful theological and ethical inquiry. While unfettered and boundary-less freedom is not appropriate in a Christian academic environment, neither is an intellectually deadly confinement of thought under coercive political and career constraints. (And, by the way, such constraints can be enforced from the left as well as from the right.)

What follows, then, for both of us, is an attempt to get free of such constraints and attempt a fresh look, however brief, at the biblical witness on this issue and the real options that lie before us.

Jesus and Women

As we look to Jesus for direction on this question we do not find explicit teaching that might settle the matter. Instead we must step back and look both at Jesus' overall teachings and his practice, especially against the backdrop of his religious context in first-century Jewish life.

An entry into the subject can be provided by considering the teachings of Jesus about lust and divorce that were the focus of the last chapter and will be considered in the next. First-century Jewish teachers, as David Garland has argued, placed all of the responsibility for the inflammation of male sexual desire on the woman. Thus the answer to the problem of lust for the morally serious man was to have as little exposure to women as possible—through a system limiting the access of women to public space and personal freedom. As Garland puts it: "The solution was therefore to avoid women, to segregate them, and to cover them up" (*Reading Matthew,* 67). Similar systems exist in some parts of the world today, especially in very conservative Muslim contexts.

Women were sequestered in a separate section during public worship in the temple, they were not to sit at the feet of rabbis for teaching as men did, they were never to touch men who were not members of their families, and they were required to cover themselves to avoid being seen by men. When sexual misconduct did happen, the focus of punishment was the woman rather than the man. An example can be seen in the story of the woman taken in adultery—presumably she did not commit adultery alone, yet the guilty man is nowhere to be seen in the story (Jn 8:1-11). Old Testament law required the death penalty for *both* parties to adultery, though a double standard favoring men was subtly insinuated into case law on this issue and certainly existed in first-century Jewish practice (Lev 20:10; Deut 22:22; see Guelich, *Sermon on the Mount,* 193; Garland, *Reading Matthew,* 66).

In his teaching in this section of the Sermon, Jesus placed responsibility for lust and adultery on the man. As Garland puts it: "Jesus does not warn his disciples about women but about themselves" (*Reading Matthew,* 67). This was revolutionary. Jesus instructed men about vicious cycles related to sexuality and placed the responsibility on them to remove the attitudes, actions and practices that deepen the descent into sin in this area of life. Likewise Jesus did not permit men to divorce their wives cavalierly. These kinds of teachings reflected a respect for the dignity of women that, rightly understood, would transform the attitudes and actions of the Christian disciple and the church as a whole. Men were not to regard women as disposable sex objects, simultaneously alluring and dangerous (Allison, *Sermon on the Mount,* 72; cf. Schrage, *Ethics of the New Testament,* 98).

In the ongoing practice of his ministry, Jesus shattered numerous taboos related to male-female contact and association. His traveling band of itinerants included women (Lk 8:1-3), some of whom helped to support the work financially and provide for Jesus' needs (Mt 27:55-56; Mk 15:40-41). He did not hesitate to touch or be touched by women in order to heal them (Mt 9:18-26; Lk 13:10-16). He allowed a woman of questionable reputation to express her love for him through anointing his feet (Lk 7:36-50). He spoke at length to the Samaritan woman at the well (Jn 4), and to a lowly Canaanite woman (Mt 15:21-28). He affirmed Mary in her desire to sit at his feet and receive his teachings along with his male followers (Lk 10:38-42) and treated both Mary and Martha as close friends. Women were the first witnesses of his resurrection and the first proclaimers of the good news (Mt 28:8-10; Jn 20:11-18). There is no evidence that Jesus ever treated women with anything other than full respect—an extraordinary practice in his context.

Why was this the approach that Jesus took toward women? We believe that it was because Jesus was concerned above all with the reign of God. He invited everyone who heard him to join in the great work of deliverance that God was inaugurating through him. While Jesus did not articulate a revolutionary overthrow of the deeply embedded patriarchy of Jewish culture, he did by his practice throw open the door to new roles and new freedom for women in service of the gospel movement, and the rest of the New Testament quietly documents their passage through some of those doors (Witherington, *Women in the Earliest Churches*).

Paul and Women

The apostle Paul dealt with the issue of gender roles in the context of how to structure the life of the early Christian communities under his care. Many hundreds of interpreters have puzzled over the nuances of Paul's perspective on this issue, and he has been read to support all of the major Christian perspectives already outlined.

The textual record is quite complicated. Egalitarians tend to notice the role of certain prominent women in proclaiming the gospel message. Priscilla, for example, is described as working alongside her husband in "explain[ing] the way of God . . . more accurately" to Apollos (Acts 18:26). She is mentioned six times in the New Testament, each time without any distinction from her husband as a fellow church leader (Acts 18:2, 18, 26; Rom 16:3; 1 Cor 16:19; 2 Tim 4:19). Lists of fellow workers and beloved brothers and sisters in Christ include women's names regularly with those of men (cf. Rom 16). Euodia and Syntyche (Phil 4:2-3) are described by Paul as women who have "struggled beside me in the work of the gospel."

Biblical egalitarians also emphasize the echoes of Jesus' radicalism in Paul's own message. Galatians 3:26-28 is a key text: "in Christ Jesus you are all children of God through faith. As many of you as were baptized into Christ have clothed yourselves with Christ. There is no longer Jew or Greek, there is no longer slave or free, there is no longer male and female; for all of you are one in Christ Jesus."

Paul consistently exulted in the breakthroughs in human community accomplished by the gospel. A "new humanity" (Eph 2:15) had been created in Christ, breaking down humanly constructed walls of division and hostility. Rich and poor, Jew and Gentile, male and female, slave and free, were becoming a new people—the church. While this does not speak to the issue of women's leadership, narrowly construed, it certainly raises the question of whether a new humanity of this type would be expected to govern itself according to traditional gender distinctions.

Egalitarians point to Paul's emphasis on spiritual gifts. It was Paul who so strongly emphasized both the gifts of the Spirit (1 Cor 12:1-11; Eph 4:11) and the fruit of the Spirit (Gal 5:22-23). Both were bestowed upon believers without any apparent gender distinction. Both gifts and fruits were intended to build up the body of Christ and advance the Lord's urgent work in the world.

Finally, even Paul's controversial discussions of public worship (1 Cor 11:2-16; 14:33-35; 1 Tim 2:11-15), pivotal to the male leadership perspective, do include some countervailing evidence. Whereas 1 Corinthians 14:34 mandates that "women should be silent in the churches," 1 Corinthians 11:4 tells women who are in fact praying and prophesying in public worship to keep their heads covered. It is hard to square even these two passages in the same book, and a number of proposals have been attempted.

A Male Leadership Perspective

The male leadership perspective might begin by questioning whether Jesus was as radical in his practice in relation to women as the egalitarians suggest. He did, after all, select twelve men to be his apostles, clearly as a symbolic affirmation/reenactment of the twelve tribes of Israel, all of which were, of course, headed by men.

But the heart of the male leadership argument about gender roles returns to the writings of Paul. It would certainly be possible to argue for an extremely conservative male leadership view by focusing heavily on the 1 Corinthians 14:33 passage as well as the 1 Timothy 2:11 passage. Indeed, such an argument would not be merely for male leadership in the church but for women's silence therein. While there certainly are some Christian groups who stake their claim here, none of the leading contemporary exponents of complementarianism do so.

Instead, the focus of the male leadership case rests heavily on Paul's arguments in 1 Corinthians 11:3-10 and 1 Timothy 2:11-15. First Corinthians 11:3 essentially makes a creation-grounded claim for the man as the head (*kephalē*) of woman (or the husband as the head of the wife). In 1 Timothy 2, Paul also makes an argument from the creation story for the authority of male over female and says that he does not permit a woman "to teach or to have authority over a man" (1 Tim 2:12). Complementarians also appeal to the so-called household code passages (Eph 5:21-33; Col 3:18-19), in which married women are taught to submit voluntarily to their husbands, who in turn are taught to love their wives in a Christlike manner. Finally, the male leadership case rests on Paul's instructions in the pastoral epistles, in which church leaders (*episkopoi*) are assumed to be (some say commanded to be) male (cf. 1 Tim 3:2).

What results is a claim for male leadership in home and church both from creation and from the perceived witness of the early church, especially Paul's writings. Complementarians claim that contemporary feminism has badly confused and distorted the God-given differences in gender and gender roles that are wired into human nature. Catholic complementarians make the case from natural law, Protestants from Scripture, but both argue that a disastrous androgyny has swept across the Western world via the feminist movement, that it has harmed male-female relations, family life, church and society, and that it must be rejected. Sifting through the wreckage, complementarians seek to reclaim the notion that male leadership—marvelously purged of abusive or domineering elements in Christ—is the divine plan for male-female relations. They pursue this vision in family life and in the church, though the society appears beyond reclamation for this perspective and thus little effort is made at this time to promote such a vision for social life.

The practical outcome of that vision for church life finds no consensus among complementarians. The official position that emerged at Southern Seminary in 1995-1996 was that women were biblically barred only from the senior pastor position. Further, male leadership and female submission in the home were stressed. These are also the two positions that were memorably codified in the 2000 revision of the Southern Baptist "Faith and Message" statement. (In practice, women faculty members in the School of Theology were forced out, and ministry positions in churches became more difficult to find.) In terms of official church life, it is interesting how limited this exclusion actually is, leaving open ordination, missionary service and all other ministerial positions in local churches—not to mention teaching in theological seminaries and Baptist universities, preaching on the lecture circuit, writing books and so on. Other denominations, and individual congregations, draw the lines at very different points, often far more narrowly. It is not unfair to say that in operational terms what complementarian perspectives all have in common is that there is *something* women should not be permitted to do in church life; but little consensus on what exactly that *something* is.

The vague sense in her religious context that women are not supposed to do certain things in Christian leadership, though it is unclear exactly what those things are, is precisely what afflicts my student Alisha—and many women like her—and casts a shadow over the pursuit of her gifts.

The treatment of male leadership in the home among complementarians has been quite striking. While strongly emphasizing distinct male and female roles, following Ephesians 5:22-33 and often bypassing the topic sentence in 5:21, "Be subject to one another out of reverence for Christ," contemporary complementarians stress the sacrificial and servanthood dimension of male leadership and authority. If men are to lead, which on this view they should, they must do so as Christ did. He lived and died for "her"—the church. He put his own preferences last. He attended to her well-being above all. He loved her as much or more than he loved himself. He was completely other-regarding and unselfish.

Many evangelical men and, it must be admitted, many evangelical women, warm to this vision of a benign, sacrificial, even heroic male leadership. Complementarian theoreticians are *not* calling for a return to the brutish male dominance of the prefeminist years. But they are wanting to claim distinctions in male and female nature, leading to distinctions in male and female roles. The male is called to lead (via servant-leadership), to take responsibility for his family and to be accountable to God for how he exercises his unique responsibility. Many evangelical men tremble at this sense of accountability but find it appeals deeply to their masculinity, while many evangelical women find that the role prescribed for them appeals deeply to their femininity. Whether evangelical men, women and families convinced of this model will find that it works for them in the long term has yet to be determined. Outside observers who caricature this approach as a return to caveman days, however, do so irresponsibly.

It should be noted that for some male leadership advocates it is actually the structure of family and marital relations that drives their approach to church life. If a man is called by the Scriptures to exercise leadership at home then it is deeply problematic for his pastor-wife, say, to exercise leadership and authority over him at church. For this reason, some complementarians handle issues of church leadership differently in cases where the woman in question is unmarried or widowed. The whole issue is rendered more complex by the interchangeability of the Greek terms for man/husband and woman/wife.

Conclusion: Is a Convergence Possible?

On the basis of the complex picture laid before us, we propose that a kingdom perspective emphasizing a reclamation and healing of male-female relations in mutual covenant and the full use of the giftedness of God's people best fits with the vision presented and practiced by Jesus.

The good news is that such a perspective need not be woven out of whole cloth. The Wesleyan Methodist, Pentecostal/charismatic and black church traditions are examples of historic Christian movements that have (at least some of the time) read the Scriptures in the fashion we are emphasizing here (see Roebuck, "Perfect Liberty to Preach the Gospel"; Gill, "Contemporary State of Women in Ministry in the Assemblies of God"; Everts, "Brokenness as the Center of a Woman's Ministry"; Poluma, "Charisma, Institutionalization, and Social Change").

In terms of church life and work, gender differences are not dissolved but gender as a determinant of roles fades from view in light of the massive goals of aggressive world evangelization and discipling of new believers, doing the healing and delivering and justice-making works of Christ, and practicing the gifts of the Spirit to edify the church, until Christ returns. The criterion for who may pursue these precious kingdom goals is simply the whole body of Christ, with specialization directed by spiritual giftedness. At Pentecost, the Spirit fell upon both men and women, as the Old Testament had promised (Acts 2:17-18; Joel 2:28-29). The last thing one wants to do at Pentecost or in the perspective created by the experience of Pentecost is to stifle gifts that might bring advances in the reign of God; too much is at stake (see Van Leeuwen, *Gender and Grace*, 34-38). If the goal of the Christ-follower is to seek God's kingdom, the primary issue is not specifying gender roles but maximizing mission, effectiveness and impact. Again, it must be emphasized that this perspective predates the feminist movement and is grounded *not on late-twentieth-century secular egalitarianism but in a gospel and kingdom focus.*

As for the exercise of authority within the church body, we want to make the simple suggestion that Paul offers a *mutual servanthood* paradigm for all relationships in the body of Christ, including that between men and women. Rightly understood, this paradigm brings rival egalitarian and complementarian positions toward convergence.

Paul knew that any functioning community must have structures of authority. Even an itinerant band of international missionaries seeking to advance the kingdom needs some structure of decision making and authority. We see that structure at work in the New Testament. Yet the overall witness of his writings both offers a servant-oriented approach to authority and refuses to locate authority fundamentally in gender. Though some dispute the claim, it seems to us that Paul did in fact recognize certain distinctions in gender, especially related to male-female needs and roles within the family (Eph 5:22-33). These distinctions disturb some contemporary observers while ringing true with others, and there is considerable debate over how to interpret the impact of Greco-Roman and Jewish culture on Paul's perspective here. However that point is resolved, Paul is best understood as subordinating even irreducible gender distinctions under the more important rubric of mutual servanthood after the model of Christ—"Be subject to one another out of reverence for Christ" (Eph 5:21). Here Paul points to the theme of our book: interpretation in accord with the lordship of Jesus Christ, his model of teaching and practice, his death and resurrection.

Leadership and authority in family life and in the church are to be offered in humility, in mutual submission and in the context of the narrative of how Christ exercised authority. As the glorious Christ-hymn of Philippians 2 puts it, in the incarnation and on the cross Jesus was self-emptying, humble, devoted to the needs of others and ultimately obedient to the authority of God the Father (Phil 2:5-11). This connects with Jesus' virtues of humility, yieldedness to God and justice that we saw in the Beatitudes. All Christians are to imitate his pattern.

Mutual servanthood places limits on the exercise of authority by any Christian in any setting. The model of Christ shapes the perspective within which all authority is employed. Any member of the Christian community can hold any other member, including leaders (or husband, or wife), accountable to conformity with Christ's example. The kingdom or gospel-advancing purpose of the church and the Christian marriage is the goal to which all are committed and thus also sets a standard for the exercise of authority. Any use of authority which might stifle spiritual gifts that could advance the kingdom is inappropriate. Meanwhile, with this great freedom to use kingdom gifts comes the responsibility to use such gifts only for the purpose for which they were given. So no merely autonomous or permissive understanding of freedom is envisioned here. Mutual servanthood employs yet constrains freedom, unleashes gifts for responsible use, directs authority, orders Christian community and participates in the kingdom. In love, mutual servanthood creates checks and balances on the exercise both of freedom and of power that preserve and advance justice. This is the best model for all relationships in the body of Christ, including those between men and women, and husbands and wives.

SECTION V:

The Central Norms
of Christian Ethics

For many generations, Christian moral thinkers have sought to identify central biblical or theological norms for Christian ethics. These are moral convictions that cut across the Christian moral life as great imperatives, applying to all realms of activity and any particular moral problem or issue. Undoubtedly the two norms most often generated by such a search are the ones we consider here: love and justice.

Our Hebraic, Jesus-centered and kingdom-focused approach offers a treatment of love and justice that is strikingly different from many standard accounts. It refuses to draw any hard-and-fast distinction between love and justice, and anchors both in the delivering activity of God in an often loveless and unjust world. They have a depth in the character and action of God as revealed in the biblical drama, culminating in the inbreaking of the kingdom, that is richer and more multidimensional than a thin Enlightenment-rationalistic or allegedly universal definition.

16

LOVE

—

You have learned that they were told, "Love your neighbor, hate your enemy." But what I
tell you is this: Love your enemies and pray for your persecutors; only so can you be
children of your heavenly Father, who makes his sun rise on good and bad like, and sends
the rain on the honest and the dishonest. . . .

There must be no limit to your goodness, as your heavenly Father's goodness knows no
bounds.

MATTHEW 5:43-44, 48 NEB

For Christians, love is the heart of living, of being human. Love is at the heart
of the life of Christ, his teaching and his death on the cross. Even on the cross,
Jesus had compassion on his mother, compassion on the two rebels crucified with
him and compassion on his enemies who were crucifying him. As Victor Furnish
says, for Jesus the love command functioned as "the hermeneutical key to the
law's interpretation" and was "an integral part of his proclamation of the coming
Reign of God." Jesus understood the imminent reign of God as establishing
"God's own sovereign power, justice, and mercy," and he called people "to turn
and receive God's proffered love and forgiveness—a love which actively seeks
out the sinner, just as the father sought out the prodigal son (Lk 15:20). God's
reign is thereby understood as the rule of love" (Furnish, *Love Commands in the
New Testament*, 328-29). Christlike love is one of the central virtues, and one of the
basic convictions, in our holistic ethic of character (see chapters two and three).

For all of us, Christians or not, love that we received during infancy and
childhood is what gave us our start as selves with personality. Love is also
what has moved us forward out of pain, powerlessness, provincialism and
confusion. Someone has loved us enough to free us from being helpless, stuck,
lonely or lost. The love we have received, even with its imperfections, has
shaped our selfhood and left its deep imprint.

Love is the norm for life. But what do we mean by love? What is the true shape of love? We present four major Christian definitions of love, which contend with each other, in order to help you sharpen your own understanding of the norm of love. We ask you to compare them and discern which one best fits true Christian ethics.

Sacrificial Love

Anders Nygren, a Swedish bishop, published *Agape and Eros* in 1932. It has become a classic and has profoundly shaped both scholarly and popular Christian understandings of love.

> Anders Nygren defines *agape*, the major New Testament word for love, as *sacrificial love*. Such love is purely unselfish, spontaneous and unmotivated by any value or benefit the other might have for us. It is not created by any value it sees in others but instead creates value in them. We love regardless of the attractiveness of the one we love, in an uncalculating, unlimited and unconditional way. This is not something we do or are able to do; instead, God initiates it as pure gift, and we merely reflect the love that shines from God through us toward others (Nygren, *Agape and Eros*, 75-81, 91, 94, 118).
>
> The method we are advocating in this book says that basic convictions and fundamental loyalties—the bottom two dimensions in the four-dimensional holistic diagram sketched in chapter three—shape the meaning of key terms. *Love* does not get its meaning merely by its definition but by its function in the narrative that shapes particular traditions. Sacrificial love as defined above fits Nygren's Lutheran understanding of the atonement (God's act of reconciliation with humanity through the life, death and resurrection of Jesus). In Nygren's understanding, the atonement is pure, unmerited gift, and there is nothing that we contribute. We are merely passive recipients of what God does for us, with passive righteousness given by grace, without any calculation of our merit. We cannot love God. God loves us.

There is powerful truth in the understanding of love as sacrificial. We all feel its appeal. Sacrificial love throws its pure white light on our usual way of loving and reveals our selfish rationalizing and calculating. It purges our complacent self-congratulating, self-justifying and boasting. It gives us much-needed humility. By comparison with pure, unselfish, sacrificial love, our usual loving can do no boasting. Sacrificial love can redeem our usual selfish kind of loving and turn selfish relationships into beautiful relationships.

When, for example, a couple begins to experience the painful, ragged rejection and repudiation of one another amidst bitter conflict, sacrificial love takes the risk of initiating reconciliation whether it expects any affirmative response or not. It speaks compassion even when compassion hurts. Thereby it can interrupt the vicious cycle of mutual recrimination. It can redeem lost or damaged love and create new love.

But as a definition of Christian love, sacrificial love has some very damaging liabilities:

1. It seems so ideal and impossible to realize that people either write it off as impractical or experience its lack with a guilty conscience (Wallwork, "Thou Shalt Love," 265-67).

2. It appears to allow no place for some self-concern or for setting boundaries to protect the self. Nygren argued that such a concern for oneself belongs to the needy natural love of eros that he rejected as sub-Christian.

3. It seems to sever the connection between love and justice, which in the biblical story fit together like hand and glove. Micah 6:8, for example, clearly puts justice, love and serving the Lord in synonymous parallelism: "What does the LORD require of you but to do justice [*mishpat*], and to love kindness [*hesed*], and to walk humbly with your God?" All the first eight verses of Micah 6 are clearly structured in synonymous parallelism; doing justice and loving kindness are here proclaimed as parallel and basically synonymous. But Nygren's understanding of love is far removed from justice, which needs calculation, reciprocity and a certain amount of coercion. This dichotomy between love and justice has often led Christians to claim that they were loving persons while they neglected justice. And it has sometimes led thoughtful Christians, such as Reinhold Niebuhr, to believe that their great concern for justice stands in stark tension with the (sacrificial) "love ethic of Jesus" (Niebuhr, *Love and Justice*, 27-29, 29-40, passim).

4. It has been used to keep oppressed people "in their place," whether it be the peasants in Martin Luther's day, blacks in the United States or South Africa, or women throughout history. Feminist ethics has reminded us that in a culture that socializes women to altruism and selfless love, the call to practice sacrificial love can be misused to tell women not to oppose patriarchal exploitation (Andolsen, "*Agape* in Feminist Ethics," 74-75).

5. If my focus is on the sacrifice I am making for others, it can give me a martyr complex and can make others mere dependents on what I paternalistically know to be best. As Richard Roach puts it, "When I feel that I know the good for someone else without allowing him to participate in the definition or attainment of that good, I become an oppressor, self-justified by an ideology" (Roach, "New Sense of Faith," 145).

6. It seems to misunderstand the significance of Jesus' death. Jesus did not sacrifice himself on the cross for the sake of self-sacrifice. He died for the sake of delivering us from our bondage to sin and into community.

Mutual Love

Daniel Day Williams' profound book *The Spirit and the Forms of Love* argues that Nygren's concept of sacrificial love is inadequate because it assumes a neoplatonic concept of God's impassibility—that God is unmotivated and unaffected by what happens in history. Instead, our thinking about love needs to employ a Hebraic/biblical understanding of *history* and the biblical *story* in which God cares about people's response to God's love and is affected by what happens in history (Williams, *Spirit and the Forms of Love*, 1-3, 9, 53-63). God deeply desires our response of love. God wants love to be *mutual love*.

Williams argues, "I use the word *agape* for God's love which the Bible sees taking form in God's election of Israel and which is finally manifest in the story of Jesus" (*Spirit and the Forms of Love*, 2-3). "The story of Jesus is the story of the only begotten Son, the beloved, now fulfilling the divine purpose through enacting the life of love in the midst of the world's need" (37). Williams shows that both Old and New Testament speak of many different dimensions of love, and do not reduce the meaning of *agape* to one ahistorical meaning as Nygren does. "The love of God is known as concern, devoted care, willingness to share in the life of a particular people to set them free and to deal with them graciously in their desires and passions, health and sickness, worship and pleasure, warfare and peace, life and death," and to make a covenant with them (Williams, *Spirit and the Forms of Love*, 22-23). "It is simply not true that the agape of the New Testament is nothing but the grace of God poured out without motive upon the unworthy. It is also the spirit of rejoicing, of friendship and of the new life with its foretaste of the blessedness of life with God and with the brethren in the full freedom of love" (Williams, *Spirit and the Forms of Love*, 44, 46). This has been confirmed by other scholars since (Furnish, *Love Commands in the New Testament*, 50, 134, 220-22, 231; A. L. Hall, "Complicating the Command," 100-109).

Love is not a one-way street running from God to us, in which God has no motive, does not seek any return of love from us and is unaffected by our love or unfaithfulness (Williams, *Spirit and the Forms of Love*, 20). Rather, God wants *mutual love*, personal communion in which we give love back to God. The New Testament doctrine of love is based first in the mutual love between God the Father and the Son in its ultimate depth as the mystery of personal communion. Furthermore, the love expressed in the life of Jesus provides the shape and content of the ethical commandment to love. "The love of God becomes the suffering, self-giving love of the merciful God for sinners, actualized when God gives his only Son to share the human lot, to suffer the limitations of human existence and to die that the world might be reconciled to him. . . . God loves his Son and he loves the world with an unshakable will to communion" (35-37).

In Williams's view, five dimensions are necessary for love:

1. *Real otherness or individuality* of the person loving and of the person being loved. Loving another must not mean that my selfhood is destroyed or absorbed in the other, or that the selfhood of the other is destroyed or absorbed in me (Williams, *Spirit and the Forms of Love*, 114-15).

2. *Freedom with limits.* "We cannot give ourselves authentically to another in love without the will to assume the demands and risks which are present." Love must "affirm and accept the freedom of the other. . . . Nothing is more pathetic than the attempt to compel or coerce the love of another, for it carries self-defeat within it." Furthermore, covenant love requires us to accept the limits that we take on when we make a promise or a commitment (Williams, *Spirit and the Forms of Love*, 116).

3. *Acting and receiving, or suffering.* "We do not love unless our personal being is transformed through the relation to the other." There can be no love without suffering, in the sense of being acted upon, being changed, moved, transformed by the action of another. "Any experience of love includes the discovery of the other through what the other suffers for, with and because of me. The evidence of love is nowhere deeper than this: 'Greater love hath no man than this: that he lay down his life for his friends'" (Jn 15:13 KJV; Williams, *Spirit and the Forms of Love*, 117).

4. *Power to change the other and be changed by the other.* Love intensifies the power to "restrain one another, to oppose our wills to the other's use of his freedom. We set conditions, pass judgments, and make demands." And the discovery that we are loved has the power to cause us to be changed. The attitudes and actions of others whom we love move us (Williams, *Spirit and the Forms of Love*, 119-20; cf. Harrison, "Power of Anger and the Work of Love").

5. *Impartial judgment and justice.* "Even the most radical assertions that the divine love is 'uncalculating' usually come with the concession that love is concern for the need of the neighbour. But how shall we discover needs except by realistic appraisal and understanding?" And that requires attention to equity and justice (Williams, *Spirit and the Forms of Love*, 121-22).

All five of these dimensions point to *mutual love in covenant community*, with respect for otherness, and with justice that "lifts the burdens of the weak and the hurt" (Williams, *Spirit and the Forms of Love*, 245). Love is not set over against justice but leads to a community-oriented affirmation of justice. "The Bible never treats justice as a lesser order than that required by love, but as the objectification of the spirit of love in human and divine relationships" (244-45, 249-50).

Williams' understanding of love has its meaning in a narrative of the Hebraic concept of *covenant* (*Spirit and the Forms of Love*, 251-52) and of the *atonement*
as the action of God's community-creating love. "We come to the deepest mystery when we see in the suffering of Jesus a disclosure of the suffering of God."
Jesus' suffering reveals both the sources of evil and of God's loyalty to us—
God's loving will to oppose those evils and seek the reconciliation of humankind (*Spirit and the Forms of Love*, 178, 181-85). The atonement is God's word of
forgiveness and God's work of creating the church as the new community, in
which we are not only passive recipients but mutually active participants in the
reconciling action. "Failure to understand that the Church exists by continual
participation in the atoning action of God in Jesus underlies many of the illusions" in peoples' usual ways of understanding the church (187-88).

Love as Equal Regard

More recently, Gene Outka has argued that we should define Christian love as
equal regard. Love means that we value all persons equally, regardless of their
special traits, actions, merits or what they can do for us. Of course, the appropriate way for me to express my love to various equally regarded people may
differ. We each love our children—Michael, Bill and David, and Holly, David,
Marie and Madeleine—equally; but with different actions suited to their widely different needs (Outka, *Agape*, 9-24).

Equal regard, as the definition of *agape*, has the advantage that it fits well
with the struggle for justice. Justice is based on equal rights, responsibilities
and opportunities for all persons. And equal regard seems less susceptible to
paternalism; all are equal. Furthermore, equal regard has a proper place for
self-regard. I, too, am a person created in the image of God and should receive
equal regard as a person (Outka, *Agape*, 70-92, 257-312). One problem is that in
the name of equal regard for myself I can easily rationalize, paying much more
attention to my own desires and needs than yours—or than the needs of needy
others in other neighborhoods and other countries. This charge has been made
against Outka by Colin Grant, who defends a version of sacrificial or "altruis-
tic" love closer to Nygren (Grant, "For the Love of God," 3-21; cf. Outka's reply, "Theocentric Agape and the Self," 35-42).

Surely equal regard is basic to any Christian understanding of love.
Stephen Pope argues that within the scholarly ranks of Christian ethicists it
has replaced sacrificial love as the dominant definition of agape (Pope,
"'Equal Regard' Versus 'Special Relations?' " 353). But it seems somehow incomplete. It is an abstract ethical principle that some believe owes more to Immanuel Kant's "categorical imperative" (always treat persons as ends-in-
themselves and never merely as means to an end) than to the New Testament's
description of agape-love (Grant, "For the Love of God," 10-14, with qualifica-

tions). Others have charged that the universality of equal regard underplays the moral importance of the special obligations we owe to family members and others in specific relations to us (Vacek, *Love, Human and Divine,* 49; Post, *Spheres of Love,* 65; Purvis, "Mothers, Neighbors, and Strangers," 19-34. Outka has replied to this charge and has also been defended by Pope. See Outka, "Universal Love and Impartiality"; Outka, "Theocentric Agape and the Self," 35-42; Pope, " 'Equal Regard' Versus 'Special Relations?'" 353-79).

Equal regard also seems to assume that the problem we have is simply to get a correct philosophical definition of our ethical norm. It seems to imply something like a moral influence theory of the atonement: In dying for all persons, Jesus gives us a moral principle that all persons are equally valuable. This is true and essential. But the problem we have goes deeper. We need to be grabbed deep down, where our unspoken motivations come from. And we need God's sacrifice for us in the cross, embracing us even in our unlovingness.

Delivering Love

Proponents of delivering love argue that love is not just a single principle, like a song sung in a monotone, but a complex drama, with different dramatic actions as the characters grow and interact. As Amy Laura Hall ("Complicating the Command," 98-100, 109-10) has argued, love has numerous dimensions of meaning in different scriptural texts, and reducing it to one principle or theme screens out other scriptural meanings that need to confront us. "A turn to Scripture itself is a corrective preferable to supplanting" one single meaning with another. By seeing four acts in the drama of delivering love, we hope to avoid a monotonic single-principle interpretation, without the opposite error of saying love means many things and nothing specific. The four acts we propose closely resemble themes Hall finds running through Exodus, Leviticus, Hosea, Luke and John.

Christian love points centrally to the drama of Jesus Christ, the paradigm of love. Christ acted with mercy toward outcasts, fed the hungry, healed the blind, taught the way, forgave the guilty, set his face toward Jerusalem and died at the hands of the Roman imperial administration. He did this not for the sake of self-sacrifice by itself but to deliver others from bondage into the community of reconciliation. We propose to identify the primary norm of love not as sacrificial love, or equal regard, but as *delivering love.* The drama behind the word *love* is the drama of *deliverance.* This connects with our understanding of the kingdom as God's delivering action.

Where in the New Testament does Jesus teach the shape of love most explicitly? There are many New Testament teachings on love; to research them, we recommend Victor Furnish, *The Love Commands in the New Testament.* But none of these spells out *the shape* of love as fully as does the parable of the compassionate Samaritan (Lk 10:25-37). The parable is Jesus' answer to the lawyer's question: "Who is my neighbor?"—itself a follow-up to the lawyer's original question of how he might attain eternal life, and Jesus' response demanding love of God and neighbor. Some New Testament scholars argue that originally the lawyer's question and the story of the compassionate Samaritan were separate stories, later brought together as they are now in Luke (e.g., Scott, *Hear Then the Parable*, 192; but see Young, *Parables*, 103). Whether this is true or not, the Samaritan story is still about the shape of love. Even without the lawyer's question, the parable is intrinsically a midrash on Leviticus 19:18—"You shall love your neighbor as yourself: I am the LORD" (P. R. Jones, "Love Command in Parable," 224-42). Either way, the question is, "Who is my neighbor?" (Blomberg, *Interpreting the Parables*, 230). The answer offers definitive instruction both on how and whom we should love (Crossan, *In Parables*, 57).

Biblical scholars have learned not to interpret each detail in a parable allegorically—for example, making the Samaritan stand for Jesus and the going into the ditch for the cross. As a radical corrective, Adolf Jülicher argued that we should focus on only one central point of a parable in order to control our interpretation. But that is now widely seen as an overcorrection, an unneeded straightjacket (e.g., Blomberg, *Interpreting the Parables*, chap. 2). Seeking some objectivity in our interpretation, we look for what Jesus' way of telling the parable seems designed to emphasize in a first-century Jewish context.

We are interpreting the parables as drama in a historical context. They were composed not originally as stories to be read in private but as dramas publicly articulated, and they made the hearers into actors, asking for their participation in seeing with a new perspective, in commitment and in practice. They were being acted out in Jesus' ministry, and they made sense in the historical context in which Jesus ministered and in the drama of Israel's history. "The parables are not simply *information about* the kingdom, but are part of the *means of* bringing it to birth. . . . They invite people into the new world that is being created, and warn of dire consequences if the invitation is refused" (N. T. Wright, *Jesus and the Victory of God*, 176).

We find four dramatic emphases in the parable of the compassionate Samaritan that surely would have struck hearers in the first century and so should be considered crucial acts in the drama of delivering love:

1. Love sees with compassion and enters into the situation of persons in bondage. Mary Patrick points out that the original hearers did not know that the parable was called "the Good Samaritan." It begins: "A man was going down from Jerusalem to Jericho when he fell into the hands of rebels." The original hearers of the drama would have identified with the man in danger. We start out with compassion for him (Patrick, *Love Commandment*, 57-58).

The contrast is then clear: A priest saw the man and passed by on the other side. A Levite saw him and passed by on the other side. But a Samaritan saw him *with compassion* and *went to him*. The Greek word for compassion literally names gut-feeling. Here is the intensity of a strong emotional response and the dramatic action that we know is a central dimension of love as it often occurs—you enter into the situation of the other.

The Greek prefixes of the verbs in Luke 10:31-33 "themselves convey graphically responses of moving away (anti-) and toward (pros-), . . . a clue about the nature of compassion." Compassion moves us to go to the other and enter into his or her situation. The priest "reacted by complete withdrawal to the other side of the road. He put all the possible distance between himself and the stranger. . . . The text describing the response of the second clerical traveler . . . may well favor the picture of the Levite drawing nearer and looking more carefully" before also passing the victim by. The Samaritan's response of seeing with compassion and going to him fits the rhetorical rule that the emphasis comes at the end of a series of comparisons—here the third member in the triad. Jesus tells the story in a way that emphasizes that compassion moves toward need and identification with that need (L. G. Jones, *Embodying Forgiveness*, 222-26; Donohue, *Gospel in Parable*, 131-32; Scott, *Hear Then the Parable*, 199-200).

Jesus emphasized the vulnerability and helplessness—not only the neediness but the inability to save himself—of the man who was left half dead. Jesus piled on details for emphasis: "fell into the hands of rebels. They stripped him of his clothes, beat him and went away, leaving him half-dead." People had their security from membership in an ethnic group that would take care of them. Each ethnic group had its distinctive dress and speech. To be stripped naked and left unconscious and unable to speak was to be both shamed and unrecognizable as a member of any ethnic or religious community, and therefore removed from group loyalty and help. "The road from high-lying Jerusalem to Jericho down the Jordan valley leads through an uninhabited rocky wilderness and is notorious even to this day for attacks by robbers. A man who had been robbed even of his clothes, seriously wounded, and left there to his fate by the robbers was bound to die miserably if he found no one to help him" (Linnemann, *Parables of Jesus*, 53; K. Bailey, *Through Peasant Eyes*, 43; Donohue, *Gospel in Parable*, 130; Hultgren, *Parables of Jesus*, 96).

Jesus was not here teaching a thin ethic of *equal regard* or a focus on *sacrificial love*; he taught compassion especially for those who are in bondage, who are vulnerable and oppressed because they are powerless. Jesus was realistic about human sin. The poor, the powerless, the outcasts, the orphans, the women, the foreigners do not receive justice. The lost sheep cannot find its way home. Therefore love has special regard for those who are in bondage to others or to their own sin.

Jeremias (*Parables of Jesus*, 205-6) speaks of "love having no boundaries" and writes: "it turns towards the very people who are poor and despised (Lk 14:12-14), helpless (Mk 9:37), and insignificant" (Mt 18:10; 25:31-46). Jeremias's biblical citations point to something more specific than simply "having no boundaries." These passages say that love is not only unbounded, but it goes out especially to those who are poor and despised and in need, in bondage. Surely this does break down boundaries and in a sense includes everyone, but the emphasis is on those who are in need of deliverance. It is the lost sheep, it is those who are sick and need a physician, whom Jesus came to deliver. Christian love sees those in bondage with compassion and enters into their situation.

2. Love does deeds of deliverance. Parables are usually short and succinct. They do not waste words. But here Jesus spent many words emphasizing the actual deeds that were done. He described deed after deed, nine in total (P. R. Jones, *Teaching of the Parables*, 222): "He went to him and bandaged his wounds, pouring on oil and wine. Then he put the man on his own donkey, took him to an inn and took care of him. The next day he took out two silver coins and gave them to the innkeeper. 'Look after him,' he said, 'and when I return, I will reimburse you for any extra expense you may have.'" When you add to this remarkable piling on of deeds the principle that the emphasis usually comes at the end of the story, it is clear that Jesus was emphasizing that compassion is seen in deeds of deliverance (cf. Donohue, *Gospel in Parable*, 132-33, Scott, *Hear Then the Parable*, 199-200, Crossan, *In Parables*, 62-63).

What characterizes these nine deeds? Jesus did not emphasize that the deeds are unselfish and sacrificial. We like to suggest that the Samaritan might have risked his own life by going to the victim, or that the Samaritan had to walk the whole distance to the inn, or that paying money (two days' wages) was a big sacrifice. But that is not what Jesus emphasized. Jesus emphasized the deeds needed to deliver from bondage. Suppose the Samaritan saw the victim and had great compassion and said, "Oh how terrible! I feel so sorry for this man." So he pulled out his knife and stabbed himself in his heart and died side by side with the victim in the ditch. It would have been sacrificial. It would have been unselfish. But it would not have delivered the victim from his bondage.

Each of the deeds that Jesus chose to emphasize is precisely what is needed to deliver the half-dead victim in the ditch from his helplessness. Wounds need washing and bandaging, the helpless man needs transporting and caring for, and this caring needs paying for (Gollwitzer, *Das Gleichnis*, 55). Jesus was teaching delivering love, not simply sacrificial love. Delivering love is not paternalistic benevolence that condescends to people and makes them into dependents. It frees them and delivers them from bondage. Jesus died not because he loved sacrifice (although his death certainly involved his self-sacrifice), but because he wanted to free us from our bondage. And delivering love involves deeds, not mere feelings or attitudes. Jones (*Teaching of the Parables*, 228-31) points out that the story is framed by the command to "do": "Do this and you will live" and "Go and do likewise." "The love command of Leviticus 19:18 itself calls for action. . . . The story of the compassionate Samaritan illuminates what it really means to accept the Lordship of Christ. . . . Compassion is something you do. When the word is used in the Gospels, it is a verb and means action."

The call for deeds of deliverance is accentuated all the more by the explicit contrast with the priest and the Levite. "The wounded man became a test of authentic religion. . . . The parable exposes any religion with a mania for creeds and an anemia for deeds, an uptightness about orthodoxy and a laxness about orthopraxy (cf. 1 Jn 3:23)" (P. R. Jones, "Love Command in the Parables," 229, 233; cf. Gollwitzer, *Das Gleichnis*, 43-45, 53-54).

3. *Love invites into community with freedom, justice and responsibility for the future.* Throughout the biblical story, deliverance is not only from sin but also *into community*. God not only *liberates* the people *from* Egypt but *delivers* them through the wilderness *to* the covenant community of Israel with specific practices and institutions of justice. Hence we have written regularly of deliverance, not only of liberation. The construction of the checks and balances of justice is crucial to the biblical narrative. Jesus emphasizes that the Samaritan picks the Jew up into his own arms, puts him on his own donkey and brings him into the community of the inn and the care of the innkeeper. More than that, he arranges community for him on into the future, paying for three weeks' care and saying he would return to pay what else remains. Establishing community on into the future is itself a crucial deed of deliverance from the hostility, alienation and aloneness that trap Jews and Samaritans in death-dealing bondage. By telling this parable, Jesus is calling Jews to have community with Samaritans. Surely this is a word for today, when Palestinians have replaced Samaritans.

This is an invitation to community with *freedom*. The Samaritan contrasts with the priest and the Levite, who stand for the political-social-religious establishment that ostracizes lepers, prostitutes, publicans, sinners, rebels, women, foreigners, the poor and especially Samaritans. To affirm community with Samaritans, the Jew must learn to allow them freedom to live their lives according to their consciences. We in a privatistic, laissez-faire society should not read freedom to mean individualistic autonomy; both Jews and Samaritans were living as part of their communities, bound to serve God, as they understood God. It means they must learn not to judge, in the sense of not condemning (Mt 7:1-5; Rom 14:1—15:13). Hence community requires that we live by forgiveness and grace rather than self-righteousness and judgmentalism.

Delivering love creates a *just* community. Throughout the Bible, the new community is always characterized by justice for the poor, the powerless and the outcast. The parable of the compassionate Samaritan is a midrash on Leviticus 19:18. Leviticus 19 is about justice. It is about the ethic of the people of Israel, which is to be an ethic of compassionate justice. In Jesus' day, Jews and Samaritans were treating each other with injustice. Jesus was saying that our enemy is also our neighbor, and therefore all the biblical teachings about love and justice mean love and justice even for our enemy. The Samaritan

> pays the innkeeper two denarii . . . and enters into a contract to pay for other bills the injured man might incur. As a paradigm for compassionate entry into the world of an injured brother or sister, this final action is indispensable. According to the law of the time, a person with an unpaid debt could be enslaved until the debt was paid (cf. Mt 18:23-25). Since the injured man was robbed and stripped—deprived of all resources—he could have been at the mercy of the innkeeper, a profession that had a bad reputation in antiquity for dishonesty and violence. The Samaritan assures the injured man's freedom and independence. (Donohue, *Gospel in Parable,* 133)

4. Love confronts those who exclude. The parable of the compassionate Samaritan confronts its hearers with their rejection of others. It is like Jesus' conclusion of his inaugural sermon in Nazareth in Luke 4: "'There were many widows in Israel in the days of Elijah . . . and Elijah was sent to none of them but only to Zarephath, in the land of Sidon, to a woman who was a widow. And there were many lepers in Israel in the time of the prophet Elisha; and none of them was cleansed, but only Naaman the Syrian.' When they heard this, all in the synagogue were filled with wrath" (Lk 4:25-28 RSV). Jesus' peacemaking led toward his own crucifixion (Moltmann, *Crucified God,* chap. 4.2; Moltmann and Stassen, *Justice Creates Peace,* 18-21).

After describing how the victim was rejected by the priest and the Levite, Jesus gave special emphasis to "Samaritan" by making it the first word in the next sentence (Marshall, *Commentary on Luke,* 449). Linnemann explains:

> It was, however, surprising and offensive for Jesus' hearers that it should be a Samaritan that was given the role of the merciful man. Between the Jews and this heretical mixed people there reigned implacable hatred. On the Jewish side it went so far that they cursed the Samaritans publicly in the synagogues, and prayed God that they should have no share in eternal life; that they would not believe the testimony of a Samaritan nor accept a service from one. This hatred was fully reciprocated by the Samaritans. Between 9 and 6 B.C. they managed to prevent a Jewish Passover by scattering dead men's bones on the temple area and so defiling it. (Linnemann, *Parables of Jesus,* 53-54)

"It would be difficult to emphasize [the importance of 'Samaritan'] too much. . . . If Jesus wanted to teach love of neighbor in distress, it would have sufficed to use . . . one person, a second person, and a third person. If he wanted to . . . add in a jibe against the clerical circles of Jerusalem, . . . he could have let the third person be a Jewish lay-person. . . . It would have been radical enough to have a Jewish person stop and assist a wounded Samaritan." For the Samaritan to be the neighbor "confronted the hearers with the necessity of saying the impossible and having their world turned upside down and radically questioned. . . . Just so does the Kingdom of God break abruptly into human consciousness and demand the overturn of prior values, closed options, set judgments, and established conclusions" (Crossan, *In Parables*, 63-64; cf. Donohue, *Gospel in Parable*, 131, 134). It is such a strong confrontation that when Jesus asked the lawyer, "Which of these three, do you think, was a neighbor to the man who fell into the hands of robbers?" the lawyer could not say, "The Samaritan." He spoke indirectly: "The one who showed him mercy" (cf. Wink, "Parable of the Compassionate Samaritan," 211-12; Hultgren, *Parables of Jesus*, 99).

Crossan argues that Jesus did not intend us to take the parables as examples of what we should do, literally, but as metaphors. The point is not that we should love our enemies as the Samaritan did, but that the kingdom comes as a surprising reversal. He almost reduces the meaning of all parables to one point: surprising reversal. As his proof, he cites the parables of the wheat and the tares, and of the unjust steward. Surely Jesus was not asking us to take the steward as a literal example and be equally unjust, he implies. We retort that on the metaphorical level, these parables do indeed indicate the shape of the kingdom in which we are to participate; do practice forgiveness of debts now, and do not condemn the tares now but practice forgiveness and let the tares grow with the wheat. The parable of the compassionate Samaritan is an "example narrative," exemplifying what we are to do (Hultgren, *Parables of Jesus*, 94; Westermann, *Parables of Jesus*, 189). Crossan's logical error is his failure to ask about the ethical content of the metaphors for the kingdom. He cites other parables to show the theme of the great reversal but fails to notice that in each of the parables he cites, those who enter the kingdom are our enemies and outcasts: a Samaritan, a publican, destitute Lazarus and the poor, maimed and blind. Clearly, Jesus is *confronting* us with the eschatological challenge of a kingdom populated with our enemies whom God loves and whom we must love. The kingdom of God is like the compassionate Samaritan, practicing delivering love. If I am to inherit eternal life, I must go and do as the Samaritan did.

Love Your Enemies

Now finally we come to the Sermon on the Mount, where Jesus taught us the character of Christian love in two very significant places: the climax of chapter five (Mt 5:43-48) and the climax of the whole central section (Mt 7:12). With our perceptions sensitized by the parable of the compassionate Samaritan, we find a pattern here in the Sermon on the Mount somewhat similar to what we found in the parable. This may be more than coincidental. Following the Jewish scholar David Flusser, the evangelical New Testament scholar Brad H. Young argues that the command to love enemies may originally have circulated as the conclusion to the parable of the compassionate Samaritan. And Peter Rhea Jones, calling this story the "love command in parable," agrees that the parable defines the neighbor to be loved to include even one's enemies. (Young, *Parables*, 104-5; P. R. Jones, "Love Command in the Parables," 296-97). The four themes of Jesus' teaching on love in the parable may also be present in the Sermon:

1. Love sees with compassion and enters into the situation of those in bondage (or enmity). In Matthew 5:43-48 Jesus taught love for our enemies. "The unanimous opinion of scholars that this word does in fact go back to Jesus himself, the evidence that the early church took it with utmost seriousness, and the strikingly unique way in which this teaching cuts against the grain of popular morality in his day as in ours indicate that the church cannot ignore Jesus' teaching of the love of enemies if it wishes to be true to itself" (Klassen, *Love of Enemies*, 7; Davies and Allison, *Critical and Exegetical Commentary*, 551n). Enemies are in a particular kind of bondage—the vicious cycle of hostility and enmity.

In this teaching (Mt 5:43-48), the transforming initiative comes second rather than third—probably because this is the climax of the six triads in Matthew 5. The transforming initiative is in verses 44-45: "But I say to you, Love your enemies and pray for those who persecute you, so that you may be children of your Father in heaven; for he makes his sun rise on the evil and on the good, and sends rain on the righteous and on the unrighteous." Jesus emphasized God's compassion in including the evil and the unrighteous in his mercy, giving his enemies sunshine and rain just as he does for the good and the righteous. When we love our enemies, we are participating in God's compassionate grace; we are children of our Father in heaven (see Davies and Allison, *Critical and Exegetical Commentary*, 1:554-55).

2. Love does delivering deeds. New Testament scholars also agree that love in the New Testament is not just an attitude or feeling, but an action, and it involves the whole person (Luz, *Matthew 1—7*, 341). In Matthew 5:44, Jesus emphasized the action of praying for enemies, and in Matthew 7:12, he emphasized that we are to *do* everything to others as we would have them *do* for us. In both cases the model is God. In all-inclusive love God regularly takes the very concrete action of giving rain and sunshine to his enemies (Mt 5:45). In mercy, God answers prayer and gives good gifts to those who ask (Mt 7:11).

Throughout the Sermon, Jesus emphasized deeds, practices, transforming in- itiatives. And we have seen that these transforming initiatives are the way of deliverance from vicious cycles of bondage and judgment. Therefore Jesus commanded transforming initiatives: when someone hits you on the right cheek, turn the other to him also. When someone wants to sue you for your shirt, then let him also have your coat. Many of us are accustomed to interpret- ing these teachings not as initiatives but merely as surrender. But we have seen these are transforming initiatives, delivering deeds, very much like the nine delivering deeds done by the compassionate Samaritan.

3. Love invites into community with justice, freedom and a future. Like the parable of the compassionate Samaritan, Jesus' teaching in Matthew 5:43-48 concerns who is included in community, who is our neighbor—is it only our friend, or is it our enemy also? The parable teaches that the Samaritan is our neighbor, a member of our community. The Sermon teaches that we are to make our enemy a member of our community. And Jesus' community practic- es delivering justice. "Go and be reconciled to your brother. . . . Settle matters quickly with your adversary who is taking you to court" (Mt 5:24-25 NIV). En- emy-love opens the possibility of a peaceable future for both the enemy and myself.

4. Love confronts those who exclude. In his teaching on peacemaking, Jesus was confronting those who nursed anger and called others fools, those who excluded outcasts, those who sought revenge, those who wanted to kill Ro- man soldiers, those who hated their enemies and loved only those who love them, and those who judged others.

Here it is important to clarify the translation of Matthew 5:48. We are used to reading it as "Be perfect, therefore, as your heavenly Father is perfect." The high-ideals/hard-teachings idealistic interpretation takes that to mean we must be morally perfect as God is morally perfect. And of course we cannot be as morally perfect as God is, so Jesus is taken to be commanding us to do something we absolutely cannot do. But three overwhelming reasons show that is the wrong understanding. Instead, it should be translated, "Be complete or all-inclusive, therefore, as your heavenly Father is complete or all-inclu- sive," or perhaps "completely all-embracing, as your heavenly Father is com- pletely all-embracing."

1. Nowhere in the Old Testament or the Dead Sea Scrolls is God called "per- fect." That would better fit Greek philosophical idealism. It makes perfect sense, however, to say God is complete or all-inclusive in love, giving rain even to God's enemies (Davies and Allison, *Critical and Exegetical Commen- tary*, 563).

2. In the context, Matthew 5:43-47, Jesus has been teaching that we should in-

clude enemies in our love as God does. He has not been teaching idealistic Greek moral perfection.

3. When Luke 6:36 gives the same teaching, it says, "Be merciful, as your Father is merciful," that is, merciful or compassionate toward enemies. The context there, in Luke 6:32-35, is all about including our enemies in our love, just as it is in Matthew.

So the teaching is not about idealistic moral perfection but about resembling God by including enemies in our mercy, compassion, loving action, as God does (Davies and Allison, *Critical and Exegetical Commentary,* 1:561-63). We cannot be morally perfect, but we can be all-embracing by doing loving deeds toward our enemies, in the grace of God, who does loving deeds toward God's enemies. In doing that, we are participating in God's grace, as God's children.

The Cross

We want to conclude this chapter on Christian love by going to the heart of the Christian gospel—the cross.

Many traditional treatments of the cross emphasize a transaction that must be made in order to appease God's wrath. While this note is certainly struck in the New Testament, it should not be taught in a way that fails to emphasize the cross as a demonstration of God's *love* in Christ.

> Beloved, let us love one another, because love is from God; everyone who loves is born of God and knows God. Whoever does not love does not know God, for God is love. God's love was revealed among us in this way: God sent his only Son into the world so that we might live through him. *In this is love, not that we loved God but that he loved us and sent his Son to be the atoning sacrifice for our sins.* Beloved, since God loved us so much, we also ought to love one another. (1 Jn 4:7-11, italics added)

The once-for-all drama of the cross has far deeper meaning than any one interpretation of the meaning of the atonement can exhaust. There is both scriptural and experiential meaning in all the classical interpretations of the atonement: Christus Victor, satisfaction, penal substitution, moral, governmental and ransom theories (Grenz, *Theology for the Community of God,* 443-61; McClendon, *Doctrine,* 197-237; Paul, *Atonement and the Sacraments,* chaps. 1-8; Volf, *Exclusion and Embrace,* 22-28, 125-29, 290-95; Weaver, *Nonviolent Atonement;* Yoder, *Preface to Theology,* chap. 12). Because the meaning is far deeper than any one theory or interpretation can exhaust, there may be room for adding what could be called an "incarnational" interpretation here.

An understanding of agape as delivering love sets the cross in the context of the incarnation, as the Gospels do. God shows love for us by *entering incarnationally into our situation of bondage,* in Jesus Christ, experiencing life as we experience it, suffering as we do and, in the crucifixion, entering even into the situation of our sinful rebellion against God, becoming vulnerable to our unloving, unjust, violent rejection of him. Our human problem is that we have separated ourselves from God by our distrust, greed and shame, and that we cannot cross the barriers and defenses we have built and return ourselves to faithful community with God. In delivering love, God acts in compassion toward us in our bondage, breaking down the barriers that we have built between ourselves and God, and between one another and ourselves. God comes into our ditch, enters incarnationally into our situation of bondage, passing right through the walls we have built, establishing fellowship and presence with us on our side of the walls, since we cannot climb our way over them to God (1 Jn 4:9-11; see also Gollwitzer, *Das Gleichnis*, 68-69).

God in Christ loves us even to the point of becoming vulnerable to our rejection of him at the cross. In so doing, God discloses and confronts the sin that we had been hiding, and establishes community with us even where we commit the worst sin that we can imagine—which stands for all other sins of rejection, injustice and violence against God and our fellow humans. Even there, God forgives us and enters into community, the presence of the Holy Spirit with us. This is truly delivering love.

The delivering love offered in the cross has continuity with the mighty works of God in the history of Israel and in *the deeds of deliverance*, healing, feeding, reconciling and confronting that Jesus did even before the cross. Jesus' death on the cross is the unique, supreme, climactic delivering deed because it discloses God's love to us and it discloses the depth of our sin. It demonstrates God's loyalty to us in the midst of our sin, betrayal, injustice and violence. It is God incarnate in Jesus Christ, crossing the barriers we have erected and entering with extreme vulnerability into our fear of death. It is God suffering, bringing us into community with God and each other, community that we ourselves could not create.

Jesus did not die merely for the sake of sacrifice, but to deliver us *into community* with himself, with God disclosed in his love to the point of death and resurrection, with the body of Christ in the Holy Spirit, and with all persons whom God loves, now and eternally. It was Jesus' confrontation of the authorities over their injustice that led them to plot his crucifixion. The resurrection and the Reign of God already begin to form a community in which Jew and Gentile, Zealot and tax collector, rich and poor, male and female, taste God's forgiveness and drink his reconciliation, and eat together as disciples who are one in Christ—a foretaste of the future Great Banquet. Delivering love does not divorce the cross from the greedy injustice and the legalistic hate that continue to cause Jesus to be crucified anew; it discloses them and acts to remedy them. It does not place the cross in a mystical realm where the reasons for the crucifixion make no contact with the oppression we know in our history or with the hope that we already see in the mustard seeds of community sprouting in our midst.

The cross itself *confronts* us mightily in our sin and betrayal, just as Jesus in his love confronted those who excluded outcasts and loved only their friends, and did not know the ways of peace. If we do not understand that love includes confrontation, we will either downplay the confronting of our sin that plays a powerful part in the drama of the cross, or we will see God as Judge split off from God as compassionate Reconciler. God's love confronts those who alienate and are alienated, and when we experience the drama of the cross, we either experience that confrontation or we are hiding ourselves from the truth.

17

JUSTICE

—

Do not store up for yourselves treasures on earth, where moth and rust consume and where thieves break in and steal.

You cannot serve God and wealth.

But strive first for the kingdom of God and his righteousness, and all these things will be given to you as well.

MATTHEW 6:19, 24, 33

In chapter six we saw that the secularizing split between the private realm of inner attitudes ruled by the gospel and the public realm of actions ruled by secular authorities marginalizes the way of Jesus and the Sermon on the Mount. It also causes many to think that the gospel is not related to the concern for justice.

The secularizing split causes a painful problem in Christian ethics and Christian living. It can be described as a skip, a hop and a jump:

1. By a conservative count, the four words for justice (two in Hebrew, and two in Greek) appear 1,060 times in the Bible. Hardly any concept appears so often. By contrast, the main words for sexual sin appear about 90 times. Yet we *skip* over the huge biblical emphasis on justice as central in God's will. The problem is exacerbated by the fact that most versions of the Bible translate *tsedaqah* as "righteousness," and the King James Version translates *mishpat* as "judgment," so people do not see the Bible's insistence on justice. *Tsedaqah* mean delivering, community-restoring justice, and *mishpat* means judgment according to right or rights, and thus judgment that vindicates the right especially of the poor or powerless.

2. Skipping over the biblical meaning of justice creates a vacuum. In *hop* secular ideologies, only too happy to fill the vacuum with their justifications of greed, racism or other sinful drives—and only too happy to claim that their

ideologies are Christian. The secular ideas of justice that hop in include the Greek aristocratic ethic with its fairly abstract "to everyone his due"; or the thin philosophical concepts of utilitarianism—"the greatest happiness for the greatest number"; or liberalism—"individual autonomy"; or Kant's "treat every person as an end in himself or herself, and never only as a means"; or Rawls's two principles of fairness—"liberty and difference that benefits the least advantaged"; or Walzer's "complex equality" and human rights; the reduction of justice to retribution or punishment; or the drive for political control that reduces justice to "the dictatorship of the proletariat"; or the drive for freedom to pursue wealth that reduces justice to "the dictatorship of the free market." None of these is adequate to communicate the will of God in the biblical teaching of delivering, community-restoring justice and righteousness. (For a judicious study of different theories of justice, see Lebacqz, *Six Theories of Justice* and *Justice in and Unjust World,* and Bounds, *Coming Together/Coming Apart;* see also Walzer, *Spheres of Justice,* summarized in Stassen, "Michael Walzer's Situated Justice.")

3. Christians then contrast the idea of "justice" from some secular source with Christian love. They hear praise of Christian love that may say how superior it is to justice, understanding justice as an abstract principle. The thousand biblical teachings on justice are ignored. So Christians then not only neglect justice, they come to believe it is inferior and unimportant. They come to have no defense against secular ideologies that fill the vacuum and seduce them into unjust practices. They become unbiblical and move in the opposite direction from the way the Bible says God is moving. Thus, unknowingly, they *jump* into the arms of the devil. As we show in this chapter, Jesus was strongly concerned for justice. "Woe to you scribes and Pharisees, hypocrites! for you tithe mint, dill, and cummin, and have neglected the weightier matters of the law: justice and mercy and faith" (Mt 23:23//Lk 11:42).

Accurate repentance requires us to go back to the first step and recover a biblical understanding of justice. We must show that the split between Jesus and justice is false. And then we must make clear how strikingly different a biblical understanding of justice is from those secular understandings that betray it, in order that we can have defenses against infiltration by ungodly interests and their ideologies. Good news: help is coming from some recent developments in New Testament scholarship. We will show from this scholarship and from Scripture that Jesus' identification with the prophets, his attack on the temple system and his proclamation and practice of the reign of God all linked him inextricably to a content-rich proclamation and practice of justice. Justice is one of the central virtues in Jesus' teaching as well as in traditional virtue theory. It is one of the basic convictions in holistic character. It is thickly embedded in the biblical narratives. It is at the heart of God's will. It is crucial for relating love and Christlikeness to a public ethic that can reflect the sovereignty of God and the lordship of Christ over all of life. It is pivotal in present-day struggles for the soul of our society.

Jesus in the Tradition of the Prophets

Jesus identified especially strongly with the tradition of the prophets of Israel. This is clear in the Gospels, and it is clear now in much New Testament scholarship. It was not so clear to previous scholarship influenced by anti-Semitism, by a liberal preference for "universal truths" rather than the historical particularity of Jesus and by lack of attention to the historical context of Israel in Jesus' day. This is being corrected. N. T. Wright begins his book on the historical Jesus by saying: "Jesus' public persona within first-century Judaism was that of a prophet, and the content of his prophetic proclamation was the 'kingdom' of Israel's God. . . . The prophetic aspect of Jesus' work is often surprisingly ignored" (*Jesus and the Victory of God*, 11). Wright argues that Jesus' mission also was as Messiah and Savior, but that we cannot understand his mission accurately if we wrench him out of the tradition of the prophets.

> Jesus was proclaiming a message from the covenant God, and living it out with symbolic actions. He was confronting the people with the folly of their ways, summoning them to a different way, and expecting to take the consequences of doing so. Elijah had stood alone against the prophets of Baal, and against the wickedness of King Ahab. Jeremiah had announced the doom of the Temple and the nation, in the face of royalty, priests and official prophets . . . all were accused of troubling the status quo. When people "saw" Jesus as a prophet, this was the kind of model they had in mind. (N. T. Wright, *Jesus and the Victory of God*, 167-68)

Murray Dempster sums it up: "In formulating his moral judgments about individual behaviours and social practices Jesus will draw on many Old Testament concepts: the affirmation that human beings are God's image bearers, the moral significance of the law and its fulfillment in real life, the prophetic spirit that aspires for justice in human affairs, the importance of covenant in creating the social bonds for an ordered society, and the jubilee reversal with the forgiveness of the debt and the debtor. . . . Who God is in his character and what God reveals about himself in his mighty acts define what is right" (Dempster, "Social Concern in the Context of Jesus' Kingdom, Mission, and Minstry," 48). And God cares deeply about justice for the poor, the powerless, the outcasts and the victims of violence. This Old Testament theme, especially strongly emphasized in the prophets, is not abandoned but continued in Jesus' teaching.

Jesus' Attack on the Temple System

A second development in New Testament scholarship is new attention to

Jesus' symbolic attack on the temple system. (For only a few examples, see Myers, *Binding the Strong Man*, 79-86; 126-27, 300-304; Sanders, *Empowerment Ethics for a Liberated People*, chap. 1; Herzog, *Jesus, Justice, and the Reign of God*, chap. 6; Bockmuehl, *This Jesus*, chap. 3; Borg, *Conflict, Holiness, and Politics in the Teaching of Jesus*, chap. 7; N. T. Wright, *Jesus and the Victory of God*, 333-36, 413-28, 490-93.) Scholars are seeing that it was not merely a "cleansing" of the temple, but a prophetic and symbolic attack on the whole temple system for practicing a cover-up of injustice; the same kind of confrontation offered by both Isaiah 56 and Jeremiah 7. These are the two passages that the Gospels report Jesus quoting when he overturned the tables of the moneychangers and "would not allow anyone to carry anything through the temple" (Mk 11:15-17 and par.).

N. T. Wright (*Jesus and the Victory of God*, 335) points out that in six different passages, Jesus prophesied the destruction of the temple. Wright disagrees with the liberal scholar John Dominic Crossan on much, but here he says that Crossan comes very close to the right answer on what caused Jesus to be crucified: "Crossan thinks, and I fully agree with him, that Jesus' action in the temple was a symbolic destruction; that these words and this action followed with a close logic from the rest of Jesus' agenda" (*Jesus and the Victory of God*, 61).

David Garland writes that Jesus' action at the temple was neither an act of violent revolution nor merely a "cleansing" or reform of the temple, but a symbolic prophetic action of protest against injustice and its cover-up (*NIV Application Commentary*, 433-39). Why would Jesus merely try to cleanse the temple when he predicts it will soon be destroyed? "If sacrificial animals cannot be purchased, then sacrifice must end. If no vessel can be carried though the temple, then all cultic activity must cease." And if money cannot be made, then the financial support for the temple and the priests will be gone. "Jesus does not seek to purify current temple worship but symbolically attacks the very function of the temple and heralds its destruction." His hostility to the temple emerges as a charge at his trial (Mk 14:58) and as a taunt at the cross (Mk 15:29).

Jesus cited two passages from the prophets as he carried out this prophetic action. Isaiah 56:7, "My house will be called a house of prayer for all nations," is part of the declaration in Isaiah 56:1-8 that God's purpose is to bless all who are being excluded, the foreigners, eunuchs and outcasts. "During his entire ministry Jesus has been gathering in the impure outcasts and the physically maimed, and has even reached out to Gentiles. He expects the temple to embody this inclusive love. . . . In Jesus' day the temple had become a nationalistic symbol that served only to divide Israel from the nations" (Garland, *NIV Application Commentary*, 438). And the court intended for the Gentiles to worship in had been taken over as a trading post.

Jeremiah 7 says we should not keep claiming we have the temple of the Lord, when we need to amend our ways and truly execute justice with each other, not oppress the alien, the orphan or the widow, or shed innocent blood and go after other gods. The temple is functioning as a cover-up for injustice, what Bonhoeffer called "cheap grace." If we continue to practice injustice while claiming God is on our side, because we have the temple (or we have the church), God will destroy the temple (or the church) and cast us out of his sight. By quoting from Jeremiah 7, Jesus

> denounces the false security that the sacrificial cult breeds. . . . The den is the place where robbers retreat after having committed their crimes. It is their hideout, a place of security and refuge. Calling the temple a robbers' den is therefore not a cry of outrage against any dishonest business practices in the temple. Jesus indirectly attacks them for allowing the temple to degenerate into a safe hiding place where people think that they find forgiveness and fellowship with God no matter how they act on the outside. Jesus' prophetic action and words attack a false trust in the efficacy of the temple sacrificial system. The leaders of the people think that they can rob widows' houses (Mark 12:40) and then perform the prescribed sacrifices according to the prescribed patterns at the prescribed times in the prescribed purity in the prescribed sacred space and then be safe and secure from all alarms. They are wrong. (Garland, *NIV Application Commentary*, 439)

Jesus, the Promised Kingdom and Justice

A third development in New Testament scholarship that helps us see Jesus' concern for justice is the awareness that Jesus often cited the prophet Isaiah, which (explicitly in the Aramaic Targum, implicitly but clearly in the Hebrew text) speaks several times of the kingdom or reign of God. This is an important clue for the meaning of the kingdom. In chapter one, we found that sixteen of the seventeen kingdom-deliverance passages in Isaiah announced that *justice* was a key characteristic of God's kingdom. The next logical step is to inquire into the meaning of justice in those passages.

> **If we look carefully, we discover that justice has four dimensions: (1) deliverance of the poor and powerless from the injustice that they regularly experience; (2) lifting the foot of domineering power off the neck of the dominated and oppressed; (3) stopping the violence and establishing peace; and (4) restoring the outcasts, the excluded, the Gentiles, the exiles and the refugees to community.**

Our aim is to display here a bit of the extensive evidence for that meaning. We will not quote *all* of the passages, but we want you to be able to see what justice and righteousness in Isaiah's "reign of God" passages mean, since Jesus announced the kingdom by referring to Isaiah. These passages were especially important in Jesus' mission and teaching. They are the word of God for us.

We begin with the kingdom passage of Isaiah 11:1-4:

> A shoot shall come out from the stump of Jesse. . . .
> The spirit of the LORD shall rest upon him. . . .
> He shall not judge by what his eyes see,
>   or decide by what his ears hear;
> But with *righteousness* he shall judge the poor,
>   and decide with *equity* for the meek of the earth. (italics added)

Here is announced the coming king (and kingdom). The king will decide not by surface appearances but by righteousness and equity. Notice that *righteousness* and *equity* have parallel meaning, just as *poor* and *meek* do. In the other delivering passages, "righteousness" *(tsedaqah)* and "justice" *(mishpat)* are parallel, as they are throughout the Old Testament. "Righteousness" carries a meaning of the kind of justice that delivers the poor and the meek, or humble, from their oppression by the powerful—who use wealth to gain privilege and to deprive the poor—into covenant community (Brueggemann, *Isaiah 1—39*, 100ff.).

In Isaiah 26:2-10 we see three of the meanings: deliverance of the poor and the needy, deliverance from domination by the high and lofty, and deliverance from violence into peace.

> Open the gates,
>   so that the righteous nation that keeps faith
>   may enter in.
> Those of steadfast mind you keep in peace—
>   in peace because they trust in you.
> Trust in the LORD forever,
>   for in the LORD God
>   you have an everlasting rock.
> For he has brought low
>   the inhabitants of the height;
>   the lofty city he lays low. . . .
> The foot tramples it,
>   the feet of the poor,
>   the steps of the needy.
> The way of the righteous is level;
>   O Just One, you make smooth the path of the righteous. . . .

> For when your judgments are in the earth,
>> the inhabitants of the world learn righteousness.

Brueggemann (*Isaiah 1—39*, 203) comments that the reason for such trust

> is Yahweh's demonstrated capacity to "bring low the heights." Yahweh's charac-
> teristic action that grounds trust is to prevail over every pretentious, arrogant,
> self-sufficient, exploitative power. This is a recurring theme to eighth-century Isa-
> iah (2:12-17). . . . Indeed, the "bringing low" is so decisive and so complete that
> even "the poor and needy," those who live politically and economically close to
> the ground, will be able to trample the ruins of the arrogant city. . . . This climactic
> action is so crucial to the argument that the poet uses three parallel lines to make
> the point (v. 6). The city is trampled by the foot, the feet, the steps. One can imag-
> ine unrestrained vindication and defiance by those long oppressed.

Isaiah 32:1 and 6-7 again show that the meaning of "righteousness" parallels
the meaning of "justice":

> See, a king will reign in righteousness,
>> and princes will rule with justice. . . .

Righteousness and justice especially concern meeting the needs of the hungry
and the poor:

> For fools speak folly,
>> and their minds plot iniquity: . . .
> to leave the craving of the hungry unsatisfied,
>> and to deprive the thirsty of drink.

And they confront the power of the domineering:

> The villainies of villains are evil;
>> they devise wicked devices
> to ruin the poor with lying words,
>> even when the plea of the needy is right.

Furthermore, Isaiah 32:16-18 shows not only the parallel meaning of justice and
righteousness, but also the intimate causal relation between justice and peace:

> Then justice will dwell in the wilderness,
>> and righteousness abide in the fruitful field.
> The effect of righteousness will be peace,
>> and the result of righteousness, quietness and trust forever.
> My people will abide in a peaceful habitation,
>> in secure dwellings, and in quiet resting places.

Isaiah 33:5 and 15 again connect justice and righteousness as parallel, asserts their confrontation of oppression and greed, and connects them with
peace:

The LORD is exalted, he dwells on high;
> he filled Zion with justice and righteousness. . . .
Those [will live] who walk righteously and speak uprightly;
> who despise the gain of oppression,
who wave away a bribe instead of accepting it,
> who stop their ears from hearing of bloodshed.

Isaiah 42 is of crucial importance. All three Synoptic Gospels tell us that when at Jesus' baptism the Holy Spirit descended on him and spoke, the words were those of Isaiah 42:1 (Lk 3:22 and parallels; see also Chilton, *Isaiah Targum,* 83n, concerning Lk 4:18ff.). This passage is crucial for Jesus' mission. Notice how strongly it emphasizes the centrality of justice for the servant's mission. It confirms the intimate connection of justice with peace and nonviolence: the servant will not break even a half-broken reed or quench a barely burning wick. Furthermore, it adds a fourth theme to the three we have already noticed: justice is not only for Israel but inclusively for "the people," "the nations," "in the earth"—that is, for the Gentiles. Here is this magnificent passage, Isaiah 42:1-7:

Here is my servant, whom I uphold,
> my chosen, in whom my soul delights;
I have put my spirit upon him;
> he will bring forth justice to the nations.
He will not cry or lift up his voice,
> or make it heard in the street;
a bruised reed he will not break,
> and a dimly burning wick he will not quench;
he will faithfully bring forth justice.
He will not grow faint or be crushed
> until he has established justice in the earth. . . .
I am the LORD, I have called you in righteousness;
> I have taken you by the hand and kept you;
I have given you as a covenant to the people,
> a light to the nations,
> to open the eyes that are blind,
to bring out the prisoners from the dungeon,
> from the prison those who sit in darkness.

Isaiah 51:1, 4-7 confirms these themes. It adds that justice depends on our having God's teaching in our hearts. And it adds that justice is delivering justice, not merely punitive justice.

Listen to me, you that pursue *righteousness,*
> you that seek the LORD. . . .
Listen to me, my people,

and give heed to me, my nation;
for a teaching will go out from me,
    and my *justice for a light to the peoples.*
I will bring near my *deliverance* swiftly,
    my *salvation* has gone out
    and my arms will rule *the peoples.* . . .
Listen to me, you who know *righteousness,*
    you people who have *my teaching in your hearts.* (italics added)

In Isaiah 53:7-9, we see again the direct connection between justice and nonviolence:

He was oppressed, and he was afflicted,
    yet he did not open his mouth;
like a lamb that is led to the slaughter,
    and like a sheep that before its shearers is silent,
    so he did not open his mouth.
By a perversion of justice he was taken away. . . .
They made his grave with the wicked
    and his tomb with the rich,
although he had done no violence,
    and there was no deceit in his mouth.

Here in Isaiah 53:9-10 is one of the places where the Aramaic paraphrase in the Targum speaks of the kingdom and of deliverance from injustice: "And he *will hand over the wicked to Gehenna and those rich in possessions which they robbed to the death of the corruption, lest those who commit sin be established, and speak of possessions with their mouth. Yet* . . . the remnant of his people . . . shall *see the kingdom of their Messiah.*"

In Isaiah 54:14 we see again how righteousness is God's action of deliverance from the injustice of domination:

In righteousness you shall be established;
    you shall be far from oppression, for you shall not fear;
    and from terror, for it shall not come near you.

Isaiah 56:1 announces the theme we have seen throughout:

Thus says the LORD:
Maintain justice, and do what is right,
    for soon my salvation will come, and my deliverance be revealed.

And then follow the wonderful six verses that Jesus cites when he attacks the exclusiveness and injustice being practiced by the temple:

Do not let the foreigner joined to the LORD say,
    "The LORD will surely separate me from his people";

and do not let the eunuch say,
"I am just a dry tree."
For thus says the LORD to the eunuchs who keep my sabbaths,
who choose the things that please me and hold fast my covenant, . . .
I will give them an everlasting name
that shall not be cut off.
And the foreigners who join themselves to the LORD . . .
All who keep the sabbath, and do not profane it,
and hold fast my covenant—
These I will bring to my holy mountain,
and make them joyful in my house of prayer; . . .
for my house shall be called a house of prayer
for all peoples.

The passage begins with "justice and right," and it declares that God's will for justice and righteousness involves including outcasts and foreigners in the community. This will become a central theme for Jesus.

The intimate connection of justice and peace is announced again in Isaiah 60:17-21:

I will appoint Peace as your overseer
and Righteousness as your taskmaster.
Violence shall no more be heard in your land,
devastation or destruction within your borders;
you shall call your walls Salvation,
and your gates Praise. . . .
the LORD will be your everlasting light,
and your days of mourning shall be ended,
Your people shall all be righteous;
they shall possess the land forever.

And we reach a climax with the Jubilee passage that was Jesus' text in his inaugural sermon in Nazareth, Isaiah 61:1, 3, 8, 10-11.

The spirit of the Lord GOD is upon me, because the LORD has anointed me;
he has sent me to bring good news to the oppressed,
to bind up the brokenhearted,
to proclaim liberty to the captives, and release to the prisoners; . . .
They will be called oaks of righteousness, the planting of the LORD,
to display his glory.
. . . For I the LORD love justice, I hate robbery and wrongdoing. . . .
I will greatly rejoice in the LORD, my whole being shall exult in my God;
for he has clothed me with the garments of salvation,
he has covered me with the robe of righteousness. . . .
So the Lord GOD will cause righteousness and praise
to spring up before all the nations.

This justice and righteousness are what God wills. More than that, they are what God does, what God enacts and carries out, as God delivers the oppressed from those who dominate them. In the reign-of-God passages especially, they are not merely human action; they are the gift of God's dynamic reign. They are the heart of what God does when he delivers, saves, ransoms and redeems his people. So it is that the King James Version of the Bible translates "justice," or *mishpat*, as "judgment," because this justice is the enactment of God's decision for justice, God's verdict for justice. But it is not enough to call this "judgment," or simply to call it "justice" or "righteousness," without clarifying the concrete ethical content of God's will and action for delivering, community-restoring justice: (1) deliverance of the poor and powerless from the injustice that they regularly experience; (2) lifting the foot of the domineering power off the neck of the dominated and oppressed, and throwing the dominator for a fall; (3) stopping the violence of military domination and establishing peace; and (4) restoring the outcasts, the excluded, the Gentiles, the exiles and the refugees to community.

Jesus' Confrontation with Injustice

Jesus came proclaiming the reign of God. The reign of God in Isaiah, as we have seen, announced God's justice as deliverance of the outcasts, the poor and the oppressed from the domination of greed and concentrated power, and the restoration of community with peace. It called for repentance for injustice. Would it not be strange if Jesus announced the kingdom but avoided these central themes of God's justice and repentance for injustice?

One can hear persons who, influenced by the secularizing two-realms split between private and public, say Jesus taught only love for individuals and not justice in relation to political and economic powers and authorities. Perhaps they think Rome was the government and the high priests were only religious. Perhaps they forget that state, church and economic wealth were not separated but very much mixed together on the same hill and in the same temple in Jerusalem, and that Rome allowed the Jewish authorities to do most of the daily ruling. When Jesus confronted the representatives of the temple authority, he was confronting the public authorities of his time.

Markus Bockmuehl points out that Jesus

> was put to death by the Romans following a plot among the aristocracy. . . .
> The priestly aristocracy of Jerusalem with their private police gangs worked
> closely together with the Roman authorities to crack down at any hint of in-
> surrection. . . . The corruption of the priestly aristocracy in Jerusalem invited
> comparison with the earlier prophetic oracles of judgement and destruction.
> . . . Of the 28 high priests between 37 BC and AD 70, all but two came from four
> power-hungry, illegitimate non-Zadokite families. . . . Recent historical study
> is making increasingly clear that the operation of the Temple . . . was in the
> hands of a vast economic and religious power network. . . . Traders had only
> very recently moved into the Court of the Gentiles at the invitation of Caiaphas.
> . . . The Mishnah gives evidence of hugely inflated price fixing for sacrificial
> doves, which were the offering of the poor. . . . The hierarchy operated agents
> and hit squads known as "men of violence" and the "big men of the priest-
> hood.". . . During those two decades (of Jesus' teenage years and adulthood)
> Annas and Caiaphas together enjoyed unrivalled power as a result of success-
> ful collaboration with the occupation forces of Rome. . . . Josephus and the rab-
> binic writings also concur in offering some most remarkable descriptions of
> the utter luxury and extravagance of the priestly aristocracy in Jerusalem.
> (Bockmuehl, *This Jesus*, 69-71)

Furthermore, the 90 percent of the population who were peasant farmers
and village-craftsmen like those in Galilee produced most of the wealth. But
the 10 percent of the people who were the economic and religio-political aris-
tocracy in the cities and their supporters siphoned off over half of the products
by taxes, tithes and charges for sacrifices and temple services. The priestly authorities, both Sadducees and Pharisees, developed teachings and religious
traditions that gave authority to this centralization of economic power. The hierarchy were in collusion with the wealthy and with the Roman empire. (See
Borg, *Conflict, Holiness and Politics in the Teaching of Jesus*, x, 7, 12-14, 20ff., 33,
passim; E. P. Sanders, *Jesus and Judaism*, 309-18; Herzog, *Jesus, Justice, and the
Reign of God*, 91-92, 94-95, 102-4, 127, 137, 150, 171-72, 191, 219, 233-35, 241-44.
The extent of this burden is being questioned by some critics.)

Did Jesus teach only individual love, or did he carry out prophetic action
and teach justice that challenged and undermined the authority of this aristoc-
racy? As we have seen in Isaiah, justice is not merely an ideal for good individuals in their private life but is a righteous demand that has the power to
confront those who have power. That is one absolutely essential contribution
of justice in a sinful world where concentration of power needs restraint,
checks and balances, and limits on greed. God's will for people cannot do
without justice. Therefore, we have systematically searched the Gospels for
Jesus' confrontation of power over their injustice.

We count forty times in the Synoptic Gospels, not including the parallel passages, when Jesus confronted the powers and authorities of his day. In addition, Jesus performed practices and gave other teachings which, even if not explicitly identified as confrontations of authorities, surely challenged the theological ideology of those in power. In our study of Jesus confronting authorities, we asked, "What are the themes of Jesus' confrontations? What wrongs does Jesus focus on when he confronts the powers and authorities?" We have found that the answers to these questions embody four themes and that these themes are remarkably consistent with the four themes of justice that we saw in Isaiah's deliverance passages.

The match with Isaiah is so striking—so complete and so exact—that we want to present the evidence extensively, so you can see it and weigh it for yourself. We hope it strikes you as forcefully as it strikes us. The evidence has led us to conclude that Jesus fulfilled the theme of justice in Isaiah's deliverance passages and, therefore, he should be understood in the context of the Hebrew Scriptures, especially Isaiah. Paying close attention to Isaiah's deliverance passages helps us compensate for the reductionistic biases of our individualistic culture and helps us notice the four themes of justice in Jesus' confrontations of the powers and authorities of his day; it gives us a new appreciation for Jesus' depth and compassion.

Our method here is to report on Jesus as presented in the Gospels and not to engage in "the quest for the historical Jesus" behind the Gospels. Nevertheless, we observe that the literature of that quest basically confirms and even highlights these themes in the Synoptic Gospels. In presenting Jesus as the Gospels witness to him, we use the symbol // to indicate a parallel teaching in the other Gospels. For example, Mark 12:1-9//Mt 21:33-46//Lk 20:9-19//Is 5:1-7 indicates that Mark 12:1-9 has parallels in Matthew and Luke, and also in Isaiah. More parallels in Isaiah could be indicated than we focus on here.

The Injustice of Greed and Justice for the Poor and Hungry

Deliverance of the poor from extortion by the powerful and from their need was a central theme of John the Baptist's preaching. John declared, "Whoever has two coats must share with anyone who has none; and whoever has food must do likewise." He told the tax collectors, "Collect no more than the amount prescribed for you," and he told soldiers, "Do not extort money from anyone by threats or false accusation" (Lk 3:1-14//Mt 3:1-10). John lived much of his life in the desert. Jesus praised him as God's prophet and said in contrast, "Those who put on fine clothing and live in luxury are in royal palaces" (Lk 7:24-30).

In several teachings, Jesus confronted the wealthy for their greed: "The ones sown among thorns . . . are those who hear the word, but the cares of the world, and the delight in riches . . . choke the word, and it proves unfruitful" (Mk 4:18-19//Lk 8:14//Mt 13:22 RSV). "How hard it will be for those who have wealth to enter the kingdom of God! . . . It is easier for a camel to go through the eye of a needle than for someone who is rich to enter the kingdom of God" (Mk 10:23, 25). To the rich ruler he said, "Go, sell what you own, and give the money to the poor, and you will have treasure in heaven" (Mk 10:17-22//Mt 19:21//Lk 18:18-25). On a different occasion he confronted Zacchaeus for his extortion as a tax collector, and Zacchaeus not only repented but declared he would restore what is just to those he extorted (Lk 19:1-10).

The parable of the unforgiving slave (Mt 18:23-35) is surely a confrontation of persons who do not forgive debts. On the one hand it concerns forgiveness from the heart of one's fellow human (v. 35). But the parable is also about forgiving the poor the large debts of money owed to their creditors, and it portrays the experience of many poor people in Jesus' time, too deep in debt to pay it back. The word for "debt" (v. 27) ordinarily means a loan of money, and "release" is the word Josephus uses to refer to the Jubilee, when he says all "debtors are freed from their debts" (Hultgren, *Parables of Jesus*, 26). Thus the parable is also a confrontation of unforgiving creditors who do not forgive debts, and it fits the theme of Jubilee that André Trocmé and John Howard Yoder have brought to our attention (Yoder, *Politics of Jesus*, chap. 3).

In confronting the Pharisees, "who were lovers of money," Jesus said to them, "You are those who justify [dikaiountes] yourselves in the sight of others; but God knows your hearts" (Lk 16:14-15). In Matthew 23:16-19, 25 (RSV) Jesus pointed to the scribes and Pharisees' fixation on gold and the manner in which they forced undue hardship on those who could not offer such expensive gifts, saying "You cleanse the outside of the cup and of the plate, but inside they are full of extortion and rapacity." Jesus identified the same pattern of injustice when he warned against the scribes who "devour widows' houses" while maintaining a facade of piety with their long prayers (Mk 12:38-44). The temple, which was supposed to support widows and orphans, had been turned into "the institution that extracts their last copper coins" (Herzog, *Jesus, Justice, and the Reign of God*, 189).

Another time, Jesus asked the Pharisees, "Why do you break the commandment of God for the sake of your tradition? For God said, 'Honor your father and your mother. . . . But you say that whoever tells father or mother, 'Whatever support you might have had from me is given to God,' then that person need not honor the father" (Mt 15:3-9//Mk 7:9-13//Is 29:13). Jesus' quotation here of Isaiah 29:13 confirms our theme of his connection with Isaiah. Similarly, Jesus defended feeding the hungry on the sabbath, quoting Hosea 6:6 and saying to the Pharisees, "If you had known what this means, 'I desire mercy and not sacrifice,' you would not have condemned the guiltless" (Mt 12:1-8// Mk 2:23-28//Lk 6:1-5). Acts of mercy to the hungry are acts of covenant justice in the Old Testament. In writing about Jesus' symbolic attack on the temple Matthew quoted Jeremiah 7, which calls for truly acting justly to the alien, the orphan and the widow (Jer 7:5-8).

Jesus' teaching "render to Caesar the things that are Caesar's, and to God the things that are God's" (Mk 12:13-17//Mt 22:15-22//Lk 20:20-26 RSV) concerns paying the tribute tax to Caesar. Ched Myers (*Binding the Strong Man*, 310) says the question was "a test of loyalty that divided collaborators from subversives against the backdrop of revolt." The tax was oppressive to the poor, and it was idolatrous for faithful Jews. Jesus was so concerned about justice for the poor and so emphatically taught service to God alone that his action of getting the Pharisees and Herodians to come up with a coin, and then holding it up and asking whose image was on it, exposed their collaboration with the Roman power structure and distanced himself from it. He was confronting the injustice of the Roman tax and the collaboration of the Pharisees and Herodians, while at the same time advocating peaceful conduct. Jesus' reply is an antithetical parallelism, in which the second line, "render to God what is God's," actually includes everything, since everything belongs to God. It means "render to Caesar only what is consistent with God's will."

In sum, Jesus fulfilled the words Isaiah spoke concerning God:

For you have been a refuge to the poor,
    a refuge to the needy in their distress. (Is 25:4)

Jesus' deliverance of the poor and needy from the greed of the powerful parallels a key theme of God's deliverance in Isaiah. The first chapter of Isaiah begins with judgment on the injustice that flows from greed:

Your princes are rebels
    and companions of thieves.
Every one loves a bribe
    and runs after gifts.
They do not defend the orphan,
    and the widow's cause does not come before them. (Is 1:23)

This is God's word. Jesus taught that God cared deeply for the poor and the powerless. He not only taught it, he enacted it. Jesus fed the poor and hungry and taught the disciples the practice of sharing with those in need. He brought the way of deliverance. The kingdom began in Jesus.

The Injustice of Domination

Reading through the Gospels, it is hard to miss the fact that Jesus often confronted the injustice of domination and sought to bring about deliverance through the practice of mutual servanthood. For example, Mk 11:27-33//Mt 21:23-27//Lk 20:1-8 is a controversial drama in which the religious leaders challenged Jesus' authority. The temple scribes, "acting as proxies for the powers that be" (Herzog, *Jesus, Justice, and the Reign of God*, 234), contended that they and the chief priest should have the authority. By asking them to name the authority by which John the Baptist prophesied, Jesus emphasized the point that God did act through prophets who were not under the control and domination of the temple authorities.

In Mk 2:3-12//Mt 9:2-8//Lk 5:18-26 Jesus healed the paralytic and declared his sin forgiven. "The healing indicates that God's power is at work, confirming the identity and role of Jesus" as God's mediator. "This incenses the scribes. . . . From their point of view, the temple is the only place where sins can be forgiven and purity restored. This is the exclusive right of priests using the sacrificial system. To protect that monopoly is their likely intent in this clash" (Herzog, *Jesus, Justice, and the Reign of God*, 124-29). Similarly, in Luke 13:10-17 Jesus is criticized by the ruler of the synagogue for healing a crippled woman on the sabbath, and he confronts him, saying, "Does not each of you on the sabbath untie his ox or his donkey from the manger, and lead it away to give it water? And ought not this woman, a daughter of Abraham whom Satan bound for eighteen long years, be set free from this bondage on the sabbath day?" The rabbis of Jesus' day agreed that the Torah could be set aside to save life, or even to heal an injury, but a chronic condition could wait (Young, *Jesus the Jewish Theologian*, 108-11). Jesus deliberately contested their reading of the Torah: he healed the woman with a chronic illness on the spot. Jesus also confronted the domination of the Pharisees over sabbath practices that prohibited feeding the hungry and healing a man with the withered arm. "But they were filled with fury and discussed with one another what they might do to Jesus" (Lk 6:6-11//Mt 12:9-14//Mk 3:1-6).

Jesus taught that "the scribes and the Pharisees . . . do not practice what they teach. They tie up heavy burdens, hard to bear, and lay them on the shoulders of others; but they themselves are unwilling to lift a finger to move them. . . . They love to have the place of honor at banquets" (Mt 23:1-6//Lk 11:46). In Matthew 12:22-37 Jesus criticized the Pharisees for bearing false witness (claiming that he cast out demons by the authority of Beelzebul and thus lacked proper authority) and told them they would be condemned on the day of judgment for the careless words they uttered. "The point here is . . . to put up a barrier against the elevation of some above others and the pride that so

naturally accompanies such differentiation. . . . Behind this emphasis lies a polemic against the *de facto* authority of the scribes and Pharisees" (Hagner, *Matthew 1—13*, 661).

We see judgment on unjust domination in Lk 12:42-46//Mt 24:45-51: "But
if that slave . . . begins to beat the other slaves, men and women, and to eat and
drink and get drunk, the master of that slave will come on a day when he does
not expect him, and at an hour that he does not know, and will cut him in pieces, and put him with the unfaithful." And Jesus is surely criticizing unjust
domination in Mk 10:42//Mt 20:25-26//Lk 22:25-26: "Among the Gentiles
those whom they recognize as their rulers lord it over them, and their great
ones are tyrants over them. But it is not so among you; but whoever wishes to
become great among you must be your servant." Domination is also a theme
in Mark 12: when Jesus asked the Pharisees and Herodians to bring him a de-
narius, "he said to them 'Whose head is this, and whose title?' They answered,
'The emperor's'" (Mk 12:13-17). The title of divinity for Caesar imprinted on
the coin was certainly a claim of domination, and Jesus' answer made clear
that God, not Caesar, is Lord.

In much of the tradition in Isaiah, other nations are identified as the oppressors from which God's people need deliverance. But Isaiah turned his prophecy
in the direction of peacemaking, redemption of the Gentiles and their inclusion
in the community. Jesus completed that turn, identifying most of the domination
as internal to Israel, rather than blaming it only on hated foreigners, and calling
for repentance for their own sins. But he also criticized the Roman authorities,
who, Jesus said, "love to lord it over" people, and who were the head of the
"domination system" (Wink, *Engaging the Powers*, 1992; Borg, *Conflict, Holiness,
and Politics*, 10, 12-14). Clearly we have seen that Jesus saw this domination as
unjust, and he taught and practiced the way of deliverance from the injustice of
domination—the way of mutual servanthood.

The Injustice of Violence

When the Pharisees warned Jesus that Herod wanted to kill him, he said, "Go
and tell that fox for me, 'Listen, I am casting out demons and performing cures
today and tomorrow, . . . and the next day I must be on my way, because it is
impossible for a prophet to be killed outside of Jerusalem'" (Lk 13:31-33). N. T.
Wright (*Jesus and the Victory of God*, 579), says, "The violent fate of prophets
must have weighed heavily upon the mind of [Jesus]," who looked on John the
Baptist as his forerunner.

Often we do not notice that Jesus criticized the scribes and Pharisees for
their violence. But the Pharisees taught separation from the impurity that
comes from the outside, and that led to zealous religious hatred against the
Romans. They were the primary people who supported the violent insurrec-

tion against Rome in A.D. 66, which led to the destruction of Jerusalem and the temple and the exile of Israel for twenty centuries. Jesus sensed their hatred of him and their propensity toward violence against prophets. He said to them, "Woe to you, scribes and Pharisees, hypocrites! . . . You are descendants of those who murdered the prophets. . . . Therefore I send you prophets, sages, and scribes, some of whom you will kill and crucify, and some you will flog in your synagogues and pursue from town to town, so that upon you may come all the righteous blood shed on earth" (Mt 23:29-36). Jesus' parable of the tenants confronted those in authority for doing violence against the Lord's servants: "Some they beat, and others they killed. Finally he sent [his son] to them saying, 'They will respect my son.' But those tenants said to one another, 'This is the heir; come, let us kill him and the inheritance will be ours.' So they seized him, killed him, and threw him out of the vineyard." Jesus concluded by predicting judgment, and the chief priests and the Pharisees "realized that he had told this parable against them" (Mk 12:1-9//Mt 21:33-46//Lk 20:9-19//Is 5:1-7).

Jesus not only predicted the destruction of the temple six times, but he called on Israel's leaders to repent for their violent spirit and instead to learn the kingdom practices of peacemaking. He wept over Jerusalem when it did not learn the practices of peace: "Jerusalem, Jerusalem, the city that kills the prophets and stones those who are sent to it! How often have I desired to gather your children together as a hen gathers her brood under wings, and you were not willing!" (Mt 23:37-39//Lk 13:34). Jesus wept over Jerusalem again later, saying, "If you, even you, had only recognized on this day the things that make for peace!" (Lk 19:41).

In addition, Jesus taught transforming initiatives of peacemaking (see chapter seven) in direct contrast to the guerrilla movements emerging in his time against Roman domination and economic exploitation. Eventually these movements of insurrection boiled over in the year 66 into massive revolt, which was crushed by Rome in A.D. 70. Jerusalem and the temple were destroyed, thus fulfilling Jesus' prophecies that if the people and the powerful leaders did not repent for their hatred of their enemies, the temple would be destroyed and people would need to flee. Because of Jesus' teachings and practices, the Christian movement became a Jewish peace movement, and Christian Jews did not participate in the revolt but instead fled Jerusalem (N. T. Wright, *Jesus and the Victory of God*, 151-60, 250-53, 268-71, 296, 385; Borg, *Conflict, Holiness, and Politics in the Teaching of Jesus*, 51-65, 70ff., 77, 79-83, 175-81).

Jesus agreed with the word of God in Isaiah: violence and war are unjust; God cares deeply for peace, and Jesus shared his Father's passion, weeping over Jerusalem because it knew not the ways of peace. Through his life he taught the way of deliverance from violence.

The Injustice of Exclusion from Community

Jesus confronted anyone who would exclude enemies from the circle of love taught in Leviticus 19:18 by teaching that we should love not only our friends but also our enemies (Mt 5:43-48). His parable of the compassionate Samaritan (Lk 10:29-37) confronted priests, Levites and anyone else who hated or excluded Samaritans or other ethnic groups from the circle of compassion. And through the parable of the prodigal son, Jesus confronted people unwilling to welcome sinners, outcasts or, perhaps, Gentiles (Lk 15:11-32).

Jesus' interchange with the Syrophoenician woman in Matthew 15 reveals his mission to extend the kingdom of God to Gentiles as well as Israelites (Mt 15:21-28//Mk 7:24-30). Similarly, in Luke 4:24-29, Jesus told the religious leaders that God sent prophets not only to Israel but also to a widow of Sidon and to a Syrian (both Gentiles). In response, the religious leaders rose up in anger, put him out of the city and were about to throw him headlong from the brow of a hill. These passages suggest that Jesus initiated the mission to the Gentiles. (Some scholars, however, debate this, noting that the book of Acts [1:4, 8; 2:1ff.] tells how the mission to the Gentiles opened widely only later, through the guidance of the Holy Spirit.)

To the moneychangers taking over the court reserved for Gentiles, Jesus quoted Isaiah 56:7: "Is it not written, 'My house shall be called a house of prayer for all the nations [Gentiles]?'" Eventually Jesus withdrew, realizing that he had provoked the Pharisees enough at this point by breaking their sabbath taboos (Mt 12:1-14). Though he continued to heal people, he asked the recipients of his healing to remain quiet about it. Matthew wrote of Jesus' actions by quoting Isaiah 42:1-4 from the Greek Septuagint translation: "I will put my Spirit upon him, and he shall proclaim justice to the Gentiles."

Confronting the exclusiveness of the Pharisees, Jesus called Matthew, the tax collector, to be part of the community of disciples. When the Pharisees murmured against Jesus and his disciples for eating and drinking with tax collectors, he told them that he came to heal the sinners and to call them to repentance rather than the righteous (Lk 5:27-32//Mt 9:9-13//Mk 2:13-17). His teaching that we should let both the wheat and the weeds grow together until the harvest (Mt 13:24-30) was set against the Pharisees' and Essenes' attempts to achieve holiness through separation from all that is impure (Borg, *Conflict, Holiness, and Politics,* chap. 3). The Pharisees were offended by Jesus' conspicuous refusal to follow their purity practices that separated people into the pure and the outcasts (Mt 15:1-9). Quoting Isaiah 29:13, Jesus replied:

> This people honors me with their lips,
>   but their hearts are far from me;

in vain do they worship me,
    teaching human precepts as doctrines.

"The Pharisees' core value is purity. . . . Jesus' core value is forgiveness, because he views God as a God of mercy" (Herzog, *Jesus, Justice, and the Reign of God*, 176-77).

In Jesus' historical situation, "the quest for holiness became the dominant
cultural dynamic of Israel's corporate life," and it meant "separation from everything impure" (Borg, *Conflict, Holiness and Politics in the Teaching of Jesus*, 66-
67). For some of the Essenes, it meant separating from society, moving to the
monastery-like life at Qumran, near the Dead Sea. For the Pharisees, it meant
tithing everything agricultural, practicing ritual cleansing and purity of table
practices and not eating with those who were unpure, including those who
did not practice such rituals and those who were outcasts or foreigners. Their
"major sanction was social ostracism" (Borg, *Conflict, Holiness and Politics in the
Teaching of Jesus*, 83-84). For them, "the holiness of the Temple required metic-
ulous observance of the Temple ritual, protecting the Temple from unclean-
ness, and excluding Gentiles from its courts" (Borg, *Conflict, Holiness and
Politics in the Teaching of Jesus*, 72ff.). This created large numbers of Jews who
were considered outcasts. Jesus reprimanded their exclusiveness, saying,
"Woe to you scribes and Pharisees! For you tithe mint and dill and cummin,
and have neglected the weightier matters of the law, justice and mercy and
faithfulness" (Mt 23:23). "Woe to you, scribes and Pharisees, hypocrites! . . .
You shut the kingdom of heaven against people" (Mt 23:13).

Jesus' dramatic practice of table fellowship with outcasts and the unclean
was a deliberate demonstration of his fundamental disagreement with the
central practice of the Pharisees—their ritual purity at meals. It was "deliberately provocative" (Borg, *Conflict, Holiness and Politics in the Teaching of Jesus*,
97). Jesus saw evil not as a foreign, outside force from which Israel could separate but as an inner loyalty and practice of which we all need to repent (N. T.
Wright, *Jesus and the Victory of God*, 459-61).

Jesus' healings on the sabbath may have been further confrontations of
Pharisaic purity practice. The man who was crippled at the pool of Bethesda
was so much an outcast that he had no one to bring him to the water, yet Jesus
healed him and restored him to community. The faith of the woman with a
flow of blood enabled her to touch Jesus' coat, and Jesus welcomed that touch,
that contact, curing her and thus restoring her to community. Often Jesus
healed illnesses by touching, a personal restoration to community, and he regularly instructed the healed person to submit to the priests in the temple or to
go back to their community.

Jesus agreed with Isaiah: exclusion was deeply unjust. Isaiah's proclamation that outcasts would return, Gentiles would be welcomed to the temple, and God would give forgiveness and restore community was God's word. Jesus taught that God cared deeply for sinners and outcasts, and during his time on earth he cared deeply for them (us) and brought the way of deliverance.

Conclusion

It is customary in making the case for social justice to spend most of one's time in the Old Testament, and especially in the prophets. We could have doubled the page length of this chapter by treating the Old Testament witness on justice in detail. We could have expanded it to a book by treating the leading philosophical theories of justice named in the introduction. Instead, here we have focused on Jesus. We have indicated why it is crucial to ground a Christian concern for justice with Jesus himself. Seeing how directly Jesus taught, embodied and fulfilled the prophet Isaiah's four themes of justice gives us a dramatic new appreciation for the concreteness of Jesus' passion for delivering justice. Jesus died for our sins, including our injustice. His confronting the injustice of the powerful was a major reason why they wanted him crucified. When we see his concern for justice—for an end to unjust economic structures, unjust domination, unjust violence and unjust exclusion from community— we cannot help but rethink our entire picture of what Jesus was about in his preaching and teaching. We cannot help but think that if he was that committed to justice in his context, we are required to be just as concerned about justice in our own.

Those who do not routinely suffer injustice frequently get lulled into a lack of concern for others who do suffer it. At the heart of Christian discipleship is overcoming that privileged lull, if that is our situation, and entering into the pain and injustice of a suffering world—the way that God our Maker and Jesus our Savior did.

Perhaps this chapter can help us see more points of contact with the practice of justice and the struggle against injustice. None of us wants to be blocked from our way of making a living and feeding our families. None of us wants to be dominated by others and violated by huge concentrations of power. None of us wants to be a victim of bullying or violent crime or terrorism. None of us wants to be ostracized or excluded from community. Fear of, or the experience of, injustice reminds us of how precious justice really is. And when we see how Jesus fought for justice and died when the powerful whom he was confronting for their injustice conspired to kill him and the disciples betrayed him, we have yet one more very profound reason for repenting and following him.

SECTION VI:

Relationships of
Justice and Love

Justice and love must characterize all of a Christian's relationships. This section considers four arenas in which these norms are put to the test: truth-telling, race, economics and creation care.

The order of these chapters moves from local to global, from personal through social to transhuman. Jesus' teachings challenge us to attend to justice and love in the most intimate personal relationships, in broad intergroup relations, in the ordering of national and international economic systems, and in the way in which we relate to the ecosystem and other creatures.

Yet it would be too simple to think of these spheres that shape life and death for all persons as ascending merely from personal to social to ecological, for each has personal and social, individual and corporate dimensions. Moreover, each needs more than only right thinking; each needs practices by Christians and churches that obey the sovereignty of God as revealed in Jesus Christ our Lord through the Holy Spirit who empowers us.

18

TRUTHTELLING

—

Again, you have heard that it was said to those of ancient times, "You shall not swear
falsely, but carry out the vows you have made to the Lord." But I say to you, Do not swear
at all, either by heaven, for it is the throne of God, or by the earth, for it is his footstool, or
by Jerusalem, for it is the city of the great King. And do not swear by your head, for you
cannot make one hair white or black. Let your word be "Yes, Yes" or "No, No"; anything
more than this comes from the evil one.

MATTHEW 5:33-37

One of the very best reasons to base a textbook in Christian ethics on the
actual teachings of Jesus, especially the Sermon on the Mount, is that it forces
us to consider moral issues that might not otherwise make it onto the agenda.
Here we have come upon exactly this situation. A reading of Matthew 5:33-37,
the fourth of the triads in the Sermon, requires us to devote our attention to the
moral issues associated with truthtelling.

Despite the attention to truth as a moral issue both in the Ten Commandments (Ex 20:16//Deut 5:20) and the Sermon, contemporary introductory
treatments of both Christian ethics and philosophical ethics rarely take on the
issue. Of the fifty-plus ethics survey texts we surveyed, only six of them (Murray, *Principles of Conduct;* Hoose, *Christian Ethics;* Hooke, *Virtuous Persons, Vicious Deeds;* Smedes, *Mere Morality;* Stone, *Ultimate Imperative;* Curran, *Catholic
Moral Tradition Today*) contain a section devoted to truthtelling or much sustained attention to the issue. The omission is a general problem in Protestant
ethics, with both mainline and evangelical texts neglecting the theme. Catholic
ethics tends to do a bit better, oriented as it is to the theme of truth by its
grounding in natural law emphases on discernment of moral truth via conscience (cf. John Paul II, *Veritatis Splendor*).

The mainline realist Christian ethicist Ronald Stone does significantly better, offering a perceptive analysis of temptations to become involved in lying that arise from nationalism and the competition of power (*Ultimate Imperative,* 99-112). This illustrates our thesis that character ethics is insufficient without a critical social theory, which John Paul has embedded in his Roman Catholic tradition and Stone has in his Niebuhrian realism about injustice arising from imbalance of power. Stone and Smedes are both prodded by their attention to the Ten Commandments to deal perceptively with the question, which supports our urging that Christian ethics make concrete biblical connection. In the Sermon on the Mount, Jesus sets the model by making concrete connection with the Ten Commandments.

The reasons for this lack of attention to truth probably vary. If ethics is understood and taught as divided into "methodology" and "issues" sections, as it so often is, truth seems to slip through the cracks. The fact that there is such a thing as moral truth, and that ethics is the quest to discern what that truth might be, is generally presupposed in Christian ethics texts and thus left undiscussed except perhaps as a case study in moral decision making (see Clark and Rakestraw, *Readings in Christian Ethics,* vol. 1, chap. 3, discussed below). When attention then turns to actual "issues" in Christian ethics, truth is left behind as abortion, euthanasia, war and the environment, for example, take center stage.

It is also true that certain issues or themes in ethics do not push their way into our consciousness until we perceive a problem. This is one reason why the biblical emphasis on justice, discussed in the last chapter, has been largely neglected in affluent white North American churches. Not being routinely victimized by injustice, the comfortable have tended not to notice the problem—but it has rarely fallen off the radar screen in the black church tradition. As far as truthtelling is concerned, we are now, unfortunately, beginning to notice the problem.

This is not to say that discussion of truthtelling and its various clever and disastrous alternatives is absent from all public discussion of ethics. As we will attempt to show in the latter part of this chapter, consideration of truthfulness as a moral issue has emerged in several critically important genres of public ethics. Those writing under conditions of oppression such as the last century's many totalitarian regimes and segregationist America, frequently reflected (and still reflect) on truthtelling. Rampant public cynicism about public communication in American political life has sparked discussion of the place of truthful speech in politics. And the burgeoning field of biomedical ethics consistently examines truthtelling within its discussion of professional responsibilities in medicine. Meanwhile, it must be said that the postmodern turn in Western intellectual life has created an environment in which the very existence of "capital T Truth" has been called into question. So it may be that truthtelling is of necessity forcing its way onto our agenda these days.

We believe that our society is in a battle for truth. Society's power relations powerfully shape the sense of truth held by Christians and non-Christians. Several forces are undermining some of our traditions that taught practices of truthtelling and promise-keeping, and we believe this is a major threat to the health of society, its interactions, its members (us) and its basic trust that is essential to shalom.

1. Families in which both parents work or where there is a single parent during the children's infancy tend to produce children who do not bond deeply with their parents or imbibe the importance of covenant relationships. *Result:* a society of people not having learned to take responsibility in the family and so shifting responsibility to "someone else."

2. The shift in work culture due to corporate mergers and downsizing of work forces in order to be more competitive leads to the idea that profits are all that matters and the ends justify the means. *Result:* "the bottom line" becomes the societal metaphor for "the result that matters and defines the issue" in many areas of life and "the net profit shown on the books."

3. The free-market ideology says that corporations should be free to do whatever they calculate is in their self-interest, and checks and balances, regulation and honest auditing are a bad interference. *Result:* the ideology of laissez-faire me-ism begins to be the model for the rest of life as well—in the realms of sexual relations, marriage, economic justice, international relations and decisions about when to tell the truth and deliver on promises.

4. Political competition is strategized by media consultants, poll-takers and even experts in how to manipulate Christians to vote for a certain party or candidate. The point of communication is often not to convey the truth accurately but to craft a vivid sound bite and manipulate the news to achieve the spin that will best enhance your power. *Result:* a well-documented steady decline in people's trust in and identification with political parties and governmental institutions as well as business corporations.

5. With the crumbling of Enlightenment-influenced universal claims of truth, and the not-yet completely constructed ways of establishing truth in a postmodern time, even church leaders fashion their messages to avoid confrontation and calls for repentance. *Result:* no real training in discipleship.

We advocate covenant ethics and the interpretation of the power realities of life in terms of their implicit as well as explicit covenants. These are some of the areas of life in which covenant ethics are relevant:

1. Parenting. Parents should see having babies as entering into a covenant to be as faithfully present to them as possible, and they should teach children regular covenant responsibilities and chores in the family, so producing healthier, more cooperative and responsible people. Welfare reform policies and corporate work-scheduling policies should value and protect the responsibility of child-raising.

2. *Business policies.* Corporations receive the benefits of an educated workforce, a large base of well-paid consumers, access to raw materials and quality supplies, and a society of law, order and peace. So it is right that they enter into a covenant to take their own responsibility for justice and societal and public welfare.

3. *Economic power.* When corporations amass enormous quantities of economic power and influence, they enter into a covenant to accept the checks and balances against corruption that long history has shown us is necessary if concentration of power is not to produce concentration of corruption.

4. *Government.* Entry into the public trust of governmental leadership is implicit entry into a covenant to foster a civic culture of honest information for the people and cooperation with investigative reporting so that the people are honestly informed. This helps the people learn to fulfill their implicit covenant of participation in the active consent of the governed and participation in the civic culture of caring about justice that has compassion for the powerless and the overlooked.

5. *Church leadership.* Entry into leadership of churches is entry into a covenant to model and spread discipleship to Jesus Christ and tell the truth, rather than simply to tell only what will not cause people discomfort or disagreement.

In sum, we advocate that society be understood as made up of implicit and explicit covenants of responsibility. We advocate that the various spheres of life be interpreted and understood in terms of the covenants of truthfulness and responsibility that are crucial for their very existence, for the basic trust necessary for a healthy society and for human flourishing. Fostering truthtelling requires a shift in understanding and in organizing the underlying power relations in society that shape our interactions so that they are accountable to basic covenants of responsibility. So Jesus, in the tradition of the prophets, consistently confronted the powers and authorities of his society, calling them to their responsibility in the covenantal traditions of Israel.

In this chapter we will follow our customary pattern by first considering what Jesus had to say about truthful speech, examining the Sermon on the Mount against the backdrop of the Old Testament. Then we will expand our search to other parts of Scripture and consider the issue of living in truth as Christian disciples. Finally we will consider possible exceptions to the mandate of truthtelling under conditions of oppression and injustice.

Jesus and Truth: "Let Your Word Be Yes, Yes"

Matthew 5:33-37 begins with Jesus restating two aspects of familiar Old Testament teaching related to oath taking: "You shall not swear falsely" and "Carry out the vows you have made to the Lord." Both restatements refer to specific aspects of Old Testament teaching (Lev 19:12; Num 30:2; Deut 23:21-23; Ps 50:14) and traditional Jewish practice that continued in Jesus' day (cf. Mt 23:16-22; 26:63, 72-74; Acts 23:12; Heb 6:16-18).

Old Testament narratives constantly depict various figures swearing oaths or taking sacred vows. Words meaning "oath" or "vow" are used scores of times in the Hebrew Bible. Abraham (Gen 21:22-34), Jacob (Gen 25:33; 28:20), Joseph (Gen 50:5), Joshua (Josh 6:26), Hannah (1 Sam 1:11), Saul (1 Sam 14:24), David (1 Sam 20:17), Ezra (Ezra 10:5) and Nehemiah (Neh 13:25) are among the Old Testament personalities who swore oaths or vows. God is also regularly depicted as making oaths and vows, including an oath to Abraham to give Israel the Promised Land and to David to maintain a king in the Davidic line (Gen 22:16-18; 26:3; Num 11:12; Deut 6:23; 29:12; Ps 132:11; Jer 11:5). The practice of making vows is also attested in the Psalms (Ps 24:4; 63:11) and the Wisdom literature (Prov 20:25; Eccles 5:4-5; 8:2; 9:2). In none of these many texts is oath taking or vow swearing in itself critiqued, though Ecclesiastes mentions that there are some who "shun" oaths (Eccles 9:2; cf 5:4-5).

Rabbinic literature carefully distinguished between oaths and vows, and discussion of the issues involved with each continues in Jewish thought today (Dreyfus, "Vows and Oaths," 716-17). In a vow a person pledges before God and in God's honor that some item or act is forbidden or required of him or her (Garland, "Oaths and Swearing," 577; Dreyfus, "Vows and Oaths," 716-17). Vows were (and are) often uttered during times of distress (Gen 28:20-22) or as an expression of thanksgiving for kindnesses received (Ps 116:16-18). Their very spontaneity makes them susceptible to rashness and thus lack of follow-through, a pattern which leads the Talmud to a generally negative stance on them despite their biblical precedent.

The rabbis divided oaths into two kinds. *Assertive oaths* involved a person swearing "that they have or have not done something, usually in a judicial context to substantiate or reject testimony" (Garland, "Oaths and Swearing," 577). People confirmed their words by a sacred oath in order to communicate that their truthfulness could be counted on. Truthfulness was (as it is today) especially important in legal contexts due to the importance of the matters under consideration and the potential injustice that can be done when lies are told in court. Such truthfulness is essential to the functioning of the judicial system and the broader practice of public justice. This is why the treatment of truthtelling in the Decalogue mentions bearing "false witness," which clearly denotes perjury in a legal context (Ex 20:16//Deut 5:20; Deut 19:18-19; Prov 12:17; 25:18). The public function of oath taking in arbitrating legal disputes is strikingly illustrated in Exodus 22:11, in which a dispute over an injured or missing animal in which there are no witnesses is to be settled simply by the accused taking an oath that he has not harmed or stolen the animal (cf. Heb 6:16-18).

Voluntary oaths, on the other hand, were broader, with a person swearing that they would or would not do something (Garland, "Oaths and Swearing," 577-78), which makes them quite similar to vows. Old Testament narratives frequently include oaths of this latter type, essentially solemn promises exchanged between people, or between a person and God. In this sense, the connotation of the word "oath" *(shebuah)* is often close to that of "covenant" *(berith)*. The seriousness of the promise was vouchsafed by the taking of an oath. Such oaths were seen as legally, morally and spiritually binding, and under no circumstances were they to be broken, even if the oath was uttered rashly or foolishly (as in the disturbing Judg 11:29-40, discussed by L. R. Bailey, "Oath," 625; cf. Mk 6:23 and Herod's rash oath resulting in John's death). "When a man makes a vow to the LORD, or swears an oath to bind himself by a pledge, he shall not break his word; he shall do according to all that proceeds out of his mouth" (Num 30:2; cf. Deut 23:21-23). In Old Testament narratives, oaths often emerged in situations of crisis or mistrust between people. Oath-taking signaled the intent of the parties involved to refrain from harming each other and to keep the promises made. Thus oaths furthered sometimes fragile trust. Here we are in the territory of our emphasis throughout this book: the importance of *covenant* and *trust* and *information integrity* in society and in our ethics.

Oath taking involved various formulaic statements intended to communicate seriousness and promise honesty, much as today. We say things like "I swear on a stack of Bibles/my mother's grave" or "Cross my heart and hope to die." Old Testament narratives offer oaths based on God's house, the Lord's life ("As the LORD lives"—1 Kings 18:10; Jer 4:2; 38:16; Hos 4:15), the Lord's name (Neh 13:25), the Lord's faithfulness (Is 65:16) or simply the Lord (Gen 24:3; 1 Sam 24:21; 2 Sam 19:7). Apparently in Jesus' day, respect for the divine name had led to oath-taking based on *symbols for God's name* rather than God's name itself, such as the temple altar, the gold of the sanctuary, heaven, earth and Jerusalem (Mt 5:34-35; 23:16-22). In each case the vow-taker swears by something holy, sacred or greater than himself (cf. Heb 6:16), perhaps in combination with making the oath in a sacred space, such as the temple (1 Kings 8:31//2 Chron 6:22), all in order to vouchsafe truthfulness of speech.

When the prophets took up the issue of oaths and vows, they attacked several problems. These included Israelites taking oaths in the name of other gods (Jer 12:16; Amos 8:14; Zeph 1:5), a stark violation of the first commandment. But the prophets also attacked oath breaking (Ezek 16:59) as well as "swearing falsely," which seems to mean making oaths that one has no intention of keeping or making statements under oath that are outright lies (Jer 5:2; 7:9, Mal 3:5;

cf. Lev 6:3; 19:12). These are the traditional teachings that Jesus noted as he began his discussion of this issue in Matthew 5:33.

This review of Jewish practice related to oaths and vows helps us get a sense of their omnipresence in Jewish religious life and culture. What exactly Jesus intended his disciples to do about it, however, is disputed. The crux of the issue lies in how we interpret the next four verses. Matthew 5:34 is normally understood as the heart of his teaching on this issue: "But I say to you, Do not swear at all." The Greek verb here is *omosai*, an infinitive rather than an imperative (though at least implicitly imperatival); when it appears again in verse 36 it is in the subjunctive. The only imperative verb is found in the climax of this teaching, verse 37—"let your word be Yes, Yes, or No, No."

Christians have traditionally understood the force of this teaching to be a (hyperbolic or literal) prohibition of oath taking or any kind of swearing (Garland, "Oaths and Swearing," 578). The church fathers Justin, Irenaeus, Tertullian and Origen believed this was Jesus' teaching (Davies and Allison, *Critical and Exegetical Commentary*, 1:535). The Quakers and Anabaptists revived this line of interpretation and refused to take any kind of oath at all, even in legal settings, often invoking much wrath upon their heads for their refusal. Other Christian groups have tended to see this teaching as enjoining honesty but not the rejection of (at least judicial) oaths, which are viewed as perhaps not good in themselves but sometimes necessary (Augustine's position, quoted in Davies and Allison, *Critical and Exegetical Commentary*, 1:535, also the stance of Luther, *Sermon on the Mount and the Magnificat*, 102-3, and Calvin, *Harmony of the Gospels*, 392-33).

Our triadic reading of the Sermon on the Mount leads us to interpret Matthew 5:34-36 as primarily illustrative of a vicious cycle related to untruthful speech. As such, prohibiting oath-taking is not where the primary emphasis should be placed in interpretation and application. What helps us get here is noticing the perversion of the practice of oath taking in Jesus' own context, starkly revealed by a passage later in Matthew. It is found in Jesus' blistering attack on Israel's religious leaders, and is worth quoting in full:

> Woe to you, blind guides, who say, "Whoever swears by the sanctuary is bound by nothing, but whoever swears by the gold of the sanctuary is bound by the oath." You blind fools! For which is greater, the gold or the sanctuary that has made the gold sacred? And you say, "Whoever swears by the altar is bound by nothing, but whoever swears by the gift that is on the altar is bound by the oath." How blind you are! For which is greater, the gift or the altar that makes the gift sacred? So whoever swears by the altar, swears by it and by everything on it; and whoever swears by the sanctuary, swears by it and by the one who dwells in it; and whoever swears by heaven, swears by the throne of God and by the one who is seated upon it. (Mt 23:16-22)

Apparently, some scribes and Pharisees were using the oath system to draw fine distinctions between oaths that must be carried out and those that need not. Jesus was naming and attacking practices that subverted the very purpose of the oath tradition. Oaths and vows, which had been intended originally as sacred guarantors of truthfulness, commitment or covenant, were now being thrown around casually or manipulated in a manner that somehow delineated binding vows and oaths from a nonbinding and deceptive imitation.

Jesus was appalled at this practice, and, as Garland put it, "the infringement on God's majesty" involved in routinely calling on God as a witness to fallible human speech (in Garland, "Oaths and Swearing," 578; cf. Gundry, *Matthew*, 93). Notice that nowhere in the Matthew 23 passage did Jesus explicitly abolish oath taking; he did attack the *corruption* of oath taking in a system of hypocritical and hair-splitting casuistry (cf. Mk 7:1-13). As Donald Hagner puts it: "It seems to be assumed that oath taking is in practice more often a means of avoiding what is promised than of performing it" (Hagner, *Matthew 14—28*, 127). And, to make things worse, this was accomplished by using symbols for God's name to fool people into believing that one's words were truthful and trustworthy.

But whether this requires disciples to interpret Jesus as commanding us to reject any oath-taking under any circumstances remains an open question. It is interesting, tracing this theme out further in the New Testament, that, in a text that closely relates to Matthew 5:33-37, James argues for a "no oath" stance (Jas 5:12), whereas Paul takes various oaths and vows and even offers oaths in traditional Jewish style to support his claims in several of his epistles (2 Cor 1:23; Gal 1:20; Phil 1:8; cf. 2 Cor 11:31). The practice is used without criticism as an illustration in Hebrews 6:13-20, and an angel swears by "him who lives forever and ever" in Revelation 10:6. Later Christian differences of opinion about oath taking are clearly foreshadowed in the New Testament itself, with those divisions apparent among biblical interpreters themselves (compare Garland, "Oaths and Swearing," 577-78, with Davies and Allison, *Critical and Exegetical Commentary*, 1:535-36).

However, if we view Matthew 5:34-36 as primarily articulating a vicious cycle, it does remind us that oath-taking, at least as a means of guaranteeing truthfulness, has an inherent danger in it. It establishes a two-tier system of speech. When I speak under oath or swear that my words are true, then you as my listener are supposed to be able to have confidence in my words. But what, then, is the status of what I say when I am not swearing or not under oath? Implicitly, at least, such words carry lesser weight. They may or may not be true. *The very existence of an oath-level of speech threatens to render (or unveil) everyday speech as less trustworthy.* The Greek-Jewish theologian Philo saw this: "The mere fact of swearing casts suspicion on the trustworthiness" of the one who swears" (in Garland, "Oaths and Swearing," 577).

The oath-level really only exists because people cannot be counted on to speak truthfully under normal circumstances. Otherwise, there would be no need for it. But if people cannot be counted on to tell the truth when not under oath, then why should they be trusted to do so when they *are* under oath? If truthfulness, in and of itself, is not valued at all times, then no one's speech can be fully trusted. And of course the whole situation is worsened beyond repair if I then introduce various exceptions or escape clauses within the oath system that I do employ, or if I sometimes use oaths cynically to fool people into believing my lies.

This is why Jesus concluded this teaching with the transforming initiative enjoining straightforward and truthful speech: "Let your yes be yes and your no be no." The way of deliverance from this vicious cycle of verbal untrustworthiness is simply to practice truthtelling all the time. Truthfulness rather than any kind of deceit is a characteristic of the inbreaking reign of God. The Swiss New Testament scholar Hans Weder catches this when he says, "In church history, again and again this teaching is reduced to the legalistic, a Christian may swear no oath." But that "passes right by the actual intention of Jesus: not on the not-swearing does he really aim, but on the truthfulness of every word" (*Die "Rede der Reden,"* 127). This interpretation is consistent with others offered in this volume—we view Jesus' teaching as dynamic instruction for how disciples can participate in the dawning kingdom, rather than as a set of new legal restrictions. Our focus must shift from whether or not we should swear oaths in court to how to become truthful people.

Jesus closes this teaching with the stark explanation: "anything more than this comes from the evil one." The resort to various vows and oaths invites a pattern of deceit and falsehood that is ultimately traceable to Satan, the father of lies (Jn 8:44), whose deceptive speech in the Garden began the human descent toward sin and death, initiating the pattern of untrustworthy speech that so characterizes the human condition.

Living in Truth as Christian Disciples

It is striking that of the thirty-one uses of the word *truth (alētheia)* in the Gospels, all but six of them are found in the Gospel of John. *Truth* is a key word in the Johannine literature, appearing as a noun twenty-five times in the Gospel and twenty times in the three letters of John (Morris, *Gospel According to John,* 260). A close reading of this strand of the New Testament literature shows several things about how the Johannine community linked truth with Jesus and with discipleship.

For John, Jesus is the embodiment of truth. He is described as "full of grace and truth" in the prologue to the Gospel (Jn 1:14). In John 14:6 Jesus identified himself with the truth: "I am the way, the truth, and the life." In preparing to take leave of his disciples, he promised the Holy Spirit, three times denoting him as "the Spirit of truth" (Jn 14:17; 15:26; 16:13; cf 1 Jn 5:6— "the Spirit is the truth").

This usage of the term "truth" suggests connections to Hebrew understandings of God's character as truthful. Hebrew words for "truth" and "truly" (*emeth* and *amen*), or phrases describing God as "the God of truth" (Ps 31:5; Is 65:16; cf. Rev 15:3), point to God's reliability, fidelity and trustworthiness. It is not just that God speaks truth but that *God is true;* that is, God is characterized by fidelity and is reliable in keeping his commitments. Thus, for John to link Jesus with truth, or for Jesus to make this connection himself, is to claim not just that Jesus spoke truthfully but that he embodied the character of the God who is "true."

Yet for John it was also true that Jesus was the ultimate bearer and communicator of truth. He revealed reality over against mere appearance, truth over against falsehood (cf. Morris, *Gospel According to John,* 259). "Grace and truth came through Jesus Christ" (Jn 1:17). In a bitter dispute with the religious leaders, Jesus described himself as "a man who has told you the truth that I heard from God" (Jn 8:40). He told the truth, but his words were rejected (Jn 8:45-46). The Spirit of truth would continue the work that Jesus had been doing, of guiding his followers "into all the truth" (Jn 16:13). Jesus said to Pilate that "for this reason I came into the world, to testify to the truth" (Jn 18:37). Pilate responded with his famous and cynical rejoinder: "What is truth?" (Jn 18:38).

Followers of Jesus know the truth (1 Jn 2:21; 4:6; 2 Jn 1:1) and tell the truth (Jn 19:35). But more profoundly, disciples are "from the truth" (1 Jn 3:19) and "in the truth" (2 Jn 1:1); the "truth abides in [them]" (1 Jn 1:2). They are made holy, or sanctified, in the truth (Jn 17:17).

Yet this mystical interpenetration of disciple and truth is threatened by any kind of disobedience on the disciple's part. The truth is something that disciples "walk" in (2 Jn 1:4; 3 Jn 1:3-4); that is, the truth is lived. Failure to live the truth raises questions about whether the truth exists in such persons (1 Jn 1:8; 2:4); that is, whether they truly love Jesus, because the one who loves Jesus keeps his commands (Jn 14:15). "If you hold to my teaching, you are really my disciples. Then you will know the truth, and the truth will set you free" (Jn 8:31-32 NIV).

It is possible that John's incessant reference to truth has at least something to do with the situation of controversy that existed between the Johannine community and Jewish religious leaders at the time the Gospel was written. In a battle over contradictory ultimate truth-claims, John was adamant that he and his community were "in the truth" and their adversaries were not. This clash of truth-claims between Christians and Jews through the centuries has had fateful consequences, which as Christians we should acknowledge with sorrow.

However, for our purposes two critical moral themes are helpfully introduced here, and in various ways they appear elsewhere in Scripture as well. First, *the truth is not simply something that is believed or spoken, but instead a way of being*. It is a path that is followed (2 Tim 2:18; Jas 5:19), a place one inhabits (2 Pet 1:12) and a commitment of the self. Truth is something that is either "in" us, or not (Gen 42:16). It dwells in our "hearts" or "inward being" (Ps 51:6), and thus emerges from our "mouths" quite naturally when we have occasion to speak (cf Mk 7:21-23; Ps 5:9; 15:2; 51:6). Truth is to be loved (Zech 8:19; 2 Thess 2:10), sought ardently (Jer 5:1, 3), rejoiced in (1 Cor 13:6) and sided with (2 Cor 13:8). A life of truth sets us free (Jn 8:32). See the virtue of purity of heart, which in chapter two we said means "integrity, a correspondence between outward action and inward thought, . . . a lack of duplicity, singleness of intention, . . . and the desire to please God above all else" (Davies and Allison, *Critical and Exegetical Commentary*, 1:456).

Second, *one's commitment to the truth is verified by deeds*. These deeds, of course, do include the nature of one's characteristic speech—whether we lie and deceive or instead speak the truth (Ps 5:9; Prov 8:7; 12:20; Jer 9:3). Commitment to the truth also includes our openness to receiving and learning from unpleasant but truthful speech, which is the foundation of growth in discipleship and critical to life in covenant community (Amos 5:10; Mt 18:15-20; Gal 2:14; 2 Tim 2:25). Openness to critical yet truthful speech undergirds the concept of continuous repentance that we have stressed from time to time in this volume as fundamental to Christian living and Christian ethics as a discipline. More broadly, throughout Scripture, as we have tried to show in many different ways, we are taught that God wants from human beings not mere intellectual assent to right beliefs but instead an entire way of life that conforms with his will.

The inbreaking of the kingdom heightens the urgency of participation in God's redemptive will as taught by Jesus Christ. It begins with rightly perceiving reality as the dawning reign of God in Jesus Christ. Following from this radically revised perception of reality is a radically revised way of living in every dimension of existence. We live truthfully when we see reality for what it is.

Part of kingdom living is a commitment to truth itself. Having shed a false apprehension of reality itself, there is no point in dabbling in falsehood in any arena of life. Discipleship involves stripping away all falseness and instead living in truth—buckling "the belt of truth" around one's waist, as Paul put it (Eph 6:14). Believing lies is the path to immorality and disobedience and must be rejected (cf. Rom 1—2). Kingdom existence includes putting away falsehood and various other sins of speech in all their manifold varieties—deceit,

guile, cunning, dissembling, misleading, boasting, flattery, cursing, verbal am-
bushing (Ps 57:4; 64:3; Jer 9:8) and malicious and wrongful speech of all kinds
(1 Cor 5:8; Col 3:9; 1 Pet 3:10; Jas 3:1-12). Finally, participation in God's reign
involves not just an individual reorientation but the creating and sustaining of
a new kind of covenant community, the church, characterized in a pioneering
way by the practice of truthful living and straightforward, yet loving, truth-
speaking (Eph 4:15; cf. Volf, *Exclusion and Embrace*, 258ff).

Truth, Covenant, Power and Fear

Most discussions of truth and ethics would by now have already offered theories related to when it is permissible to lie, but we want to focus on what Jesus
focused on rather than on possible exceptions!

However, in the final section of this chapter we do acknowledge the need
to consider possible exceptions to truthtelling. But we reject the customary approach of simply considering the possible legitimacy of certain lies as an abstract issue in ethical methodology.

For example, in Clark and Rakestraw's fine volume of readings in Christian
ethics, a case is batted around by several authors concerning the legitimacy of
lying to the Nazis about whether Jews are being hidden (vol. 1, chap. 3). The
case is drawn from *The Hiding Place*, the much-loved book by the Dutchwom-
an Corrie ten Boom about her family's involvement in rescuing Jews during
the Holocaust.

The first real test of the family's convictions about truthtelling occurs when
Nazi soldiers come to the door of Corrie's niece, Cocky, in search of her brothers (rather than Jews, at this point), attempting to seize them for forced labor
in Germany (ten Boom, *Hiding Place*, chap. 7). Corrie's niece believes that lying
is in no case morally permissible for Christians and so, after a bit of evading
and dissembling, simply tells the Nazis that the young men are under the
kitchen table (which they are, but in a hidden space under a trapdoor). The Nazis do not see the door and assume that she is simply toying with them. They
leave angrily but without the men. The niece views the incident as divine vindication of her absolute stance forbidding lies under any circumstance, while
Corrie sees her niece as having endangered family members unnecessarily. A
lie, she thinks, would be permissible in that situation; in fact, rescue activity
has already involved them in regularly "do[ing] a lie" (ten Boom, *Hiding Place*,
91). It makes no sense to Corrie to have made the principled decision to temporarily live a lie in order to save innocent lives and then to risk those same
lives by telling the Nazis the truth.

In the Clark and Rakestraw anthology, this case is used to discuss the question of whether absolute moral norms can conflict, and if so, how one resolves
such conflicts. Robert Rakestraw takes a position he calls *unqualified absolutism*

to argue that moral norms in no cases can really conflict, and that "no lie can ever be justified" (*Readings in Christian Ethics*, 123), presumably including lying to the Nazis to save Jews. An excerpt from Helmut Thielicke argues for a position called *conflicting absolutism*, in which moral norms do conflict in certain extreme cases, and that when they do, there is no sin-free course—we must choose the lesser evil, which would justify lying to the Nazis (Clark and Rakestraw, *Readings in Christian Ethics*, 130). Norman Geisler takes a *graded absolutism* stance, arguing that moral norms do conflict but when they do we must choose the weightier norm and in doing so cannot be said to have sinned. Thus lying to the Nazis was "not evil but good" (*Christian Ethics*, 137).

While this kind of discussion has genuine value, we believe that the most important issue raised by the "lying to the Nazis" case is *the covenantal and power dimension of the ethics of truthtelling*. This will be our way into the discussion of possible exceptions to the norm of truthtelling. Notice how the form and function of moral norms, as considered in chapter five, bears on this discussion.

Theological foundations. We have already seen that God is a God of truth and is identified with truth in Jesus Christ. Truth flows from the divine being (Ps 43:3). God fights for the cause of truth (Ps 43:5) and speaks only truth (Ps 119:160; Is 45:19). "All his works are truth" (Dan 4:37). God's "eyes" look for truth in human life (Jer 5:3). All that we have said above about the relationship of Jesus and truth applies here.

God makes oaths to selected human beings and made a covenant with Israel and, through Jesus, with the church. God keeps the covenants that he makes, and he expects covenant-fidelity of those who make vows to him. God also expects and demands that human beings relate in covenant fidelity to one another. Further, God made human beings in the divine image and demands that appropriate respect be demonstrated as we relate to each other.

Principles. One aspect of that covenantal respect is that we tell people the truth when we speak to them. When we tell someone something, we are implying (implicitly communicating, just by the very act of speech) that we respect them and will tell them the truth. If we speak to them as if we were telling them the truth, we owe them the actual truth. A covenantal web, one might say, binds me together with the person to whom I am speaking. There can be no human community without the trust that follows from consistent truthtelling (Hicks, "Truth," 867). On the basis of the fundamental principle of covenant fidelity, we commit to the particular principle of truthtelling.

Rules. This principle generates the rule that we must not lie to one another. It generates other subrules, too, such as declaring all relevant income on our taxes, telling the cashier if he gives me too much change at the grocery store, and so on. All of these rules are intended to serve the principle of truthtelling.

Thus, on the basis of God's character and will we are to commit to this principle and to construct various rules that apply that principle to specific cases. The principle of covenant-keeping undergirds our commitment to truthtelling, as it does to promise-keeping, marital fidelity and other principles.

However, *situations arise in a sinful and unjust world in which gross imbalances or misuses of power subvert or even destroy the implicit covenant that exists in communities.* These kinds of situations sometimes place severe pressure on the principle of truthtelling. Most discussions of possibly compelling moral exceptions to the principle of truthtelling, if examined closely, share this same feature. This point is neglected in ethics texts that do discuss truth as a moral issue.

Howard Thurman discussed with acute and poignant clarity what it was like to try to be a truthful person under oppression. His reflections were clearly rooted in his own experience as a black man in segregationist America, though he frames his discussion more broadly (*Jesus and the Disinherited*, chap. 3). Shining a light into the inner consciousness of the oppressed, Thurman showed that powerlessness makes it next to impossible to relate truthfully to the powerful. "Through the ages, at all stages of sentient activity, the weak have survived by fooling the strong" (*Jesus and the Disinherited*, 58). Thurman, like many other African American writers, documents the stealth and cunning that developed in the slave community as just such a survival strategy for blacks in America. Yet this survival-by-deception exacts its own costs—it is degrading, it threatens to destroy one's moral sensitivity and ability to draw moral distinctions, and finally it may turn one's very self into a "deception" (*Jesus and the Disinherited*, 64-65).

Reflecting on Jesus' teaching in Matthew 5:33-37, Thurman concludes that liberation for both oppressor and oppressed is ultimately found in "a complete and devastating sincerity" on the part of the oppressed, as they refuse to validate the oppressor's power by bowing to it any longer (*Jesus and the Disinherited*, 70). Of course, the very act of living and speaking truth in a context of oppression risks abuse and even death; but in the end it shows the promise of puncturing the oppressors' sense of prerogative and superiority and opening the way for an eventual "relationship between human beings," a great triumph for human dignity (*Jesus and the Disinherited*, 73). Thurman's words here presaged the approach of the later civil rights movement in a remarkable way.

Cheryl Sanders, professor of Christian ethics at Howard University Divinity School, also deals with the issue of truthtelling ethics under oppression in an African-American context. She discusses the practice among slaves of lying to get food (*Empowerment Ethics for a Liberated People*, 14-15). Slaves knew that under *just* conditions, it would be wrong to steal or to lie, and—this is critically important—*they did not tolerate theft and lying among themselves.* They believed that "such behavior would constitute an imitation of white immorality to the detriment of black solidarity and well-being" (*Empowerment Ethics for a Liberated People,* 15). In other words, in the context of gross injustice, in which every human right of the slave was routinely violated, in which their labor was stolen from them and the very system involved a great lie about their humanity, and in which their very survival was threatened by starvation, "stealing was a necessary response." Sanders, unfortunately, calls this "situation ethics," but our discussion in chapter five helps us see that this is instead a principlist ethic: rules against lying and stealing are based on the principle of respect for human rights in covenant community.

Like the context of the Nazis and Corrie ten Boom, the gross violation of the conditions of covenant community under slavery creates a kind of moral emergency in which the principle of the right to food and the right to life override the rule against lying. But the rule against lying is still obligatory, and therefore slaves must not lie to each other and must live for the day when conditions of justice and basic human rights are (re)established and blacks and whites will once more live in covenant community. Sanders's own discussion makes clear that the overriding principle is the right to life, not a mere situational ethic.

Václav Havel, the Czech president who spent years in prison as a truth-speaking dissident under communism, authored a collection of essays called *Living in Truth*. Certainly truthtelling is not the only theme of this volume. But Havel, like so many wise observers (and victims) of life under totalitarian regimes in twentieth-century Europe, documented with great profundity how truth is among the first casualties of political repression. Bonhoeffer, Solzhenitsyn, Orwell, Mandela, King, Wiesel and many other literary and political heroes of the twentieth century paid a considerable price for speaking the truth in their contexts.

The Croatian expatriate theologian Miroslav Volf offers rich reflections on this same theme in his recent work titled *Exclusion and Embrace*. Volf begins with a stark acknowledgment that under totalitarian regimes truth is concealed, defined, redefined, controlled and suppressed by the "Party" or the "State." Yet no state has proven capable of utterly destroying the will to know and speak the truth that is so fundamental to the human person. There will always be those who commit themselves to know, remember and articulate what really happened or what is now happening—the ultimate revolutionary act in conditions of oppression. That commitment to know and speak the truth is costly; it invites suffering and death. It must also be done in the right spirit, for truth can be remembered and spoken in such a way as to invite further violence and victimization. But still the choice must be truth. Seeking and speaking truth may be risky but is much to be preferred to the alternative, that is, to strategies of fraud and falsehood, cunning and deception. The oppressed do sometimes embrace such strategies as a means of survival or to find ways to break the hold of the oppressors over the public definition of truth, but in so doing risk "enthron[ing] precisely the enemy" they seek to fight (Volf, *Exclusion and Embrace,* 236). Reflecting on the dramatic scene of Jesus before Pilate, Volf sees here a clash between "the truth of power" and "the power of truth"; though Christ ends up hanging on the cross, his death ultimately marks the victory both of truth and of life (*Exclusion and Embrace,* 268).

Dietrich Bonhoeffer himself, in one of the most famous (and controversial) treatments of this issue ever offered, argued from a Nazi prison that truthtelling is a covenantal and contextual reality (*Ethics,* 363-72). His argument is worth lingering over.

Bonhoeffer claimed that the obligation to tell the truth is bounded by the particular relationship we have to the person with whom we are speaking. We would call this a *covenantal* approach to truthtelling to indicate that it is tied to the obligations that exist by virtue of the kinds of relationships we have with others.

Bonhoeffer begins his essay "What Is Meant by 'Telling the Truth'" by pointing out that we first learn what it means to tell the truth as children in relation to our parents. Bonhoeffer says, "The truthfulness of a small child lies open before the parents, and what the child says should reveal to them everything that is hidden and secret" (*Ethics,* 363).

But Bonhoeffer says the reverse is not the case. Parents do not tell children everything, and they should not, because children would not understand and might be too frightened or troubled if they knew everything parents worry about. So he concludes that "telling the truth" means something different according to the particular relation in which we stand (*Ethics,* 364).

Incidentally, we would say it is nevertheless very important that a parent tell the truth to children. This is where children learn honesty—first of all from their parents. And it is where they learn the trusting, covenant relationship between parents and children that enables them later to establish trusting, covenant relationships with other persons. So we must tell the truth to children, and not injure their trust, even though we limit what we say to what fits their capacity and right to know, as Bonhoeffer rightly indicates.

But still, telling the truth means something different according to the particular relation in which we stand. When I relate to a friend, I have a covenant obligation to speak honestly. I need friends who will speak truth honestly to me and not just flatter me. When I go to a restaurant and order food, I enter into an implicit covenant to pay for my food and to conduct myself quietly and politely. The workers in the restaurant have entered into a covenant to give me food that is not spoiled or contaminated with disease.

Bonhoeffer said that you have to ask in what way a person is entitled to demand truthful speech from others. Speech between parents and children is different from speech between government and subject, friend and foe. He must have been thinking of his relationship to the Nazi government, which at that very time was killing Jews. Bonhoeffer helped Jews escape. To save the lives of Jews, he had to conceal the truth and finally to tell lies to the governing authorities. He meant that he did not owe the same kind of truth to the ruling authorities that he owed to his parents.

The covenant between parents and children requires one kind of truth. The covenant between friends, or between customer and restaurant owner, each demand a different kind of truth. A farmer owes truth about tomatoes to his customers, but he is not obligated to tell them all about his inner life in the same way he is obligated to tell that to his wife. To do so would be a kind of shamelessness that violates covenant obligations in family life. Bonhoeffer had no covenant with Nazis to tell them the truth about Jews whom they wanted to kill.

Bonhoeffer pointed out that Immanuel Kant "declared that he was too proud ever to utter a falsehood; indeed, he unintentionally carried this principle *ad absurdum* by saying that he would feel himself obliged to give truthful information even to a criminal looking for a friend of his who had concealed himself in his house" (*Ethics*, 369n; see Kant, *Critique of Practical Reason*, 346-50). Bonhoeffer was here referring to Kant's famous story of the axe-murderer looking for his victim. It is a remarkable foreshadowing of what would happen *en masse* in Nazi Germany some 150 years later. Kant's claim is that the decision maker would bear no moral responsibility for telling the truth to the madman—he is absolutely obligated to do so and not to lie under this or any circumstance.

Bonhoeffer differs. He uses an example to illustrate his own perspective:

> A teacher asks a child in front of the class whether it is true that his father often comes home drunk. It is true, but the child denies it. The teacher's question has placed him in a situation for which he is not yet prepared. He feels only that what is taking place is an unjustified interference in the order of the family and that he must oppose it. What goes on in the family is not for the ears of the class in school. The family has its own secret and must preserve it. The teacher has failed to respect the reality of this institution. The child ought now to find a way of answering which would comply with both the rule of the family and the rule of the school. But he is not yet able to do this. He lacks experience, knowledge, and the ability to express himself in the right way. As a simple no to the teacher's question the child's answer is certainly untrue; yet at the same time it nevertheless gives expression to the truth that the family is an institution *sui generis* and that the teacher had no right to interfere in it. The child's answer can indeed be called a lie; yet this lie contains more truth, that is to say, it is more in accordance with

reality than would have been the case if the child had betrayed his father's weakness in front of the class. According to the measure of his knowledge, the child acted correctly. The blame for the lie falls back entirely upon the teacher. (*Ethics,* 367-68)

Bonhoeffer said that to learn how to tell the truth you have to learn not only to have good character but also about the kinds of social contexts in which we are relating to others and the responsibilities we have in different contexts. "The ethical cannot be detached from reality, and therefore continual progress in learning to appreciate reality is a necessary ingredient in ethical action" (*Ethics,* 365). Parents need to teach children "the differences between the various circles in which they are to live and the differences in their responsibilities" (*Ethics,* 364). He was very likely pointing to the need to teach children that they did not owe full truth to Nazi officials. There are things that we must keep secret from others.

We would say we have no covenant with such evil authorities to tell them such truth as will help them do their evil. By contrast, when a government is legitimate, does justice and has the consent of the people, then we have an obligation to assist the government in doing justice and to tell them the kind of truth that one owes a legitimate government. Our commitment to justice and our consent to the government bring us into a covenant with the government. We tell the truth about our income so that the government can collect legitimate taxes, and we tell the truth about criminal activity that we know about so the government can do its job stopping unjust actions. And the government has a covenant with the people to tell the truth, to allow the newspapers and television to tell the truth as they understand the truth, and to allow the churches to tell the truth as they understand the truth. The government has no authority to control what the media or the churches tell as the truth.

This covenantal understanding is very different from saying that we are free to calculate when telling the truth or a lie is to our advantage. Such self-interested calculation has the great danger of opening the door to approving many kinds of lies. In a society in which everyone is always calculating whether to tell a lie, trust breaks down and people learn to do only what is in their own selfish interest. People also learn to lie to God and to deceive themselves. A covenantal approach guards against the practice of lying while also being sensitive to contextual and relational realities, the most extraordinary of which involves the descent into social evil.

Bonhoeffer's stance can be supported by numerous biblical texts that explicitly or implicitly offer divine approval to acts of deception or even dishonesty in conditions of oppression, injustice or war. The most important of these is the story of the Hebrew midwives Shiphrah and Puah lying to Pharoah in order to save the lives of the male Hebrew babies (Ex 1:19); God responded by blessing them with children of their own. Rahab the prostitute lied to protect Israelite spies (Josh 2:4-6; cf. Heb 11:31). Jael deceived Sisera in order to kill him (Judg 4:17-21). Elisha deceived the Aramean army, leading to their capture (2 Kings 6:18-20—for an effort to hold to a "no exception" position based on a different interpretation of these texts, see Murray, *Principles of Conduct,* chap. 6).

Interesting strategies have sometimes been employed by serious Christians attempting to fulfill their obligations both to the truth and to other people. Quakers on the Underground Railroad, for example, often preferred to state the exact truth but with silent *mental reservations.* For example, "I do not know the whereabouts of any escaped slaves" (mentally adding: "at this very minute"). The mental reservations debate is actually quite extensive in the literature on truthtelling. Sissela Bok, who has offered excellent philosophical reflections on lying, is extremely critical of this approach (*Lying,* 37-39). Yet it can be viewed as a valiant effort to avoid lying even to save a life—breaking the rule for the deeper principle of the sacredness of human life. If those are the stakes involved, one can see the value of the mental reservation approach. One would certainly not be wise, however, in making such a practice routine, as it would very likely undermine truthfulness and reinforce self-deception. This is where we believe our covenantal approach is more adequate: it limits such mental reservations to unjust power relations where we have no covenant to tell the truth because of a deeper principle.

From the other side of a relationship of unbalanced power, recent work in biomedical ethics strongly emphasizes the obligation of medical professionals to speak truthfully to patients. This is generally called the "principle of veracity" in bioethics texts. It represents an acknowledgment on the part of health care professionals that by their access to specialized medical knowledge they hold considerable power over patients, power which could readily be abused (and has been in the past), often out of a well-intentioned effort to spare a patient unnecessary suffering. It is now understood that there exists a covenant between medical professional and patient that includes the obligation of truth-telling (Beauchamp and Childress, *Principles of Biomedical Ethics,* 283-92). With rare exceptions, patients should be given as much information as they wish to know about their medical condition and prospects for treatment. While there is some debate in medical ethics and nursing ethics about various issues here—the role of families in disclosing information to patients, the sensed obligation to help patients maintain hope, obligations in relation to third-party payers, the issue of maintaining privacy of medical records and so on—the principle of veracity is itself now widely accepted. Greater sensitivity to the power of medical professionals has imposed moral obligations intended to improve the conditions of decision making for patients and their families.

Conclusion

Telling the truth is a human obligation under God's sovereignty emerging in our various covenantal relations with others, sharpened considerably for those committed to participation in the dawning reign of God. There are times when fear hinders us from truthtelling, though in many cases the fear is simply that of loss of face or minor personal embarrassment. Such fears are not adequate reasons for withholding the truth; Jesus teaches that we can live in trust in God, in whom we find our true worth. We must avoid a moral casuistry that justifies ever more questionable lies. For the great majority of us, the main issue is learning to renounce the casual resort to lies and instead live in truth. As Ronald Preston has put it: "[M]ost of the time people tell lies when they should not. The temptation comes suddenly, perhaps to get out of an awkward situation or to practice some petty fraud or deception, and they succumb. In order to have the discernment to know when a lie is called for, one needs to be habitually truthful ("Lying," 363).

Yet challenges emerging in situations of political oppression or social evil, as we have seen, raise compelling questions. The Scriptures remind us of occasions in which "truth has perished" (Jer 7:28) or "stumble[d] in the public square" (Is 59:14). In such times justice, righteousness and human life itself can become supremely threatened. Those who hold power are called especially to live in truth and to be aware of the many temptations they face to resort to duplicity, dishonesty and truth's suppression. Those, on the other hand, who are threatened and oppressed may be permitted in times of moral emergency to suspend truthtelling temporarily in some contexts in order to honor central covenant obligations—and to work clandestinely, if necessary, for a just and peaceful public square in which truth may be freely spoken once again.

19

RACE

For where your treasure is, there your heart will be also. The eye is the lamp of the body. So, if your eye is healthy, your whole body will be full of light; but if your eye is unhealthy, your whole body will be full of darkness. If then the light in you is darkness, how great is the darkness!

MATTHEW 6:21-24

No respectable white North American Christian leader would today express opposition to racial reconciliation. In recent years both mainline and evangelical leaders have repeatedly affirmed the goal of racial reconciliation (Lee, "Racial Reconciliation Tops NAE's Agenda," 97; Sojourners, *Who Is My Neighbor?* 6-8). Catholic churches, being by very name and practice inclusive (catholic), have long done better overall but not always in particular. Mainline churches have long claimed support for racial reconciliation and have, in fact, provided many of the troops who battled committedly in the struggle for civil rights and against segregation and discrimination. Numerous racial reconciliation initiatives are now underway in various largely white evangelical church and parachurch bodies (Blackmon, "Racial Reconciliation Becomes a Priority for the Religious Right"; Sojourners, *Who Is My Neighbor?* 50-51).

Yet, with rare exceptions (notably in the Pentecostal world—see Macchia, "From Azusa to Memphis," 203-18; Daniels, "Dialogue Between Black and Hispanic Pentecostal Scholars," 219-38), few would argue that progress has been dramatic. On the contrary, evidence of a gulf between white and black Christians of similar theological stances, including largely white and largely black evangelical Christian denominations and agencies, remains obvious (see Emerson and Smith, *Divided by Faith?*).Voting patterns in the 2000 presidential election, for example, clearly illustrated a profound gap in political loyalties between black and white Christians. Only 8 percent of black Americans (61 percent of whom describe themselves as born-again Christians, and 49 percent of whom attend church on a given Sunday, according to Barna Research Group statistics) voted for the self-identified (white) evangelical candidate of the Republican party, George W. Bush. No group protested the post-election certification of Bush's presidency after the contested outcome in Florida more vigorously, and no group questioned his legitimacy as president more deeply.

This is not a discussion of racial politics in Florida or the 2000 election. But what happened then and there provides a clue both to the normative shape of Christian understandings of race and to our current struggle as U.S. Christians to achieve the elusive goal of racial reconciliation both in church life and in the nation. It may not be too much to say that until Christians truly understand the divergent voting patterns of black and white evangelicals (among other political realities) we will have no chance whatsoever of achieving genuine racial reconciliation. It makes a vivid marker of all that divides us.

Our thesis here is that justice rather than reconciliation is the better rubric under which to consider issues of race. More precisely, we want to argue that both biblically and in the context of historic patterns of racial injustice in the United States, the concept of reconciliation is empty of content unless it is built upon the sturdy foundation of justice. If reconciliation is understood as the repair of broken relationships and the restoration of trusting and intimate community between persons or groups, then justice is its first step. There can be no racial reconciliation unless there is first the redress of race-based or race-linked injustice, just as there can generally be no reconciliation between alienated persons or groups until or unless previous and current wrongs are constructively addressed (for a similar approach, see Shearer, *Enter the River*).

While the language of racial reconciliation continues to carry the day in most Christian circles, seemingly unquestioned, it is precisely over issues of racial *justice* that white and black Americans tend to disagree most vigorously. Indeed, at times it seems as if white and black Americans live in "two nations," in Andrew Hacker's pregnant phrase, not just disagreeing about issues of racial justice but *experiencing* those issues in fundamentally contrary ways (compare the title of Shipler's book, *A Country of Strangers*). If this is the case, as it certainly seems to be, then talk of racial reconciliation between white and black Christians is premature and may be actually destructive of progress in race relations in our churches and our nation.

In this section, then, we will attempt to apply Jesus' understanding of justice to the arena of race, focusing particularly on concrete racial injustices that continue to plague African Americans, while remembering as we conclude that this is just one of many historic and contemporary contexts of racial injustice and race-based conflict, both in the United States and around the world. We are particularly aware of the importance of seeing racial injustice truly and accurately. Our holistic method emphasizes that loyalties to friends, groups and usual practices, as well as economic investments, shape the way we see things. Whites tend to have more white friends and relatives; Latinos and Latinas tend to have more Latin friends and relatives; blacks tend to have more black friends and relatives. Personal experience as well as objective polls tell us that people do see things differently according to their group memberships. Immediately after Jesus has talked about where our heart loyalties are (Mt 5:21), he points to the contrast between the healthy and unhealthy way of seeing: our heart loyalties shape our seeing far more than we can be consciously aware of. We need to develop a healthy and accurate way of seeing what is happening in our society.

As a caveat, we must note that in this chapter we focus almost exclusively on the concrete racial injustices that continue to plague African Americans and on the issue of white-black racial reconciliation. We do recognize that racial injustice and the broader issue of interethnic relations are far broader problems both here and around the world than this focus might indicate. We regret that here we cannot, for example, grapple with the particular issues raised by Latino/a authors, Native Americans and Asian-American voices related to race relations in the United States. As primary author of this chapter, I (Dave Gushee) have chosen this approach in part due to my own geographical context, in which racial divisions are still largely along black-white lines, and in part due to space constraints. But also it can be argued that the American history of slavery and its heritage have shaped race relations more powerfully and more distinctively than the other forms of racial injustice. Until we heal that history, we are unlikely to heal the other forms. So it may be that my own geographical context may be, in an ironical kind of way, a gift for sensing the challenge. Our references to the two highly readable *Sojourners* study books point to more ethnically diverse perspectives.

Race and the Injustice of Violence and Death

We have argued in chapter seventeen and elsewhere in this book that Jesus rejected various forms of unjust violence and made perfectly clear that his mission was a nonviolent one. The question to consider here is whether in the American setting race is linked to the injustice of violence and, by extension, premature death. The answer is clearly yes. The following are several death- and violence-related issues experienced quite differently by white and black Americans, issues which raise legitimate justice concerns not generally noticed or taken seriously by white Americans.

Violent crime. Black men are seven times more likely to die as murder victims than are white men, and black women are four times more likely to die in this way than white women (U.S. Census Bureau, *Abstract 2000*, table 134). Blacks are more likely than whites or Hispanics to be victimized by violent crimes in general ((U.S. Census Bureau, *Abstract 2000*, table 341). They are *less* likely to receive prompt police attention when victimized or to sense that their victimization is of as much concern as the victimization of whites (Sojourners, *America's Original Sin*, 22-29). The experience of life in some of our urban neighborhoods is simply inconceivable and certainly would be beyond intolerable to those who have never set foot there. As former student residents of urban New York and Philadelphia, we do speak with some experience in this regard but recognize that our experience does not approach that of permanent residents of our nation's most blighted areas.

Hate crimes. Recognizing that violent crimes rooted in racial hatred constitute a particularly devastating attack on personal security and American values, legislators in many states, and at the national level, have in recent years pressed for legislation imposing especially severe penalties on such crimes. FBI hate crimes statistics demonstrate that blacks are victimized by reported hate crimes more than any other group, whether racial, ethnic, religious or sexual (U.S. Census Bureau, *Abstract 2000*, table 338). Occasional hate crimes, such as the July 1999 shootings in the Chicago area by a man affiliated with the White Nationalist Party, remind us of the continued existence of raw race hatred in the underbelly of American society. The brutal and clearly racially motivated murder of James Byrd in Texas highlighted in a tragic way the continued existence of crimes motivated by racial hatred. Black Americans tend to favor legislation directed specifically at hate crimes (which ultimately passed in Texas in May 2001), while white Americans are less likely to.

The death penalty. While African Americans are disproportionately victimized by violent crimes, including the stunning difference in murder rates cited above, they are less likely to support the death penalty than are white Americans. The reason is not so obscure. The consistent experience of injustice in the judicial system undermines the confidence among blacks that the death penalty will be fairly meted out. The evidence for racial discrimination in sentencing and application of the death penalty is by now nearly indisputable—both race-of-victim and race-of-offender inequities are well-documented (see Death Penalty Information Center webpage <www.deathpenaltyinfo.org>, and chapter nine). That is, a black victim is less likely to be requited for their victimization by the sentencing of his or her murderer to death; and a black convicted of murder is more likely to be sentenced to death, all things being equal, than a white convicted of murder. This may have something to do with the fact that 98 percent of district attorneys in counties using the death penalty in the United States are white.

Environmentai degradation. Poor, largely minority (especially black) communities are far more likely to be sites for toxic waste dumps and other environmentally hazardous industries than are suburban or largely white neighborhoods. This issue, sometimes called "environmental racism," remains largely unknown to white Americans. Clearly the problem has as much to do with the lack of political and economic power of black Americans as it does with historic patterns of racial discrimination. When everyone says "not in my backyard," whose backyard loses out? The backyard belonging to the one lacking the power to prevent it. Or, alternatively, it ends up in the backyard of the one so lacking in alternative means of economic advancement that the economic gains expected from a dangerous new industry or waste dump are judged as being worthy of the environmental risks involved.

Life expectancy. According to the most recent complete federal government statistics (1998), black women can expect to live five years less than white women. Black men can expect to live nearly seven years less than white men (U.S. Census Bureau, *Abstract 2000*, table 115). While the gap has closed somewhat in recent years, never in the history of this statistic have black Americans come close to matching white Americans in life expectancy. Sources of this difference in life expectancy are various, including disease, hypertension, stress, obesity, anxiety, poor medical care, lack of insurance and the greater likelihood of victimization by violent crime. It is hard to imagine a more fundamental justice concern than life expectancy.

Race and the Injustice of Economic Deprivation

The second area of injustice Jesus addressed was greed and economic oppression. His concern for economic justice reminds us to consider whether race in America is linked to economic injustice. The answer to that is obvious; the only question is where to begin.

Economic indicators. Black Americans continue to lag behind white Americans in every indicator of economic well-being. As of 1998, the median income for a black household was $25,351 and for a white household $40,912, meaning that a black family earns $619 for every $1000 earned by a white family (derived from U.S. Census Bureau, *Abstract 2000*, table 736). While some of this disparity relates to the tragically high pattern of single-parent families in the black community, this does not account for the whole of the difference. In terms of income distribution, of those making under $15,000 per year in 1998, 16 percent of white households and 32 percent of black households fell within this category (U.S. Census Bureau, *Abstract 2000*, table 736). According to the official government definition of poverty, 36.4 percent of black children are poor compared to 14.4 percent of white children (U.S. Census Bureau, *Abstract*

2000, table 755). As of 1998, 46 percent of blacks owned their own home, while 72 percent of whites owned homes (Cose, "Good News About Black America," 33). Finally, the unemployment rate as of 1998 was 8.9 percent for blacks and 3.9 percent for whites (U.S. Census Bureau, *Abstract 2000*, table 645). None of these statistics speak to the issue of causation. They do point to systemic injustice in the distribution of income and economic benefit in American society.

Welfare reform and antipoverty programs. The year 1996 saw the highly contested passage of national welfare reform legislation. This legislation ended any federal entitlement to income support for the poor. The late 1990s saw a booming economy that softened the predicted massive increase in human suffering due to this national policy change. However, tougher economic conditions since late 2000 have begun to tell a different story. Further, it must be remembered that ending welfare does not constitute an antipoverty program. The best state efforts in this area, such as those in Wisconsin under former Governor Tommy Thompson, have mixed welfare reform with aggressive job training, child care, transportation and other efforts needed to move people from welfare to work. Such efforts cost money, sometimes more money than welfare did. Whites, including most white Christians, are not known for their aggressive advocacy of government spending on such initiatives. Quite the contrary—the majority tend to oppose such spending. Black Christians notice this.

Affirmative action. Affirmative action began in the late 1960s as an effort to redress unconscious and unintentional discrimination against women and minorities. The earlier civil rights laws of the 1960s were directed at intentional and de jure discrimination, such as voting, housing and hiring policies that overtly excluded blacks and women. Affirmative action was intended as the next step, aiming to deal with the advantages (and disadvantages) created by deeply embedded social structures that passed along preferred status to whites in hiring and advancement in business as well as in admissions to colleges and universities. The idea was to take aggressive, "affirmative" steps to "level the playing field" and get blacks, Hispanics, women and other disadvantaged groups in the door of institutions that had previously excluded them. Enforcement of the civil rights laws would prevent intentional discrimination, affirmative action would proactively prevent unintentional discrimination—and would begin to redress the accumulated disadvantages passed along through the generations to minority groups.

Affirmative action does not retain universal support among black Americans, for a variety of reasons—the most common concern is that it undermines both black self-confidence and white confidence in the competence of their black colleagues (McWhorter, *Losing the Race;* cf. Carter, *Reflections of an Affirmative Action Baby;* Ezorsky, *Racism and Justice*). But if support for affirmative action has weakened among black Americans, it has dropped dramatically among many whites. Many whites are unwilling to acknowledge the continued existence of structured social inequality or the advantages that accrue simply by being white in a white-dominated society. Thus they are unwilling to support a policy based on this reading of reality. While affirmative action can be legitimately debated as to its scope and form, whites betray a lack of concern for justice and lack of perspective on social life when they deny the reality of structural injustice and its link to race (Sojourners, *Crossing the Racial Divide*, 70-71). White Christians, in particular, may be indicted for failing to look beyond their own racial interests to the interests of others (Phil 2:4), especially the historically disadvantaged.

Education. Many of the most intense battles in our society are fought over issues related to education. Racial injustice in education clearly exists. Perhaps its most devastating form is the atrocious state of many of our urban schools. No child can easily succeed in a school that is unsafe, overcrowded, poorly led or falling apart. Yet that is the reality of many of our schools, and it simply reflects the reality of their surrounding neighborhoods and of political unwillingness to invest in education for those whose parents lack clout and connections.

Many African Americans have made a major, determined effort to overcome discrimination by the traditional method of educational advancement, in spite of bad schools in poorer areas and lack of money to afford college education. In spite of these and other drawbacks, in 1960, six years after the *Brown* v. *Board of Education* decision had begun to desegregate schools, 18.7 percent of recent black high school grads were in college, which approached the white level of 24.3 percent. By 1970, with more enforcement of and public support for civil rights laws, and new grants and loans assisting persons of all races who had economic need in affording college, the percent of recent black high school grads in college had jumped to 26.7. Government support for college education also assisted white high school grads; their percent had jumped even more, to 33.9. By 1975, black high school grads basically tied whites: 32.5 percent of blacks and 33 percent of whites who had graduated from high school were in college. This was a remarkable accomplishment, and a tribute to blacks' drive for education as well as to policies making college accessible.

But in the 1980s there was a backing down in government grants and loans for college attendance (as well as job training), and in enforcement of civil rights laws, and the percentage of recent black high school grads in college did not continue to rise; it dropped to 26.5 in 1985, by comparison with white high school grads, 35 percent of whom were in college. The decrease in government support slowed the white climb as well, but their rate did climb some, to 39.8 percent in 1990, by which time blacks were at 33.7 percent—statistically the same as they had achieved in 1975. By 1992, whites had climbed a bit farther, to 42.7 percent, but blacks were still stuck at 34.3 percent. With the improving economy in the 1990s, and more government support for civil rights laws, this number began to climb again. Whites were up 4 percent by comparison with 1990, and blacks were up dramatically, to within 4 percent of whites (U.S. Census Bureau, *Abstract 1994*).

Other educational issues are also debated, including the place of the study of black Americans and black history in the overall curriculum and the fact that educational attainment still does not yet eliminate the disparity in economic outcomes between black and white Americans. (A higher percentage of blacks than whites live in poverty at every level of educational attainment—U.S. Census Bureau, *Abstract 2000*, table 761.) For a time, racial injustices and efforts to redress them tore American school systems and communities apart—one thinks of the central role of the *Brown* v. *Board of Education* case (1954) which ordered school desegregation, and the fallout in places like Little Rock's Central High School and all over America.

Today there seems to be more hope of common ground between white and black Americans on some of these educational issues than on many other issues, as evidenced by President Bush's oft-stated concern for the improvement of public schools. Yet in his case (and here the president stands in as a paradigm for many others) this concern for the schools is not linked to any broader vision for the amelioration of economic injustice and its link to race.

Race and the Injustice of Domination by the Powerful

Jesus confronted those who dominated others. He was critical both of the dominating power of Roman political/military leaders and of Jewish religious leaders. Authority is an indispensable dimension of community life, to be sure, but Jesus taught that authority must be exercised as servanthood.

Power imbalances. Accustomed as we are to social power, white Americans are not normally inclined to notice the very fact of radical imbalances of power in our society. In many sectors, the United States remains a white-dominated society—despite the increasing diversification of our national population. This does not mean that blacks and other racial "minorities" lack formal or even functional opportunity to ascend to positions of leadership; it does mean, however, that this ascent remains relatively unusual and has not affected the fact that the face of social power in much of our nation remains largely white. Perhaps the single best example of the phenomenon remains the fact that the White House has been occupied solely by white men throughout our entire history. This is extraordinarily symbolic of the distribution of power in the United States. Blacks have been largely excluded from what sociologist Daniel

Bell calls "the public household" of American life, a fact visibly symbolized by their absence from the ultimate American household.

Criminal (in)justices. It is hard to imagine a more fundamental power than the right to arrest, imprison and execute. Strenuous efforts have been made across our nation in recent decades to ensure that this power is exercised without regard to race; but black Americans, in our view accurately, continue to view the criminal justice system as a primary example of unjust and dominative power. The issues range across the board: police harassment, excessive use of force, brutality, racial profiling, differential treatment in law enforcement when victimized, differential treatment in the courts and so on (see Goldberg, "Color of Suspicion"; Kennedy, "Suspect Policy"). Reflecting on the causes of serious racial disturbances in Cincinnati in early 2001, Michelle Cottle wrote, "Police brutality has become America's preoccupying racial trauma—the distinct trauma of a society whose efforts to overcome racial segregation far outpace its efforts to overcome racial injustice" ("Boomerang," 27). More broadly, as Megan Twohey has written, "The nation's criminal justice system is the hottest civil rights arena today" ("Broken Promises"). And today's struggles occur against the backdrop of a horrible history. Whites must remember the history of the use and abuse of the criminal justice system to sustain and enable our own form of apartheid until it was forcibly dismantled in the 1960s.

Race and the Injustice of Exclusion from Community

One key form of dominative power is the power to exclude from full participation in community. Radical inclusion in community was a key theme in Jesus' ministry, as we have argued. Jesus included the ill and outcast, women and children, various kinds of "sinners" and even Gentiles. He created a new kind of community of disciples and forgiven sinners that shattered boundaries of all types. The exclusion from community wounds the excluded deeply, both at an emotional level and a practical level. Whether it is the child excluded on the playground or the worker not invited to a meeting that ought to involve her, exclusion from participation in community is a profound injustice and one consistently addressed in Scripture. When it comes to the relation between race and exclusion, we have no trouble finding issues worthy of address:

Housing discrimination. While it is now illegal to discriminate on the basis of race in the real estate business, residential apartheid, as Andrew Hacker calls it, continues to exist to a considerable degree. Many residential areas in our nation are nearly or entirely monoracial. The pressures that keep black Americans out of predominantly white areas are by now mainly subtle ones of social ostracism and varieties of evasion, though outright intimidation and other violations of civil rights and housing laws do still occur—such as the continued survival of "racial covenants" in certain neighborhoods. Numerous studies indicate that many whites grow uncomfortable if the black proportion of their neighborhoods reaches 8 percent; anything more than that passes the "tipping point" at which "white flight" often begins and the neighborhood rapidly turns over (Hacker, *Two Nations*, 36). As a white person, it is hard to imagine the sense of humiliation and rejection that the white flight phenomenon must signify to black Americans. On the other hand, many leading areas, such as the larger Los Angeles area where Glen lives, are wondrously multiethnic and thereby much enriched.

Voting rights. The issue of black voting rights was officially settled in 1965 with the Voting Rights Act. However, the enormous controversy that surrounded the 2000 presidential election revealed that more subtle voting rights issues still remain and that these issues do indeed have a racial component. At the very least, black Floridians, on the whole, experienced more trouble exercising their franchise than did white Floridians—primarily, it appears, due to antiquated equipment and inadequate provisions to accommodate voters in some overwhelmingly black districts. An outside firm was hired to purge suspected erroneous voter-registrants, and it purged mostly minorities—in very many cases wrongly. One may or may not see a conspiracy here, but surely at least it shows the same second-best, second-class treatment of blacks and other nonwhite groups that so frequently characterizes life in this nation. Another voting rights issue has to do with what by now must be viewed as the unjust exclusion of convicted felons who have served their time from ever voting again in most states; an exclusion which currently affects 13 percent of all black men in America (Cose, "Good News About Black America," 39).

Exclusion from churches and other voluntary associations. Barely forty years ago, churches, country clubs and other voluntary membership organizations routinely excluded blacks and sometimes other nonwhites and Jews from participation or membership. This is now against the law. However, informal exclusion continues to occur. In west Tennessee, where I live, it continues to be the case that white churches sometimes make it abundantly clear to black visitors that they are not welcome. I counsel with college students who work in ministry in such churches and wrestle with how to respond when they discover, to their shock, that the Great Commission is not viewed as applicable to "them"—at least, not "here." Meanwhile, we continue to hear of country clubs and other bastions of elite society that have yet to admit their first black member.

Remembered Wrongs Inadequately Addressed

One final kind of injustice needs at least brief mention here—the injustice of inadequately addressing prior wrongs.

Many fine books recently have been written on the complex cluster of issues having to do with redressing national, corporate and political wrongdoing (Rotberg and Thompson, *Truth v. Justice;* Barkan, *Guilt of Nations;* and especially Shriver, *Ethic for Enemies*). War crimes tribunals, most famously the Nuremberg tribunals after World War II, have been established in order to bring perpetrators to justice. Discussion of reparations related to World War II itself is still ongoing, over fifty-five years since the end of the war. South Africa set up a Truth and Reconciliation Commission to deal with the crimes and wrongs of the apartheid era. Over twenty nations in various continents have acted similarly after a regime change made a truthful accounting possible. How best to deal with historic injustices in a world where justice is never perfect is a vexing question indeed. Should the goal be to arrive at a truthful accounting, to bring perpetrators to justice, to gain symbolic or material compensation for victims, or to achieve communal healing and reconciliation?

While each of these goals can be defended, no one can reasonably argue that the best way to deal with a history of horrific injustice is to ignore it. Sweeping such evils under the rug is not an option. It certainly does nothing to contribute to truth or to justice or to reconciliation or to anything approaching the reign of God. Our own perspective is that generally a combination of approaches, all grounded in truthtelling, is the best approach. But this is much easier said than done, and varying situations demand varying approaches (for an excellent overview of these issues, including a fascinating perspective on the value of truthtelling, see Todorov, "In Search of Lost Crime"; also Wink, *When the Powers Fall*).

When truthtelling is applied to the issue of racial injustice in America, white Americans frequently respond with impatient frustration to any claim that our tortuous history in regard to race should be confronted at all. Those who bring up this history are blamed for "making trouble"—it would be better just to "let sleeping dogs lie." But, of course, failure to face the wrongs of the past almost always signals a lack of readiness to live in justice and, yes, reconciliation, today. As the editors of *The New Republic* put it with reference to American atrocities in Vietnam:

> The more we learn about the past, the better we comprehend it. . . . Surely "healing" is not accomplished by an indifference to truth. Or is the ascendancy of "healing" as an American ideal owed precisely to its indifference to truth, to its emotional efficiency, to its promise of an instant absolution and a swift "moving on"? ("Anti-Hero," unsigned editorial, May 14, 2001)

No agency or representative of the United States has ever offered a full and truthful accounting of the evils of white racism or formally apologized for the institution of slavery or for what followed emancipation: the century of de jure segregation and what Orlando Patterson rightly calls "the demonization, terrorization, and humiliation" of black Americans by official and unofficial representatives of white society (*Rituals of Blood*, 223). President Clinton in 1997 offered an official apology for the infamous Tuskegee syphilis experiments, but of course that particular outrage was just one of many. Talk of some form of reparation for slavery, while flaring up from time to time, remains peripheral. Meanwhile, southern states continue to wrestle with the symbolism of the Confederacy, with many whites displaying no sensitivity whatsoever to the pain aroused by symbols such as the Confederate flag.

My own experience with the Southern Baptist Convention's effort to repudiate its own racist history in 1995 attests to the difficulties, the limits and yet the value of such an effort. Our resolution on racial reconciliation, widely covered in the media in June 1995, did not undo four hundred years of history or make all things right. Some whites hated the statement. Some black respondents decried it as "too little, too late." It was too little, and it was certainly too late, but as a participant in its drafting I can attest that it was heartfelt and genuine, at least for its drafters. Confession is an aspect of justice and a precursor to reconciliation. It can open the door to forgiveness and salve those wounds that otherwise make reconciliation impossible. Conversely, the refusal to deal appropriately with prior wrongs is an aspect of injustice. It continues to plague black-white relations in America.

We do not want to leave the impression that we consider the entirety of the black experience in America to be a sordid tale of victimization. Quite the contrary: as Ellis Cose has written, "Now is a great time—the best time ever—to be black in America" ("Good News About Black America," 30). African Americans have made enormous efforts to overcome the heritage of domination and economic exploitation. The untold heroes are in the millions. In spite of the oppression of white-led systems, structures and culture, millions of white allies have done their bit, or more, toward redeeming a sordid heritage, also in mostly unsung ways.

We do not want to overlook the concerns raised by responsible black authors about significant internal problems within black families (most profoundly, Patterson, *Rituals of Blood*, chap. 1), or predominantly black communities and "black America" as a whole (see Gates and West, *Future of the Race*; McWhorter, *Losing the Race*). Nor do we believe that racism is an entirely white-on-black phenomenon. Nor, finally, do we agree that all concerns raised by some African American leaders as justice issues are in fact justice issues. To converse honestly about these dimensions of our ongoing struggles about race in America, however, requires for whites a price of admission, we believe, because by centuries of discrimination and insensitivity we have long earned suspicion of our motives and of our commitment. And that price of admission is serious attention to the ongoing experience of racial injustice. As Ellis Cose says:

> Despite all the progress of the last several decades, we continue to talk about black America as a place and a people apart. And despite the lip service we pay to the concept of equality, we look with equanimity, even pride, upon a statistical profile of black Americans that, were it of whites, would be a source of horror and consternation. ("Good News About Black America," 40)

It also requires conversation, learning, sharing stories, establishing friendships and becoming allies. Andrea Ayvazian, Beverly Daniel Tatum and Rodolpho Carrasco give some very practical and healing suggestions in "Can We Talk?' and a "'New School' of Racial Healing" in *Crossing the Racial Divide* (Sojourners, 62-67). One of the deeper and often hidden realities for whites is subconscious shame about two realities in our history. First, being "white" has connotations of being identified with white racism, with white superiority claims and white oppression, and we do not want to identify with that or talk about it. Second, our families did not come to these shores as "whites," but as Celts, Irish, Italians, Germans, Greeks, Bulgarians, Russians, Scandinavians, Jews and so on. As such, we once had some rich ethnic family narratives and memories of the pilgrimage from the old country to the land of "liberty and justice for all," or however your family narrative runs.

Becoming known as "white" involved suppressing some of that rich ethnic heritage in order to conform to a dominating white culture and fit in. This white culture bleaches out the richness of heritage; "white" is not the name of a family narrative that I can affirm or be proud of or talk about; it carries the subtle shame not only of the history of white racism but also the subconscious shame of having repressed our German, Scandinavian or Huguenot heritage in order to fit in. And that shame blocks whites from asking blacks or Latinos or Koreans about their own family narratives and ethnic experience. It causes us to project an assumed generic narrative on others that makes us miss the rich diversity of others in our acquaintance. It causes a subtle conspiracy of silence about what we project as potentially embarrassing topics. But everybody has a story that would be interesting to talk about. We suggest that we all, including "whites," start talking openly, though with some sensitivity, humility and humor, about our own family narratives and ethnic foibles, and ask others, including blacks, Hispanics, Native Americans and so on, if family narratives have also been a part of their history. It really is surprising how quickly friendships and deeper sharing and good humor can open up. (For more on this, see Hulteen in Sojourners, *Crossing the Racial Divide*, 18-19, and Thandeka, *Learning to Be White*.)

Scripture and Race

We have focused our discussion on black-white relations in America because, as Donald Shriver puts it, white racism is America's "oldest civic injustice"

(*Ethic for Enemies,* 171) and its impact lingers to this day, as we have attempted to show.

Yet we do not wish to leave the impression that racial prejudice and injustice began in Jamestown in 1609. No, the God-given diversity of the human family was twisted by sin into the destruction of human community long before the first slaves reached our shores.

The Bible both records the conflicts between human people-groups and offers rich normative resources for racial justice and reconciliation. Let us consider these briefly.

The story of the election of Israel from among the peoples of the earth to be God's chosen people has been interpreted in ways both constructive and destructive to the cause of racial justice and reconciliation. Some voices within the Jewish tradition, though a definite minority, as well as some who have appropriated the story of Israel into their own self-understanding as one or another "new Israel" (white American settlers, Afrikaners in South Africa, etc.) have read Israel's election as divine affirmation of ethnic/racial superiority.

Yet this is a gross misunderstanding. Scripture repeatedly affirms that the people of Israel were chosen from among the nations not because of their superiority but because of their insignificance. Statements like these abound: "It was not because you were more numerous than any other people that the LORD set his heart on you and chose you—for you were the fewest of all peoples" (Deut 7:7). Election was an act of divine grace.

And election was linked to Israel's covenant fidelity. Indeed, its identity and continued status as a people uniquely related to God is inextricably linked to its way of life as a witness to God's will: "Now therefore, if you obey my voice and keep my covenant, you shall be my treasured possession out of all the peoples. Indeed, the whole earth is mine, but you shall be for me a priestly kingdom and a holy nation" (Ex 19:5-6).

The crowd fleeing the Egyptians was actually "mixed" (Ex 12:38), not ethnically homogeneous. It can be said that the exodus-Sinai experience rather than a common ethnicity crystallized the fugitives' identity as a people. Covenant fidelity makes one a part of the people of God. This hunch is confirmed by the numerous provisions of the law opening up membership in the Jewish community to those aliens willing to live by the terms of the covenant. Numerous commands in the Pentateuch include resident aliens—while a distinction is consistently drawn between them and other Israelites, the statutes apply to both with few variations (cf. Lev 17:8-15; Deut 26:11-13). We later see that several people not of Israelite extraction but faithful to the covenant gain an honored place in the biblical narrative—Ruth for example, who enters the lineage of David and thus of Jesus the Messiah. Isaiah also makes it clear that the Gentiles are to be welcomed.

Stark distinctions *are* drawn between the Israelites and other peoples, but these distinctions are religio-moral rather than racial. Constantly, the people are called to keep themselves separate from other peoples, but the concern is idolatry rather than any kind of racism as we might think of it. The separatism that is called for appears never to have been fully achieved, and one of the central themes of the Old Testament is Israel's struggle toward an exclusive Yahwistic monotheism and away from a local syncretism encouraged by intermarriage and neighborly ties.

The closest the Old Testament ever gets to crossing over the line between religious and racial separatism is in the postexilic books of Ezra and Nehemiah. In Ezra, for example, the desperate community of returned exiles is depicted as divorcing their foreign wives and sending away the children of those marriages. They do so in order to regain God's favor (cf. Ezra 9—10) by preserving the holy "seed" (Ezra 9:2 NRSV; not "race" [NIV]; Heb *zerah*) from *religious* rather than *racial* contamination, though the distinction is perhaps clearer to us than it would have been to this book's first readers.

Several prophets add an important theme to Israel's self-understanding when they affirm that God is in fact intensely related to other peoples. Amos strikes an astonishingly universalistic note in saying: "Are you not like the Ethiopians to me, O people of Israel? says the LORD. Did I not bring Israel up from the land of Egypt, and the Philistines from Caphtor and the Arameans from Kir?" (Amos 9:7). The book of Jonah concerns God's successful effort to bring about the repentance of the hated Assyrians, despite the reluctant prophet's best effort to avoid being of use in that cause. Warnings of judgment abound in relation to other nations (cf. Amos 1:3—2:5) but so do numerous promises that the nations will one day be brought into a joyful covenant relationship with God (cf. Is 2:3-4; Zech 8:20-22).

All this being said, it is still true that as we move toward the New Testament era some in the ancient world were not able to discern the distinction between religious and ethnic particularism among the Jewish people, and some Jews left the impression of believing in their ethnic superiority over Gentiles. The tension between Jews and Gentiles is one of the striking themes of the New Testament. How that tension was handled provides rich resources for Christian thinking about racial justice and reconciliation today.

Jesus clearly undertook his ministry within a Jewish context and worked primarily with fellow Jews. And yet the Gospel accounts make clear that in his itinerant ministry he roamed well beyond Jewish territory. Much of his work was focused in Galilee rather than the heart of Jewish life in Judea, and he also visited non-Jewish areas such as the cities of Tyre and Sidon, the Decapolis across the Sea of Galilee, Perea and, most significantly perhaps, Samaria. Everywhere he went, he offered essentially the same ministry of preaching, teaching, healing and exorcism.

Within Jewish territory, Jesus did not hesitate to talk to any who crossed his path, including officials of the hated Roman occupation. His encounter with a centurion elicited this exclamation: "I tell you, not even in Israel have I found such faith" (Lk 7:9). In reference to Jesus' teaching, the parable of the compassionate Samaritan is rightly interpreted not only as a clarion call to active compassion but also as a ringing repudiation of anti-Samaritan religio-racism. And in the Great Commission (Mt 28:16-20) Jesus instituted a global mission for the early church, calling his followers to make disciples of all nations (*ethnoi* = peoples). At Pentecost, the Holy Spirit began the work of sending the disciples to all the language-groups (Acts 1:4, 8; 2:1-13; and the whole book of Acts shows the Holy Spirit working in the hearts of an increasingly diverse assortment of Gentiles. See especially Stagg, *Book of Acts;* Dempster et al., *Called and Empowered*).

The early church struggled mightily to cross the Jew-Gentile barrier once and for all as its mission spread throughout the Mediterranean world. Whether Gentiles should be included in the community of Christ-followers at all (cf. Acts 10), or to what extent they would have to take on historic biblical and cultural markers of Jewish identity to be included in Christian community (cf. Acts 15, Gal 2), were major and deeply controverted decisions among the earliest Christians. While signs of real struggle and difference of opinion are obvious, the ultimate outcome is clear—the Christian faith and community would be an international and interethnic reality. A vision of a new kind of humanity took root, one in which historic ethnic barriers were put to death (Eph 2:16) and Christians of all ethnic backgrounds formed a new household (Eph 2:19), a family of faith with Jesus Christ at its head. The book of Acts reveals that the early church did in fact become such a multiethnic community, with leadership provided by Africans, Asians and Europeans, and of course by both Jews and Gentiles (DeYoung, "Racial Reconciliation and the Twenty-first Century Church").

This is the vision on the issue of race that Scripture leaves with all who read it rightly. Christians do take community seriously, and any serious community requires boundaries, but with both the Old and the New Testament we must affirm that Christian community boundaries are to be religio-moral rather than racial-ethnic. It is possible to be excluded from Christian community on the basis of heterodoxy (grave theological error) or heteropraxy (grave moral error) but not, to coin a phrase, heteroethnicity. That some Christians have not understood this, and still do not understand this, constitutes one of the gravest offenses possible against the gospel (for further resources, see McKenzie, *All God's Children;* Okholm, ed., *The Gospel in Black and White*).

Racial Justice and Reconciliation: On the Frontiers

Today the United States is more ethnically diverse than any society in history.

The 2000 census revealed, among other things, a sharp rise in the number of Hispanic Americans, who now have pulled even with African Americans in the population at around 35 million each. There has been a dramatic increase in the number of people identifying themselves as mixed-race, reminding us that the very concept of "race" is socially constructed; and California has become the first state in which whites do not constitute a simple majority of the population. While white racism is America's original sin, and its predominant victims were first native Americans and then black Americans, America in the twenty-first century will offer a much more complex and multidirectional set of challenges and opportunities (for a similar analysis, see Patterson, "Race Over," 6; and Sojourners, *America's Original Sin*).

The northern Virginia area, for example, where I grew up, was overwhelmingly white in the 1960s and 1970s with a small and rather segregated black population. Now it is among the most diverse regions in the land, a veritable ethnic smorgasbord of men, women and children from most nations on earth. As the next northern Virginia generation grows up in this environment, cross-ethnic dating and intermarrying will undoubtedly create the kind of interethnic community that our nation's racists have always feared and sought to prevent.

And yet there will remain pockets of the nation in which racial issues look pretty much like they always have. In much of the rural and small-town South, such as my own Jackson, Tennessee, community, to speak of "race" is still to speak primarily of a black-white reality—at least for now. It is still to witness sometimes subtle, sometimes not-so-subtle white-black racial tensions in the public schools, the town councils and the grocery stores—not to mention the churches. Here it is still possible to speak quite accurately of "white" and "black" churches. Most white Southern Baptist churches in town have not a single black member, and most black Baptist churches not a single white member. We sing some of the same songs but do not sing them together. And efforts to cross the color line, at least in the white churches, remain harrowing in some places. It is beyond shameful.

It seems to me that in this region of the country, in any case, and perhaps elsewhere, the courageous and pioneering spirit of the civil rights crusaders of the 1960s is still needed in crossing this last frontier of racial integration. I find that spirit in some of my students, who can be found quietly building bridges across racial lines. Pioneers of this type can be found across the nation.

Martin Luther King's most poignant phrase was perhaps "the beloved community." This phrase makes for a good place to circle around to the thesis we have been exploring here. We have argued that racial reconciliation may be the wrong conceptual tool, at least for now, with which to understand the racial situation in the United States. Instead, we have said that *ra-*

cial justice should be our primary paradigm. When we consider black-white relations at least, using categories of justice derived from Jesus' teaching, we discover numerous areas in which injustice prevails. Reconciliation, if it is to happen at all, must come as a consequence of white Americans taking racial injustice toward black Americans seriously and responding with concrete political and social action.

According to Michael Emerson and Christian Smith, this is precisely what white evangelicals have been unable or unwilling to do. Their sociological study of evangelical attitudes toward race reveals a pervasive individualism and what they call a *relationalism* in white attitudes. Whites they interviewed were almost invariably unwilling or unable to recognize the social dimension of race relations in America, in part due to an individualistic understanding of sin and salvation. A handful of scattered individuals may be racists, these interviewees granted, but there is no systemic racial problem in America. If this is so, then the only thing a white evangelical can do about race relations is to avoid personal prejudice and try to get along with everyone they encounter (Emerson and Smith, *Divided by Faith?* 38).

If, as Emerson and Smith boldly claim, "this is the white American evangelical perspective on race" (cf. Blackmon, "Racial Reconciliation Becomes a Priority"), we have one of the clues we need as to the misdirection, and even failure, of efforts at racial reconciliation emanating from white Christian Americans. An inability or unwillingness to recognize systemic racial injustice makes real racial reconciliation all but impossible. We would argue here that this blind spot is rooted not only in white social isolation from blacks and theological individualism, as Emerson and Smith claim, but also in a broader misreading of the meaning of the life and message of Jesus Christ. We think he has everything to do with justice; most of our white coreligionists do not. Their understanding of the gospel has trained them not to notice injustice.

There is one nuance to be added at this point. Within the black community one finds some thinkers and leaders who have puzzled over this justice/reconciliation issue and appear to have come out in a different place from the one we are advocating here. For seventeen years, Spencer Perkins and his white friend Chris Rice attempted an experiment in racial reconciliation through living in intentional interracial community in Jackson, Mississippi. Out of this effort to incarnate "racial healing for the sake of the gospel," as they called it, Perkins and Rice wrote a significant book (*More Than Equals*) and edited a magazine whose title, *Reconcilers*, indicates the vision for race relations that they were pursuing before Perkins' untimely death in early 1998.

In Perkins's last public speech, he described his journey toward an emphasis on grace, forgiveness and reconciliation with "white folks." At the close of this speech Perkins clarified his stance on the relationship between forgiveness and justice in the following way:

> Nothing that I have been learning about grace and forgiveness diminishes my belief in Christians working for justice. . . . I know many tired soldiers who, like me, have fought for social justice most of their lives. Nothing in the Scriptures even hints that these modern-day prophets of justice should soften their message. But I know that some of them have carried an extra weight of resentment against people they consider oppressors. . . . Although we must continue to speak on behalf of those who are oppressed and warn oppressors, my willingness to forgive them is not dependent on how they respond. Being able to extend grace and to forgive people sets us free. ("Playing the Grace Card," 43)

This clarifies something very important. As Howard Thurman pointed out many years ago, there is a significant difference that exists in the moral situation facing the historic oppressor and the historically oppressed. When Perkins talks of grace and forgiveness, he primarily speaks to the need for black Christians to forgive their white oppressors, both for blacks' own spiritual/moral well-being and for the sake, ultimately, of effectiveness in achieving racial justice itself (Perkins, "Playing the Grace Card," 44). Perkins describes this conviction not as an easy conclusion but as the outcome of a fierce struggle within himself. This choice for grace despite all obstacles is really quite extraordinary, and yet it characterized the work of Martin Luther King and the leadership of the civil rights movement as well. Looking back on the entire history of postemancipation politics among black Americans, Donald Shriver has wondered, "Is there, in the culture of a significant segment of African Americans, a predisposition toward, an ingrained *gift* for, injecting forgiveness into their political relations with the white majority of this country?" (*Ethic for Enemies,* 177).

Perhaps there is. If so, it is an astonishing gift to offer to white Americans. But it is not a gift that white Christians can either take for granted or piggyback on. The problem is that when white evangelicals speak of forgiveness and reconciliation they normally do not do so out of the experience of *solidarity* with blacks in suffering for justice but instead as a *substitute* for that work of justice. Chris Rice was and is an exception to that pattern, and this is why his own talk of reconciliation has had more viability—and he still speaks of justice quite vigorously as well (see Rice, "More Than Family"). In short, while black Christians are morally entitled to emphasize the ultimate aim of reconciliation, white Christians are generally not thus entitled. Our calling is to join in the struggle for justice; only within that context can we then, later, speak credibly of reconciliation (cf. Barndt, *Dismantling Racism*).

As we close, then, we do not back away from our thesis but instead find it confirmed. Martin Luther King's vision of the "beloved community" reminds us that out ahead of us remains the goal of full and joyful reconciliation across black-white (and all) racial lines. The dream is, as King said, a beloved (and loving) community, in which men and women of all races genuinely love one another as Jesus has loved us. Yet the path to such a community is not *around* the hard work of justice but right *through* it—exactly the path that King himself took, as even a cursory reading of his published works reveals (see Washington, *Testament of Hope*). The church, which has lagged so shamefully behind as the nation has taken steps toward racial justice, needs to make up that lost ground and then move on to the next frontier, the one King lived and died for—the beloved community.

20

ECONOMICS

■

Do not store up for yourselves treasures on earth, where moth and rust consume and

where thieves break in and steal; but store up for yourselves treasures in heaven, where

neither moth nor rust consume and where thieves do not break in and steal. For where

your treasure is, there your heart will be also. . . . No one can serve two masters; for a slave

will either hate the one and love the other, or be devoted to the one and despise the other.

You cannot serve God and wealth.

MATTHEW 6:19-21, 24

The challenge of developing a Christian moral vision for economic life has been with the church since its very beginning. Few issues in Christian ethics have generated a literature as massive or as polemical (for a helpful recent survey-anthology, see Atherton, *Christian Social Ethics*). Few issues are so thoroughly addressed in Scripture, including the teachings of Jesus. And few are so directly applicable at every level of Christian moral engagement—individual and family life, church practices and public ethics.

In this chapter, in keeping with our method, the bulk of our attention will go to the teachings of Jesus, beginning in the Sermon on the Mount and then extending outward to the rest of what Jesus has to say in the Gospel accounts. We will then consider several of the most significant issues in contemporary economic ethics and consider how the broader biblical witness ought to shape our response.

It is important to note both the unity and the diversity of the biblical witness on this issue, as on most moral issues of any significance. The challenge for interpreters is to take the diversity seriously while emerging from the process of reading Scripture with some kind of synthesis offering concrete guidance for disciples of Jesus Christ today (cf. Wheeler's careful discussion of ethical methodology and exegesis, *Wealth as Peril and Obligation*, chaps. 1-2). This is what we will attempt to do here.

You Cannot Serve God and Wealth: Mammon and the Sermon

Matthew 6:19 begins the third major section of the Sermon on the Mount (6:19—7:12). Biblical scholars disagree on which verses should be grouped as units. Betz (*Sermon on the Mount*, 423) gives up on grouping them and simply sees eight separate teachings. Others group them in clusters but disagree on precisely how to do that. We will attempt to show that Matthew 6:19-34 contains two distinct but related triads both relevant to this topic. We see them as triads eleven (Mt 6:19-23) and twelve (Mt 6:24-34) of the Sermon.

All scholars agree that Matthew 6:19 begins a new unit. It begins with a traditional or proverbial teaching, a negative imperative. Literally translated, it reads: "Do not treasure up for yourselves treasures on earth." The play on words, "treasure up treasures," connotes hoarding out of pride, greed and stinginess.

The vicious cycle is then clear: "where moth and rust consume and thieves break in and steal" (cf. Jas 5:1-6). Material possessions have always been susceptible to decay and theft, but Jesus' first-century listeners would have been acutely aware of the problem. Thieves could dig right through the walls of most homes and steal any strongbox in which precious possessions might be stored. Some dealt with this problem by hiding valuables in caves or burying them in the ground, but both clothing and coins could easily be ruined in such hiding places (Keener, *IVP Bible Background Commentary*, 63). The folly of accumulating excess goods in such circumstances is obvious.

The transforming initiative is found in the imperative (Mt 6:20): "But treasure up for yourselves treasures in heaven." This text is quite similar to a saying found in the apocryphal book of Tobit: "If you have many possessions, make your gift from them in proportion; if few, do not be afraid to give according to the little you have. So you will be laying up a good treasure for yourself against the day of necessity" (Tobit 4:8-9). The concept of treasures in heaven is also mentioned elsewhere in Jesus' teaching (Mt 19:21//Mk 10:21//Lk 18:22; Mt 13:44; Lk 12:33) and in the epistles (1 Tim 6:19; Jas 5:3). The idea is that a life of economic generosity trades earthly treasures for divine approval in this life and the next, an exchange of "treasures" well worth making.

This first explanation is linked to two others: "where your treasure is, there your heart will be also" (Mt 6:21) and "If your eye is healthy, your whole body will be full of light" (Mt 6:22). These comments illustrate our claim that Jesus did not teach impossible ideals but transforming initiatives that participate in the deliverance of the kingdom.

"Heaven," for Matthew, is "the sphere of God's rule where his will is done. . . . To have one's treasure in heaven means to submit oneself totally to that which is in heaven—God's sovereign rule. It is this motif that follows Mt. 6:19-

21 in 6:22-23, 24, 33, not to mention the parallels in 5:8, 7:21, and 12:34" (Gue-lich, *Sermon on the Mount*, 327-28). The contrast Jesus was drawing was not be-tween this life and the life after, but between this life characterized by profound, misery-causing injustice and God's coming reign characterized by salvation, justice, peace and joy in God's presence. The transforming initiative is to invest one's treasures in God's reign of justice and love through practices of economic generosity and justice-making.

This teaching does not "idealistically" reject personal property or the hold-ing of any possessions (as has sometimes been argued), but instead "treasur-ing up treasures"—stinginess, greed, hoarding and lack of generosity. The reference to vision is critical here. The ability to "see" the coming eschatologi-cal era and to respond with appropriate deeds constitutes "messianic salva-tion" (Gundry, *Matthew*, 113). As well, the "evil eye" in Jewish teaching connotes stinginess and greed and the "healthy" (or "single") eye connotes generosity (Gundry, *Matthew*, 113-14; Davies and Allison, *Critical and Exegetical Commentary*, 1:638). Matthew 6:22-23 pulls these two themes together and could perhaps be restated something like this: "If in view of the coming es-chaton you see your neighbor's need rightly and respond generously, your en-tire self blazes with the light of God's presence; but if you close your eyes to your neighbor's need, your self is full of the darkness of God's absence, and that darkness is very great indeed." That then leads us back to Matthew 6:21: Either path you choose reveals the true condition of your heart.

A genuinely "impossible ideal" would be to do what so many (including Christians) in wealthy cultures such as our own do: piling up wealth and ex-travagant possessions for themselves while at the same time claiming to give as generously to the needy as they "can," and living extravagantly while claiming not to be affected by such spending choices in their "hearts." Jesus' teaching is far more realistic: invest your possessions generously in God's reign of justice and mercy, and you will find your heart is invested there as well.

Sondra Wheeler points out that a transformed economic praxis such as Jesus teaches here "*follows* from faith, the reasonable response of one who per-ceives in Jesus the advent of the kingdom" (*Wealth as Peril and Obligation*, 68). In other words, disciples do not live simply and give generously in order to be counted worthy of being disciples. Instead, because we are disciples of Jesus and are invested in his eschatological project it naturally follows that we reori-ent our lives in every area, including economic life. This claim fits with the theme we have attempted to pursue throughout this volume—kingdom ethics is grace-based, rooted in an invitation to participate in the inbreaking of God's reign through Jesus Christ. Disciples are those who believe the story of Jesus the Messiah, enter it and live accordingly.

We have said that scholars are in much disagreement about how to group

the teachings in this section, and that our new awareness of the triadic structure might help. Gundry and Betz both treat Matthew 6:24—"No one can
serve two masters"—as independent of either the preceding or the succeeding verse, but Schweizer (*Good News According to Matthew*, 213), Davies and
Allison (*Critical and Exegetical Commentary*, 1:626, 641), Blomberg (*Matthew*,
124), Guelich (*Sermon on the Mount*, 367-68), Luz (*Matthew 1—7*, 398), Hagner
(*Matthew 1—13*, 159) and Lambrecht (*Out of the Treasure*, 159) treat 6:24 as belonging with 6:19-23. If the majority is right, we may then see the admonition
against worry in Matthew 6:25-30 as the traditional teaching plus explanation, 6:31-32 as the vicious cycle and 6:33-34 as the transforming initiative.
The grammatical and rhetorical structure would fit the pattern we proposed
in chapter 6, except that the traditional teaching includes three imperatives:
"do not worry . . . look . . . consider."

Alternatively, the triadic pattern might suggest that we cluster Matthew
6:24 with what follows in 25-34, and see verse 24 as the traditional teaching
that begins the triad. This is what we think more likely fits. It would work out
in the following way.

The first part of Matthew 6:24 reads: "No one can [is able to] serve two masters; for a slave will either hate the one and love the other, or be devoted to the
one and despise the other." This statement takes the form of a traditional Jewish wisdom proverb (Guelich, *Sermon on the Mount*, 333; Davies and Allison,
Critical and Exegetical Commentary, 1:642; Betz, *Sermon on the Mount*, 456). Hillel
is reported as saying, "the more possessions, the more care" (Hagner, *Matthew
1—13*, 159). The idea that one cannot serve God and money "was far-flung in
antiquity" (Allison, *Sermon on the Mount*, 145). As expected in the traditional
teaching part of a Matthean triad, it is negative, and it is not an imperative.

The vicious cycle is named directly in the last part of Matthew 6:24: "You
cannot [literally: are not able to] serve God and wealth [mammon]." Those who
attempt to do so are like those slaves who attempt to serve two imperious masters—they are placed in an impossible position. Only one master can be served.
The effort to evade this fact of existence is simply a futile self-deception.

Matthew 6:25-33 then offers four exhortations: "do not worry," "look at the
birds," "consider the lilies," and "strive first for the kingdom." If "do not worry" is counted as part of the transforming initiative, it breaks our normal pattern, for it is a negative verb rather than an imperative; in every other case in
the Sermon, negative verbs are associated with the vicious cycle element rather than the transforming initiative. And it fits with the vicious cycle just
named: attempting the impossible by serving both God and mammon, one
ends up in the condition of being anxious about possessions.

The thrust of the transforming initiative is found in the latter three imperatives, climaxing in the exhortation to "strive first for the kingdom of God and

his righteousness." These imperatives teach us to give ourselves over to trusting participation in the dynamic, gracious, delivering presence of God. In looking at the provision God majestically offers for the flora and fauna we are called away from anxiety to trust in God the Creator-Sustainer-Redeemer. When we make the critical life decision to devote our "eyes" and "heart"—our selves—to participation in the reign of God we break loose from the vicious cycle of "mammonism" and are set free to live for justice with singleness of purpose. Not only does this decision make us fully useful as instruments of kingdom work, it is both wise and reasonable as well. As Jesus reminds us, worry never added a day to life or clothed and fed anybody. "Today's trouble is enough for today" (Mt 6:34). Trust God for "daily bread," and devote yourself to the kingdom.

The thematic consistency of this entire passage (Mt 6:19-34) is summarized nicely by Guelich:

> Since God's sovereign rule and all the benefits for our material needs come from God to us, this passage suggests by implication that we can become a part of God's redemptive force in history by sharing these benefits with those who are in need. . . . Part of the presence of the Kingdom is indeed material blessings. Therefore, we can hardly live under God's reign, receive his blessings, and not use them to help alleviate the evil of hunger and need elsewhere. . . . Not only do we recognize that all we have comes from God, but we also recognize that sharing that with others to remove their suffering is to defeat the enemy and to "seek the Kingdom . . . on earth as in heaven." (*Sermon on the Mount,* 373)

It is important to read the exhortation against worry in light of the emphasis on economic generosity and the economic justice that characterizes God's reign ("strive first for the kingdom of God and his *dikaiosynē* [righteousness/ justice]"). Seeing this can help comfortable Westerners avoid reducing Jesus' moral teaching on economic life to something like the following understanding, so common in our churches: "Enjoy your material comforts and try not to worry too much if you don't have everything you want."

Instead, in a context characterized by extraordinary economic exploitation in Jesus' own day and long economic depression in Matthew's time, Jesus was teaching about the kind of compassionate and merciful justice that delivers the poor from poverty and restores them into community. This is a justice teaching, not a psychological teaching. And it is a discipleship teaching, a summons to serve God's compassionate reign through acts of justice-advancing compassion toward the most economically vulnerable and oppressed.

Evidence from elsewhere in the Sermon on the Mount helps confirm this reading. In Matthew 6:1-18, on the "practice of piety," which is better translated as the "practice of righteousness/justice" (Greek *dikaiosynē*—see chapter twenty-two), Jesus reaffirmed the giving of alms (charity) to the poor, attacking the prideful quest to be noticed but not challenging the central Jewish practice of almsgiving in any way. In Matthew 5:42 Jesus called his disciples to "give to everyone who begs from you." And in the Lord's Prayer (Mt 6:9-13), where Jesus taught us to pray for God's reign to come, God's will to be done, on earth as it is in heaven, and for the bread we need for the day, Jesus also taught forgiveness of debts and linked this practice inextricably with God's forgiveness of our "debts" before him (see chapter twenty-two). This reference appears to be linked to the Old Testament theme of debt-forgiveness in the Jubilee year (Lev 25, 27), as J. H. Yoder was among the first to point out (*Politics of Jesus*, chap. 3; but compare N. T. Wright, *Jesus and the Victory of God*, 295).

In short, working only with the Sermon on the Mount to this point, we see certain essentials of a Jesus-centered economic ethic. Seeing the inbreaking reign of God when most do not, the follower of Jesus is overjoyed at the opportunity to participate in the kingdom's dynamic advance in every area, economic life included. Living simply, not hoarding wealth for ourselves and trusting God to meet our basic material needs are practices that free us to offer generosity to and seek justice for and with the poor and hungry and, in general, to follow Jesus. Finally, in turning our hearts and eyes in this direction we ourselves enjoy the added benefit of a remarkable personal liberation that yanks us free from greed, acquisitiveness and a fruitless worry over treasures that will all too soon pass away.

Jesus and Money Elsewhere in the Gospels

Even outside the Sermon on the Mount, the Gospels offer an abundance of testimony concerning Jesus' teaching about money, wealth, poverty and greed. It is especially important to review this because North American Christians have developed and refined a variety of evasion strategies for (not) dealing with these teachings. Our defenses are so firmly entrenched that it is very difficult for us to simply listen to these texts without qualifying, spiritualizing or dismissing them. Let us refuse to do that here. We will consider five major themes of Jesus' teaching about money as found in the rest of the Gospels.

1. Possessions are intrinsically insignificant beyond the basic sufficiency provided by our gracious God. We have already seen in the Sermon on the Mount that Jesus calls his listeners to trust God rather than worry about food, drink and clothing. This has seemed to many interpreters as a "hard saying" or "counsel of perfection." It does not seem like such an impossible ideal, however, when one considers Jesus' emphasis on investing in God's kingdom and justice so that all have basic needs cared for (Mt 6:33).

In Luke 12:13-15 we read the story of the man asking Jesus to settle an inheritance dispute the man is having with his brother. Jesus refuses to get involved in estate arbitration and warns his listeners: "Take care! Be on your guard against all kinds of greed; for one's life does not consist in the abundance of possessions."

It must be emphasized that having a basic sufficiency of food and drink, clothing, shelter and medical care is *not* insignificant. Both by his teachings (cf. Mt 25:31-46) and by his actions of feeding and healing, Jesus affirmed the need to feed, clothe and house the human body. Jesus must not be interpreted as a gnostic or dualistic dreamer who cared nothing for the human body and its needs. Money and possessions have value as a resource for ourselves and for helping others in need (Wheeler, *Wealth as Peril and Obligation,* 132-33).

The spiritual and moral problem develops when people ascribe undue significance to possessions. It is easy for us to think of this as a uniquely contemporary problem; we are deluged with skillful advertising that tells us a series of lies about the great significance of this or that food, television, gadget or car. But the fact that Jesus addressed the issue shows that finding "one's life" in the "abundance of possessions" is a human problem rather than a modern problem alone. The issue has to do with treating possessions, as Joel Green puts it, "as an alternative landmark according to which one might define one's life, and thus as a peril to eternal life" (*Gospel of Luke,* 489 n. 34).

2. Misreading the value of possessions stimulates greed. It is no coincidence that Jesus employed images related to sight when speaking of the problem of treasuring up treasures on earth. For in a sense this is fundamentally a problem of vision—that is, moral perception. Misperceiving the value of possessions leads one to moral decisions characterized by greed, which can be defined as *an excessive desire for money and the things money can buy.*

Jesus attacked the Pharisees as "full of greed and self-indulgence" (Mt 23:25; cf. Lk 11:39, "greed and wickedness"; in Lk 16:14 they are described as "lovers of money"). We have already seen in Matthew 6:24 the intrinsic conflict between love of God and love of wealth. Greed is a spiritual and moral disorder. Rooted in a fundamental misunderstanding of the value of possessions and of the role that possessions can play in a person's life, greed misleads men and women into ascribing inordinate value to that which is not worthy of it. When wealth, or the possessions wealth can buy, ascends into a position of inordinate value, it is both a form of idolatry and a pitiful delusion contrary to the best interests of the human being. Seeing wealth as an occasion for idolatry is a major Old Testament theme, especially in the prophets, and Jesus (as well as other New Testament writers) picks up and develops this theme (Wheeler, *Wealth as Peril and Obligation,* 123-24, 129).

The delusional nature of greed is illustrated in a terrifying way by the parable of the rich fool (Lk 12:16-21). Here a wealthy farmer-landowner is blessed with an especially abundant harvest. Unwilling to sell the excess produce on a saturated market and unable to find a place to store all this grain and, apparently, his many other "goods" (Lk 12:18), he embarks on the ambitious project of tearing down all his barns to build larger ones. That very night, he gets a rude surprise: "You fool! This very night your life is being demanded of you. And the things you have prepared, whose will they be?" (Lk 12:20). Jesus concluded, "So it is with those who store up treasures for themselves but are not rich toward God" (Lk 12: 21). To live in greed or to love possessions is to stake one's life on the transitory and vain, to reject God and God's will, and thus to invite divine judgment.

3. Greed encourages a lifestyle of luxury, pride, hoarding, self-indulgence, oppression and lack of generosity. Something else is illustrated by this story. The problem with greed is not just that it is a personal spiritual disorder, but that it leads to sins against one's neighbor, in particular hoarding and lack of generosity. The clear implication of the story of the rich fool is that he should have responded to God's overabundant provision by sharing with those less fortunate. Some might have been able to eat who otherwise would not. This would have stored up treasures in heaven; instead the landowner chose treasures on earth, only to have them rudely snatched away. His greed blinded him to the obvious moral responsibility to aid his neighbor.

We have already seen that Jesus, in continuity with both Old Testament and rabbinic Judaism, taught enjoining extensive almsgiving and economic generosity. People whose hearts are given over to God give to their neighbor with open-heartedness, in so doing offering devotion to God. The account of the great judgment in Matthew 25:31-46 makes entrance into eternal life contingent upon feeding the hungry, welcoming the stranger, clothing the naked and visiting the sick and imprisoned. Here we see that generosity encompasses both giving *material goods* and *service* to those in need.

This dynamic is central to Jesus' intention when he calls followers to sell their possessions. In Luke 12:33, a passage that largely parallels Matthew 6:24-34 in the Sermon on the Mount, Jesus is reported to have also said: "Sell your possessions, and give alms." Luke 14:33 reads: "None of you can become my disciple if you do not give up all your possessions."

The most familiar of these passages is the story of the rich young ruler (Mt 19:16-30//Mk 10:17-31//Lk 18:18-30). Here Jesus encountered what appeared to be an earnest seeker. He was honest in his search to find out "what must I do to inherit eternal life?" (Mk 10:17). He claimed to have kept the moral teachings of the Decalogue since youth, as Jesus suggested (in good Jewish fashion) was required of him. And Jesus never challenged him on this point, instead saying: "You lack one thing; go, sell what you own, and give the money to the poor, and you will have treasure in heaven; then come, follow me" (Mk 10:21). The man was shocked by this demand and went away grieving, because he had many possessions. Jesus then warned his disciples about the dangers of wealth and said, "It is easier for a camel to go through the eye of a needle than for a rich man to enter the kingdom of God" (Mk 10:25).

This teaching is evaded or spiritualized to death in suburban churches. The man is described as "having the wrong priorities" or "having a wrong attitude toward money." True enough, perhaps, but evasive of the central point: *the man's attachment to his possessions both manifested an inordinate love for them which blocked generosity to the poor and led him to say no to following Jesus.* Jesus really did ask the man to sell all that he had, to give it all to the poor and to embark on a new life of itinerant kingdom poverty with the community of disciples. Those who followed Jesus frequently did exactly this, selling their possessions, giving the money to the poor and/or contributing it to the common purse that supported Jesus' movement and ensured that all had their basic needs met (cf. 1 Jn 3:17-18; Acts 4:32-37; 5:1-11; 2 Cor 8:13-15; Garland, *Reading Matthew,* 396ff; Hays, *Moral Vision of the New Testament,* 464). And Jesus really did say that wealth poses a mortal spiritual threat. No exegetical gymnastics related to an imagined "Needle's Eye" gate in Jerusalem (a fabrication first suggested in the eleventh century!) can save us from the obvious import of the text (Garland, *Reading Matthew,* 401).

These familiar exegetical contortions might be humorous were there not so much at stake. Wealthy or comfortable readers would be better off taking Jesus at his word, and believing that wealth—acquired by work or by inheritance, by luck or by labor—presents profound spiritual dangers. This does not mean that no person of wealth can enter into eternal life; Jesus did not make this claim. It does mean that people in positions of considerable wealth should take careful heed of the state of their souls as evidenced by their practices.

This is also the significance of the unforgettable story of Lazarus and the rich man in Luke 16:19-31. Here a stark contrast is drawn between the rich man (not given a name, in an ironic reversal of social realities; see Green, *Gospel of Luke,* 606) and the poor beggar, Lazarus. The rich man has a superfluity of the most luxurious clothing and sumptuous food and drink. Poor Lazarus has nothing. He has been tossed outside the gates of the rich man and is given nary a scrap. At death, their conditions of suffering and privilege are reversed, with no explicit explanation—the rich man is in torment, Lazarus in Abraham's bosom. It is hard to avoid the conclusion (not that many have not attempted it) that it was the inebriated unconcern of the rich man for his suffering neighbor that led to his eternal downfall. In his luxury and greed he had abandoned the most basic obligations of generosity.

4. The deceptive allure of wealth can choke discipleship and imperil the soul. In the parable of the sower and the seed (Mk 4:3-20//Mt 13:3-23//Lk 8:4-15), Jesus outlined four kinds of responses to the "word of the kingdom" (Mt 13:19). What is germane for our purposes is the third type of soil/response, the "thorny." Both Matthew 13:22 and Mark 4:19 say that the seed sown among thorns represents the person whose growth is "choke[d]" by, among other things, *apatē tou ploutou* (NRSV, "the lure of wealth," better translated in the NIV as "the deceitfulness of wealth"). Jesus was saying that there is a type of listener who begins to respond to the kingdom's joyful news but whose progress is choked off by worldly concerns and the deceitfulness of wealth and possessions. *Deceitfulness* is precisely the right term, for deception involves misrepresenting reality—concealing or distorting the truth about something for the purpose of misleading others. Wealth has a kind of power of deceit; it can fool people into seeing in it a kind of earthly salvation ("life") that simply cannot be found there. A marvelous line from the Tennessee Williams classic *Cat on a Hot Tin Roof* captures this nicely:

> The human animal is a beast that eventually has to die. And if he's got money he buys and he buys and he buys. And the reason why he buys everything he can is because of the crazy hope that one of the things he buys will be life everlasting— which it can never be.

All that we have reviewed thus far reminds us of why Jesus warned about wealth: the temptation to misread the value of possessions, the consequent greedy spirit, a way of life characterized by luxury, self-indulgence and lack of generosity, the threat of wealth choking off growth in discipleship—all of these are clear teachings of Jesus that also find confirmation in everyday life if we look with discernment on the world around us.

5. Jesus identified with the poor and promises abundance and justice in a coming "great reversal." Perhaps it is not surprising, in view of all of the foregoing, that Jesus—while the bearer of a message for any person in any context—identified with the poor and hungry, directed his attention to the needs of the poor, celebrated the receptivity of the poor to God and (in Luke, especially) promised the poor a coming time of abundance and justice that contrasts with their current state of need and oppression.

We have already touched on several of these themes in earlier chapters, in discussing the meaning of the reign of God and how Jesus positioned his ministry in relation to that reign. We have shown that the Old Testament hope of the kingdom of God included a vision of justice, of which economic justice for the poor and hungry was an inextricable part. In inaugurating his ministry (Lk 4:18-21), Jesus appropriated Isaiah 61 and its messianic promise of "good news for the poor," release for the captives and freedom for the oppressed (cf. Mt 11:5).

Jesus ministered among the poor throughout his brief sojourn here, feeding them, healing them and addressing systemic injustice that kept them in their wretched condition (see chapter seventeen). His parables frequently involve the inclusion of the previously excluded poor (cf. Lk 14:15-24). He enjoined almsgiving for the poor, as we have seen. Zaccheus the tax collector sought to show his good faith to Jesus by giving his ill-gotten gains to the poor (Lk 19:8). Jesus' disciples and his band of itinerants appeared to practice almsgiving when they had means (cf. Jn 12:5-6; 13:29). Jesus attacked and sometimes poked fun at the luxurious (cf. Lk 7:25; 19:16-31) and contrasted their superfluous possessions with the meager lot of the poor.

In Luke, Jesus promised a future time of abundance for the poor, in which they inherit the kingdom of God and finally eat to their fill (Lk 6:20-21), while those currently rich find themselves on the outside looking in. The same theme, as we have seen, takes parabolic form in the story of the rich man and Lazarus. This has been called "the great reversal" (Verhey, *The Great Reversal*; cf. Kraybill, *Upside-Down Kingdom*) or, more technically, "transposition" (Green, *Gospel of Luke*, 264), and it is one of the most radical dimensions of Jesus' teaching, and not just on economic issues (cf. Lk 1:46-55; 14:7-24; 18:9-14, 22-24). It stands in continuity with the prophetic promise of abundance and prosperity for all in the time of God's reign, a joyful contrast with the perennial misery and injustice of poverty in the midst of plenty.

Key Themes in Christian Economic Ethics

Jesus' teaching on the economic practices and attitudes of kingdom people has obviously been enormously influential in shaping Christian behavior and belief through two millennia. Yet Christian economic ethics has developed themes from other strands of Scripture and has been required to address a range of moral concerns arising in various historical contexts. Further, to be quite honest, Jesus' bracing teachings have often been ignored or evaded.

In this final section, let us touch on several of the most significant themes and issues in Christian economic ethics more broadly considered. We will name the issue, articulate our basic stance amidst competing alternatives, and along the way point to some of the most significant literature available.

Property rights, work and the nature of ownership. Some interpreters of Jesus' teachings, including Leo Tolstoy, have concluded that Christians cannot support the concept of a right to private property, so critical to most economic systems and especially to capitalism. They find nothing in Jesus' witness on this issue to undergird the concept and much that points in the direction of economic disinvestment. Others are so committed to liberal capitalism as to find the issue unworthy of debate. We reject both poles and argue here for a qualified right to private property subordinate to the primary norm of economic justice as an aspect of God's reign.

Here we need to read Jesus against the backdrop of central Old Testament themes, beginning with the creation story. In Genesis 1:28-30 God the Creator of all that exists declared that the plants and fruit have been given to humanity for food; later, after sin entered the picture and God responded with the Flood, this provision was extended to include animal life (Gen 9:3-4). The point is that *all material goods, beginning with the most basic—food—should be viewed as God's good gifts, divine provision for all humankind.* The Catholic tradition labels this concept the "universal destination of goods" (*Catechism of the Catholic Church,* #2402ff.). It is a nice image—God the gracious sender, the human family as a whole the addressee. The human task is to exercise our God-given dominion over such goods in such a way that they are rightly distributed to all to whom they are addressed.

This is the fundamental mandate of economic ethics—just distribution. Hundreds of Old Testament passages, beginning in the Pentateuch, seek to prevent and finally decry distributive economic injustice. The prophets announced God's judgment upon Israel for its manifold sins in this critical arena (for a compendium of these passages, see Sider, *Cry Justice* and *Rich Christians in an Age of Hunger*). It is one of humanity's cardinal sins, and not only Israel's—this division into have and have-not, those who have a chance at earning their fair share and those who die of hunger, sleep in the streets or succumb to preventable diseases. The fight for distributive economic justice amidst varying levels of injustice is (sadly) a perennial aspect of human responsibility and a key dimension of the Christian ethical task.

Yet this does not mean that individuals and collectivities are not permitted to own and even delight in their respective portion of earthly goods, experiencing such bounty as divine blessing (see J. Schneider, *Godly Materialism*). This is the case as long as this ownership is understood as bounded by deeper theological and ethical realities: the universal destination of goods, moral limits on how wealth and property are acquired, the obligation of stewardship and the quest for distributive economic justice. Underlying these particular norms is the concept of God's provision and ultimate "ownership" of all created goods and, in a sense, of the human subjects who temporarily manage them (cf. Wogaman, *Economics and Ethics,* chap. 3; J. Schneider, *Godly Materialism,* esp. chap. 3).

The right to private property is best grounded in a theological understanding of work, personal and familial responsibility, and human freedom. The dominion/stewardship mandate (Gen 1:28) requires human beings to exercise responsibility over the creation. This involves various forms of work, which, after the fall, became arduous and difficult (Gen 3:19)—yet work itself remains rooted in God's design for human life. Work reflects and advances human dignity as our vocations become an outlet for creativity, self-development and even joy, an avenue to contribute to the common good and a means of providing for ourselves, our families and those we can bless with our generosity (*Catechism*, 2427-28; cf. John Paul II, *Laborem Exercens*). The ability to keep, enjoy and develop the fruit of our labor as private property enhances the incentive to work and is legitimate as long as we also meet our public ethical responsibilities. The eighth commandment, prohibiting theft (Ex 20:15), helps seal the biblical case for a right to private property (otherwise, there would be no need for a provision against theft), yet it is important not to forget these deeper theological considerations in our understanding of this issue (cf. Wogaman, *Economics and Ethics*, chap. 3).

This understanding of the meaning of work helps to provide nuance to our concept of distributive economic justice. Some have argued that economic justice consists in rough equality of outcome—that all economic actors should at the end of the day enjoy roughly comparable economic well-being. But this notion, superficially attractive, ultimately founders because it fails to take the mandate to work with adequate seriousness. Nor is it supported by a close reading of the Old Testament's rich witness on economic life. Nor, finally, does it take into account the distorting effect of sin on human decision making.

Instead of equality of outcome, the better statement of the Christian norm of economic justice can be found in this definition offered by Stephen Mott and Ronald Sider: *"Justice demands that every person or family has access to the productive resources (land, money, knowledge) so they have the opportunity to earn a generous sufficiency of material necessities and be dignified, participating members of their community"* (Mott and Sider, "Economic Justice," 40, italics in the original). A just economy creates wealth, including that found in adequately remunerative work to all who are able to work. Its number one priority in wealth-creation, however, is not extravagant bounty for the few but access to economic opportunity and participation in economic community for the many. While there may be some who for various reasons choose not to participate vigorously in economic life and thus will undoubtedly live in meager circumstances, a just economy generates employment for that great majority of able-bodied persons who do desire gainful work.

Secondarily, all actors in a just economy will do their part to make adequate provision for a decent and dignified existence for those who are unable to provide for themselves, such as the disabled, orphaned children, the abandoned, the mentally ill, the very old and so on (for the abundance of biblical texts on this theme, see Mott and Sider, "Economic Justice," 40-42; e.g., Ex 23:10-11; Lev

19:9-10; 25:47-53; Deut 14:28-29; Ruth 2). Given the frailty of human bodies and human social life, societies will always contain a percentage of people who cannot provide adequately for themselves. A just society does all it can to reduce this number to the bare minimum, but first private and then public efforts must be undertaken to meet the needs of those who cannot care for themselves. The exact mix of, and nature of, public and private relief and empowerment ventures is the subject of vigorous debate (cf. Olasky, *Tragedy of American Compassion;* Blank, *Do Justice;* Wogaman, *Economics and Ethics;* Sider, *Just Generosity;* Gushee, *Toward a Just and Caring Society;* Copeland, *And the Poor Get Welfare*), but that debate must not obscure the basic biblical mandate that the community as a whole has responsibilities in meeting the needs of the helpless poor as effectively as possible.

Christians need to learn practices of economic spending, sharing and empowerment that lead the way here. Indeed, this whole chapter points to the need for a faithful embodiment among disciples of the vision of economic justice that Jesus teaches. Only such practices can enable us to shake off the misperception of reality that is fed to all of us in advertising and other cultural outlets. (For descriptions of such practices, see Dawn Nakano and Thad Williamson, "Piece by Piece," in Sojourners, *Who Is My Neighbor?* 155-57, describing churches banding together to support each other in achieving change; Jack Nelson-Pallmeyer, "By Their Spending You Shall Know Them," in the same book, 142-43, suggests ten practices to help church members think creatively about their own spending; compare also Ron Sider's classic statement in *Rich Christians.*)

The economic systems debate. The foregoing discussion leads into the much-debated issue of economic systems. That is: should Christians endorse one or another economic system as "the Christian economic system"?

World history has seen a wide variety of economic systems: agrarian feudalism, laissez-faire industrial capitalism, Marxist Communism, state socialism, democratic socialism, mixed or balanced economy, and now free-market globalization, to name a few. In their own time, each one of these ways of organizing economic life has found Christian theologians and church leaders willing to endorse it as divinely ordained. By now most of these endorsements look foolish indeed.

The history of Catholic economic ethics is instructive here. Throughout the medieval period the Church was deeply wedded to the structure of agrarian feudalism. It responded to early capitalism without enthusiasm and was distressed by many of the changes in Western political and cultural life that capitalism unleashed. It much preferred a static feudal hierarchy over bourgeois liberal capitalist democracy.

Yet modern Catholic social thought (beginning with the papal encyclical

Rerum Novarum in 1891) turned in a more creative direction. This tradition of teaching, renewed periodically over the past century, has attempted to bring broad Christian moral norms to bear in evaluating the ongoing development and practice of economic life (see O'Brien and Shannon, *Catholic Social Thought*). This tradition paralleled the Protestant Social Gospel movement in the late nineteenth and early twentieth centuries (cf. Rauschenbusch, *Christianity and the Social Crisis*) in decrying the obvious injustices and human degradation produced by laissez-faire capitalism. Their combined protests, as well as various political movements, finally helped to produce an environment amenable to modest government regulation and reform in the early part of the twentieth century. After 1929, the crisis caused by the Depression resulted in radically more interventionist government approaches, many of which were supported by both mainline Protestants and the Catholic Church.

The modification of laissez-faire capitalism into a regulated, "mixed" or, better, "balanced" capitalism has characterized most Western nations since that time; the exact shape and extent of the balance has rarely left the top of the political debate in any nation or era, and has consistently attracted the attention of Christian economic ethicists (see Wogaman, *Great Economic Debate*). What Wogaman makes clear is that we should not reduce the debate to only two extremes—laissez-faire capitalism and centrally directed socialism. That does not reflect the real world, and it stultifies our ethical awareness. The real debates are where to place the balance in a balanced economy, and how much attention to give to the need for conservation. For brief descriptions of a covenant ethics approach, see Sojourners, *Who Is My Neighbor*, 24, 40-49, 53; and Mount, *Covenant, Community, and the Common Good*, chaps. 4-5.

Marxism and its various communist incarnations were met with constant suspicion in the Catholic social teaching tradition. In hindsight, and in light of considerable mainstream Protestant flirtation with Communism, especially in the 1930s, Catholic resistance to communism looks exceptionally prescient. Catholic leaders, as seen in various encyclicals produced throughout communism's brief but bloody run, rightly evaluated the disastrous worldview assumptions of communism and predicted that its atheism ultimately would produce a moral relativism that would cheapen human life in dangerous ways (cf. Pius XI, *Quadragesimo Anno*, a 1931 encyclical). Communism ultimately provided nightmarish confirmation of these predictions: those seeking communist utopias were willing to do so "by any means necessary" (Lenin), ultimately producing some hundred million corpses (Courtois et al., *Black Book of Communism*) from Russia to China to Cambodia and elsewhere.

Yet Catholic social teaching has not offered an uncritical embrace of liberal capitalism as practiced in Western industrialized nations and now, under their hegemony, around the world. North American evangelical economic thought has rarely had trouble recognizing and celebrating the fact that liberal capitalism at its best maximizes personal autonomy, encourages innovation, meets the basic human needs of most people in society, generates numerous jobs and produces great wealth. Yet conservative evangelicals, at least, have tended to downplay numerous systemic problems associated with contemporary liberal capitalism. These include persistent and sometimes devastating income and wealth inequality both within and between nations, gross concentrations of economic and political power both stemming from and contributing to the exploitation of the poor by the rich, the stimulation of an ethos of consumerism and acquisitiveness with deeply problematic cultural and moral ramifications (see B. Anderson, "Capitalism and the Suicide of Culture"), ruthlessness in economic relations, production of morally odious products of various types and environmental devastation (see chapter twenty-one; for the best recent overview of these issues, see de Vries, *Champions of the Poor*).

Catholic social teachings have been willing to name these problems quite forthrightly and have consistently called for appropriate government regulation of free-market economies so as to reduce distributive injustice. The encyclicals also have pleaded with individuals and institutions to remember the universal destination of goods, the biblical mandate for economic generosity and the simple humanity of those who suffer economic deprivation. Such documents have offered special concern since the 1960s for the plight of the "Two-Thirds World," in which billions of people live in relative or absolute poverty and never enjoy the economic development promised by wealthy nations or multinational corporations. This has been a persistent theme in "unofficial" Catholic and mainline Protestant economic ethics as well (see Wogaman, *Economics and Ethics*, chap. 9; Stackhouse et al., *Christian Social Ethics in a Global Era*; Cobb, *Sustaining the Common Good*; Simons, *Competing Gospels*) and beginning in the 1970s attracted evangelical attention and debate (Gay, *With Liberty and Justice for Whom?*). Meanwhile, most liberation theologians have made ameliorating the "developing" world's miseries the center of their theological-ethical project (Gutiérrez, *Theology of Liberation*).

The real debate in Christian economic ethics at this point is essentially over an analysis of the sources and extent of existing economic injustice and the right mix of strategies for addressing such injustice. No one argues for communism, though some of us do still find Marx's analysis of the ways economic self-interest blinds people to the sources of their own political/economic convictions quite trenchant (never better presented than by Reinhold Niebuhr, *Moral Man and Immoral Society*, chaps. 5-6). And many of us, including the authors of this volume, do argue for more aggressive government involvement in constructive economic empowerment efforts (Gushee, *Christians and Politics Beyond the Culture Wars*; Sider, *Just Generosity*). We also support dramatically revised international economic policies on the part of wealthy nations in order to reduce our sometimes predatory involvement in international economic life, unjust consumption of resources and environmental damage (see Daly and Cobb, *For the Common Good*). The fact that most North American believers continue to be "rich Christians in an age [a world] of hunger" (Sider, *Just Generosity*) remains an appalling contradiction that followers of Christ Jesus ought to address with utmost seriousness, however complex the problems.

Business ethics, stewardship and Dave Ramsey. North American Christians do pay a fair amount of attention to issues of economic life; however, little of that attention follows the path we have just suggested. The most popular treatments of economic life assume the moral goodness of capitalist economics and attempt to navigate the ethical waters from within this system.

Business ethics, for example, which I (David) have had several opportunities to teach, is standard fare now in business schools and economics departments. Business ethics courses and the texts that service them (cf. Velasquez, *Business Ethics*; cf. Rae and Wong, *Beyond Integrity*; Chewning et al., *Business Through the Eyes of Faith*) generally explore moral dilemmas emerging from the cut-throat world of even our own modified capitalism. Sometimes these texts and courses raise searching questions about the very system within which moral dilemmas arise; more often, however, they fall prey to a complacent acceptance of systemic realities and a kind of reductionism in which the goal is to find some thin understanding of procedural justice or legal obligation to generate norms for the Christian in business. Rarely do they challenge the uncritical embrace of corporate culture or "The American Dream" that characterizes the lives of millions of baptized Christians.

As for the churches, most continue to use the language of stewardship when speaking of financial matters. Christians are called to be good stewards, it is argued, of the material bounty that God provides. At times this well-placed concern for stewardship reduces to a call for generous giving, even tithing, to the local church. Much debate can be found about the ongoing validity of the tithing mandate, given its relatively thin Old Testament basis and the lack of explicit affirmation of the tithe in the New Testament. We think that giving sacrificially to God's kingdom work is a clear biblical mandate but regret that the notion of economic stewardship is so frequently reduced to legalistic debates over tithing.

Dave Ramsey, Larry Burkett and a handful of other financial gurus have become extraordinarily popular in North American evangelical circles. Essentially, these men offer debt-laden, confused Christians foundational principles for the practice of economic self-discipline. Listening to Ramsey's syndicated radio show, one is struck by the mess that many believers make out of their lives by mishandling their personal finances. Frequently the problem is that listeners have been sucked into the consumerism that constitutes in many ways our national religion, and now, up to their eyeballs in debt, are attempting to avoid bankruptcy, divorce or insanity. More positively, these thinkers do sometimes offer wealthy Christians strategies for maximizing their opportunity to do good with their money, an important moral theme in its own right (see Wheeler, *Wealth as Peril and Obligation;* Blomberg, *Neither Poverty nor Riches,* 247-52).

Mention of consumerism reminds us of where we started. Christians living in the wealthiest and most powerful nation in the world, the powerhouse of global capitalism, are daily subjected to the most sophisticated enticements ever devised—enticements not just to buy certain products but to *buy into* a certain way of looking at and living life. It is a way of life that ascribes inordinate value to the acquisition of material goods and indeed thrives based on the creation of new "needs" and then cut-throat competition to fulfill those "needs." If Christian ethics is following Jesus, it must involve a clear-eyed analysis and finally repudiation of an economic ethos that ratifies the "deceitfulness of wealth" and makes Mammon the national idol.

This is no mere theoretical preference. As I write I think of lives ruined by this ethos: those who deteriorate into essentially soul-less creatures pursuing the latest goodies with zombie-like intensity; those who have no access to adequate work and no way to provide for their families; those around the world who live in squalor and misery; those whose lives could be turned around by a small commitment on the part of unhappily prosperous people who will never pause from their quest for the latest redemptive gadget to consider the needs of the least of these. This latter is a condition that has been called "affluenza," and according to Jesus, it is terminal.

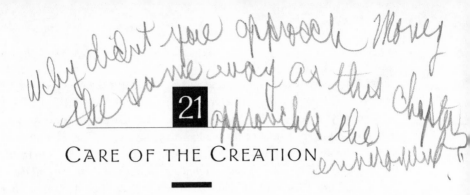

Why didn't you approach Money the same way as this chapter approaches the environment?

21

CARE OF THE CREATION

Do not store up for yourselves treasures on earth, where moth and rust consume and where thieves break in and steal, but store up for yourselves treasures in heaven. . . . For where your treasure is, there will your heart be also. . . .

Look at the birds of the air: they neither sow nor reap nor gather into barns, and yet your heavenly Father feeds them. Are you not of more value than they? . . . Consider the lilies of the field, how they grow; they neither toil nor spin. . . . But if God so clothes the grass of the field, which today is alive and tomorrow is thrown into the oven, will he not much more clothe you—you of little faith? . . .

But strive first for the kingdom of God and his righteousness, and all these things will be given to you as well.

MATTHEW 6:19-33 NRSV

Richard Cartwright Austin was trying to write a doctoral dissertation while pastoring a small rural church in the Appalachian area of Virginia. But the noise and pollution of nearby strip-mining for coal kept interrupting his writing. In strip-mining, the surface of the ground is ripped open, the coal is extracted, and the surface is ruined. With every rainfall thereafter, more acid washes out, so that for generations the land is no longer suitable for farming or natural growth, and the streams are too acidic for fish. Austin's parishioners' lives were being directly affected by this strip-mining—some worked for the coal company, but most were farmers whose land was being ruined. The threat to God's creation and the injustice to his parishioners pulled Austin out of his study and into organizing the community to resist the strip-mining. Eventually, he became a national leader in efforts to control strip-mining and to promote energy conservation. They achieved striking success in the form of laws requiring that the land be restored after it was stripped.

Although there have been Christian saints and heroes through the ages for whom Christian discipleship connected with care for the creation (e.g., Francis of Assisi, John Wesley), awareness of a growing crisis hit Christian ethicists shortly before 1970, and a renewal of Christian concern for the environment in the midst of the ecological crisis began. The first evangelical works on care of the creation took book form in 1971: Francis Schaeffer, a mentor for many conservative evangelicals, published *Pollution and the Death of Man*, and Eric Rust, biblical theologian and philosopher at Southern Baptist Theological Seminary, published *Nature—Garden or Desert?* In 1972, Rust's colleague in Christian ethics, Henlee Barnette, published his groundbreaking work *The Church and the Ecological Crisis*. Barnette argued strongly that God intends humans to be stewards of creation, and he alerted Christians to the rapidly mounting crisis of the creation.

Many denominations now have environmental offices. Presbyterian social ethicist Dieter Hessel edits *The Egg: An Eco-Justice Quarterly.* Wesley Granberg-Michaelson, a leading voice for "Justice, Peace, and the Integrity of Creation" in the World Council of Churches became general secretary of the Reformed Church of America. In self-consciously evangelical circles, ecological concern is also expanding exponentially: Roy and D'Aun Goble founded the Christian Environmental Association, which quickly recruited Gordon Aeschliman (formerly with Evangelicals for Social Action) as president. The organization has become Target Earth International and focuses on serving the earth and the poor (see their website at <www.targetearth.org>). Evangelicals for Social Action also spawned the Evangelical Environmental Network, which publishes *Creation Care* (formerly called *Green Cross*).

Dimensions of the Ecological Crisis

A hundred years ago nature was still resilient and forgiving; now "we stand astride global threats to nature's capacity both to produce for its human members *and* to regenerate itself" (Rasmussen, *Earth Community, Earth Ethics*, 5). A generation ago, we grew up thinking of nature as the woods, a seashore or a park where we might go for a walk or camping trip. The threat was that we might leave the beauty of nature dirty with paper, garbage or tin cans, or might leave some hot ashes that could start a fire. So Girl Scouts, Boy Scouts and Smokey Bear taught us an ethics of cleaning up after ourselves and putting out sparks. Now the threat has reached a drastic new level. Our earth is no longer resilient and forgiving, but weakening and receding, like a dying person. Industry is such a powerful and all-consuming engine that it is eating up the whole earth like a strip-mining machine and killing off species by the thousands. It is no longer "nature" out there and us as "visitors" for a day or two. Because of the power of our machines, we are now the largest part of nature, and we are dependent for our health on what we are destroying. Our machines and our industry are the main force that consumes, pollutes and destroys what God has given us. It is not nature out there and us here, but us as part of creation, and the rest of creation on which we depend for human life.

Jesus focuses our perception on two factors:

1. *God cares.* In Matthew 6:19-34, Jesus makes absolutely clear that God cares for the birds of the air and the lilies of the field, and that we are placed in the midst of this community of God's caring. Many of Jesus' parables point to God's caring for the growth of seeds, for the fields, for the gift of rain and sunshine to all persons. Just as Jesus' teaching on divorce said God's covenant in Genesis established the norm, so his parables treat God's creating and caring for us and the rest of creation as the norm for our awareness of God's present reign. God has created us in a limited community, the earth, and God continues to care for that community. It is not *us* over against *nature* or *the environment;* we are *part of God's created community* of the earth, and we are dependent on this earth community for our lives, just as it is now dependent on us for its life.

2. *Greed does not work.* As we discussed in the last chapter, in Matthew 6:19-34 Jesus devotes two triads to making it clear that investing our money in hoards of wealth and serving wealth (mammon) create a powerful vicious cycle. Where our money is invested shapes how our hearts are tuned. And how our hearts are tuned shapes how we see (Mt 6:21-23). Therefore, it is crucial to put our treasures in God's reign and God's justice. In Matthew 6:22-23, the sound eye is the generous eye, and the unsound eye is the greedy eye (Davies and Allison, *Critical and Exegetical Commentary,* 1:638-41). This fits our four-dimensional model of holistic ethics: If we put our treasures in greed and shape our incentives so that greed for ever more treasures is rewarded, then our loyalties and our perceiving will focus on greed, and we will consume exponentially more each year in a limited earth that is a one-time gift from God. Jesus says that if we try to serve both God and greed, we will hate the one and love the other. The way we have been destroying the creation at breakneck speed constitutes firm evidence that we love the short-term wealth and hate God's care for the creation.

In the economy of nature and in the longest stretches of human history (hunt-er-gatherer society), all creatures consume only renewable resources—fruit, nuts, plants, fish and animals, seeds, grass, berries, bark and so on. Industrial so-ciety, however, draws from stored energy to use both renewable and nonrenew-able resources (and renewables at a nonrenewable rate). But as Hawken notes, this newfound capacity for what we came to call progress means that "every day the worldwide economy burns an amount of energy the planet required 10,000 days to create. Or, put another way, 27 years worth of stored solar energy is burned and released by utilities, cars, houses, factories, and farms every 24 hours." It hardly takes rocket scientist intelligence to read "unsustainability" writ large here, if such a way of life goes on for very long, in earth terms, or if very large numbers of persons pursue it even a short while (Rasmussen, *Earth Community, Earth Ethics*, 59, citing Paul Hawken).

In our four-dimensional model of holistic ethics in chapter three, we saw that a crucial dimension of character is *how we perceive the context*. The priest and the Levite *saw* and passed by on the other side, but the compassionate Sa-maritan *saw with compassion* and took the needed action. A key variable that shapes our perceiving is how we see *the threat* (the cause of what is wrong). If we want to see the threat to God's creation with compassion, we cannot pass by on the other side. But our spiritual reality is that we are tempted to practice denial of facts that demand repentance and change. And the inertia of percep-tion means that we are slow to perceive the meaning of trends. We assume, un-consciously, that things will continue mostly as they were before. The reality, however, is that things can't continue. "If current trends continue, we will not" (Rasmussen, *Earth Community, Earth Ethics*, 10).

> When the [twentieth] century began, neither human technology nor human numbers were powerful enough to alter planetary life-systems. . . . Nor was it the case that "every natural system on the planet [was] disintegrating.". . . Soil ero-sion was not exceeding soil formation. . . . Species extinction was not exceeding species evolution. Carbon emissions were not exceeding carbon fixation. Fish catches were not exceeding fish reproduction. Forest destruction was not exceed-ing forest regeneration. Fresh water use was not exceeding aquifer replenish-ment. Half the world's coastlines, the most densely populated human areas, were not imperiled. An ominous, if bland, word thus appears. . .—"unsustainability." It wasn't there at century's beginning, at least in people's consciousness. Neither were "carrying capacity," "the integrity of creation," and "sustainable develop-ment." We stand astride global threats to nature's capacity both to produce for its human members *and* to regenerate itself. (Rasmussen, *Earth Community, Earth Ethics*, 4-5, citing Paul Hawken)

Sherlock Holmes solved a murder mystery by noticing that at the time of the crime, the family dog did not bark. It clued him that the murderer was not a stranger but a member of the family. In our case the perpetrator of the crime is not a stranger but a member of the family of nature. We humans are not something apart from nature but a part of nature. God created us that way, and God created the nonrenewable resources of nature like oil, natural gas and chromium as a one-time gift. We could share them so future generations will have some, or steal them for one huge binge by the present generation. And our family dog—economics—does not bark.

> Take classic texts in the study of economics. Take macroeconomics, especially, the branch of economics that analyzes mass structures, dynamics, and scale. Take a look at the index and note what isn't there. Typically there is no entry for "environment." Or for "natural resources," "pollution," or "depletion." There is no entry for "sustainability" either, or even the hot topic, "sustainable development." These spaces are blank. These dogs don't bark. These clues give away the case. (Rasmussen, *Earth Community, Earth Ethics,* 111)

The industrial economy depends for its life on all these missing variables, but it systematically excludes them from its calculations as it consumes what will not grow back and pollutes in ways that destroy, while ignoring the organic functioning of the Earth. The incentives are wrong. Jesus focuses us realistically on how we shape our economic incentives: "Where your treasure is, there will your heart be" (Mt 6:21).

The earth functions organically, steadily working to heal and renew what gets disturbed. But the industrial system functions consumptively, not building healing or renewing into its equations or its practices. The industrial system is growing with exponential speed, and the mismatch is like a massive cancer metastasized throughout the organic body of someone who thought life would go on for many more years but suddenly learns that the growth within does not match that expectation.

In the United States *air pollution* has been increasing. Nitrogen oxides increased 11 percent between 1970 and 1997. From 1995 to 1998, sulfur dioxide emissions (resulting in fine particulate pollution or soot) increased more than 9 percent. Estimates are that soot results in fifteen thousand premature deaths every year. More than one in three Americans live in areas with unhealthy air, especially in poorer neighborhoods. Between 1985 and 1995 there was a 45.3 percent increase in asthma deaths. By 2020 asthma sufferers are projected to double to 29 million, with one family in five forced to live with the disease (<www.creationcare.org>). Asthma is probably not caused by pollution, but pollution increases its rate of fatality. Air pollution causes damage to farm crops and forests from acid rain, loss of fish and other aquatic species from acidification, and reproductive failures caused by mercury in fish and in birds that eat fish. Mercury contamination has forced the authorities to issue warnings about the dangers of eating large quantities of certain fresh-water fish.

Several forms of childhood cancers have risen sharply in the last fifteen years in the United States: brain tumors are up more than 30 percent, leukemia is up 10 percent, and testicular cancer is up 60 percent. Cancer is now the second leading cause of childhood death. We do not know how much of this is caused by air pollution and hazardous wastes, but we know many harmful chemicals have tested as carcinogens. One in four children live within one mile of a *hazardous waste site*. Clearly, it is not just about "nature"; it is about creation, and the threat is to us humans as part of creation as well as to "the rest of creation."

Smog and heat inversions are local models of a planet-wide threat: *global warming*. Life as we know it can exist only in a narrow range of temperatures. But carbon dioxide, carbon monoxide and methane produced in massive amounts by autos, trucks and industries burning fossil fuels cause a layer of "greenhouse gases" that trap heat in the lower atmosphere like the heat in a greenhouse. This raises the temperature of the planet. *Deforestation* also contributes to global warming, since trees are crucial for converting carbon dioxide back into oxygen. Surface temperatures in recent decades have been moving upwards on the average of 0.1 degree per decade. In December 2001, the World Meteorological Organization announced that 1998 and 2001 were the two warmest years since global records began to be kept 140 years ago. "Temperatures are getting hotter, and they are getting hotter faster now than at any time in the past" (*Los Angeles Times*, December 19, 2001, A23). Scientists from the Intergovernmental Panel on Climate Change (IPCC), considered the most authoritative body on the issue of global climate change, conclude:

> Studies using tree rings and coral reefs have shown that the decade of the 1990s has been the warmest decade in at least the past 1,000 years. Ice core dating spanning 420,000 years demonstrates that current CO_2 and CH_4 (methane) levels are the highest they've ever been. . . . Projections from the 1995 IPCC report indicate that by the year 2100 the average global temperature could rise anywhere from 1.0 to 3.5 degrees Centigrade (1.8-6.3 degrees Fahrenheit). Temperature changes, which would normally take 50,000-100,000 years, could occur in 50-100 years. It is this incredibly rapid rate of change that creates the serious danger posed by global warming: . . . a dangerous rise in sea level, flooding coastal areas and low-lying islands; an abrupt shift northward of arable land in the northern hemisphere; massive extinctions of both flora and fauna unable to adapt to such quickly changing conditions; millions and millions of environmental refugees, and increased conflicts over shifting resources. The total effect could create profound disruptions in every aspect of human culture, and result in a great deal of suffering throughout God's Creation. (As reported by <www.creationcare.org>)

Disagreement with the consensus view on global warming has been generated by a handful of scientists in the pay of the oil industry, especially S. Fred Singer (see Gelbspan, the Union of Concerned Scientists; and Environmental

Defense). One effort seeks to divert attention in two ways: (1) It shifts the focus from surface temperatures to temperatures up in the troposphere. But of course icebergs melt, crops wither and deserts spread because of warming trends on the earth's surface, not up in the troposphere. (2) It selects the warmest year of the seventies (1979) and the coolest year of the nineties (1996) to claim the tropospheric temperatures slightly declined. In fact, even its data show that, if you begin anywhere from 1965 to 1978, and compare with the average from 1980 to 1997, the temperature increases about 0.4 degrees. And the dramatic upward trend occurs in the last years the data measure (1992-1998).

Resource depletion is the exhaustion of nonrenewable resources and the overuse of renewable resources at rates faster than they can be renewed. This is the ecological equivalent of "living beyond our means," in this case, beyond the means of the planet's natural wealth. Nonrenewable resources do not grow back when they are used up. They include fossil fuels (oil, coal, natural gas) and industrially significant minerals (iron, manganese, nickel, chromium, copper, silver, tin, bauxite and so on). They are being used up at accelerating rates.

Deforestation, either through lumbering or deliberate burning of rainforests for grazing cattle, is currently progressing at an average rate of a football field per minute! Forests that it took nature centuries to grow are destroyed in the blink of an eye—and the burning adds carbon dioxide to the air, increasing global warming. The loss of habitats for animal life also results in species reduction, a loss of *biodiversity*. Thus, one process, deforestation, has a major negative effect on multiple dimensions of the ecology (World Resources Institute). The rapid *loss of biodiversity* through the extinction and radical reduction of species of plants and animals threatens the whole interlinked ecosystem. A healthy ecosystem depends on the complex interaction of a great variety of life forms, each of which fills an ecological "niche" that other species depend on for their lives. Human and industrial "development" and consumption that do not take ecosystemic impact into account have led to a startling loss of species—at a rate of about one plant or animal species becoming extinct daily (Hessel, *After Nature's Revolt*, 1; Nash, *Loving Nature*, 54-58).

Human *overpopulation* is a sensitive area for many Christians because some advocate unethical means to curtail it. But opposition to such means cannot responsibly translate into unconcern for the problem itself. It took humanity until 1650 to reach a total population of one-half billion. By 1930 there were 2 billion humans on the planet. Just thirty years later, in 1960, there were 3 billion. Only fifteen years later, there were 4 billion. "Now another Mexico City is added every sixty days, another Brazil each year." But not every addition causes the same amount of trouble for the earth. "The estimated 50 million people added to the U.S. population over the next forty years will have roughly the same negative global consumption impact as 2 billion people in India"

(Rasmussen, *Earth Community, Earth Ethics,* 38-39). Chicago alone "consumes as much as one South Asian nation of 97 million people (Bangladesh)." Currently, there are about 6 billion people in the world (although by the time you read this book it will be more). Earlier projections indicated that this would increase to ten to eleven billion by 2025 and could reach fourteen billion by 2100, but worldwide efforts are reducing these projections. Many predict food riots, especially if current consumption rates and patterns are continued (Nash, *Loving Nature,* 44-50; Bratton, *Six Billion and More*). Population growth has stopped in some relatively advanced nations, which has caused some in those nations to be concerned. But from the perspective of care of the creation, including care of the world's people, it is the relatively advanced nations where growth most needs to stop, because their population consumes so much more of the resources that are running out.

The maldistribution of goods and services through unjust economic patterns of production and consumption creates wealth for a small percentage of the human population not only at the cost of 1.2 billion human beings living on only one dollar a day and 2 billion on two dollars a day, but also at the cost of the whole creation as well. We are thoroughly interconnected as part of God's creation: economic injustice increases ecological degradation and ecological degradation causes human suffering, and will cause suffering for the rest of history in a dangerous downward spiral. For example, when poor farmers in Latin America are forced off their lands by export agribusiness, they burn down rainforests in order to find new land to farm, increasing the rate of deforestation. Ecological degradation has a greater impact on poor and marginalized peoples than on the wealthy and powerful.

One dimension of eco-*injustice* is *environmental racism.* For much of its history, the environmental movement has been largely white and middle class, perceived by the poor and persons of color (or other marginalized persons) as concern for pretty animals and scenery at the expense of their empowerment. This is changing. Consciousness is being raised about the racial and economic elements of environmental exploitation. Hazardous waste dumps and other ecological hazards are more likely to be located in poor neighborhoods than elsewhere. Further, the economic deprivation of minorities makes it increasingly likely that they have to take jobs with greater environmental health hazards. And the concentration of racial and ethnic minorities in inner-city slums cuts them off from nature, to the detriment of both (see Schwab, *Deeper Shades of Green;* Goldman and Fitton, *Toxic Wastes and Race Revisited;* Chavis and Lee, *Toxic Wastes and Race in the United States*).

Each of these dimensions is connected to the others in multidimensional ways. The complex interweaving of our ecological crisis with the economics of the "hydrocarbon society" and the concentration of power in transnational corporations hovering above the laws of any one nation leads to several temptations. The first temptation is despair that anything can be done. While it may be too late to avoid all consequences of our ecological degradation of the last two centuries, it is not too late to minimize consequences that cannot be wholly avoided. Despair demonstrates lack of faith in God and is a convenient way to shirk responsibility for correcting the systemic evils that have brought us to this crisis. Another temptation is to trust in a miraculous "techno-fix," a massive technological breakthrough that will solve all of our ecological troubles without any changes in current patterns of production, consumption and conservation. While research into new technologies has a necessary role, especially research into alternate energy sources that decrease our reliance on oil and coal and are far more ecologically sustainable, any long-term solutions to the ecological crisis will require massive changes in the global economy: The so-called First World must change to simpler lifestyles that consume far less energy and that share the world's resources in a more just manner. We must learn to "live simply that others may simply live."

Approaches to an Ethic of Creation Care

We group the different ethical approaches into three types based on two variables in our holistic model: the *ultimate loyalty* and the view of the relation of *God* to the creation.

1. Anthropocentric approaches. These place humans at the center of concern. God may have created the universe, but he did so for our sake and has now handed the dominion over to humans. We are now in charge and should use it for our benefit. Because humans are intrinsically connected with the rest of the natural order, even anthropocentric approaches can be concerned about the ecological crisis because of its negative impact on humanity, especially the poor. Further, a major passion for ecological health may arise from the duties we owe to *future generations* of humans (Baier, "For the Sake of Future Generations"; Parham, *Loving Neighbors Across Time*). Indeed, although powerful vested interests often try to label environmental concern as intrinsically harmful to human well-being ("the 'tree-huggers' care more about cute furry animals than about jobs for humans"), often the short-term interests of humanity and almost always our long-term interests coincide with the well-being of the rest of creation.

Different, however, is the anthropocentric utilitarian approach. Its premise is that land, air, water and the other living creatures have worth only according to their utilitarian value for humans. Calvin Beisner's *Where Garden Meets Wilderness* interprets the Creation command that we are "to till and keep" the garden (Gen 2:15), as meaning that we are "to cause the earth to serve man."

He mentions the Fall into sin in Genesis 3 but draws no implications that we need to build in some limitations on consumption and greed. Similarly, his section on redemption draws only one implication—that we are restored to the mandate from Creation that we are to use nature for our purposes. His idiosyncratic interpretation of Scripture claims that biblical justice is not concerned about unfair distribution of wealth. He affirms, *in principle*, the biblical commands taught in *Earthkeeping in the Nineties: Stewardship of Creation* (Wilkinson), which he calls "the most important and substantive evangelical environmentalist book to date." But then he says the biblical principles do not tell us what to do and should not cause us to adopt limits to our consumption. Most especially, we should avoid government action to encourage or require conservation. Instead, we should trust the market to tell us when we should conserve. Thus his agnosticism about what obedience to biblical imperatives means leads to the assertion that the market is what we should obey.

Beisner admits that the earth has only a limited quantity of oil, natural gas and other nonrenewable resources. Yet he asserts repeatedly that the more we use, the more we have. He gives three kinds of evidence for this surprising claim:

1. He claims the United States produces more resources than it consumes. Yet over half the oil that the United States consumes is imported, and this proportion is growing each year because we are running out of oil. We ship dollars to other countries so they will ship us oil, thus causing a consistently growing imbalance of payments, an increasing indebtedness to other countries and a distortion of our geopolitical priorities. Furthermore, the word *produce* is a sleight of hand, not peculiar to Beisner. By "producing" oil he means pumping it out of the ground so it can be used up. We actually produce no oil at all; God did that millions of years ago as a one-time gift. When it is used up, it does not grow back.

2. He claims that world oil reserves have risen from 100 billion barrels in 1943 to 10 trillion barrels in 1989. "Ten trillion" is an error, however. There were only one trillion, as he has since admitted (*Creation Care*, winter and spring, 1998). "World Petroleum Trends 1996" reports that "1995 saw the tenth successive decline in remaining worldwide oil reserves (to 939 billion barrels)." Furthermore, by choosing 1943 as the year of comparison, he biased the case. That was before extensive exploration. Once major exploration was begun, the easy discoveries were made. In the 1940s, approximately five hundred barrels of oil reserves were discovered per foot of wildcat drilling in the continental United States. By the 1960s only thirty barrels were discovered per foot of drilling. In the 1990s the amount was less than five barrels (Meadows, *Beyond the Limits*, 72). In spite of the search technology being much better, each new discovery comes much harder and less often— and with less oil—clear evidence that we are running out of oil to discover.

3. He argues that "falling long-term real prices of petroleum" tell us we are not running out. But as we all know, market prices rise and fall according to the supply of oil *this week*, not next year, and not next generation. The problem we face is not a shortage this week; it is that world consumption is doubling each thirty years, a rate at which the known reserves will be used up in about twenty-five years, permanently, not to grow back for future generations. When confronted by the fact of the declining oil reserves, he claimed it was because market prices are not high enough to encourage drilling; when the market says we need more oil, they will drill more. Thus again he relies on the market to trump ethics. The problem, however, is not a lack of drilling, it is that even with much improved technology, the drilling is coming up dry. This is a dramatic sign of the inadequacy of trust in unlimited market consumption to solve our problems.

Surely the free market is better than the communist system, but it does need some regulations and incentives. A football game has some rules and regulations, and incentives to score in prescribed ways, and this hardly prevents the players from being free to compete. Without rules, the competition would be chaos and result in untold injuries and even deaths. Similarly, a market needs rules and incentives to make business ethical. That does not prevent competition; it prevents chaos, injuries and deaths. Jesus' teaching on treasures, hearts and eyes raises a question: where does an ideology that perceives biblical teaching and scientific data as dictating no restraint on greed have its heart and its treasures? Without help, without incentives for conservation, the market will not tell us we are in trouble until the year we bump against the limit and there is a shortage of oil; by then it will be too late to do anything about our having used up almost all the oil we were given by our Creator.

2. Biocentric approaches. These approaches give no special status to human beings, considering them just one species among others on earth. All of earth's living creatures not only have *intrinsic worth or value*, but *equal intrinsic worth or value*. If biocentrists speak of God, they tend to speak of God pantheistically as identified with or part of the earth or the universe. Some world religions, such as Hinduism, Buddhism and Native American spiritualities, have traditionally espoused some version of biocentrism. In the secular environmental movement, such a perspective was made famous by naturalist Aldo Leopold's *A Sand County Almanac* (1948). Perhaps the most persuasive current philosophical version is neo-Kantian Paul W. Taylor's *Respect for Nature: A Theory of Environmental Ethics* (1986). Taylor denies human superiority in any morally relevant way; for example, humans may be smarter, but horses are faster. All living creatures have *equal* inherent worth and should be viewed as members of one "community of life" and a system of interdependence. Other versions of biocentric ethics develop James Lovelock's "Gaia hypothesis" that the planet forms a living whole of which all its constituent parts, living and nonliving, are a part (Lovelock, *Gaia* and *Ages of Gaia*).

Members of so-called New Age and deep ecology movements have adapted the Gaia thesis into a pantheistic nature spirituality of wholeness and interconnection to Gaia, the earth. The New Age movement includes mystical elements from traditional Native American religions and elements from Eastern religions and neo-pagan groups like the Wiccans. All of these views tend to reverence nature as holy in itself and sometimes worship nature. Some Christians have made the mistake of associating ecological concern with neo-pagan New Age movements. The Christian movement to care for the creation is radically different. Christians worship only the Creator and not the creation, and they ground their ethics solidly on biblical teaching about God's care for his creation. There have been a few attempts to form Christian versions of biocentric ethics, drawing on the nature mysticism of Francis of Assisi or the ethic of "reverence for life" proposed by Albert Schweitzer. Matthew Fox and Thomas Berry have attempted to reconstruct Christian spirituality along biocentric lines, but to do so they have had to downplay the transcendence of God, any sense of humans as the only creatures "in the image and likeness of God," and sin and the need for redemption, emphasizing instead creation's original blessing, human goodness, divine immanence and a spiritual equality of all creatures (see Berry, *Dream of the Earth;* Fox, *Original Blessing*).

3. Theocentric approaches. These reject the anthropocentric utilitarian and "wise management" approaches in which only humans have intrinsic worth, as well as the radical egalitarianism of the various biocentric approaches. They insist that *God* is the center of value and that God's creatures, including humans, have value only within God's created community. The key is that God is not split off and disconnected from creation. Making God that distant tends to separate worship and service of God from care for God's creation as a peripheral "issue." Rather, God is Creator and is continuously, dynamically involved in caring for the creation, as Jesus teaches concerning God's ongoing care for the birds of the air and the lilies of the field. God is the "I am," who hears the cries of the people and sees our need and has come to deliver, promising: "I will be with you" (Ex 3:6-15). God is the Holy One, dynamically present to redeem. Therefore worshiping God directly involves us in caring for the creation, as God is so involved in caring for the creation and for us as responsible parts of the creation.

A non-Christocentric version of theocentrism is James Gustafson's approach. Drawing from a theologically liberal version of the Reformed tradition, Gustafson emphasizes God's sovereign power, arguing that what is good for humans does not always take precedence over the larger scope of God's plans. Further, believing that science should inform and even revise Christian theology, Gustafson has abandoned traditional Christian eschatological hopes, believing that the law of entropy will lead to an ultimate heat death for the universe. Thus, his ecological ethic has much in common with biocentric viewpoints, except that he allows for humans to give priority to their own species insofar as they reflect God's valuing of different parts of creation more than others (Gustafson, *Ethics from a Theocentric Perspective* and *Protestant and Roman Catholic Ethics*).

Process and feminist approaches usually differ from biocentrism, teaching that God, the Creator, transcends the creation in the sense that God is greater than the Creation and is eternal. But they criticize views of transcendence that separate God from creation: God is dynamically active in the creation, caring for it, developing it and moving it toward its future. While stressing the interconnections and worth of all life they do not posit the equality of all life forms. (For environmental ethics informed by process theology, see Cobb, *Is It Too Late?* and *Sustainability;* McDaniel, *Of God and Pelicans*.)

"Eco-feminists" see intrinsic connections between the domination of women by men and the domination of nature (often personified as female) by "man." Elizabeth A. Johnson, *Women, Earth, and Creator Spirit*, provides perhaps the most "orthodox" variety of Christian eco-feminism to date. Eco-feminists who place less emphasis on God's transcendence and more on God's relationality, and sometimes move partially toward biocentrism, include Sallie McFague, *The Body of God: An Ecological Theology* and *Super, Natural Christians: How We Should Love Nature;* Rosemary Radford Ruether, *Gaia and God: An Ecofeminist Theology of Earth Healing;* and *Women Healing Earth: Third-World Women on Ecology, Feminism, and Religion*.

The *earthkeeper stewardship* ethic is partly anthropocentric, in that human interests and responsibilities are central, and partly theocentric, in that humans are mandated by God to care for creation. *Earthkeeper stewards* affirm the basic ecological tenet that humans are biologically related to and dependent on the earth's ecosystems. So, although economic growth is necessary, they recognize limits to economic growth and the need for economic reorganization into a system that is *sustainable* and just (i.e., it meets the needs of the poor while preserving the resources of the earth and living within its carrying capacity). Examples are the pioneers Rust and Barnette, and Tony Campolo, *How to Rescue the Earth Without Worshiping Nature;* Calvin B. De-Witt, *Caring for Creation: Responsible Stewardship of God's Handiwork;* Douglas John Hall, *Imaging God: Dominion as Stewardship* and *The Steward: A Biblical Symbol Come of Age;* and Loren A. Wilkinson, *Earthkeeping in the Nineties: Stewardship of Creation*. Although other, more radically theocentric approaches appreciate the insights of the earthkeeper form of stewardship ethics, they tend to see the concept as too anthropocentric to deal with either the wealth of biblical materials on God's stewardship and care of the creation or the depth of the ecological crisis.

A broad subset of theocentric ecological ethics emphasizes a *covenantal* perspective. Such ethicists note that God made a covenant with all creation after the flood and that Israel's covenant included duties to the nonhuman creation, both in terms of cultivated plants and livestock and in terms of "wild nature." God's dynamic involvement in caring for the creation is revealed in the biblical narratives of God's care, and our caring for the creation does not replace God but participates in God's continuing to care. For an evangelical theological perspective see R. Young, *Healing the Earth*; Granberg-Michaelson, *Ecology and Life*—an evolution in his thought from his earlier "earthkeeper stewardship" approach; and Bouma-Prediger, *For the Beauty of the Earth*. Rasmussen's significant work *Earth Community, Earth Ethics* is influenced by Bonhoeffer's Christocentric and incarnational ethics. See also Nash, *Loving Nature*; Moltmann, *God in Creation*; Murphy, *The Cosmic Covenant*; and each of Austin's books. We see our own ethic as a covenantal and trinitarian version of a theocentric approach.

Biblical and Theological Reflections on Creation Care

Having discussed the question of how the threat should be defined and how God's relation to the creation should be described, we may now turn to key biblical sources with sharper questions in mind. Christian discussions of creation often concentrate on Genesis 1—2. We sharpen the focus a bit, seeing creation through an explicitly Christocentric lens:

> For [God] has rescued us from the dominion of darkness and transferred us to the Reign of his beloved Son, in whom we have redemption, the forgiveness of sins. He is the image of the invisible God, the firstborn over all creation. For by him [Christ] all was created: in the heavens and on earth, visible and invisible, whether thrones or powers or rulers or authorities; all was created by him and for him. He is before all and in him all holds together. And he is the head of the body, the church; he is the beginning and the firstborn from the dead, so that in everything he might have the supremacy. For God was pleased to have all his fullness dwell in him, and through him to reconcile to himself all, whether on earth or in the heavens, by making peace through his blood, shed on the cross. (Col 1:13-20; trans. Michael Westmoreland-White)

This great Christ hymn speaks of a reconciliation of all creation by the one who made all creation and in whom all creation is united. It does not speak precisely of the *redemption* of all creation. The term *redemption* is predicated only of "us" (i.e., followers of Jesus) and specifically defined as the forgiveness of sins. Although the whole creation is "fallen" and under "the dominion of darkness," the nonhuman creation is not sinful. Only humans need forgiveness of sins. But human sinfulness has created alienation between humanity and the rest of creation (Gen 3:14-19; 9:1-6), and this passage promises reconciliation, an end to that alienation (see Ball, *Planting a Tree*, 12-19).

Likewise in Romans 8:18-25 we are told that *all creation* waits with "eager longing" for the revealing of God's children. The creation has been "subjected to futility," and with human salvation it will be set free from bondage and decay. Currently, Paul tells us, the whole creation is groaning like a woman in childbirth, just as we are groaning as we anticipate our adoption as God's children, the redemption of our bodies. The human salvation that Christ's atoning work is now accomplishing is inextricably interwoven with the release of the rest of creation from its sufferings as a result of human sin—sufferings that we have described above.

In the light of such explicitly cosmic pictures of Christ's work of salvation, Genesis 1:1—2:3 cannot be taken in the exploitive direction of those who argue for the anthropocentric-utilitarian human *domination* of creation. In this hymn-like description of God's creative work, each stage of creation is called *good*. The "dominion" given to humans in Genesis 1:26-29 does imply a human preeminence, a theme echoed in such passages as Psalm 8, but it opposes a theology of domination (Brueggemann, *Genesis*, 73ff.). We have also seen in our chapter on Jesus and justice that Jesus, standing in the tradition of the Torah and the Prophets, considered domination to be a major dimension of injustice. To interpret Genesis 1:26 as permission for human domination is to fail to recognize the injustice of domination and the impossibility of dominating nonhuman creation without also dominating portions of humanity as well. As Sider points out, Christians can believe they have permission to plunder or neglect the environment only by failing to love Jesus very much (in LeQuire, *Best Preaching on Earth*, 37).

In the Noachic covenant (Gen 9:8-17), God is portrayed as making an unconditional pledge in perpetuity to all humanity, to all other creatures and to the earth itself, never again to destroy them by flood. This covenant, along with the story of Noah's ark itself, implicitly recognizes that human well-being is inextricably intertwined with the well-being of all creatures in their ecosystems (Nash, *Loving Nature*, 100-101). The rainbow in the clouds is an unstrung war-bow—God's covenant of peace and pledge not to war against the creation (Austin, *Hope for the Land*, 32).

Israel's covenantal laws included obligations to plants, to livestock and to wild nature. These obligations are especially strong in the sabbath and Jubilee traditions that formed so much of Jesus' perspective on justice. For example:

> For six years you shall sow your land and gather in its yield; but the seventh year you shall let it rest and lie fallow, that the poor of your people may eat; and what they leave the wild beasts may eat. You shall do likewise with your vineyard, and with your olive orchard. Six days you shall do your work, but on the seventh day

you shall rest, so that your ox and your donkey may have relief, and your home-born slave and the resident alien may be refreshed. (Ex 23:10-12)

Notice that the sabbath day and sabbath year are concerned for both humans and animals, domestic animals and wild animals, slaves and resident aliens (immigrants), and for the earth itself. Is it any wonder that Jesus objected so strenuously to the misuse of the sabbath to harm rather than help the poor? Likewise the Jubilee legislation (Lev 25:8-10) provided that after every seven sabbath years (i.e., forty-nine years), the fiftieth year would be a year of "liberation for the land and all its inhabitants." As in the sabbath year, the land would lie fallow (enabling it to renew its life-giving properties), land would be redistributed along the roughly equal lots into which the Promised Land was originally divided among Israel's tribes; and slaves (acquired through debt or war) would be set free and given capital to start afresh. Thus, both the land itself and extreme concentrations of wealth and poverty over the generations were to be prevented. Such legislation was both a radical "antipoverty" program and a concern for the land itself. In Isaiah, God rails against those who violate this legislation by buying up all the land and creating homelessness. The result of such injustice will be a radical loss of the land's fertile productivity (Is 5:8-10).

There were other ecological provisions in Israel's covenant as detailed by the Torah. When the Israelites went to war, they were forbidden to cut down fruit trees—the scorched earth policies common to siege warfare (Deut 20:19-20). This sensitivity to God's care would have prevented the ecological damage of Sherman's march from Atlanta to the sea, the napalm bombing of Vietnam and the Iraqi destruction of Kuwaiti oil wells during the 1991 Persian Gulf War, to say nothing of the ecological devastation that would be caused by nuclear warfare. Likewise, Deuteronomy 22:6-7 allows the eating of a mother bird or her eggs, but not both. Deuteronomy 25:4 forbids muzzling oxen while mowing grain, despite how annoying that is to the farmer. Deuteronomy 22:10 likewise forbids yoking an ox and an ass to the same plow because such a cruel mismatch would overwork one animal and frustrate the other. And the roots of Jesus' great transforming initiative for peacemaking, "Love your enemies and do good to those who hate you" (Lk 6:27) are found in Exodus 23:4-5: "When you come upon your enemy's ox or ass straying, you shall take it back to him. When you see the ass of someone who hates you lying helpless under its load, however unwilling you may be to help it, you must give him a hand with it" (NEB).

The portraits of eschatological redemption in the prophets include concern for the natural world. Hosea 2:18-23 includes the promise of a covenant with the beasts of the field and the birds of the air (as well as abolishing bow, sword and battle). Isaiah's vision of the Peaceable Kingdom includes peace between animals (Is 65:17-25). The land was a gift from God; if the people took good care of the land and followed God's commands, the land would be fruitful (Deut 11:11-17; Jer 11:5). Because of their deceit, injustice and violence, the land mourned and was defiled (Hos 4:1-3; many passages in Jeremiah). Notice the many biblical teachings on the sin of greed (Mt 6:19-33; Lk 12:15; Col 3:5; 2 Pet 2:3, 14; Jas 4:1-3). With redemption comes restoration of the land (Ezek 47:9-12; Jer 33:11).

Transforming Initiatives and Christian Practices

Think imaginatively. How can we take a step of commitment, a step of repentance, a step of discipleship that participates in God's caring for the creation? Steven Bouma-Prediger says we can cultivate the virtues of respect and receptivity, self-restraint and frugality, humility and honesty, benevolence (mercy) and love and justice (*For the Beauty of the Earth,* 137-65). These resemble the virtues we saw in the Beatitudes. We cultivate those Christian virtues by our regular practices and our investments.

One step is for the church to preach and teach, and practice what it preaches. We hope this chapter, and the bibliography at the end of the book, can provide some resources. A church will be much more persuasive if it practices what it teaches. Lead the church to take energy conservation measures, and talk about them in sermons, Sunday school classes and small groups. We know a church that had a vacation Bible school each year for adults as well as children in which one of the week-long workshops was a practical class in energy-saving, taught with concrete, practical projects. Participants actually implemented the practices in their homes. It was fun, and it saved them a lot of money for gasoline, heating and electricity.

> This is the theme we learn from Jesus: "Where your treasure is, there will your heart be also." Jesus was a realist. Jesus did not teach an idealistic ethic in which the point is to have good ideals while maintaining the same economic incentives and investments. We need to change where our money is invested and what the financial incentives are for practicing modesty, conservation and generosity. This suggests an approach to the care of creation that differs from much that one reads. In the church Bible school class, we learned how to save gasoline, heating, air-conditioning and electricity, and *we calculated how much money we were saving, which we could do better things with, including giving to kingdom causes.* We lined up our economic incentives with our ecological ethics. As Jesus predicted, our hearts followed our financial practices, and so did our perceiving.

Your church can take several simple actions to save money from utility expenditures, or get an energy audit and thus implement its care for the creation. Articles by Andy Rudin, whose profession is helping churches reduce their energy bills, are thoroughly practical: see *Green Cross* (summer 1997), 12; (fall 1997), 12; *Creation Care* (summer 1998), 12; (summer 2000), 16ff. When your church conserves, it can also teach members to do similarly at home.

By living where you are within walking or bicycling distance from your work or school, or near a bus route, and buying a high-mileage car if a car is a necessity, you can cut your gasoline bill to a quarter of what it was. It saves a lot of time—you can read on the bus, and it is hard to do that while driving on the freeway! By turning down your thermostat a few degrees in daytime and more at night or when you go out, and closing drapes or shades when it is cold outside, you can cut your heating bill in half. Cooking, baking or air conditioning use far more electricity than lights or computers; by not preheating your oven, and turning it off a few minutes before the baking is finished; and by turning on air-conditioning only when you really need it, and turning off lights and computers when you are not using them, you can cut your electricity bill in half. We have done these things.

How about naming a carpooling committee for church? When I (Glen) was a teenager, I was a leader of the church youth fellowship. I organized carpooling to come to the meetings. It created the expectation you would come, since someone had agreed in advance to pick you up. It created the practice of calling potential members and visitors to see if they would like a ride, thus making them feel wanted. It created group belonging and fellowship together, plus a witness to participating in God's caring for the creation. The group grew 400 percent. Why not organize something like this for everyone in the church who might be interested?

Limiting family size not to what the family can afford but to what the world can afford is a clear moral duty. If some desire a large family, they can adopt some of the many abandoned children of their nation and the world. If we hope to avoid the draconian measures China has taken to limit families, we need to use moral leadership to encourage voluntary limits. Ethically appropriate birth control and practices of sexual responsibility are needed ecological practices in our age.

At the beginning of the twentieth century, Los Angeles had a public transportation system of three thousand electric trolleys that radiated seventy-five miles from the city's center and produced no smog. However, as in forty-five cities, the Los Angeles trolley system was bought up by General Motors, with help from Standard Oil, in order to get people to depend on cars and buses, and after they got rid of the electric trolleys, sold back (Commoner, *Poverty of Power*, 177ff.). It worked: Los Angeles became infamous for its dependence on over 9 million motor vehicles and for its traffic jams. The smog was horrible, ruining health, comfort and beauty. Greater Los Angeles had some of the dirtiest air in the United States. In Pasadena, only two miles from the San Gabriel Mountain Range, on most days one could not even see the mountains.

Only with Mayor Tom Bradley did Los Angeles begin to rebuild its public transportation system. State and federal laws set standards for clean air. The Air Quality Management Control Board (from whose website, <www.aqmd.gov>, much of this information comes) developed an emissions trading program that allows factories that can cut their pollution to get a financial reward, while those for whom cutting pollution would be too expensive pay a fee. This creates "the flexibility to choose the most cost-effective means of achieving annual reductions in air pollution. Other facilities are issued permits spelling out specific requirements for equipment and operations that emit pollution." Employers are required to develop an effective plan to encourage employees to ride buses or bicycles to work, or to carpool. "Despite an increase in population from 1950 to 1990 from 5 million to 13 million, the ozone pollution has decreased from 70 particles per 100 million to 30." Stage II smog alerts, which a decade ago occurred fifteen or twenty times a year, almost never occur now. In Pasadena you can see the beautiful mountains almost every day.

Europeans know that gasoline consumption has many social costs. It creates smog and health problems. It creates acid rain and damage to forests. It requires large imports of oil and thus creates large trade imbalances and national indebtedness to oil-providing countries. It consumes the dwindling supplies, so the next generation will not have oil. Therefore European nations reflect these social costs in the price of gasoline by charging higher taxes for purchasing and consuming gasoline. The tax income then goes to support Europe's excellent public transportation systems. Hence there are incentives for using public transportation, for living closer to work, for purchasing more gas-efficient cars and fewer SUVs and vans, and for more walking and thus better health. It is what Jesus said: "Where your treasures are, there will your hearts be." Wise policy arranges incentives so people are more likely to do what is good for health, justice and the community.

What Europeans know is equally true in the United States. But ideological interests have resisted such policies. On September 23, 1987, a full-page ad appeared in *The New York Times*. Bold letters declared at the top: "Good News! Over the past 13 years, American car makers have doubled their average fuel economy." The page was a large graph with one line curving from the lower left to the upper right. It showed that in 1974 average fuel economy per automobile was 13.2 miles per gallon. By 1985 it had exactly doubled to 26.4. At the bottom, the ad declared, "We think that says something for American technology." What the text did not point out was that the progress was required by law, mandating that the auto companies improve the average mileage for their fleet of cars by one mile per gallon each year.

The president of Ford Motor Company had said it was the kind of regulation companies prefer, if they have to have regulation. They knew well in advance what the goal was, so they could plan, and they had the freedom to reach the goal with whatever mixture of compacts and luxury cars they wanted. We think that says something for proper regulation that allows a degree of freedom. What else the ad did not point out was that in the last three years, the chart showed that the progress had stopped: the mileage in 1985 was 26.4; in 1986 it was 26.6; in 1987 it was 26.6. And the next years, off the chart, efficiency began dropping. Why? Was engineering skill failing? No—the auto companies had successfully persuaded President Reagan that regulation was a bad idea, and he had canceled the future application of the law. So no more progress was made thereafter, in spite of American technology. Someone has calculated that had the law stayed in effect, by the year 2000 we would have saved the amount of petroleum found in the huge deposit in the North Slope of Alaska multiplied by two. Since then, the American auto companies successfully lobbied to have SUVs and vans count as trucks and thus be unregulated for mileage efficiency, and then persuaded Americans to buy more vans and SUVs than cars. So average fuel economy is actually plummeting, in spite of the know-how of American technology. We think that says something about having your heart where your treasures are.

In the United States, some incentives do exist for more energy-efficient appliances and energy conservation. More incentives like this are desperately needed. Up in the stratosphere, ozone forms a shield that protects earth's animals, plants and human populations from dangerous radiation from space. Certain airborne chemicals, called chlorofluorocarbons (or CFCs), when released into the atmosphere, eventually make their way into the upper atmosphere where they destroy the ozone layer. These CFCs, found especially in certain aerosol propellants and refrigerators, have caused severe ozone depletion in the upper atmosphere. This has increased skin cancers dramatically (Zurer, "Ozone Depletion's Recurring Surprises"). But this is also a drama of hope: after prodding by scientists and citizens, governments have agreed internationally to outlaw CFCs, and ozone depletion is being reversed. The question is whether it is this trend, or the SUV trend, that will most characterize the laws of the world's wealthiest and most energy-consuming nation in years to come.

SECTION VII:

A Passion for God's Reign

In this concluding section we discuss prayer and political engagement as practices that both reflect a passion for God's reign.

While most treatments of Christian ethics address Christian engagement in public life, very few consider prayer. Yet they are inextricably linked, as we show in this section, and both receive attention by Jesus in the Sermon on the Mount.

Our concluding chapter reinforces the focus on kingdom practices by reviewing the many concrete practices that have been proposed during the course of this book.

Every word of this book has been crafted as an expression of our passion for God's reign, which reflects Jesus' passion for God's reign, and which, we hope, will stoke your passion for that reign of justice, peace, salvation-deliverance, joy and God's remarkable presence. This is the deepest hope of the Hebrew Bible and the boldest claim of the New Testament—that God's promised reign has broken through in Jesus Christ.

22

PRAYER

—

Beware of practicing your piety before others in order to be seen by them; for then you have
no reward from your Father in heaven. . . . When you are praying, do not heap up empty
phrases as the Gentiles do; for they think that they will be heard because of their many
words. Do not be like them, for your Father knows what you need before you ask him.

MATTHEW 6:1, 7-8

We have suggested that attending to Jesus and the Sermon on the Mount raises pivotal concerns for ethics that would otherwise be overlooked. Nowhere is that more true than here. Basing our Christian ethics on Jesus' teaching in the Sermon brings the link between prayer and ethics to our attention and causes us to notice other aspects of the New Testament witness we might otherwise miss.

It is hard to think of a more neglected issue in Christian ethics than prayer. No Christian ethics survey text that we can find deals with prayer at all. And, not surprisingly, it is completely off the radar screen in secular introductions to ethics, as even a cursory review of that literature reveals.

The inattention among scholars to prayer and its link with ethics both reflects and deepens the split between heart and mind, between "pious spirit" and "real world," that characterizes so much of Western Christianity. It is as if "piety" can be found in one compartment of the faith, and "life" in another; but human beings are not fragmented in this way, and there is no warrant for this kind of thinking in Scripture.

We have argued throughout this volume that the Christian moral life is grounded in an eschatological drama about the dawning reign of God in Jesus Christ. It is a drama of God's difficult, costly, but ultimately-to-be-victorious effort to reclaim the rebellious creation from the grip of sin and Satan. In his earthly ministry, Jesus was the pioneer and trailblazer of this reclaiming of the world for God. It is striking that despite the exalted claims the New Testament makes for Jesus' identity, no effort to hide Jesus' strenuous life of prayer is ever made. Indeed, prayer was an integral part of the life of the kingdom-inaugurating Son, as we shall show. The Gospels give us a Spirit-led picture of Jesus. Examination of Jesus' teachings and narratives related to prayer should help us overcome the prayer/ethics split and root both in the biblical narrative of God's reign.

The "Practices of Righteousness" (Mt 6:1-18)

Matthew 6:1-18 constitutes four separate triads (triads 7-10—see chapter six to review our proposal related to the Sermon on the Mount's structure) related to practices of righteousness common in Jewish life. These four parallel teachings concern almsgiving (Mt 6:2-4), praying (Mt 6:5-6, 7-8) and fasting (Mt 6:16-18). The second of the two triads on prayer is expanded with the inclusion of the famous "Lord's prayer" (Mt 6:9-13) and commentary on its emphasis on forgiveness (Mt 6:14-15).

In this section it is easy to see the triadic structure that we have been proposing is characteristic of Jesus' teaching as presented by Matthew in the Sermon on the Mount. The entire section begins with a general introduction offering a thesis statement about the nature of true righteousness *(dikaiosynē):* "Be careful not to do your 'acts of righteousness' before men, to be seen by them. If you do, you will have no reward from your Father in heaven" (Mt 6:1 NIV).

With that introduction, Jesus then moves on to consider "the three main pillars of Jewish piety—prayer, fasting, and almsgiving" (Gundry, *Matthew,* 101). In each case the discussion begins with reference to one or the other of these traditional practices. Each verb is in the subjunctive. Each sentence begins with "whenever" *(hotan),* except for 6:7, which is in a sense a continuation of 6:5:

6:2 "Whenever you give alms"

6:5 "Whenever you pray"

6:7 "And in praying"

6:16 "Whenever you fast"

According to the thesis/antithesis reading of the Sermon, we should now see an attack on the practices of almsgiving, praying and fasting. Yet we have already shown that Jesus and his itinerant band gave to the poor (see chapter twenty); Jesus prayed consistently, though usually in solitude (Mt 14:23; Mk 1:35; 6:46; Lk 5:16; 6:12; 9:18, 28-29; 11:1; 22:40-42); and at least for one extended period of time at the outset of his ministry, Jesus fasted in the wilderness, alone (Mt 4:1-11//Mk 1:12-13//Lk 4:1-13). It is true that Jesus was attacked for the lack of a regular practice of fasting among his band of itinerant disciples (Mt 9:14-17); one text implies that they also were perceived as not particularly prayerful in comparison, for example, with John the Baptist and his followers (Lk 5:33).

Perhaps the clue we need as to why Jesus and his movement would be viewed in this way can be found right here in his own teachings. In critical interaction with the piety of his own time, Jesus offers a warning in each triad about succumbing to the vicious cycle of practicing almsgiving, prayer and fasting for show and at the same time expecting a reward from God. The public practice of an exaggerated piety, Jesus taught, is spiritually deadly. The vicious cycles are denoted as follows:

6:2 "do not sound a trumpet before you"

6:5 "do not be like the hypocrites; for they love to stand and pray in the synagogues and at the street corners, so that they may be seen by others"

6:7 "do not heap up empty phrases as the Gentiles do"

6:16 "do not look dismal . . . for they disfigure their faces so as to show others that they are fasting"

In each case the warning begins with a "do not," followed by a picturesque and bitingly hyperbolic description (Keener, *IVP Bible Background Commentary*, 61; Gundry, *Matthew*, 102) of what exactly not to do. Each warning concludes with the dreadful outcome of receiving no reward from God (at Judgment Day, presumably) if one is practicing piety for public acclaim. Those who practice their piety to be seen by others have received all the reward they will ever see—they have been "paid in full" (Mt 6:2, 5, 16). The warning is quite similar to what Jesus said a little later about "treasures on earth" versus "treasures in heaven" (Mt 6:19-21; see chapter twenty). Essentially, he taught that human beings get a choice between serving God with purity of heart or using God as a means to serving the idol of prestige.

Finally, Jesus offered commands concerning what to do about almsgiving, prayer and fasting. These constitute the transforming initiative aspect of his teaching.

6:3 "do it [give alms] in secret"

6:6 "go into your room and shut the door"

6:9 "pray then in this way"

6:17 "put oil on your head and wash your face"

Each of the basic imperatives is followed by the exact same explanation:

6:4, 6, 18 "Your Father who sees in secret will reward you."

Remember our fundamental claims about the structure of Jesus' teaching in the Sermon on the Mount: he first notes a traditional Jewish teaching or practice and interacts with it rather than abolishes it; he then diagnoses patterns of sin, vicious cycles, that block obedience to God's will in that area; finally he gives a transforming initiative that will break through these vicious cycles and enable a liberating obedience to occur. This last element of the triad is always realistic rather than idealistic, achievable rather than a high ideal, and an invitation to participation in God's grace rather than something intended merely to shame us with recognition of our sinfulness.

That is what we find here related to these practices of righteousness. If Jesus had taught that we should continue to do our praying/fasting/almsgiving in extravagant public displays but have our whole self focused only on God and not on what others are thinking, that would have been a hard, idealistic, shame-inducing teaching. But to pray simply and in secret, give in secret and fast in secret is not an impossible or idealistic teaching. Any of us can do these three things. Jesus offered a realistic way of deliverance from the unsustainable and spiritually devastating double-mindedness of seeking rewards from both God and people. After all, as Jesus said just a bit later, "No one can serve two masters" (Mt 6:24).

Specific Christian practices demand reconsideration in view of these teachings. Let us consider as one example the issue of charitable giving and the way in which Jesus' teaching eviscerates our normal patterns of behavior. Similar points could be made about public prayer and fasting.

Christians routinely give charitable gifts and donations. Jesus never says we should not do so. But how many major gifts, say, to build a building on a college campus, are *anonymous*? The structure of most funding and development campaigns hinges on a scheme of escalating honors and awards based on the seriousness of the giving involved. The Century Club, the Gold Medallion Club, the President's Circle and so on—significant givers gain heightened recognition, access and sometimes power. They get to put their names, or the names of loved ones, on buildings. Meanwhile, they are publicly recognized for their selfless giving!

Development officers and fundraisers know the same thing Jesus knew— that people crave recognition. Each of us wants to be counted as significant, to be honored for something special about us. In the midst of life's tenuousness and the fragility of the human ego, we draw strength and security from various recognitions, titles and honors. We surround ourselves with symbols of our own worth and honor one another with the same. Academic life is rife with this pattern. People tend to carry their earned or honorary titles with pride, and life is structured based on a ranking system established to denote with precision the exact academic pecking order (distinguished professor, senior professor, full professor, associate professor, assistant professor, instructor, adjunct professor, lowly guest lecturer!). We cease to be just people, or just learners, or just colleagues, or just Christians, but instead exist in a ranked hierarchy so extravagant as to make Thomas Aquinas's angels blush.

The difference between the development officer (or the academic system) and Jesus is quite simply that Jesus invites us to find our significance in God and in God's reign alone and to dispense with the quest for "salvation" through any kind of earthly recognition. Most cunningly, Jesus reveals and then rejects the particularly tempting mixed motives one finds in religious life. *For it is only in religious life that people can bring the quest for human recognition together with the apparent practice of religious commitment.* If I give generously to the Elks Club or the Green Party, that's one thing; but if I give generously to First Christian Church, that's quite another. In the latter setting I can simultaneously receive deeply satisfying human recognition and be honored (both by other people and possibly in my own mind and heart) for my single-minded and selfless devotion to God. Christian development officers and fundraising campaigns *depend* on the uncanny allure of these two towering objects of devotion—Self and God—and on our self-deceptive unwillingness to admit our mixed motives. Jesus topples the idol of Self and proclaims God's reward to be dependent on us doing the same.

Trust, Prayer and the Reign of God

How is it, then, that we as disciples can get free of the desire for human recognition and thus do all our "practices of righteousness" for God alone? A clue can be found in the eight references to God as "your Father" in this brief passage (Mt 6:1-18). These reflect the extraordinary intimacy and trust that Jesus experienced with God and invited his disciples to experience. The practice of acts of righteousness without any shred of hope of earthly recognition is only possible in a relationship with God characterized by the experience of divine grace and intimate presence.

It is precisely this joyful experience of God's presence that Isaiah promised would be one of the marks of God's kingdom. When the Messiah comes, "the spirit of the LORD shall rest upon him" (Is 11:2). The "spirit from on high" will be "poured out on us" (Is 32:15). The "light of the LORD" is another symbol for God's renewed presence: "I will turn the darkness before them into light" (Is 42:16). "Arise, shine; for your light has come, and the glory of the LORD has risen upon you . . . the LORD will be your everlasting light" (Is 60:1, 20). References to Jesus as light and the inexpressible incarnation of God's presence abound in the New Testament. The experience of God's presence through the outpouring of the Holy Spirit then becomes one of the main themes of the book of Acts and much of the rest of the New Testament.

In short, Jesus was saying this: the time of God's reign is at hand. The light of God's presence is dawning for his people and for all nations. Celebrate the inbreaking reign of God. Receive God's renewed grace with ecstatic gratitude. Dwell in God's presence. Participate in what God is doing even as you enjoy his presence. Dallas Willard writes that when Jesus gave forgiveness and healing, and invited people to base their own lives on the rule of God "at hand," of course they had no general understanding of what was involved, but they knew Jesus meant that he was acting with God and God with him, that God's rule was effectively present through him.... Jesus' words and presence gave many of his hearers faith to see that when he acted God also acted, that the governance or "rule" of God came into play and thus was *at hand*. They were aware of the invisible presence of God acting within the visible reality and action of Jesus, the carpenter rabbi. (*Divine Conspiracy*, 19, 21)

And trust in God. It may be that the fundamental issue raised by Jesus' teaching in this section is simply *trust*. In a vicious world where daily life for most was a struggle for survival, a world where Jewish visionaries and iconoclasts ended up dead, Jesus taught that God was a Father who *could* be trusted, *must* be trusted and in light of the evidence of God's inbreaking reign, *should*, right now, be trusted. Jesus' own trust in God was so visible during his life as to be a source of mockery at his crucifixion. As he hung on the cross, it was said of him: "He trusts in God; let God deliver him now, if he wants to" (Mt 27:43). The resurrection then marks the decisive vindication of Jesus' eschatological trust in God.

Jesus called his followers to share this same trust, and still does. The basic dividing line in the human family may well be between those who believe that there is a God who can be trusted and those who do not. And, as Alexander Solzhenitsyn put it in another context, that dividing line runs not between groups or states "but right through every human heart" (*Gulag Archipelago*, 615). We struggle to trust God, even those of us who are Christians, and so we hedge our bets through the kinds of "self-insurance" schemes Jesus here dismisses.

The same theme can be found implicitly throughout the Sermon on the Mount. Trusting in God and heavenly reward, we can bear persecution patiently (Mt 5:11-12). Trusting in God, we can let go of our anger and resentment, and risk the vulnerability of attempting reconciliation (Mt 5:21-26). Trusting in God, we can bear to speak truthfully without evasion or falsehood (Mt 5:33-37). Trusting in God, we can attempt nonviolent transforming initiatives and enemy-love (Mt 5:38-48). Trusting in God, we can dispense with both the spiritual and moral temptations of acquisitiveness (Mt 6:19-34). Trusting in God, we can reject a blind judgmentalism and instead look honestly at our own lives and forgivingly at others (Mt 7:1-5). Trusting in God, we can build our entire lives on God's will and the quest for God's kingdom (Mt 6:33; 7:24-27).

Finally—trusting in God, we can continue in secret yet persistent prayer, just like Jesus himself.

Jesus withdrew for forty days of prayer and fasting at the outset of his ministry (Mt 4:1-11). He prayed before choosing his twelve apostles (Lk 6:12-16). He went to deserted places and mountains alone or in very small groups to pray (Mt 14:23; Mk 1:35; 6:46; Lk 5:16). On the night before his death he prayed extensively with his disciples, and then in agonized hours at Gethsemane he prayed as he awaited his arrest (Mk 14:32-42). He offered anguished prayers while on the cross (Lk 23:34).

Yet Jesus taught us not to fill the air with many fancy words (Mt 6:7). This must mean that much of Jesus' deep and extensive prayer life was not just speaking *to* God, but *listening* for God's will. And surely we see the evidence of that in the Gospels. Jesus was closely in touch with God's Spirit and so what we see in Jesus is the Holy Spirit speaking to us in Jesus. We advocate a prayer life that does give God thanks, and does make requests, as the Lord's Prayer does, but also a prayer life that listens for God's will, God's presence. Ask God, and God will give guidance. The practice of listening prayer has a long and deep heritage in the history of the church.

You go into your room or somewhere where you can have privacy and quiet. As William Spohn writes, "A definite time and a quiet, private place are necessary to pray freely and without interruption, as Jesus did when 'he withdrew from there . . . to a deserted place by himself'" (Mt 14:13; Spohn, *Go and Do Likewise,* 138). You sit in a relaxed position, with your eyes closed, so not too many outside distractions interrupt you. Most important, you "enter meditation receptively in the confidence that [you] are seeking God only because God has already found" you (Spohn, *Go and Do Likewise,* 138).You may first begin with a Scripture reading, or you may begin with a request or a concern for God. You ask God to guide your thoughts. And then you simply sit quietly, waiting, listening.

Sometimes anxieties will come into your mind: worries about relationships, about work, about your own priorities. You do not fight them; you offer them up to God. You ask God if there is some guidance for them. Sometimes a word comes to you, or a picture. Sometimes it is a new awareness of something you could do today that would be in line with God's will, and that otherwise you would not have thought of. Sometimes it is a picture of what a person with whom you have some antagonism is really concerned about: it may not be so much directed at you, as at that person's own suffering, need or sense of life's purpose. You learn, as Paul says, to rejoice with your enemies when they rejoice and to mourn with them when they mourn (Rom 12:15). That means you are concerned for your enemies' valid concerns, even if you cannot affirm their actions.

You may do this in the early morning before the rush of the day makes you more task-oriented. Sometimes your priorities for the day come into your mind, and you let them be examined by God in God's presence. The result may be a change in priorities, or an acceptance of your limits that you have not been accepting. You yield your life and your concerns to God. The virtues of yieldedness, surrender and humility in God's presence are the base of the spiritual life and of the character that seeks the reign of God.

Others may find time during or before the lunch break, or at night when you can review what there was to be thankful for during this day, and what there was you could learn from and do better next time. Let all this be examined in God's compassionate and forgiving presence. And give thanks for the mustard seeds of God's reign, present in very small but grace-giving ways.

This may not come easily at first. But slowly, or maybe even suddenly, you will experience a closer relation with the presence of God. Some of the insights that you have read in this book have come out of this experience of patiently waiting in the presence of God. It may transform your life.

We also recommend that you find another person, or a group, that practices prayer, and share some of your experiences—and frustrations—with growing a life of listening prayer. In what follows, we will suggest a possible discipline to try for a while in relation to the Lord's Prayer.

Jesus taught his followers to be confident in prayer. At times, his teaching on prayer seems to promise consistent satisfaction of our requests (Mt 21:21-22). In the Sermon on the Mount (Mt 7:7-11), the divine Father image is again employed to encourage complete trust in God. Jesus said:

> Ask, and it will be given you; search, and you will find; knock, and the door will be opened for you. For everyone who asks receives, and everyone who searches finds, and for everyone who knocks, the door will be opened. Is there anyone among you who, if your child asks for bread, will give a stone? Or if the child asks for a fish, will give a snake? If you then, who are evil, know how to give good gifts to your children, how much more will your Father in heaven give good things to those who ask him! (Lk 11:9-13)

And yet Jesus also taught in a bold and striking way the need for persistence in prayer in the face of disappointment and a lack of answers. Two parables reinforce the theme—the story of a man who has to be roused out of bed to get some bread for a persistent friend (Lk 11:5-8) and the story of the persistent widow and the unjust judge (Lk 18:1-8). This latter parable compares God to a judge who "neither feared God nor had respect for people." He ignored the pleas for justice offered by a persistent widow, but finally relented simply to get rid of her: "yet because this widow keeps bothering me, I will grant her justice; so that she may not wear me out by continually coming." Jesus concluded: "And will not God grant justice to his chosen ones who cry out to him day and night? Will he delay long in helping them? I tell you, he will quickly grant justice to them."

Faith in God is trust in God's character, sovereignty and ultimate triumph. In view of the brokenness of the world, Satan's continued victories and life's many disappointments, the legitimacy of trust in God will always be an open question. Meanwhile, men and women will be tempted to place their trust in idols. Inherently vulnerable, we will scramble for objects of trust, however ridiculous they are when viewed in the cold light of day. Multiple divinities, Ouija boards, horoscopes, palm reading, 401(k)s, mutual funds, football teams, lovers, good luck charms and superstitions of all types bear witness to this desire for worthy objects of trust.

We think that it is precisely this issue of trust that makes sense of the most enigmatic verse in the entire Sermon on the Mount: "Do not give what is holy to dogs; and do not throw your pearls before swine, or they will trample them under foot and turn and maul you" (Mt 7:6). Scholars generally try to interpret this verse in one of two ways. Many interpret it in light of the teaching against judging in the preceding section (7:1-5; Schweizer, *Good News According to Matthew*, 167-68; Gundry, *Matthew*, 122ff.; Guelich, *Sermon on the Mount*, 363; Blomberg, *Matthew*, 128ff.; Davies and Allison, *Critical and Exegetical Commentary*, 626). The obvious problem with this link is that it seems to contradict what Jesus had just taught, now saying that we should actually judge who are dogs and pigs and deny them what is holy. But this makes little sense, so others propose that Matthew 7:6 is simply an independent saying with no discernible link to what comes before or after (Hagner, *Matthew 1—13*, 171; Betz, *Sermon on the Mount*, 454; Luz, *Matthew 1—7*, 418ff.).

We propose that the triadic pattern we have seen to be so consistent also applies here. It suggests a different context and gives a strong clue to the meaning. It very much connects with our emphasis here on prayer as a test of whom one trusts.

Matthew 7:6, we suggest, is actually the first element in a triad that continues through 7:11. It was a traditional teaching in Jewish life, especially in recent Jewish life at the time of Jesus' ministry, not to allow Jewish holy things or places to be corrupted by pagan Gentiles. Scholars are agreed that Jesus has Gentiles in mind with his reference to dogs and pigs.

A look at rabbinic literature clearly shows a consistent naming together of dogs and pigs as symbols of non-Israelites (Luz, *Matthew 1—7*, 419). For Jews, both dogs and pigs were unclean animals. Stray dogs could be particularly vicious, even turning on those who tried to feed and care for them (Keener, *IVP Bible Background Commentary*, 64). Thus they made apt symbols of the heathen world, especially as it impinged upon the Jewish people in Judea as an oppressive power (in the form of the occupying Romans) or as a culturally seductive power (in terms of Hellenization, which was much advanced in Judea; see Witherington, *New Testament History*, chaps. 1-3).

The vicious cycle follows: if you give what is holy or valuable to dogs or pigs, they will trample them underfoot and tear you into pieces. So we have some kind of coded warning here about what Gentiles will do to those who make their holy or valuable things vulnerable to them.

The transforming initiative is found in the *next* section (Mt 7:7-8, with explanation in 7:9-11), which we have already quoted, and which we now suggest actually begins with 7:6. The imperative verbs are *ask, seek* and *knock*. They are all positive initiatives, not negative commands, which we find consistently characteristic of the climactic element of Jesus' triads. Instead of giving what is holy or precious to (Gentile) dogs and pigs, Jesus says, we should give our trust to God.

The meaning of the transforming initiative is this: give your trust, your loyalty and your prayers, to your Father in heaven alone. It is not only about prayer; it is about how trustworthy, how merciful and how caring the Father in heaven really is. He knows how to give good gifts. He alone deserves your trust and loyalty. Just as Matthew 6:1-18 tells us to trust God rather than human recognition or prestige, and Matthew 6:19-33 tells us to trust God rather than Mammon, this passage teaches us to give our trust and loyalty to God rather than to Gentile rulers and their sycophants.

The temptation to give loyalty, trust and indeed collaboration to Rome was a very present temptation in Jesus' time. Living under the thumb of Rome, some responded by organizing or dreaming of violent revolution, which Jesus clearly rejected (as we have argued in chapters seven and eight), and which led to extraordinary calamity in the Jewish-Roman War of A.D. 66-70. The other primary temptation, however, was to accommodate to Rome through collaboration, as did large elements of the Jewish power structure and the economic elite in Jesus' day. Oppression distorts power relationships and tempts the oppressed to either rebellion or collaboration, as history consistently demonstrates. We suggest that just as Jesus warned against the Zealot option of hatred and insurrection, he was here warning against the more subtle temptation to find security (and wealth, privilege and prestige) in cozying up to Rome. Rome cannot be trusted; do not offer your "prayers" there, or she will turn and tear you to pieces. Jesus made this case in a kind of code language, much like Revelation does when dealing with Rome as well. Instead of trusting in Roman dogs and pigs, trust God.

Incidentally, this reading helps us make more sense of the seemingly sublime optimism of Jesus' teaching about prayer in Matthew 7:7-11. It is easy to conclude that Jesus rather cruelly fostered a pious illusion when he promised that all our prayers will be answered with good things, when so obviously many are not. Jesus himself prayed in Gethsemane that "this cup" would pass from him, and he did not receive an affirmative answer. In the context of the full triad, though, Jesus was saying that God was faithful as the Roman/Gentile power structure was not. They will trample you under foot and tear you to pieces; but God gives good gifts. Trust God, not Rome. Only God deserves your allegiance. Jesus was not saying that you will get everything you ask for in prayer. He was saying that God is faithful and deserves our trust, as the Roman power structure does not.

The Lord's Prayer

We have delayed our consideration of the Lord's Prayer until now in order to give the more neglected dimensions of Jesus' teaching about prayer, almsgiving and fasting appropriate attention. Now let us consider this famous prayer itself.

The Lord's Prayer in Matthew is introduced with the same threefold structure of the rest of the Sermon on the Mount:

6:7 "When you are praying"

6:7 "Do not heap up empty phrases as the Gentiles do"

6:9 "Pray then in this way"

The prayer itself, as we find it in Matthew 6:9-13 (cf. Lk 11:1-4), is deceptively simple. Jesus asked us to use few words in praying, precisely the opposite of the heaped-up phrases and elaborate showmanship of public prayer that he had just rejected. His disciples were instructed to talk intimately with God as children would with their father, making their requests known in simple, clear, everyday language, confident that God already knows what they need in any case (Mt 6:8). One hears in this model prayer at least as much silence as speech. Disciples turn to their heavenly Father in quiet confidence, listening as well as speaking. The fact that they are to pray "Our Father" reminds us of the corporate nature of this prayer—disciples do pray individually, but it is not insignificant that Jesus taught his followers to pray as a community in this model prayer (Gundry, *Matthew*, 106).

The content of the disciples' petitions is to have a sevenfold structure, just as the *fourteen* triads have a two-times-seven structure. The first three petitions pray for God's delivering rule to happen on earth. Nowhere is the kingdom-centered thesis we have been pursuing in this volume more clearly supported than here. Contrary to our natural human tendencies, prayer is to begin not with self-concern but with kingdom concern. "This prayer is not for getting what we want but rather for bending our wants toward what God wants" (Willimon and Hauerwas, *Lord, Teach Us*, 19). The only kind of people who can meaningfully pray like this are those who are learning to make the "kingdom of God and his righteousness" (Mt 6:33) their primary aim in life. Their deepest desire is for God to reign here on earth as he does so gloriously in heaven. That being the case, they gladly make petitions for God's reign their first order of business. They pray in three different ways for the same kingdom goal:

6:9 "Hallowed be your name"

6:10 "Your kingdom come"

6:10 "Your will be done"

To pray that God sanctify or hallow God's name is to plead that a rebellious world no longer reject its Creator, who has revealed himself by name (Ex 3:13-14). To know God's holy name is, in Old Testament perspective, to know God (Davies and Allison, *Critical and Exegetical Commentary*, 1:603). The Hebrew Scriptures sternly warn the Jewish people against profaning the holy name or bringing it into disrepute among the nations through living wrongly (Ex 20:7; Jer 34:16; Amos 2:7). To first-century Jews God's name was so holy as to be unutterable. And yet despite all this, that holy name was defamed in countless ways every day, both by those who called on it and by those who rejected the God of Israel. Thus Jewish prayers recognized and anticipated that in the time of God's reign God's name would be hallowed as it should (cf. Is 29:23; Ezek 36:23; 39:7). When God fully rules, at last people will pay him the homage he deserves (Jeremias, *Prayers of Jesus*, 98). Here Jesus echoed that traditional hope and implied that the time of its fulfillment was at hand. If you decide to try a few weeks of listening prayer as suggested above, consider asking God on Sunday, or the first day, to give you an idea concerning how God's name could be hallowed in your day—through what you are inspired to do, or what you pray someone else might do. A vision of a small, thoughtful initiative that you could take might come to you. A yearning for God's name to be hallowed might come to you.

To pray for God's kingdom to come and God's will to be done on earth is to acknowledge that the world is rebellious and in need of redemption, and to pray for God's deliverance and human obedience. Jesus himself pioneered the way by being totally devoted to practicing God's will (Gundry, *Matthew*, 106). The kingdom must be understood as essentially consisting of God's will being done on earth as it already is in heaven; the phrases stand in poetic parallelism, and the meaning fits. Disciples are to pray for the hallowing of God's name, the coming of God's reign and the doing of God's will in the hope that such prayers will move God to act speedily to bring this magnificent outcome to its full culmination (Davies and Allison, *Critical and Exegetical Commentary*, 1:604).

When we pray in this way, quietly, honestly and yearningly, usually we receive a painful awareness of the clash between God's reign and our world's destructive patterns and processes. Your kingdom come—in the Middle East. Your will be done—in our feuding church. Your kingdom come—in the life of that family in our church that is suffering just now. The more we pray for God's kingdom to come, the more clearly and compassionately we see the wrong, the injustice, the violence and the sadness in the world's patterns and power arrangements. And the more we become engaged in seeking our part along with others in correcting some part of those wrongs, the more clearly we see their contradiction of God's reign, and the more intensely and richly we pray for God's reign truly to come.

On Monday, or your second day of listening prayer, you might spend some time considering how God's kingdom might come in the world's life, and then in your life, in the next twenty-four hours.

As we pray, we may become acutely aware of areas in our own life in which our will is out of alignment with God's, our behavior out of keeping with the reign of God. And so we are moved to repent and to pray, Your kingdom come—in my thought life. Your will be done—in my marriage. Your kingdom come—in my use of money. Your will be done—in the way I speak to my children. To pray the Lord's prayer is to "cleanse the mind, purify the heart, and align one's will with God's will" (Davies and Allison, *Critical and Exegetical Commentary,* 1:588). When the kingdom becomes the refiner's fire we use to examine our lives in the presence of God, the dross of all that does not fit with the reign of God is, through confession, purged.

There is thus a strong *participatory* strand in this aspect of the prayer; indeed, in the entire prayer. Jesus, the trailblazer of the reign of God, gathers his disciples around him to teach us how to be most fit for kingdom existence. As we pray for God's name to be hallowed, God's kingdom to come and God's will to be done, we become coworkers in kingdom labors. We have opportunity to participate in the coming of God's reign, in God's delivering love. This understanding of God's grace as an invitation to participate in kingdom work is so much richer and more dynamic than the unfortunate notion of divine grace as sheer gift dumped gratuitously upon the souls of unworthy people who can only respond passively to something they had nothing to do with. Grace is certainly gift, and we are certainly unworthy; but what grace demands is not just gratitude but active participation in God's redemptive work in the world. So on Tuesday, or your third day of listening prayer, ask God's guidance for how you might be able to do God's will in a way you might not have thought of, or would not have been empowered to try, if you had not listened in God's presence.

The latter four petitions in the Lord's prayer ask for God to deliver us from four concrete threats to life and to our participation in kingdom work:

6:11 "Give us today enough bread for the coming day"

6:12 "Forgive us our debts (as we forgive our debtors)"

6:13 "Do not bring us into a time of trial/temptation"

6:13 "Deliver us from the evil one"

The first petition, for daily bread, marks a recognition of the physical needs of the human being. We each have basic food, shelter and clothing needs, and unless they are met, we are unable to do much else. This petition reflects the overwhelming poverty of many of Jesus' listeners, both then and today. Those among us who have pantries and refrigerators stuffed with food can hardly imagine having to pray for just enough bread for the coming day. The very modesty of this request raises acute questions about our own acquisitiveness and overdeveloped sense of what we "need," as discussed in chapters twenty and twenty-one. It also demands our attention to the physical needs of those around us. Several commentators also make the interesting suggestion of another level of meaning here—that along with the obvious material dimension of this petition Jesus was also praying for the eschatological "bread" of eternal salvation and the consummation of the kingdom (Jeremias, *Prayers of Jesus*, 100-101). On Wednesday, or your fourth day, you could read this paragraph again, and then, in listening prayer, open your mind so God might give you a vision of human need that you could help meet during the next twenty-four hours.

The emphasis on forgiveness has both a material and spiritual dimension; the same Aramaic word was used for both material and relational "debts." As to the former, disciples of Jesus lend without expecting anything in return (Mt 5:42), and this openhandedness should extend to debt-forgiveness. Several parables speak to debts and their forgiveness (cf. Mt 18:21-35; Lk 7:41-50), and indebtedness was clearly one of the most oppressive economic problems of Jesus' context (see also Yoder, *Royal Priesthood*, chap. 3).

The broader issue of forgiveness of wrongs both committed and suffered is clearly in view as well. Both here and in the explanation that follows, Jesus emphasized forgiveness as strongly as possible. We receive God's forgiveness only if we forgive others their sins against us. Krister Stendahl has pointed out that four texts in three Gospel accounts (Mt 6:12-15; 18:15-35; Mk 11:20-25; Lk 17:3-6) all suggest, in the original source, that the power of our prayer depends on the practice of our forgiveness (cited in Davies and Allison, *Critical and Exegetical Commentary*, 1:616-17). If we forgive, we shall be forgiven, but if we do not forgive, we shall not be forgiven.

Jesus was realistic about the vicious cycles of bondage to the power of sin in human life. We will inevitably sin against both God and neighbor, and our neighbors will sin against us. In the light of God's presence, we come to realize how deeply selfish, unfaithful, hostile, greedy, angry, vengeful, hateful, lustful, hypocritical, pretentious, anxious, prideful and untruthful we are. Commitment to the reign of God reorients us, but this does not mean we will no longer fail. God forgives the repentant our "indebtedness" to himself. But in turn, we are required to forgive others their "debts" just as freely.

Kingdom progress is blocked in so many sectors of life—marriage, parenting, international relations—by unforgiveness. This is why Jesus makes forgiveness such a central theme. Kingdom people do not carry unforgiven grudges in their backpacks. They travel light in order to be of the greatest possible use to God. This understanding of the centrality of forgiveness does not resolve all the complex and sometimes agonizing issues that arise, but does establish the fundamental stance that disciples of Jesus Christ are to take (cf.

Shriver, *Ethic for Enemies;* Smedes, *Forgive and Forget;* Tutu, *No Future Without Forgiveness;* Lampman, *God and the Victim;* L. G. Jones, *Embodying Forgiveness;* Volf, *Exclusion and Embrace*). On Thursday, or your fifth day of listening prayer, you could ask to be made aware of a part of your life where you could use some forgiveness, and of another person in your relationships who could use some forgiveness from you or from someone else whom you could help do some forgiving. Just relax and ask for God's presence, and for God to give you a word of forgiveness that you can take to heart, or that you can speak to someone else.

The last two petitions request deliverance from times of trial or temptation, and ultimately from the evil one, who (rather than God) is the active agent in such times (cf. Jas 1:13; Davies and Allison, *Critical and Exegetical Commentary,* 613). The word *peirasmos* (Mt 6:13), historically translated "temptation," can just as easily mean "trial," which may be the better understanding here—and of course, temptation is itself one form of trial. Keener suggests the best understanding is this: "let us not sin when we are tested" (*IVP Bible Background Commentary,* 62). On Friday, or your sixth day of listening prayer, you can confess to God some temptation in your life, admit you cannot solve it yourself, and ask for God to make you aware of how the vicious cycle works and how you can be delivered. Or you can pray for someone else's empowerment to avoid temptation, and a supporting word may come to you to mention to that other person.

Jesus taught his disciples to pray to be spared from succumbing to evil during times of trial and to be delivered from the evil one. Could it be that he had his own harrowing time of temptation in the wilderness in mind? There Satan tried Jesus' own sense of mission with various temptations, most notably perhaps the temptation to seize earthly power by evil or violent means (cf. Mt 4:8-10 and Yoder, *Politics of Jesus,* chap. 2). In Gethsemane, Jesus urged his disciples to pray that they would not fall into temptation (Mt 26:41). The theme is picked up by James (Jas 1:12), who describes as "blessed" anyone who successfully withstands temptation. Paul expresses concerns in Galatians and 1 Thessalonians about his flocks' enduring trials presented by "the tempter" (1 Thess 3:5; cf. Gal 6:1; 2 Thess 3:2-3), but he also expresses confidence that God will provide the needed strength (1 Cor 10:13).

The New Testament again and again shows Jesus doing battle with a living Satan who was the chief enemy of his mission, as evidenced by dozens of references to his struggle with "the evil one." The picture seems to be of the real possibility that followers of Jesus, kingdom people, can be picked off by the tempter and thus have their kingdom impact ruined, especially during times of persecution and distress (cf. Gundry, *Matthew,* 109). Jesus teaches us to pray that we be spared such failure amidst current or future trials. On Saturday, or your seventh day of listening prayer, ask that you be made aware of God's delivering action in your life or the life of someone else. It may give you new imagination of how you can participate in God's dynamic presence to deliver.

We have suggested a seven-day experiment with listening prayer, guided by the seven petitions of the Lord's Prayer. We suggest you try this for several weeks. Listening prayer is like soccer; you get better at it with regular practice. If you continue this practice, you will find that God does not always speak on your schedule. Some days, no word may come, or only what seems like a quite routine word. But your heart will gradually yield. Or the word that does come will not always be on the topic you thought you were asking about. Again, give thanks for the mustard seeds. Give thanks for what does come to you. And share your experience with someone else. You may strengthen each other.

William Spohn writes helpfully of meditation on Scripture, a prayerful way of Bible study and meditation using empathy to enter into parables and stories.

> Every biblical story has room for one more character: the believer whose story it is also. . . . Identifying with the scene can help us pray out of emotions or aspects of ourselves that have been kept buried and can strip away the posture of formality that often inhibits our relation to God. It also gets us to improvise and to see how the Lord responds.
>
> The five senses help the imagination bring home the actual details of the scene . . . . For example, in the three scenes that make up the parable of the Prodigal Son, we could place ourselves in the pigsty with the younger brother and imagine what he is experiencing [and smelling]. Or we could imagine the joy of the father when he first catches sight of the son for whom he has waited so long; then we could shift to what the son feels as he sees the father run out to meet him on the road. It should not be difficult to taste the resentment that sours the older brother as he listens to the bustle of preparation for the feasts and smells the roasting fatted calf.
>
> Meditation means chewing, savoring and enjoying a word or phrase until the savor is gone; only then do we move on to another aspect. The point is to dwell in the image-shaped emotion and to pray from that place to God. This savoring is helped by recalling analogous situations from personal history and returning to them in an unhurried fashion. (*Go and Do Likewise*, 136-41)

Sometimes a breakthrough, an insight or a feeling comes that would be good to write into a journal. Glen, who is right-handed, prefers to keep his journal in his computer, because that way his left hand and right brain are more engaged, and he is more connected with his deeper and more imaginative feelings. Dave is naturally left-handed and so can write feelingly just by nature. (In this book, you may detect Glen's linear, analytic logic combined with Dave's feeling, compassionate presence, and appreciate the teamwork.) Part of the practice is "to become more present to your emotions, for they are the ties that link to God" (Spohn, *Go and Do Likewise*, 139). Glen's sister, who is right-handed, actually journals left-handed in order to help her connect as a whole person. You may not be impressed with this diversion into intimate personal self-disclosure, but we are illustrating that journaling should be as uninhibited, as present to feelings and even humor and illogic, as it can, if it helps you be present to God's presence where you had not expected it. (Glen is writing this paragraph at four o'clock in the morning, meditating while his inner censor is still half asleep and he can be more present to inspiration of the Spirit. He does that often; the early morning is so quiet, both outside and inside himself.)

Spohn echoes our experience when he writes, "As the practice of meditation deepens, it often leads to contemplation, when words fail and a simple reverent attention to God is all that satisfies. Here the presence of God is entered directly and simply, even though a certain amount of distraction may be occurring at a more superficial level" (*Go and Do Likewise*, 139). In Spohn's quiet way, or in the more dramatic way of Pentecost, in private meditation or in group worship, there may be an experience of the presence of the Holy Spirit with power, that empowers us with an experience and a message and the courage to share it, as a witness. Donald Gee writes of Pentecost: "What should be carefully noted is that the pouring out of the gift of the Holy Spirit upon these people was a definite experience. They did not simply believe a doctrine about the Holy Spirit; neither did they 'take it by faith' and hope for some future grace and gift; they received right on the spot something of a perfectly positive nature. And everybody knew it." It gave them the empowerment to make changes in their lives and to be witnesses, and it showed itself in fruits of more faithful living (Gee, *God's Grace and Power for Today* and *Is It God?*).

But you will also experience dark times, when you are not so present to God and the experience of God's Spirit. Then biblical meditation by itself can do its work quietly while you wait for a new time of presence. Sometimes this means you have decided on a course of action or you are engaging in a practice that you really do not want God to interfere with. The presence of the Spirit may be restored only when you are open to repentance in a new way. Or you may come to a period of doubt. Then paradoxically meditation may enable you to sense God's pressing on you in your experience of God's absence, or your absence from God. Your experience of the emptiness or dryness of life lived in God's absence is your experience of God's presence in absence, showing you what you are missing, calling for a turning. This is like the people of Jesus' day, wishing for God's presence but experiencing God's absence until Jesus brought the presence. But life has rhythms, sometimes with significantly more sense of God's presence, and sometimes with a "vacation" of ordinariness and absence or laxness. Furthermore, different ones of us have different makeups and different kinds of spiritual lives. Many people do better in regular group Bible study, group discussion and group prayer, and simply do not enjoy private meditation. Or a love for meditation may come at a later stage in life.

Conclusion: Ethics and Prayer Revisited

We argued at the outset of this chapter that the link between prayer and Christian ethics needs much more attention than it normally receives. We think that the discussion we have just offered suggests the following twelve points of contact between prayer (as Jesus taught it) and ethics:

- Prayer deepens our commitment to the narrative of the kingdom of God.
- Prayer binds us more thoroughly to God the gracious Father and to Jesus the faithful Son.
- Prayer connects us more closely with other brothers and sisters who also are giving their lives to the reign of God.
- Prayer aligns our will with the will of God and the contours of God's reign.
- Prayer gives us opportunity to participate in the coming of God's reign through petitioning God for that coming.
- Prayer alerts us to Satan's wiles and fortifies us for resistance in times of trial.
- Prayer deepens our trust in God and our consequent willingness to take risks for the kingdom.
- Prayer purifies us of mixed allegiances that threaten our fidelity to God.
- Prayer trains our hearts to seek heavenly rather than earthly rewards.
- Prayer keeps us from investing ourselves in unworthy idols in quest of an illusory security.
- Prayer keeps us from cozying up to unjust earthly powers in order to protect ourselves.
- Prayer aids our moral discernment and decision making process by establishing kingdom practices as the plumblines.

In short: prayer as Jesus taught it is asking for God's delivering grace to rain down upon the earth, and at the same time making the grateful choice to participate in that delivering grace ourselves.

23

POLITICS

—

You are the salt of the earth; but if salt loses its saltiness, what can make it salt again? It is good for nothing, but to be thrown out and trampled under foot by the people.

You are the light of the world. A city that is built upon a hill cannot be hidden. Nor do they light a lamp and put it under a bushel, but upon the lampstand, and it gives light to all in the house.

So, shine your light before the people, so that they may see your good deeds and give glory to your Father in heaven.

MATTHEW 5:13-16 AUTHOR'S TRANSLATION

Do not give what is holy to dogs; and do not throw your pearls before swine, or they will trample them under foot and turn and maul you . . . In everything do to others as you would have them do to you; for this is the law and the prophets.

MATTHEW 7:6, 12

$\mathcal{A}$s we move toward the conclusion of our exploration of Christian ethics as Jesus taught it, we reach back to Matthew 5:13-16, the famous passage on salt, light and deeds. Upon the foundation of this brief passage entire theologies of Christian mission, social action and political engagement have been constructed, some far more credible than others. We too find this text critically important in ascertaining Jesus' teaching on the action his disciples must take toward and in the world if they are to participate in the gracious deliverance God is undertaking in Jesus Christ. Thus we will explore its particular meaning and then broaden the search for resources for a Christian public theology. Our essential claim will be the following: *Jesus taught that participation in God's reign requires the disciplined practices of a Christ-following countercultural community that obeys God by publicly engaging in working for justice and refusing to trust in the world's powers and authorities.* Aspects of this claim will be developed in this chapter, with the rest held for our concluding chapter on moral practices.

And we also reach forward to the climactic verse, "In everything do to others as you would have them do to you; for this is the law and the prophets" (Mt 7:12).

Interpreting the Passage

In Matthew 5:13-16 three descriptive claims are made concerning followers of Jesus. The first is that they are "the salt of the earth," the second that they are "the light of the world" and the third that they are to do "good deeds." We believe that all three are equally important and thus will discuss this passage as a salt, light and deeds triad, rather than merely "salt and light," as the passage is traditionally read.

Related to these three descriptive claims is the clear implication—and in one case a direct statement—of the disciples' responsibilities related to each of the elements of salt, light and deeds. Disciples are the "salt of the earth," and they must by implication retain their "saltiness." The Markan version of this passage concludes "Have salt in yourselves" (Mk 9:50; cf. Lk 14:34-35). As the light of the world, disciples are directed to "shine [their light] before others" (Mt 5:16). As for deeds, the entire Sermon on the Mount as well as the rest of Jesus' teaching focuses on doing the deeds of obedience. A key text comes near the end of the Sermon: "Not everyone who says to me, 'Lord, Lord,' will enter the kingdom of heaven, but only the one who does the will of my Father in heaven" (Mt 7:21).

1. Salt. W. D. Davies suggests that "it is perhaps best to think of the parable as originally spoken with the challenge of Qumran in mind" (Davies, *Setting of the Sermon on the Mount,* 214ff., cf. 249-56, 457). An intense argument raged within first-century Jewish life about the requirements of morality under the covenant, especially in the context of Roman occupation and the pressures of Hellenization. Moral practice ranged from profound corruption and worldliness, such as that which could be found in the Herodian court (see Mt 14:1-12), to the compromises with the Roman power structure made by the Sadducees, to the serious but flawed moral effort of the Pharisees, to the revolutionary visions of the rebels, all the way to the experiment in moral purity conducted by the separatist Qumran or Dead Sea community.

The Dead Sea community at Qumran was deeply troubled by the way much of Israel was living a morally corrupted life and so withdrew from that life into a rigorous monastic community in order to live in covenant fidelity. They were "salty" in two senses: they were living in a way very different from the world, and they were living by the Dead Sea, which was literally very salty. Jesus was saying that his disciples must live lives different from the morally corrupted life of the world. Like the members of the Dead Sea community, they should be very "salty," very different from the world, because they were followers of Jesus and loyal to God. Also—and this is critical—they must repent when they live in a manner conformed to the world rather than to God's way (cf. Mt 3:8, 10; 4:17). But Jesus was also saying that his followers should be salty—different from the world—in a different way from the Dead Sea community.

The text contains a warning against the salt becoming tasteless (probably by being polluted with gypsum and other impurities, a process which in reality and in this metaphor is irreversible) and thus losing its *reason for being*. The same note related to "saltiness" is struck in parallel passages in the other Gospels (Mk 9:50; Lk 14:34-35). Jesus' followers are supposed to be salty, which indicates that in actuality it is moral goodness that adds "spice" to the world, rather than moral evil—which in a very real sense can be described, as banal (Arendt, *Eichmann in Jerusalem*).

Some interpreters try to figure out what Jesus meant by "salt" by choosing a use that salt must have had in Jesus' time. This, however, is not a sure route to right understanding, because salt had several different uses. Simply choosing one of the several possible meanings of salt as the clue to meaning can lead to the speculative reading of someone's favorite point into what Jesus said (Hagner, *Matthew 1—13*, 99). In the Old Testament, salt is associated with the following meanings: *purity* (Ex 30:35; 2 Kings 2:19-23); *covenant loyalty* (Lev 2:13; Num 18:19, 2 Chron 13:5; Ezra 4:14); *an element to be added to sacrifices* (Lev 2:13); *a seasoning* for food (Job 6:6). *A preservative* is the least likely meaning; it is not mentioned in the Hebrew Scriptures, but by Ignatius, well after the time of Jesus (Davies and Allison, *Critical and Exegetical Commentary*, 1:472).

We get much surer guidance by focusing on the second sentence, "if salt loses its saltiness, . . . it is good for nothing, but to be thrown out and trampled under foot." There are several reasons why this gives us surer guidance:

1. This part of the teaching has the unusual distinction of being in both Mark and the special sayings source "Q" that scholars believe Matthew and Luke used, so even skeptical scholars think it offers doubly convincing evidence as coming from Jesus (Davies and Allison, *Critical and Exegetical Commentary*, 1:474).

2. It suggests a special context of meaning—a polemic against losing your special identity by losing your distinction from the world. Salt lost its taste and became no better than the sand people walked on by becoming corrupted with other chemicals and with sand. The Greek word for "becoming tasteless" can just as well mean "becoming foolish," and this represents

more accurately the Hebrew and Aramaic that likely lay behind it (Guelich, *Sermon on the Mount*, 121, 126; Jeremias, *Parables of Jesus*, 168). Furthermore, in some rabbinic texts salt is associated with wisdom (Davies and Allison, *Critical and Exegetical Commentary*, 1:473), so losing saltiness would mean becoming foolish.

3. This meaning strikingly parallels the concluding teaching of the Sermon, so that this introduction and the conclusion serve as bookends (what New Testament scholars call an *inclusio*), enclosing the beginning and end of the main section of the Sermon:

(a) It parallels the emphasis on foolishness versus wisdom in Matthew 7:24, 26: salt becoming foolish is like the foolish builder who builds on sand and has his house destroyed.

(b) It parallels the emphasis on the way not to become foolish: do the deeds that Jesus teaches (Mt 5:16; 7:24, 26).

(c) It parallels the consequence: to be thrown out and "trampled under foot" (the same word meaning "trampled" is used in Mt 5:13 and 7:6), and suggests eschatological judgment, as Matthew 7:26 also does.

(d) It may parallel the metaphor of sand: salt that has lost its taste and become foolish and good for nothing but to be trampled on is like sand (which we trample on all the time); the foolish builder builds on sand (Mt 5:13; 7:26).

(e) It also parallels Jesus' teachings on becoming like the Gentiles (Mt 5:46-47; 6:7, 32) and the hypocrites (6:2, 5, 16; 7:5, 22-23), and so having no eschatological reward.

So we conclude that "losing your saltiness" means losing your identity that distinguishes you from the foolish world—being corrupted by the world because you do not do the deeds Jesus teaches.

It means acting in such a way that you give your loyalty to another Lord and become worldly. This would then fit the most frequent Old Testament meanings for salt—purity and covenant loyalty—as well as seasoning (that has not lost its distinctiveness and become like sand).

2. Light. The significance of the metaphor of light is clear. Two particular images of light are used in the passage. The first is the famous "city built on a hill" (Mt 5:14), an image that rhetoricians from Winthrop to Reagan have found compelling. The second is the image of the lamp on the lampstand in a home (Mt 5:15). In both cases Jesus made the obvious point that light penetrates darkness and cannot—and of course, should not—be hidden. Otherwise the very purpose of light is defeated.

In using light imagery, Jesus drew deeply on the rich resources of the Old Testament tradition related to the presence of God, as we have discussed in chapter one on the characteristics of the kingdom of God. As early as the creation story God is identified as the source of light (Gen 1:3), and God's presence is identified with a bright shining light (Is 60:1-3). Isaiah speaks of the "light of the LORD" (Is 2:5). Israel is called to be the light of the nations (Is 49:6). God's word is also identified as light (Ps 119:105), and to undertake deeds of obedience is to walk in the light (Ps 112:4, cf. 1 Jn. 1:7). David Garland argues that Isaiah 2:2-5 and 49:6 serve as the Old Testament backdrop to this particular image of an eschatological city on the hill (Jerusalem), blazing with the light of God's salvation, presence, justice and peace, and drawing people of all nations up the hill and into its gates—people seeking to share in the glorious shalom experienced there (*Reading Matthew;* cf. Lohfink, *Jesus and Community,* 66).

Davies suggests that Jesus was here disavowing the separatism of the Dead Sea community, one of whose favorite images of itself was as the "sons of light" in contrast with the world's "sons of darkness." A separatist or withdrawal strategy by definition makes for a hiding rather than a displaying of the light. Light can only penetrate darkness if it is not hid under a bushel basket (or in caves near the Dead Sea). Likewise, the background of this text in Isaiah 2:2-5 must be kept firmly in mind to forestall any separatism to which we might be inclined today. Disciples are a "city on a hill" in the Isaiah 2 sense only if we invite and draw people of all nations "up the hill" and through the gates into an experience of shared eschatological community. Much as the neon sign of a hotel invites the weary traveler to rest, so is our light to be an invitation. "What is meant is precisely that according to God's will Jesus' followers will transform the whole of humanity through their lives. More and more people will join the community of those who orient themselves on the will of God" (Lohfink, *Jesus and Community,* 66, quoting Luise Schottroff).

The early Christian movement was small. Among the earliest disciples there must have been doubts as to whether that little band could make a difference. But Jesus was saying that the impact of this movement would spread surprisingly. That is also the point of the parables of growth (mustard seed, etc.)—much would happen from modest beginnings. Also implicit was the idea that the reign of God would happen not only through what Jesus did, but through what the community of disciples did as together it functioned as a city on a hill (Lohfink, *Jesus and Community,* 67-69).

3. Deeds. Usually people speak of this teaching as twofold, "salt and light." But the climax of the whole teaching is clearly in the last verse, in which the emphasis is on deeds that give glory to God (Hagner, *Matthew 1—13,* 100). To mention salt and light and leave deeds out is to tilt the passage toward cheap grace or "easy believism" that does no deeds of following Jesus. Therefore we emphasize that the teaching is threefold: "salt, light and deeds." We offer the following reasons for seeing the teaching as threefold and the emphasis on deeds as the climax:

- The Gospel of Matthew has about seventy-five threefold teachings and almost no twofold teachings. It would be odd if this teaching were only twofold.

- The only command or imperative in the whole teaching in the original Greek comes in the third part, "*shine* your light before people that they may see your good deeds." Emphasis in Jesus' teaching, as we have seen, can almost always be found where the imperative verb is found. Incidentally, the Greek imperative is an active verb—"shine your light"—not a passive, "let your light shine," as usually translated. Shine your light by actively doing God's deeds.

- Also, the third teaching is the first mention of "your Father in heaven," clearly a climax.

- The emphasis here in the beginning on good *deeds* mirrors the teaching in the end of the Sermon on hearing these words and *doing* them (Mt 7:24). So when we see the emphasis here on deeds, we see how the whole Sermon is symmetrical.

- The climax clarifies the meaning-content of the salt and deeds. Doing good deeds is the content of being the salt of the earth and the light of the world. What makes the salt keep its saltiness is the good deeds that show God's light to people.

- It pulls together all the previous verses: The Greek for "people" (*tōn anthrō-pōn*) in verse 13, the Greek for "light" in verse 14, and the different Greek word for "light" or "shine" in verse 15, are all brought together as "shine your light before the people" in the climactic verse 16.

This interpretation is fully consistent with the vision of Isaiah 2:2-5 upon which Jesus appears to have based this teaching. The nations come to the mountain of the Lord "that he may teach us his ways and that we may walk in his paths" (Is 2:3). Those ways are then described in the moving and unforgettable imagery of peace and justice: "they shall beat their swords into plowshares, and their spears into pruning hooks" (Is 2:4). Disciples of Jesus—like their Master—participate in the fulfillment of this eschatological vision through their deeds of peacemaking, their justice-doing, their feeding of the hungry and their care for the sick. It is the joy of this way of life and its fruit that draws men and women to the city on the hill—to the community of disciples.

To sum up: we have argued that the teaching on salt, light and deeds found in Matthew 5:13-16 has the following essential meaning:

1. *Saltiness:* being an alternative community different from the world, not conformed to the world;

2. *Light:* being a caring community that does not withdraw from the world but instead serves the whole human family, beckoning outsiders and weary ones, bringing light to the dark places inhabited by outcasts and the wretched of the earth;

3. *Deeds:* being a disciple-making community that lives out Christ's actual commands in joyful obedience.

As such, and only as such, can the church be a useful participant in God's kingdom-building activity. In the remainder of this chapter, we will focus on fleshing out a social ethic of salt, light and deeds, with the majority of the latter discussion held until our final chapter.

Toward a Christian Social Ethic of Salt, Light and Deeds

Some have offered the odd argument that Jesus—in the Sermon on the Mount, and elsewhere—was not interested in social or political matters but solely in inner attitudes or the state of the human heart. We have already shown that Jesus was vitally interested in deeds that shine light in the world, not only in inner attitudes. As such, his teaching is inevitably "social" and "political." We believe that limiting our ethics, our obedience, to inner attitudes is a morally disastrous argument. In the discussion that follows, drawing on the work of theologian/ ethicist H. Richard Niebuhr and others, we will unpack some of the implications of the salt, light and deeds triad for the church's mission in the world, including its social and political witness. We contend that the church has a threefold mission, corresponding not only with salt, light and deeds, but with the Trinitarian nature of God. (This logic is developed in Stassen, Yeager and Yoder, *Authentic Transformation,* 222-46.) While this is not by any means intended as a complete presentation of a Christian political ethic, we hope it helps to point the way to some of its key elements. Resources noted along the way will be helpful to those interested in further discussion of these issues.

Salt: the church as pioneering model for human community. Let us summarize what we argued concerning the "salt of the earth" language in Matthew 5:13.

Jesus was calling his disciples to a morally rigorous way of life, clearly distinct from that of the corrupt world. The church must be a repentant community, ever on its knees in acknowledgment of ways in which it has conformed to the world rather than to Christ. That is always the first step if we are to function as salt in society.

In reflecting on the implications of this we are reminded of Niebuhr's very helpful image of the church as a *pioneering community*, which takes a new path different from the world, goes out ahead of the world and provides leadership to the whole human family through its own faithful following of God's will:

> The Church is that part of the human community which responds first to God-in-Christ and Christ-in-God.... It is that group which hears the Word of God, which sees God's judgments, which has the vision of the resurrection. In its relations with God it is the pioneer part of society that responds to God on behalf of the whole society, somewhat... as science is the pioneer in responding to pattern or rationality in experience and as artists are the pioneers in responding to beauty. (Niebuhr, "Responsibility of the Church for Society," 130)

To respond to God is always to pioneer because God's will is always ahead of where society is. God's rule cannot be reduced to the way things are; it includes judgment and change. This is especially clear when we remember that God is not just an idea or a doctrine, or the possession of any church or institution, but God is living, dynamic Holy Spirit (Jn 4:24), who brings us to judgment and calls to repentance and change. Disciples are those who pioneer in saying yes to God and in being changed by the power of the Holy Spirit. They contrast sharply with those who reject divine judgment and cling defensively to ways of life contrary to God's will.

We know that the contemporary church is an inconsistent pioneer-model of faithfulness. In the wake of many scandals that have rocked the churches, and in the light of the ideological captivity of much church teaching, the church can hardly be a pioneer without leading in the act of repentance. But that has always been part of what it means to be "salt."

The mission of Christ and the church as representative of society parallels what the German theologian-martyr Dietrich Bonhoeffer wrote of both Christ and the church as representative or deputy (*Stellvertreter*—one who walks in the place of others: Bonhoeffer, *Ethics*, 224). It was Bonhoeffer who confessed his own sin powerfully during the Nazi period as a representative of German society, and thereby influenced German churches and West Germany to confess their sin publicly after the war (*Ethics*, 110ff.)—a key step in the remarkable moral reclamation of German society (Shriver, *Ethic for Enemies*).

Some readers will be familiar with the heavy attention given in the mainstream American media to the pronouncements of the Southern Baptist Convention annual meeting each June. It appears to have been the 1995 resolution on racial reconciliation that began the trend. Though far too late, it clearly and unequivocally renounced the denomination's historic acquiescence to slavery and participation in racist practices. This document served as a vivid example of the church as repentant community and as such was generally warmly received and stimulated some productive national conversation about race.

Southern Baptist Convention resolutions and statements since that time, however, have generally not followed the same pattern and have tended to be characterized by finger-pointing rather than repentance. It is no surprise that their impact has thus been more polarizing than light-spreading, tending to produce a defensive rather than reflective reaction in the society as a whole. Repentance is disarming, whereas attacks produce counterattacks. The church as pioneer is there with the rest of society, participating in the change that is sought, rather than standing aloof on the sidelines or pointing fingers from the bleachers (Walzer, *Company of Critics*).

The church as salt, pioneer or model also points toward the theme that runs throughout Mennonite ethicist John Howard Yoder's writings—the church as model and as *alternative community*. It points strongly toward the koinonia (community) nature of the church, a community of disciples obeying the particular ways of God revealed in Christ. A major way the church transforms society is by being a model, a pioneer, of what it means to live in love, justice, inclusiveness, servanthood, forgiveness—and confessing its own need for forgiveness.

Here Yoder brings a special insight that points to the character of the church as pioneer community:

> Not only are there lessons for the outside world from the inner life of the Christian church as a society; a comparable creative impulse should radiate from the church's services to the larger community. The most obvious examples would be the institutions of the school and the hospital, both of which began in Christian history as services rendered by the church . . . to the entire society. . . . The witness of the church to the state must be consistent with her own behavior. . . . A racially segregated church has nothing to say to the state about integration. . . . Only a church doing something about prisoner rehabilitation would have any moral right to speak—or have any good ideas—about prison conditions or parole regulations. (Yoder, *Christian Witness to the State*, 19-22)

The church as community also helps to correct the autonomous individualism that fragments our society, thus functioning as a critical pioneer of this important aspect of social existence. Larry Rasmussen works out the implications accurately:

> Even irrepressible dreamers know that nothing is ever real until it is embodied . . . . What counts with God and one another is not "opportunity," or even vision,

but incarnation. What carries power and promise and generates conviction and courage is concrete community. . . . Very practical theological and technical attention must be given to what the churches do with their own institutional property and moneys. . . . It means attending to how governance happens in these ranks, the quality of our treatment of one another within the household of faith, the mirroring of the vision of inclusive, egalitarian membership in each locale. It means attending to the way the earth and things of the earth are cared for in this open enclave of creation. (Rasmussen, *Moral Fragments and Moral Community*, 152-53)

Rasmussen describes our need for community and diagnoses the causes of its fragmentation in "calculating market logic" and interest-based association. We associate with people and churches just like we patronize department stores—based on calculated self-interest. The domination of market logic is seen in "divorce, distrust, suspicion, and general alienation" (*Moral Fragments and Moral Community*, 53). And because we lack community, we lack moral formation. To resist and transform these powerful forces of fragmentation, we need pioneering community (Roof and McKinney, *American Mainline Religion*, 99, 251). So long as churches are merely associations of autonomous individuals and not pioneering communities, we will be weak puffs of air against the winds of fragmentation.

To become such communities, churches need *shared practices* that transform social experiences, that form and transform people morally, that provide a meaningful sense of membership and that support critical teaching of the difference between obedience to the subtle powers and authorities of our society and obedience to the rule of God.

Light: the church as caring community for the human family. In exegeting Matthew 5:14-16, we identified several dimensions of the concept of disciples as "the light of the world." Against the backdrop of the use of the term *light* in the Old Testament, especially Isaiah 2:2-5, we focused on the church's vocation to be that community in which the salvation, presence, peace and justice of the Lord of light are experienced and into which all human beings are invited. The church is called to a role of service to the world, bearing witness to the love of God and caring for all persons, but especially society's broken, needy and outcast.

H. Richard Niebuhr can be helpful to us once again here. He synthesizes several of these themes in the image of the church as *pastor*. He intends the New Testament meaning of pastor; that is, a shepherd who is distinguished not by authority but by caring, especially for *the lost, the outcast, the needy and the vulnerable*. He argues that the church responds to Christ by being a shepherd, a seeker of the lost, the friend of sinners, the lowly and the brokenhearted.

The caring or pastoral mission of the church is thus the logical implication of a key dimension of the sovereign reign of God over all things. This is God as Creator and Ruler. All are included in God's rule and God's love, all of society, including members of the church and outcasts, friends and enemies, the powerless and the powerful, the orphans and the powers and authorities. God sends showers of rain and sunshine on the just and unjust alike (Mt 5:45). The response to God's universal mercy is universal caring, a caring that Jesus incarnated by going first "to those excluded from human solidarity and who felt themselves excluded from God's solidarity" (Bauckham, *Bible in Politics*, 146). This was a critical part of the content of his kingdom-inaugurating ministry.

The ministry of *caring directly for the church's own members* seems so obviously essential for any church that one wonders at the need to emphasize it. But the grace dimension of the universal sovereignty of God requires special emphasis on God's caring for all diverse kinds of people within a church. Any gathering of sons and daughters of Adam and Eve is filled with people who sense that there is an inner circle from which they have been barred because of their particular faults, shortcomings, practices, vices, virtues, beliefs, inadequacies, history, class, race, gender and other unknown reasons. People try to present their acceptable frontside in the gathering and hide their backside. Membership, then, is only partial and is partially alienating.

In our culture, as we have said, we especially need community. God's grace reemphasizes the need for transforming churches to become forgiving and inclusive communities (Rom 12:1-13; 14:1—16:20). God's rule requires that we look sensitively for those whose gifts are not being called out, for groups of people not being encouraged to participate, for needs within the community still to be met.

Recently I (David) had a sobering conversation with a fellow church member. Ours is a relatively small church, and the experience of Christian community is often rich. Yet one night I was reminded of how little we know about people we see each week. I had been teaching about issues of family life and found myself in what I thought would be a brief postmessage conversation with a divorced mother of three, a faithful member of our congregation but not one whom I knew well.

A brief talk was not enough, and so we moved to an office where the congregant had more privacy and time to unburden herself. I learned of her financial troubles, her growing difficulty retaining control over her kids, her lingering bitterness over her divorce and her fight against a sense of despair. I had known none of this prior to our talk. I was able to follow up on at least one dimension of her need but was aware of the inadequacy of these efforts and was once again astonished at the need so often hidden within the church. Glen had this experience in many surprising ways after he had been a pastor about a year. People began to trust him and tell of hidden pain, tragedy, abandonment and injustice that he had not suspected when he looked over a room of seemingly happy, friendly fellow church members.

As light of the world and pastor to society, *the church is also called to offer direct aid to those outside the congregation*. We must do so, of course, within the limits of our resources and wisdom. But the church can make an enormous contribution to the kingdom as it undertakes these kinds of efforts. Numerous works in recent years have chronicled such efforts by the church, both historically and today (Sider, *Cup of Water, Bread of Life*). Churches are participating in efforts that are genuinely transforming some of the most troubled neighborhoods in our nation. Churches are also leading the way in establishing relationships with those formerly dependent on welfare and mentoring them toward self-sufficiency (Sherman, "Getting to Work"; Carlson-Thies, "Welfare Reform and the Evangelical Church"). These and many other examples both demonstrate what is possible for the church to do on its own and the range of public and private partnerships that the church must undertake to maximize its impact.

These direct-aid mercy ministries lead almost inevitably to *broader social and political concern*, and one can imagine few better paths to such concern. Out of its pastoral concern for human beings in need, "the church has found itself forced to take an interest in political and economic measures or institutions" (H. R. Niebuhr, "Responsibility of the Church for Society," 129). Often the needy are also the powerless, and they need caring communities to intervene for their rights. Both kinds of pastoral action, direct and indirect, are needed if the church is to be faithful to God who is universal sovereign, ruling not only in the church but in all of the world.

For example, one church Glen attended invited the county Association for Retarded Persons to establish a weekday School of Hope for retarded adults in the church basement. This was direct aid, a caring service the church could help to provide. Gradually church members grew in awareness and open-heartedness toward their new students' needs, their remarkable accomplishments and their joy in finally having a school.

Then an issue of city policy arose that would affect the mentally retarded. Members of the church who had never engaged in such civic action before gathered in the city hall and spoke to the mayor and city council on behalf of the powerless whom they had come to know. And they won. Then some began to ask why these adults had never had any school when they were children; why they had never received the right to a public education, when they needed an education even more than others did. Without schooling, they were helpless, could not become personally independent, care for themselves or be economically productive. With school they could. So one church member, a parent of a handicapped child, who had joined the Board of the County Association for Retarded Persons, joined with a few other parents in the state association to sue the state for the right to education for children of several varieties of handicaps, including mental retardation. Again they won. The state agreed for the first time to educate thousands of its citizens who had received no schooling before. This too was pastoral. It was action that grew out of the church's caring for people.

In recent decades the issue of Christian political engagement has exercised the attention of great sections of the church, especially in North America (Cerillo and Dempster, *Salt and Light;* Cromartie, "Evangelical Kaleidoscope"; Gushee, *Christians and Politics;* Thomas and Dobson, *Blinded by Might;* Wallis, *Soul of Politics).* Our reading of the Sermon on the Mount and of Jesus' entire ministry both leads us to endorse certain kinds of political engagement but also to situate such engagement within a broader approach to the public witness and social ministry of the church. It also leads us—like several other recent evangelical observers (Thomas and Dobson, *Blinded by Might;* Horton, *Beyond Culture Wars;* Boice, *Two Cities, Two Loves)*—to call for a rethinking of this intense political engagement in our current American context.

Political activism carries unique dangers for the church while offering real, but limited, kingdom opportunities. The danger is to become too close to a particular political ideology and to accommodate Jesus' call to discipleship to a worldly power strategy or power center. We should not give our trust and loyalty to the political left or right. Instead, we should give practical attention to what government can do best and what churches and private groups can do best to transform the lives of the poor. The challenge for Christians is to ground political efforts in a healthy understanding of church, state, society and the reign of God (Mott, *Biblical Ethics and Social Change;* Yoder, *For the Nations).* The plumb line for measuring policies must be the biblical narrative and the principle of justice of doing for all others what we would have others do for us (Mt 7:12).

We place social and political action and advocacy within the framework of the church's role as caring pastor to society—and within the framework of the teachings of Jesus which ground this vision. At our best, Christians vote, lobby, campaign, meet with political leaders and become such leaders themselves as a natural outflow of our pastoral concern for the social good under the sovereignty of the God who loves all persons. We are alerted to brokenness, need and injustice through ministry with people or awareness of their needs, and care for such persons then moves us, in part, toward politics. Meanwhile, we are also animated by the rich eschatological vision of the Scripture as we imagine the inbreaking of the holistic shalom that God intends—the city on a hill in which God's way is lived out. Thus we are both *pushed* into politics through hands-on ministry and *pulled* into politics through our intoxication with the biblical vision of the kingdom.

Approaching politics through caring pastoral action and compassionate and merciful pastoral moral vision also affects very deeply the way in which we conduct ourselves in the public struggle over justice for the needy and outcasts. The authentic pastor seeks not domination but service, not status but a role in helping to meet real human needs and to encourage others to do the same. This approach also shapes the tone of our engagement. As pastor, the church nudges, encourages, exhorts, sometimes chastises, but does not seek to destroy enemies or to inflame social hostilities (see Hunter, *Culture Wars;* Wuthnow, *Christianity and Civil Society*).

We believe that one good example of Christian political engagement in this style on the current scene is to be found in the American Catholic Church. Let us reflect on its public witness for a moment (cf. Wald, *Religion and Politics in the United States*, 280-303).

For centuries the Catholic Church exercised cultural and even political hegemony over Western European nations. During the medieval period Catholic leaders grew accustomed to directing the course of political events. Indeed, they became habituated to significant political power, sometimes with spiritually and morally disastrous consequences (the Crusades, the Inquisition).

As the Catholic Church lost hegemony over Europe—through the Protestant Reformation, the Enlightenment, and many other historical developments—it struggled for a long time with keeping the frustration out of its public voice. There was the same sense of being aggrieved over privileges lost that one typically hears from voices on the Christian Right in the United States. But by the late nineteenth century the Catholic Church had found a new tone. It would continue to express concern for public affairs, for the governance of nations and the international community. *But it would do so by offering thoughtful and constructive public reflection in the interests of the common human good under the sovereignty of God the Creator.* It would also do so by offering itself sacrificially/pastorally in service to those in need.

The name of one important Catholic encyclical, *Mater et Magistra* ("Mother and Teacher," 1961), illustrates these crucial points quite nicely. "Mother and Teacher" is precisely the tone taken by this document as well as by the whole body of contemporary Catholic social teaching. The Church is concerned not mainly about its own power or interests but in a motherly/pastoral way about the whole of the world and all who dwell therein. She will serve the world with all of her love and all of her energy.

This is the official Catholic approach today, and it is at times amazingly fruitful despite inevitable occasions of failure. Can Protestants learn something from it? Here is the model:

- a church that acts on behalf of the well-being of society regardless of whether the society is particularly appreciative or not—as opposed to a Christian public witness marred by a sense of aggrieved entitlement to both respect and privilege;

- a church that offers sophisticated Christian moral instruction in a respectful public language that communicates its values in a way that a wide variety of people can understand and embrace (Weigel, *Soul of the World*, chap. 4; cf. Audi and Wolterstorff, *Religion in the Public Square*, 34-35, 111-12)—as opposed either to a withdrawn sectarianism or a hateful attack-dog politics of either left or right (see Wallis, *Soul of Politics*, chap. 2);

- a church that focuses its activism on the well-being of the whole society, in particular those trampled on by the current cultural and political order, rather than on its own narrow interests;

- a church that respects religious liberty and appropriate church-state boundaries in a pluralistic democracy rather than yearning for establishment or theocracy (Hollenbach, *Justice, Peace and Human Rights; Claims in Conflict*);

- a church that retains its independence, its saltiness, refusing to align itself with any particular politician or party, so that it might serve God and the common good, rather than being drawn inexorably either left or right under the influence of political power;

- a church that lays down its life for its society, like a mother for her children—or like a pastor—rather than fighting religious culture wars to the bitter end.

A major element in this transformation of the Catholic moral witness has been the Church's coming to terms with its role as a disestablished participant in a pluralistic liberal democracy. John Courtney Murray was a key figure in helping the American Catholic Church make the transition to seeing disestablishment as a blessing rather than a curse (J. C. Murray, *We Hold These Truths*; Hittinger, "Catholic Theology of John Courtney Murray").

This insight came several centuries earlier to those in the Anabaptist tradition whose earliest experiences involved suffering at the hands of confessional states in which religious and political power were fused. Anabaptists on the Continent (such as Menno Simons), in England (Richard Overton), and America (Roger Williams, John Leland) became key advocates for religious liberty and the disestablishment of religion (Kramnick and Moore, *Godless Constitution*). The tradition they represent is important for us to consider here.

Anabaptist convictions on this issue were grounded not solely in harsh experience but also in biblical exegesis. Anabaptists were (and are) convinced that Jesus' Great Commission to the church (Mt 28:16-20) must be read as a call to evangelism, teaching and other means of persuasion and exhortation into the Christian faith—rather than coercion, which only creates false and hypo-critical "faith." Coerced faith is not Christian faith. At least not if Christian faith follows Jesus. On the basis of Christ's command that the church be the light of the world, they argued vigorously for the church's freedom and right to spread its message via such legitimate means as preaching and teaching. They chose to die at the hands of those states that sought to stifle their Chris-tian witness, rather than allowing themselves to be silenced. When persecuted for their convictions, Anabaptists did not fail to offer a prophetic critique to the state, just as Jesus did, in declaring such persecution an unjust misuse of gov-ernment power. Anabaptists regularly declared that Christ is Lord over the government as over every institution in human life, and disciples "must obey God rather than any human authority" (Acts 5:29; Bonhoeffer, *Ethics*, 188-213).

Anabaptists were very clear about the need for the church as "salt" to keep its distance from government while as "light" still engaging the government. Members of this tradition are generally resistant to the blandishments and se-ductions of government. They embrace the legitimate work of limited gov-ernment doing justice in its proper sphere, which does not include the inculcation of religious belief or the suppression of what some would view as heresy. In part influenced by Jesus' parable of the wheat and the tares (Mt 13:24-30), Anabaptists fully expect that right and wrong, truth and falsehood, virtue and vice will exist and intermingle until Christ returns, and that it is not for human governments to root out and destroy what we or they might view as displeasing to God.

In the North American context, it is easy to see how a commitment to reli-gious liberty fits with the church's role as caring pastor for all people—but dis-tressing to see how some Christians continue to be tempted to abandon such liberty in return for the establishment of a favored version of Christianity (Martin, *With God on Our Side*). The true pastor is concerned not just with the religious majority but with the rights of the one person who marches to the beat of a different drummer. It is unkind, uncaring, unjust and unbiblical for Christians to be unconcerned with the rights of religious minorities in our public schools, our communities, our nation or around the world. The United States was the very first nation to embrace full religious liberty in the context of religious pluralism, and Anabaptist Christians played a key role in initiating this innovation that is now appropriately recognized as part of the basic pack-age of human rights and liberties that must be honored by any state, especially those claiming to be democratic (Gamwell, *Meaning of Religious Freedom*, pt. 4).

Contemporary Reconstructionists/theonomists, "Christian America" ad-vocates, or others who seek to establish a confessional state (Bahnsen, *Theono-my in Christian Ethics*; Martin, *With God on Our Side*, 353-57) are, we believe, fundamentally in error in terms of Scripture and both Christian and secular history, and we count it fortunate indeed that they lack the power to work their will in our society today. Their perspective reflects an enduring temptation in the history of Christianity and, as we have seen in recent years, in Islam as well. As light of the world, we invite people into a relationship with Christ and into the joyful way of life of covenant community—we *invite*, and never *coerce*, anyone who is interested to come and join our "city on a hill," in which God's shalom is beginning to be experienced.

Deeds: the church as disciple-making community obeying Christ's commands. We have argued in this chapter that the famous "salt and light" command of Jesus is actually a salt, light and deeds triad. The mission of the church is trinitarian—being faithful to God as Holy Spirit, Creator-Sustainer and Beloved Son. Christian disciples are distinguished from the world (salt) and at the same time illuminate (light) the world through their good deeds *(kala erga)* in obedience to the way of the Son, Jesus Christ. When we actually do such good deeds we cause onlookers to "give glory" to God—that is, to praise God and to recognize the divine goodness, power and plan. Thus the disciples' good deeds are part of our prayer: "thy kingdom come, thy will be done." This is true, not only in terms of the direct impact of those deeds but also through their evangelistic impact on a watching world. Being salt and light, when understood concretely, consists of a particular set of practices undertaken by the community of disciples in obedience to the teachings of Jesus Christ our Lord. Those practices are the theme of our next and final chapter.

24

PRACTICES

*Not everyone who says to me, "Lord, Lord," will enter the kingdom of heaven, but only
the one who does the will of my Father in heaven. . . . Everyone then who hears these words
of mine and acts on them will be like a wise man who built his house on rock. The rain fell,
the floods came, and the winds blew and beat on that house, but it did not fall, because it
had been founded on rock. And everyone who hears these words of mine and does not act
on them will be like a foolish man who built his house on sand. The rain fell, and the floods
came, and the winds blew and beat against that house, and it fell—and great was its fall!*

MATTHEW 7:21, 24-27

The content of the Christian faith is ever and always a matter of dispute. In every generation, men and women of faith bow their heads in prayer, revisit sacred Scripture, and plumb church tradition and other sources in an effort to come to terms with the meaning of the faith to which they have committed themselves.

This book is at one level "merely" an introduction to Christian ethics, an academic discipline. If you have read it closely thus far you have learned much about that discipline. But at another level, even more precious to us as its authors, this book constitutes a proposal concerning the very content of Christian faith and the shape of normative Christian existence.

Christian teachers, scholars and leaders inherit a sacred trust. Just like our counterparts in earlier generations, we are commanded to "guard the good treasure entrusted" to us (2 Tim 1:14). It is indeed an awesome responsibility to interpret and articulate the Christian faith. We are aware that our words matter and that we will be held accountable for them before God (Jas 3:1-12).

At the heart of what motivated us to write this book was the conviction that the moral witness of Jesus Christ our Lord has been neglected, misunderstood and even evaded—not only in Christian ethics as a discipline, but in the general presentation of the Christian faith in thousands upon thousands of churches in our nation and around the world. The result is nothing less than the malformation of Christianity, a faith torn loose from its foundation on the rock of the teachings and example of Jesus Christ.

We dare not claim that every aspect of our moral analysis and every proposal we have made in this volume carries the authority of Jesus Christ. That would be absurd and completely contrary to our emphasis on self-correction and continual repentance. However, we hope that we have demonstrated that the witness of Jesus Christ himself, anchored firmly in Jesus' own historical context and yet in its own way timeless, can and must be at the heart of Christian existence—and that therefore it merits the closest and most careful study. It is this we have sought to offer in this volume.

We believe that Jesus was the One the Father sent to reclaim a rebellious creation and inaugurate the long-delayed reign of God. And we believe that the "church" must be defined as that community of men and women who follow after Jesus, the trailblazer and pioneer of God's reign. We have written to serve that God and edify that church.

At the conclusion of the Sermon on the Mount, which certainly includes Matthew 7:24-27 but can be seen as extending back to 7:12, Jesus claims in various ways that the appropriate response to his teachings is simply to practice them. *Discipleship—and therefore, the Christian faith—is about doing the words of Jesus.* Listen as we offer a brief consideration of the various ways he says this same thing in the last section of the Sermon on the Mount:

Matthew 7:12. "In everything do to others as you would have them do to you; for this is the law and the prophets." Jesus here claimed that the moral content of the entire biblical witness can be summarized as an ethic of other-regard demonstrated through deeds. This Golden Rule fires the moral imagination as its inexhaustible implications for neighbor-love are considered.

Matthew 7:13-14. "Enter through the narrow gate . . . for the gate is narrow and the road is narrow that leads to life, and there are few who find it." Christian existence is a path that is followed, a way of living that is practiced. The road is narrow; many miss it. This is a terrifying warning, and one that makes no sense if the Christian faith is understood merely or even primarily as intellectual assent to convictions about Jesus, as an inspiring and encouraging personal relationship with him, or as a forensic transaction gaining us admission to heaven.

Matthew 7:15-20. "You will know them by their fruits." Many "false prophets" claim allegiance to Jesus Christ or to God the Father. Jesus here simply imposed a practices test—you will know who belongs to me by the fruit that they produce in life. This text is often, and not illegitimately, employed in discussions of character (the good tree/good fruit connection). But its fundamental point is that discipleship involves a way of life concrete enough that its fidelity to Jesus' way is obviously either present or absent.

Matthew 7:21-23. "Not everyone who says to me, 'Lord, Lord' will enter the kingdom of heaven, but only the one who does the will of my Father in heaven." Jesus then went on to reject "evildoers" who manage to prophesy, cast out demons and do "many deeds of power" in his name. Such spiritual fireworks are worthless apart from practicing his teachings. It is sobering to consider whether one might be included among those who will be rejected as falsely proclaiming Jesus' lordship.

Matthew 7:24-27. "Everyone who hears these words of mine and acts on them will be like a wise man who built his house on rock." Dietrich Bonhoeffer famously asked, in the context of Nazi threats and enticements, "Who stands fast?" Jesus here taught that those who will stand fast are only those who hear his words and do them. Only such people build upon a foundation that can endure.

It is hard to know what else Jesus could have said to have made his point more clear. Let us restate it one more time: *according to Jesus, there is no authentic Christianity, discipleship or Christian ethics apart from doing the deeds he taught his followers to do.* A fuller summary, influenced in part by a careful reading of the Great Commission (Mt 28:16-20) would be this: the "deeds" dimension of Jesus' teaching enjoins concrete obedience to Jesus' commands, deed-teaching and disciple-making. Disciples of Jesus study, obey, teach and train others in the deeds Jesus taught and practiced. They do so, we must recall, as a joyful response to, and participation in, God's gracious deliverance and inauguration of the kingdom through Jesus Christ.

In making this proposal we are joining a small band of other Christian scholars and church leaders who believe much of the church long ago tragically got sidetracked from this focus on Jesus and his concrete teachings.

Larry Rasmussen, for example, writes that the church was first understood as, and even called, "the people of the Way" (cf. Acts 9:2; 18:25-26; 19:9, 23; 24:14, 22), and yet fairly early in its history this vision was misplaced *(Moral Fragments).* Similarly Catholic theologian Avery Dulles advocates this "community of disciples" model as the most adequate: "The way of Jesus is the way of the disciple, and discipleship consists in walking the way with Jesus." He points out that in the book of Acts, "all Christian believers are called disciples, and the Church itself is called the community of disciples." Here and elsewhere in the New Testament, Christianity is represented as a way of life by which one follows Jesus (Acts 9:2, 22:4), who is himself the Way (John 14:6)" (Dulles, *Models of the Church,* 210-11).

Jesus identified with the tradition of the prophets of Israel, with their teachings, with their call to repentance, faith and justice, their promise of the coming redemption, even with the opposition they encountered. The church, then, pointing to the particular way of the incarnate Jew, Jesus, needs to interpret him in that prophetic and Jewish context. It needs to correct tendencies that ignore Jesus' concrete context and that reduce his teaching to a pale reflection of our culture.

A key dimension of that work of correction is simply a focus on the actual deeds that Jesus embodied and taught. We have emphasized Christian ethics as *practices*—not merely ideals, and not only rules or principles that ought to be done, but practices that are actually and regularly done, embodied in action (see our definition of practices in chapter five, and see also Bass). Here it is absolutely crucial to be concrete rather than abstract, in order that Christian ethics not be emptied of its actual content. Though this is by no means an exhaustive list, let us review what we have proposed in this book by naming some concrete practices taught by Jesus or appropriate applications of his approach to contemporary realities:

- Disciples develop a holistic ethic of character, attending critically to their passions and loyalties, way of moral reasoning, perceptions and basic-conviction theological beliefs; they live humbly before God, mourn what is wrong in themselves and the world, surrender themselves to God, hunger and thirst for God's delivering justice, offer compassionate action, forgiveness, healing and covenant steadfastness to those in need, give their whole self over to God, make peace with their enemies and persist and even rejoice under persecution (Mt 5:3-12; chapters two and three of this work).

- Disciples ground their moral decisions and way of life in biblical authority, reading the entire canon as Jesus did—through a prophetic grid that heightens emphasis on God's grace, the moral aspects of Old Testament law, the content of righteousness as deeds of justice, mercy and love, and an awareness of the inner wellsprings of all action (Mt 5:17-20; chapter four).

- Disciples practice Jesus' teaching in the context of belief in the grand biblical narrative, especially the account of the inbreaking kingdom within which Jesus undertook his ministry; this account of God's character, will and action in history then grounds the development of particular moral principles, rules and judgments within the situations presented by life (Mt 5:17-20; chapters one and five).

- Disciples read Jesus' moral teaching not as high ideals, hard sayings, counsels of perfection or evidence of our sinfulness, but as concrete instruction for living; they focus where Jesus did, on the particular transforming initiatives that enable disciples to break humanity's vicious cycles, which block obedience to the will of God the Creator and Redeemer.

- Disciples do not murder or bless violent killing; instead, they humble themselves, take peacemaking initiatives and act to prevent violence in personal, social, national and international life (Mt 5:21-26, 38-48; chapters seven to nine).

- Disciples value life at its vulnerable beginning and vulnerable end, acting to prevent abortion, embryo destruction, reproductive cloning, narcissistic genetic modification and euthanasia (Mt 5:21-26; chapters ten to twelve).

- Disciples honor God's intentions for male-female relations by treating one another with respect, encouraging mutual submission and a gospel/kingdom focus in gender relations and confining the expression of genital sexuality to celibate singleness or monogamous covenant marriage (Mt 5:27-30; chapters thirteen and fourteen).

- Disciples understand marriage as a binding covenant, marry wisely, seek reconciliation in times of marital conflict, divorce with extreme rarity, and guard and honor the joyful permanence of their marriages (Mt 5:31-32; chapter fifteen).

- Disciples live out delivering love and justice in every relationship, especially with regard to the most vulnerable, the excluded, outcast, powerless and oppressed (Mt 5:43-48; chapters sixteen and seventeen).

- Disciples speak truthfully rather than deceptively or dishonestly; they keep covenant and live in truth, withholding it only in rare moral emergencies under conditions of social evil (Mt 5:33-37; chapter eighteen).

- Disciples work for justice in race relations and economic life, living in relative economic simplicity, avoiding idolatrous acquisitiveness, consumerism, greed and injustice and feeding the hungry and poor as both a personal and social practice (Mt 6:19-34; chapters nineteen and twenty).

- Disciples exercise creation care in numerous ways, such as energy conservation, limiting family size and resource use, supporting public transit and appropriate government regulation (Mt 6:19-34; chapter twenty-one).

- Disciples practice almsgiving, fasting and prayer without seeking human recognition for their piety; they pray in a manner designed to deepen their commitment to, and participation in, God's reign (Mt 6:1-18; 7:6-11; chapter twenty-two).

- Disciples retain their distinctiveness as Christ-followers while graciously engaging the world with a pioneering, pastoral, service-oriented and transforming presence (Mt 5:13-16; 7:6-12; chapter twenty-three).

- Disciples study, reflect upon and obey the teachings of Jesus, and seek to train others to do the same (Mt 7:12-27; chapter twenty-four).

One way to tell whether one's ethic is concrete or abstract is to articulate its key norms and then ask whether or not it is possible to evaluate whether one is acting in conformity with them. On this test, Jesus' teaching was concrete, which is why we have sought to be just as concrete in this volume. Either one is feeding the hungry or one is not. Either one is faithful to one's spouse or one is not. Either one is speaking truthfully or one is not. Certainly ethics does include other, less easily evaluated dimensions: interior attitudes, depth of passion and commitment, purity of intention and so on. But much Christian ethics has misunderstood Jesus' teachings as a call for us to focus on these harder-to-evaluate dimensions rather than on his actual concrete teachings. Or, worse, the church has sometimes taught or indicated that Jesus never intended his teachings to be actually obeyed: instead, they are merely ideals for us to strive for. Meanwhile, we actually end up living according to the cut-throat and "realistic" rules of everyday life, because *some* set of norms must govern every life.

Sociologist Robert Wuthnow has said in an interview that a major reason why mainline churches are hemorrhaging members is that in their reaction against conservative religious legalism their moral teaching has become too vague. Struggling, searching and expressing doubt seems to be the main message being communicated to congregants. Sermons often move from a simple structure to a more complex one, and the moral conclusion is hidden in many words. Dean R. Hoge writes that

> ecclesiastical and creedal statements have been written abstractly enough, or with enough internal pluralism, to include all shades of theology in the denomination. . . . One problem with this policy in any denomination is lack of identity. The question Who are we? or What do we believe? is not satisfactorily answered by a recitation of diverse viewpoints current in the church. Evangelism is barely possible when the identity of the church and its gospel are difficult to state clearly. Today it is no accident that many middle-class Protestants are hesitant to discuss their own Christian beliefs with other persons. (Hoge, *Division in the Protestant House*, 126)

By contrast with mainline churches, Roof and McKinney report the results of their study of American church life: "Almost all of the churches that retained distance from the culture by encouraging distinctive life-styles and belief grew." They "were 'identifiable' religiously and culturally, known for their distinctive beliefs and moral teachings; they offered an experiential faith centered around belief in salvation through personal commitment to Christ." Evangelicalism—defined as consisting of those who describe themselves as born again, have encouraged others to believe in Jesus Christ, and have a high view of biblical authority—has grown significantly. Orthodox Judaism, with its concrete teachings, biblical authority and focus on the sovereignty of God, also has grown.

Roof and McKinney report that evangelical churches are distinguished from mainline churches by their having four times as high a percentage of their adults in religious education, twice the percentage of members in worship and twice the giving, and they are twice as likely to have grown 25 percent in membership in the past five years (Roof and McKinney, *American Mainline Religion*, 20-24). And they teach more concretely, less abstractly. This does *not* necessarily mean that they teach the full scope of discipleship as Jesus taught and embodied it. It does not mean that every church growing in numbers is growing in authentic discipleship. But it does mean that vitality and strength of identification with the church community do seem to require more concrete, specific and frequent teaching, with a sense of vision and identity.

Daniel Buttry's book describing the revitalization of a church advocates concrete teaching "directed toward shaping the life of discipleship and the community of the church," and "occasionally a national or global issue cries out for biblical challenge." He quotes Martin Luther King, who echoes Dietrich Bonhoeffer: "If you preach the gospel in all aspects with the exception of the issues which deal specifically with your time, you are not preaching the gospel at all" (Buttry, *Bringing Your Church Back to Life*, 83; cf. Gushee and Long, *A Bolder Pulpit*, chap. 1).

In my (David's) study of Christian rescuers of Jews during the Holocaust, the centrality of concrete deeds in any authentic Christian faith became overwhelmingly obvious to me. The Nazis wanted to kill Jews—they were certainly concrete in their intentions and performed that particular horrific deed some six million times. Jews wanted to survive and did what they could to save their children and themselves. But survival most frequently required the concrete help of non-Jewish Gentiles/Christians (Gushee, *Righteous Gentiles of the Holocaust*, chaps. 3-4).

It was not enough to pray for Jews. It was not enough to hope for the best for Jews, to wish someone would help Jews, to have feelings of compassion toward Jews or to dream of a world in which neither Jews nor anyone else would be murdered. Nor was it enough to have the intention of helping Jews, to talk about helping Jews or to make plans to help Jews. Nor, for that matter, was it enough to believe in Jesus, go to church, receive the sacraments, read the Bible or say the "sinner's prayer." What had to happen was for Christians to welcome needy Jewish strangers into their homes, to provide this much food and that much money, offer hiding places and hygienic services and medical care and false identification and transportation and protection, and to do such things indefinitely at constant risk.

That minority of Christians most likely to do such deeds of mercy most often came from families and faith traditions in which concrete, hands-on caregiving and justice-making were both taught and modeled (Gushee, *Righteous*

Gentiles of the Holocaust, chaps. 5-6). That preparation served them well when they were tested in the crucible of the Holocaust.

Jewish theologian Irving Greenberg writes: "Religion is as religion does—all the rest is talk" ("Third Great Cycle of Jewish History," 10). He writes in the shadow of the Holocaust, but his comment reflects a commitment that goes deep to the core of the Jewish tradition—the same tradition, that is, that nurtured Jesus the Christ and that informed his amazingly concrete moral instruction. Jesus taught that his disciples are to be salt and light and can only be this as they obey him—through doing the personal, ecclesial, social and political deeds that he taught. As they do, they bring glory to God and advance God's reign, which is the whole purpose of Jesus and all who would follow him.

As Hans Weder puts it in *Die "Rede der Reden" (The Speech of all Speeches):* "In our context one speaks happily of the witness character of good works, of the active proclamation of the church. . . . In Matthew the movement to the world happens in no other form than in the form of good works. For something other the world has no understanding" (89).

And "for something other" the Messiah himself has no appreciation.

BIBLIOGRAPHY

Achtemeier, Elizabeth. "Righteousness in the Old Testament." In *Interpreter's Dictionary of the Bible.* Volume 4. Edited by Keith Crim. Nashville: Abingdon, 1976.

Aiken, Henry David. *Reason and Conduct: New Bearings in Moral Philosophy.* New York: Knopf, 1962.

Allison, Dale C. *The Sermon on the Mount: Inspiring the Moral Imagination.* New York: Herder & Herder, 1989.

American Baptist Churches. *Our Only Home: Planet Earth.* Ecology and Racial Justice Program, National Ministries, ABCUSA, Box 851, Valley Forge, PA 19482-0851 (a Bible study on the ecology policy statement of the American Baptist Churches USA).

American Jewish Congress. "Statement on Capital Punishment." Adopted at the 66th Annual Meeting, May 6, 1972.

Anderson, Brian C. "Capitalism and the Suicide of Culture." *First Things* 100 (February 2000): 23-30.

Anderson, Ray S., and Dennis B. Guernsey. *On Being Family: A Social Theology of the Family.* Grand Rapids, Mich.: Eerdmans, 1985.

Andolsen, Barbara Hilkert. "*Agape* in Feminist Ethics." *The Journal of Religious Ethics* 9, no. 2 (1981): 69-83.

"Anti-Hero." (Unsigned editorial.) *The New Republic,* May 14, 2001, p. 11.

Arendt, Hannah. *Eichmann in Jerusalem.* New York: Penguin, 1962.

Atherton, John, ed. *Christian Social Ethics.* Cleveland: Pilgrim, 1994.

Audi, Robert, and Nicholas Wolterstorff. *Religion in the Public Square: The Place of Religious Convictions in Political Debate.* New York: Rowman & Littlefield, 1997.

Austin, Richard Cartwright. *Baptized into Wilderness: A Christian Perspective on John Muir.* Environmental Theology 1. Atlanta: John Knox Press, 1987.

———. *Beauty of the Lord: Awakening the Senses.* Environmental Theology 2. Atlanta: John Knox Press, 1988.

———. *Hope for the Land: Nature in the Bible.* Environmental Theology 3. Atlanta: John Knox Press, 1988.

———. *Reclaiming America: Restoring Nature to Culture.* Environmental Theology 4. Abingdon, Va.: Creekside, 1990.

Bahnsen, Greg L. *Theonomy in Christian Ethics.* Phillipsburg, N.J.: Presbyterian & Reformed, 1984.

Baier, Annette. "For the Sake of Future Generations." In *Earthbound: New Introductory Essays in Environmental Ethics.* Edited by Tom Regan. New York: Random House, 1984.

Bailey, D. S. *Homosexuality and the Western Christian Tradition*. London: Longmans Green, 1955.

Bailey, Kenneth E. *Through Peasant Eyes*. Grand Rapids, Mich.: Eerdmans, 1980.

Bailey, Lloyd R. "Oath." In *Mercer Dictionary of the Bible*. Edited by Watson E. Mills. Macon, Ga.: Mercer University Press, 1990.

Bailie, Gil. *Violence Unveiled: Humanity at the Crossroads*. New York: Crossroad, 1995.

Baker, William H. *On Capital Punishment*. Chicago: Moody Press, 1973, 1985.

Ball, Jim. *Planting a Tree This Afternoon: Global Warming, Public Theology, and Public Policy*. Wynnewood, Penn.: ESA, 1998.

Barkan, Elazar. *The Guilt of Nations: Restitution and Negotiating Historical Injustices*. New York: Norton, 2000.

Barna Research Group, accessed 4/21/01 at <www.barna.org>.

Barndt, Joseph. *Dismantling Racism: The Continuing Challenge to White America*. Minneapolis: Augsburg/Fortress, 1991.

Barnette, Henlee H. *The Church and the Ecological Crisis*. Philadelphia: Westminster Press, 1972.

——. *Crucial Problems in Christian Perspective*. Philadelphia: Westminster Press, 1970.

——. *Introducing Christian Ethics*. Nashville: Broadman, 1961.

——. "My Millennium." *Louisville Courier-Journal*, September 8, 2000.

Bass, Dorothy, ed. *Practicing Our Faith*. San Francisco: Jossey-Bass, 1997.

Bauckham, Richard. *The Bible in Politics*. Louisville, Ky.: Westminster John Knox, 1989.

——. *The Climax of Prophecy: Studies on the Book of Revelation*. Edinburgh: T & T Clark, 1993.

Baumann, Clarence. *The Sermon on the Mount: The Modern Quest for Its Meaning*. Macon, Ga: Mercer University Press, 1985.

Baumeister, Roy F., and Joseph M. Boden. "Aggression and the Self: High Self-Esteem, Low Self-Control, and Ego Threat." Chapter 5 of *Human Aggression: Theories, Research, and Implications for Social Policy*. Edited by Russell G. Geen and Edward Donnerstein. San Diego: Academic, 1998.

Beale, G. K. *The Book of Revelation: A Commentary on the Greek Text*. Grand Rapids, Mich.: Eerdmans, 1999.

Beaman, Jay. *Pentecostal Pacifism: The Origin, Development, and Rejection of Pacific Belief Among Pentecostals*. Hillsboro, Ore.: Center for Mennonite Brethren Studies, 1989.

Beates, Michael S. "God's Sovereignty and Genetic Anomalies." Chapter 3 of *Genetic Ethics: Do the Ends Justify the Genes?* Edited by John F. Kilner. Grand Rapids, Mich.: Eerdmans, 1997.

Beauchamp, Tom L., and James F. Childress. *Principles of Biomedical Ethics*. 5th ed. Oxford: Oxford University Press, 2001.

Beckwith, Francis J. *Politically Correct Death*. Grand Rapids, Mich.: Baker, 1993.

Bedau, Hugo A., et al. *In Spite of Innocence: Erroneous Convictions in Capital Cases*. Boston: Northeastern University Press, 1994.

Beisner, Calvin. *Where Garden Meets Wilderness*. Grand Rapids, Mich.: Eerdmans, 1997.

Bellah, Robert, et al. *Habits of the Heart*. New York: Harper & Row, 1985.

Benson, Peter, et al. *A Fragile Foundation: The State of Developmental Assets Among American Youth*. Minneapolis: Search Institute, 1999.

Benvenutt, Sherilyn. "Anointed, Gifted and Called: Pentecostal Women in Ministry," *Pneuma* 17, no. 2 (1995): 229-36.

Berger, Kathleen S. *The Developing Person Through Childhood and Adolescence*. New York: Worth, 1993.

Berns, Walter. *For Capital Punishment*. New York: Basic Books, 1979.

Berry, Thomas. *The Dream of the Earth*. San Francisco: Sierra Club Books, 1988.

Bethge, Eberhard. *Dietrich Bonhoeffer: A Biography*. Rev. ed. Minneapolis: Fortress, 2000.

Betz, Hans Dieter. *The Sermon on the Mount*. Minneapolis: Fortress, 1995.

Birch, Bruce. *Let Justice Roll Down: The Old Testament, Ethics, and the Christian Life*. Louisville: Westminster John Knox, 1991.

Birch, Bruce C., and Larry L. Rasmussen. *Bible and Ethics in the Christian Life*. Rev. ed. Minneapolis: Augsburg Fortress, 1989.

Blackmon, Douglas A. "Racial Reconciliation Becomes a Priority for the Religious Right." *Wall Street Journal*, June 23, 1997, pp. A1, A8.

Blank, Rebecca. *Do Justice*. Cleveland: United Church Press, 1992.

Blomberg, Craig L. *Interpreting the Parables*. Downers Grove, Ill.: InterVarsity Press, 1990.

———. *Matthew*. New American Commentary. Vol. 22. Nashville: Broadman & Holman, 1992.

———. *Neither Poverty nor Riches*. Grand Rapids, Mich.: Eerdmans, 1999.

Blount, Brian K. *Then the Whisper Put on Flesh: New Testament Ethics in an African American Context*. Nashville: Abingdon, 2001.

Bockmuehl, Markus. *This Jesus: Martyr, Lord, Messiah*. Downers Grove, Ill.: InterVarsity Press, 1994.

Boice, James Montgomery. *Two Cities, Two Loves: Christian Responsibility in a Crumbling Culture*. Downers Grove, Ill.: InterVarsity Press, 1996.

Bok, Sissela. *Lying*. New York: Vintage, 1979.

Bonhoeffer, Dietrich. *The Cost of Discipleship*. New York: Macmillan, 1963.

———. *Ethics*. New York: Simon & Schuster Touchstone Edition, 1995.

———. *Gesammelte Schriften* III. Munich, 1960.

———. *Letters and Papers from Prison*, enlarged edition. New York: Macmillan, 1972.

Bonner, Raymond, and Ford Fessenden, "States Without the Death Penalty Have Better Record on Homicide Rates." *New York Times*, September 22, 2000, p. A1.

Borg, Marcus. *Conflict, Holiness, and Politics in the Teaching of Jesus*. Harrisburg, Penn.: Trinity Press International, 1998.

Bornkamm, Günther. *Jesus of Nazareth*. Minneapolis: Fortress, 1995.

Boswell, John. *Christianity, Social Tolerance, and Homosexuality*. Chicago: University of Chicago Press, 1980.

Boulton, Wayne G., et al. *From Christ to the World*. Grand Rapids, Mich.: Eerdmans, 1994.

Bouma-Prediger, Steven. *For the Beauty of the Earth: A Christian Vision for Creation Care*. Grand Rapids, Mich.: Baker, 2001.

———. "Why Care for Creation? From Prudence to Piety." *Christian Scholar's Review* 27 (spring 1998): 277-97.

Bounds, Elizabeth. *Coming Together/Coming Apart: Religion, Community, and Modernity*. New York: Routledge, 1997.

Bratton, Susan P. *Six Billion and More: Human Population Regulation and Christian Ethics.* Louisville, Ky.: Westminster John Knox, 1992.

Brown, Francis, S. R. Driver, and Charles A. Briggs. *The New Brown, Driver, Briggs, Gesenius Hebrew and English Lexicon.* Peabody, Mass.: Hendrickson, 1979.

Brown, Raymond E. *The Gospel According to John.* Vol. 1. Garden City, N.Y.: Doubleday, 1966.

Brueggemann, Walter. *Genesis.* Atlanta: John Knox Press, 1982.

————. *Isaiah 1—39.* Louisville, Ky.: Westminster John Knox, 1998.

————. *Isaiah 40—66.* Louisville, Ky.: Westminster John Knox, 1998.

————. *The Prophetic Imagination.* Philadelphia: Fortress, 1978.

————. *A Social Reading of the Old Testament Prophetic Approaches to Israel's Communal Life.* Edited by Patrick D. Miller. Minneapolis: Augsburg Fortress, 1994.

————. *Theology of the Old Testament.* Minneapolis: Augsburg Fortress, 1997.

Buchanan, Allen, et al. *From Chance to Choice: Genetics and Justice.* Cambridge: Cambridge University Press, 2000.

Bultmann, Rudolf. *Jesus and the Word.* New York: Scribner's, 1958.

Burkett, Larry. *Debt-Free Living.* Chicago: Moody Press, 1999.

Buttry, Daniel L. *Bringing Your Church Back to Life.* Valley Forge, Penn.: Judson Press, 1990.

————. *Christian Peacemaking: From Heritage to Hope.* Valley Forge, Penn.: Judson Press, 1994.

Caddick, Alison. "Bio-Tech Dreaming." *Arena Magazine,* August 1999, p. 12.

Cahill, Lisa Sowle. *Between the Sexes.* Philadelphia: Fortress, 1985.

————. *Love Your Enemies: Discipleship, Pacifism, and Just War Theory.* Minneapolis: Augsburg Fortress, 1994.

Cahill, Lisa Sowle, and James F. Childress, eds. *Christian Ethics: Problems and Prospects.* Cleveland: Pilgrim, 1996.

Caird, G. B. A. *A Commentary on the Revelation of St. John the Divine.* New York: Harper & Row, 1966.

Calvin, John. *A Harmony of the Gospels Matthew, Mark and Luke.* Vol. 1. Grand Rapids, Mich.: Eerdmans, 1972.

————. *Institutes of the Christian Religion.* Vol. 1. Edited by John T. McNeill. London: SCM Press, 1956.

Campolo, Tony. *How to Rescue the Earth Without Worshiping Nature.* Nashville: Thomas Nelson, 1992.

Cannon, Katie. *Black Womanist Ethics.* Atlanta: Scholars Press, 1988.

Carlson-Thies, Stanley. "Welfare Reform and the Evangelical Church." In *Christians and Politics Beyond the Culture Wars.* Edited by David P. Gushee. Grand Rapids, Mich.: Baker, 2000.

Carson, D. A. *Matthew.* Expositor's Bible Commentary 8. Grand Rapids, Mich.: Zondervan, 1984.

Carter, Stephen. *Catechism of the Catholic Church.* Liguori, Mo.: Liguori Publications, 1994.

————. *The Culture of Disbelief.* New York: Anchor, 1994.

————. *Reflections of an Affirmative Action Baby.* New York: Basic Books, 1991.

Cavanaugh, William T. *Torture and the Eucharist: Theology, Politics, and the Body of Christ.* Oxford: Blackwell, 1988.

Cerillo, Augustus, Jr., and Murray W. Dempster. *Salt and Light: Evangelical Political Thought in Modern America.* Grand Rapids, Mich.: Baker, 1989.

Chapman, Audrey. *Unprecedented Choices: Religious Ethics at the Frontiers of Genetic Science.* Minneapolis: Fortress, 1999.

Chavis, Benjamin F., Jr., and Charles Lee, eds. *Toxic Wastes and Race in the United States: A National Report on the Racial and Socio-Economic Characteristics of Communities with Hazardous Waste Sites.* Commission for Racial Justice, United Church of Christ, 1987.

Chewning, Richard C., et al. *Business Through the Eyes of Faith.* San Francisco: Harper & Row, 1990.

Childress, James. Review of Walzer, *Just and Unjust Wars.* In *The Bulletin of the Atomic Scientists* 38, no. 8 (1978): 44-48.

Chilton, Bruce. *A Galilean Rabbi and His Bible: Jesus' Use of the Interpreted Scripture of His Time.* Wilmington, Del.: Michael Glazier, 1984.

———. *God in Strength: Jesus' Announcement of the Kingdom.* Freistadt: Plöchl, 1979.

———. *The Isaiah Targum: Introduction, Translation, Apparatus and Notes.* Wilmington, Del.: Michael Glazier, 1987.

———. *Pure Kingdom: Jesus' Vision of God.* Grand Rapids, Mich.: Eerdmans, 1996.

Chilton, Bruce, and Craig Evans. *Studying the Historical Jesus: Evaluations of the State of Current Research.* Leiden: E. J. Brill, 1994.

Chilton, Bruce, and J. I. H. McDonald. *Jesus and the Ethics of the Kingdom.* Grand Rapids, Mich.: Eerdmans, 1987.

Clapp, Rodney. *Families at the Crossroads.* Downers Grove, Ill.: InterVarsity Press, 1993.

Clark, David K., and Robert V. Rakestraw, eds. *Readings in Christian Ethics.* Vols. 1 and 2. Grand Rapids, Mich.: Baker, 1996.

Cobb, John B., Jr. *Is It Too Late? A Theology of Ecology.* Rev. ed. Denton, Tex.: Environmental Ethics Books, 1995.

———. *Sustainability: Economics, Ecology, and Justice.* Maryknoll, N.Y.: Orbis, 1992.

———. *Sustaining the Common Good.* Cleveland: Pilgrim, 1994.

Cole-Turner, Ronald, ed. *Human Cloning: Religious Responses.* Louisville, Ky.: Westminster John Knox, 1997.

Collins, Francis S., et al. "Heredity and Humanity." *The New Republic,* June 25, 2001, pp. 27-29.

Colson, Charles, and Nancy Pearcey. *How Now Shall We Live?* Wheaton, Ill.: Tyndale House, 1999.

Commoner, Barry. *The Poverty of Power.* New York: Bantam, 1977.

Comstock, G., and H. Paik. "The Effects of Television Violence on Antisocial Behavior: A Meta-Analysis." *Communication Research* 21, no. 4 (1994): 516-46.

Comstock, Gary David. *Gay Theology Without Apology.* Cleveland: Pilgrim, 1993.

Copeland, Warren R. *And the Poor Get Welfare.* Nashville: Abingdon, 1994.

Cornes, Andrew. *Divorce and Remarriage.* Grand Rapids, Mich.: Eerdmans, 1993.

Cose, Ellis. "The Good News About Black America." *Newsweek,* June 7, 1999, pp. 30-40.

Cottle, Michelle. "Boomerang." *The New Republic,* May 7, 2001, pp. 26-29.

Cottrell, Jack W. "Abortion and the Mosaic Law." In *Readings in Christian Ethics* 2:32-35. Edited by David Clark and Robert Rakestraw. Grand Rapids, Mich.: Baker, 1996.

Countryman, William L. *Dirt, Greed, and Sex: Sexual Ethics in the New Testament and Their Implications for Today*. Philadelphia: Fortress, 1988.

Courtois, Stéphane, et al. *The Black Book of Communism*. Cambridge, Mass.: Harvard University Press, 1999.

Craigie, Peter. *The Problem of War in the Old Testament*. Grand Rapids, Mich.: Eerdmans, 1978.

Cromartie, Michael. "The Evangelical Kaleidoscope: A Survey of Recent Evangelical Political Engagement." In *Christians and Politics Beyond the Culture Wars*. Edited by David P. Gushee. Grand Rapids, Mich.: Baker, 2000.

Crossan, John Dominic. *In Parables*. New York: Harper & Row, 1973.

Culpepper, Alan. *Anatomy of the Fourth Gospel*. Philadelphia: Fortress, 1983.

Curran, Charles E. *The Catholic Moral Tradition Today*. Washington, D.C.: Georgetown University Press, 1999.

Curran, Charles E., and Richard A. McCormick. *Readings in Moral Theology, No. 8*. New York: Paulist, 1993.

Daly, Herman E., and John B. Cobb Jr. *For the Common Good*. Boston: Beacon, 1989.

Danby, Herbert, trans. *The Mishnah*. London: Oxford University Press, 1933.

Daniels, David D. "Dialogue Between Black and Hispanic Pentecostal Scholars: A Report and Some Personal Observations," *Pneuma* 17, no. 2 (1995): 219-38.

Davies, W. D. *The Setting of the Sermon on the Mount*. Cambridge: Cambridge University Press, 1964.

Davies, W. D., and Dale Allison. *A Critical and Exegetical Commentary on the Gospel According to St. Matthew*. Vol. 1. Edinburgh: T & T Clark, 1988.

Davis, John Jefferson. *Evangelical Ethics*. 2nd ed. Phillipsburg, N.J.: Presbyterian & Reformed, 1993.

Dawn, Marva. *Sexual Character*. Grand Rapids, Mich.: Eerdmans, 1993.

De La Torre, Miguel A. *Reading the Bible from the Margins*. Maryknoll: Orbis, 2002.

de Vries, Barend. *Champions of the Poor*. Washington, D.C.: Georgetown University Press, 1998.

Death Penalty Information Center, accessed 4/21/01 at <www.deathpenaltyinfo.org>.

Dempster, Murray. "'Crossing Borders': Arguments Used by Early American Pentecostals in Support of the Global Character of Pacifism." *European Pentecostal Theological Association Bulletin* 10, no. 2 (1991): 63-80.

———. "Pentecostal Social Concern." In *Called and Empowered: Global Mission in Pentecostal Perspective*. Edited by Murray W. Dempster, Byron D. Klause and Douglas Petersen. Peabody, Mass.: Hendrickson, 1992.

———. "Reassessing the Moral Rhetoric of Early American Pentecostal Pacifism." *Crux* 26, no. 1 (1990): 23-36; see also the dialogue between Dempster and Beaman in *Proclaim Peace* (1997): 31-57 and 82-93.

———. "Social Concern in the Context of Jesus' Kingdom, Mission, and Ministry." *Transformation* 16, no. 2 (1999): 43-53.

Dempster, Murray W., Byron D. Klause and Douglas Petersen, eds. *Called and Empow-*

ered: Pentecostal Perspectives on Global Mission. Peabody, Mass.: Hendrickson, 1992.

DeWitt, Calvin B. *Caring for Creation: Responsible Stewardship of God's Handiwork.* Grand Rapids, Mich.: Baker, 1998.

DeYoung, Curtiss Paul. "Racial Reconciliation and the Twenty-first Century Church." *The Clergy Journal* (July 1999).

The Didache. Translated by James A. Kleist. In Ancient Christian Writers 6:15-25. New York: Newman Press, 1948.

Dieter, Richard C. "The Death Penalty in Black and White: Who Lives, Who Dies, Who Decides." Washington, D.C.: Death Penalty Information Center, 1998.

————. "Executive Summary: The Dealth Penalty and Human Rights." Washington, D.C.: Death Penalty Information Center, 2002.

Dittes, James E. *Bias and the Pious.* Minneapolis: Augsburg, 1973.

Dittes, James E., and David E. Switzer. *Driven by Hope: Men and Meaning.* Louisville, Ky.: Westminster John Knox, 1996.

Donagan, Alan. *The Theory of Morality.* Chicago: University of Chicago Press, 1971.

Donohue, John R., S.J. *The Gospel in Parable.* Minneapolis: Fortress, 1988.

Dreyfus, Dennis W. "Vows and Oaths." In *The Oxford Dictionary of the Jewish Religion.* Edited by R. J. Zwi Werblowsky and Geoffrey Wigoder. Oxford: Oxford University Press, 1997.

Driedger, Leo, and Donald Kraybill. *Mennonite Peacemaking: From Quietism to Activism.* Scottdale, Penn.: Herald, 1994.

Dulles, Avery, S.J. *Models of the Church.* New York: Doubleday, 1987.

Dupont-Sommer, A. *The Essene Writings from Qumran.* Translated by G. Vermes. Gloucester, Mass.: Peter Smith, 1973.

Easterbrook, Gregg. "Medical Evolution: Will Homo Sapiens Become Obsolete?" *The New Republic,* March 1, 1999, accessed at <www.tnr.com>.

Edwards, George L. *Gay/Lesbian Liberation: A Biblical Approach.* Philadelphia: Westminster, 1985.

Elliott, Delbert S., Beatrix A. Hamburg, and Kirk R. Williams, *Violence in American Schools.* Cambridge: Cambridge University Press, 1998.

Emerson, Michael D., and Christian Smith. "Divided by Faith?" *Christianity Today* special section, October 2, 2000, pp. 34-55.

————. *Divided by Faith? Evangelical Religion and the Problem of Race in America.* New York: Oxford University Press, 2000.

Environmental Defense Fund. "The View from Earth Day 2000: Thirty Years of Global Warming." Available at <www.environmentaldefense.org>.

Erdahl, Lowell. *Pro-Life/Pro-Peace.* Minneapolis: Augsburg, 1986.

"Euthanasia: Introduction." In *Readings in Christian Ethics,* 2:95-101. Edited by David Clark and Robert Rakestraw. Grand Rapids, Mich.: Baker, 1996.

Everett, William. "Vocation and Location: An Exploration in the Ethics of Ethics." *Journal of Religious Ethics* 5 (spring 1977): 91-114.

Everts, Janet Meyer. "Brokenness as the Center of a Woman's Ministry," *Pneuma* 17, no. 1 (1995): 237-44.

Ezorsky, Gertrude. *Racism and Justice: The Case for Affirmative Action.* Ithaca, N.Y.: Cornell University Press, 1991.

Farley, Benjamin W. *In Praise of Virtue: An Exploration of the Biblical Virtues in a Christian Context*. Grand Rapids, Mich.: Eerdmans, 1995.

Farley, Margaret A. *Personal Commitments: Beginning, Keeping, and Changing*. San Francisco: Harper & Row, 1986.

Fasching, Darrell. *The Ethical Challenge of Auschwitz and Hiroshima*. Albany: State University of New York Press, 1993.

———. *Narrative Theology After Auschwitz*. Minneapolis: Fortress, 1992.

Fee, Gordon D. *Gospel and Spirit: Issues in New Testament Hermeneutics*. Peabody, Mass.: Hendrickson, 1991.

———. "The Kingdom of God." In *Called and Empowered: Pentecostal Perspectives on Global Mission*. Edited by Murray Dempster, Byron D. Klause and Douglas Petersen. Peabody, Mass.: Hendrickson, 1992.

Feinberg, John S. "A Theological Basis for Genetic Intervention." Chapter 15 of *Genetic Ethics: Do the Ends Justify the Genes?* Edited by John F. Kilner. Grand Rapids, Mich.: Eerdmans, 1997.

Feinberg, John S., and Paul D. Feinberg. *Ethics for a Brave New World*. Wheaton, Ill.: Crossway, 1993.

Ferguson, John. *The Politics of Love: The New Testament on Nonviolent Revolution*. Nyack, N.Y.: Fellowship Publications, 1979.

Fletcher, Joseph. *Situation Ethics*. Philadelphia: Westminster Press, 1966.

Fowl, Stephen, and L. Gregory Jones. *Reading in Communion: Scripture and Ethics in Christian Life*. Grand Rapids, Mich.: Eerdmans, 1991.

Fox, Matthew. *Original Blessing*. Santa Fe: Bear Publishing, 1983.

Frankena, William. *Ethics*. Englewood Cliffs, N.J.: Prentice-Hall, 1973.

Freston, Paul. "Evangelicals and Politics in the Third World." In *Christians and Politics Beyond the Culture Wars*. Edited by David P. Gushee. Grand Rapids, Mich.: Baker, 2000.

Friedrich, Johannes, Wolfgang Pöhlmann and Peter Stuhlmacher. "Zur historischen Situation und Intention von Rm 13, 1-7." *Zeitschrift für Theologie und Kirche* (1976).

Friesen, Duane K. *Artists, Citizens, Philosophers: Seeking the Peace of the City—An Anabaptist Theology of Culture*. Scottdale, Penn.: Herald, 2000.

Furnish, Victor Paul. *The Love Commands in the New Testament*. Nashville: Abingdon, 1972.

Gamwell, Franklin I. *The Meaning of Religious Freedom*. Albany: State University of New York Press, 1995.

Garland, David E. *Mark: The NIV Application Commentary*. Grand Rapids, Mich.: Zondervan, 1996.

———. "Oaths and Swearing." In *Dictionary of Jesus and the Gospels*. Edited by Joel B. Green, et al. Downers Grove, Ill.: InterVarsity Press, 1992.

———. *Reading Matthew*. New York: Crossroad, 1995.

Gates, Henry Louis, Jr., and Cornel West. *The Future of the Race*. New York: Knopf, 1996.

Gay, Craig M. *With Liberty and Justice for Whom?* Grand Rapids, Mich.: Eerdmans, 1991.

Gee, Donald. *God's Grace and Power for Today: the Practical Experience of Being Filled with the Holy Spirit*. Springfield, Mo.: Gospel, 1936.

————. *Is It God?* Springfield, Mo.: Gospel, 1972.

Geen, Russell G., and Edward Donnerstein, eds. *Human Aggression: Theories, Research, and Implications for Social Policy.* San Diego: Academic, 1998.

Geisler, Norman. *Christian Ethics.* Grand Rapids, Mich.: Baker, 1989.

Gelbspan, Ross. "The Theory of Global Warming Is Scientifically Credible." In *Global Warming: Opposing Viewpoints,* pp. 47-53. Edited by Tamara L. Roleff, Opposing Viewpoints Series. San Diego: Greenhaven, 1997.

George, Timothy. *Theology of the Reformers.* Nashville: Broadman, 1988.

Gill, Deborah M. "The Contemporary State of Women in Ministry in the Assemblies of God," *Pneuma* 17, no. 1 (1995): 33-36.

Goldberg, Jeffrey, "The Color of Suspicion." *New York Times Magazine,* June 20, 1999, pp. 51-57, 64, 85-87.

Goldingay, John. *Approaches to Old Testament Interpretation.* Downers Grove, Ill.: InterVarsity Press, 1981.

————. *Models for Interpretation of Scripture.* Grand Rapids, Mich.: Eerdmans, 1995.

Goldman, Benjamin A., and Laura Fitton. *Toxic Wastes and Race Revisited: An Update of the 1987 Report on the Racial and Socioeconomic Characteristics of Communities with Hazardous Waste Sites.* Washington, D.C.: Center for Policy Alternatives, 1994.

Gollwitzer, Helmut. *Das Gleichnis vom barmherzigen Samariter.* Neukirchen: Neukirchenerverlag, 1962. Translations in the text by Glen Stassen.

Gorman, Michael J. "Why Is the New Testament Silent About Abortion?" *Christianity Today,* January 11, 1993, pp. 27-29.

Gottwald, Norman. *All the Kingdoms of the Earth: Israelite Prophecy and International Relations in the Ancient Near East.* New York: Harper & Row, 1964.

Granberg-Michaelson, Wesley. *Ecology and Life: Accepting Our Environmental Responsibility.* Dallas: Word, 1988.

————. *A Worldly Spirituality.* New York: Harper & Row, 1984.

Grant, Colin. "For the Love of God: Agape." *Journal of Religious Ethics* 24, no. 1 (1996): 3-21.

Green, Joel B. *The Gospel of Luke.* Grand Rapids, Mich.: Eerdmans, 1997.

Greenberg, Irving. "The Third Great Cycle of Jewish History." New York: CLAL, 1981.

Grenz, Stanley. *Sexual Ethics.* Nashville: Word, 1990. This has also been published in a new edition as *Sexual Ethics: An Evangelical Perspective.* Louisville, Ky.: Westminster John Knox, 1997.

————. *Theology for the Community of God.* Nashville: Broadman & Holman, 1994.

————. *Welcoming but Not Affirming.* Louisville, Ky.: Westminster John Knox, 1998.

Grenz, Stanley, with Denise Muir Kjesbo. *Women in the Church.* Downers Grove, Ill.: InterVarsity Press, 1995.

Gudorf, Christine. *Body, Sex, and Pleasure.* Cleveland: Pilgrim, 1994.

Guelich, Robert. *The Sermon on the Mount: A Foundation for Understanding.* Waco, Tex.: Word, 1982.

Gundry, Robert H. *Matthew.* 2nd ed. Grand Rapids, Mich.: Eerdmans, 1994.

Guroian, Vigen. "An Ethic of Marriage and Family." In *From Christ to the World.* Edited by Wayne G. Boulton et al. Grand Rapids, Mich.: Eerdmans, 1994.

Gurr, Ted. *Why Men Rebel.* Princeton, N.J.: Princeton University Press, 1970.

Gushee, David P. *The Righteous Gentiles of the Holocaust.* Minneapolis: Fortress, 1994.

Gushee, David P., ed. *Christians and Politics Beyond the Culture Wars: An Agenda for Engagement.* Grand Rapids, Mich.: Baker, 2000.

———. *Toward a Just and Caring Society.* Grand Rapids, Mich.: Baker, 1999.

Gushee, David P., and Robert H. Long. *A Bolder Pulpit.* Valley Forge, Penn.: Judson Press, 1998.

Gustafson, James. *Christ and the Moral Life.* New York: Harper & Row, 1968.

———. "Context vs. Principle: A Misplaced Debate in Christian Ethics." *Harvard Theological Review* 58 (1965): 171-202.

———. *Ethics from a Theocentric Perspective.* 2 vols. Chicago: University of Chicago Press, 1981, 1984.

———. *Protestant and Roman Catholic Ethics.* Chicago: University of Chicago, 1978.

———. *A Sense of the Divine.* Cleveland: Pilgrim, 1994.

Gutiérrez, Gustavo. *A Theology of Liberation.* Maryknoll, N.Y.: Orbis, 1988.

Hacker, Andrew. *Two Nations: Black and White, Separate, Hostile, Unequal.* New York: Ballantine, 1992.

Hagner, Donald A. *Matthew 1—13.* Word Biblical Commentary 33A. Waco, Tex.: Word, 1993.

———. *Matthew 14—28.* Word Biblical Commentary 33B. Waco, Tex.: Word, 1995.

Hall, Amy Laura. "Complicating the Command: *Agape* in Scriptural Context." *Annual of the Society of Christian Ethics* 19 (1999): 97-113.

Hall, Douglas John. *Imaging God: Dominion As Stewardship.* Grand Rapids, Mich.: Eerdmans: 1986.

———. *The Steward: A Biblical Symbol Come of Age.* New York: Friendship, 1982.

Hall, Kermit L. ed. *The Oxford Guide to United States Supreme Court Decisions.* Oxford: Oxford University Press, 1999.

Hampton, Robert L., Pamela Jenkins, and Thomas P. Gullotta, eds. *Preventing Violence in America.* New York: Sage, 1996.

Harak, G. Simon, S.J. *Virtuous Passions: The Formation of Christian Character.* New York: Paulist, 1993.

Harrison, Beverly. "The Power of Anger and the Work of Love." In *Making the Connections.* Boston: Beacon, 1988.

Harvey, John Collins. "Distinctly Human." *Commonweal,* February 8, 2002, pp. 11-13.

Hauerwas, Stanley. *A Community of Character.* Notre Dame, Ind.: University of Notre Dame, 1981.

———. *Peaceable Kingdom: A Primer in Christian Ethics.* Notre Dame, Ind.: University of Notre Dame Press, 1983.

Hauerwas, Stanley, and Charles Pinches. *Christians Among the Virtues.* Notre Dame, Ind.: University of Notre Dame Press, 1997.

Havel, Václav. *Living in Truth.* New York: Faber & Faber, 1990.

Hays, Richard B. "Justification." In *Anchor Bible Dictionary,* 3:1129-33. New York: Doubleday, 1992.

———. *The Moral Vision of the New Testament: Community, Cross, New Creation.* New York: HarperCollins, 1996.

Hengel, Martin. *Crucifixion in the Ancient World and the Folly of the Message of the Cross.* Philadelphia: Fortress, 1977.

Herzog, William, II. *Jesus, Justice, and the Reign of God.* Louisville, Ky.: Westminster John Knox, 2000.

Hessel, Dieter, ed. *After Nature's Revolt: Eco-Justice and Theology.* Minneapolis: Fortress, 1992.

Heth, William A., and Gordon J. Wenham, *Jesus and Divorce.* Nashville: Thomas Nelson, 1984.

Hicks, P. A. "Truth." In *New Dictionary of Christian Ethics and Pastoral Theology.* Edited by David J. Atkinson et al. Downers Grove, Ill.: InterVarsity Press, 1995.

Hittinger, Russell. "The Catholic Theology of John Courtney Murray." *Weekly Standard,* January 4/11, 1999, pp. 32-35.

Hoge, Dean R. *Division in the Protestant House.* Philadelphia: Westminster Press, 1976.

Holland, Suzanne. "To Market, to Market: Cloning as an ART?" *Second Opinion* 6 (Park Ridge Center), June 4, 2001.

Hollenbach, David. *Claims in Conflict: Retrieving and Renewing the Catholic Human Rights Tradition.* New York: Paulist, 1979.

———. *Justice, Peace and Human Rights: American Catholic Social Ethics in a Pluralistic World.* New York: Crossroad, 1988.

Holmes, Arthur. *The Idea of a Christian College.* Rev. ed. Grand Rapids, Mich.: Eerdmans, 1987.

———. "The Just War." In *War: Four Christian Views.* Edited by Robert G. Clouse. Downers Grove, Ill.: InterVarsity Press, 1991.

Hooke, Alexander E. *Virtuous Persons, Vicious Deeds.* Mountain View, Calif.: Mayfield, 1999.

Hoose, Bernard, ed. *Christian Ethics: An Introduction.* Collegeville, Minn.: Liturgical Press, 1998.

Horowitz, George. *The Spirit of Jewish Law.* New York: Central Book, 1963.

Horton, Michael S. *Beyond Culture Wars.* Chicago: Moody Press, 1994.

House, H. Wayne. "In Favor of the Death Penalty." In *The Death Penalty Debate.* Edited by H. Wayne House and John Howard Yoder. Waco, Tex.: Word, 1991.

Hull, Gretchen Gaebelein. *Equal to Serve.* Grand Rapids, Mich.: Baker, 1998.

Hultgren, Arland J. *The Parables of Jesus.* Grand Rapids, Mich.: Eerdmans, 2000.

Hunter, James Davison. *Culture Wars.* New York: Basic Books, 1991.

International Bonhoeffer Society, *Newsletter* 67 (June 1998): 1ff.; 68 (October 1998): 15ff.

Jacob, Edmond. *Theology of the Old Testament.* New York: Harper & Brothers, 1958.

Janzen, Waldemar. *Old Testament Ethics: A Paradigmatic Approach.* Louisville, Ky.: Westminster John Knox, 1994.

Jeremias, Joachim. *The Parables of Jesus.* Rev. ed. London: SCM Press, 1963.

———. *The Prayers of Jesus.* Philadelphia: Fortress, 1978.

Jervis, Robert. *Perception and Misperception in International Politics.* Princeton, N.J.: Princeton University Press, 1976.

John Paul II. *The Gospel of Life.* New York: Random House, 1995.

———. *Laborem Exercens (On Human Work).* 1981. In *Catholic Social Thought.* Edited by David J. O'Brien and Thomas A. Shannon. Maryknoll, N.Y.: Orbis, 1992.

———. *Veritatis Splendor (The Splendor of Truth)*. Boston: Pauline, 1993.

Johnson, Elizabeth A. *Women, Earth, and Creator Spirit*. New York: Paulist, 1993.

Johnson, Luke Timothy. *Scripture and Discernment*. Nashville: Abingdon, 1996.

Johnstone, Megan-Jane. *Bioethics: A Nursing Perspective*. 3rd ed. London: Harcourt Saunders, 1999.

Jones, L. Gregory. *Embodying Forgiveness*. Grand Rapids, Mich.: Eerdmans, 1995.

Jones, Peter Rhea. "The Love Command in Parable: Luke 10:25-37." *Perspectives in Religious Studies* 6 (1979): 224-42.

———. *Studying the Parables of Jesus*. Macon, Ga.: Smyth & Helwys, 1999.

———. *The Teaching of the Parables*. Nashville: Broadman, 1982.

Jordan, Clarence. *Sermon on the Mount*. Valley Forge, Penn.: Judson Press, 1974.

———. *The Substance of Faith and Other Cotton Patch Sermons*. Edited by Dallas Lee. New York: Association Press, 1972.

Juhnke, James, and Carol M. Hunter. *The Missing Peace: The Search for Nonviolent Alternatives in United States History*. Scottdale, Penn.: Herald, 2001.

Justin Martyr, *First Apology*. In *The Ante-Nicene Fathers*, vol. 1: *The Apostolic Fathers with Justin Martyr and Irenaeus*. Edited by A. Cleveland Coxe. Grand Rapids, Mich.: Eerdmans, 1956.

Kant, Immanuel. *Critique of Practical Reason and Other Writings in Moral Philosophy*. Edited and trans. by Lewis White Beck. Chicago: University of Chicago Press, 1949.

Kass, Leon. "Preventing a Brave New World." *The New Republic*, May 21, 2001, pp. 30-39.

Kassian, Mary A. *The Feminist Gospel*. Wheaton, Ill.: Crossway, 1992.

Kaveny, M. Cathleen. "Jurisprudence and Genetics." *Theological Studies* 60 (March 1999): 135-47.

Keener, Craig S. *And Marries Another*. Peabody, Mass: Hendrickson., 1991.

———. *The IVP Bible Background Commentary: New Testament*. Downers Grove, Ill.: InterVarsity Press, 1993.

Keil, T., and G. Vito, "Race and the Death Penalty in Kentucky Murder Trials: 1976-1991." *American Journal of Criminal Justice* 20 (1995): 17ff.

Kennedy, Randall. "Suspect Policy." *The New Republic*, September 13/20, 1999, pp. 30-35.

King, Martin Luther, Jr. *Strength to Love*. Minneapolis: Fortress, 1981.

Kissinger, Warren S. *The Sermon on the Mount: A History of Interpretation and Bibliography*. New York: Scarecrow, 1975.

Klassen, William. *Love of Enemies: The Way to Peace*. Philadelphia: Fortress, 1984.

Kotva, Joseph J., Jr. *The Christian Case for Virtue Ethics*. Washington, D.C.: Georgetown University Press, 1996.

Kramnick, Isaac, and R. Laurence Moore. *The Godless Constitution*. New York: W. W. Norton, 1996.

Kraybill, Donald B. *The Upside-Down Kingdom*. Scottdale, Penn.: Herald, 1978.

Kroeger, Catherine Clark, and James R. Beck. *Women, Abuse, and the Bible: How Scripture Can Be Used to Hurt or to Heal*. Grand Rapids, Mich.: Baker, 1996.

Lambrecht, Jan. *Out of the Treasure: The Parables in the Gospel of Matthew*. Grand Rapids, Mich.: Eerdmans, 1992.

Lampman, Lisa Barnes, ed. *God and the Victim*. Grand Rapids, Mich.: Eerdmans, 1999.

Land, Steven J. *Pentecostal Spirituality: A Passion for the Kingdom.* Sheffield: Sheffield Academic, 1994.

Lapide, Pinchas. *The Sermon on the Mount.* Maryknoll, N.Y.: Orbis, 1986.

Lazareth, William H. *Christians in Society: Luther, the Bible and Social Ethics.* Minneapolis: Fortress, 2001.

Lebacqz, Karen. "Appropriate Vulnerability: A Sexual Ethic for Singles." In *Readings in Christian Ethics.* Vol. 2. Edited by David Clark and Robert Rakestraw. Grand Rapids, Mich.: Baker, 1996.

———. *Justice in an Unjust World.* Minneapolis: Augsburg, 1987.

———. *Six Theories of Justice.* Minneapolis: Augsburg, 1986.

Lee, Helen. "Racial Reconciliation Tops NAE's Agenda." *Christianity Today,* April 3, 1995, pp. 97.

Lehmann, Paul. *Ethics in a Christian Context.* New York: Harper & Row, 1963.

Leopold, Aldo. *A Sand County Almanac.* New York: Oxford University Press, 1948.

LeQuire, Stan, ed. *The Best Preaching on Earth: Sermons on Caring for Creation.* Valley Forge, Penn.: Judson, 1996.

Liebman, James S., Jeffrey Fagan and Valerie West. "A Broken System: Error Rates in Capital Cases, 1973-1995." *University of Columbia School of Law,* September 12, 2000.

Lind, Millard. *Yahweh Is a Warrior: The Theology of Warfare in Ancient Israel.* Scottdale, Penn.: Herald, 1987.

Linnemann, E. *Parables of Jesus: Introduction and Exposition.* London: SPCK, 1966.

Lloyd-Jones, Martyn. *Studies in the Sermon on the Mount.* Grand Rapids, Mich.: Eerdmans, [1960] 1996.

Lohfink, Gerhard. *Jesus and Community.* Translated by John P. Galvin. Minneapolis: Fortress, 1984.

Lohse, Eduard. *Theological Ethics of the New Testament.* Translated by M. E. Boring. Minneapolis: Fortress: 1991.

Lovelock, James E. *The Ages of Gaia.* New York: Oxford University, 1988.

———. *Gaia.* New York: Oxford University, 1979.

Luther, Martin. "Of Secular Authority: To What Extent It Can Be Obeyed." In *Martin Luther: Selections from His Writings,* pp. 363-402. Edited by John Dillenberger. Garden City, N.Y.: Anchor Books, 1961.

———. *Sermon on the Mount and the Magnificat.* Vol. 21 of *Luther's Works.* Philadelphia: Fortress, 1956.

Luz, Ulrich. *Matthew 1—7: A Continental Commentary.* Minneapolis: Augsburg, 1989.

Macchia, Frank D. "From Azusa to Memphis: Evaluating the Racial Reconciliation Dialogue Among Pentecostals," *Pneuma* 17, no. 2 (1995): 203-18.

MacIntyre, Alasdair. *After Virtue.* 2nd ed. Notre Dame: University of Notre Dame Press, 1984.

Marshall, Christopher D. *Beyond Retribution: A New Testament Vision for Justice, Crime, and Punishment.* Grand Rapids: Eerdmans, 2001.

———. *Crowned with Glory and Honor.* Telford, Penn.: Pandora, 2001.

Marshall, I. Howard. *Commentary on Luke.* Grand Rapids, Mich.: Eerdmans, 1978.

Martin, William. *With God on Our Side*. New York: Broadway, 1996.

Maston, T. B. *The Bible and Family Relations*. Nashville: Broadman, 1983.

Mathewes-Green, Frederica. "If Wombs Had Windows." *ESA Advocate* 15, no. 5 (1993): 12.

———. *Real Choices: Offering Practical Life-Affirming Alternatives to Abortion*. Sisters, Ore.: Multnomah Publishers, 1994.

———. "Why Women Choose Abortion." *Christianity Today*, January 9, 1995, pp. 21-25.

McArthur, Harvey K. *Understanding the Sermon on the Mount*. New York: Harper & Brothers, 1960.

McClendon, James William, Jr. *Doctrine: Systematic Theology*. Vol. 2. Nashville: Abingdon, 1994.

———. *Ethics: Systematic Theology*. Vol. 1. Nashville: Abingdon, 1986.

———. "Three Strands of Christian Ethics." *Journal of Religious Ethics* (spring 1978): 54-80.

———. *Witness: Systematic Theology*. Vol. 3. Nashville: Abingdon, 2000.

McClendon, James William, Jr., and James M. Smith. *Convictions: Defusing Religious Relativism*. Valley Forge, Penn.: Trinity Press International, 1994.

McDaniel, Jay B. *Of God and Pelicans: A Theology of Reverence for Life*. Louisville, Ky.: Westminster John Knox, 1989.

McFague, Sallie. *The Body of God: An Ecological Theology*. Minneapolis: Fortress, 1993.

———. *Super, Natural Christians: How We Should Love Nature*. Minneapolis: Fortress, 1997.

McKeating, Henry. "The Development of the Law on Homicide in Ancient Israel." *Vetus Testamentum* 25 (1975): 46-68.

———. "Sanctions Against Adultery in Ancient Israelite Society." *Journal for the Study of the Old Testament* 11 (1979): 57-72.

McKenzie, Steven L. *All God's Children: A Biblical Critique of Racism*. Louisville, Ky.: Westminster John Knox, 1997.

McNeill, John J. *The Church and the Homosexual*. 4th ed. Boston: Beacon, 1993.

McWhorter, John H. *Losing the Race: Self-Sabotage in Black America*. New York: Free Press, 2000.

Meadows, Donella, et al. *Beyond the Limits: Confronting Global Collapse, Envisioning a Sustainable Future*. Post Mills, Vt.: Chelsea Green, 1992.

Megivern, James. *The Death Penalty: An Historical and Theological Survey*. New York: Paulist, 1997.

Meilaender, Gilbert C. *Bioethics: A Primer for Christians*. Grand Rapids, Mich.: Eerdmans, 1996.

———. "The Distinction Between Killing and Allowing to Die." In *From Christ to the World*, pp. 404-6. Edited by Wayne G. Boulton et al. Grand Rapids, Mich.: Eerdmans, 1994.

———. "On Removing Food and Water: Against the Stream." In *Readings in Christian Ethics*, 2:109-15. Edited by David Clark and Robert Rakestraw. Grand Rapids, Mich.: Baker, 1996.

———. *The Theory and Practice of Virtue*. Notre Dame, Ind.: University of Notre Dame Press, 1984.

Melton, J. Gordon, ed. *The Churches Speak on Capital Punishment*. Detroit: Gale Research, 1989.

Milbank, John. *Theology and Social Theory: Beyond Secular Reason.* Cambridge, Mass.: Blackwell, 1995.

Miller, Richard B. "Just-War Criteria and Theocentric Ethics." In *Christian Ethics: Problems and Prospects.* Edited by Lisa Sowle Cahill and James F. Childress. Cleveland: Pilgrim, 1996.

Mollenkott, Virginia Ramey. "Reproductive Choice: Basic to Justice for Women." In *Readings in Christian Ethics,* 2:26-31. Edited by David Clark and Robert Rakestraw. Grand Rapids, Mich.: Baker, 1996.

Moltmann, Jürgen. *The Crucified God.* New York: Harper & Row, 1974.

———. *God in Creation: A New Theology of Creation and the Spirit of God.* New York: Harper & Row, 1985.

———. *The Way of Jesus Christ: Christology in Messianic Dimensions.* Translated by Margaret Kohl. San Francisco: HarperCollins, 1990.

Moltmann, Jürgen, and Glen H. Stassen. *Justice Creates Peace.* Louisville, Ky.: International Baptist Spirituality Series # 13, 1988.

Moore, George Foot. *Judaism in the First Centuries of the Christian Era.* Vol. 2. New York: Schocken, 1971.

Moreland, J. P. "James Rachels and the Active Euthanasia Debate." In *Readings in Christian Ethics,* 2:102-8. Edited by David Clark and Robert Rakestraw. Grand Rapids, Mich.: Baker, 1996.

Morris, Leon. *The Gospel According to John.* Rev ed. Grand Rapids, Mich.: Eerdmans, 1995.

Mott, Stephen Charles. *Biblical Ethics and Social Change.* New York: Oxford University Press, 1982.

Mott, Stephen, and Ronald J. Sider. "Economic Justice: A Biblical Paradigm." In *Toward a Just and Caring Society.* Edited by David P. Gushee. Grand Rapids, Mich.: Baker, 1999.

Mount, Eric. *Covenant, Community, and the Common Good: An Interpretation of Christian Ethics.* Cleveland: Pilgrim, 1999.

Mouw, Richard J. *The God Who Commands: A Study in Divine Command Ethics.* Notre Dame, Ind.: University of Notre Dame Press, 1990.

———. *Uncommon Decency: Christian Civility in an Uncivil World.* Downers Grove, Ill.: InterVarsity Press, 1992.

Murphy, Charles M. *The Cosmic Covenant: Biblical Themes on Justice, Peace, and the Integrity of Creation.* London: Sheed & Ward, 1992.

Murray, John Courtney. *We Hold These Truths.* New York: Sheed & Ward, 1960.

Murray, John. *Principles of Conduct.* Grand Rapids, Mich.: Eerdmans, 1957.

Musto, Ronald G. *The Catholic Peace Tradition.* Maryknoll, N.Y.: Orbis, 1986.

Myers, Ched. *Binding the Strong Man.* Maryknoll, N.Y.: Orbis, 1997.

Nash, James A. *Loving Nature: Ecological Integrity and Christian Responsibility.* Nashville: Abingdon, 1991.

National Conference of Catholic Bishops. *Economic Justice for All.* Washington, D.C.: United States Catholic Conference, 1986.

Neuhaus, Richard John. *America Against Itself: Moral Vision and the Public Order.* Notre Dame, Ind.: University of Notre Dame Press, 1992.

Niditch, Susan. *War in the Hebrew Bible*. New York: Oxford, 1993.

Niebuhr, H. Richard. *The Meaning of Revelation*. New York: Macmillan, 1941.

———. "The Responsibility of the Church for Society." In *The Gospel, the Church, and the World*, pp. 111-33. Edited by Kenneth Scott Latourette. New York: Harper, 1946.

Niebuhr, Reinhold. *Love and Justice: Selections From the Shorter Writings of Reinhold Niebuhr*. Edited by D. B. Robertson. Louisville, Ky.: Westminster John Knox, 1992.

———. *Moral Man and Immoral Society*. New York: Scribner's, 1932.

———. *The Responsible Self*. New York: Harper & Row, 1963.

Nissinen, Martti. *Homoeroticism in the Biblical World*. Minneapolis: Augsburg Fortress, 1998.

Nuland, Sherwin B. "The Principle of Hope," *The New Republic*, May 27, 2002, <www.tnr.com>.

Nussbaum, Martha C. "Brave Good World." *The New Republic*, December 4, 2000, pp. 38-48.

Nygren, Anders. *Agape and Eros*. Translated by Philip S. Watson. Philadelphia: Westminster Press, 1953.

O'Brien, David J., and Thomas A. Shannon, eds. *Catholic Social Thought*. Maryknoll, N.Y.: Orbis, 1992.

Ogletree, Thomas W. *The Use of the Bible in Christian Ethics*. Minneapolis: Fortress, 1983.

Okholm, Dennis L., ed. *The Gospel in Black and White: Theological Resources for Racial Reconciliation*. Downers Grove, Ill.: InterVarsity Press, 1997.

Olasky, Marvin. *The Tragedy of American Compassion*. Washington, D.C.: Regnery, 1992.

Ottati, Douglas, and Douglas Schuurman, eds. "Covenantal Ethics." *The Annual of the Society of Christian Ethics 1996*, 245-310.

Outka, Gene. *Agape: An Ethical Analysis*. New Haven, Conn.: Yale University Press, 1972.

———. "Theocentric Agape and the Self: An Asymmetrical Affirmation in Response to Colin Grant's Either/Or." *Journal of Religious Ethics* 24, no. 1 (1996): 35-42.

———. "Universal Love and Impartiality." In *The Love Commandments: Essays in Christian Ethics and Moral Philosophy*, pp. 1-103. Edited by Edmund N. Santurri and William Werpehowski. Washington, D.C.: Georgetown University Press, 1992.

Parham, Robert A. *Loving Neighbors Across Time: A Christian Guide to Protecting the Earth*. Birmingham, Ala.: New Hope, 1992.

Paris, Peter. *The Spirituality of African Peoples: The Search for a Common Moral Discourse*. Minneapolis: Fortress, 1995.

Patrick, Mary W. *The Love Commandment: How to Find Its Meaning for Today*. St. Louis: CBP Press, 1984.

Patterson, Orlando. "Race Over." *The New Republic*, January 10, 2000, p. 6.

———. *Rituals of Blood*. New York: Basic Civitas, 1998.

Paul, Robert S. *The Atonement and the Sacraments*. Nashville: Abingdon, 1960.

Pelikan, Jaroslav. *Divine Rhetoric: The Sermon on the Mount as Message and as Model in Augustine, Chrysostom, and Luther*. Crestwood, N.Y.: St Vladimir's Seminary Press, 2001.

Pelikan, Jaroslav, ed. *Luther's Works*. Vol. 21. St. Louis: Concordia Publishing House, 1956.

Perkins, Spencer. "Playing the Grace Card." *Christianity Today,* July 13, 1998, pp. 41-44.

Perkins, Spencer, and Chris Rice. *More Than Equals: Racial Healing for the Sake of the Gospel.* Downers Grove, Ill.: InterVarsity Press, 1993.

Peters, Ted. *For the Love of Children.* Louisville, Ky.: Westminster John Knox, 1996.

———. *Playing God?* London: Routledge, 1997.

Petersen, Douglas. *Not by Might nor by Power: A Pentecostal Theology of Social Concern in Latin America.* Oxford: Regnum, 1996.

Peterson, James C. *Genetic Turning Points: The Ethics of Human Genetic Intervention.* Grand Rapids, Mich.: Eerdmans, 2001.

Pieper, Josef. *The Four Cardinal Virtues.* New York: Harcourt, Brace & World, 1965.

Piper, John. "Divorce and Remarriage." Unpublished paper, Bethlehem Baptist Church, Minneapolis, July 21, 1986.

Piper, John, and Wayne Grudem, eds. *Recovering Biblical Manhood and Womanhood.* Wheaton, Ill.: Crossway, 1991.

Pius XI. *Quadragesimo Anno (After Forty Years).* 1931. In *Catholic Social Thought.* Edited by David J. O'Brien and Thomas A. Shannon. Maryknoll, N.Y.: Orbis, 1992.

Pojman, Louis P., and Francis J. Beckwith. *The Abortion Controversy.* London: Jones & Bartlett, 1994.

Poluma, Margaret M. "Charisma, Institutionalization and Social Change," *Pneuma* 17, no. 2 (1995): 245-50.

Pope, Stephen J. "'Equal Regard' Versus 'Special Relations'? Reaffirming the Inclusiveness of Agape." *The Journal of Religion* 77, no. 3 (1997): 353-79.

———. "Love in Contemporary Christian Ethics." *Journal of Religious Ethics* 23, no. 1 (1995): 167-97.

Porter, Jean. *The Recovery of Virtue: The Relevance of Aquinas for Christian Ethics.* Louisville, Ky.: Westminster John Knox, 1990.

Post, Stephen G. *Spheres of Love: Toward a New Ethics of Family.* Dallas: Southern Methodist University Press, 1994.

Potter, Ralph. *War and Moral Discourse.* Atlanta: John Knox Press, 1969.

Preece, Gordon R., ed. *Rethinking Peter Singer.* Downers Grove, Ill.: InterVarsity Press, 2002.

Prejean, Helen. *Dead Man Walking.* New York: Random House, 1993.

Preston, Ronald. "Lying." In *The Westminster Dictionary of Christian Ethics.* Edited by James F. Childress and John Macquarrie. Philadelphia: Westminster Press, 1986.

Purvis, Sally B. "Mothers, Neighbors, and Strangers: Another Look at Agape." *Journal of Feminist Studies in Religion* 7, no. 1 (1991): 19-34.

Rae, Scott B. *Moral Choices.* Grand Rapids, Mich.: Zondervan, 1995.

Rae, Scott B., and Kenman L. Wong. *Beyond Integrity.* Grand Rapids, Mich.: Zondervan, 1996.

Rae, Scott B., and Paul M. Cox. *Bioethics: A Christian Approach in a Pluralistic Age.* Grand Rapids, Mich.: Eerdmans, 1999.

Rakestraw, Robert. "The Persistent Vegetative State and the Withdrawal of Nutrition and Hydration." In *Readings in Christian Ethics,* 2:116-31. Edited by David Clark and Robert Rakestraw. Grand Rapids, Mich.: Baker, 1996.

Ramsey, Dave. *Financial Peace*. New York: Viking, 1997.

Ramsey, Paul. *Ethics at the Edges of Life: Medical and Legal Intersections*. New Haven, Conn.: Yale University Press, 1978.

————. *Fabricated Man: The Ethics of Genetic Control*. New Haven, Conn.: Yale University Press, 1970.

Rasmussen, Larry. *Dietrich Bonhoeffer: Reality and Resistance*. Nashville: Abingdon, 1972.

————. *Earth Community, Earth Ethics*. Maryknoll, N.Y.: Orbis, 1996.

————. *Moral Fragments and Moral Community*. Minneapolis: Augsburg Fortress, 1993.

Rauschenbusch, Walter. *Christianity and the Social Crisis*. Louisville, Ky.: Westminster John Knox, 1991.

Reiss, Albert J., Jr., and Jeffrey A. Roth, eds., *Understanding and Preventing Violence*. Washington, D.C.: National Academy Press, 1993.

Rice, Chris. "More Than Family." *Sojourners*, September/October 1999 <www.sojo.net>.

Roach, Richard R., S.J. "A New Sense of Faith." *Journal of Religious Ethics* 5, no. 1 (1977): 135-54.

Roberts, Samuel K. *African American Christian Ethics*. Cleveland: Pilgrim, 2001.

Roebuck, David. "Perfect Liberty to Preach the Gospel: Women Ministers in the Church of God," *Pneuma* 17, no. 1 (1995): 25-34.

Roof, Wade Clark, and William McKinney. *American Mainline Religion*. Rutgers, N.J.: Rutgers University Press, 1990.

Rotberg, Robert I., and Dennis Thompson. *Truth v. Justice: The Morality of Truth Commissions*. Princeton, N.J.: Princeton University Press, 2000.

Rudy, Kathy. *Sex and the Church*. Boston: Beacon, 1997.

Ruether, Rosemary Radford. *Gaia and God: An Ecofeminist Theology of Earth Healing*. New York: HarperCollins, 1992.

Ruether, Rosemary Radford, ed. *Women Healing Earth: Third-World Women on Ecology, Feminism, and Religion*. Maryknoll, N.Y.: Orbis, 1996.

Rust, Eric. *Nature—Garden or Desert? An Essay in Environmental Theology*. Dallas: Word, 1971.

Ryrie, Charles. "Biblical Teachings on Divorce and Remarriage." In *Readings in Christian Ethics*. Vol. 2. Edited by David Clark and Robert Rakestraw. Grand Rapids, Mich.: Baker, 1994.

Sanders, Cheryl. *Empowerment Ethics for a Liberated People*. Minneapolis: Fortress, 1995.

Sanders, E. P. *Jesus and Judaism*. Philadelphia: Fortress, 1985.

Satinover, Jeffrey. *Homosexuality and the Politics of Truth*. Grand Rapids, Mich.: Baker, 1996.

Scalise, Charles J. *Hermeneutics as Theological Prolegomena: A Canonical Approach*. Atlanta: Mercer University Press, 1994.

Scanzoni, Letha Dawson, and Nancy A. Hardesty. *All We're Meant to Be*. 3rd ed. Grand Rapids, Mich.: Eerdmans, 1992.

Schaeffer, Francis A. *Pollution and the Death of Man: The Christian View of Ecology*. Wheaton, Ill.: Tyndale House, 1971, 1979.

Schmidt, Thomas E. *Straight and Narrow?* Downers Grove, Ill.: InterVarsity Press, 1995.

Schnackenburg, Rudolf, ed. *Bergpredigt: Utopische Vision oder Handlungsanweisung?* Düsseldorf: Patmos, 1982.

Schneider, John. *Godly Materialism*. Downers Grove, Ill.: InterVarsity Press, 1994.

Schneider, Keith. "The Regulatory Thickets of Environmental Racism." *New York Times*, December 19, 1993.

Schrage, Wolfgang. *The Ethics of the New Testament*. Philadelphia: Fortress, 1988.

Schwab, Jim. *Deeper Shades of Green: The Rise of Blue-Collar and Minority Environmentalism in America*. San Francisco: Sierra Club Books, 1994.

Schweizer, Eduard. *The Good News According to Matthew*. Atlanta: John Knox Press, 1975.

Scott, Bernard Brandon. *Hear Then the Parable*. Minneapolis: Fortress, 1989.

Sharp, Gene. *The Politics of Nonviolent Action*. New York: Porter Sargent, 1974.

Shearer, Jody Miller. *Enter the River: Healing Steps from White Privilege Toward Racial Reconciliation*. Scottdale, Penn.: Herald, 1994.

Sherlock, Richard, Richard G. Wilkins and Steven Clark. "Mediating the Polar Extremes: A Guide to Post-*Webster* Abortion Policy." *Brigham Young University Law Review* (1991): 403-88.

Sherman, Amy. "Getting to Work: Church-Based Responses to Welfare Reform." *Prism* 6, no. 1 (1999): 12-16.

Shipler, David K. *A Country of Strangers: Blacks and Whites in America*. New York: Knopf, 1997.

Shriver, Donald W., Jr. *An Ethic for Enemies: Forgiveness in Politics*. New York: Oxford University Press, 1995.

Sider, Ronald J. *Cry Justice*. New York: Paulist, 1980.

——. *Cup of Water, Bread of Life*. Grand Rapids, Mich.: Zondervan, 1994.

——. *Just Generosity: A New Vision for Overcoming Poverty in America*. Grand Rapids, Mich.: Baker, 1999.

——. *Rich Christians in an Age of Hunger*. 20th anniversary ed. Dallas: Word, 1997.

Siker, Jeffrey S. *Scripture and Ethics*. New York: Oxford University Press, 1997.

Simmons, Paul. *Birth and Death: Bioethical Decision-Making*. Philadelphia: Westminster Press, 1983.

Simons, Robert G. *Competing Gospels: Public Theology and Economic Theory*. Alexandria, Australia: E. J. Dwyer, 1995.

Singer, Peter. *Practical Ethics*. 2nd ed. Cambridge: Cambridge University Press, 1993.

Sleeper, C. Freeman. *The Bible and the Moral Life*. Louisville, Ky.: Westminster John Knox, 1992.

Smedes, Lewis B. *Forgive and Forget*. San Francisco: HarperSanFrancisco, 1984.

——. *Mere Morality: What God Expects from Ordinary People*. Grand Rapids, Mich.: Eerdmans, 1983.

——. *Sex for Christians*. Rev. ed. Grand Rapids, Mich.: Eerdmans, 1994.

Smith, Wesley J. "'Futile Care' and Its Friends." *Weekly Standard*, July 23, 2001, pp. 27-29.

Soards, Marion L. *Scripture and Homosexuality*. Louisville, Ky.: Westminster John Knox, 1995.

Sojourners. *America's Original Sin: A Study Guide on White Racism*. Washington, D.C.: Sojourners, 1995.

——. *Crossing the Racial Divide: American's Struggle for Justice and Reconciliation*. Washington, D.C.: Sojourners, 1998.

———. *Who Is My Neighbor: Economics As If Values Matter*. Washington, D.C.: Sojourners, 1994.

Solzhenitsyn, Aleksandr. *The Gulag Archipelago*. New York: HarperCollins, 1992.

Spencer, Aída Besançon. *Beyond the Curse*. Peabody, Mass.: Hendrickson, 1985.

Spiegel, James S. "Can a Christian Be Morally Pro-Life and Politically Pro-Choice?" *Christian Scholar's Review* 30, no. 1 (2000): 107-15.

Spohn, William C., S.J. *Go and Do Likewise: Jesus and Ethics*. New York: Continuum, 1999.

———. *What Are they Saying About Scripture?* Ramsey, N.J.: Paulist, 1984.

Stackhouse, John G., Jr. *Can God Be Trusted?* New York: Oxford University Press, 1998.

Stackhouse, Max L. *Covenant and Commitments: Faith, Family, and Economic Life*. Louisville, Ky.: Westminster John Knox, 1997.

Stackhouse, Max L., et al. *Christian Social Ethics in a Global Era*. Nashville: Abingdon, 1995.

Stagg, Frank. *The Book of Acts: The Early Struggle for an Unhindered Gospel*. Nashville: Broadman, 1955.

Stassen, Glen H. "Critical Variables in Christian Social Ethics." In *Issues in Christian Ethics*. Edited by Paul Simmons. Nashville: Broadman, 1980.

———. "The Fourteen Triads of the Sermon on the Mount." *Journal of Biblical Literature*, 2003.

———. "Individual Preferences and Role Constraints in Policy-Making; Senatorial Response to Secretaries Acheson and Dulles." *World Politics* (October 1972); reprinted in Chittick, *The Analysis of Foreign Policy Outputs*. Charles Merrill, 1975.

———. *Just Peacemaking: Ten Practices for Abolishing War*. Cleveland: Pilgrim, 1998.

———. *Just Peacemaking: Transforming Initiatives for Justice and Peace*. Louisville, Ky.: Westminster John Knox, 1992.

———. "Michael Walzer's Situated Justice." *Journal of Religious Ethics* (fall 1994).

———. "A Social Theory Model for Religious Social Ethics." *Journal of Religious Ethics* (spring 1977).

Stassen, Glen H., ed. *Capital Punishment: A Reader*. Cleveland: Pilgrim, 1998.

Stassen, Glen, D. M. Yeager, and John Howard Yoder. *Authentic Transformation: A New Vision of Christ and Culture*. Nashville: Abingdon, 1996.

Steele, Shelby. *The Content of Our Character: A New Vision of Race in America*. New York: HarperCollins, 1990.

Steffen, Lloyd. *Life/Choice: The Theory of Just Abortion*. Cleveland: Pilgrim, 1994.

Stern, Fritz. *The Politics of Cultural Despair: A Study in the Rise of the Germanic Ideology*. Berkeley: University of California Press, 1974.

Stone, Ronald. *The Ultimate Imperative*. Cleveland: Pilgrim, 1999.

Swartley, Willard. *Israel's Scripture Traditions and the Synoptic Gospels*. Peabody, Mass.: Hendrickson, 1994.

———. "War and Peace in the NT." In *Aufstieg und Niedergang der römischen Welt* 2.26.3. Edited by Wolfgang Haase. Berlin: Walther de Gruyter, 1996. 2298-2408.

Swift, E. M., and Don Yaeger. "Unnatural Selection." *Sports Illustrated*, May 14, 2001, pp. 86-94.

Taylor, Paul W. *Respect for Nature: A Theory of Environmental Ethics*. Princeton, N.J.:

Princeton University Press, 1986.

ten Boom, Corrie. *The Hiding Place.* New York: Bantam, 1971.

Thandeka. *Learning to Be White: Money, Race and God in America.* New York: Continuum, 1999.

Thomas, Cal, and Ed Dobson. *Blinded by Might: Can the Religious Right Save America?* Grand Rapids, Mich.: Zondervan/HarperCollins, 1999.

Thurman, Howard. *Jesus and the Disinherited.* Richmond, Ind.: Friends United Press, 1981.

Todd, James. "Participation: An Overlooked Clue." *Encounter* 34 (1973): 27-35.

Todorov, Tzvetan. "In Search of Lost Crime." *The New Republic,* January 29, 2001, pp. 29-36.

Tödt, Heinz Eduard. "Kirche und Ethik: Dietrich Bonhoeffers Entscheidungen in den Krisenjahren 1929-1933." In *Kirche: Festschrift für Günther Bornkamm.* Tübingen: J.C.B. Mohr, 1980.

———. *Theologische Perspektiven nach Dietrich Bonhoeffer.* Gütersloh: Christian Kaiser, 1993.

Tooley, Michelle. *Voices of the Voiceless: Women, Justice, and Human Rights in Guatemala.* Scottdale, Penn.: Herald, 1997.

Trimiew, Darryl. "The Limits of Virtue Theory for African American Christian Ethics." Unpublished paper, Society of Christian Ethics Annual Meeting, January 2001.

———. *Voices of the Silenced: The Responsible Self in Marginalized Community.* Cleveland: Pilgrim, 1992.

Trull, Joe. *Walking in the Way.* Nashville: Broadman & Holman, 1997.

Tutu, Desmond. *No Future Without Forgiveness.* New York: Doubleday Image, 2000.

Twohey, Megan. "Promise Unrealized." *National Journal,* December 16, 2000.

Union of Concerned Scientists. *Myths and Facts About Global Warming.* Washington, D.C.: Union of Concerned Scientists, 2000.

U.S. Census Bureau, *Statistical Abstract of the United States 2000.* Washington, D.C.: U.S. Government Printing Office, 2000.

U.S. National Conference of Catholic Bishops. *The Challenge of Peace.* Washington, D.C.: U. S. Catholic Conference, 1983.

Vacek, Edward Collins, S.J. *Love, Human and Divine: The Heart of Christian Ethics.* Washington, D.C.: Georgetown University Press, 1990.

Van Leeuwen, Mary Stewart. *Gender and Grace.* Downers Grove, Ill.: InterVarsity Press, 1990.

VandenBos, Gary R., and Elizabeth Q. Bulatao, ed. *Violence on the Job: Identifying Risks and Developing Solutions.* Washington, D.C.: American Psychological Association, 1996.

Velasquez, Manuel G. *Business Ethics.* 4th ed. Upper Saddle River, N.J.: Prentice-Hall, 1998.

Verhey, Allen. *The Great Reversal: Ethics and the New Testament.* Grand Rapids, Mich.: Eerdmans, 1993.

———. *Remembering Jesus: Christian Community, Scripture and the Moral Life.* Grand Rapids, Mich.: Eerdmans, 2002.

Vermes, Geza. *Jesus the Jew.* Minneapolis: Fortress, 1981.

———. *The Religion of Jesus the Jew.* Minneapolis: Fortress, 1993.

Villafañe, Eldin. *The Liberating Spirit: Toward an Hispanic American Pentecostal Social Eth-*

ics. Grand Rapids, Mich.: Eerdmans, 1993.

———. "The Politics of the Spirit: Reflections on a Theology of Social Transformation for the Twenty-First Century," Presidential Address for the Society of Pentecostal Studies, *Pneuma: The Journal of the Society of Pentecostal Studies* 18, no. 2 (fall 1996): 161-70.

Volf, Miroslav. *Exclusion and Embrace.* Nashville: Abingdon, 1996.

Von Rad, Gerhard. *Old Testament Theology.* Vol. 1. Edinburgh: Oliver & Boyd, 1962.

Wald, Kenneth D. *Religion and Politics in the United States.* 2nd ed. Washington, D.C.: Congressional Quarterly, 1992.

Wallis, Jim. *The Soul of Politics.* New York: The Free Press and Orbis Books, 1994.

Wallwork, Ernest. "'Thou Shalt Love Thy Neighbor As Thyself': The Freudian Critique." *Journal of Religious Ethics* 10, no. 2 (1982): 264-319.

Walzer, Michael. *The Company of Critics: Social Criticism and Political Commitment in the Twentieth Century.* New York: Basic Books, 1988.

———. *Just and Unjust Wars.* New York: Basic Books, 1977.

———. *The Revolution of the Saints: A Study in the Origins of Radical Politics.* Cambridge, Mass.: Harvard University Press, 1965.

———. *Spheres of Justice.* New York: Basic Books, 1983.

Washington, James M. *A Testament of Hope: The Essential Writings of Martin Luther King, Jr.* San Francisco: Harper & Row, 1986.

Watson, Paul, Tyler Marshall and Bob Drogin. "On the Trail of the Real Osama bin Laden." *Los Angeles Times,* September 15, 2001, A16-17.

Watts, Rikki. E. *Isaiah's New Exodus in Mark.* Grand Rapids, Mich.: Baker Academic, 1997.

Weaver, J. Denny. *The Nonviolent Atonement.* Grand Rapids, Mich.: Eerdmans, 2001.

Weder, Hans. *Die "Rede der Reden": Eine Auslegung der Bergpredigt Heute.* 2nd ed. Zurich: Theologischer Verlag, 1987. Excerpts for this volume translated by Glen Stassen.

Weigel, George. *Soul of the World: Notes on the Future of Public Catholicism.* Grand Rapids, Mich.: Eerdmans/Ethics and Public Policy Center, 1996.

Wennberg, Robert N. "The Right to Life: Three Theories." In *Readings in Christian Ethics,* 2:36-45. Edited by David Clark and Robert Rakestraw. Grand Rapids, Mich.: Baker, 1996.

West, Cornel. *Race Matters.* New York: Random House, 1994.

Westermann, Claus. *Genesis 1—11: A Commentary.* Minneapolis: Augsburg, 1984.

———. *The Parables of Jesus in the Light of the Old Testament.* Minneapolis: Fortress, 1990.

Westmoreland-White, Michael L. "Reading Scripture in the Baptist Vision: James Wm. McClendon, Jr. and the Hermeneutics of Participation," *Perspectives in Religious Studies* 27:1 (spring 2000), 61-69.

———. "Setting the Record Straight: Christian Faith, Human Rights, and the Enlightenment." In *The Annual of the Society of Christian Ethics* (1995): 75-96.

Wheeler, Sondra. "Making Babies?" *Sojourners,* May 1999, p. 14.

———. *Wealth as Peril and Obligation.* Grand Rapids, Mich.: Eerdmans, 1995.

Whitehead, Barbara Dafoe. *The Divorce Culture.* New York: Knopf, 1997.

Wilkinson, Loren, ed. *Earthkeeping in the Nineties.* Rev. ed. Grand Rapids, Mich.: Eerdmans, 1991.

Willard, Dallas, *The Divine Conspiracy: Rediscovering Our Hidden Life in God*. San Francisco: HarperSanFrancisco, 1998.

Williams, Daniel Day. *The Spirit and the Forms of Love*. New York and Evanston: Harper & Row, 1968.

Willimon, William H., and Stanley Hauerwas. *Lord, Teach Us*. Nashville: Abingdon, 1996.

Wilson, Jonathan. *Gospel Virtues*. Downers Grove, Ill.: InterVarsity Press, 1998.

Wink, Walter. "Beyond Just War and Pacifism: Jesus' Nonviolent Way." *Review and Expositor* 89, no. 2 (1992).

————. *Engaging the Powers: Discernment and Resistance in a World of Domination*. Philadelphia: Fortress, 1992.

————. "The Parable of the Compassionate Samaritan: A Communal Exegesis Approach." *Review and Expositor* 76 (1979): 199-218.

————. *When the Powers Fall: Reconciliation in the Healing of Nations*. Minneapolis: Fortress, 1998.

Winwright, Tobias. "From Police Officers to Peace Officers." In *The Wisdom of the Cross: Essays in Honor of John Howard Yoder*, pp. 84-114. Grand Rapids, Mich.: Eerdmans, 1999.

Witherington, Ben, III. *New Testament History*. Grand Rapids, Mich.: Baker, 2001.

————. *Women in the Earliest Churches*. Cambridge: Cambridge University Press, 1988.

Wogaman, Philip. *Christian Ethics*. Louisville, Ky.: Westminster John Knox, 1993.

————. *Christian Moral Judgment*. Louisville, Ky.: Westminster John Knox, 1989.

————. *Economics and Ethics*. Philadelphia: Fortress, 1986.

————. *The Great Economic Debate*. Philadelphia: Westminster Press, 1977.

Wold, Donald J. *Out of Order*. Grand Rapids, Mich.: Baker, 1998.

Wolfe, David A., Christine Wekerle and Katreena Scott. *Alternatives to Violence: Empowering Youth to Develop Healthy Relationships*. New York: Sage, 1997.

Wood, John. *Perspectives on War in the Bible*. Macon, Ga.: Mercer University Press, 1998.

World Resources Institute. *Deforestation: The Global Assault Continues*. World Resources Institute: 2001. For extensive information, see their website <www.wri.org>.

Wright, Christopher J. H. *Walking in the Ways of the Lord: The Ethical Authority of the Old Testament*. Downers Grove, Ill.: InterVarsity Press, 1995.

Wright, N. T. *Jesus and the Victory of God*. Minneapolis: Fortress, 1996.

Wuthnow, Robert. *Acts of Compassion*. Princeton, N.J.: Princeton University Press, 1991.

————. *Christianity and Civil Society*. Valley Forge, Penn.: Trinity Press International, 1996.

Yoder, John Howard. "Against the Death Penalty." In *The Death Penalty Debate*. Edited by H. Wayne House and John Howard Yoder. Waco, Tex.: Word, 1991.

————. *Body Politics*. Nashville: Discipleship Resources, 1992.

————. *The Christian Witness to the State*. London: Wipf & Stock, 1997.

————. *For the Nations: Essays Public & Evangelical*. Grand Rapids, Mich.: Eerdmans, 1997.

————. *Nevertheless: Varieties and Shortcomings of Religious Pacifism*. Scottdale, Penn.: Herald, 1992.

———. *The Politics of Jesus*. Grand Rapids, Mich.: Eerdmans, [1972] 1994.

———. *Preface to Theology: Christology and Theological Method*. Grand Rapids, Mich.: Brazos, 2002.

———. *The Royal Priesthood: Essays Ecclesiological and Ecumenical*. Grand Rapids, Mich.: Eerdmans, 1994.

———. *The War of the Lamb*. Forthcoming.

———. *When War Is Unjust*. Minneapolis: Augsburg, 1984.

Yoder, Perry. *Shalom: The Bible's Word for Salvation, Justice, and Peace*. Nappanee, Ind.: Evangel, 1998.

Young, Brad H. *Jesus the Jewish Theologian*. Peabody, Mass.: Hendrickson, 1995.

———. *The Parables: Jewish Tradition and Christian Interpretation*. Peabody, Mass.: Hendrickson, 1998.

Young, Richard A. *Healing the Earth: A Theocentric Perspective on Environmental Problems and Their Solutions*. Nashville: Broadman & Holman, 1994.

Zurer, Pam. "Ozone Depletion's Recurring Surprises Challenge Atmospheric Scientists." *Chemical & Engineering News*, May 24, 1993.

Author Index

Subject Index

abortion, 31, 34, 37, 47, 57, 58, 59, 60, 63, 68, 75, 100, 108, 147, 237
  and the church, 230-32
  on demand, 224, 228, 231, 235
  elective vs. spontaneous, 220
  as murder, 221
  and Scripture, 215-20
  selective, 255
  as violence against women, 235
  and women's oppression, 228
  See further chap. 10
absolutism, contextual, 109-10
action(s), 71, 244
  God's delivering, 25, 34, 62, 229
actuality principle. *See* person
adoption, 233, 236
adultery, 199, 234, 271, 279, 293
advanced directives, 243
affirmative action, 394
agent(s), moral, 90, 249
air pollution, 431-32
allowed to die, 244, 245, 250
Anabaptist(s), 15, 68, 132, 375
analogy, moral, 101-2
anthropocentric, 430-37, 439
antitheses, 84, 133
appropriate vulnerability, 303. *See also* ethics, sexual
authoritarianism, 61, 66, 76, 126, 183
authority, authorities, 26,

33, 75, 76, 79, 165, 178
  in just war theory, 159-60
  of Scripture, 95
  sources of, 81-90, 190-91, 254 (*see further* chap. 4)
  state, 204, 209
  as unjust, 204, 209
autonomy, autonomous, 63, 183, 259, 314
  female, 228
  patient, 242-45
artificial nutrition and hydration, 247
baptize, baptism, 37, 69, 73, 97
Beatitudes, 36, 66, 70, 140, 195, 212, 443
beliefs. *See* convictions; doctrines
beneficence, 54
Bible. *See* Scripture
biocentric ethics, 437-38
biodiversity, loss of, 433
biomedical ethics, 370
biopharming, 255-56
biotechnology, 147
  and economics, 257-58
  See further chap. 12
birth control, 304-6, 444
  nonabortive, 236
capital punishment. *See* death penalty
capitalism, 258, 419-20, 422-24
care, caring, 77, 78, 227
  God's, 429
casuistry, 224
celibacy, 303
character, 13, 17, 52, 56, 57, 61, 63, 64, 68, 73, 74, 75, 76, 99, 121
  dimensions of, 59
  ethics of, 70
  of God, 38, 42, 272
  holistic, 60, 69
chastity, 128

child abuse, 195
childbearing (meant for marriage), 303-5
childlessness as tragedy, 216
choice(s), moral, 74, 83
Christ, Jesus Christ, 14, 15, 20, 34, 36, 45, 70
Christ followers, 12. 14, 15, 30, 60, 251, 467
Christian identity, crisis of, 11
Christian life, 69, 74, 109
Christian pacifism
  defined, 166
  varieties of, 167
Christlikeness, 59, 61, 64, 70
christomorphic, 36, 37
church(es), 11, 13, 15, 39, 49, 57, 61, 66, 73, 82, 91, 118, 165, 201, 224, 225
church, mission of, 59, 62, 67, 70
civil rights movement, 66, 139
class, 77, 78. *See also* wealth, poverty, economic justice
clean/unclean, 44
cloning, 61, 252, 256-57, 262-64
  reproductive, 256
commands, divine, 121
common good, 52, 57
community, communities, 15, 21, 25, 32, 39, 53, 56, 57, 60, 61, 63, 64, 69, 70, 72, 74, 77, 87, 136, 137, 151, 174, 196, 222, 227
  of care/service, 473
  countercultural, 429, 473
  divergent, 52
  equal participation in, 42
  exclusion from, 363-65
  of faith, 50, 88, 89, 145, 231, 294

Scripture Index

538